THE POSSIBILITY OF LITERATURE

The Possibility of Literature is an essential collection from one of the most powerful and distinctive voices in contemporary literary studies. Bringing together key compositions from the last twenty-five years, as well as several new pieces, the book demonstrates the changing fate of literary thinking over the first decades of the twenty-first century. Peter Boxall traces here the profound shifts in the global conditions that make literature possible as these have occurred in the historical passage from 9/11 to Covid-19. Exploring questions such as 'The Idea of Beauty', the nature of 'Mere Being' and the possibilities of rereading, the author anatomises the myriad forces that shape the literary imagination. At the same time, he gives vivid critical expression to the imaginative possibilities of literature itself – those unique forms of communal life that literature makes possible in a dramatically changing world and that lead us towards a new shared future.

PETER BOXALL is Goldsmiths' Professor of English Literature at the University of Oxford. He has published a number of books on the novel, including *Twenty-First Century Fiction* (2013), *The Value of the Novel* (2015) and *The Prosthetic Imagination* (2020, winner of the Modern Language Association James Russell Lowell Prize). He is currently writing a book entitled *Fictions of the West*.

THE POSSIBILITY OF LITERATURE

The Novel and the Politics of Form

PETER BOXALL
University of Oxford

Shaftesbury Road, Cambridge CB2 8EA, United Kingdom

One Liberty Plaza, 20th Floor, New York, NY 10006, USA

477 Williamstown Road, Port Melbourne, VIC 3207, Australia

314–321, 3rd Floor, Plot 3, Splendor Forum, Jasola District Centre, New Delhi – 110025, India

103 Penang Road, #05–06/07, Visioncrest Commercial, Singapore 238467

Cambridge University Press is part of Cambridge University Press & Assessment, a department of the University of Cambridge.

We share the University's mission to contribute to society through the pursuit of education, learning and research at the highest international levels of excellence.

www.cambridge.org
Information on this title: www.cambridge.org/9781009314299

DOI: 10.1017/9781009314305

© Peter Boxall 2024

This publication is in copyright. Subject to statutory exception and to the provisions of relevant collective licensing agreements, no reproduction of any part may take place without the written permission of Cambridge University Press & Assessment.

When citing this work, please include a reference to the DOI 10.1017/9781009314305

First published 2024

Printed in the United Kingdom by TJ Books Limited, Padstow Cornwall

A catalogue record for this publication is available from the British Library

Library of Congress Cataloging-in-Publication Data
NAMES: Boxall, Peter, author.
TITLE: The possibility of literature : the novel and the politics of form / Peter Boxall.
DESCRIPTION: Cambridge, United Kingdom ; New York, NY : Cambridge University Press, 2024. | Includes bibliographical references.
IDENTIFIERS: LCCN 2023056531 (print) | LCCN 2023056532 (ebook) | ISBN 9781009314299 (hardback) | ISBN 9781009314305 (ebook)
SUBJECTS: LCSH: Fiction – History and criticism – Theory, etc. | Politics in literature. | Politics and literature.
CLASSIFICATION: LCC PN3331 .B69 2024 (print) | LCC PN3331 (ebook) | DDC 809.3–dc23/eng/20240226
LC record available at https://lccn.loc.gov/2023056531
LC ebook record available at https://lccn.loc.gov/2023056532

ISBN 978-1-009-31429-9 Hardback

Cambridge University Press & Assessment has no responsibility for the persistence or accuracy of URLs for external or third-party internet websites referred to in this publication and does not guarantee that any content on such websites is, or will remain, accurate or appropriate.

In memory of Laura Marcus
1956–2021

I dwell in Possibility.

Emily Dickinson

Contents

List of Figures *page* ix
Acknowledgements x

Introduction: The Possibility of Literature 1

PART I ON WRITERS

1 A Sort of Crutch: Race and Prosthesis in Herman Melville's Fiction 29

2 Samuel Beckett: Towards a Political Reading 47

3 A Leap Out of Our Biology: History, Tautology and Biomatter in DeLillo's Later Fiction 63

4 A More Sophisticated Imitation: Ishiguro and the Novel 87

5 A Cleaving in the Mind: Kelman's Later Novels 104

6 Zadie Smith, E. M. Forster and the Idea of Beauty 117

PART II ON LITERARY HISTORY

7 The Threshold of Vision: The Animal Gaze in Beckett, Sebald and Coetzee 149

8 The Anatomy of Realism: Cervantes, Coetzee and Artificial Life 169

9 Back Roads: Edgeworth. Bowen. Yeats. Beckett 187

10 Blind Seeing: Deathwriting from Dickinson to the Contemporary 206

11 Mere Being: Imagination at the End of the Mind 227

PART III ON THE CONTEMPORARY

12 Imagining the Future in the British Novel   255
13 Shallow Intensity: Neoliberalism and the Novel   275
14 To Carry Now Away: Happy Days in the Anthropocene   291
15 On Rereading Proust   308

Notes   340
Bibliography   372
Index   389

Figures

6.1	Rembrandt van Rijn, *Woman Bathing in a Stream*, 1654	*page* 141
6.2	Rembrandt van Rijn, *The Anatomy Lesson of Dr Tulp*, 1632	144
14.1	Caspar David Friedrich, *Two Men Contemplating the Moon*, 1830s	303
15.1	Sandro Botticelli, *The Trials of Moses* [detail], 1481–1482	328

Acknowledgements

James Baldwin, in his preface to the 1984 edition of *Notes of a Native Son*, thanks his friend and publisher Sol Stein for encouraging him to gather together a volume of his previously published essays. 'It was Sol Stein', he writes, 'high school buddy, editor, novelist, playwright, who first suggested this book'. He had never himself thought of the discrete pieces as a book. 'Once they were behind me', he says, 'I don't, in fact, think that I thought of them at all'. Without Sol, *Notes of a Native Son* would not exist, but Baldwin's thanks are somewhat ambivalent. 'Sol's suggestion had the startling and unkind effect of causing me to realize that time had passed. It was as though he had dashed cold water in my face'.

In collecting the essays in this volume, I too have realised that time has passed. To return in this way to my earlier writing self is to be reminded of a whole past which I was not aware that I carried about within me. I have no ambivalence, though, in thanking Ray Ryan – publisher, editor, literary critic, wise counsellor and friend – for suggesting this volume and for supporting it with his unique generosity and energy.

The majority of the essays collected here have previously been published, the oldest in 2002. That essay was written in the late 1990s when, much to my dismay, I barely needed to shave. A number of the other essays were written, in response to particular occasions or invitations, in the course of the following two decades, in the 2000s and the 2010s. Many have been written more recently, either for forthcoming publication elsewhere or for the purposes of this volume. Three essays – 'Mere Being', 'Happy Days in the Anthropocene' and 'On Rereading Proust' – have not been and will not be published anywhere else. I have dated each essay, to give a sense of the contexts in which they were written. Where an essay has not yet come out, or is not being published elsewhere, I have given the date of composition. In all other cases, I have given the year of publication. I have lightly edited earlier essays but have not sought to update them, so they bear the mark of their time. On occasion, I have inserted new footnotes to earlier essays, and in these cases, I have included the footnotes in square brackets.

Acknowledgements

To look back over a quarter of a century of writing is to find oneself recovering moments and discussions that had fallen into cracks in the mind. Mostly, it is to remember how many people are involved in the expression of every idea one has and to see that all thinking about literary possibility is a shared enterprise. Each of these essays carries echoes of conversations I have had over the years with students, friends, colleagues and loved ones. One of the great pleasures of working on this book has been to find these voices, conversations and friendships preserved; it has also made me newly conscious of the debts that I owe. Reading the earlier essays here brought back to me what a brilliant and diligent PhD supervisor I had in Drew Milne. I can feel also the constant presence of the people with whom I have the longest and closest working relationships: Laura Marcus, Nicholas Royle, Peter Nicholls and Andrew Hadfield. Many friends have read these essays in draft, and made them immeasurably better as a result. In particular, I have benefitted from the advice of Nicholas Royle (again), Tom Healy, Pam Thurschwell, Michael Jonik, Lara Feigel, Kate Briggs, Daniela Caselli, Devorah Baum, Arthur Bradley and Polona Osojnik. My niece Mae Losasso has read my work with great generosity and brought to it her characteristic fine intelligence. My partner, Hannah Jordan, is my first, closest, and most illuminating reader.

I have given the more recent pieces here as papers in several places – in Antakya, Turkey, in Fribourg, Switzerland, at the Huntington, California, at the Association for the Study of Australian Literature and at Brown University, Stanford University, Edinburgh, Bristol, Oxford, Warwick, Lancaster, Birmingham, UCL and Sussex. Audiences at all these talks helped me to develop and revise my thinking. In particular I would like to thank Tim Bewes, Thangam Ravindranathan, David Wills, Branka Arsić, Ian Duncan, Margaret Cohen, Andrew Bennett, Ayça Vurmay, Berkem Saglam, Niklas Fischer, Ankhi Mukherjee, Santanu Das and David James.

Over the decades that these essays were written, my three children, Ava, Laurie and Iris, were born and have, miraculously, grown up. Every thought I have tried to have here, about the kind of shared life that literature makes possible, has its origins in my love for them and for my partner, Hannah. My first and last thanks are reserved for them.

***

I would like here to acknowledge the editors and publishers who have published previous or forthcoming versions of the essays collected here. In each case, the version published in this volume is different from that published elsewhere.

'A Sort of Crutch: Race and Prosthesis in Herman Melville's Fiction' is forthcoming in *The Oxford Handbook of Melville* (Oxford: Oxford University Press, 2024), eds. Michael Jonik and Jennifer Greiman. 'Samuel Beckett: Towards a Political Reading' appeared in *Irish Studies Review*, vol. 10, no. 2, 2002. 'A Leap Out of Our Biology: History, Tautology and Biomatter in DeLillo's Later Fiction' appeared in *Contemporary Literature*, vol. 58, no. 4, 2018. 'A More Sophisticated Imitation: Ishiguro and the Novel' appeared in *The Cambridge Companion to Kazuo Ishiguro* (Cambridge: Cambridge University Press, 2023), ed. Andrew Bennett. 'A Cleaving in the Mind: Kelman's Later Novels' appeared as 'Narrative Limits: Kelman's Later Novels' in the *Edinburgh Companion to James Kelman* (Edinburgh: Edinburgh University Press, 2010), ed. Scott Hames. 'Zadie Smith, E. M. Forster and the Idea of Beauty' is forthcoming in *The British Novel of Ideas: George Eliot to Zadie Smith* (Cambridge: Cambridge University Press, 2024), eds. Rachel Potter and Matt Taunton. 'The Threshold of Vision: The Animal Gaze in Beckett, Sebald and Coetzee' appeared in the *Journal of Beckett Studies*, vol. 20, no. 2, 2011. 'The Anatomy of Realism: Cervantes, Coetzee and Artificial Life' appeared in *Anglistik: International Journal of English Studies*, vol. 26, no. 2, 2015. 'Back Roads: Edgeworth. Bowen. Yeats. Beckett' appeared in *Beckett and Ireland* (Cambridge: Cambridge University Press, 2010), ed. Sean Kennedy. 'Blind Seeing: Death Writing from Dickinson to the Contemporary' appeared in *New Formations*, vol. 89–90, 2017. 'Imagining the Future in the British Novel' appeared in *The Cambridge Companion to British Fiction, 1980–2018* (Cambridge: Cambridge University Press, 2019). 'Shallow Intensity: Neoliberalism and the Novel' appeared as 'Neoliberalism' in *The Cambridge Companion to Twentieth-Century Literature and Politics* (Cambridge: Cambridge University Press, 2023), eds. Christos Hadjiyiannis and Rachel Potter.

I would also like to acknowledge permission to reproduce the illustrations in the volume. Thanks to the National Gallery London, and the Mauritshuis in The Hague, for permission to reproduce the Rembrandt images. Thanks to the Galerie Hans, Hamburg, for permission to reproduce the Caspar David Friedrich.

Introduction
The Possibility of Literature

The phrase 'the possibility of literature' harbours two distinct forms of possibility. It refers in one of its senses to the conditions which make literature possible – the forces which dictate whether and in what ways literature can come into the world. And in the other it concerns the forms of possibility that literature itself creates, the possibility that it summons into being. The word 'of' is the pivot around which these two meanings turn.

The essays that are collected here are all centrally concerned with the hinge that is made by this 'of'. How far is literary expression a reflection of its conditions of possibility (as these are referred to in the first sense of the phrase)? How far can literature itself float free of these conditions in order to critique or reimagine the world that it represents? How does the genitive 'of' instantiate this double imperative, binding the possibilities that determine and delimit literary thinking to those that it invents?

In addressing these questions, these essays trace a selective and symptomatic history of the conditions of literary thinking, as they have played themselves out over the first decades of the twenty-first century. I wrote the oldest essay in this volume – 'Samuel Beckett: Towards a Political Reading' – at the turn of the twenty-first century, when I was in my late twenties. This essay, which grew out of a PhD thesis I completed in 1997, was already approaching this question of literary possibility – a problem which I belatedly realise I have been thinking about throughout my writing life. How, it asks, can we address the political power of Beckett's imagination – how can we give critical expression to the radical utopianism of his rejection of the world as it is – when that power is drawn so explicitly from its equally radical refusal of its own possibility. 'To be an artist' a young Beckett famously declared, in what had the feel of a kind of antimanifesto, 'is to fail as no other dare fail'.[1] Can we erect a literary politics upon this failure, a failure whose only possible achievement is that it radicalises itself ever more fully, so that it can only become potent through its heightened impotence, and can only succeed by failing better?

To ask this question at the turn of the current century was to ask it at a time when the broader critical consensus in the Anglo-American academy about what constituted a literary politics was coming unstuck. William Davies and Helen Bailey, in their 2021 volume *Beckett and Politics*, cite my essay as part of what they call a 'first phase' of criticism which addressed what has come to be known as a 'political Beckett', and which oriented itself in relation to that broader paradigm shift in our understanding of literary politics.[2] Before the arrival of this 'phase' – a first wave, perhaps, of 'political Beckett', but a third wave of Beckett criticism more generally – there was an uneasy agreement, among very different kinds of critic, that Beckett's writing constituted a rejection of the very possibility of political engagement or commitment. A first wave of critics who saw in Beckett's work the expression of a fundamental universal condition gave way, in the nineteen eighties, to a second wave which found in Beckett something very nearly the opposite, not a basic ground of human being, but the ontological groundlessness which it was a central task of later twentieth-century literary and critical theory to expose.[3] The critics in the first wave were often implacably opposed to those in the second, as proponents of each tended to face each other across the territory that was contested in what was known as the 'theory wars'. But for both groups of readers, Beckett's work was not, strictly speaking, political. It either eschewed political commitments in favour of a revelation of an underlying condition which was above, or beneath, or immune to, mere political life. Or it dismantled political life into the undecidable, unrepresentable, or unnamable conditions of being that are revealed to us in the deconstructive tendencies of literary expression.

So, to propose a 'political reading' of Beckett in the early 2000s was to push against an orthodoxy about literary politics that survived the great divides of the twentieth-century theory wars; but it was to do so, as I have said, at a moment when that orthodoxy was already coming undone. The political commitments of later twentieth-century literary theory tended to take place under the sign of the 'post' – the post that recurred in poststructuralism, in postcolonialism and in a host of other 'posts' which gathered under the umbrella term postmodernism. It was this collective function of the post (a prefix which became at this time kind of signifier in its own right) that Kwame Anthony Appiah had in mind, when he asked, in an influential 1991 essay of that title, 'Is the Post- in Postmodernism the Post- in Postcolonial?'. Appiah's answer to this question, broadly speaking, was yes. Postmodernism, he argued, involved what he called a 'clearing of the space', a 'distancing of the ancestors' (p. 342) in which the historical content of modernity is perceived to have been overcome, or 'transcended'.[4] This clearing, this overcoming of history, takes place, for Appiah, as a result of the emergence of a global public sphere, and of the globalization of capital. 'Postmodern culture', he writes, 'is global – though that emphatically does not mean that it is the culture of every person in the world' (p. 343). It is global because capital is global, and so the overcoming that we see in postmodern culture is the overcoming that we see too in the emergence of late stage capitalism. The experience of postness comes about as a result of the 'incorporation of all areas of the world and all areas of even formerly "private" life into the money economy' (p. 344). It is global capital, in its radical fungibility, that clears space, that frees us from our entrenchment in local places and histories, as it 'turns every element of the real into a sign' (p. 344). Postmodernism, as most theorists who have employed the term have recognised, is thus bound up in a close association with global capitalism, an association which causes difficulties for anyone seeking to contrive a postmodern politics that is not complicit with a western political economy. How does a postmodern cultural form, which has come about as a symptom of late capitalism, act as a critique of the operations of capital? This is a question that attends all thinking of postmodernism, and it is inescapable too, Appiah suggests, when we find that same prefix at work in postcolonial theory. When an attempt to think the aftermath of western colonial power is conducted through the shared logic of the post – when, as Appiah puts it, 'postcolonial meets postmodern' (p. 356) – we find that the very experience that the postcolonial thinker is seeking to recuperate, to recover from the western imperium, is put under the erasure that is the defining feature of the post. 'For the *post-* in postcolonial', Appiah writes, 'like the *post-* in postmodern, is the *post-* of the space-clearing gesture' (p. 348).

This space-clearing 'post' is the medium in which late twentieth-century critical thought takes place, its 'structure of feeling', its 'cultural dominant'.[5] It is powered, of course, by a wide range of theoretical forces and political commitments that are transformative in their own right, and which often do not themselves partake of the logic of the post. But it is one of the peculiarities of this period in western intellectual history that a diverse set of languages and thought forms – from deconstruction to the various strands of third wave feminism to theories of the rhizome – are subsumed under the sign of the post. Only such a peculiar effect could explain the illusion of a common ground between a thinker such as Fredric Jameson, whose career is spent trying to develop a language for a postmodern Marxism, and a thinker like Francis Fukuyama, who acts as a theoretical enabler for the more rapacious versions of Anglo American neoconservatism that emerged in the wake of Reagan and Thatcher. When Jameson writes, in his 2003 essay 'The End of Temporality', that the postmodern period sees the 'wholesale liquidation of futurity, of which the revival of Hegel's "end of History" was only an intellectual symptom', he no doubt has Fukuyama in mind, along with the common ground they seem to (but in fact do not) share.[6] Fukuyama's 'end of history', drawing on Alexandre Kojève's, is premised on the conviction that the 'countries of post-war Western Europe' – 'that is, those capitalist democracies that had achieved a high degree of material abundance and political stability' – are 'societies with no fundamental "contradictions" remaining'.[7] In the last decade of the twentieth century, Fukuyama writes, the liberal democracies of the west were 'emerging victorious' as all other forms and systems of government fell away, and we achieved a universal consensus on the rectitude of the 'liberal *idea*'. 'That is to say', he writes, 'for a very large part of the world, there is now no ideology with pretensions to universality that is in a position to challenge liberal democracy' (p. 45). This triumph of western democracy spells the end of history, because it means that there is no real alternative to liberalism, and so history, understood as a struggle between competing world views, is over. Of course, Fukuyama breezily concedes, 'many things could be improved'. We could 'house the homeless', for example, or 'guarantee opportunity for minorities and women' (p. 46). But nevertheless, despite these minor flaws in this best of all possible worlds, 'we cannot picture to ourselves a world that is *essentially* different from the present one, and at the same time better' (p. 46). Under these circumstances, we can see that the formation, in 1957, of the 'European Community' was 'an appropriate institutional embodiment of the end of history' (p. 67).

Jameson's 'post' and Fukuyama's thus yield oddly congruent pictures of historical finitude, even if the two thinkers come from diametrically opposed positions. 'In our grandparents' time', Fukuyama writes, 'many reasonable people could foresee a radiant socialist future in which private property and capitalism had been abolished' (p. 46). For both Fukuyama and for Jameson, such a future is no longer available. 'Few periods' Jameson writes, 'have proved as incapable of framing immediate alternatives for themselves, let alone of imagining those great utopias that have occasionally broken in the status quo like a sunburst'.[8] Fukuyama's liquidation of futurity comes about through the post-ideological consensus that, as he puts it in an article published, unironically, on 11 October 2001, the 'west has won';[9] Jameson's from his theoretical conviction that the 'historical tendency of late capitalism' is towards what he calls a 'reduction to the present', a weakening of historicity, a waning of affect.[10] It is a symptom of the post, of postness as a cultural dominant, that such different thinkers should arrive at a condition that feels so much the same, a condition of frictionlessness, of historical vapidity, in which it is difficult to gain any material purchase. And it was in this broader late century context that it proved so difficult to arrive at a reading of Beckett's work that could escape the sense that his writing was itself empty of historical content, was itself an expression of the end of history. Beckett's work, of course, conspires with this difficulty, and is in deep sympathy with a critical sensibility which is tending towards historical exhaustion, towards waning and weakening. Molloy speaks for many of Beckett's borderline creatures when he says that he lives in 'a world at an end, in spite of appearances' – a world in which 'I too am at an end'.[11] Molloy offers himself as a 'last man' – a version of the 'last man' that appears in the title of Fukuyama's book, and who, Fukuyama writes, 'reportedly emerges at the end of history' (p. 300). In *Molloy*, or in an empty late work such as *The Lost Ones*, Beckett presents us with dying worlds, which resist any attempt to tie them to a historical moment or a geographical space, and which tend to collapse critical thinking into itself, to confront it with its own limits. Indeed, it is hard to think of a more thoroughgoing depiction of critical and political exhaustion than *The Lost Ones*, in which the world consists of a 'cylinder' containing a global population of 'searchers' who are dying one by one, until we are left with one last searcher, a last man: 'There he opens then his eyes this last of all if a man'.[12] The searching of the searchers, despite its relentlessness, appears so futile, so facile, so empty of content, that it has the effect of emptying out any kind of critical inquiry that it might itself provoke, or that we might bring to it. Beckett's work appears not only to resist criticism, but to cause critique itself to malfunction. This is what Adorno means when he writes, in an influential early response to Beckett's 1956 play *Endgame*, that 'interpretation of *Endgame* cannot pursue the chimerical aim of expressing the play's meaning in a form mediated by philosophy'.[13] 'Understanding *Endgame*', Adorno says, 'can only mean understanding its unintelligibility, concretely reconstructing the fact that it has no meaning' (p. 243). It is what Derrida means, too, when he explains that he can't write about Beckett because he writes 'in my language, in a language which is his up to a point, mine up to a point'. Derek Attridge presses him on this feeling, that Beckett is 'too close' to him, that he in some way occupies the inside of his own language. 'Is there a sense', Attridge asks, 'in which Beckett's writing is already so "deconstructive", or "self-deconstructive", that there is not much left to do?'. 'No doubt', Derrida replies, 'that's true'.[14]

The reception of Beckett's work is bound up at the turn of the century with the critical logic which draws Derrida together with Jameson, Adorno and Fukuyama, into a false perception of historical finitude, what Adorno himself would call a 'reconciliation under duress' in which the rush to the post appears to have overcome the historical content of modernity.[15] But it is abundantly clear that this sensibility, this structure of critical feeling, so millenarian in character, does not survive the turn of the millennium. However fictional calendrical conventions are, historical change tends to become interwoven with them, with the passage from decade to decade, from century to century; and the entry into the twenty-first century coincided with a profound shift in the texture of western historical experience – a shift which is manifest in the quite dramatic expiry of 'postness' as an explanatory category. Fukuyama's conception of belatedness, of coming after the end, involved his sense that there are no longer any fundamental contradictions remaining at the heart of western democracy. In this he draws, again, on Kojève, and on the latter's claim that the modern western state has completed the '*real* process of historical evolution, in the course of which man *created* new Worlds and *transformed* himself by creating them'. With the completion of this process, Kojève writes, we are able to 'reveal *the* World – that is, to reveal being in the *completed* totality of its spatial-temporal existence'.[16] It was always a bizarre quirk of the late century historical mood that such a complacent and imperialist conception of historical completion could have become entangled with the postness at work in formulations not only of postmodernism but of postcolonialism, postfeminism and so on; but the early years of the current century destroyed this unlikely alliance, and revealed to us, in the plainest possible way, the contradictions that persist in the concept of western democracy, and that always underlay the various strands that went into the perception of postness, of the overcoming of a historical period of modernity. The dawning of the new millennium produced a recognition, widely felt, that history is not after all over, or at least that the end of a collection of historical structures and apparatuses (the dominance of postness being one of them) did not herald the end of everything, but rather saw the beginning of some new things, some different things.

It is conventional to date the arrival of this recognition in the western political imagination to 11 September 2001 – a date on which, like Woolf's 'December 1910', everything changed ('All human relations have shifted', Woolf writes, 'and when human relations change there is at the same time a change in religion, conduct, politics, and literature').[17] It was difficult at the time, and it remains difficult now, to accord to the terrorist attacks that took place on that day a proper historical scale. Jean Baudrillard, in a typically extravagant essay written a few months after the attacks, conceives of the event in the very terms, of historical finitude, that it seems to me to contest. 'We must' Baudrillard writes, 'assume that the collapse of the towers – itself a unique event in the history of modern cities – prefigures a kind of dramatic ending and, all in all, disappearance both of this form of architecture and of the world system it embodies'.[18] Baudrillard cannot address the event outside the millenarian tendencies that shape his own thinking, so he sees the collapse of the World Trade towers as the symbolic manifestation of some death drive in western power itself (a death drive which was always native to that power, and bound up with its unending persistence). 'Seeing them collapse themselves', he writes, 'as if by implosion, one had the impression that they were committing suicide in response to the suicide of the suicide planes' (p. 47). Such a response to the 9/11 attacks seems to me both offensive and exaggerated ('What has critique become', Bruno Latour asks, when a 'marshal of critique' can claim 'that the Twin Towers destroyed themselves under their own weight, so to speak, undermined by the utter nihilism inherent in capitalism itself?').[19] It is strikingly at odds with J. M. Coetzee's less grandiose assessment of their world historical significance, when he describes them, in the guise of one of his late alteregos, as 'the pin-pricks of terrorism'.[20] This question of scale was one of the challenges that the attacks presented, in their immediate aftermath, to our models of global politics and international relations. How might we find a credible means of measuring their magnitude? How might we decry this grotesque murder of innocent people, while situating it in relation to the wider global balance of power? Baudrillard's response suggested how unsuited his theoretical language was to that task, and how little purchase the language of 'dramatic ending' had on the consequences of the event. The attacks quite obviously did not signify the disappearance of the world system of late capitalism. But neither, as Coetzee knows when he uses the term, can they be seen as pin-pricks. Aside from their gravity in their own right as acts of terror, they represented and initiated a historical change whose consequences are still unfolding.

This shift, as it has played out over the two decades since the attacks, has taken many forms, all of which bear, as historical events always do, an uncertain and contingent relation to any single historical cause. The military response to the attacks – the invasion of Afghanistan and Iraq by the US led 'coalition of the willing' – has not only inflicted untold damage in the middle east, but has contributed to a much wider shift in the global balance of power.[21] The failure to secure a UN resolution to authorise the war in Iraq has had a lasting negative impact on the legitimacy of the United Nations, and the disastrous consequences of the wars in both Iraq and Afghanistan have exacerbated that impact. Tony Blair's support for US aggression, which was instrumental in securing the invasion without a UN mandate, was predicated on his stated belief in the benign power of global capital.[22] But the consequences of the wars that he enabled have caused even the zealous Blair to express doubts about the future viability of the global west. He wrote an essay, in response to the catastrophic withdrawal of the US from Afghanistan in 2021, that betrayed this crisis of Blairite faith, and that gave a peculiarly eloquent testimony to the damage that the wars he enabled have done to the very concept of western hegemony, in whose name they were fought. Both Blair and George W. Bush insisted that the wars in Iraq and Afghanistan were prosecuted in order to install democracy in the middle east – to continue that march towards the universalising of the liberal idea that Fukuyama celebrates in 1992. As Bush was fond of putting it, 'freedom' itself was 'on the march!'.[23] But Blair concedes, in 2021, that the belief in any such cause – scarcely credible when he championed it in 2001 – seems in the wake of the US withdrawal to be blatantly delusional. 'Today', he writes, on 21 August 2021, 'we are in a mood that seems to regard the bringing of democracy as a utopian delusion and intervention, virtually of any sort, as a fool's errand'.[24] As a result, he goes on, 'the world is now uncertain of where the West stands', and Blair himself fears that we are at 'a moment when the West is in epoch-changing retreat' (np).

The historical passage from the terrorist attacks in 2001 to the US withdrawal from Afghanistan in 2021 has seen this dramatic weakening of US hegemony – and interwoven with it has been a series of other failures that have made that late twentieth-century picture of an unassailable west look like the fantasy it always was. The global economic crash of 2008 fatally undermined the strand of neoliberal economics that saw the market as an engine for the production of wealth, and for the resolution of those contradictions that Fukuyama thinks have already vanished in the wake of the globalization of liberal democracy.[25] The models of globalization that drove centrist governments in the west throughout the later decades of the twentieth century were predicated on the idea that national boundaries would weaken, as we moved towards global communities, legitimated not by national sovereignty but by international trade. The 2008 crash upended that cultural logic, as national governments were forced to shore up their own economies, and to intervene in the market, whose freedom from any form of state control had been, since the collapse of the Bretton Woods agreement in 1973, the founding principle of the neoliberal project.[26] The historical tendency away from nation states and towards larger federations underwritten by global capital originated in the wake of the second world war with the establishment of bodies such as the United Nations in 1945, NATO in 1949, and, in 1957, the European Community, which Fukuyama and Kojève see as the 'institutional embodiment of the end of history'. The 2008 crash is part of a reversal of that historical logic, a reversal which takes us towards the UK's vote to leave the European Union in 2016, and the rise of ever more rampant right-wing nationalism in the US and across Europe. The collapse of the Soviet Union and the fall of the Berlin Wall seemed to many in the west, at the end of the twentieth century, to presage the inevitable growth of a global market place and the steady erosion of the nation state, but the first two decades of the twenty-first century have seen the failure of virtually every element of that neoliberal project. This reversal leads to Blair's fear, in August 2021, that the west is 'in retreat'; and it has an influence, too, on the first major conflict in Europe since 1945. Russia's invasion of Ukraine in February 2022 is, among other things, a manifestation of the expiry of the global US, and a sign that we are in the midst of a tectonic shift in the global balance of power between Russia, China and the west.

Under these circumstances, it is easy to see why the logic of the post, of the overcoming of historical contradictions, has not survived the turn of the century. It has been central to the experience of western cultural life in the current century that the dominant narratives that we have fashioned with which to expound the cultural logic of late capitalism are no longer serviceable (a failure which makes of the 'we' itself, which I continue to evoke throughout these essays, a kind of conundrum: who is this 'we', this 'our', this 'us'; what are the terms which govern such a community; who is included in it, who expelled; and what legislative or discursive forms can legitimate it?). Postmodernism was framed, by one of its most influential early theorists, as a movement based on a scepticism towards grand narratives ('The grand narrative', Jean-François Lyotard writes, 'has lost its credibility, regardless of what mode of unification it uses').[27] But, against the grain of Lyotard's own thought, postmodernism itself became, unmistakably, a grand narrative, a lingua franca which ascribed a kind of homogeneity to the diverse elements of contemporary life it encompassed. With the lapsing of the languages of postmodernism, with the peeling away of an estranged form of capitalism from the cultural languages that seemed to articulate it, we have found ourselves in a condition of near compulsory inarticulacy – an inarticulacy which is radicalised by the other dominant context for twenty-first-century cultural life, a context that dwarfs all others. That is, the phenomenon of climate change. As thinkers from Timothy Morton to Wai Chee Dimock to Ursula Heise to Timothy Clark have demonstrated, the climate emergency presents the most significant challenge to our critical capacities, a challenge that unsettles the fundamental terms in which we have conceived of the relation between the human and the planet, between culture and nature.[28] And yet despite, or perhaps because of the enormity of the threat that eco-crisis presents to our capacity to picture or inhabit the world, our critical literary forms have been strangely slow or reluctant to answer this demand. This is what Amitav Ghosh means when he writes that the 'climate crisis' is 'a crisis of culture and of the imagination' – that the 'currents of global warming' are 'too wild to be navigated in the accustomed barques of narration'.[29] It is what Richard Powers means when he urges us, speaking through his fictional alter-ego Mia Erdmann, to contemplate the sublime multiplicity of an ecology that lies outside of the terms in which human imaginative forms have framed it. 'When our stories yearn for a vanished world, green and pleasant', Erdmann writes, 'they do so out of sheer terror, however suppressed, at the real look of the energy bazaar that truly surrounds and encloses us'.[30] It is the task of our critical institutions, as it is the task of our literary forms, to overcome that terror, to find a way of seeing the world, shorn of its human forms. 'The real, bedrock deal', she says, 'is vegetative, fungal, invisible: superbugs, extremophiles, bacteria that thrive on acid and salt, that never see the sun, that live in suspended animation 320 degrees below Fahrenheit, or mass in a spoon of soil in concentrations beyond anyone's ability to number'. What kind of literature, what kind of philosophy, might approach such a world? 'What', Erdmann asks, 'would a literature that knew all this look like?' (p. 63–63).

Erdmann's question, asked in Powers' 2005 story, is our question, the question that has dominated critical thinking over the course of the last two decades, the question that has lain behind all of the essays collected in this volume. What kind of critical imagination can address a world which appears no longer to conform to the forms with which it has been made legible to us? However little we know about the world now, we know that it is not Kojève's world, the world that is created by us, and that can 'reveal being in the *completed* totality of its spatial-temporal existence'. It is a world that appears estranged from the forms in which we have imagined it and thought about it, and so the imperative that has driven twenty-first-century critical theory has been to discover new forms, new critical languages, new literary possibilities. With the failure of US hegemony, as Noam Chomsky puts it, we are led to ask whether 'another world is possible', and how to 'create constructive alternatives of thought'.[31] As the terms that have oriented twentieth-century thinking and imagining lapse – as our ecosystems become alien to us, as the idea of the west as a global organising principle falls into crisis, as the organising power of the post wanes – we have collectively sought a new language, a language that might replace or supersede the rhetoric of the 'post'. But that collective effort has been thwarted, at every stage, by the contradictions that it seeks to overcome. How does one supersede the language of the post, a language that is already grounded in a logic of supersession, a logic of supersession that has failed?

One response to this problem has been to look for forms of postness that might come after the waning of the post, a kind of mise-en-abime of belatedness in which our critical terms enter into infinite regress. We have tried on the various languages of the 'post-post', as we might try on an outlandish suit. We have experimented with something like a 'late post', as in Jeremy Green's *Late Postmodernism*, in which postness (as an expression of the logic of late capitalism) has itself entered into a late phase.[32] We have flirted with the idea of 'post-critique', most influentially in Rita Felski's elaboration of that term, in which we 'articulate a positive vision for humanistic thought' (p. 186) by trying to cure ourselves of the scepticism with which postmodern critique (as a hermeneutic of suspicion) has been associated.[33] These forms of post-postness then become bound up with other attempts to get past the exhaustion of postmodern thinking, by deploying terms such as 'metamodernism', or the 'new sincerity' (a movement, like Felski's post-critique', through which we try to escape the collapse into inarticulacy by repurposing a value system that predates the post).[34] But it is difficult to resist the feeling that these new terminologies lack conviction, and that they are symptoms of, rather than a redress to, the sense that the western academy has lost its critical authority, as the intellectual and political co-ordinates of the contemporary moment resist any kind of systematic theoretical or epistemological articulation. As John Guillory has recently argued, it is difficult not to see in the emergence of post-critique – in what he calls the 'rejection of disciplinary methods of reading in the postcritical moment' – a 'crisis of legitimation' and a 'crisis of faith'.[35] The urgent call, from many different strands in contemporary thought, for a 'decolonisation' of the university, is in part a response to this perception, this sense that the western university itself as a knowledge producer is irredeemably entangled with a colonial, fossil fuelled passage in world history that has passed, and so cannot itself be the vehicle either of renewal or of supersession, without making an epistemological leap that far exceeds the rhetoric of the post, or of the post-post. The troubling complicity between postmodernism and postcolonialism that Appiah sees in 1991 grows in the 2000s into a much broader scepticism about the capacity of our critical institutions themselves to outlive the passing of the European colonial age. Hamid Dabashi writes, in *Europe and Its Shadows*, that '"Europe" is a metaphoric moment that has exhausted its epistemic possibilities and has now positively imploded onto itself – and we need to move beyond it'.[36] Given that, as Priyamvada Gopal has recently argued, the 'Western university form' is a 'widely established colonial institution' which has been historically responsible for 'colonial knowledge gathering', it seems clear that for the university to produce new paradigms for critical thinking it needs to undergo a fundamental 'reckoning', as Gopal puts it, 'with its own self-constitution in the crucible of empire'.[37]

Without such a reckoning, without a refashioning of the cultural apparatuses of the west whose full scope and significance is not yet clear, our available critical languages struggle to achieve the kind of overarching articulacy that was arguably last seen in Jameson's *Postmodernism: Or the Cultural Logic of Late Capitalism*. The theorist who has come closest in the last decade to Jameson's capacity for articulating an encompassing cultural logic – Sianne Ngai – does so in a way that demonstrates, itself, something like the immanent failure of such a language to capture twenty-first-century experience. Ngai composes a set of new 'aesthetic categories' that are partly grounded in Jamesonian Marxist critique, and that have been more influential than any other aesthetic-critical formations proposed in the current century; but these categories cannot help but replicate a sense of their own malfunctioning. Most notably in her analysis of the 'gimmick', as what she calls an 'aesthetic response' to 'mature, crisis prone capitalism' (p. 33), Ngai's work exposes, and draws upon, the peculiar vacuity of its own procedures.[38] The gimmick, she argues, is a species of device that is both too efficient and not efficient enough. Its tricksiness derives from its capacity to seem effective, even wonderfully or magically so, while revealing that its wondrousness is also, and at the same time, defective, deceptive, unsatisfying. In this respect, Ngai shows, the gimmick is expressive of the operations of capital, which also seems to nourish where it starves, or better nourishes and starves at the same time. 'Overperforming and underperforming, encoding either too much or not enough time, and fundamentally gratuitous yet strangely essential, the gimmick is arguably

Introduction 13

a miniature model of capital itself' (p. 6). It is a mark of Ngai's singular critical power that she can harness this contradiction in the constitution of the gimmick, in order to deploy it as a means of examining what she calls, quoting Alberto Toscano and Jeff Kinkle, a 'social theory of capitalism as a totality' (p. 33); but it is a feature of the explanatory power that she finds in the gimmick that it partakes, itself, of the contradictions of the gimmick, that it is, itself, 'gimmicky'.[39] The theory of the gimmick, she acknowledges, is one that exhibits an excess of coherence, while threatening, as a result of that very excess, to become incoherent, as the gimmick will always be too explanatory and not explanatory enough. This is not a failure of Ngai's category – or if it is it is one that can only, in accordance with Beckett's logic, fail better – as it is an intrinsic part of its function to discover its coherence in its incoherence. When critique is bound up with capital in its 'mature' phase, Ngai's work suggests, then critique itself exhibits an antinomial relation between the overly expressive and the inexpressive, the perceptible and the imperceptible, the full and the empty.

This, then, is the fate of critique today, and in the first decades of the twenty-first century. Felski searches for a form of 'humanistic' thinking that might counteract the implosion of critique by reanimating older critical categories; Gopal calls for a dismantling of the terms on which the colonial university has been founded in order, in Dabashi's words, to 'move beyond' the shadow of European imperialism; Ngai employs a critical device that is itself a symptom of the operations of twenty-first-century capital as the only means of diagnosing our aesthetic response to those operations. These three responses map out the conditions of possibility of literary critical thinking now; and they set the terms, too, for the thinking conducted in the essays gathered together in this volume. Each of the pieces collected here – written at different times, and in response to different occasions – bears the mark of the limits to critique that I have sketched out in this introduction, the limits against which Ngai, Felski and Gopal conduct their own thinking, the limits that Amitav Ghosh and Mia Erdmann find in the failure of our literature to address the climate emergency. The essay on Beckett's politics – the earliest essay in the collection, and published here as Chapter 2 – reads for the continued existence of possible worlds in Beckett's work, even as the flow of his writing is towards the denial of such possibility. And then each of the other essays collected here presses against some element of resistance, some limit to thought. The essays address a range of writers – from Cervantes to Maria Edgeworth to Emily Dickinson; from Herman Melville and W.B. Yeats, to Henry James, Marcel Proust and Virginia Woolf; from Philip Roth and

Don DeLillo to James Kelman, Kazuo Ishiguro and Zadie Smith – a range of writers whose work makes these limits to the possibility of critique palpable. How is Melville's imagining of the prosthetic body limited and disfigured by what Toni Morrison calls 'whiteness as ideology' (Chapter 1)?[40] How does Ishiguro articulate the relation between the human and the machine in a posthuman environment, without recourse to reactionary categories of the human (Chapter 4)? How does the university as an institution examine or sustain the idea of aesthetic beauty, without simply reproducing beauty as a reactionary ideological category (Chapter 6)? How do new and experimental forms of realism and fictional representation press against the given boundaries between human and animal, and between human and non-human (Chapters 7 and 8)? How can we give critical expression to forms of counter-history, without simply translating those forms into the dominant language they seek to resist (Chapter 9)? How can we see or imagine an ontological ground to shared life – what Wallace Stevens calls 'mere being' – when our ways of seeing and thinking lead us to organise life into categories that can never be politically neutral or transparent (Chapter 11)?[41] How are we to imagine the future, when futurity itself appears estranged from our existing experience of duration, our languages of tensed being (Chapter 12)? How do we measure the relation between the superficial and the profound, the shallow and the intense, when cultural forms under late capital have elided that opposition, and rendered shallowness itself intense, and intensity shallow (Chapter 13)? How can we know or experience happiness when eco-crisis has made of the terms of human happiness a kind of sick joke, as well as an agent of toxicity (Chapter 14)? The closing essay offers rereading as a figure for the kind of work that literary criticism must do today – rereading as a continual attempt to approach a kind of literary possibility that continually eludes us. Does rereading allow us to repurpose a literary tradition, to make it expressive of and responsive to our own deranged contemporaneity? Or does rereading simply mark and perform the necessary inadequacy of our critical and aesthetic forms, their helplessness before the reading to come, the world to come, which will always evade our apparatuses for thinking, seeing and knowing?

In putting these questions, in relation to the various writers they address, these essays trace the conditions of possibility for a critical literature, as they unfold over the first two decades of the century, and in the wake of the 'post'. They enact, in the limits of their own articulacy, the ways in which a form of historical and temporal continuity – the persistence of history past Jameson's and Fukuyama's end of history – is flung free of the forms in which we might narrate it. In doing so, they suggest that the forms and institutions in which the possibility of literature finds itself enshrined – from our aesthetic categories, to the university as a custodian of critical thought – have inclined in these years towards a kind of atrophy. The tendency of critical expression, under these circumstances, is towards what Beckett calls the 'ideal tautology', the speech act, in Wittgenstein's terms, whose accuracy and truthfulness relies on its absolute vacuity.[42] The tautology, Wittgenstein writes, 'lacks sense'.[43] It has 'no truth-conditions, since it is unconditionally true' (p. 41). 'In a tautology', he says, 'the conditions of agreement with the world – the representational relations – cancel one another, so that it does not stand in any representational relation to reality' (p. 41). We can rely on the tautology to agree with itself, to enact a perfectly sealed form of self-reference. This is what Lauren Hartke discovers, in Don DeLillo's turn of the century novel *The Body Artist*, as she reflects on a box of breadcrumbs. 'She looked at the bread-crumb carton' the narrator says, 'for the first true time, really seeing it and understanding what was in it, and it was bread crumbs'.[44] It is what Jeff Lockhart thinks, in DeLillo's 2016 novel *Zero K*, as he is exiled to a minimalist cell in the desert at the end of the world. 'The ceiling was low, the bed was bedlike, the chair was a chair'.[45] The tautology exhibits the capacity of words to mean what they say. A chair is, unquestionably, a chair. Peter is inescapably Peter ('this is who you are' Althusser writes, 'you are Peter!').[46] But the increasing prevalence of the tautology in the Anglophone fiction of the later twentieth and twenty-first centuries is a mark not of a successful speech act, but of one which is tending towards emptiness, one which is losing its representational grip on reality. This is what Snowman, the protagonist of Margaret Atwood's 2003 novel *Oryx and Crake*, finds when the words that he learned in his youth no longer conform to the dystopian, posthuman world in which he now lives. He keeps lists of words that he wants to preserve – '*Mesozoic*', say, or 'valance', or 'serendipity'.[47] 'He can see the word', he thinks, 'he can hear the word'. But the word does not touch anything beyond itself. 'He can't attach anything to it'. 'This is happening too much lately', he thinks, 'this dissolution of meaning, the entries on his wordlists drifting off into space' (p. 43). As the world, in these late fictions, slides beyond the grasp of language, language itself becomes an empty piece of machinery, a stopped clock, whose only reference is to itself, its own sign system. 'The world shrinking down,' as the protagonist of Cormac McCarthy's novel *The Road* puts it, 'about a raw core of parsible entities':

> The names of things slowly following those things into oblivion. Colors. The names of birds. Things to eat. Finally the names of things one believed to be true [....] The sacred idiom shorn of its referents and so of its reality. Drawing down like something trying to preserve heat. In time to wink out forever.[48]

Atwood, DeLillo and McCarthy recognise here that the climate emergency, and the associated crisis of the human, has opened a gulf between language and the world – a gulf that is at the heart too of J. M. Coetzee's writing. Contemporary crisis requires us to attempt to see past what Coetzee calls 'the great Western discourse of man versus beast, of reason versus unreason', and thus to recognise that 'reason' itself 'is not the being of the universe nor the being of God'.[49] Instead, he writes, it looks 'suspiciously like the being of human thought', 'the being of a certain spectrum of human thinking' (p. 67). To think outside this spectrum, as the climate emergency requires us to do (as Powers' Erdmann requires us to do) is to see that reason itself is a kind of self-reference machine. 'For', Coetzee writes, 'seen from the outside, from a being who is alien to it, reason is simply a vast tautology' (pp. 69–70). Climate crisis makes language appear tautologous; this is what DeLillo sees, in his play *The Word for Snow*. When global warming turns white spaces green, the only referent of snow will be the word, snow. 'The word for snow will be the snow'.[50] It is what Jacques Derrida sees when he declares, with his own distrust of the capacities of critical reasoning, that 'critique and non-critique are fundamentally the same', that critique and non-critique have become oddly tautologous.[51] How, Coetzee asks, can we imagine a critical literature, when words themselves have lost their relation to the world, when Wittgenstein's 'representational relation' has failed? In a line which Timothy Bewes takes as an epigraph to his own recent attempt to imagine a future for critique, Coetzee writes that we are living at a moment in which 'the bottom has dropped out'.[52] 'There used to be a time', Coetzee's Elizabeth Costello says, when we knew how language related to reality. 'We used to believe that when the text said, "On the table stood a glass of water", there was indeed a table, and a glass of water on it, and we had only to look in the word-mirror of the text to see them' (p. 19). But at some unspecified point, some cataclysmic version of Woolf's December 1910, Costello says, all that changed. 'The word-mirror has broken, irreparably it seems [....] The words on the page will no longer stand up and be counted, each proclaiming "I mean what I mean"'. 'There used to be a time' she says, 'when we could say who we were. Now we are just performers playing our parts. The bottom has dropped out' (p. 19). The failure of this binding between word and world has inaugurated us, Bewes writes, into a 'postfictional age', an age in which the conventions that had allowed us to employ imaginative speech acts in order to orient ourselves to the world have lapsed – an age in which, in the words of Bewes's other epigraph, taken from Deleuze, 'the link between man and world is broken'.[53] Where Charles Dickens was writing at a time, for Bewes, when 'fiction is a fully operative category' (p. 44), a writer such as W. G. Sebald is writing in a 'postfictional universe', in which the capacity of language to oversee shared being – the Forsterian 'question of connection' – has failed. In Sebald's writing, 'it is no longer possible to distinguish the person writing from the person represented, the actions described from the act of description' (p. 43). Something has 'happened', between Dickens and Sebald, 'such that the kinds of social, economic, and ethical connections presupposed in Dickens's works are no longer possible'. In the passage from Dickens to Sebald, 'the fictional conceit has collapsed' (p. 43).

All of the essays collected here register some version of this collapse. The continued possibility of critical literary thinking takes place in its shadow – and not only in relation to writers that postdate whatever it is that has happened to cause the word mirror to shatter, the bottom to drop out. As both Coetzee and Bewes acknowledge, the historical location of this shift is elusive, and its effects are retrospective. It may be that, 'in Dickens', as Bewes puts it, the 'conceit is intact', and fiction is 'fully operative' (p. 44); but for us, reading Dickens, this is no longer so. To read Dickens now, is to read him under the conditions of fictional possibility that obtain now, just as Coetzee can see that to read Cervantes is to read him in our own time, the time in which words, for Coetzee, will no longer stand up and be counted. It is to read him as Simón and his adopted son David read him, in Coetzee's late trilogy of novels known as the *Jesus* books. As a young child, David teaches himself to read, miraculously, by studying an abridged copy of *Don Quixote*, and demonstrates to his surrogate father, Simón, his new skill. Simón 'chooses a page at random' from the book, and instructs the boy to 'read':

> 'God knows whether there is a Dulcinea in this world or not,' reads the boy, 'whether she is fatansical or not fatansical.'
> 'Fantastical. Go on.'
> 'These are not things that can be proved or disproved. I neither engendered her nor gave birth to her. What is engendered?'
> 'Don Quixote is saying that he is neither the father nor the mother of Dulcinea. Engendering is what the father does to make the baby. Go on'.[54]

This scene of reading takes place in the world that Coetzee imagines in the *Jesus* books – a strange, evacuated world, whose inhabitants have been 'washed clean' of their commitments and connections to each other, a purgatorial world of critical disorientation and emotional detachment that resembles, unmistakably, our own. In evoking Cervantes here, in a fictional world the status of whose reality is so uncertain, Coetzee stages a dialogue with the writer who, more than any other, established the terms in which fictional possibility is interwoven with the relation of writing to reality. Coetzee has called him the 'first of all novelists', who writes of a 'world where a living play of feelings and ideas is possible'.[55] But in David's reading, the tension between the fantastical and the not fantastical is calibrated according to the world in which David lives, a world where the relation between the imaginary and the real obeys something like Bewes's postfictional imperatives. It is to read him under circumstances in which the opposition between critique and non-critique has become obscure, and the critical languages we have for overseeing the productive exchange between mind and world (the exchange 'in the course of which man *created* new Worlds and *transformed* himself by creating them') have fallen into abeyance.

These are the circumstances that prescribe critical thinking today, and that oversee the possibility of critique in the essays that are collected here; but while these essays exhibit and demarcate the limits of critique, they also, and at the same time, work towards a form of literary possibility that continually exceeds those limits, even if it does so by entering into a zone of inarticulacy, a kind of speechlessness or unnamability. This excess, this entry into a region of poetic nonexpression threaded into expression itself, is at work even, or perhaps particularly, in those writers who are most concerned to deny its possibility. Coetzee's fiction stands as a rebuke to the conditions of literary possibility, a demonstration of the ways in which the literary imagination is bound up with the limits of what he calls human reason. Reason cannot free itself, Coetzee's Costello suggests, from the tautology of reason. 'Of course', she says,

> reason will validate reason as the first principle of the universe – what else should it do? Dethrone itself? Reasoning systems, as systems of totality, do not have that power. If there were a position from which reason could attack and dethrone itself, reason would have occupied that position; otherwise it would not be total.[56]

Reason can gain no access to non-reason, to a way of thinking that is not under its sway. Reason tends to absorb non-reason into itself, as critique, in Derrida's terms, tends to 'situate the non-critical in a place which would no longer be opposed to, nor even perhaps exterior to, critique'.[57] There is no place outside of 'systems of totality' from which to view the totality; and yet Coetzee's oeuvre, from beginning to end, is a demonstration of the porousness of the totality, when it is given expression in fictional form. His own narratives are machines for the production of a voice that does not belong within the sign systems that they create, a voice that occupies, in part, that position from which reason could attack and dethrone itself. It is the nature of fiction, the nature of literature, to bring that position into view, to show us that nonreason is a constituent part of our reasoning apparatuses, and so the province of a kind of critical thinking that is unique to literature, that happens every time literature happens.

We can see this happening – we can see literature happening – as David reads Cervantes's words in the strange, postfictional limbo that is the territory of Coetzee's late work. 'God knows whether there is a Dulcinea in this world or not'. 'I neither engendered her nor gave birth to her'.[58] These words, declaring the absolute undecidability of Dulcinea's existence, and the inoperability of our gendered rhetoric of conception and parturition, exceed any of the semantic fields from which they might emerge. Do they belong to Cervantes? Do they belong to Coetzee? Or to Simón, for whom they are read? Or to David, who reads them? Or to we who read David reading them? What language are they written in? Are they written in Cervantes's Spanish? Are they written in Coetzee's English? Are they written in the halting Spanish that David and Simón speak, the language which they adopt when they arrive in their limbo after their first language, whatever it was, has been 'washed away'? Simón asks David to copy down what he has read. 'Write down' he says, '"God knows whether there is a Dulcinea in this world or not"'. David obeys, and 'shows him his exercise book. *Deos sabe si hay Dulcinea o no en el mundo*, he reads: the line of words marches steadily from left to right' (p. 218). What kind of fiction is this? What kind of description? The steadily marching line of words, written in one language and then bewilderingly in another, emerging from one century and then another, one semantic field and then another, falls continually into a kind of unworded realm, a realm that cannot be subsumed under any given regime of signification, but that continually prises sign systems apart, that continually opens onto the outside of any system to which it might belong.

This capacity of literary writing to exceed its own terms is the engine of literary possibility, as it is conceived in the essays collected here. It is the force that is contained in the 'of' – the genitive that ties the conditions that make literature possible to the possibility that literature itself engenders. Literary possibility blasts open the limits that determine it as, for Walter Benjamin, it is the task of historical materialism to 'blast open the continuum of history';[59] but this excessive force emerges not from a *denial* of its determining conditions, not as a negative theology or an article of imaginative faith, but from those conditions themselves. This is the hinged nature of the 'of', which looks, like Benjamin's angel, two ways, which binds while it frees, frees while it binds ('I' Donne's poet writes, 'Except you enthral me, never shall be free').[60] Coetzee does not invent some 'being' that stands outside the 'vast tautology' of reason, does not grant some imaginary agent the power to see the 'universe', as Coetzee puts it in *Diary of a Bad year*, outside the 'paradigms of thought we bring to it'.[61] He no more gives us a consolatory version of the world, or of humans' place in it, than Samuel Beckett does – a writer who is one of Coetzee's key points of reference. Coetzee and Beckett are both concerned to provide us with pictures, in Beckett's phrase, of 'How It Is', rather than of how it might or ought to be. Beckett's *The Lost Ones* is as unenchanted a picture of the world as one can easily imagine, a world caught in the grip of that historical current towards finitude and futility that I have traced here in the passage of critique past its own conditions of possibility. The world of *The Lost Ones* is all that is the case, a total system, from which nothing is missing. 'In the cylinder alone', the narrator says, 'are certitudes to be found and without nothing but mystery' (p. 216). The searchers look for whatever it is they look for, turning restlessly around the sealed periphery of the cylinder, searching with their 'famished eyes', climbing up and down ladders in order to explore 'niches' that are secreted in the 'unbroken surface' (p. 220) of the walls. They search and climb in obedience to a set of elaborate rules which 'in their precision and the submission they extract from the climbers resemble laws' (p. 207). But whatever ethical spirit animates those laws, whatever erotic or intellectual longing compels the searchers to search, remains to us obscure. We cannot see beyond the limits of the totality. There is nothing behind the veil. There are no possible worlds, only this one, and there is no 'being', in Coetzee's terms, who can see it from 'outside'. To imagine such a being – a critical reader, say, who might come to some measured conclusions about the purpose of life in this place – is to meet with the remnants of Beckett's comedy, to experience, like Winnie in *Happy Days*, a 'brief … gale of laughter' when we 'happen to see the old joke again'.[62] When the narrator ponders what 'an intelligence' would be 'tempted to see' (p. 212) in this spectacle of searching – when he asks what 'a thinking being coldly intent on all these data' (p. 214) would make of life in the cylinder – he reduces thinking, critical intelligence, to a kind of comic fatuity, one which we struggle, even now, as we are coldly intent on yet another 'reading' of *The Lost Ones*, to cure ourselves of.

For Beckett, as for Coetzee, critique becomes fatuously mystical when it is bound up with a theological investment in the outside, the beyond. But even if this is so, it is a shared characteristic of their aesthetic that the possibility of a critical literature – of a critical reading – persists as an element of their picturing of a totality that has no outside. In the world of *The Lost Ones*, the narrator tells us, there is a history of religious belief, a history which has been characterised by doctrinal differences which are slowly ebbing away, as history itself moves towards its inevitable but unthinkable end. 'From time immemorial', he says, 'rumour has it or better still the notion is abroad that there exists a way out' of the cylinder:

> Regarding the nature of this way out and its location two opinions divide without opposing all those still loyal to that old belief. One school swears by a secret passage branching from one of the tunnels and leading in the words of the poet to nature's sanctuaries. The other dreams of a trapdoor hidden in the hub of the ceiling giving access to a flue at the end of which the sun and other stars would still be shining. Conversion is frequent either way and such a one who at a given moment would hear of nothing but the tunnel may well a moment later hear of nothing but the trapdoor and a moment later still give himself the lie again. The fact remains none the less that of these two persuasions the former is declining in favour of the latter but in a manner so desultory and slow and of course with so little effect on the comportment of either sect that to perceive it one must be in the secret of the gods. (pp. 206–207)

This is an extraordinarily mobile passage, one which performs, right in front of us, the capacity of language to create its own surplus that is the condition of literary possibility. It reads, in part, as an extension of a tradition of theological satire that has roots in Swift. The partisans of the secret passage and the hidden trapdoor are descendants of the big-endians and little-endians of *Gulliver's Travels*. For them, Dante's struggle towards the light of divine and earthly love is rendered merely comic. The 'flue' to which Beckett's trapdoor leads is taken from the moment at the end of the *Inferno* when Dante and Virgil emerge from darkness into an illuminated place where the sun and other stars were shining. 'We climbed', the poet says,

> he first and I behind, until,
> through a small round opening ahead of us
> I saw the lovely things the heavens hold,
> and we came out to see once more the stars.[63]

All three volumes of the *Divine Comedy* end with this movement towards the light, and all three endings are lit by their heavenly final word, 'stelle'.[64] But if the searchers' struggle towards that starlight persists in *The Lost Ones*, it does so only as a feature of the process by which the light dies. 'Its fatuous little light', the narrator says, 'will be assuredly the last to leave them' (p. 207), as the passage of history is the desultorily slow dawning of the recognition that our own epistemological and theological paradigms are artificial, tautologous. 'Thus by insensible degrees the way out transfers from the tunnel to the ceiling prior to never having been' (p. 207). The cancelling of the paradigms of knowledge and belief are here equated with the end of history, and the last man. But what is so compelling about this passage, what makes it such a provocation to critical reading, is that its narration of the historical trajectory towards finitude continually escapes that narrative, continually exposes and exceeds the limits of that historical paradigm. Religion dies in the cylinder, 'in accordance with the notion requiring as long as it holds that here all should die' (p. 206). It is the nature of entropic systems to dwindle and die. As Lucky tells us in *Waiting for Godot*, despite the existence of a 'personal God quaquaquaqua with white beard quaquaquaqua outside time without extension' who 'loves us dearly with some exceptions for reasons unknown but time will tell', it is 'established beyond all doubt' that 'man in short man in brief in spite of the strides of alimentation and defecation is seen to waste and pine waste and pine'.[65] Religion dies; 'but it does so with so gradual and to put it plainly so fluctuant a death as to escape the notice even of a visitor' (p. 206). Even a visiting 'intelligence' looking on at the cylinder, even a 'thinking being' coldly intent on anatomising this system, could not put their finger on the moment that this death occurs. The death of religion, the death of history, is so slow, so gradual, so fluctuant, that in order to perceive it, you have to be in the secret of the gods. You cannot see it from your position inside the cylinder, inside the paradigm, inside the tautology. In order to see the process by which belief dies, you have to occupy the very position that the death of belief is slowly, gradually, fluctuantly revealing to be non-existent.

This is emphatically not to say that Beckett's writing, or Coetzee's, summons faith from atheism, praise from burial. There *is* no way out, no exit from the cylinder and no mystical outside that is the province of an intelligence or of a thinking being. But what *The Lost Ones* does demonstrate, as clearly, as coldly as it is possible to demonstrate, is that the languages that allow us to see the world in which we live, that allow us to describe it to ourselves and each other, include within them, as a part of their constitution, an unworldliness, or otherworldliness, that cannot be eradicated, and that it is the vocation of literary thinking to animate. The narrator describes to us the world of the cylinder, and the rules that govern the society of searchers that live there, in such a way that we can see that the 'needs of the cylinder' are met, 'so all is for the best' (p. 216). The echo here of Leibniz, and behind that of Voltaire, suggests that the tautological adequacy of description here eradicates the possibility of other worlds.[66] This desperate hell is the best of all possible words, the only possible world. But it is the brilliance and the singularity of *The Lost Ones* to see that the narrative refusal of possible worlds is the very mechanism that opens the cylinder to possibility. The narrator appears to change his mind, towards the close of the narrative, to rethink. The turbulent climate in the cylinder, the vibrating movement from extreme heat to extreme cold that obtains there, suggests to him that perhaps the end of history has not yet arrived after all, and so the world that we see is not quite yet all that is the case. 'The persistence of the twofold vibration suggests that in this old abode all is not yet quite for the best' (p. 223). We can read best, here, as worst (as the narrator of *Worstward Ho* commands himself to 'say that best worst').[67] Best and worst become interchangeable, at this limit to expression, and so the deferred arrival of the best of all possible worlds is the only flicker we have of hope for a better one. But it is not actually the case that the narrator changes his mind here, or has some volte-face concerning the texture of historical finitude in the cylinder. It is the discovery of this text that continuation is woven into finitude, that the picture of a history that is already over summons that very historical surplus that indicates to us that history continues, even if it does so in a way that has no language for itself, no duration, no tense. The continuation of history takes place in that outside to the cylinder that the narrative itself equates with the refusal of its existence, that impossible space from which it is possible to see, without seeing, the slow death of belief, among the little people of searchers, the dying of that fatuous little light. 'Its fatuous little light will assuredly be the last to leave them always assuming they are darkward bound' (p. 207).

This peculiar tension between 'assuredly' and 'assuming' opens the fracture that runs through the cylinder of *The Lost Ones*, the fracture that testifies to the possibility of literature as it is conceived throughout the essays collected here. The certainty of death, the absolute refusal of any way out of the predicament of being as it is encountered in the cylinder, owes its certainty, its assuredness, to the assumptions that structure that predicament. As the most insistent refrain of *The Lost Ones* has it, the 'certitudes' that are to be found 'in the cylinder alone' are certain only 'if this notion is maintained', only within the 'paradigms of thought' that we bring to it.

The task of reading Beckett's work, outside of the critical consensus with which I opened this introduction, is one which requires us to dwell in the opening that occurs when, for an unmeasured instant, the paradigms that structure thinking give way, and we see that the non-existent outside of the cylinder is a structuring principle of its inside, of the languages with which we encounter it. As Coetzee puts it, in his own essay on Samuel Beckett, 'Something opens and then almost immediately closes again. In that split second a revelation takes place. It is trying to be understood (language creaks under the strain) how the universe works, what the laws are'.[68] To read the possibility of literature, as I do in these essays, as it is at work in writing from Cervantes to Coetzee, from Edgeworth to Dickinson to Woolf, from Melville to James to Roth, is to approach this split second revelation, this sense that we can see in the darkness of a world that lies outside the spectrum of human thinking. Few writers, of course, approach this opening, this split second, with the austerity that we find in Beckett, and that is reflected in Coetzee. Beckett stands as a limit case, a test of the possibility of literature at its furthest edge. But the terms in which Beckett binds and liberates critical possibility to and from its refusal points towards a form of critique, a form of literary thinking that might survive the historical moment we have reached now, in which it has become so difficult to see the opposition between critique and non-critique. It is this form of critique that is put into a kind of motion, when David reads from his abridged copy of Cervantes in Coetzee's *Childhood of Jesus*, and we see deep into the join between the fantastical and the not fantastical. It is this form of critique that is at work when Toni Morrison rereads Melville, and finds in him a brief and difficult suspension of whiteness as ideology. It is what we see, in Emily Dickinson, when her poetry allows her to 'grow accustomed to the Dark', to discover that the darkness of unknowing is threaded into the light of thought, so that 'What I see not, I better see'.[69] It is what we see, in Virginia Woolf's last novel *Between the Acts*, when an amateur village pageant recreates the history of England, playing it out on a 'natural stage' in the grounds of a country house in 1939, as the forces of history propel us towards world war. Woolf's novel anatomises the join between history and fiction, as they conspire to write us into our being; but it turns, at its heart, around the recognition that literature makes briefly perceptible a kind of being, a kind of between, that has not been conscripted to any fiction, or any history. As one of the actors in the pageant says to its author, 'You've stirred in me my unacted part'.[70]

It is this unacted part, this visible darkness, that these essays seek to bring to critical expression, as a way of approaching the continued possibility of literature in our time. But if this is so, if this volume offers a theory of literary possibility in the wake of 'theory', it does so in the understanding that such possibility evades any given theoretical or political apparatus. There is no 'post' to append to any descriptors of our cultural life that could capture this kind of possibility, and no new critical vocabulary that could render it legible. Rather, the only kind of theory that these essays can lay claim to is a constellatory theory, in the sense in which Walter Benjamin uses that term, a theory that emerges from the disaggregation of its elements. 'Resolute refusal of the concept of "timeless truth" is in order', Benjamin writes in *The Arcades Project*. But such a refusal does not consign us to fatuity, or non-criticality. Truth is not a 'merely contingent function of knowing, but is bound to a nucleus of time lying hidden within the knower and the known alike'.[71] It is this nucleus of time that Benjamin sees contained within the literary image, as it flashes upon us, in that split second interval that Coetzee finds in Beckett. 'It is not', Benjamin writes, 'that what is past casts its light on what is present, or what is present casts its light on what is past; rather, image is that wherein what has been comes together in a flash with the new to form a constellation' (p. 463). Cervantes does not cast his light on Coetzee, or Coetzee his on Cervantes; rather, this coming together forms a constellation, a literary moment of being that lies outside of what Marcel Proust calls the 'field of possibilities'.[72] 'The image that is read –', Benjamin writes, 'which is to say, the image in the now of its recognizability – bears to the highest degree the imprint of the perilous critical moment on which all reading is founded' (p. 463).

The essays that are collected here bear the imprint of our perilous critical moment in the images that they recover, the fleeting forms of nonbeing that stir, unacted, in the collective literary mind. They testify at once to a kind of inarticulacy, a theoretical insufficiency in relation to the world before us, and to a continued, ravening thirst for the kind of knowing, the kind of truth, that literary writing promises. The volume concludes with an essay on Proust – 'On Rereading Proust' – that is a testament both to that inarticulacy, and to that thirst. Proust shows us that literature is never consigned to a given reading, never yields to a theory, as all literary knowing awaits the reading to come. As Marcel realises, at the orchestral close of *A la recherche*, literature calls always to a rereading, in which 'this life that we live in half-darkness can be illumined, this life that at every moment we distort can be restored to its true pristine shape'.[73] It is the constellatory image, Benjamin writes, in his own essay on Proust, that bears the mark of this truth, forever offering itself to us, forever withholding itself from us. The image in Proust contains its own separation, its own falling into the disunity of which it is made, while also, at the same time, harbouring a 'rejuvenating force' that might overcome that disunity, in a sudden moment of pristine clarity. 'When the past is reflected in the dewy fresh "instant," Benjamin writes, 'a painful shock of rejuvenation pulls it together once more'.[74] Half-darkness is the province of illumination in Benjamin's Proust, as it is the province of literary possibility in the essays collected here. We are living in what Emily Dickinson calls a time of 'larger – Darknesses'; critical thinking takes place now in what she calls the 'Evenings of the Brain'.[75] We are at a moment when our given critical forms cast only a dusky and intermittent light. But in Dickinson, in Proust, in Beckett, in Coetzee, literary thinking takes place in the dark, or the half-dark. The literary image makes of darkness a kind of illumination, a lighter blindness, so that, as we look into the obscurity of our own present,

> Either the Darkness alters –
> Or something in the sight
> Adjusts itself to Midnight –
> And Life steps almost straight.[76]

2023

PART I

On Writers

CHAPTER 1

A Sort of Crutch
Race and Prosthesis in Herman Melville's Fiction

Is it possible to speak without a prosthesis?

This is a question that occupies much of Herman Melville's fiction, not only in his great novel of prosthetic imagining, *Moby Dick*, but across his fiction. From *Typee* to *Bartleby the Scrivener*, to *Benito Cereno*, to the late and unfinished *Billy Budd*, one can see Melville's work as an extended examination of the means by which voice attaches itself to its apparatuses.

Consider, for example, *Billy Budd*. This is a story, above all else, about the mechanics of speech. Billy is an example of what Melville calls a 'Handsome Sailor' – a beautiful, 'welkin-eyed' (p. 104) specimen of manhood, who attracts all those (men) around him and who establishes good will and harmony in any ship in which he sails. The chief characteristic of the handsome sailor in general, and of Billy's 'masculine beauty' in particular, consists in a certain affinity between the inside and the outside of being.[1] 'The moral nature', Melville's narrator says, 'was seldom out of keeping with the physical make' (p. 104). Billy's handsome exterior – what Ishmael calls his 'clayey part'[2] – is 'lit' by that true moral nature that shines within him: 'the bonfire in his heart made luminous the rose-tan in his cheek' (p. 129). Billy's skin is eloquent, like that of John Donne's Elizabeth Drury, whose blush 'spoke in her cheeks' so that 'one might almost say, her body thought'.[3] This accord between inner nature and bodily extension is mirrored, we are given to understand, in Billy's voice. Captain Graveling (the good captain of the *Rights-of-Man*, the merchant ship in which we first meet Billy) is notable for a 'certain chime in his voice' which 'seemed to be the veritable unobstructed outcome of the innermost man' (p. 105); Billy too has some such chime. 'He was illiterate', the narrator says. 'He could not read, but he could sing, and like the illiterate nightingale was sometimes the composer of his own song' (p. 110). Billy's voice, like Captain Graveling's, is 'unobstructed'. It does not pass through the medium of written language, of which Billy knows nothing, but expresses itself, unmediated, with the full-throated ease of Keats's nightingale. But,

29

of course, the fatal element of Melville's tale lies in a flaw in Billy's speech, a 'vocal defect', which acts to obstruct the flow from the innermost man to his outer form. Billy has a stutter. 'Under sudden provocation of strong heart-feeling his voice, otherwise singularly musical, as if expressive of the harmony within, was apt to develop an organic hesitancy, in fact more or less of a stutter or even worse' (p. 111).

Everything that happens in *Billy Budd* is determined by this defect, through which the connection between voice and thought is broken, so Billy's musical voice is reduced to what Avital Ronell calls a 'technosputter' that 'profiles the mechanical effect of language', a language which 'conveys', as Barbara Johnson puts it, 'only its own empty, mechanical functioning'.[4] Billy's stutter marks what Johnson calls a 'deadly gap in his ability to speak' (p. 94), one that reveals itself under the 'provocation' of social injustice, of a prevailing tendency for words not to mean what they say, for the passage between the inner and the outer to be 'obstructed' by devious and ill intent. The particular instance of stammering around which the novel turns – the moment when Billy's inability to get his words out leads to tragedy – is provoked by the ill will of Billy's shipmate Claggart, whose jealousy of Billy (and implicitly his thwarted desire for him) drives him, like Shakespeare's Iago, to poison the ship's captain against him. Claggart also speaks in a tuneful voice – his voice is 'musical' (p. 125), it is 'silvery and low' (p. 143) – but where Billy's speech is the mark of his transparent honesty and ingenuousness, Claggart's is the smooth, insinuating voice of the dishonest manipulator. Claggart stands before Billy and Captain Vere and accuses Billy, falsely, of fomenting a mutiny against the captain. Vere, like everyone else, is drawn to Billy. He has a protective, paternal feeling for him and does not believe the accusation against him. As Billy stands, dumbly bewildered by Claggart's brazen treachery, Vere tries to encourage him, tries to ease him into a state where he can speak for himself, can deny the accusation against him. 'There is no hurry, my boy', he says. 'Take your time, take your time' (p. 145); but the kindness of the words, 'so fatherly in tone' (p. 145), only congests Billy further, leading him to 'strain forward in an agony of ineffectual eagerness to obey the injunction to speak and defend himself' (p. 145). The corruption of Claggart's voice breaks the immediacy of Billy's, and as his voice becomes paralysed, unable to pronounce his evident innocence, so his body becomes prosthetic, automatic, mechanised. While he cannot speak to defend himself, his body acts as if of its own accord, with no bidding from the morally paralysed Billy. 'The next instant, quick as the flame from a discharged cannon at night, his right arm shot out, and Claggart dropped to the deck'

(p. 145). Billy's body acts without the direction of his mind, and in so doing it produces a dramatic prosthetising effect on Claggart, as both men demonstrate the disastrous effects of a breach between inner being and outer, between mind and spirit. Claggart is immediately despatched by the blow, in a fashion that not only kills him, but renders him into an object, a 'body' which is estranged from any form of life: 'the body fell over lengthwise, like a heavy plank tilted from erectness. A gasp or two, and he lay motionless' (p. 145). The smooth passage between mind and voice that makes Claggart such a masterful manipulator is broken at the same time as he succeeds in breaking Billy's. As Captain Vere puts it, in tying Billy's innocent tongue as he does, Claggart himself is condemned to a 'lasting tongue-tie' (p. 152).

It is the central aim of *Bully Budd* to examine the role of narrative voice in navigating this relation between a moral interior and the outside world in which the conscious being is required to act. The novel has the subtitle 'An Inside Narrative', because it asks how far narrative is able to cleave to an inside, to be true to it, while also making it appear on the outside of things, on the visible surface. Billy's innocence, his illiteracy and the childish simplicity which leads the crew to name him 'Baby Budd' rest on his unawareness of any gulf between thought, speech and action. Billy partakes of the same transparency that Voltaire ascribes to his naif Candide, when he opens *Candide* with the resonant remark that 'his mind could be read in his face'.[5] But it is with precisely the gulf between mind and face, between thought and speech, that Melville's novel is concerned, and with the perception that between inner being and social action there intervenes a discursive fabric which is fully integrated with neither. After Claggart's death, Vere convenes a 'drum-head' court, composed of members of the ship's crew, which is charged with the task of determining whether Billy is innocent or guilty. Vere and his fellow jurors are intuitively convinced of Billy's innocence. He is a 'fellow creature innocent before God, and whom we feel to be so'. 'I too feel that', Vere says, 'the full force of that. It is nature' (p. 153). Nature would find Billy innocent, but, Vere says, it is not with natural justice that the drum-head court is concerned but with justice as it is codified in British martial law (as Victor Hugo's Javert is concerned not with the spirit but with the letter of the law).[6] Vere puts a series of heightened rhetorical questions to the court. 'Do these buttons that we wear', he asks, 'attest that our allegiance is to Nature?' (p. 153). 'Though the ocean, which is inviolate Nature primeval, though this be the element where we move and have our being as sailors, yet as the King's officers lies our duty in a sphere correspondingly natural?' No, he says.

Our allegiance is not to nature, it is 'to the King'. Our duty does not lie in a natural sphere – 'So little is that true, that in receiving our commissions we in the most important regards ceased to be natural free agents' (p. 153). In acting as the mouthpiece of the law, Vere says, the court itself becomes prosthetic, renouncing that immediate organic correspondence between spirit and material, between nature and culture, that made Billy a 'Handsome Sailor'. Even though Billy has done nothing wrong, even though the crime that the court is adjudicating on consists not in Billy's spontaneous defence of himself but in Claggart's corruption of the language of natural justice, the court can only compound that tragedy by acting against the call of nature, and in favour of the unjust diktats of the law. And it is this law that the court must serve, because we do not speak as ourselves, or as natural beings, but as social beings, socially constructed. 'For suppose condemnation to follow these present proceedings', Vere says:

> Would it be so much we ourselves that would condemn it as it would be martial law operating through us? For that law and the rigor of it, we are not responsible. Our vowed responsibility is in this: That however pitilessly that law may operate in any instances, we nevertheless adhere to it and administer it. (p. 153)

The law is an artificial and not a natural construct, and so abiding by it, enforcing it, requires us to forsake that harmony between moral nature and physical make that grants Billy his masculine beauty. It reduces us to voiceless apparatuses through which the law speaks. This is the thought that animates not only *Billy Budd* but all of Melville's fiction. Billy is the manifestation of a desire to speak without a prosthesis, to speak as a 'natural free agent', to free himself from what Nicholas Royle has called the 'veering' that is at work in Captain Vere's administration of the law (in which, Royle writes, the homophone of Vere's name 'signifies 'truth' and 'faith' but also (as 'Bartleby the Scrivener' encourages us to suppose) a *veering about*').[7] This is the desire too of Ahab. The man who is a patchwork of prostheses, who walks on a whalebone leg, is ravaged and compelled by a desire to free himself from all attachments and encumbrances, to live as pure, unalloyed spirit. It is the desire of Bartleby, the pale scrivener, who would prefer not to. He would prefer not to copy out legal documents for his employer. He would prefer not to duplicate himself, or extend himself, or adumbrate himself. He would prefer not to eat ('I prefer not to dine today', he says, 'It would disagree with me; I am unused to dinners').[8] He would prefer not to live, if living involves a prosthetic addition to the starveling mind. Ishmael speaks for all of these refusers of the prosthesis when he says that 'whether by day or by night, and whether asleep or awake, I have a way of always keeping my eyes shut'.[9] To see the social world is to accept that it is composed according to laws that we ourselves have not agreed upon, that we were not consulted on, that we abhor. It is to accept that one's identity is an alloy of what one is and what one is not, so it is best to keep one's eyes shut if you are Ishmael, to prefer not to see if you are Bartleby, to attempt through main force to make the bony world conform to your way of seeing if you are Ahab, to think like an unborn child if you are Baby Budd. 'Because', Ishmael says, 'no man can ever feel his identity aright except his eyes be closed; as if darkness were indeed the proper element of our essences, though light be more congenial to our clayey part' (p. 55).

Narrative voice in Melville, Melville's 'inside narrative', is generated by contact with this darkness that is the 'proper element of our essences' and which lies like a seam of imaginative possibility between unextended and extended being. The refusal of a prosthesis, combined with the recognition that the law of social being requires that we overcome such refusal, is the contradictory impulse of Melville's fiction, an impulse for which he finds an origin, as he does for so much of his literary thinking, in Shakespeare.[10] The desire of Melville's protagonists to speak without a prosthesis derives from Hamlet's discovery of a form of narrative voice that emerges, inchoate, almost unmade, from the Elizabethan stage. When Hamlet sets out to contrive a device through which to prove the truth or falsehood of his dead father's claim – that he was murdered by his brother Claudius, so that Claudius could usurp his throne and marry his wife Gertrude – it is to this naked narrative voice he turns. The spectral father's accusation won't become manifest in the form of a voice – of another prosthetic addition to spirit. Rather, it will come in the form of an inside narrative, a narrative that emerges only in the darkness of a pure imaginary, the unformed possibility of literary being. He will stage a play within a play, Hamlet thinks, and so draw on the underground space beneath speech and language, that dark place from which all forms of action arise but which itself is unenacted, like Virginia Woolf's 'unacted part'.[11] He will coax the truth not from words but from the underside of words, 'For murder, though it have no tongue, will speak / With most miraculous organ'.[12] The play within the play does not shine a light on the truth but makes the darkness in which the truth is embalmed – the abyssal ground that opens between outer play and inner – briefly, spectrally visible. This is the dark in which Ishmael lies, when he closes his eyes. It is the darkness in which the poet of Shakespeare's sonnets learns to see ('When most I wink, then do mine eyes best see').[13] It is the night, 'brightly dark', in which those writers who have a sidelong affinity with Melville are able to see – the night of Dickinson's verse ('What I see not, I better see'),[14] or that of the strenuous refusers of prostheses in Beckett's fiction (think of Malone, whose only true gift is that he is able to 'close my eyes, close them really, as others cannot').[15]

Melville's protagonists, Ishmael, Billy, Bartleby, all belong to this minor tradition of dark seers – figures who see without light, who speak not with what Katie Chenoweth has called a 'prosthetic tongue' but only with Hamlet's 'most miraculous organ'.[16] But if the refusal of the prosthesis is common to Melville's speakers, it is in his short 1855 novel *Benito Cereno* that this refusal reaches its most intense pitch, and here too that the implicit stakes of the prosthetic voice, as it is imagined throughout Melville's fiction, become explicit. It is in *Benito Cereno* that it becomes most clear that, for Melville, to think about prosthetics is to think about race.

Benito Cereno is the story of a revolt aboard a slave ship named the *San Dominick* – a revolt that Michael Rogin has called 'the only successful mutiny in all of Melville's fiction'.[17] We see the revolt through the eyes of the protagonist, Amasa Delano, who is the captain of a 'large sealer and general trader' named the *Bachelor's Delight*. The story opens as Delano discovers the *San Dominick* floundering at the mouth of the 'harbor of St. Maria – a small, desert, uninhabited island toward the southern extremity of the long coast of Chili' (pp. 34–35). Delano boards the *San Dominick*, to help it make safe passage into the harbour, and the story follows Delano's attempt to make sense of the spectacle that he finds on board the ship, a spectacle that unfolds for the reader in the same manner, and under the same time signature, as it unfolds for Delano. Delano finds the ship in disarray. The African slaves (who the narrator calls the *San Dominick*'s 'living freight') are not fettered but are free to move around the ship, where they mingle with the Spaniards who make up the crew. In this mingling, Delano finds a 'spectacle of disorder' (p. 58) that he can't easily fathom, a disorder that seems to him of a piece with the 'sad disrepair' (p. 37) of the ship, the tattered sails, the barnacled hull, and most of all the dilapidated stern piece and the shrouded figurehead (the stern piece depicts a 'dark satyr in a mask, holding his foot on the prostrate neck of a writhing figure, likewise masked'; the figurehead is wrapped in canvas, 'either to protect it while undergoing a refurbishing, or else decently to hide its decay' (p. 37)). The chaos and disorder on board the ship alarms and bewilders Delano, but the most perplexing element of the scene, for him, is the attitude of the ship's captain, Benito Cereno. Delano finds Cereno standing listlessly in the midst of the chaos, among the 'noisy indocility' of the Africans. He is 'dressed with singular richness', adorned in the garb of European aristocratic authority and colonial power. But as all is in ruin around him he seems to show no concern, no agency, no captaincy. Instead, like Bartleby, he appears hardly present at this scene of bedlam. Bartleby is a 'poor, pale, passive mortal';[18] Cereno, in his effeminate finery, 'stood passively by, leaning against the main-mast, at one moment casting a dreary, spiritless look upon his excited people, at the next an unhappy glance toward his visitor' (p. 39).

Delano can't make sense of the scene before him, because he has no language for black power, and so cannot even begin to imagine that Cereno's passivity, his 'cloudy languor' (p. 41), might represent white power overthrown, or the transfer of power from white to black, from Spaniard to African. Neither can Delano begin to understand the true relation between Cereno and his 'body servant' Babo, the African who attends closely at all times to Cereno, never letting him out of his sight or his reach. Delano, seeing the scene through his fixed conception of white supremacy, can only interpret Babo's intense proximity to Cereno as a form of exaggerated devotion, and so is utterly blind to the fact – hidden in plain sight – that Babo, the leader of the revolution, is violently controlling Cereno's every move. Babo stands by Cereno's side not in order to support him but to force him, on pain of death, to uphold the story that has been hastily devised in order to hide from Delano, the inconvenient visitor, the truth of the revolt. As the story follows Delano's misreading of the scene before him, it is the framework of Delano's shifting conception of power and agency that becomes the central drama of the narrative – a drama which turns on the nature of voice, and more specifically of prosthetic voice. When Delano first encounters Cereno and Babo on the deck of the *San Dominick*, he finds them in a kind of embrace that is unmistakably that of puppet and puppet master – an embrace through which Cereno is forced, like a ventriloquist's dummy, to tell Babo's cover story, according to which the disorder on the ship, and the death of the ship's officers, is due not to rebellion but to an outbreak of disease. Cereno himself appears to have fallen victim to that disease – his 'distempered spirit was lodged', Delano thinks, 'in as distempered a frame' (p. 40) – and one of the symptoms of this distemper is a cough that renders Cereno nearly speechless. 'His voice', Delano thinks, 'was like that of one with lungs half gone, hoarsely suppressed, a husky whisper' (p. 40), so when he is called upon to speak, when Delano asks him to give an account of the disorder on board the ship, it is Babo who gives him a voice, who provides the vocal strength that is missing in his own frame. Cereno tries to tell the fabricated story he has agreed on with Babo, but when he comes to explain what it was that 'eventually brought about our chief causes of suffering', his whispery voice gives way, and Babo has to operate him like a dummy – as the law operates through the drum-head court in *Billy Budd*. Cereno has a 'sudden fainting attack of his cough', Delano sees, and 'his servant sustained him, and drawing a cordial from his pocket, placed it to his lips':

> He a little revived. But unwilling to leave him unsupported while imperfectly restored, the black with one arm still encircled his master, at the same time keeping his eye fixed on his face, as if to watch for the first sign of complete restoration, or relapse, as the event might prove. (pp. 43–44)

This is a remarkable moment in *Benito Cereno* – a remarkable moment in the passage of Melville's fiction. Babo, an African slave in the very process of overthrowing his European oppressor, holds the body of white power before him, his arm encircling his 'master', cradling him, presenting that body to the white American who stands before him, so that it might cover him, mask him and speak for him. And from this moment on, the story anatomises Delano's reading of the relations between Cereno and Babo, as they present themselves to him in the form of successive tableau – stilled and laden images in which the bodies of each, of Babo and Cereno, are held against each other by tensely strung lines of force that Delano can't fathom. For the long hours that Delano is on board the *San Dominick*, he is entranced by the sight of the two men, at once drawn to some erotic bond between them and fascinatedly repelled by the restrained violence that he can see before him, in plain sight, but for which he cannot account. He watches as Babo 'supports' Cereno, as he 'sustains him', as 'master and man stood before him, the black upholding the white'. He watches Cereno 'painfully turning in the half embrace of his servant' (p. 45); he watches as, every time Cereno's husky voice seems on the point of giving way, Babo offers him a sip of that sinister 'cordial' that allows him to continue to speak. In the most famous scene in the story – and one of the most famous scenes in Melville's work as a whole – Delano watches as Babo shaves Cereno, pressing his razor against his master's neck, in an attitude of servility that contains within it the most naked demonstration of violent threat. 'Now master', Babo says, as he presses Cereno's head back, and 'gently further back in the crotch of the chair', exposing his neck to the blade. 'Now master', he says, as the 'steel glanced nigh the throat', and as the 'razor drew blood, spots of which stained the creamy lather'. 'See, master', Babo says, 'you shook so – here's Babo's first blood' (pp. 72, 73).

Delano watches these scenes – enthralled, almost drugged himself, as if he has taken a sip of Babo's cordial – and continues to read them as signs of Babo's faithful service to Cereno, as evidence of the 'beauty of that relationship which could present such a spectacle of fidelity on the one hand and confidence on the other' (p. 45). He continues to read the relation between the two men in this way, even as his stay on the *San Dominick* draws to its close and he prepares to leave, to board the boat that will return him to his ship, and leave Cereno to the ministrations of Babo. He is standing, 'his foot in the first act of descent into the boat' (p. 83), preparing to 'overstep the threshold of the open gangway' (p. 84), when Cereno appears before him for one last time, 'an unwonted energy in his air', attended, as ever, by Babo:

> With instinctive good feeling, Captain Delano, withdrawing his foot, turned and reciprocally advanced. As he did so, the Spaniard's nervous eagerness increased, but his vital energy failed; so that, the better to support him, the servant, placing his master's hand on his naked shoulder, and gently holding it there, formed himself into a sort of crutch. (p. 83)

This is, in a sense, the climax of the story. Delano sees the pressure that Babo is exerting on Cereno – his pressing of Cereno's hand to his own naked shoulder, his body braced against Cereno's in a last effort to prevent Cereno from escaping from the *San Dominick* with Delano. He sees the pressure, the two bodies leaning into each other, but he reads the force that Babo exerts as that of a 'crutch' – as a prosthetic support of Cereno's liberty, ability and mastery, rather than a counterweight to it. Cereno reaches towards Delano, from the midst of Babo's embrace, and 'fervently took the hand of the American' (p. 83), and even then, even as the truth of Cereno's captivity swells beneath the thin surface of the cover story, Delano won't relinquish his conception of Babo as a prosthetic for white power. He sees Babo blocking the passage between himself and Cereno; 'And so', he thinks, in his free indirect speech

> still presenting himself as a crutch, and walking between the two captains, [Babo] advanced with them towards the gangway; while still, as if full of kindly contrition, Don Benito would not let go of the hand of Delano, but retained it, across the black's body. (p. 84)

This is the moment when Delano's credulity is strained to breaking point, the moment when his conception of Babo as a crutch for Cereno trembles on the brink of expiry, as Cereno reaches towards him over Babo's body with a pleading hand; and then, quickly, the pretence is over, and the taut pressure that has held these bodies in place throughout the story finally snaps, finally gives way. Delano leaves the boat, and in a suddenly accelerated narrative blur, Cereno breaks free of the grasp of Babo and jumps after him, leaping across the threshold between the *San Dominick* and the *Bachelor's Delight*. Babo, his mask removed, leaps into the boat too, intent on murdering his oppressor. 'At that moment', the narrator says,

> across the long-benighted mind of Captain Delano, a flash of revelation swept, illuminating in unanticipated clearness, his host's whole mysterious demeanour, with every enigmatic event of the day, as well as the entire past voyage of the San Dominick. (p. 85)

The extended moment on the threshold is the hinge in the story, between Delano's duped acceptance of the cover story, in which Babo is a loyal servant, and the revelation of the true state of affairs, in which Babo is a mutineer holding Cereno captive, exploiting him as a white mask to cover the fact of black insurrection. After this hinge moment, the narrative accelerates ('All this, with what preceded, and what followed, occurred with such involutions of rapidity, that past, present, and future seemed one' (p. 85)), and we pass from the strange becalmed suspense of the first movement of the story to the rapid narration of the second, in which Delano and his crew suddenly spring into action. The revolution is put down, Cereno is saved, Babo is imprisoned, and then hung. Order is restored. The elements of the situation aboard the *San Dominick* that resisted Delano's view, that were uninterpretable to him, are all cleared away, as the rapid dramatic narrative (and then Cereno's post facto legal 'deposition') 'served as the key to fit into the lock of the complications which precede it', so 'as a vault whose door has been flung back, the San Dominick's hull lies open today' (p. 100).

Benito Cereno turns around this hinge, so that what before was dark now is light. But even if this is so, even if the overt drive of the narrative is towards this kind of revelation, one cannot read this short novel without seeing that its real investment, the latent but deeply thrilling desire of the work, is not in the story with which it closes, the story that opens wide the door of the vault and restores Cereno's authority, but in the 'inside narrative' which remains untold. The inside narrative of the novel is the story of a revolutionary uprising which succeeds in overthrowing European mastery, and in establishing a political condition of freedom from white authority, a freedom that is so radically different from an existing rhetoric of power that Delano cannot see it even when it is right in front of him, even when Babo holds the steel of his razor against the skin of his deposed master's neck. It is for this reason – because the real erotic and aesthetic investment of Melville's work lies in the possibility of a black emancipation which flows against the current towards the restoration of white power – that the climax of the story comes when it does, as Babo stands before Delano, pressing Cereno's hand to his shoulder, his whole body braced against him, acting as a 'sort of crutch'. This is a moment at which the relation between being and the loaded political terms in which being finds expression is at its most suspended – a moment when we can see into the join where we meet with our extensions, where voice is attached to its prostheses. When this moment is over, when Delano is enlightened by his 'flash of revelation' (p. 85), he simply replaces one myth of white supremacy with another. Babo is no longer the obedient slave, and becomes instead the black threat which white power must suppress in order to sustain itself. The flow of the story relies on this substitution; but at this stretched hiatus, as Babo offers himself as a crutch to Cereno, the story extends a moment in which neither narrative – that of servility or of threat – is quite operative. For this unmeasured span of narrative time, the portents which have overloaded the narrative – the stern-piece depicting a masked satyr with his foot on the neck of his masked victim; the ominous figurehead draped in canvas – become eloquent of another balance of power, another means of organising bodies in space. Push becomes strangely confused with pull; Babo pressing Cereno's hand to his own naked shoulder speaks of an amalgam of political and erotic forces, a torsional relation between black and white, that evades the available languages of power. The masks that proliferate through the story are not here removed – or not yet removed. Delano will soon see with the 'scales dropped from his eyes' (p. 85) – he will soon see Babo 'not as if frantically concerned for Don Benito, but with mask torn away, flourishing hatchets and knives, in ferocious piratical revolt' (p. 85). The opaque scales will fall from Delano's eyes, Babo will remove the mask of servility, the canvas covering the figurehead will be 'whipped away' to reveal its 'chalky comment' (p. 86) in the form of the denuded white skeleton of the murdered slave owner Aranda. But for this suspended period on the threshold, the story's masks tremble on the verge of another kind of speech. At this balanced, precarious junction in the story, Melville's narrative makes an opening for a voice to speak, a voice of black power, black self-determination, that does not require a white mask to make itself heard, or that is able to mask itself in its own being, as Billy's voice makes an unobstructed passage between his innermost self and his clayey tenement, so that it was as if his body thought.

Such a voice, though, such a thinking body, does not arrive. The conclusion of the story rests on Babo's speechlessness, his inability or refusal to speak. Seeing that his revolution had been foiled, 'seeing all was over',

Babo 'uttered no sound and could not be forced to. His aspect seemed to say, since I cannot do deeds, I will not speak words' (p. 102). He renounces speech, as Bartleby too prefers not to clothe his resistance in speech, and the closing paragraph sees Babo 'dragged to the gibbet at the tail of a mule', where he 'met his voiceless end' (p. 102). The muteness of black resistance is the content of the story, and the conclusion of the plot, as white power reasserts itself; but it is also, and more subtly, an element of its form, as the balance between voice and voicelessness reappears in the internal narrative dynamics of the text. The prosthetic relation between Babo and Cereno is reproduced, in the most precise and delicate way, in the prosthetic relation between the narrative voice, which has no body or perspective of its own, and Delano's free indirect speech, which it adopts at all times as a sort of crutch. It is one of the most marked peculiarities of this peculiar work that the narrative agent that sees and knows – the agent for which the hull of the San Dominick has always lain open – is bound to the agent who does not know and does not see, so that the narrative voice itself partakes of Delano's ignorance and racist credulity. It is not just that the narrative sees through Delano's racist eyes and mind – as in the moment that Delano admires the African mothers on board the ship as they tend to their infants: 'There's naked nature, now, pure tenderness and love, thought Captain Delano, well pleased' (p. 61). It is that the narrative voice itself speaks *as* Delano, as if it has no other organ of expression. Who is speaking, for example, when, during the extraordinary shaving scene, Babo's masterful barbering is offered as evidence of the natural propensity to serve of African peoples? 'There is something in the negro', the narrator declares, 'which, in a peculiar way, fits him for avocations about one's person' (p. 70). As Babo shaves and tends Cereno, the narrator reflects that Babo exhibits a 'certain easy cheerfulness, harmonious in every glance and gesture, as though God had set the whole negro to some pleasant tune' (pp. 70–71). There is no 'thought Captain Delano' here, no marker of a difference between Melville's narrator and the free indirect speech of his character, so not only does the narrative voice partake of Delano's racism, but it also enters into his galactically gullible misreading of the scene before him. Even though it speaks from a position of knowledge, the narrative voice cannot free itself from the prosthetic voice of Delano, any more than Babo can speak in his own voice, so the undercurrent of revolutionary possibility that thrills through the story remains unvoiced, not only by Babo, but by the narrative itself. It is as if, in Toni Morrison's terms, Melville's novel is a manifestation of the perception that black power is itself 'unsayable'.[19] It is Melville's great achievement, Morrison writes, to grasp an 'extraordinary and unprecedented idea that had its fullest manifestation in his own time in his own country'. 'That idea', she writes, 'was the successful assertion of whiteness as ideology' (p. 178). When Ishmael thinks, in *Moby Dick*, that 'the whiteness of the whale appalled me', it is this whiteness as ideology that is so appalling, whiteness as a kind of power that has no outside, no evident apparatus of visibility, and so a power that seems unassailable.[20] It was Melville's gift to see how 'gigantic' the problem of white power is; it was his 'task', Morrison writes, to 'question the very idea of white progress, the very idea of racial superiority of whiteness as the privileged place in the evolutionary ladder of humankind, and to meditate on the fraudulent, self-destroying philosophy of that superiority, to "pluck it out from under the robes of senators and judges," to drag the "judge himself to the bar"' (p. 180). But what Melville finds, in undertaking this 'dangerous, solitary, radical work' – what makes the whiteness of the whale so truly appalling – is that whiteness is so fundamental to the language of 'humankind' that to speak against whiteness as ideology requires us to speak without words, to 'say the unsayable'. It is this 'unspeakable' denunciation of white power, she writes, that 'has remained the "hidden course" of Melville's work, the '"truth in the Face of Falsehood"'. 'To this day, no novelist has so wrestled with its subject', or devoted such energy to the 'effort to say something unsayable' (p. 180). 'To this day', Ishmael says, in Morrison's quotation, 'I almost despair of putting it into comprehensive form' (p. 179).

In allying whiteness, in this way, with the sayable, and blackness with the unsayable, Morrison's reading of Melville situates him at the beginning of a critical tradition that reaches from W. E. B. Du Bois, to Frantz Fanon, to James Baldwin, to Gayatri Spivak, to David Marriott – a critical tradition that is dedicated to anatomising the terms in which black experience finds expression. This is a tradition that is bound up, from the beginning, with a prosthetic logic, in which coming to consciousness involves the alloying of being, the fusing of the self with the not-self. Du Bois articulates this experience, most famously, in 1903, when he offers an early account of what he calls a 'double-consciousness'.[21] To be black in America, he writes, is to be 'born with a veil, and gifted with second sight', a double form of seeing which means that one is 'always looking at oneself through the eyes of others', and 'measuring one's soul by the tape of a world that looks on in amused contempt and pity' (p. 8). It is to feel that one has 'two souls, two thoughts, two unreconciled strivings; two warring ideals in one dark body, whose dogged strength alone keeps it from being torn asunder' (p. 8). Writers who come after Du Bois – Fanon, Baldwin – powerfully reject the terms in which Du Bois conceives of this double-consciousness, even as they tend, knowingly, to extend and replicate them. To think that one's own experience involves the adopting of the language and visual forms of another – and to think, what is more, that one is equated with the negative term in that binding, the unsayable element of the sayable, the invisible element of the visible – this is intolerable to Fanon. In his furious rejection of Sartre's conception of negritude, Fanon refuses the idea that his 'effort' to 'reclaim my negritude' was 'only a term in the dialectic'.[22] He will not accept that 'it is not I who make a meaning for myself, but it is the meaning that was already there, pre-existing, waiting for me' (p. 102). He is not a negative term in the dialectic, Fanon writes. Rather, 'black consciousness is immanent in its own eyes'. 'I am not a potentiality of something', he writes, 'I am wholly what I am' (p. 103). 'My negro consciousness does not hold itself as a lack. It *is*.' Fanon refuses the Orientalist logic whereby, as Edward Said puts it, 'European culture gained in strength and identity by setting itself off against the Orient as a sort of surrogate and even underground self'.[23] He is wholly who he is, as Baldwin's Rufus, in his 1963 novel *Another Country*, is wholly himself: 'Rufus was aware of every inch of Rufus', Baldwin's narrator writes, 'He was flesh, bone, muscle, fluid, orifices, hair and skin'.[24] But even as Fanon and Baldwin assert the immanence of being, this assertion becomes bound up in a logic of objectification that robs being of the very vitality that both writers so strenuously assert. Rufus's assertion of his identity with himself – with the material of his own body – comes as the prose rushes towards his suicide. In one of the most intense passages in the history of the twentieth-century novel, Rufus throws himself from a bridge into the Hudson. 'All right', he screams as he falls, 'all right you motherfucking Godalmighty bastard, I'm coming to you' (p. 93). Plunging into the water, he thinks to himself that 'he was black and the water was black' (p 93). Immersion in his blackness affords a fullness of being, but it also leads to a deathly, suicidal nonbeing, as Fanon too finds that being wholly who he is not only an extension, but also what he calls an 'amputation'. 'Unable to be abroad with the other, the white man who mercifully imprisoned me', Fanon writes, 'I made myself an object' – but becoming a thing is an excision, a loss of being rather than, or as well as, a gain. 'What else could it be for me', Fanon writes, 'but an amputation, an excision, a haemorrhage that spattered my whole body with black blood'.[25] As he later thinks, sitting in a cinema, watching representations of black life on the screen ('I cannot go to a film', he says, 'without seeing myself' (p. 107)), it is this amputation that he cannot tolerate. 'I feel in myself a soul as immense as the world, truly a soul as deep as the deepest of rivers, my chest has the power to expand without limit' (p. 108).

With this power inside him, he will not allow himself to become either an object, or the negative term in a dialectic. 'I am a master', he writes, 'and I am advised to adopt the humility of the cripple'. 'With all my strength', he writes, 'I refuse to accept that amputation' (p. 108).

For Fanon and Baldwin, writing in the middle of the twentieth century, for David Marriott, at the turn of the twenty-first, the question of how black life matters involves a negotiation between these two poles – between accepting prostheses which misrepresent you, or refusing them, which renders you mute or thing-like. As Baldwin writes, in a phrase which Marriott takes as an epigraph to his chapter on Fanon, 'one is always in the position of having to decide between amputation and gangrene'.[26] You cut off the body which has been poorly grafted to you, or you let it remain so it rots and poisons you. 'The idea of going through life as a cripple', Baldwin writes, 'is more than one can bear, and equally unbearable is the risk of swelling up slowly, in agony, with poison'.[27] But while one can see the persistence of this contradiction, from Du Bois to Baldwin to Marriott, it is the case too that one can see in these writers the staking out of another kind of being, neither amputated nor gangrenous, one which also has its hesitant growth in Melville's prosthetic imagination. At the heart of Baldwin's writing is a certain 'region', what he calls in *The Fire Next Time* a 'region in my mind', a space, terrible in its own way, that remains apart from all the structures that define and interpellate you.[28] If you want to go there, Baldwin writes, you have to be able to 'go behind the white man's definitions'.[29] This is the region that briefly opens in Baldwin's novel *Another Country*:

> A region where there were no definitions of any kind, neither of colour, nor of male and female. There was only the leap and the rending and the terror and the surrender. And the terror: which all seemed to begin and end and begin again – forever – in a cavern behind the eye.[30]

A region of the mind, a cavern behind the eye, a vanishing ground, behind all definitions; this is the centre around which Baldwin's writing turns, and it is the space, too, that Melville searches for, in *Moby Dick,* in *Billy Budd,* in *Benito Cereno*. Not so much in an attempt to say the unsayable, but as a reaching towards the underside of the said, the inside narrative from which all forms of utterance derive, but which does not itself yield to the prostheses of voice and language. Morrison writes that Melville harnesses his enormous imaginative power in an attempt to speak 'truth in the face of falsehood'. His 'struggle is gigantic', she says, because the attempt to speak that truth involves nothing less than the lifting away of the language of human being itself, a language which is inextricably bound up in in falsehood, in whiteness as ideology. That is why 'he cannot' succeed in that struggle, and 'nor can we'.[31] We cannot speak, Morrison writes, without adopting the prosthetic voices bequeathed to us by the history of humanism, as the court in *Billy Budd* cannot talk except through the prosthesis of a corrupt law. We cannot speak expect by assuming a human guise, a guise which has been fashioned, through the history of European and North American imperialism, from the assertion of white supremacy. The great force of thought that gathers in *Moby Dick* is dedicated to this lifting away, this peeling back of whiteness, so that we might reach towards the 'fathom deep life of the whale' (p. 164) – the inhuman mind that is secreted behind the 'immensely amplified' forehead, the 'mere handful' of brain 'hidden away behind its vast outworks', 'lying in strange folds, courses and convolutions' like 'the innermost citadel within the amplified fortifications of Quebec' (p. 387). The struggle in *Moby Dick* is the struggle away from whiteness towards Baldwin's cavern behind the eye, towards that Shakespearian, Dickinsonian dark that Ishmael can see when he shuts his eyes, that one can best see when one's eyes do wink, that we better see when we see not. And for Morrison, the power of this struggle lies in its failure, in the force with which it demonstrates to us how saturated Melville's culture is – and Morrison's is in the later twentieth century, and ours is in the early twenty-first – in whiteness as ideology. But even if this is so, if the struggle towards a lit darkness is a necessarily failed one, Morrison writes, Melville, for all his furious, impotent power, generates a delicate machine for looking towards what Dickinson calls 'another way – to see'.[32] 'But in non-figurative language', Morrison says, 'he identifies the imaginative tools needed to solve the problem: "subtlety appeals to subtlety, and without imagination no man can follow another into these halls"'.[33]

This subtlety is everywhere in Melville, even when his writing is at its most amplified, its most unrestrained. *Moby Dick*, in all its seething enormity, is an appeal to subtlety; but it is in his short novels, and particularly in *Benito Cereno*, that this appeal is most naked, and that the delicate crafting of a counternarrative to whiteness comes closest to the surface of his prose. The narrative voice that speaks in *Benito Cereno* is cloven to the free indirect speech of Captain Delano. This cleaving, as I have said, is one of the striking peculiarities of the work. The narrator himself (if such a figure can be said to exist) remarks on it. 'The nature of this narrative', the narrator declares at the close of the story, 'besides rendering the intricacies in the beginning unavoidable, has more or less required that many things, instead of being set down in the order of occurrence, should be retrospectively, or irregularly given' (p. 100). The binding of narrative voice to Delano's perspective has rendered the narrative intricate, retrospective, irregular. The narrator (such a figure *cannot* be said to exist) does not intervene to order, to regulate and to clarify what to Delano appears out of time, irregular and opaque. He (she? it?) does not do so, because the real content of this story is the borderlessness of whiteness ('to analyse it', Ishmael thinks, 'would seem impossible' (p. 168)) for those who are immersed in a racist ideological project that has slavery as its imperative. The narrator adopts the prosthetic of Delano's voice, as a response to the muteness of black resistance to white supremacy – the muteness of the 'gigantic', 'colossal' African Atufal ('how like a mute Atufal moves' (p. 49), Babo says), the 'voicelessness' of Babo himself (p. 102). But even as narrative voice cleaves in this way to the language of white oppression, the true beauty of this story, and the specific gravity of that cleaving, is that the narrative summons its own revolutionary counterlogic, not by speaking against Delano, but by working at the underside of his voice. Morrison writes that Melville invents the 'imaginative tools' to 'solve the problem' of whiteness; here, in *Benito Cereno*, the tool is the capacity of narrative voice to allow a revolutionary refusal of whiteness to cleave to the underside of the voice of white supremacy itself. 'Murder' Hamlet says, 'though it have no tongue, will speak / With most miraculous organ' (p. 669) – the organ of uninstantiated dramatic possibility as it resides outside of the confines of any given play. It is this possibility, this capacity of narrative voice to speak without a tongue, that gives miraculous expression to the revolt in Melville's tale – the revolt that is the libidinal and political centre of the work, and that, even if put down, permanently undoes the will to power of the slave trader Benito Cereno. Cereno cannot recover from his encounter with Babo, from that moment when Babo presses Cereno's hand to his naked shoulder (gently? violently?), and when he offers his own body as a prosthetic extension of Cereno's. After this moment, Cereno wilts, and slowly, quietly dies, to the perplexity of the ever-obtuse Delano. 'You are saved', Delano says to Cereno in their last conversation, in a line that Ralph Ellison takes as an epigraph to *The Invisible Man*. 'You are saved; what has cast such a shadow upon you?' (p. 101).[34]

Cereno's reply, 'The negro', the last word that he speaks, brings Cereno to the same silence that he has inflicted on his 'living freight': 'There was silence, while the moody man sat, slowly and unconsciously gathering his mantle about him, as if it were a pall' (p. 101). Cereno wraps himself in his own graveclothes, as Babo wraps Aranda in canvas on the figurehead of the San Dominick, and his story, like Babo's, 'ended in muteness' (p. 101). In that climactic moment on the threshold of the ship, as Cereno and Babo stand together, prosthetic extensions of each other, the narrative exposes some underside to white power, some shadow that both sustains and undoes it. To give expression to that underside is the revolutionary desire that Fanon expresses, at the heart of *Black Skin, White Masks*. 'Like a magician', he writes, 'I robbed the white man of "a certain world," forever after lost to him'. Fanon might be talking of Delano, when he writes that 'the white man has never understood this magic substitution' (p. 97). It is some such substitution that is carried in Cereno's last word, his last act of racism; but the last word in *Benito Cereno*, spoken not by a tongue, but by the most miraculous organ of narrative voice, goes to Babo. 'I feel in myself', Fanon writes, 'a soul as immense as the world'. 'My chest has the power to expand without limit' (p. 108). It is this immensity, this limitlessness, that Melville's novel leaves us with, in its last image of Babo, the last evocation of Babo's subtle revolutionary mind ('his brain, not body, had schemed and led the revolt' (p. 102)). Babo is murdered, 'the body was burned to ashes'; 'but for many days, the head, that hive of subtlety, fixed on a pole in the Plaza, met, unabashed, the gaze of the whites' (p. 102). Subtlety appeals to subtlety, as Babo's gaze challenges us to meet it. Melville's novel cannot contain that subtle mind, as Babo's own body cannot contain the power that dwells within it, and that eludes any prosthetic extension. 'His slight frame', the narrator says, in the closest that the novel comes to an articulation of its real revolutionary desire, was 'inadequate to that which it held' (p. 102). The inadequacy of that frame, and the swelling, unworded power that it cannot contain, is the legacy of *Benito Cereno*, and its call to the future.

2022

CHAPTER 2

Samuel Beckett
Towards a Political Reading

I

Beckett's work has come to mark the far limits of apolitical writing.[1] His perceived longing for silence, for voicelessness and placelessness, his indeterminate nationality, his relentless, ascetic refusal of all forms of belonging, his paring down of reference to the point that his writing seems barely to refer to the world at all, have all led critics to suggest that his writing constitutes an abdication from, a denial of, or an indifference to the political.[2] His writing witnesses and performs the emergence of a voice from the wreckage of politics, a voice which does not need political forms of representation to clothe it or embody it or make itself heard. What Beckett offers us is an aesthetic that defies, outlasts, or negates the political. Part of its value is that it allows both writer and reader to escape from politics into the thin but clear air of a pure aesthetics.

In insisting here, contrary to this prevailing critical current, that Beckett's work has a political content and value, I am not suggesting that the historical emphasis on his apoliticism has been entirely misplaced. My intention here is not to disavow the movement in Beckett's work towards indifference, or to make light of the kinds of freedom from political determination and location that many critics have suggested that Beckett's work offers. I do not wish to make the reductive claim that Beckett is in some direct sense a 'political writer' (whatever that may mean), or to argue that beneath the ironic and restless surface of his work he has really been committed to a political cause all along. On the other hand, neither do I wish merely to preserve his apoliticism within a critique that insists that even apoliticism is in some sense political. I do not seek simply to valorise Beckett's rejection of the political as itself a political gesture. This is not only too pat a resolution to the nuanced political and critical difficulties posed by Beckett's writing, it is also a dangerous manoeuvre in its own right. If all forms of activity, even that of resistance to the category of the political, can be effortlessly co-opted into the political, then the meanings of the terms politics and resistance are at risk of being effaced. My call for a political reading of Beckett's aesthetics follows rather from the conviction that certain limits have been imposed on our understanding of Beckett's work both by a widespread over-emphasis on his political neutrality and by the ways in which his indifference has been read and articulated.

These limits can be regarded as constricting the reception of Beckett's work in two more or less opposite ways. Firstly, it has proved difficult to gain a clear understanding of the *difficulties* that Beckett encounters in his drive towards an apolitical, culturally displaced neutrality. An interpretive orthodoxy that insists upon the indifference of Beckett's writing is hard pressed to account for its violence, for its strangely bloody-minded determination, and for its sheer stamina in the face of repeated failure. This contradiction in Beckett's writing between determined commitment and resigned indifference is of course very familiar, and emerges in many guises throughout his oeuvre, most famously perhaps in the figure of Beckettian silence. Just as Beckett's longing for calm neutrality involves him in frenzied struggle, so his desire for silence leads him to produce copious amounts of speech. Prevailing assumptions that have underpinned the reception of Beckett's work, however, have tended to produce readings which have sought to resolve or foreclose these contradictions, rather than to examine them in their contradictory state. The silence, indifference or neutrality that is taken to be Beckett's goal is removed from the contradictory and agonistic textual environment that determines the conditions of its possibility, and is read as a kind of truth that leaks or springs or emerges from the text as if by magic. This concern to represent Beckett's works as having given voice to a pure aesthetic silence has led many critics to leap over the difficult, knotted, peristaltic texture of the writing into a plane of indifferent serenity, and in so doing to convert an aesthetic of failure into an aesthetic of success. The cultural conditions that have given rise to the celebration of Beckett's apoliticism have limited critical access to the boundary that his work establishes, and violently contests, between statement and denial, affirmation and negation, voice and silence, despite the fact that these pairings have become the keywords of the critical industry. The writhings and contortions endured by Beckett's narrators and characters are orchestrated around a relentless confrontation between a poetic demand for a right to silence and a political demand for speech. The political texture and significance of this confrontation has been partly obscured by the critical impulse to regard it as being already over. A powerful and often latent tendency to privilege poetic silence over political compromise has made it an uneven contest that has been prematurely decided.

The second way in which criticism of Beckett's work has been limited by the emphasis on his apoliticism is in its approach to his cultural specificity. A crucial element of Beckett's apoliticism is his universality. From the earliest days of Beckett criticism, this has been grasped as the most significant and characteristic feature of his writing. He was celebrated by his first readers as a writer who, by virtue of writing about no place, no time and no one, has produced a universal voice that speaks for everyone, that presents and diagnoses a generalised cultural condition. There are good reasons for this reluctance to pay attention to the relation between Beckett's writing and the specific cultural context from which it emerges. Such a boundary has seemed unapproachable not only because Beckett's work doesn't seem to have very much of the world in it but also because many of the fragile poetic structures that Beckett creates are partly built around concealing it. His works contain elaborate forms of resistance to cultural location of any sort, and the attempt to understand how culture may present Beckett with some kind of constraint or lure often risks the clumsy demolition of these delicate textual defences. The narrator of *Worstward Ho*, in commanding himself to narrate, enjoins himself to predicate 'A place. Where none.'[3] The forbidding abruptness of this rejection of the placedness of Beckett's writing belongs to the sparse terrain of Beckett's later prose, but the protection of the writing against the possibility of its own worldly existence is present in Beckett almost from the beginning. It is difficult to gain a purchase in the brief space between the acceptance and denial of location, of 'place', without threatening to misread or misrepresent this anxiously self-cancelling movement.

Perhaps the most convincing illustration of just how difficult it is to approach the relation between Beckett and the world is provided by those moments in Beckett criticism in which specific cultural references in his work are acknowledged. It is one of the oddities of Beckett studies that the prevailing interpretive insistence on his transcultural universality has run alongside, and tended to absorb, a minor but tenacious and long-standing scholarly interest in those points where Beckett's work betrays its cultural origins and points of reference. As early as 1977, Vivian Mercier suggests that his sketch of the national, class and denominational conditions that underlie Beckett's writing would probably already seem familiar to his readers.[4] Since at least then, the claim that Beckett's writing emerges from, and contains a certain nostalgic reference to, a white, male, protestant, Irish, impoverished bourgeois culture is recognised and undisputed by the majority of his readers. This residual cultural content, however, is almost always read as a patina, or a trace, or a dash of local colour, that has no bearing or influence on his universality. When a biographical or train-spotterish interest is betrayed in the odd cultural details that pepper Beckett's writing, it is shrouded in anxious caveats that assure the reader that such details are of signal unimportance in the wide and empty expanses of the Beckettian poetic terrain. Even those works, such as Eoin O'Brien's *The Beckett Country*, that expressly set out to examine the cultural content of Beckett's writing are at great pains to stress that such content offers no obstacle to his freedom from its claims. O'Brien warns that 'an obsessional diligence in identifying realities, could blight the beauty of Beckett's imagination – the "soul-landscape"'.[5] This anxiety, that a connection between Beckett's imagination and the socio-political world may end up tainting an otherwise pure art form, leads O'Brien to some fairly curious contortions. The whole thrust of his encyclopaedia of Irish references in Beckett's writing is geared towards suggesting that his work is more concerned with 'outer reality' than his critics had previously been willing to acknowledge, and yet this corrective spirit is erased and effaced in the very midst of its ardour. O'Brien claims that

> Much of the apparently surrealistic in Beckett's writing is linked, sometimes forcefully, often only tenuously, with the reality of existence, and much of this actuality emanates from Beckett's memories of Dublin, a world which he renders almost unrecognisable as he removes reality from his landscape and its people (while also annihilating time) in his creation of the 'unreality of the real'.[6]

Whilst O'Brien's work does not present itself as a critical analysis of Beckett's cultural location, but rather as an illustrated reader's guide to Beckett's Ireland, the tension here between a literal minded urge to reveal Beckett's worldliness and a reluctance to trespass on the sanctity of his artistic freedom from the world, emerges in many more engaged critiques. Indeed, it is telling that O'Brien's unusual (and oddly compelling) book has achieved a strange influence in Beckett criticism, perhaps because in its bluntness it allows a difficulty that has been collectively repressed to return. James Knowlson, whose 1996 biography of Beckett displays a similarly contradictory attitude towards Beckett's relation with his cultural contexts, suggests that O'Brien's book is 'among the most important to appear on Beckett in the past two decades because it seems likely that it might encourage a shift back in Beckett criticism to consider how Beckett deals with "outer reality"'.[7] The reception of *The Beckett Country* in Beckett criticism might suggest that O'Brien's research resonates with a general inchoate awareness of a more engaged, located and culturally specific Beckett, which, despite James Knowlson's optimism, it remains beyond the hermeneutic powers of the mainstream to articulate fully.

The two limitations that I have sketched out, then, mark out what I suggest is a double failure to articulate, a failure that is endemic to the critical environment in which Beckett is read. On the one hand, a deeply ingrained conviction that a narrative voice has the capacity to move beyond the cultural language that contains it has made it very difficult to approach those moments in Beckett's work in which his tendency towards 'lessening' and 'worsening' has brought him up against a political limit beyond which he cannot pass. On the other hand, it has proved equally difficult to interpret the residual cultural specificity of his writing, a specificity which his aesthetic economy itself strives to undermine and erase. Criticism has struggled, for many reasons, to give adequate expression both to Beckett's trying-and-failing to be free from the world and his trying-and-failing to refer to it. Consequently, it has failed also to illuminate the politics both of Beckett's drive to negate the political world and of his drive to find a way of belonging to it. It is in the relation between these two contradictory drives that I suggest Beckett's politics can be found – a politics which couples ferocious resistance to the capitalist machinery of appropriation and exploitation with a poignant mourning for a worldly paradise that may always have been lost. The received perception of Beckett's writing as being virtually empty of significant reference to the world is a symptom of a more general blindness to the promises and constraints that culture offers it and imposes upon it. Read without the blinkers of critical insistence upon his apolitical universality, Beckett's writing can be seen to be held together by a delicate tracery of reference to the cultural and political landscape of Ireland and Europe, a pattern which shapes and is shaped by the systole-diastole of his rhythmic movement between resistance to and longing for a homeland. The relentless struggling onwards which characterises Beckett's work is not driven solely by an abstract compulsion or categorical imperative, but by a difficult and ambivalent relationship with a material political geography, whose specific cultural meanings both constrain and partly produce the constantly self-effacing spaces of his writing. In his movement towards negativity and poetic indifference, Beckett does not simply slough the skin of his Protestantism, or of his Irishness, or of his gender, or of his sexuality, or of the history of middle-class colonial ambivalence that is his familial scene and his cultural heritage. The semi-autobiographical drama of cultural belonging and alienation that partly determines Beckett's narrators' and characters' wanderings is written into the very fibre of his fictional and dramatic spaces. The material space of and between Ireland, England and mainland Europe, that provides the early prose with its setting and its impetus, does not give way to an empty and infinitely malleable space in the move from *Murphy* to *Watt*.[8] *Watt*'s progression from the ground to the first floor of Mr Knott's establishment, the global perambulations of Mahood in *The Unnamable*, the agonised crawling of the millions through the mud of *How It Is*, the restless circling of Vladimir, Estragon and Krapp, the spitty mastication of Mouth, the pacing of May in *Footfalls* and the virtually still stirrings in *Stirrings Still* and *Nohow On* are all choreographed partly by reference to an Irish and European political geography that will not go away.

II

It is partly because Beckett's politics emerge in this way from his negotiation of the demands of reference to a political geography, that the failures of critical articulation discussed earlier have come about. It is difficult to imagine how Beckett's writing may be constrained by geopolitical fields of force, when the language for describing and exploring the dialectical relation between fictional spaces and their material referents is scarcely available to us.[9] In a theoretical environment in which all space appears to be textual, and susceptible to limitless rewriting, remoulding and reimagining, it seems that Beckett, the epitome of the disengaged and unlocated writer, should be at liberty to imagine any space, or absence of space, that he desires.

Certainly, Beckett criticism has reflected the prevailing emphasis upon the freedom to produce and reproduce literary spaces that detach themselves from a referential relationship with a material geography beyond their horizons. Beckett's critics have tended either to situate his work in the space of the human condition, a space which happily requires no cultural or political co-ordinates, or, more recently, to focus on the textual mechanics by which his writing undermines and negates the condition of placedness. While the first of these tendencies has been largely directed towards the containment of Beckett's radically negative aesthetic within the boundaries of a humanist ideology, the second is much more given to an analysis of Beckett's writing as ideology critique. The tension between these two tendencies leads to a divergence in Beckett studies, in the late eighties, between the humanist school led by Hugh Kenner, Martin Esslin and Ruby Cohn, and a theoretically more adventurous group of critics headed by Steven Connor, Leslie Hill and Mary Bryden. Whatever else this forking may have signified or achieved, one of its effects has been to break the consensus which had effectively tamed and subsumed Beckett's negativity. As a result, the 'theoretical' Beckett that emerged in the nineties, in a shape largely determined by readings of Blanchot, Deleuze and Derrida, made the possibility of a political Beckett much more imaginable. There is a shift, in this development, from Beckett as the stoic poet of the status quo, to Beckett as restless, insurgent and mutely transgressive. Despite this shift, however, Beckett's politics have remained imaginable, rather than articulable, and efforts to bridge this gap have proved, in the estimation of some of the critics who have attempted it, half-hearted and more or less unsatisfying (Leslie Hill, in the aftermath of his searching exploration of Beckett's politics, concludes that 'in a very real sense I can't say what I mean by politics').[10] One reason for this has been the difficulty of reaching an understanding of how Beckett's negativity is bound up with his stubbornly residual referentiality. The occasional essays and reflections on Beckett by Blanchot and Deleuze, which have been so influential in the recent wave of criticism, are geared towards exploring the means by which Beckett opens up ruptures and discontinuities in the text through which a naked and extracultural voice or image can be heard or seen.[11] This work has been extremely revealing about the characteristic ways in which Beckett's writing invokes a utopian literary space which is detached from the world, but it has proved exceptionally difficult to read such detachment as having any sort of critical capacity. The negativity of Beckett's vision is so extreme, and so unlimited, that it becomes impossible to read it as being dialectically engaged with any positive term. It is not simply that Beckett's writing opens literary spaces of freedom from the socio-political world, but that he creates spaces which disrupt and exceed the limits of written space. Beckett's writing opens up something akin to a black hole, a rupture in the universe of writing through which the image or the narrative voice escapes and is lost, and which destroys the world of the work by the action of its negativity.

This sense that Beckett's writing performs such an extreme form of negation, and produces such pure, uncontaminated literary spaces, naturally suggests a close relationship between Beckett and theorists such as Blanchot. In many ways, Beckett's writing can be read as a perfect enactment of Blanchot's thought. It is difficult to imagine a more ideal manifestation of Blanchot's Space of Literature than the placeless place of *The Unnamable*, or than the rotunda of *Imagination Dead Imagine*. There is, however, a certain awkwardness between Blanchot and Beckett, an awkwardness which stems from their sheer proximity. In giving such direct expression to the negative narrative voice that Blanchot envisages in texts such as *The Space of Literature* and *The Infinite Conversation*, Beckett's work threatens to collapse or undermine Blanchot's thinking at the very moment that it verifies it. The purity of Beckett's negativity tends to unsettle the intricate play of limits upon which Blanchot's thinking is based. Blanchot's analysis of the means by which the literary work allows a voice to be heard speaking from the outside, from the realm of death and silence that exists beyond the furthest limits of life, relies on a conception of the work as in some way limited. The space of literature is as vast, unlimited and empty as the space of death, but despite this vastness, or even because of it, the literary work which offers a glimpse of this limitless space is itself limited, inadequate and partial. Just as living a life is the only way that we can approach death, so writing a book that is of the world is the only way that we can approach the space of literature that lies beyond the world and beyond the book. The literary work, Blanchot writes, builds a 'delicate and endless bridge' that, impossibly, arches over the far limit between life and death, between voice and silence.[12] The thinking that Blanchot employs to approach these contradictions in the literary work between limitation and limitlessness derives much of its energy from what might be thought of as a modernist tension between the aesthetic imagination and the socio-political world with which it is partly engaged. Stephen Dedalus forges the uncreated conscience of his race in the smithy of a soul which is supersaturated, as his friend Cranly comments, with a religion in which he says he disbelieves.[13] His action of rewriting and reimagining, his movement towards a literary space which transcends the political world, is profoundly engaged with that which is being rewritten. The book exists in the world, and is bound up with writing the world, but it opens within itself a fissure through which an other space, an uncreated space, can be glimpsed. In Beckett's writing, however, Blanchot suggests this structure is no longer in play. Beckett's apprehension of the negative space of writing is immediate, rather than generated by the contradiction between the imagination and the world. Blanchot comments, in his review of *The Unnamable*, that this novel negates itself so completely that it should not even be regarded as a book. Rather it is a

> direct confrontation with the process from which all books derive – with the original point at which the work is inevitably lost, that always destroys the work, creates endless idleness in the work, but with which too, if anything is to come of it, an ever more primal relationship has to be established.[14]

As a result of this 'direct confrontation' with a vanishing point of origin, the play between limits and limitlessness that characterises Blanchot's reading of modernist aesthetics gives way to a devastating revelation of an unlimited negativity. The negative voice in Beckett's work resounds so powerfully that the delicate contradictory structures that surround and support the narrative voice in much of Blanchot's thinking fall away. Blanchot reads the development of Beckett's prose as working towards this moment at which the narrative voice removes itself from world, text and pronoun, into a magisterial, accomplished negativity. The first two novels of Beckett's trilogy, Blanchot suggests, are flawed because Malone, Molloy and Moran have certain residual connections with a recognisable reality. The Unnamable narrative voice, however, has, 'dropped out of reality' (p. 197). When we reach *The Unnamable* we gain admission to a textual geography that has nothing of the world in it. But this point in Beckett's writing, precisely because it seems so perfectly to enact Blanchot's thought, ends up undermining it and somehow becalming it. The stillness of Blanchottian neutrality depends upon choppy contradiction for its value, just as the success that issues from the literary work is locked into a tightly choreographed relation with the failure that dismembers it ('Writing', Blanchot says, in a discussion of André Breton, 'is a harrowing experience, which can be pursued only under the veil of failure. And yet, while the experience is the infinitely hazardous movement which cannot succeed we call what issues from it success').[15] Beckett's success, though, is so all encompassing that it becomes completely indistinguishable from failure. Read through Blanchot, his writing is both the most successful and the most failed of artistic practices. The release of the voice from text and pronoun leads to a freedom that, in its excess, becomes incarceration, to a plenitude that becomes penury, and to a plenum that is also a void. The 'breakthrough' that Beckett achieves in *The Unnamable* leads directly to what has become the famous 'impasse' that some claim stalls his prose writing for the rest of his career. As Beckett has apocryphally commented to Israel Schenker, when there is 'no 'I', no 'have', no 'being', no nominative, no accusative, no verb', there is 'no way to go on'.[16]

This identity of success and failure is problematic for Blanchot's reading, because it suggests a vanishing point to his thinking, at which much of his work is undone. Blanchot assumes a close relation between success and failure, but he prioritises one term over the other; the narrative voice that speaks from a negative zone beyond the text is prior to the text, and the movement towards the place from which this non-speech issues is 'what makes art an important activity.'[17] The means by which the voice speaks is generated by the material of the text, but it must not tip over to betray an identity with it. It is in the extremes of the Beckettian experimentation with the narrative voice that this tipping can be seen to occur. In Fredric Jameson's terminology, it may be that this tension between Blanchot and Beckett can be mapped onto the movement from the contradiction to the antinomy. For Jameson, the contradiction is a modernist 'category', and the antinomy is a postmodern one.[18] In the contradiction, the antithetical term has a certain amount of negative energy which is stored within the movement of the contradiction, and which has a utopian transformative potential. The terms both oppose each other, and betray a certain identity which allows antithesis to remain locked into thesis whilst exhibiting its negative resistance and irreducibility to that which it opposes. In the antinomy, however, the terms become so absolutely opposed to each other that such dialectical activity becomes impossible. The 'nondialectical categories' float away from each other into an opposition the completeness of which they demonstrate by 'effortlessly turning into each other at the slightest pretext' (p. 7). Where, in the contradiction, both the identity and the opposition between the terms are partial, in the antinomy they are complete. An example that Jameson provides is the antinomial relation between absolute change and absolute stasis. When the concept of absolute change is thought to its limit, the completeness of its opposition to absolute stasis leads to and is indistinguishable from a complete identity with it. That which constantly changes becomes, by its very constancy, that which is constantly the same; 'where everything now submits to the perpetual change of fashion and media image, nothing can change any longer' (p. 18). It is this movement from modernist contradiction to postmodern antinomy that leads, for Jameson, to the 'free play of masks or roles without content or substance' that is characteristic of 'postmodernity itself' (p. 18). Where the contradiction is anchored and rooted, with each of its feet planted in 'a different irreconcilable world' (p. 5), the antinomy has freed itself from such rootedness into the homogenised space of dizzying change and constant play that is characteristic both of postmodernism and of late capitalism. Paradoxically, what is lost in this movement towards the constantly changing is the capacity to conceive of change. For Jameson, the 'persistence of the Same through absolute Difference... discredits change'. It is in this respect that

> the antinomy really does result in the blocking or the paralysis of thought, since the impossibility of thinking another system except by way of the cancellation of this one ends up discrediting the utopian imagination itself. (p. 18)

Blanchot's identification of a neutral narrative voice that speaks from beyond the text is dependent on the contradiction that Jameson regards as a modernist category. It is the energy that subsists within Blanchot's contradictions that flings the voice clear of the work, and opens the work to the voice. In Beckett's writing, however, the modernist contradiction can appear to slide over into the postmodern antinomy. The voice is no longer generated by the dialectical movement of the text, but frees itself into a utopian no place that is also a profoundly anti-utopian acceptance of the limits of the status quo. In Beckett's work everything changes, but everything stays the same. Everything oozes, but it's never the same pus from one moment to the next. The nakedness of his literary space is both a refusal of all that there is, and an acceptance of all that there is. Difference tips over into sameness, outside into inside, ending into beginning. It is impossible to distinguish, in this antinomial world, between resistance and resignation.

III

Such mercurial and rhythmic movement between absolute difference and sudden identity is one of the characteristics of Beckett's writing that has made it very difficult to critique. It has also made it exceptionally resistant to political readings. The process whereby the utopian drive is insistently collapsed back into a representation of the status quo, is equally the process by which the critical and transformative capacities that are perhaps central to a political aesthetic are dismantled. Where critics have attempted to wrest a political significance or potential from Beckett's writing, they have tended to work within the limited terms of his antinomial aesthetic practice. Seamus Deane, for example, is quick to emphasise the collapse of opposites in Beckett's work. His writing presents 'an infinity from which there is no escape'. In Beckett, 'the compulsion to stop is also a symptom of the dedication to going on'. There is 'neither a way out nor a way in', and the 'beginning is not a point of entry'.[19] Deane explicitly contrasts this looping, circular, hermetic and self-cancelling writing with Joyce's work, which he suggests is locked in a dialectical engagement with historical and philosophical structures which gives it a cultural grip that Beckett lacks. Where Joyce's work is 'heavy with the weight of history', Beckett's 'is weightless' (p. 130). Freed from the gravitational demand of reference to anything outside itself, Beckett's oeuvre orbits effortlessly and emptily in a referential vacuum, like a galaxy. Its ending curling into its beginning, its outside slipping into its inside, it multiplies and reduces its internal resonances in obedience to a law that is established only within the terms of its own endlessly collapsing textual systems. It is this weightlessness alone that allows for a reading that might suggest a relation between Beckett's writing and Irish politics. Beckett's emptiness can be read as a parallel to what Deane describes as Ireland's 'nullity':

> Ireland, with its dead language, its deadening politics, its illiberal legislation, is the historical correlative of the personal state of nirvana-nullity for which Beckett's people crave. Silent, ruined, given to the imaginary, dominated by the actual, it is a perfect site for the metaphysics of absence. (p. 131)

The parallels between Beckett's fictional geographies and the cultural landscape of Ireland in no way suggest that Beckett's work is 'set' in Ireland – Deane stresses that Beckett ruthlessly 'repudiates' this null space. He insists that 'it is not important to decide whether or no the landscape that [Beckett's characters] travel through is a version of the Irish landscape' but he claims that it is nevertheless

> useful to recognise that it has no historical presence and therefore does operate successfully as a site of absence, as a place many people have passed through without leaving a trace. Ireland's nullity is thus converted by Beckett into an image of desolation, a zone in which his creatures journey and discover that its 'illimitable' space is like infinity from which there is no escape. Because there is no escape, there is only repetition. (p. 131)

So, Beckett's writing can be read as a response to Irish political conditions, but only by virtue of the absence in Beckett's writing of any 'historical presence' that may situate it in relation to Ireland. The characteristic predicament in which Beckett's narrator is banished from the world into an unlocated and self-cancelling narrative practice is also a wilful protest against the colonial conditions that have led to the estrangement of the Anglo-Irish imagination from the contested landscape of Ireland. For Deane, such a dismantling, such an undoing of attachment to our political referents in a movement towards an empty infinity that is also a narrow impasse, is what the political in Beckett has become.

The limits of this approach to a Beckettian political aesthetic are narrow, and yield only a vanishing kind of politics, one which, in Hill's terms, emerges from the difficulty we would have in saying what it means. It may be that Beckett's starved landscapes could be read as a metonym for the Irish landscape, but without the biographical context that might lead to this work of interpretation, Beckett's negativity could be read as performing its task of resistance in any cultural arena. It is also difficult to see how this opportunistic and peripatetic writing of resistance or critique can maintain any more than a superficial critical or oppositional valency, if it is to be read purely as a writing of inauthenticity and dismantlement. Universal resistance, resistance to any context that might offer a field of interpretation, opens equally onto universal compliance, as the work of Martin Esslin demonstrates. The negativity which might become resistance to colonisation in an Irish context, or resistance to forms of political unfreedom in Eastern Europe, can just as well become compliance with those same forms of unfreedom when it is read within the norms of the western canon. I would suggest, however, that to cast Beckett's writing as detaching itself in this way from any specific context, is fundamentally to misread its engagement with those contexts it partly resists. It is true that Beckett's oeuvre consists in an extended writing of undoing. Few writers have worked harder than Beckett to produce a literature that erases itself, that cancels itself in the throes of its own negation. But one should not read from this that he succeeds in producing an aesthetic that has given voice to silence, or that has articulated a condition of pure cultural detachment. In his 1983 work *Worstward Ho*, Beckett's narrator seems to reflect fairly explicitly on the fate of an oeuvre which has sought to eradicate itself, to drive itself inexorably to the point of its own disappearance. The narrator sets out worstward and leastward with ironic bravura, but finds that the text in which he seeks diminishment offers up a limit rather than a vanishing point. The narrative is geared towards discovering a language which will 'worsen' and 'lessen' the text itself, an antinomial language which will swallow being up into nothingness, success into failure and ending into beginning, in order to leave no trace of itself behind. But rather than such a self-cancelling language, the narrator discovers what is described as 'the unworsenable' and 'the unlessenable'.[20] A point is reached at which the narrator concedes that the text cannot become any worse, or any less. The moment this concession is made is a catastrophic one in Beckett's oeuvre. The Beckett narrator has spent the entirety of his narrating life denying that this limit exists, but amidst the dense contradictions of this late work, he approaches an acknowledgement of the limitations that are imposed on the power to negate by the act of narration itself.

The limit that becomes visible in this text, and that runs like a jagged fault line through the entire oeuvre, unsettles and recalibrates the antinomial logic that has shaped our understanding of Beckett's politics. It is the release of the narrative voice from the material, cultural and textual conditions of its possibility, its exceeding of the furthest limits, that leads to the reversal whereby resistance becomes indistinguishable from complicity. Blanchot's suggestion that a (Mallarméan) modernist poetics might yield the 'extreme moment in which negation is founded and completed', freed from any connection with that which it negates, threatens in Beckett's writing to bring negation to a frictionless identity with affirmation.[21] Similarly, in Deane's model of Beckett's writing as a negative reflection upon an Irish colonial predicament, it is the freedom of his negative vision from any material or cultural limits that spins his resistance off into an enclosed and self-referring orbit. Ending becomes indistinguishable from beginning, for Deane, in Beckett's work, because the notional beginning and the notional end are thought to their abstract extremes. But the limit that I suggest becomes clear in *Worstward Ho*, that which is unworsenable and unlessenable, intrudes upon this effortless identity of contraries. The narrator of *Worstward Ho* may claim, with some urgency, that 'back' should be understood to be in some sense the same as 'on' ('Back is on', the narrator says, 'No more from now now back and now back on. From now back alone. Back for back on');[22] but the event that this late story turns around is the failure of the text to achieve such identity. The narrator works with ever more elaborate algebraic and alchemical deftness to conjure 'back' into 'on', and 'on' into 'back', but movement forward remains the opposite of movement backwards, as the two words and the two directions refuse to collapse into one another. The intense labour of translation itself points insistently to the difference between the terms which seek equivalence; the opposites will not turn into each other, maxima will not turn into minima and a step forward will not become a step back, because the story turns around a battered but persistent limit-boundary between an anarchic creative imagination, and its material conditions of possibility. This residual referential relationship between the story and the world, in its extreme reduction, is that which is unlessenable in *Wostward Ho*. It is the finest and lightest of sutures, which nevertheless prevents the heavy anti-matter of Beckett's fictional world from spinning off into its own empty infinity. This flimsy relation prevents the fault-line that runs through Beckett's writing from opening into a chasm which might separate Beckett's writing from the world, and in which his politics might be swallowed up.

The political reading of Beckett's work envisaged here would approach this limit-boundary, as it stretches throughout the oeuvre, in order to understand the politics both of Beckett's relentless resistance to it as a constraint on the freedom of his imagination, and his equally relentless attempt to find a way of writing this limit, of accepting and integrating it into the economy of his writing. His writing is in some sense a vain struggle not to refer, but it is also and at the same time an attempt to make reference to a landscape that is loved and mourned, and this ambivalence lies at the very heart of his work. It is through a reading of the excruciating mechanics by which Beckett's work simultaneously refers and resists reference, simultaneously affirms and denies a partly autobiographical cultural being, that Beckett's politics can begin to emerge. Beckett's writing, as both Blanchot and Deleuze have suggested, is dedicated to opening up the holes, gaps and absences that inhabit the writing of the self. Few writers have produced a literature that so delicately and ruthlessly unpicks the text, in order to release the voice into the 'place without a place where the work is silent'.[23] This negative drive, however, is always in process, always in motion and always incomplete. The displaced narrative voice does not free itself into indifference, but is rather engaged at every level with a voice that belongs, with a kind of violent nostalgia, to the world. The work of undoing is bound to that which it undoes, by bonds both of necessity and desire, and as such reflects back critically upon it. By virtue of this bondage, Beckett's writing leaves us, in all its indeterminacy, its partiality, its uncertainty, with two 'unlessenable' cultural conditions – that of belonging to the world, and that of being estranged from it. It is in the mortal struggle between these contradictory conditions that Beckett's writing yields a double politics. It is a writing of what exists, a struggle to determine the limits and possibilities of reference available to Beckett, as he writes through the later decades of the twentieth century, and to us, as we find ourselves at the threshold of the twenty-first. In this sense, it is a writing which articulates with extraordinary exactitude the difficulties and curious pleasures of placing or finding one's body (Lefebvre's 'fleshy body' complete with 'spatial qualities' and 'energetic properties') in a word from which it is violently estranged.[24] It is also a writing of what does not exist, a writing of refusal, a writing of inexhaustible resistance, a writing of negation. It is an extraordinarily powerful expression of a utopian negativity, an expression and enactment of the processes by which the creative imagination, ever on the point of expiry, exceeds itself, distinguishes itself, displaces itself.

I suggest that an understanding of Beckett's politics requires a critical language that reads these two forms of writing, both in their separation and in their entanglement. As the unavailability of this language over the last fifty years of Beckett studies might suggest, however, the critical conditions for its development have long been unfavourable. In order for the movement in Beckett's writing between reference and negation of reference to become articulable, we need to have a clearer access to the material limits that operate on the creative imagination. As a result of the transparency or the invisibility of these constraints, the utopian function slides over, in Beckett's writing, into the abandonment of commitment. The contradictory mechanics of modernist self-fashioning appear to give way, in the move from Joyce to Beckett, to an undialectical writing of disengagement that becomes exemplary, for some, of postmodern literary production. A reading of Beckett's politics that can shed light on the ways in which the utopian function persists in his writing, as a critique of the material conditions of possibility, will require and produce a rethinking and reimagining of the relationship between writing and politics in the twentieth century more generally.

Molloy comments, in a typically sanguine mood, that 'one is what one is', but he undermines this fatalistic acceptance of sameness with oneself with the tantalising qualification 'partly at least'.[25] This statement and qualification might be seen as a miniature of the sinuous shifting between tautology and difference in Beckett's writing, between a condition of unadulterated and irredeemable sameness in which there is nothing to be done, and a condition of implacable difference between imaginary self and political self which leads to a loss of transformative tension between mind and world. But what is most striking about Molloy's phrase is the word 'partly'. Sameness is written into difference in such a way that both separation and identification can only be partial. An understanding of the cultural and material conditions that generate and determine this partiality may lead to a clearer analysis of Beckett's politics, and may suggest new ways of thinking about the function and scope of a utopian negativity in post-war European culture more generally.

2002

CHAPTER 3

A Leap Out of Our Biology
History, Tautology and Biomatter in DeLillo's Later Fiction

I   Stasis

Lauren Hartke, the protagonist of Don DeLillo's turn of the century novel *The Body Artist*, proposes a relation between historical time and the experience of being in a body, as this experience takes a new shape in the dawning millennium. The novel ends with Lauren standing by an open window in her remote house by the sea, in order to expose herself to the elements, to feel the mingled currents moving in the salty air. 'She threw the window open', the narrator says. 'She didn't know why she did this, then she knew. She wanted to feel the sea tang on her face and the flow of time in her body, to tell her who she was'.[1]

This moment is exemplary of DeLillo's singular late style, a style which combines a sparsening, a paring back of linguistic excess, with access to a new, shifted temporal and spatial dimension, a new way of experiencing one's own being. In the stripped, stilled prose that he crafts, from *The Body Artist* to *Zero K*, there is a particular diminishment, a starving to nothing; but this reduction yields also a kind of expansion, an odd experience of surfeit won from deficit that is a property, I will argue here, of the tautology as an insistently recurring feature of DeLillo's style, and of his literary thinking. To understand this strange and elusive late phase in DeLillo's career it is necessary to develop a means of responding to the exhausted aridity and also the lifted profusion that is found within the horizons of the DeLillian tautology – to glimpse the differently embodied life, the adjusted relation to the body in empty space and stretched time, that it harbours.

Consider, to begin with, three characteristic late pieces – *The Body Artist*, 'The Starveling' and *Point Omega*.

In the first, *The Body Artist*, a woman, mourning for her dead husband, locks herself away in a remote house in the country, where she is visited by Mr Tuttle, a peculiar, partial figure who sits at a strange, inward angle to the forms in which he comes to presence – to his stunted, diminished body, and his evacuated, circling language. This spectral, stuttery figure, who is perhaps a simple projection of the woman's grief, might or might not help the woman to re-enter the flow of communal life after her husband's death.

In the second, 'The Starveling', a man who has devoted his life to going to the movies, multiple times each day, meets a woman, also a fanatical movie-goer, a peculiar, partial figure who appears to be starving herself – to be undertaking a dedicated programme of self-erasure – such is her commitment to the film world, such is the nourishment that she finds in the act of sitting in the dark, watching a lit screen. The man accosts the starveling, awkwardly, in the bathroom of a cinema, where he tries, and apparently fails, to draw her into a fiction of his own devising.

In the third, *Point Omega*, a man visits a retired intellectual in a hideaway in the desert, where he tries to persuade him to take part in a film that would comprise simply of unedited scenes in which the retired intellectual talks in unscripted gusts, standing by a wall. The two men are visited in the desert by the intellectual's daughter, a peculiar, partial figure who finally manifests this partiality by vanishing into thin air. The scenes in the desert are bookended by a prologue and an epilogue set in the city, in which a man who repeatedly and compulsively watches a super-slowed screening of Hitchcock's *Psycho* meets an unnamed woman, a peculiar, partial figure, who may be a version of the intellectual's daughter, as she may be a version of the Starveling, or a version of Mr Tuttle. These bookends might or might not help us to decode the daughter's disappearance, to attend to the detailed process of her unbecoming.

These three pieces have many elements in common, many crossovers and shared reference points. They are all vanishingly scant, not just in page length or word count, but in temperament, in their capacity to evoke their absence from the scene of their own becoming. They are all obsessively concerned with the processes by which an unravelling or self-erasing mind is held within the matrices of space and time, and within the webbing of the body itself. And they all unfold this obsession through a precise attention to screens and other representational surfaces and forms – to the ways in which we use such surfaces to perform to ourselves the fragility of our own enmeshment in the embodied protocols of shared space, and of shared time. But the family likeness exhibited by these pieces that I am particularly concerned with in this essay is a certain attitude they all adopt towards the tautology, a certain possibility they all glimpse, obliquely, shimmering within the closed horizons of tautological utterances. The pieces share a rhythm which is peculiar to DeLillo's late style, an eerie, circling, self-cancelling movement which is modelled on the tautology, even when it is not itself strictly tautologous. This fascination with the tautology is not in itself new – DeLillo's work has been concerned with the tautology from the beginning – but in the late fiction tautology becomes newly expressive, and captures a starved intellectual vibrancy that is particularly tuned to his post-millennial turn.

Take the opening of *Point Omega*, and the oddly accumulating drifts of prose with which this emptying novel begins:

> There was a man standing against the north wall, barely visible. People entered in twos and threes and they stood in the dark and looked at the screen and then they left. Sometimes they hardly moved past the doorway, larger groups wandering in, tourists in a daze, and they looked and shifted their weight and then they left.
>
> There were no seats in the gallery. The screen was free-standing, about ten by fourteen feet, not elevated, placed in the middle of the room. It was a translucent screen and some people, a few, remained long enough to drift to the other side. They stayed a moment longer and then they left.[2]

At the heart of this opening is the bare perception that people enter rooms and then leave them – a condition of habitation, of dwelling, that is perhaps unusually visible in gallery spaces, where the timed presence of the self in the room is an exposed part of the experience, rather than a by-product of some other compulsion. People entered, and then they left; these opening lines make this observation not once, not twice, but three times. This is the metrical insistence of DeLillo's late style (think of the rhythmically spare opening of *Cosmopolis*: 'Sleep failed him more often now, not once or twice a week but four times, five').[3] The prose accumulates, repeating itself around a central, naked proposition, and strangely, almost magically, the more the prose accumulates, the more naked, the more elemental the condition it describes becomes. 'It was a translucent screen and some people, a few, remained long enough to drift to the other side'. The drifting of the prose around the translucent screen here interrupts itself – 'some people, a few', – hesitating, qualifying the description of the process by which people come in and then leave. The insertion of the qualifier 'a few' should give us more information, should embroider or ornament or advance the description of people coming, and then leaving. But instead it simply elongates the scantness, dwelling a bit longer in the condition of some people, a few, entering and leaving a room, stretching the sinews of the prose, expanding it, only to allow us to see into its emptiness, its bareness.

This accumulating diminishment is not, as I say, itself tautological. But it shares something with the tautology, and prepares the ground for the increasing insistence of tautological structures, as they appear in *Point Omega*, and across DeLillo's late work. One can feel, throughout *Point Omega*, the presence of the tautology, always just under the skin of the prose. When the film-maker, Jim Finley, describes the only film he has made as 'an idea' for a film, for example, the tautology suddenly surfaces. 'I'd done only one film' he says. 'I did it, I finished it, people saw it but what did they see? An idea, they said, that remains an idea' (p. 32). The film is driven by an idea that is an idea. And watching film, in *Point Omega*, is itself oddly tautological. The slowed Hitchcock film, the anonymous man thinks in the epilogue, is mesmerisingly beautiful and painfully revealing, because it opens a space in which 'everything is so intensely what it is' (p. 147). The film depicts or creates an environment in which things are what they are; and it produces also a sense that we ourselves, the viewers, become ourselves too, are placed within the frame of our own being. The film requires you to 'see what's here, finally to look and to know that you're looking' (p. 7). As the same anonymous man puts it in the prologue, 'The film made him feel like someone watching a film' (p. 13); or as Jessie, the disappearing daughter from the desert episode, puts it, the film inducts you into its own stalled time frame. 'The whole point of nothing happening', Jessie thinks: 'the point of waiting just to be waiting' (p. 60).

Once one has become sensitized to it, one recognises that *Point Omega* as a whole is infested with tautological statements – as it if it is structured by the tautology, or powered by it. Finley asks who the intellectual, Elster, worked with, when he advised the US government, helping to 'conceptualize' the Iraq war – 'to apply overarching ideas and principles to such matters as troop deployment and counterinsurgency' (pp. 23–24). 'Who was there' at the meetings, Finley asks, 'Cabinet-level people? Military people?' (p. 65). These are the questions that will power Finley's film, the intellectual standing against the wall, talking about the process by which ideas might be applied to warfare; but Elster's answer collapses the question back on itself, suggesting, perhaps, that Finley's second film will be as tautological as his first, that ideas will remain ideas, and will not escape their own involuted circuitry. 'Who was there?', Finley asks, and Elster replies 'Whoever was there. That's who was there' (p. 65). This might appear to be a non-answer, an evasion, but Finley's response resonates with the drive of the tautology in *Point Omega*, and in DeLillo's later work more generally – the sense that the tautology contains something, a truth that cannot be arrived at by other means. 'I liked this answer', Finley thinks. 'It said everything. The more I thought about it, the clearer everything seemed' (pp. 65–66). The tautology seems the preserve of a kind of truth in *Point Omega*, a clarity or transparency; and when one tunes oneself to this clarity, one can find it running through the heart of DeLillo's slim prose works published since *Underworld*, the tonic or keynote of his late thinking. *The Body Artist* works to shape a passage of clear light, a sliver of lucid, pristine space and time, in which one might examine the unstuck fibres of still being, the separated components of unmoving time and space to which grief delivers us; and it is the tautology that grants us access to this slowed clarity. Lauren Hartke, left in an empty house after her husband's death, finds herself shadowed by herself, attended by her own abandoned presence in a fashion that confronts her, repeatedly, with blank self-reference, closed tautological self-awareness. 'She climbed the stairs', the narrator says, 'hearing the sound a person makes who climbs the stairs' (p. 33). Or she regards a box of bread crumbs that she keeps in the pantry for feeding the birds, seeing it with a clarity, a bright shining thereness, that is won from her slowed, elemental condition, her capacity to see things in themselves. 'She looked at the bread-crumb carton' the narrator says, 'for the first true time, really seeing it and understanding what was in it, and it was bread crumbs' (p. 35). And when Lauren discovers Mr Tuttle, the odd, partial figure, manifestation of her mourning, who has been secretly living with her in the house, we find that he speaks and thinks in flurried tautologies, that his speech patterns follow that combination of stutter and tautology that his name itself suggests. Lauren asks him to 'say some words', and his response is to repeat her request back to her, as in a mirror, or as a form of heightened self-awareness, Echo and Narcissus, but also in a bound, tautological form, one that seals the utterance off, makes it unassailable. 'Say some words', Lauren says, and Mr Tuttle replies 'Say some words to say some words' (p. 55). Or when Lauren displays the night sky to Mr Tuttle, tracing 'a constellation with her finger', his response is a strange, closed remark that seems to deny or negate the sublimity of the sight: 'the word for moonlight is moonlight' (p. 82). This is a response that cancels out awe, that collapses language on itself; but it is one that satisfies Lauren, as Elster's answer satisfies Finley. 'This made her happy', Lauren thinks. 'It was logically complex and oddly moving and circularly beautiful and true' (p. 82).

Across these late works, the tautology functions in this way, combining a kind of diminishment, a receding to nothing, with a blankly expanded awareness, a transparent clarity. As the anonymous man in *Point Omega* says of the slowed Hitchcock that 'the film made him feel like someone watching a film', so the protagonist of 'The Starveling', Leo Zhelezniak, considers his own dedication to the cinema as 'being at the movies to be at the movies' (a condition, he thinks, that 'probes his deeper recesses').[4] In this story, as in *Point Omega* and *The Body Artist*, the tautology names a fascination with the screen, or with the artwork more generally, as an agent of disappearance. Being at the movies, standing in a gallery, entering into a space of aesthetic detachment or philosophical rigour, this is bound up with the vacuity of the tautology, the emptying out of self-reflection. The starveling of 'The Starveling' starves because she is immersed in a drama of reflection, a mirroring or duplicating of the self which, even as it gathers being within its expressive repletion, leads to a hollowing out of being, a peculiar, circling stasis. In another of the near tautologies that run through the story, Zhelezniak thinks to himself that the starveling is a 'scant being, trying to find a place to be' (p. 199). The tautological doubling of being – the starveling is a being who must continually struggle to be – is undermined by, or attended with a scantness, a scantness which is a function of the tautology, even as it seems to evade it. She is a being who is already condemned to be, but she has not yet found a place (in fiction or in life) in which to undertake or carry out her being. In these late works, one might suggest, it is the very completion of the tautology, the very perfectedness of the speech act, or of the expressive gesture, that has produced this diminishment, this vacuity. As Wittgenstein puts it in the *Tractatus*, the tautology produces a representational deficit out of its very completeness. The tautology he writes, is 'unconditionally true'; but 'in a tautology', he goes on, 'the conditions of agreement with the world – the representational relations – cancel one another, so that it does not stand in any representational relation to reality'.[5] Because the 'tautology leaves open to reality the whole – the infinite whole – of logical space', it is unable to 'determine reality in any way' (p. 42). Or as Roland Barthes puts it, in *Mythologies*, the tautology emerges where language has 'failed', meaning, for Barthes, that 'tautology creates a dead, a motionless world'.[6] The slightness of DeLillo's late works follows from this tautologous logic. He produces here a style which is so transparent, which has become so nearly itself, that it carries a death within it (as Barthes says that the tautology is a 'death', a 'saving aphasia' (p. 152)). As with the vanishing effect of repetition – in which a repeated word becomes eerily unfamiliar and inexpressive even as it fills the field of comprehension – the purer an act of expression becomes, the smaller the gap between a word and its meaning, the fuller it becomes, and the emptier.

II Counter

The tautology is a recurrent feature of DeLillo's post-millennial prose. But if we are to respond fully to its signifying power in late DeLillo – if we are to understand its function as a feature of his late style – we have to acknowledge that DeLillo's interest in tautology, as I have already said, is not confined to his sparse late phase, but is a feature of his writing more generally. It is clear to any close reader of DeLillo's prose that his interest in the tautology stretches back a long way – that it is found, indeed, at the heart of his earliest writings. There is something uncanny about the appearance of Lauren's sense of doubled self-awareness thirty years before *The Body Artist* was published, in DeLillo's 1971 novel *Americana*. Lauren climbs the stairs, 'hearing the sound a person makes who climbs the stairs'; David Bell, the protagonist of *Americana*, has much the same epiphany when considering how it feels to stay in an anonymous motel. The motel has 'one hundred hermetic rooms', Bell thinks, and 'postcards of itself at the desk'. 'Repeated endlessly on the way to your room', he says, 'you can easily forget who you are here; you can sit on your bed and become *man sitting on bed*, an abstraction to compete with infinity itself'.[7] The novels that DeLillo wrote in the seventies, as he was shaping his aesthetic sensibility, are pitted with tautologies, just as his late works are, as if his work turns around the unmoving, static time of the tautology itself. The philosophical comedy, for example, *Great Jones Street*, in proposing a rock star as a minimalist guru of inwardness and diminishment, returns repeatedly to the tautological utterance, declaring that 'silence is silence', or claiming at one point, of a tape recording of Bucky Wunderlick's own late work, that 'the effect of the tapes is that they are tapes'.[8] And *End Zone*, perhaps the most philosophically honed of the early novels, is dedicated to an investigation of screened off places, bare refuges, shaped by tautological thinking, in which a 'thing' can become 'unalterably itself'.[9] If *Point Omega* is centrally concerned with the difficult relationship between philosophy and the military – with what happens when one applies 'ideas' to warfare – then *End Zone* is already investigating this relationship, already fashioning empty, desert spaces, in which to test the relationship between ideas expressed in words, and heavy bodies moving in space with violent intent. The football players around whom the novel turns – Gary Harkness and Taft Robinson – are slabs of muscle, dedicated to training and competition, but they are also monkish, quietist philosophers from Japanese Noh or late Beckett. They retreat to measured, bare rooms, in which they meditate on 'static forms of beauty', a 'certain play of shapes'. 'I like to measure off things and then let them remain', Taft says to

Harkness, 'I try to create degrees of silence' (p. 239). The training grounds are a retreat, in which football payers sit in monastic cells, reflecting on how bodies take up space and time, and how they enter into alignment or collision. But the result of their reflections does not help us to make connections between ideas and warfare, between ideas and sport, between sport and war; the work of metaphor here does not lead to transformative poetic thinking, but rather to the strange, stalled tautology that resurfaces time and again in DeLillo's work. The burden of Harkness and Taft's discussion of football is the discovery that football 'is not swimming or track or some kind of extracurricular thing [....] It's football. It's *football*' (p. 233). And what we learn about warfare really amounts to Alan Zapalac's declaration that 'Warfare is warfare' ('I reject the notion of football as warfare', he says. 'Warfare is warfare. We don't need substitutes because we've got the real thing' (p. 111)). If, as Daniel Grausam has argued, 'what the novel is literally about' is 'football as nuclear war, and nuclear war as football, and what makes it possible to speak about one in the language of the other' (p. 109), then the collapse into tautology suggests that such analogy continually fails, that language falls into self-reference, even as it reaches for translation, for metaphoricity.[10]

So the appearance of the tautology in DeLillo's post-millennial work is not a late invention, but a feature of his style and of his thinking that has been present in his work from the beginning. But if this is so, it is also the case, I suggest, that the tautology functions in a different way in DeLillo's late phase than it does in his early phase or his middle phase, and further that the shifts in the poetic and philosophical shape of the tautology are closely bound up with the texture and quality of DeLillo's late style. This shift has to do at its heart with the way that DeLillo understands history, and with the way that his writing depicts and performs the pressure that history exerts upon the body, as it exists in space and in time. The tautology in DeLillo's work has always, from its earliest manifestations, carried something apocalyptic with it, some foretaste or intimation of the end of history, the end of the world. If, as Grausam suggests, *End Zone* stages the representation of the cold war as a 'historical, rather than an ontological and linguistic, problem' (p. 110), then in part the novel suggests that the logic of the cold war tends to a kind of historical stasis, the historical completion that is carried in the collapsed movement of the tautology. DeLillo's work has always been attuned to the possibility that the arms race, and the global expansion of US military, economic and cultural power that it entails, leads to self-reference, the production of a public sphere which absorbs its own margins. The combination of coldwar politics and global capital leads to the increasing obliteration of difference, what Nick Shay in *Underworld* thinks of as 'cold war ideologies of massive uniformity', a 'furtive sameness', a 'planing away of particulars'.[11] When DeLillo pictures athletes living in Quonset huts in the desert, meditating on the bare elements of football, its 'boosh boosh boosh', its 'thwack thwack thwack', he is presenting us with a scenario in which this furtive sameness has been realised, in which particulars have been planed away, nuance burned off.[12] The failure of metaphorical relations between one thing and another, between football and war or between a thing and the idea we might have of it, is in part a realisation of a situation in which things tend to become simply themselves, in which bodies are reduced to their stark being as bodies – a draining of difference and heterogeneity that is a symptom of late twentieth-century politics and aesthetics. As a character named Viktor notes at the end of *Underworld*, nuclear proliferation and global capital leads to a situation in which things cannot deviate from the picture or idea we have of them. 'Believe everything', Viktor says, 'Everything is true'. 'The bomb makes everything true' (p. 802). The tautology is the privileged term in DeLillo of for this kind of truth, this disappearance of dissent or nuance. When tautological speech acts surface in *End Zone*, when we arrive at the hard-won realisation that football is football, or that warfare is warfare, or, at one point, that shit is shit (p. 89), the prose is enacting a historical tendency for monocular vision, a sense that we are being hemmed into a truth that is both all encompassing and historically drained, culturally nullified. But, if the tautology in early and mid DeLillo is a symptom of cultural self-reference, of a failure of dialectics, it is also the case that the tautology is employed here as a means of discovering historical difference in the midst of a furtive sameness, of giving articulation to a historical principle that lives on, as we find ourselves propelled towards a cultural end point, or end zone. The bleached situation in *End Zone* in which bodies occupy elemental space and slowed time is a response to a growing ahistoricism, a growing awareness that the dialectics of history are creeping towards a standstill; but the static forms of beauty that *End Zone* crafts are also themselves bursting with a mute historical significance that lies within the horizons of the tautology, waiting to be activated. Taft's body, its packed power and speed, has a history within it, Harkness thinks, a history that is carried in the simple angles that the body makes with itself. 'Taft's speed had a life and history of its own', Harkness says. 'Hip-width. Leg-length. Tendon and tibia' (p. 191). 'History', Harkness says earlier in the novel, 'is the placement of bodies' (p. 45). History is latent in the way that bodies occupy rooms, in the junction that wall makes with ceiling, in the way that the body is disposed within geometrical space. 'History', Harkness says, 'is the angle at which realities meet' (p. 46). The tautology in *End Zone* might stage a recognition that there has been a dwindling of the imaginative faculties, a narrowing of the expressive range. Language has been reduced to a bare trace of what is already here. But this very reduction preserves a kind of potential, allowing a pent, restless history that is working on these bodies, moving them into position, to stir in the separated fibres of the language, waiting for something to happen to release it. The tautology is not only the sign of a spent cultural imagination – it is also the prelude to a new era, a new movement, in which one can discern, even as the historical current takes us towards the end of history, the stirrings of what DeLillo has called a 'counternarrative', the expression of historical resistance and refusal.[13]

Throughout the sweep of DeLillo's work, from *Americana* and *End Zone* to *Underworld*, the tautology can be seen working in this way. It is a syntactical form which suggests and enacts a blank identity, needlessly or gratuitously displaying an object's identity with itself; but it also refuses the identity that it witnesses. The very reaching for the self-same produces, in the stuttering repetition of the tautological utterance, the difference that it seeks to eradicate. Samuel Beckett recognises this contradiction, and recognises too its centrality to a mode of modernist aesthetics, when he discovers it operating in Proust's synthesising imagination. 'Proust', Beckett writes, 'recognises the dual significance of every condition and circumstance of life'. Nothing is simply what it is, because all things carry a trace of what they are not, or not yet, as an integral part of their being, and as a condition of their coming to language and to thought. 'The most ideal tautology', Beckett goes on, 'presupposes a relation and the affirmation of equality involves only an approximate identification, and by asserting unity denies unity'.[14] Beckett finds this enactment of different and disunity within the declaration of the identical and the united at the heart of the Proustian experience of lost time, and it is this historical and temporal paradox at work within the tautology that drives DeLillo's historical imagination – an imagination which has clear affinities with Proust and Joyce, and with Beckett. For the DeLillo of *End Zone*, of *Libra*, of *Mao II* and *Underworld*, the historical forces that drive us towards repetition and stasis also carry an undertow, a historical surplus, or what Percival in *Running Dog* calls a 'historical counterfunction'.[15] It is the task of DeLillo's poetic imagination, as well as the content of his historical thinking, to give this counterfunction, this counternarrative, some form of expression; and it is the gift of the tautological utterance, in DeLillo, to harbour this counter force, to bring it to thought. The urge towards the pale and the diminished, that urge one can see so clearly in the static beauties of *End Zone*, is there throughout DeLillo's writing; but it merges with and yields a historical potency, a roiling gathering of historical power that drives thought, as it shapes the body's occupation of space and time. The experience of American political and economic power leads to homogeneity, to closed redundancy. The opening of DeLillo's most historically muscular work tells us so: 'He speaks in your voice, American'.[16] America summons us all to live in its image, at the close of the twentieth century (what DeLillo calls 'the American century'), at the height of US global dominance.[17] 'He' and 'you' become tautologous terms, as we are fashioned by an economic force that shaves away difference and singularity, as the third person is equated with the second, and with the first. But it is the double gift of *Underworld*, what Beckett would call its 'dual significance', to present the tautologous relationship between he and you as both a sign of historical exhaustion, and the occasion for a great unfolding of historical difference, a testimony to the power of history to exceed its own limits, to break its own frame, to discover the counterthought vibrating in the most complacent of orthodoxies, or the most violent of tyrannies. The power of the historical current which 'flows forever onward' towards stasis[18] – the tendency towards apocalypse that powers DeLillo's novels up to *Underworld* – is balanced by the gathering of seething historical material that moves within the novel's closed horizons, within its American voice, that does not have an official language, but that is caught in the novels' undertow, the backwash of counterhistorical force that is held within the very self-referring language which attests to homogeneity, which performs its historical inevitability. The tautology, in these novels, harbours a counterhistorical force, that makes the sentences tremble with a mute significance, what Grausam calls a meaning 'beyond simple signification' (p. 105), even if does not have a revolutionary language with which to express itself.

The end of *Underworld* coincides in a fashion with the end of the American century, and also with the end of DeLillo's mid career, the period that John Duvall has recently called 'major DeLillo'.[19] There is something symphonic and cataclysmic about the climax to that great novel, but its final word, 'Peace' (p. 827), suggests also that it ends in historical death. Nick Shay thinks to himself, in the final pages of the novel, that he begins to 'feel something drain out of me. Some old opposition, a capacity to resist' (p. 801), and it is hard not to see this feeling as a kind of historical running out, an exhausted reconciliation. If it is the case that something happens to the tautology in DeLillo's writing after *Underworld*, if a shift in the function of the tautology in *The Body Artist* and *Point*

Omega is related to the emergence of a late DeLillian aesthetics, then it is hard to resist the sense that this is because the historical power that drives the tautology from *Americana* to *Underworld* has drained away, with the end of the American century, and with the final word of DeLillo's magnum opus. The tautology has always operated in DeLillo's writing, but as it appears in *The Body Artist*, in *Point Omega*, and in his late short fiction, it feels different, less an engine of historical difference, and more the mark of an unreconciled reconciliation, a version of the incomplete completion that Edward Said has characterised as a feature of late style, the impossible stretching of a time that has already come to an end, the persistent afterimage that both Philip Roth and Margaret Atwood have recently characterised as 'posthumous' art.[20] As Lauren Hartke regards a carton of bread crumbs and realises that they are bread crumbs, as Leo Zhelezniak goes to the movies to go to the movies, as Mr Tuttle observes that the word for moonlight is moonlight, as the 'Scholar' in *The Word for Snow* declares that 'The word for snow will be the snow',[21] these works turn around the awed possibility that words have nothing inside them. We find ourselves, with Lauren, 'shadow-inching through a sentence [seeing] a word in its faces and aspects' (p. 48), and what we see is the word, the word shorn of its surplus, its counterforce. In *End Zone* we see the failure of the metaphorical relation between football and warfare, between ideas and bodies, as the occasion for the unfolding of a historical possibility – scant in its appearance but massive in its latent implications; in *Point Omega*, we find ourselves in a desert space, in which the bright, unfaltering light admits of no shades of meaning, no difference at work in the heart of the self-same. Elster wants to apply ideas to the Iraq war, to find a frame within which to philosophise or metabolise the first conflicts of the twenty-first century, the aftereffects of the global US; but the novel seems to suggest that such a frame is unavailable, that ideas and things fall away from each other or into each other, that they cannot enter into a transformative relation with one another. Things remain simply what they are, or not, resistant to the shaping force of history, immune or indifferent to the shape of a sentence or a decade. Jessie's disappearance does not yield a counternarrative, or make any historical friction. 'I could not think around the fact of her disappearance', Jim says late in the novel. 'At the heart of it, in the moment itself, the physical crux of it', there is 'only a hole in the air' (p. 104). Historical possibility is narrowed down to the bare elements of being, where oppositions become indistinguishable from tautologies, where everything is 'funnelled down' to the predicament in which Jessie is here or gone, 'one body, out there somewhere, or not' (p. 124).

III Lift

This draining of the tautology might appear to be a feature of late aesthetics, of irreconciled reconciliation. But what I want most centrally to argue here is that, even as these works unfold a distinct late style, and even as this late style finds a certain resonance with a postmillennial historical evacuation or disorientation, they bear within their own stark passages the seeds of a different kind of body time, an emerging historical and biopolitical possibility that is peculiar to these late works, and that has not yet come fully to expression, or found its place in the 'physical crux' of the moment. As David Cowart puts it, this is not 'mere tautology', but the container of 'poetic nuance', 'dreamy and ethereal and otherworldly'.[22] The evacuated insides of DeLillo's late tautologies – which hold within them a glacial world that has echoes of Woolf's stilling of the temporal current, her making of the moment 'something permanent'[23] – carry a surplus which is utterly unprecedented, which demands not only a new way of thinking about time and futurity, a new way of framing and measuring duration, but also a new form of embodiment, a new way of thinking about how time passes through the body, how the moving stream of consciousness finds itself embedded in matter, in body and in place. If the tautology in DeLillo's earlier novels contained a form of countercurrent, a set of historical possibilities that pushed against the apocalyptic tendencies of late twentieth-century literature and thought, the tautology in the postmillennial works feels altogether different, not a turbulent counterforce but a pool of stilled time and stilled thought in the midst of a post-historical calm; not a harbinger of apocalypse but post-apocalyptic, posthumous. But even as these works slow and still, as the increasingly insistent appearance of the tautology sounds our arrival at a kind of completion, something stirs within the bounds of self-reference, something that has not before been available to thought, and that lifts, weightlessly, on an invisible thermal.

In *The Body Artist*, in *Point Omega*, this emergent possibility, so slight and delicate that it is barely perceptible, is registered not as a corrective to a post-millennial vacuity or exhaustion – not as the summoning of narrative historical continuity from the teeth of the end of history – but as a feature of it, a part of its own unfolding logic. *The Body Artist* closes with the suggestion, as she stands by the open window and feels 'the flow of time in her body' (p. 124), that Lauren's period of mourning is drawing to an end, that she is now ready to re-enter the stream of collective time. This offers the possibility that Lauren will retune herself to the human space and time from which grief has exiled her, that she will humanise herself again, as Elster is humanised by the loss of his daughter Jessie in *Point Omega*. But if *The Body Artist* conforms in one sense to this narrative of recovery, it is balanced in another around the discovery of a different model of duration altogether, a different conception of futurity that does not belong to sequential narrative, but that finds itself moving in the unworlded intervals of the novel's pared back sentences, in the semantic pauses and lapses that work in the midst of Mr Tuttle's tautologies. It is this other form of duration, this other relation between time and the body, that generates the novel's poetry, that confers its moments of weightless lift, and that produces, as if out of nothing, the perception of a different model of life, a different way of patterning and encountering the movement of consciousness. 'You are made out of time', Lauren tells herself, as she tries to fathom the static movement of Mr Tuttle's mind, and of his syntax. 'This is the force that tells you who you are. Close your eyes and feel it. It is time that defines your existence' (p. 92). Time drives the movement of being, just as it shapes the passage of a sentence; but, Lauren realises, Mr Tuttle's tautologies evade this narrative momentum. 'This is the point', Lauren thinks, 'He laps and seeps, somehow, into other reaches of being, other time-lives' (p. 92). His time life belongs not to the narrative of mourning and recovery – the pieties of healing time that are so alienating and insulting to all who experience grief – but to that static movement that Lauren discovers in the depths of her mourning, that is found in the circular truths of Mr Tuttle's gnomic utterances, or in the 'brief but deep dimensions' that Lauren can hear in the synthesised voice of a telephone answering machine ('*Please / leave / a / mess/age / af/ter / the / tone*' (p. 67)). It is not in the human voice, or in the human experience of narrative sequence, that this other kind of being resides, but in the nonhuman, in the stone, or in the animal. Think of Elster in the desert, reflecting on his Teilhard de Chardin, on the end of history, the disintegration of consciousness into matter. We are entering a posthistorical moment, he thinks to himself, at which we are ready for what he calls a 'leap out of our biology', a time when we need to recognise that consciousness is not calibrated to a human spatial or temporal scale, but extends beyond us, into other worlds, and other time lives. 'Ask yourself this question', he says to Finley:

> Do we have to be human forever? Consciousness is exhausted. Back now to inorganic matter. That is what we want. We want to be stones in a field.[24]

Or think of Lauren, catching the flight of a bird out of the corner of her eye:

> She saw something rise past the window, eerie and birdlike but maybe not a bird. She looked and it was a bird, its flight line perfectly vertical, its streaked brown body horizontal, wings calmly stroking, a sparrow, not wind-hovering but generating lift and then instantly gone.[25]

In following the lift of the bird, the prose exceeds its own representational register, lifting out of the domain of shared worlds, and into some other drama of passing time, some thought-time-body assemblage that cannot be contained within the official sequences, the narrative protocols. 'She saw it mostly in retrospect', Lauren thinks, of the lift of the bird, this uncaptured movement of animal life, 'because she didn't know what she was seeing at first and had to re-create the ghostly moment, write it like a line in a piece of fiction' (p. 91). This is fiction reaching through or past itself, to an experience that is always doubled, an echo or a counter-thought or a picture of itself, but also unoccurring, yet to happen, still bodiless in the space of undreamt futurity. In one of those eerie moments of self-quotation that run through DeLillo's oeuvre, that give it a timeless quality, Lauren reaches for the sense that the flight of the bird does not belong to sequential narrative time, but is suspended in the latent tense of DeLillo's prose – a tense that lends the prose a certain negative religiosity, the 'post-secular' form of 'resacralization' that both Amy Hungerford and John McClure find in DeLillo's work.[26] James Axton thinks to himself, in DeLillo's 1983 novel *The Names*, that we find it hard to remember air travel, that we cannot properly recall the 'windy blast of aircraft', or 'the white noise of flight'. 'It is dead time', he thinks. 'It never happens until it happens again. Then it never happened'.[27] Lauren, in her postmillennial hideaway, catches this same sense of the unoccurring nature of narrative time, and of birdflight. 'Maybe it wasn't a sparrow at all', Lauren thinks, 'and how would she ever know for sure unless it happened again, and even then, she thought, and even then again' (p. 91). This is the time of Lauren's mourning, this time that she shares with the alien, animal life of the bird – a time stalled between happening and happening again, edging into thought only as the movement of a certain kind of fiction, a stretched, stilled prose, working at the limit of its expressive capacity, finding semantic flight as an effect of the redundancy of the tautology.

To think with the animal, to think like a stone, to take a 'leap out of our biology', these late works suggest, requires us to find a different conception of time life, one held not outside but within the bounds of a self-referring language. *Point Omega* seeks to open this space, as a poetic principle at work within the sentences themselves, as does *The Body Artist*. But it is in DeLillo's 2016 novel *Zero K* that the unmoving quality of tautological prose, as it offers a means of imagining a differently timed and tensed body, reaches its definitive late-stage expression. In this novel, the encounter with a different time life that is implicit in *The Body Artist* and *Point Omega* – the search for a different way of experiencing the flow of time in the body – is given the most literal expression. Here, the leap out of our biology – the search for what Henry James earlier called a mode of art that might grant the writer an 'extension', 'another go' at existence – takes the form of cryogenic suspension.[28] The novel, split into three parts, tells the story of an estranged father and son – Ross and Jeff Lockhart – struggling to come to terms with their differing responses to the promise of unending life offered by new medical technology, a 'scientific process that will keep body tissue from decomposing'.[29] The novel's first section is set in a scientific compound called the Convergence, lost in the bare landscapes of the Eurasian desert, where bodies are placed into suspended animation – the body frozen, as Jeff's stepmother Artis puts it, to be enhanced and perfected at some later date, 'reassembled, atom by atom', and then 'reborn into a deeper and truer reality' (p. 47). This first section – austere, alienated – extends the desert scenes of *Point Omega* into science fictional territory. The Convergence, part scientific installation, part avant-garde artwork, is dedicated to realising the transformed futurity that remains an idea in *Point Omega*. The vast underground structure houses the pods that project deanimated bodies into an unimaginable future; and it also works, like the bookends of *Point Omega*, as a gallery space, an aesthetic reflection on the end of the world, complete with free floating video screens that depict rushing disasters, tornados, floods, atrocities, self-immolations. Where the earlier novel seeks to retune the relationship between consciousness and matter, to find consciousness somehow returned to the landscape as stones in a field, the Convergence is conceived as a 'new generation of earth art, with human bodies in states of suspended animation' (p. 16). The buildings themselves are buried in the landscape, 'designed to fold into themselves (pp. 4–5), to 'blend into' the 'stark terrain' (p. 4), and in secreting themselves in this way, they seek to produce a new continuity between mind and material. 'One of our objectives', a Convergence scientist explains, 'is to establish a consciousness that blends with the environment' (p. 64). In response on the one hand to the threat of eco-crisis, nuclear war, population explosion, and other catastrophic end-states, and on the other to the emergence of new prosthetic and information technologies, the Convergence offers to disintegrate and reintegrate the terms in which we conceive of life, inhabitation, dwelling. 'We want to stretch the boundaries of what it means to be human', another scientist says, 'stretch and then surpass. We want to do whatever we are capable of doing in order to alter human thought and bend the energies of civilization' (p. 71).

The Convergence is dedicated to 'making the future. A new idea of the future' (p. 30), and in taking itself into this unmade space, a place 'outside the limits' (p. 31), where we will 'emerge from the capsules' as 'ahistorical humans' (pp. 129, 130), it feels cold, inhuman. Balanced against this frozen time, the novel's third section details Jeff's return from the Convergence to New York, his re-entry to shared space and time, the rush and bustle and hum of city life. As *The Body Artist* and *Point Omega* play the human against the antihuman or posthuman, so in *Zero K*, the far reaches of dismantled life in the Convergence are counterweighted by an immersion in the reality of human longing. The disarticulated forms of humanity contained in the underground chambers of the Convergence – the ranks of prosthetic bodies in pods, the screens which display pictures of a world at an end in the empty corridors – are mirrored, in this third section, but rescaled, humanised. The screens showing natural disasters re-emerge as the touchscreen in the back of a New York taxi, giving information about the weather. The variously malfunctioning humans preparing for the hinterland of ahistorical nonbeing in the Convergence appear as historical people seeking to live with damage, to find a way of focusing it as a principle of embodied being. There is a school child with special needs, a 'girl who could not take a step without sensing some premeditated danger', 'Light brown hair, sunlit now, a natural blush on her face, an intent look, tiny hands, six years old' (p. 191); there is a boy on a bus, 'thick bodied, an oversized head', overcome with awe at the sight of a New York sunset, a 'tide of light' (273) flooding the Manhattan grid. In mirroring the elements of which it is made in this way, in setting the desert against the city, decommissioned bodies against those still struggling to become, the novel seems to oppose an experience of collective, loving life, against the abstracted, technologised life of the Convergence. Do not think of difficulty, of biological failing, as an error to be written out of the code, the novel seems to suggest, but learn to live with, in and at a human scale. Do not medicalise, prostheticise, cryogenise, but, like the fearful school girl, learn to 'play a game, make a list, draw a dog, take a step' (p. 191).

This description of the novel might suggest that *Zero K* moves beyond the scant horizons of DeLillo's other post-millennial novels, even as it shares their concerns. Indeed, DeLillo himself has commented on this sense that the later novel feels more expansive, more fully realised than its direct predecessors. He wrote in 2016 that '*Zero K* is a leap out of the bare-skinned narratives of *Point Omega* and *The Body Artist*'.[30] Where the two earlier novels encamp in borderline spaces, shacks in the geographical and aesthetic desert, *Zero K* embeds and realises itself. The Convergence, even as it shares the desert setting with *Point Omega*, builds a world that more closely resembles the scientific installation 'Field Experiment Number One', in DeLillo's 1976 novel *Ratner's Star*; and the New York sequences from the third section of *Zero K* have some of the vibrant lyricism, the embodied hues, of the Bronzini episodes in *Underworld*. But if this is so, I think it is also the case that the return to fuller blooded life in this novel, the leap out of the bare skin of the late prose, is itself a distinctly late stage development – with some structural resemblance to the wintry renaissance that we find in Samuel Beckett's late novel *Company*. In balancing the human against the posthuman, New York against the Convergence (what DeLillo calls the 'twin identities' of the novel),[31] I do not think there is any simple renunciation of the bare theoretical and philosophical rigour of the late work, or any settled sense that the reaching towards an ahistorical future in the novel's first section is counteracted or repudiated by the historically rich humanity of the third. Rather, in playing lyrical pictures of human singularity (a striving girl with an intent look and small hands and flushed face) against an abstracted picture of a humanity at the stretched limits of its self-conception (the body of Artis, encased in a pod, lit ethereally from within (p. 258)), the novel is searching for a distinct, late stylistic means of picturing a humanity that has reached a historical tipping point, a humanity whose most intimate self-congress is being shaped by an encounter with a leap beyond its own determining conditions, a leap out of its own biology.

The mark of this search – and the stylistic feature which balances the human lyricism of this novel against its investigation of the posthuman limits of historical being – is the tautology, the grammatical symptom in DeLillo of stretched, abstracted self-reference, a mind at the limits of reflection. The tautology, or partial forms of tautology, surface throughout the novel – Artis' elusive assertion that 'I'm someone who's supposed to be me' (p. 52), for example, echoes the hunger of the Starveling for *dasein*, the struggle of another scant being to find a place to be – but the tautology emerges most definitively early in the novel, at a moment which recurs throughout the narrative, and which offers itself as a centre to the work, the lynchpin that holds together its twin identities. As Jeff arrives at the Convergence, he is struck by its sparseness, regardless of the technology, the money. The kitchen is basic – 'It was called a food unit and this is what it was' (p. 20) – but it is his first survey of his bedroom that brings the prose gradually, inevitably, towards the redundancy of the tautology:

> The room was small and featureless. It was generic to the point of being a thing with walls. The ceiling was low, the bed was bedlike, the chair was a chair. (p. 20)

This is the revelation that lies at the heart of this novel – the encounter with a limit condition in which a chair is a chair, in which things are what they are. The prose arrives here in the sealed space that Beckett discovers in his own late historical, late stylistic works. Jeff's room comes straight out of one of Beckett's late pieces for television – a work such as *Ghost Trio*, in which a man is locked in a sealed room, whose features – walls, floor, bed, door – are shown by a dispassionate camera, and described, in all their unornamented thereness, by a toneless extradiegetic voice. The room in the Convergence is a feature of a world at an end, a world in which the difference that powers imaginative forms has lapsed. But if the tautology marks this end state – and if the lyricism of the third section might be read as a reaction to this white blankness – it is also the case that the tautologous room returns repeatedly, not only as the mark of Elster's exhaustion of consciousness, but also as the basis itself for a mode of lyrical rethinking, a lifted leaping out of a closed horizon. As Beckett's closed rooms also open themselves – through the virtue of such radical closure – to the dimensions they seem to deny, so Jeff's room at the convergence expresses both an end state, and the terms of a new mode of consciousness, a 'new way', as Jeff and Artis both put it, 'to think and see'.[32] The voice in Beckett's *Ghost Trio* commands us, once we have looked carefully at the 'kind of wall', the 'kind of floor', to 'look again'; the room is not as closed as it seems, or perhaps it is both open and closed, because, as the stage directions elusively declare, door and window are 'imperceptibly ajar'.[33] As the Beckettian tautology both asserts and denies unity, so the boundaries of Beckett's rooms are at once sealed and porous, and so, too, Jeff's room in the convergence marks both the end of a certain historical principle, and the terms in which we might learn to 'go on', in which we might learn to 'look again'.

The recurrence of the tautologous room, and the tendency for its closed boundaries to open onto other dimensions, can be traced throughout the scenes set in the Convergence – most strikingly as Artis prepares to enter into her own death, or afterlife. She could date the onset of her condition, she tells Jeff – the illness that leads to her decision to suspend her animated life – to a moment, after an eye operation, when she is suddenly granted access to the thingness of things, to the density of reality compressed into the most exposed and bare of surfaces – 'the familiar room', as she puts it, 'now transformed' (p. 45). She looks at the room and finds, in its revealed thereness, not the redundancy of the tautology, but a sudden release into poetic surplus that the tautology harbours. 'What was I seeing?' she says – 'I was seeing what is always there. The bed, the windows, the walls, the floor' (p. 44). But the seeing she is granted here reveals to her 'the brightness of it, the radiance'. The window frame, she says, is 'white, simply white', but this is a new kind of white. 'I had never seen white such as this, a white of enormous depth, white without contrast, I didn't need contrast, white as it is' (p. 46). This is a white that Beckett calls 'all white in the whiteness'.[34] To see this whiteness, to see this radiance, requires us, Artis goes on, in a near quotation of Lauren in *The Body Artist*, to see *not* as humans see, but to look at the world as if we were an animal, or a stone, beings and objects that, in Heidegger's famous account, are respectively 'poor in world' and 'worldless'.[35] Looking at a bird outside the widow, looking into the eyes of the elusive animal, the animal in flight, Lauren thinks to herself that 'she thought she'd somehow only now learned how to look' (p. 21), that 'this must be what it means to see if you've been near blind all your life' (p. 22), and as Artis sees into the dimensions of her empty room, she has the same thought. 'Is this the reality we haven't learned how to see?' she asks, 'Is this the world that only animals are capable of seeing? The world that belongs to hawks, to tigers in the wild?' (p. 46).

Artis offers another way to see the empty room – she allows, DeLillo suggests, a 'poetic breeze to whisper through the novel',[36] a lifted surplus to move in her strangely cancelled utterances – and the remaining passages in the Convergence seek to tune themselves to this expanded awareness, this sense that austerity, scantness, might open onto life extension, rebooted consciousness. Jeff becomes absorbed in intense self-reflection as he adjusts to the rhythms of the Convergence. 'I could not chew and swallow without thinking of *Chew and Swallow*'. 'Every act had to be performed with the words intact'. 'Maybe', he thinks, 'I could blame the *room*, my room, the introspective box' (p. 89). As he contemplates the various gallery spaces in the convergence – there is a huge gallery which contains only a 'small human figure' (p. 148), a near empty space in which 'the gallery itself is the art, the space itself, the walls, the floor' (p. 148); there is a 'sloped gallery' (140) containing three suspended bodies in pods, 'humans as mannequins' (p. 146) – Jeff reaches back to his room, the sealed space, as the key to the reworlding that the Convergence promises. 'Mannequined lives', Jeff thinks. 'I thought about my room, small and tight but embodying an odd totalness' (p. 146). If the refashioning of bodies opens here into some experience of totalness, the 'total object', as Beckett puts it, 'complete with missing parts'[37] – or the 'infinite whole' that Wittgenstein finds in the tautology[38] – then this largeness emerges from the experience of scantness, of tightness, the plainness that DeLillo has investigated in his postmillennial fiction, at the level of the sentence, at the level of the syntax. But the work of the tautology here is not confined to the austere spaces of the Convergence. To understand the balance of this novel, to respond to the push and pull between its twin identities, it is necessary to see that the tautology is at work not only in the bare white spaces of the lab, but also in the rich, coloured sequences in New York, the lyrically intense counterpoint to the cryogenic alienation, the frozen abstractions that might 'compete with infinity itself'.[39] Jeff visits his father in his New York town house, and sits in the father's room, decorated with abstract art, the room to which the father retreats in order to 'grow old'. This relationship is at the human heart of the novel – how a son measures the span and heft of his life against that of his father – but as they sit together in the painterly room, the room of mortal dimensions, one can feel the presence of Jeff's room in the Convergence, the thing with walls, interfering with the signal, offering another horizon or framework to the conversation. There was the subject of inheritance between them, Jeff thinks – would he come to live here himself, after his father's death? – 'Then the was the sparsely furnished room itself bearing a measure of such express intent that a person might feel that his presence was a violation' (p. 185).

The dying father's room contains an image of the deathless son's introspective box; and throughout the New York scenes, one can feel this resonance, this vibration, this sense that the expanded range of the visible, the radiance of a mode of nonhuman seeing that the Convergence demands, is a feature of the human principle, the engine of its lyricism, rather than its antidote. Jeff takes his girlfriend's son, Stak, to a gallery in New York, and again, one senses the presence of the Convergence in the city, the thinness of the partition that divides embodied human life from its extended, abstracted forms. The New York gallery, like the bare gallery in the Convergence – like the bare gallery that opens and closes *Point Omega* – produces a rigour, a naked awareness, that fringes all acts of apprehension in late DeLillo. 'The huge gallery area', Jeff says, is 'nearly bare', and 'the one prominent object on display lent a significance to the simplest movement, man or woman, dog or cat' (p. 217). This calls irresistibly to the gallery in the Convergence, the bare walls and floor, containing only a single object, a human figure, the 'fact of life, one small body with beating heart in this soaring mausoleum' (p. 149). But the gallery in New York contains not human life, but stone, that 'material object', which, Heidegger writes, is 'worldless'. The single artwork on display is a 'large rock, one rock' (p. 214), 'a chunk of material that belongs to nature, shaped by forces such as erosion, flowing water, blowing sand, falling rain' (p. 216). Jeff gives Stak a key to interpret this particular sight, in the form of a passage from Heidegger (from a short text entitled 'The Way Back into the Ground of Metaphysics'). 'Man alone exists', Heidegger writes, 'Rocks are, but they do not exist. Trees are, but they do not exist. Horses are, but they do not exist' (p. 213).[40] As both Alexander Pope and Johann Wolfgang von Goethe put it, 'the proper study of mankind is man'.[41] But the presence of the rock in the gallery space here suggests that *Zero K*, in what Heidegger calls the 'effort to go back into the grounds of metaphysics',[42] requires us to see this rock outside of the bounds of the human, beyond the human lyricism that DeLillo's prose so effortlessly summons – that we need now to think with the bird, with the stone, to think outside the terms of our own 'world picture'.[43] If we are to grasp the lyrical thrust of DeLillo's portrait of a girl who is afraid to take a step, the girl with tiny hands and an intent look on her flushed face, we need to see that she is *paired* here with that girl in the gallery space in the Convergence, a child's body emptied and abstracted. When Jeff sees the child in the Convergence, he thinks to himself, in an echo of Elster's Chardinan reflections, that she is a picture of exhausted consciousness. 'Even if I knew the reason for her presence and her pose' he says, 'it would defy all meaning. Meaning was exhausted in the figure itself, the sight itself' (p. 149). The six year old girl in New York, striving to draw a picture of a dog, to take a step, is in some sense the opposite of this abstracted form; but the logic of the novel, the thrust of its close examination of the texture of distributed life, of Jane Bennett's 'vibrant matter', is to see that our understanding of life now has to encompass the prosthetic, cryogenic abstraction of being as a principle of embodied striving – has to respond to the layering here of two gallery spaces, one displaying a child, one displaying a stone.[44]

As Jeff looks at the deanimated bodies in the Convergence, he thinks to himself that they represent 'lives in abeyance', the 'empty framework of lives beyond retrieval' (p. 141). It is the poetic task of DeLillo's late novels to approach this empty framework, this picture of life at or beyond its edge, brought to us in the bounded utterances of tautological prose. But if these novels seek to approach this region, as they do so they discover another life world, another time life, that lies beyond the ground of metaphysics, that is shared by child, and stone, and bird. In the brief middle section of the novel, that intervenes between the Convergence and New York, DeLillo gives a form of expression to the deracinated thoughts of Artis, as she stands suspended in the pod. These thoughts take the form of circling, stalled sentences, tautological utterances that cannot break free of their own circuitry. The words Artis speaks are reduced to words that declare their existence as words, like those words with nothing inside them that we find in *The Body Artist*. 'I am made of words' (p. 158), Artis says, in one of those DeLillian utterances that seek to exhaust themselves, to cancel themselves out. This is the language of life extended beyond the bounds of the human, into the exhausted, self-referring swirls of words that DeLillo first intuits in Mr Tuttle's broken syntax, the words that exist after consciousness has become exhausted. But if we are to grasp the picture of extended, prosthetic life that DeLillo is reaching for in his late work, and most fully in *Zero K*, we have to see that this closed language, this language reduced to a picture of itself, is a poetry that points towards a future, as Artis puts it, that is 'beyond imagining', that requires us to rethink what it is we mean by the imagination, an imagination which might outlive its own dying, or the lapsing of its human forms. Even as the middle section of the novel reduces itself to dead repetition, to the emptiness that is the closest we can come to the language of a consciousness that has outlived itself, the phrases themselves produce a peculiar, wriggling surplus, a language time that exceeds the words that are trying to depict themselves as words, shorn of their meaning – a language time that bridges the novel's twin identities, in which the lived time of the human might meet with the dead time of the Convergence. 'It is only when I say something that I know that I am here' (p. 161), Artis says, from the spectrally extended space of her pod. Words produce the being they witness, as Beckett finds in the grim narration of disappearing life in *How It Is*: 'I say it as I hear it'.[45] But here, as Artis enacts the reduction of consciousness to its verbalisation, the narrowing down of disembodied thought to the bare moment of its expression, she performs the movement of mind beyond the utterance that houses it, demonstrating that thought and word do not and cannot fully coincide, but always open a gap, a space which is the lifted ground to being in these late works. Try reading that sentence – 'It is only when I say something that I know that I am here' – without feeling a distance from and within the words, without realising that the sentence happens not in its midst but at its outsides, in the lapses that separate the components, as in Lauren's answer machine, or the laps and seeps in which Mr Tuttle enters other 'reaches of being' – those very spaces beyond the sentence that the sentence itself denies. It is as language tries to narrow itself down that we realise the opening that language always is, the movement of consciousness beyond its own limits that is the very genetics of thought, the sign of a mind moving within and beyond the matter through which it knows itself.

DeLillo wrote in 2016 that it is the task of novels to 'reveal consciousness'; but he suggested, at the same time, that writing *Zero K* had taken him to the far edge of the consciousness that prose fiction is able to reveal, a place beyond the closed room, 'beyond the man or woman seated at the writer's desk'.[46] It has led him to a late historical scenario at which consciousness has reached an omega point, tipping over into matter, or code. 'Will advancing technology revitalise consciousness', he asked, 'or drown it forever?'.[47] These late works depict an imagination that is facing the possibility of its own death, a human consciousness that might be drowned forever, either by cataclysmic flood, or by the technological overcoming of the limits of the human itself. If the approaching realities both of ecocatastrophe and of technological transformation are to be survived, these late works suggest – if the lowering horizons of our age are to open onto a revitalization, a leap out of our biology – then we must find a way to give expression to a consciousness that is already moving beyond the terms in which we recognise and humanise ourselves. We have to learn how to see the empty syntactical and biomaterial frameworks that lie at the fringes of our forms of apprehension – the featureless body in the pod that is a late shadow of, and an early precursor to, the intent girl summoning the courage to take a step.

2018

CHAPTER 4

A More Sophisticated Imitation
Ishiguro and the Novel

I'll have grounds / More relative than this.
William Shakespeare, *Hamlet*.[1]

We are never "at home": we are always outside ourselves.
Michel de Montaigne, *Essays*.[2]

There is a moment in Kazuo Ishiguro's 2021 novel *Klara and the Sun* which offers itself as a prism through which to read Ishiguro's long conversation with the novel form.

The moment comes in a scene, three quarters of the way through the novel, in which the protagonist and first-person narrator Klara makes a critical discovery about the nature of artistic representations. This discovery is intimately related to the various forms of artificial life with which the novel is centrally concerned. Klara is an automaton whose sole purpose in life is to act as an 'Artificial Friend' (or AF) to her owner, a teenaged girl named Josie. But if Klara is the most obviously artificial persona in this novel, she is part of an environment which has become more generally artificial, manufactured and simulacral. Children need AFs in the world of the novel – an oddly skewed version of a North American suburb – because life has become so technologically mediated that there are few places left in which young people might socialise with each other, and so make real friends. Children do not go to school, but are educated at home on their mobile devices (in a somewhat eerie enactment of home schooling during the 2020 pandemic). Their education and their social life are empty, a tinny replica of shared life, and the children themselves are biologically engineered, made in the laboratory. Wealthier families subject their children to a form of genetic enhancement known as 'lifting', which makes enhanced students more readily able to learn the lessons given to them by their avatar professors. The genetically modified children learn in artificial educational environments from simulacral educators, and it is the job of AFs like Klara to assuage the loneliness and isolation that such radically alienating social engineering produces.

This biomedical adaptation of children like Josie to the artificial environment of the novel – reminiscent, of course, of Ishiguro's earlier novel *Never Let Me Go* – comes at a great cost. Being 'lifted', we learn, does not only render these children strangely evacuated and out of focus, but it is also dangerous. Josie had an older sister, named Sal, who died of the procedure. Josie herself, from the beginning of the novel, is seriously and possibly terminally ill, also as a side effect of the lifting process. Josie is so weak that she is more or less housebound; but despite her illness she makes regular trips to the nearby city, where she visits the studio of a local artist named Mr Capaldi in order to sit for a 'portrait'. There is something fishy both about this portrait, we are led to suspect, and about the portraitist, something obscurely connected to Josie's illness, and to her artificiality. Josie's boyfriend Rick (the only 'unlifted' child we meet) is suspicious of him. 'This guy', Rick says, 'this artist person. Everything you say about him sounds, well, *creepy*'. 'All he seems to do' he says, 'is take photos up close. This piece of you, that piece of you. Is that really what artists do?'.[3] Josie's housekeeper Melania – a tough talking immigrant worker of unspecified ethnicity – also expresses her distrust, perhaps more plainly. 'That Mr Capaldi', she says, is 'one creep son bitch'. Klara, confused by Melania's virulence, replies 'but housekeeper, isn't Mr Capaldi just wishing to paint Josie's portrait?', and Melania only intensifies her hostility: 'Paint portrait fuck. AF, you watch close Mr Son Bitch or something bad happen Miss Josie' (p. 177).

It is when Klara and Josie, and Josie's mother and father, pay a visit to Mr Capaldi in his studio that the moment I am interested in here arrives. Klara's mother and Josie say to Mr Capaldi that they want to see the portrait he has made of her. 'It's kind of scary', Josie says, 'but I'd like to take a peek'. Mr Capaldi, though, is a little hesitant, a little reluctant. 'You must understand', he says, 'it's still a work in progress. And it's not easy for a layperson to understand the way these things slowly take shape' (p. 196). Josie is forbidden to look at the portrait, but Klara, with Melania's emphatic instructions in her mind, breaks into the studio, to see it for herself:

> I turned the corner of the L and saw Josie there, suspended in the air. She wasn't very high – her feet were at the height of my shoulders – but because she was leaning forward, arms outstretched, fingers spread, she seemed to be frozen in the act of falling. Little beams illuminated her from various angles, forbidding her any refuge. (p. 204)

The 'portrait' of Josie, we realise at this moment, isn't a portrait at all. Klara had already intuited this, she says to Mr Capaldi and to Josie's mother. 'I'd suspected for some time', she says, 'that Mr Capaldi's portrait wasn't a picture or a sculpture, but an AF' (p. 207) – an automaton like Klara herself. Through all of Josie's trips to sit for Mr Capaldi, as he photographed the various disaggregated 'pieces' of her, Mr Capaldi had not been making a *representation*, but rather a new version of her, one that might take her place when she herself dies, a victim of her own genetic artificiality. As Mr Capaldi says, 'What you have to understand is this. The new Josie won't be an imitation. She *really will be Josie. A Continuation* of Josie' (p. 208, Ishiguro's emphasis). Mr Capaldi has made a new automaton body to replace Josie's when she dies; and he explains to Klara that she too is part of the portrait that he is making, that Klara's own real purpose is to act as a replacement, a continuation, of Josie's mind, of her personality. 'That Josie you saw up there', Mr Capaldi says to Klara, 'is empty'. Klara must 'inhabit' her. 'We want you to inhabit that Josie up there with everything you've learned' (p. 209). 'You're not being required simply to mimic Josie's outward behaviour. You're being asked to continue her' (p. 210). 'The second Josie won't be a copy', Mr Capaldi says to Josie's mother. There's 'nothing inside Josie that's beyond the Klaras of this world to continue' (p. 210). 'She'll be the exact same and you'll have every right to love her just as you love Josie now' (p. 210).

This moment is the crux around which Ishiguro's novel turns, a moment which one can only begin to address by placing it in dialogue not only with Ishiguro's wider oeuvre but with the novel form as a whole. Rebecca Walkowitz, in a seminal essay on Ishiguro published in 2001, before either *Klara and the Sun* or *Never Let Me Go* were written, might have been addressing this moment, *avant la lettre*, when she says that Ishiguro's novels 'register this dialectic, between the narratives that generate identities and the narratives that describe them'.[4] How, Ishiguro asks, are we to find or guard the line, in a fictional world, between an act of imitation and an act of creation – that is, between mimesis and prosthesis, between representing a missing thing, and being the thing that is missing? When Klara says, in her first-person narrative voice, that she 'saw Josie there, suspended in the air', how are we to read the referring power of the proper name 'Josie'? Do we sustain a difference, within the name itself, between the living child Josie and the prosthetic replacement of Josie that Mr Capaldi has made? I saw Josie there, Klara says, and we hear her saying that the doll Josie she saw was so like the real Josie, such a 'sophisticated imitation' of her, that it felt as if she was looking at Josie herself.[5] Or do we hear, in that single name being used to refer at once to Josie and this imitation of her, this replacement, this *continuation*, the suggestion that there is no difference between the real Josie and the artificial Josie, that 'Josie' is artifice, is fiction, pure and simple, and so the distinctions between first order and second order versions of her collapse at the moment that her status as fiction, as an *effect* of fiction, is revealed?

Ishiguro asks this question at this moment in *Klara and the Sun*, and in asking it he poses a question about the nature and history of the novel form – a form he has always worked with in a highly self-conscious fashion, so that one never forgets, when reading Ishiguro, that he is working in the wake of a crowded host of ancestors. Ishiguro's fiction is always haunted in this way – he mobilises multiple literary and national traditions with every stroke of his pen – but this episode of the portrait is perhaps unusually rich in associations, unusually powerful in its evocation of the imaginative apparatus of prose fiction itself. To place a character in a fiction in front of his or her represented likeness, in order to ask whether the original or the copy has ontological primacy; this is to mobilise a tradition of fictional portraits that reaches back through the history of the novel. It is to employ a device that knows it is a device, and that knows that it is a device which has been employed, at every key moment in the history of fictional representation, to anatomise the texture and mimetic potency of the device itself. As Klara stands in front of the portrait of Josie – as these different forms of artificial life confront one another under the technological and political conditions that determine representation in *Klara and the Sun* – we can feel Ishiguro weighing the balance, in 2021, between prosthesis and mimesis, pressing at the ways in which the technological, political and material production of the real is related to our capacity for crafting representations. And as we feel Ishiguro approaching this difficult, shifting ground, we can see, ranged behind this meeting between the portrait and its subject, earlier stagings of this encounter, each of which speaks in its own terms of the relation between the prosthetic and the mimetic, between life and the representation of life.

Take, for example, the centrality of the painted portrait to Thomas Pynchon's 1965 novel *The Crying of Lot 49*. This work sits at a junction in the history of prose fiction in part because it articulates the revolutionary power of the aesthetic representation to overcome that which is represented. The novel's protagonist Oedipa Maas feels herself to be ensnared in a series of interlocking representations that have no reality underpinning them – to be trapped, as she sees it, in a simulacral tower – and the vertiginous sense that Pynchon's novel is approaching its own status as a groundless representation is concentrated in a moment at which Oedipa stands in front of a painting which depicts other women, other Rapunzels, trapped in their own towers. The painting, *Embroidering Earth's mantle* by Remedios Varo, depicts a 'number of frail girls' locked in a tower, embroidering a tapestry which spills out of its frame, so that 'all the waves, ships and forests of the earth were contained in this tapestry, and the tapestry was the world'.[6] The imagined portrait here bears the weight of an epistemological revolution – the revolution which came to be known as postmodernism – which tends to invert the relationship between original and copy, between fiction and the real. To read Ishiguro's portrait against Pynchon's, and Varo's, is to approach the balance between the material and the informational, as this has shifted in the passage from the later twentieth to the early twenty-first century, and from the postmodern moment to whatever has come to replace it. And then behind Pynchon's portrait, we can see other portraits reaching back, to modernism, and then before that to nineteenth-century realism, and before that to the earliest manifestations of the modern novel form.

Consider, for example, the moment in Edith Wharton's *The House of Mirth*, when Wharton's protagonist Lily Bart feels herself to be a continuation of Joshua Reynold's portrait of Mrs Lloyd, or the twinned moment in Henry James's *The Wings of the Dove* when Milly Theale is overwhelmed by her resemblance to Bronzino's portrait of Lucrezia Panciatichi. Both of these moments follow closely the contours of the meeting between Josie and her portrait in *Klara and the Sun*, but in Wharton and in James this meeting is given its epistemological weight by the tension, at the turn of the twentieth century, between a realist and a modernist world view. In Wharton's novel Lily Bart materialises her affinity with the Reynolds portrait, quite literally, when she poses as Mrs Lloyd during an evening of *tableaux vivantes* – becoming a living picture, just as Josie's portrait is a living picture of Josie. 'She had shown her artistic intelligence', Wharton's narrator says of Lily's performance,

> in selecting a type so like her own that she could embody the person represented without ceasing to be herself. It was as though she had stepped, not out of, but into, Reynold's canvas, banishing the phantom of his dead beauty by the beams of her living grace.[7]

Lily is not an imitation of Mrs Lloyd, any more than Mrs Lloyd is an imitation of Lily. As Lily stands static on the stage, allowing her body to assume the posed attitude of Mrs Lloyd, the two are *continuations* of each other, sharing their being with each other, as Josie shares her being with her prosthetic twin. It is in becoming Mrs Lloyd, Lily's pseudo lover Lawrence Selden thinks, that she becomes 'the real Lily Bart', 'the Lily we know' (p. 133). Lily's reality is enhanced, for Selden, by this intimately shared relation between being and representation; but in Wharton, as in Henry James, this struggle between life and artifice does not quite lead to the overcoming we see in Pynchon, but stages rather a kind of struggle between a modernist aestheticism and a real which it cannot fully either accommodate or eject. Lily's sharing of her being with a portrait is the uncertain climax of Wharton's novel – a moment of deeply compromised freedom that is quickly forsaken as Lily heads towards poverty, unfreedom and death; and in James's *Wings of the Dove*, Milly Theale achieves a similarly vexed form of epiphany, in her identification with the portrait of Lucrezia. It is as she stands in front of the Bronzino, as she finds herself replicated in the compositional fields of an Old Master, that she is granted some ecstatic understanding of the nature of her being, some revelation in which she comes to understand both that she is herself a representation and that, like Ishiguro's Josie, she is dying, that there is some underlying connection between aestheticism and death. 'She found herself', the narrator says, 'looking at the mysterious portrait through tears':

> The lady in question, at all events, with her slightly Michelangelesque squareness, her eyes of other days, her full lips, her long neck, her recorded jewels, her brocaded and wasted reds, was a very great personage – only unaccompanied by a joy. And she was dead, dead, dead.[8]

James's entire novel is concentrated in this moment, as *The House of Mirth* is concentrated in the coming together of Lily and Mrs Lloyd. The emergence of James's and Wharton's modernism is materialised in this politically weighted encounter between a fictional character and a painted portrait, one which is itself staged as a corrective to or conversation with earlier such encounters. It is impossible not to see in Lily's affinity with Mrs Lloyd an after-image of Oscar Wilde's living picture in *The Picture of Dorian Gray*. Dorian's portrait has what Wilde's narrator calls a 'strange affinity' with the life that it represents and substitutes, but Wilde imagines this affinity not as incipient modernism but rather as a late Gothicism, in which the death that James sees as a function of aesthetic representation is altogether more ghoulish.[9] The eeriness of the bond between the portrait and its subject that one can feel in Ishiguro, in Wharton and in James, is given its full rein in Wilde (and in a mass of nineteenth-century gothic works by Bram Stoker, Charles Maturin, Sheridan Lefanu, E. T. A. Hoffman, Edgar Allan Poe and others).[10] And it runs, too, throughout the realist tradition, where the capacities of the novel to depict life truly are insistently shadowed by a fascination with the painted portrait, its particular fidelities and duplicities. Consider the painting, concealed spookily behind a wooden panel, of 'an upturned dead face' which opens George Eliot's *Daniel Deronda*, and which is the hinge around which the entire novel turns (the painting prefigures Gwendolen's view of her husband's face as she watches him drown towards the novel's close: 'there was the dead face – dead, dead').[11] Or think of the central episode of the portrait, earlier in the nineteenth century, in Jane Austen's *Emma*. Emma adopts an artificial friend (an early version, perhaps, of Ishiguro's Klara), in the form of the cheerful Hartfield resident Harriet Smith. Emma has no real feeling for Harriet, the narrator suggests, and their manufactured friendship is a sign of Emma's faulty and partial understanding both of people around her and of herself. This gulf, between the novel's world and that world as Emma sees it, is given its most condensed form in the portrait that Emma decides to paint of Harriet, with the intention of dazzling the local vicar, Mr Elton, with her beauty. The delicious comedy of this episode turns around the fact that Harriet, focalised through Emma's own skewed forms of perception, is already an artificial figure, and so Emma's amateur and deliberately mistaken likeness of Harriet is not so much a bad portrait as it is another version of Harriet, a *continuation* of the ways in which the novel sees her (or fails to see her). Each of the central characters expresses a view on Emma's artistry, and in eliciting these critiques the portrait serves as an index of the novel's reality effect, a means of testing how ways of seeing, ways of representing, relate to a notional real Harriet, lying somewhere beyond the limits of the text. Emma's doting valetudinarian father Mr Woodhouse fails to understand that the painted Harriet is not susceptible to the common cold: 'The only thing I do not thoroughly like is, that she seems to be sitting out of doors, with only a little shawl over her shoulders'.[12] The schoolmasterly Mr Knightley simply refers Emma to the errors in her portrait: 'You have made her too tall, Emma' (p. 38). Mrs Weston sees the gap between Harriet and Emma's flattering portrait, but her love for Emma leads her, in Procrustean fashion, to blame the subject for failing to conform the portrait, rather than the other way around. 'Miss Woodhouse has given her friend the only beauty she wanted', she says. 'The expression of the eye is most correct, but Miss Smith has not those eye-brows and eye-lashes. It is the fault of her face that she has them not' (p. 38). Mr Elton, of course, artificially in love with the painter of the portrait rather than its subject, is overflowing with feigned admiration for the picture: 'It appears to me a most perfect resemblance in every feature.

I never saw such a likeness in my life [....] Oh it is most admirable! I can't keep my eyes from it. I never saw such a likeness' (p. 38, 39).

Austen's experiments with representational forms in *Emma* are central to the development of her model of realism; and they themselves call back to an earlier moment in the history of the novel form. In balancing Harriet against Emma's depiction of her, Austen enters knowingly into a dialogue with Cervantes, the writer who had done most before her to examine the relation between representation and life, and who is one of the originators of the tradition of living pictures that I am tracing here. The relation between Harriet and her portrait has an origin in those repeated moments in *Don Quixote* when Quixote fails, as a result of his credulous infatuation with books of chivalry, to distinguish between fantasy and reality. When Austen crafts a form of realism that gains access to the failures of Emma's perception – that allows us to feel the broken bond between Emma's ways of seeing and the world that lies beyond her apprehension – we can see, behind Emma, the scrawny figure of Cervantes's knight errant, tilting at windmills. The failure to distinguish properly between Harriet and her portrait that Mr Woodhouse suffers when he thinks a portrait might catch a cold; that the ridiculous Mr Elton suffers when he picks the portrait up with a 'tender sigh', exclaiming 'what a precious deposit' (p. 39); that Emma herself suffers when she confuses 'improving' Harriet in the portrait with improving her in life (p. 34): all of these failures summon the spectre of Quixote, the light and mirror of knight errantry, slaying imaginary giants, brandishing his sword at wineskins. Austen's blurring of boundaries between Harriet and her portrait reaches right back to the blurred boundaries, in *Quixote*, between puppets and the characters they represent in a puppet show – the confusion between life and the 'pasteboard' representation of life that results in Don Quixote striding up to the stage to 'rain blows upon the puppet heathenry' with 'swift and unparalleled fury'.[13]

When Ishiguro imagines Klara standing in front of Mr Capaldi's prosthetic version of Josie – the artificial friend, the pasteboard puppet – he activates this novelistic tradition of portraiture, this long examination of the ways in which representations diverge from and unite with the people and things they represent. One can feel, at work in this encounter between Josie, Klara, and Mr Capaldi's 'imitation' of Josie, a history of the novel's struggle to make of represented forms a new kind of reality. As Ishiguro asks how far contemporary forms of artificial life can replace or stand in for human life we can see behind this question the forms invented by Pynchon, by James and Wharton, by Wilde, by Austen, by

Cervantes – fictional forms which are a record of the material historical forces which determine both how our representations imitate the world, and how they serve to create it. In *Klara and the Sun*, and throughout his work, it is one of Ishiguro's singular gifts to create this effect, this sense that a given act of imagination comes about in a layered relation with the other imaginative acts which inform it, which enable it, which constrain it. From the early 'Japanese' works *A Pale View of Hills* and *The Artist of the Floating World*, through his intricate study of Englishness in *Remains of the Day* and the dislocated dreamwork of *The Unconsoled*, to his skewed science fictions *Never Let me Go* and *Klara and the Sun*, Ishiguro has worked this strange magic, this capacity at once to imagine, and to reveal the hidden historical determinants of the imagination, its richly embedded conditions of possibility.

Ishiguro's work is always attentive, in this way, to the history of form, always conscious of the histories and traditions that attend every act of imagination; and the most recurrent means by which he explores and articulates these histories is through his fictional recreation of the work of art itself. As *Klara and the Sun* is centrally interested in the capacity of the portrait either to represent or to create life, so his work more generally sets out to explore the machinery of the work of art, and how the precise mechanics of aesthetic representation relate to the political and historical realities that the artwork witnesses. In the early 'Japanese' novels, for example, this exploration is conducted in relation to painting, and particularly in relation to the ways in which a painted canvas is bound up with the world that the canvas represents. *The Artist of the Floating World* – Ishiguro's second novel – concerns the artist, Masuji Ono, whose paintings, it is suggested, served a propagandist function in the build up to World War II. Ono is retired as the narrative begins in October 1948, and he spends the novel looking back, on his career as an artist, and on the disastrous consequences of Japan's military intervention in the war (not the least of which, for Ono, is the loss of his own son, who died as a combatant). As in so much of Ishiguro's fiction, Ono's reflections on the war, on his family, on his painting, are conducted through a kind of thick filter, an emotional stuntedness and a distorted perspective which makes it difficult to see clearly the world that Ono reflects on, and so to make accurate judgements about it. But the task and pleasure of reading the novel is to see through Ono's confusions and blindnesses, to understand what kind of reckoning he is trying to make, with his early political investment in Japanese nationalism, his relation to his authoritarian father, his own weaknesses and failures as a father to his dead son and living daughters.

And at the heart of this reckoning is Ono's attempt to understand how his painting contributed to Japan's entry into the war. He painted a work named 'Eyes to the Horizon' in the thirties, he remembers, which featured a soldier who 'held out his sword, pointing the way west towards Asia', under the slogan 'Japan must go forward'.[14] He fears that this painting, and others that he made in the thirties, had a material influence on the course of history, and the pathos of the novel is bound up with his slow and partial attempt to take responsibility for that influence, and to come to terms with his errors of political and aesthetic judgement. But what is so peculiar and haunting about Ono's reflection on his role in the escalation of Japanese militarism is that it cannot float free from his own inability to separate the aesthetic components of his artwork from the political ones. The novel's particular, enveloping sadness arises in large part from Ono's failure to understand that political reality is a brutal and coarse thing, and that it is not shaped, or at least not directly, by the delicacies of the painter's art. His regret is not the regret of a propagandist – who necessarily paints in broad brush strokes – but of an artist still convinced that real material change might be brought about by his old teacher's determination to 'change fundamentally the identity of painting as practised in our city' (p. 144), or to 'bring European influence into the Utamaro tradition' (p. 202). It is hard for Ono to understand his failings as an artist, as a citizen, as a father, when he can't focus the relation between the artwork and the realities it touches on, when, as he himself puts it, he is prone to make 'a naïve mistake about what art can and cannot do' (p. 172).

The Artist of the Floating World is centrally concerned with this question, how to calibrate what it is that art does, how art relates to forces that are larger than it and beyond its control. In the Japanese novels, it is painting that is the focus of this question, and then as Ishiguro's work develops he expands to explore other artworks and other genres as they engage with the political contexts that determine them. In his 1995 novel *The Unconsoled* – perhaps the most sustained and powerful analysis of the political purchase of the artwork that he has made – the medium is not painting but music. The protagonist, Ryder, is a world-famous pianist, who has arrived in an unnamed Middle European city to give a recital that is of crucial importance to the entire community. From the beginning, the narrative suffers that same miscalibration, that same derangement of scale, that we find in *Artist of the Floating World*, but here it is much more extreme, as the fabric and texture of the fictional world becomes immeasurably more fissile and warped, more subject to dreamlike transformations and incongruences. The city itself is both entirely unknown to Ryder, and some half-forgotten version of his childhood home; the people he encounters are both strangers and intimate friends. Two strangers he meets, a woman named Sophie and her child Boris, are his lover and adopted son, even though they never cease, at the same time, to be strangers. The city swirls around Ryder in this confused amalgam of the familiar and the strange, and at the heart of the confusion, of the drastic lack of proper focus, is the question of Ryder's role as a musician, and the purpose that his upcoming recital should serve. Ono's teacher wants to 'change fundamentally the identity of painting as practised in our city'; Ryder's visit to the city of *The Unconsoled* is bound up with some obscure responsibility that he has to cure all of the community's ills – to heal a sickness which has infected the souls of the inhabitants – by bringing about some fundamental change to the identity of music, as it is practised by the city's leading musical lights. The leaders of the community, wildly improbably, are concerned not with parking restrictions or refuse collection or local taxation levels, but with the finer technicalities and demands imposed by the difficult music of the contemporary avant-garde. The disgraced conductor and former head of the community Christoff complains to Ryder that it is difficult to achieve political change in the community, to bring the city back to some semblance of order, when the musical literacy of the inhabitants has been allowed to fall so low. 'But the modern forms!', Christoff says, they're too difficult, too demanding for the person in the street to master. 'How can people like this, untrained, provincial people, how can they ever understand such things, however great a sense of duty they feel towards the community'.[15] The confusion that attends Ryder's relation to his environment, that estranges him from his family and from himself, this is part of some wider malaise, it is suggested, some failure of scale and meaning that it is Ryder's task to correct, through his mere talent as a musician. He will take to the stage at the climax of his visit to the city, he will give a perfect rendition of one of the more demanding pieces by the imaginary composers of the day, by 'Kazan' or 'Mullery', and the community will magically be healed, brought back to clarity, reality, legibility, by the sheer beauty of his 'crushed cadence', or his 'vented rest' (p. 186).

Ishiguro's test of the function and purpose of art is almost always conducted through this failure of scale, this misreading or warping of the relation between art and reality. Music takes on an exaggerated or misconceived importance in *The Unconsoled*, as painting does in *The Floating World*. The clones in *Never Let Me Go* have to demonstrate their capacity to 'be creative' in order to prove that they have souls, as the portrait in *Klara and the Sun* is required not to represent its subject but to become it.[16]

But if this is the case, perhaps the most singular characteristic of Ishiguro's work is that such misreadings do not produce a malfunction of the artwork itself – or do not *only* produce such a malfunction – but rather open onto an encounter with its very conditions of possibility. Ishiguro's fiction binds itself to other art forms in ways that distort and dismantle those forms, but he does so, always, in order to approach the difficult, vanishing space that underlies form itself, the space from which the possibility of the artwork arises, and into which it always threatens to disappear.

In *The Unconsoled*, for example, the oddity of the scenario, the dreamlike predicament that Ryder finds himself in, seems like it should result in a general collapse of the reality effect. The very prospect of a musician visiting a city whose entire social and political life revolves around the finer technicalities demanded by its avant-garde composers – the technicalities that the musician himself is required to demonstrate in a recital on stage before the entire community – is itself, unmistakably, a dream, an unreality. When Christoff bemoans to Ryder the paucity of the citizens' musical understanding we know we are in the world of a dream, and more specifically in the world of a dream as imagined in Franz Kafka's fiction. The skewed forms of community here – townsfolk holding debates about musicology in the darkened space of a cinema, while others sit around playing cards – are a reflection of those legal debates in *The Trial*, or the theological debates in a darkened church, or the conversations about portraiture between K and a court painter that take place in the painter's cramped attic room (which opens, weirdly, directly onto the courtroom itself).[17] The community discussions of musicology in *The Unconsoled* are tuned to a Kafkan wavelength, and so too is the lager furniture of Ishiguro's novel, its locale, its atmosphere. The dislocated, alienated city of *The Unconsoled* belongs in *The Castle*, or *The Trial*. Passages pass through the novel, connecting spaces which should remain remote from one another in the sudden and uncanny contiguity that Deleuze and Guattari have so powerfully identified as the folded terrain of Kafka's thinking.[18] Just as Ishiguro activates a history of fictional portraiture in *Klara and the Sun*, so in *The Unconsoled* he reanimates Kafka's work with a deeply uncanny intensity, and he does so in part in order to push a Kafkan dreamwork beyond its own limits. The desire of the narrative is in a sense to bring the very possibility of narration, and its relation to the world that we live in, to the point at which it collapses. As in all of Ishiguro's work, the connections that Ryder has with others feel empty, broken, breached by a distance that cannot be crossed, as Ryder cannot properly enter into a relation with his artificial lover Sophie, or his surrogate son Boris, or his elderly parents, who are supposedly coming to the city to watch him play but remain just beyond his grasp, just out of reach around every corner. The narrative mechanism that might allow Ryder to fully inhabit the world of the novel, to closely meet with the people he loves, is too broken for this to happen, just as Ono in *The Artist of the Floating World* cannot quite make contact with his own past, or focus the political legacy of his art, and just as the clones in *Never Let Me Go* can't understand or formulate their relation to their own artificial personhood. In *The Unconsoled* even the positioning of narrative perspective, the bond between narrative voice and the bodies and places that the voice calls to being, is too dismantled, too dreamlike, too Kafkan, to sustain a coherent imagined world, to embed Ryder in his relation to himself and to others. Early in the novel, for example, Ryder drives a character named Stephan to a meeting with another character named Miss Collins. Ryder stays in the car, while he watches Stephan walk to the entrance of Miss Collins' house, and press the doorbell. 'The door was opened by an elderly, silver haired woman' – Miss Collins herself. 'The door closed behind him', Ryder says, 'but by leaning right back in my seat I found I could still see the two of them clearly illuminated in the narrow pane to the side of the front door' (p. 56). Ryder can still see them even though they are in the house and he is outside, across the street; and when they start speaking, Ryder can somehow hear what it is that they are saying, through some strange and impossible narrative telepathy. And then, as they walk together further into the house, Ryder can follow them still, from his position in the car, his gaze effortlessly telescoping out, sliding beyond itself into the interior of the building: 'I watched her lead Stephan through a small and tidy front parlour, through a second doorway and down a shadowy corridor decorated on either side with little framed water colours. The corridor ended at Miss Collins's drawing room – a large L-shaped affair at the back of the building' (pp. 56–57).

Such disruptions in the narrative architecture of the novel should have the effect, as I say, of bringing the building of the narrative crashing down, reducing it to a pile of rubble. But it is the particular magic of Ishiguro's work, both in *The Unconsoled* and throughout his oeuvre, that it does not, that the distances, the failures of communication and narrative orthodoxy that recur in all of his fictions, lead not to narrative malfunction, but to some contact with the substance of prose fiction itself, the space that the narrator of *The Unconsoled* shares so closely with Kafka's narrative voices. When Ryder cannot focus his relations with his son, or his lover, or his parents, this does not lead to a loss of narrative investment in those relations, but instead to a singular access to the foundational possibility of narrative relation as such, to the imagined grounds upon which such relations are built. It is this access that generates Ishiguro's pathos, his peculiarly intense uncovering of the terms in which we long for others. We never see Ryder's parents, as we never understand the nature of Ryder's relation with Boris; but this dislocation does not prevent the narrative from producing an extraordinarily powerful sense of the keening loss that a father feels for a son with whom he cannot communicate, or the loss that a son feels for parents who are dead or otherwise out of reach. Ryder starts to realise, towards the end of the novel, that his parents are not going to attend his performance after all, that they are not going to watch him play or witness his talent, as he so longs for them to do. 'I was sure, this time, at last, that they would come', Ryder says. 'Surely it wasn't unreasonable of me to assume that they would come this time' (p. 512). As he understands that they are not coming, that they will never come, he says, 'I collapsed into a nearby chair and realised I had started to sob' (p. 512). This sobbing – like the overwhelming sadness that namelessly engulfs him as he stands before Boris, the simulacrum of a son, and knows that he can't reach him, can't feel for him, can't console him – this grief never finds a place within him, within an achieved narrative persona. He 'realised' he had started to sob, as if it were someone else doing the sobbing, not him. Not him. But it is the discovery of *The Unconsoled* that these emotive ties are not bound to subject positions, and do not require a reality effect to generate them, but are at work in the process of imagining itself, are there already in the undifferentiated stem cells of fictional life.

This access to the unmade ground of fiction, the place from which narrative being emerges, is Ishiguro's particular gift as a novelist, and it determines too his conversation with the novel as a form, the conversation I have been tracing here. When Ishiguro reanimates Kafka in *The Unconsoled*, or when he summons the ghost of fictional portraits past in *Klara and the Sun*, he draws our attention to the ways in which the novel form, over the course of its history, has negotiated the shifting terms of our relations to ourselves and to others. Ishiguro's conversation with Kafka in *The Unconsoled* is shaped by the material historical forces which bear differently, on Kafka and on Ishiguro, as both reach for an articulation of the narrative bonds which tie us to ourselves and to others. Similarly, *Klara and the Sun* enjoins us to reflect on how the relation between representation and life figures differently in the various portraits that it calls to thought, in Cervantes, in Austen, in Wilde or Wharton or Pynchon. Both the evolving history of prose fiction, and the shifting political and technological conditions for the production and reproduction of life, are given a form of articulation in the dialogue that Ishiguro stages between Klara's artificiality and the artificiality at work in Wharton's Lily Bart, or Austen's Emma, or Cervantes's Don Quixote. But even as Ishiguro conducts this examination of the evolving historical conditions which determine our access to our artificial extensions, he opens this strange channel, this strange continuity, seamed within the novel form itself, between Klara and Emma, between Ryder and K. Ryder remains at a distance from himself in *The Unconsoled*, just as Ono in *The Floating World* cannot build a bridge between his post-war and his pre-war view of the world. For both Ryder and Ono their art – their music, their painting – is a mark of that estrangement. Music in *The Unconsoled* contains a fugitive form of life within it that cannot come to expression or taxonomy. Beneath the 'outer structure' of Ishiguro's music, Ryder says, there are 'peculiar life-forms hiding just under the shell' (p. 492). These are the unspeciated life forms, the estranged 'imaginary animals' that are drawn by the clones of *Never Let Me Go* in order to prove to their creators that they have souls.[19] But if the imagined artwork in Ishiguro's fiction gives expression to this kind of alienation, this refusal of speciation, it also preserves, even in its dismantlement, an underlying logic of attachment, a particular bond between being and representation that is a common inheritance of the novel form.

It is at a climactic moment in *Klara and the Sun* that we can see this logic of attachment most clearly. As so often in Ishiguro's fiction, this is a climax that happens out of time, that happens too early, and in the wrong place. Josie's mother has planned to take Klara and Josie on an outing to see a nearby waterfall, but on the morning of the trip, the mother decides, tyrannically and cruelly, that Josie is too ill to leave the house, that she must be confined to her sick bed. In another twist of the cruel knife, the mother insists that she and Klara should take the trip regardless, as if Klara has already taken Josie's place, already become the mother's daughter. When the two arrive at the waterfall, as they are sitting together at a picnic table, the mother begins properly to explore this possibility for the first time, to ask herself if Klara might really be able to act as a prosthetic replacement of her daughter – as a *continuation* of her daughter. 'Okay, Klara', she says. 'Since Josie isn't here, I want *you* to be Josie' (p. 103). In one of the uncanniest moments in all of Ishiguro's fiction, Klara says that she will try, try to walk like her, talk like her, to 'give a more sophisticated imitation' of her (p. 103). If Josie were sitting here instead of Klara, the mother says, 'how would she sit? I don't think she'd sit the way you're sitting'. No, Klara replies, 'Josie would be more … like this'. 'That's good', the mother says. 'That's very good':

> 'But now I want you to move. Do something. Don't stop being Josie. Let me see you move a little.'
> I smiled in the way Josie would, settling into a slouching, informal posture.
> 'That's good. Now say something. Let me hear you speak.'
> 'I'm sorry. I'm not sure…'
> 'No. That's Klara. I want Josie.'
> 'Hi, Mom. Josie here.'
> 'Good. More. Come on.'
> 'Hi, Mom. Nothing to worry about, right? I got here and I'm fine.' (p. 104)

This is a moment of intense proximity to what the novel does, to how it works, to its imitation of being that is also a continuation of being. It is a moment that reveals the deep uncanniness of aesthetic mimicry – the uncanny spell that binds Edgar Allan Poe's narrator when he looks at a painting in which the 'absolute *life-likeness* of expression [...] confounded, subdued, and appalled me'.[20] Josie's mother, leaning forward – rapt and revealed, Klara thinks, so she 'can see the cheekbones of her face very pronounced beneath her skin' – exhibits a kind of dismantled grief at this picturing of her daughter that is Ishiguro's signature effect. This is the grief that Ryder feels, as he realises he is sobbing for his dead parents, the grief that Ono feels for his son killed in the war. This is the grief of a mother for her dead daughter, Sal, and for her daughter, Josie, who is in the process of dying. In all its uncanny power, it is a wadded grief, wreathed about in artificiality, seen through the dark window of a mother's willingness to replace the person she most longs to hold to her, to never let go. Ishiguro's novel gives us this artificiality in the most naked imaginable terms, an artificiality revealed not only at the level of the plot, but in the syntax, in the tinny affectlessness of the language. But, magically, almost miraculously, the artificiality opens onto something unguardedly, boundlessly, edgelessly real. 'Hi, Mom. Josie here'. This is Josie talking, insofar as Josie has ever talked. This is a voice back from the dead, back from the condition of never having been. This is a more sophisticated imitation, more sophisticated than any imitation has the right or the power to be, because it is not an imitation at all. There is no join, no seam, between Klara speaking and Josie speaking. As the mother leans forward, the mother who can't express her grief, who can't distinguish between the dead daughter and the living, who can't console Josie for the loss of her sister or for the loss of her own health; as the mother leans forward and speaks to Klara, she is speaking to Josie. She is not speaking to someone like Josie, or to an imitation of

Josie, but to Josie. 'I'm sorry Josie', she says. 'I'm sorry I didn't bring you here today' (p. 105). The question that Ishiguro's novel asks – can Klara save Josie? can artificial forms save life rather than replace it or imitate it? – is answered here, too early and too late, as the novel voice speaks at once for Josie and Klara, for both the artificial and the real, the living and the non-living. The beauty of this moment is that Josie's mother makes the apology, the act of loving contrition for their distance and unreality that so many of Ishiguro's parents and lovers and children long to make. Its sadness lies in the fact that, in receiving that apology, in hearing and accepting it as she does, Josie can only conform to the artificiality for which it seeks to atone, can only demonstrate that none of us are quite at home in ourselves, or in each other.

It is at this moment, this moment when Ishiguro's embrace of artificiality touches most closely on his pathos, that we glimpse the ground of the novel form itself, the ground that Ishiguro unearths in his conversation with Kafka, with Wharton, with Austen, with Cervantes. This is an oddly collapsing ground, made at once of the necessarily estranged difference between being and the forms in which it knows itself, and of the magical overcoming of such difference. The voice that speaks here is the voice of the novel, the voice that can reveal to us the terms in which we encounter ourselves, but only by installing a prosthetic distance at the heart of that self-encounter. 'Don't worry', the novel says to us here, speaking at once as Klara and as Josie. Don't worry, I can forgive you for your distance and your failure to be, and that forgiveness can be real. But the reality of such forgiveness relies on the revelation that the consolation it offers us is a fiction, a fiction deeply at work in the world, at work in all our perceived realities. 'I wish I could stop you getting sick', the mother says to Josie, to Klara, 'I wish you were here. But you're not'. 'Don't worry Mom', the daughter says, appearing magically from the other side of an impassable divide, 'I'm going to be fine' (p. 195).

2023

CHAPTER 5

A Cleaving in the Mind
Kelman's Later Novels

James Kelman's novels of the twenty-first century – *Translated Accounts* (2001), *You Have to Be Careful in the Land of the Free* (2004), and *Kieron Smith, Boy* (2008) – together suggest the emergence of a distinct form of political fiction.[1]

All three novels extend the commitments of Kelman's earlier prose – the novels *A Disaffection*, *The Busconductor Hines*, *A Chancer*, *How Late It Was How Late*, the short fictions collected in *Not Not While the Giro*, *Greyhound for Breakfast* and elsewhere; but the most recent novels combine aesthetic and political radicalism, in a way which disturbs and refigures the dominant terms in which we have understood the relation between aesthetics and politics.

The question of literary politics – of how fiction is political – was shaped, through the later decades of the twentieth century, by the debate between Theodor Adorno and Georg Lukács concerning the distinction between committed and autonomous art. This debate, famously, turns around role of realism in establishing what Adorno calls the 'true relation of art to reality' – the relation on which a literary politics rests.[2] For Lukács, it is the task of realism both to represent reality, and to offer a critical response to its depravities, a task that abstract, formalist art can only fail to perform. The literature of the twentieth century, Lukács writes in his essay 'Franz Kafka or Thomas Mann' (published in German in 1957), presents us with a 'choice between an aesthetically appealing, but decadent modernism, and a fruitful critical realism'.[3] Seeing Thomas Mann as the exemplar of the latter, and Franz Kafka of the former, Lukács makes a distinction between an abstract, autonomous aestheticism, which constitutes a 'flight from reality', and a committed realism, which seeks to overcome such abstraction, and to intervene in the process by which reality is represented and formed.[4] 'The crucial question', he writes, 'is whether a man escapes from the life of his time into a realm of abstraction [...] or confronts modern life determined to fight its evils and support what is good in it'.[5] Political literature rests on a commitment to faithfully representing reality for Lukács; for Adorno, on the other hand, it is in abstraction itself that the political force of twentieth-century literature lies. It is in Kafka and Beckett, Adorno writes, that we find the most powerful excoriations of the 'modern world'. 'Kafka and Beckett', he says, in his influential 1965 essay 'Commitment', 'arouse the fear which existentialism merely talks about'.[6] It is in decommissioning the realism of committed art, in 'dismantling appearance', that these writers 'explode from within the art which committed proclamation subjugates from without, and hence only in appearance'.[7] In its abstraction, in its 'total dislocation, to the point of worldlessness', the modernism of Kafka and Beckett 'compels the change of attitude which committed works merely demand'.[8] It is in severing apparent ties to the world that modernist writing can make its most powerful protest against it, and so, ironically, 'every commitment to the world must be abandoned to satisfy the ideal of the committed work of art'.[9] When abstraction is our only available refusal of the way things are, then 'politics has migrated into autonomous art'.[10]

This debate maintains an opposition between the committed and the autonomous that was perhaps always false, and whose falsity was perhaps always exposed by a writing like Kelman's, which blends a commitment to local realities and dialects with an abstraction that affiliates him, in the critical imagination, with Kafka and Beckett. *A Disaffection*, for example, reads as a marriage of the localism of a writer such as Lewis Grassic Gibbon, with the comic disintegrations of *Molloy*.[11] But if this is so, it is in his novels of the twenty-first century – in the overwhelming abstract violence of *Translated Accounts*, the comic caricature of *You Have to Be Careful in the Land of the Free*, the immersive narrative voice of *Kieron Smith, Boy*, that Kelman's work looks past that opposition, towards a new way of conceiving the capacities of a dismantled mind to attach itself to the realities that have deformed it. Adorno writes that all abstract art carries within it a trace of the reality that is has abstracted. 'There is no material content', he writes, 'no formal category of artistic creation, however mysteriously transmitted and itself unaware of the process, which did not originate in the empirical reality from which it breaks free'.[12] This is no doubt true; but the distinction that both Adorno and Lukács maintain between committed and autonomous art occludes the junction at which abstraction is bound to the realities it disdains.[13] As a result, the Adorno of 'Commitment' locates the power of abstraction only in its negative mode, only were reality is missing, and so cannot approach that ground where the displaced mind meets with its compulsions towards place – the ground that is the very homeland of Kelman's political imagination.

In his more recent novels, Kelman has anatomized this ground, this relation between realism and abstraction, by adopting a range of different realisms, and different narrative styles. Both *Kieron Smith, Boy* and *You Have to Be Careful* might appear to belong more readily than *Translated Accounts* to the tradition of Glaswegian working-class fiction that Kelman extends in his later twentieth-century novels.[14] Their political force stems both from their engagement with this tradition, and from their formally inventive testing of the limits of a certain kind of narrative perspective, the kind of interior monologue that was developed by the modernist avant-garde. When Jeremiah in *You Have to Be Careful* describes himself, repeatedly, as an 'unassimilatit' and 'nonintegratit' alien, he suggests a number of political positions at once.[15] His refusal (or inability) to integrate in the 'land of the free' is part of the novel's broad satire on the incapacity of the US to tolerate cultural difference in a period of xenophobic paranoia after 9/11; that he should express and experience his non-assimilation in a 'skarrisch' dialect suggests that this critique of US hegemony is conducted from the perspective of a local culture and a local idiom that shapes and colours Jeremiah's thinking and his language. But the radical embeddedness of the narrative within Jeremiah's own head suggests that the alienation that he describes is a philosophical as well as a cultural one, that the narrative performs his incapacity to get outside the coils of his own exhausting interiority, as much as it does his failure to find himself at home in American freedom.

Both *You Have to Be Careful* and *Kieron Smith, Boy* owe something to a tradition of realism which sets out to depict a cultural location of experience with great precision or authenticity – a writing, by Kelman's own account, that 'derives from my own background, my own socio-political experience'.[16] Both are also, however, indebted to an avant-garde tradition which traces a narrative interiority divorced from the 'empirical reality' that both Lukács and Adorno associate with autonomous art. Their politics, then, arises both from a determination to maintain fidelity to local conditions and idioms – in a resistance to the colonising force of Englishness that have led some to position Kelman's writing in a postcolonial tradition – and from the inventiveness of their experiments with narrative voice.[17] *Translated Accounts*, however, seems to produce and require an entirely different kind of political rhetoric, and as a result might seem to develop a kind of praxis that is very different not only from Kelman's other novels of the decade, but from his oeuvre more generally. This work does not locate itself in a recognisable social space at all, nor does it house itself within the secure confines of any particular narrative perspective. Rather, it moves across a range of protocols for the reporting or gathering of witness accounts, giving a picture of a violence and alienation that is utterly generalised and unlocated. The political task of this work is not to write back to a centre from a specific margin, or to find a language for a particular kind of social experience, but rather to suggest or articulate a collapse of the forms of sovereignty and subjecthood that have allowed for the very possibility of private experience and interior narration. These accounts resemble nothing so much as Beckett's *Fizzles*, transplanted to Guantanamo Bay, or Abu Ghraib. Beckett's narrative practice fizzles out into snatches of prose (entitled 'He is barehead', or 'Old earth');[18] Kelman's disintegrates into sections of computerised code drawn from some displaced military administration (entitled 'her arms folded', or 'old examples').[19]

The different political categories and traditions to which these novels belong, then, are characterised by the way in which narrative agents are engaged with specific historical and cultural conditions, and by the possibilities for critique and transformation that arise from such engagement. Kieron and Jeremiah suggest a kind of cultural politics in that their idiom offers to reshape the language from within, to force written English to accommodate rhythms of speech and thought that have been excluded from the public sphere; the nameless narrators of *Translated Accounts* suggest the difficulty of any political action or identification under political conditions that are recognisable only in their anonymous generality. While Kieron and Jeremiah invent a singular language which arises from the movement of their thought, the nameless narrators of *Translated Accounts* remain buried somewhere beneath an unstyled prose, their words and thoughts translated and edited by an unrevealed bureaucracy. If there is a politics arising from *Translated Accounts*, it might seem that this is a politics which presides over the end of politics, a kind of flat dystopian refusal of the political possibilities of fiction. But my central contention here is that this separation, this kind of categorisation of political aesthetics, is precisely what these three novels taken together offer to rethink. The apparent sharpness of the distinction between them at the level of form belies a rich seam of shared concerns – with translation, with editing, with the temporality and spatiality of narration – that crosses the formal divide that separates them, and gestures towards a new category of political fiction.

Perhaps the most striking mark of this shared concern is the tendency for the formal distinctions themselves, between *Translated Accounts* on one hand and *Kieron Smith, Boy* and *You Have to Be Careful* on the other, to give way under pressure. Everything I have been saying about the novels so far assumes that narrative dispersal in *Translated Accounts* is set against an intense narrative focus or singularity in *Kieron* and *Careful*, but one of the remarkable things about these novels is that the very radicalism of their treatment of narrative perspective produces a kind of reversal, in which singularity becomes strangely bound up with multiplicity, in which the sealed narrating subject in *Kieron* and *Careful* betrays a peculiar continuity with the dispersed narrators of *Translated Accounts*. This effect is at work throughout the three novels, but can be seen particularly sharply, I would suggest, in the seventeenth passage in *Translated Accounts*, entitled 'split in my brain'. This 'account' bears witness to some kind of interrogation scene, in which the anonymous first-person narrator suffers a terrible but unspecified violence, as a result of which the 'back of my head was broken', and a 'split had formed in my brain'.[20] This opening of a kind of cleaving in the mind suggests the splitting and fracturing of narrative perspective that is the most striking formal aspect of the novel. The compelling and disturbing thought that the 'back' of the narrator's head is 'broken', that the violence which saturates these texts has opened a rift in the sealed unit of the head itself, allows for the leakage of narrative identity and positioning, the loss of a stable subjecthood, to which the novel more generally attests. This kind of undoing or separating of the mind strikes a perhaps surprising resonance with the poetry of Emily Dickinson, allowing a slant of nineteenth-century light into this scene of twenty-first-century brutality and torture. The split that forms in the broken narrator's mind in *Translated Accounts* shares a seam with that cleft that opens in Dickinson's poetry in 1864:

> I felt a Cleaving in my Mind –
> As if my Brain had split –
> I tried to match it – Seam by Seam –
> But could not make them fit –
>
> The thought behind, I strove to join
> Unto the thought before –
> But Sequence ravelled out of Sound –
> Like Balls – opon a Floor –[21]

The extraordinary, almost unthinkable disorientation that Dickinson conjures here, in which the disjoining of thought from thought causes 'sequence' to 'ravel out of sound', catches perfectly the unravelling of sequence and sound in *Translated Accounts*. But what is striking about the experience of cleaving, both in Kelman and in Dickinson, is that it bears out the uncanny continuity between separation and fusion that is carried by the word itself. The narrator in Kelman's novel experiences a distance and alienation from his (her?) own thinking that feels like a consequence of the rift that has opened at the back of the head. He thinks ungrammatically and nonsequentially about the question of freedom – 'freedom not being a true freedom which I knew even then. If based on a degree of exploitation'.[22] These displaced thoughts, he admits, are 'self-evident things', but the intuition of this evident contradiction between freedom and exploitation is a difficult knowledge to own, he thinks, because it is a (translated) knowledge that cannot quite fit in the broken mind, a 'knowledge that lay beyond the edge of my brain' (p. 133). This strange unavailability of his own administered thought, however, does not simply produce a distance from self, a leaking of thought beyond the horizons of the cleft mind; rather it also produces and requires a kind of falling inward, a fusing together of distance and proximity, a relocation of the beyond to the within. The narrator says, either of himself or of his interrogator, that 'His voice was at such a distance'; but this sense of remoteness leads him to move not only outwards, but also inwards towards seclusion and interiority (p. 132). 'Soon', he says, 'I had entered into my own self'. As he looks at the limits of the room in which he is incarcerated, he finds that 'I stared way beyond', but the cleaving in his mind configures the beyond as a within, allowing him to conceive a 'method of inclosing myself in nothing but myself' (p. 132, pp. 132–133, p. 133). 'I was staring at the ceiling', he says, 'and it was as a mirror, I saw myself, staring out at the mountains beyond'. 'The place itself', he says, 'was round me and inside attempting to overthrow, take control' (p. 133).

The displaced, dispersed, broken narrators of *Translated Accounts* experience in this way a peculiarly intense interiority, which is a function and a consequence of their dispersal. The experience of translation, editing and violent distance from self is also an 'entering into my own self'. This cleaving at the boundary in *Translated Accounts* – this sense that the thresholds of the novel are at once open and closed – is what determines the singular kind of communication that occurs between Kelman's late novels, the continuity that crosses the sealed and porous horizons of all three works of the 2000s, and that opens onto a new fictional politics. The splitting that occurs in 'split in my brain' finds a kind of echo in both *Kieron Smith, Boy* and *You Have to Be Careful*, as if the tension in *Translated Accounts* between singularity and multiplicity crosses the formal divide between the novels, playing itself out in an inverted reflection in the later two works. In both *Kieron* and *Careful*, the perhaps dominant narrative effect is a conjuring of double-voicing from the insistence on an extreme monovocalism. Virtually every sentence in both novels exhibits this effect to some degree or other. Throughout *Kieron Smith, Boy*, for example, the movement of Kieron's thought is followed with such suppleness, such closeness, that the narrative finds itself paradoxically taken beyond itself, in the same way that the narrator in *Translated Accounts* encounters 'knowledge that lay beyond the edge of my brain'. Kieron's intimately interiorised narrative voice lends a voice to others – not only to other people, to his father, his mother, his granda, but also to animals, boats, things – as the apparent lack of any mediation of Kieron's thought leaves us unable to distinguish between his imagining or remembering of occurrences, and those occurrences themselves. Kieron describes a scene in which his mother and brother discover that their house has mice: 'My maw went potty and started greeting', he says.

> Me and Mattie scattered them and chased them but we could not catch them and did not know what to do. My maw was shouting in a high voice. Ohh ohhh![23]

This peculiar giving over of the narrative voice to the cries of Kieron's mother suggests already the capacity of the narrative to transform an intimacy with Kieron's interiority into a kind of exteriority, as his voice becomes one with that of his mother. But as the narrative continues, these cries themselves become merged with or rhyme with others, suggesting a growing sense of narrative dispersal. A few pages later, Kieron tells a story about going to the river with his dad to see the boats. As he enters the scene in his imagination ('ye had to go round a corner and round a river-street and then back down and there was the river and the boat was there') he remembers the sound of the fog horns of the boats on the river, as he heard them from his bedroom (p. 5). 'Ye heard the horn sometimes', Kieron says

> and ye were in bed, it was creepy, ye were maybe asleep but ye still heard it, if it was coming out of nowhere, that was how it sounded, ooohhhhh ooohhhhh, ooohhhhh, ooohhhhh, oooooohhhhhhhhhh, and a big low voice. Just creepy. (p. 5)

This moment is a multiply occupied one, which pulls the narrative in a number of directions. The ooohhhhhs of the boat, coming out of nowhere, catch at the ohhs of Kieron's mother remembered just previously, suggesting a kind of accent or idiom that the boat and the mother share, and this difficult, displacing rhyming adds to the other forms of dislocation that are at work here – the sense that the 'big low voice' of the boat has drowned out Kieron's own voice, the sense that the narrative lays the scene at the river over the scene in which Kieron lies in his bedroom, thinking of the river. And these delicately cloven, woven strands are given an extra twist when Kieron goes on to describe seeing a boat emerge from the fog, as he stands at the riverside with his dad:

> And the yellow was coming out, all bright through the fog, and it was all lights, ye could not even see the funnels or the top parts because with the fog all hiding it. But there it was the ship out from the fog, ooohhhhh ooohhhhh, it was the special one. (p. 5)

As the boat slides into visibility, it gives rise to these cries, these 'ooohhhhh's which are beautifully unreadable, at once the voice of the boat, the voice of the people at the quayside watching the boat, the cries of Kieron's mother as she flees from the mice, and the sound of Kieron himself, at the scene or looking back on the scene, marvelling at the specialness of a boat sliding yellowly out of the fog.

This kind of effect, this splicing of the single and the double, is at work in every sentence both of *Kieron* and of *Careful*, and in both novels this cleaving produces a remarkable fluidity, in which separate spatial and temporal narrative structures enter into a new kind of proximity, a new kind of conjoint and disjunct configuration. In *You Have to Be Careful*, as Jeremiah sits planted in a jazz bar on his last evening in 'Uhmerka', his mind wanders across times, places, and accents, and as the narrative follows his thought it produces an extraordinary blending or melding of cultures and subject positions. Towards the end of the evening, Jeremiah finds himself in conversation with an American couple named Norman and Rita, and Jeremiah is 'blethering on', telling them stories about his job as a security guard. He remarks at one point that, as a 'wean', he had been told he should 'never comment to strangers except on particular issues', and remembers that

> My boss at the Security agency used to say something along the same lines ... General conclusions are de rigeur in Security operations, that was what he telt me. Universal blethers lead to moral imperatives and naybody wants into that sort of stuff, especially in uniform. He said it with his ayn accent.[24]

This is a freighted moment in the novel, a moment at which Jeremiah recognises that his boss at the Security agency spoke with an accent, presumably 'Uhmerkan', that is at odds with Jeremiah's own rendering of the scene. Jeremiah's thinking his way into the language of his boss tends to remake it, to cast a 'Skarrischness' over it, just as the accounts in *Translated*

Accounts are modelled and edited by invisible processes. The nature of the narrative structure in *Careful*, the absence of anything other than Jeremiah's perspective, means that this merging of Scottish and American, of boss and worker, produces a remarkably intimate kind of hybridity in which it becomes difficult or impossible to find the boundaries between places and between subject positions. A little while later in Jeremiah's conversation with Norman and Rita, Norman upbraids Jeremiah for his use of swear words. Jeremiah is telling them that gambling is a 'stupit stupit crazy mental fucking game', and Norman, we are told, sighs, and tells Jeremiah that his language is 'a little hard on the ears':

> I do apologize.
> You get excited, said Rita.
> Ye're right, I do.
> People use that language in Skallin? said Norman. (p. 389)

Even though the narrative has taken the form of dialogue here, in which Jeremiah's memory or experience of the scene resembles omniscient narration, Norman's use of the word 'Skallin' reminds us that Jeremiah is translating here, that one must imagine another version of this conversation in which Norman speaks in his 'ayn accent' (whatever that is). As Jeremiah's own speech and thought is inflected by a range of Americanisms, so the America that he encounters is rephrased, insistently, as a kind of Scotland, as the 'land of the free' becomes strangely contiguous with the land of Jeremiah's birth, the land to which he is trying half-heartedly to return.

It is in *Kieron Smith, Boy* that this kind of hybridity, this merging of different temporalities and geographies of narration, is at its most poetically and politically inventive. Here, as in *Translated Accounts* and *Careful*, the capacity to gather together disjoined spaces and subject positions produces at once a coming together and a kind of dispersal, a cleaving as destructive, in its way, as the split that opens in the narrator's head in *Translated Accounts*. This simultaneous gathering and dispersal expresses itself most delicately in the relation that is established between the narrator as narrator (Kieron addressing us as readers, from some unspecified time and place of narration), and the narrator as character (Kieron as a boy, climbing his ronepipe, doing his round, or catching a fish). The classic form that this relation takes is perhaps most clearly and influentially modelled in Charles Dickens's novel *Great Expectations*, in which Pip as character, lost in the uncertainties and the naiveties of youth, slowly grows towards the maturity and wisdom of Pip as narrator, whose ethical clarity can be felt as a counterweight to his character's confusion throughout the narrative.

The model is adapted time and time again, and in the service of various aesthetic regimes – by Charlotte Brontë in *Jane Eyre*, by Proust in *A la recherche*, by Beckett in his middle trilogy, by Don DeLillo in his great wheeling novel *Underworld*. But, in *Kieron Smith, Boy*, Kelman takes this model to the limits of its possibility, forging in the process a new kind of narrative practice. The immediacy of the narrative, its total immersion in the moving thought of the narrator, leads one to imagine, for large parts of the novel, that there is no distinction here between the place of narration and the narrated place. There is no narrative frame that establishes such a distinction, and no temporal plot that takes us from character towards narrator. Rather, for the most part narrator and character occupy almost the same thought, as if they are woven into each other's minds. Take for example the wonderful, harrowing scene in which Kieron borrows his brother's bicycle and has it stolen by a 'man':

> It was just a man done it. A man done it and was a complete thief. I would never do nothing ever ever again, just never ever, never never ever. If something ever happened to me and was ever ever good. Nothing ever could be ever again. If God would save me. It was not my fault. I would make a promise. (p. 219)

Here, the narrative mood, the telling of the story of the stolen bicycle, folds into a continuous present, in which the prose is caught completely in the spirals of Kieron's panic and despair. It is not simply that the narrative reproduces with great immediacy Kieron's overwhelming misery – caught with wonderful precision in the repeated 'never never ever'. What is striking here is that the future from which this scene might conceivably be narrated is banished with astonishing vehemence, leaving us in a narrated present which divorces itself from the flow of time, a present in which 'nothing ever could be ever again'. But despite this tendency for the narrative to become immersed in the scenes it narrates, the figure of the narrator, of some older Kieron who no longer inhabits the language or the body or the mind of Kieron as character, insistently and repeatedly asserts itself, producing an odd sense of evacuation from the scenes that are evoked with such a vivid presence. Even the first sentence of the novel suggests such an evacuation. The novel opens with the assertion that 'In the old place the river was not far from our street' (p. 1), declaring from the outset that the scenes in the Glasgow tenement that make up the first sections of the novel belong to an older time, that for all their presence they are in the past, remembered from a vantage point in which Kieron has already left the city, is already marooned in the schemes. As the narrative continues, this switching between a continuous present and a narrated past becomes ever more fluid, a kind of dance in which narrator and narrated join and separate in the moving breath of the sentence. Take the opening scene in which Kieron catches a fish:

> If a fish came by ye saw it and just waited till it came in close. If it just stayed there over yer hands, that was how ye were waiting. It was just looking about. What was it going to do? Oh be careful if ye do it too fast, if yer fingers just move and even it is just the totiest wee bit. Its tail whished and it was away or else it did not and stayed there, so if ye grabbed it and ye got it and it did not get away. So that was you, ye caught one. (p. 1)

Here, the narrative enters and slips clear of the scene it narrates with a beautiful sinuousness, opening and closing the distance between narrator and narrated in obedience to a snaky, slippery rhythm. The narrative mood is set with Kieron's description or remembrance of a time when he would catch fish in the 'old place' ('the park had a great pond in it', he says, 'with paddleboats and people sailed model yachts. Ye caught fish in it too' (p. 1)). The opening of the above quotation – 'If a fish came by' – suggests that the fishing we are imagining here is not a specific scene, but the kind of fishing that Kieron used generally to do. But as the scene moves on, the fish shifts from the general to the specific, no longer the kind of fish that Kieron used to try to catch, but an actual fish, sliding into Kieron's grasp, just as his remembered boat slides into visibility out of the fog. 'What was it going to do?' and 'Oh be careful' plunge us back into the scene of the catching itself, in which the fish is not yet caught, in which the delicate, subtle action of trapping this moving creature requires of the narrator a stealth and speed of movement rather than an accurate recall, a kind of movement that is registered in the syntax itself, which seeks to catch at its own fugitive prey. And this takes us to the sentence in which experience and reportage, the remembered past and the continuous present, are brought side by side, into a kind of resonance which seems to require a new tense, to place before and after, here and there, into a new kind of relation to each other: 'Its tail whished and it was away or else it did not and it stayed there, so if ye grabbed it and ye got it and it did not get away'. Here 'its tail whished' produces the sudden accelerating movement of the fish in two time frames at once, both in the present and in the past. It can be paraphrased both as something like 'sometimes the fish would swish its tail and get away and sometimes it would not', and as 'be careful, because the fish might swish its tail, and then it will get away' – and the narrative does not allow us to prioritise the one over the other, creating a strange, stretched merging of past, present and future. The last sentence, 'so that was you, ye caught one', has a certain bathos to it, as the narrator resumes his distance from the scene, denying the lived excitement of 'it did not get away', but it does nothing to protect the narrator from this singular involvement with the scene he narrates. The narrator's retrospective distance from his narrative has already, on this first page, been annihilated, and the rest of the novel takes place in that strange, untensed continuity that is summoned here in the catching of a fish.

It is this continuity, I suggest, that is shared by all three of Kelman's post-2000 novels, and that summons a new kind of thinking about the writing of commitment. This continuity does not suggest a community to which Kelman's writing strives to give a voice. Rather, the forms of collectivity that are imagined in these works are closely, intimately entwined with a sundering, a cloven alienation between narrator and narrated, between here and there, between Scotland and America. These novels are built around the seam that Dickinson discovers, in 1864, between broken sequence and fractured identities. In *Kieron Smith, Boy*, as in Dickinson's poem, the failure to find a join between 'the thought behind' and 'the thought before' produces a 'cleaving in the mind', a malfunctioning of the machine that produces sequential meaning. The difference that opens and closes between narrator and narrated in *Kieron Smith, Boy* produces a split between self and self that breaks the novel, leaving it open, as in *Translated Accounts*, somewhere at the back. Looking at a photograph of himself, or thinking of the seductive possibility that, secretly, he might be a 'pape', Kieron comes back time and again to his inability to match himself to himself, 'Seam by Seam'. Looking at his face, or thinking of his face, he wonders 'if it was me'. 'I could not see if it was me', he thinks. 'Ye thought ye knew your face', he says, speaking to us, speaking to himself, 'but when ye tried to see it in yer head ye could not' (pp. 133, 134). The breath of difference from self that the narrative finds in the most intimate expression of self means that one can never inhabit one's face completely – never, never, ever – that one always feels that awful opening at the back made by state violence in *Translated Accounts*, the opening that suggests, with Arthur Rimbaud, that one is always perhaps another ('I is another', Rimbaud writes; 'I witness the unfolding of my own thought').[25] 'Maybe', Kieron thinks as he listens to his mother saying his name – as he hears and remembers his mother say 'Oh Kieron' – 'Maybe I was another boy' (p. 41).

This production, in Kelman's recent writing, of a difference from self in the most intimate heartland of the self, destabilises any simple sense that he is giving here an authentic account of a specific subject position, or that he is seeking to give a voice to a previously marginalised community or historical experience. He is not writing back from margin to centre here, not least because his writing produces a wonderfully eloquent testimony to the stubborn refusal of thinking and writing, remembering and imagining, to stay confined within the boundaries of any subject position, or of any historical or geographical field, either on the margins or at the centre. But this poetic exploration of the difficulty of finding a position from which to speak, or a face which one might inhabit, never amounts to an abandonment of political commitment, and does not follow the contours along which we have mapped committed and autonomous writing since the Frankfurt school. *Kieron Smith, Boy*, *You Have to Be Careful in the Land of the Free* and *Translated Accounts* all engage with forms of political and sociohistorical reality, and all explore the means by which such forms are experienced, remembered and recorded. What results is a forensic examination of the forces and pressures that are exerted on the contemporary imagination as it strives to conjure a sense of personhood from the conflicting violences – national, post-national, economic – that dismember us. These novels produce some of the sharpest analyses we have of the ways that such forces position us in the early years of the twenty-first century; but they also offer one of the most delicate poetic responses to such forces, as the possibility of a kind of becoming emerges, untensed and almost unworded, from the very violence that has cloven the subject apart. It is with the broken mind of *Translated Accounts* that these novels think their way towards that 'knowledge' that 'lay beyond the edge of my brain'.

2010

CHAPTER 6

Zadie Smith, E. M. Forster and the Idea of Beauty

> The eye's object *is* different from the *ear's*.
> Karl Marx, *Economic and Philosophical Manuscripts*.[1]

I Para

'One may as well begin with Jerome's emails to his father'.[2]

One may as well begin here – with the opening sentence of Zadie Smith's 2005 novel *On Beauty*.

This, as quickly becomes evident to most readers of Smith's novel, is a haunted, doubled beginning, the extension of a prior beginning, and so not really a beginning at all. Smith's beginning is not quite her own, but is a reprisal of E. M. Forster's opening to his 1910 novel, *Howards End*: 'One may as well begin with Helen's letters to her sister'.[3]

This opening gesture is one which is designed to announce, from the outset, that the work it inaugurates is one which deals with *ideas*. It is not solely or primarily concerned to tell a story, it suggests, but to reflect on what story telling is, and on how the novel goes about performing it. In this it shares something with the opening of Ian McEwan's novel *The Children Act*, published nearly a decade later, in 2014: 'London. Trinity term one week old. Implacable June weather'.[4] This opening, like that of *On Beauty*, is a borrowing from an earlier opening, in this case from Charles Dickens's 1853 novel *Bleak House*: 'London. Michaelmas Term lately over, and the Lord Chancellor sitting in Lincoln's Inn Hall. Implacable November weather'.[5] McEwan wants to write a novel about the relation between fiction and the law, and so he makes this opening obeisance to Dickens's great novel about the relation between fiction and the law. This act of *hommage* allows McEwan to call on Dickens's authority as a novelist, but it also, and more importantly, sets aside some of his own novel's commitment to verisimilitude, to realism, to storytelling. Zadie Smith, in a conversation with McEwan ('a writer', Smith says, 'as unlike me as it is possible to be') suggests that she shares with him some version of this investment in ideas which lie behind or underneath the novel's own fabric.[6] Part of the 'joy' of being a novelist, she proposes to McEwan, 'is that it allows you to write about writing', that it allows you to step back from the scene you are describing in order to expose the machinery that allows for the description. McEwan agrees: 'The dream, surely, Zadie, that we all have, is to write this beautiful paragraph that actually is describing something but at the same time in another voice is writing a commentary on its own creation' (p. 122).

This double-voicing – this installing of a critical distance at the heart of the imagined world – is part of the cost of writing a novel which seeks to think about ideas in general, and about the idea of beauty in particular. McEwan's imaginary beautiful paragraph owes its beauty to its distance from itself, its capacity at once to 'describe something', and to undermine or evacuate that description by revealing the writerly scaffolding on which it rests. It is some such distancing, some such dismantling of the machinery of description, that is subtly at work in the openings both of *The Children Act* and of *On Beauty*. In order to think, these openings suggest, the novel needs from the outset to sabotage its own realism, to declare that it speaks not of a fictional world that exists its own right, but rather of one that lies upon a revealed, examined apparatus of imagining. This sabotaging, this rending of the fabric of realism, is what J. M. Coetzee has in mind when he reflects, in his anti-novel *Elizabeth Costello*, on the antipathy of realism to ideas. 'Realism', Coetzee writes, in his guise as Costello, 'has never been comfortable with ideas'. It 'could not be otherwise', Costello says, because 'realism is premised on the idea that ideas have no autonomous existence, can exist only in things'.[7] For a work of realism to approach an idea, Coetzee and Costello suggest (jointly and severally), the idea in question has to renounce its being as an idea, and become a thing embedded in the imagined world – not the idea of the thing but the thing itself; not the idea of beauty, but beauty itself. In a work of realism, 'ideas do not and indeed cannot float free: they are tied to the speakers by whom they are enounced, and generated from the matrix of individual interests out of which their speakers act in the world' (p. 9).

Smith's opening, and McEwan's, set these novels from the outset at slight odds with the realist mode, in order to allow the ideas they contain to float a little free from that 'network of individual interests' upon which realism rests. 'There is first of all the problem', Coetzee writes in the opening line of *Elizabeth Costello*, 'of the opening, namely, how to get us from where we are, which is, as yet, nowhere, to the far bank' (p. 1). For the problem of the opening to be fully overcome, it has not to announce itself as a problem. The opening must not allow itself to be distracted by the idea of the opening. Coetzee draws our attention to the problem of his opening, in part because he is writing a novel which seeks to dismantle the apparatus of the novelistic imagination, in order to reveal its workings. It is troubling to find ourselves, on opening a book, cast into a place that is 'as yet nowhere' – the vanishing ground that attends all acts of inauguration, and that we have to disavow if we are to feel ourselves truly to have begun – so openings tend to hide that nowhere. 'London', the opening might declare, 'Michaelmas term lately over', and we are in a place, and a time, and we can begin. Phew. But Coetzee, Smith and McEwan all demonstrate that the novel that seeks to approach an idea has to take the risk of letting that nowhere in, even at the beginning, even with the progenitive breath. This is something that George Eliot too knows – Eliot, the novelist who has perhaps thought harder than any other writer with the novel form. It is what she has in mind in the epigraph that precedes the opening of her great work *Daniel Deronda* (an opening before the opening, what Beckett calls the 'threshold of my story, before the door that opens on my story'):[8] 'Men', Eliot's epigraph declares, 'can do nothing without the make believe of a beginning'.[9]

It is a characteristically Eliotian manoeuvre, at once to declare the impossibility of a beginning and to enact it. At once to demonstrate that beginnings are necessarily a fantasy (how can one conceive of a beginning without conjuring some impossible time before the beginning, from which the beginning emerges?) and to concede that we can't do without them, that they happen all the time. Every day. Eliot's procedure involves her in sustaining the vivid outlines of an imagined world, while at the same time putting the forces that hold that world in place in a form of suspense, so that the covering of life goes clear, and we can see into its hidden insides. Smith's opening – its reliance on Forster's earlier opening, which itself reflects on what it is to begin – is conducted in this same spirit. And like Eliot, with her steadfast commitment to the epigraph, Smith's opening is fenced about with other beginnings, false openings, thresholds and postscripts. Before the beginning comes an epigraph, from H. J. Blackham's *Six Existentialist Thinkers* – 'We refuse to be each other' (np).[10] Before that there is a page of acknowledgements, and before that a dedication, 'For my dear Laird' (np). And, as the beginning is preceded by a pre-beginning, so the end is extended beyond the end, in the form of an 'author's note' that is included in the back pages of the text (pp. 445–456). It is not uncommon, of course, to include such paratexts, to build an architecture around the work, in which the author speaks in their own voice, to thank their friends, to acknowledge their debts, to present the work as a gift to a loved one. But in the case of *On Beauty* these stutterings and aftershocks are not cleanly separated from the body of the text, but instead partake in the novel's examination of its own procedures (as Forster's famous epigraph to *Howards End*, 'Only connect…', stands in an uncertain relation to the occurrence of the phrase in main body of the text).[11] As the opening does not quite open, but reflects on openings, so the dedication does not quite or simply dedicate, and the acknowledgements don't simply acknowledge. Rather (and in the long tradition of novelistic paratexts) they stretch out that ground that Coetzee touches on at the opening of *Elizabeth Costello*, the nowhere place that is the boundary of the novel's territory – and in so doing they hold to the light some of the central concerns around which the novel turns.

This preparation, in the paratexts, for the thinking that the novel sets out to do, is paired with a series of interlocking references, in which Smith lays out the intellectual and aesthetic terrain with which her novel is in dialogue. In the acknowledgements, Smith declares the debt to Forster that is implicit in the novel's opening:

> It should be obvious from the first line that this is a novel inspired by a love of E. M. Forster, to whom all my fiction is indebted, one way or the other. This time I wanted to repay the debt with *hommage*. (np)

On Beauty is an *hommage* to Forster, and more specifically, although she does not declare it here, to *Howards End*. But in the acknowledgements and the closing note, Smith also draws our attention to a layered matrix of other visual and literary intertexts, which give the novel its shape. She thanks Simon Schama in the acknowledgements for the 'monumental' book *Rembrandt's Eyes*, which, she says 'helped me to see paintings properly for the first time' (np).[12] And then, in the closing author's note, she switches from art criticism to the art itself, itemising the paintings, by Rembrandt and others, that have provided the visual scaffolding of her text: two of Rembrandt's self-portraits, which hang in the Hague and in Munich; Rembrandt's *Anatomy Lesson of Dr Nicolaes Tulp*, which is also in the Hague; Rembrandt's *Hendrickje Bathing*, in London; Rubens's *Study of African Heads*, in Brussels; Hippolyte's *Erzulie*, in Haiti (pp. 445–456). Rembrandt's painting, as illuminated by Schama, provides one of the structuring principles of *On Beauty* – and then to this weave of Forster and Rembrandt Smith adds another thread, from which she draws the title of her own work. 'Thank you', she writes in the acknowledgements, 'to Elaine Scarry for her wonderful essay 'On Beauty and Being Just', from which I borrowed a title, a chapter heading and a great deal of inspiration' (np). Scarry's reflection on beauty, published in 1999, provides a philosophical foundation to Smith's novel, and then, in a repeat of the mirroring between Schama's criticism and Rembrandt's art, the title 'On Beauty' appears again, in the closing 'author's note', where it names not an essay but a poem, from the 2006 collection *To a Fault*, by Nick Laird (p. 445).[13] In thanking Laird for allowing her to take her title from his poem, this last acknowledgement of debt brings together all three of the paratexts written in Smith's voice. The 'Nick Laird' who appears in the 'author's note' as the author of the poem 'On Beauty', we assume, is also the 'Laird' of the dedication, the 'dear Laird' for whom the novel is written. He is also, we further assume, the 'Nick' who appears in the acknowledgements as 'my husband'. It is her husband, she writes, 'whose poetry I steal to make my prose look pretty'. 'It's Nick who knows that 'time is how you spend your love', and that's why this book is dedicated to him, as is my life' (np).

It feels like a peculiar thing to do, to quote from an author's acknowledgements to their spouse. It seems almost like a trespass, an infringement of Smith's privacy. But I find myself compelled and authorized to commit this trespass (as have other critics who have written on the novel), because, as I have said, the paratexts to *On Beauty* are demonstrably and performatively entangled with the text.[14] The patterned resonances between the dedication, the acknowledgements and the author's note at once establish the guiding concerns of the novel, and act formally to animate them, to put them into a kind of literary motion. One of the central questions that the novel asks is how artworks think, and how those of us who would attend to the singularity of the artwork should tune ourselves to that thinking. The dispute around which the novel turns – between the conservative art historian Montague Kipps and the critical theorist Howard Belsey – concerns this question. How should we respond to the beauty of the artwork (and particularly, for Kipps and Belsey, the painting of Rembrandt)? How do we make aesthetic beauty meaningful? Is it our duty and task as readers or viewers to humbly appreciate and glorify the beauty of art, as Kipps contends? Or should we adopt a hermeneutic of suspicion, as Belsey insists, one which allows us to see how the artwork has been complicit with the ideological dissemination of power – to recognise, as Belsey puts it, that 'prettiness' is 'the mask that power wears' (p. 155)? The juggling between acknowledgements and author's note works to frame this question. When we contemplate beauty in these pages, are we looking through Rembrandt's eyes, or Schama's? Are we reading something like Laird's poem 'On Beauty', or something more like Scarry's essay *On Beauty*? If 'prettiness' is a 'mask', does it cover Laird's poetry or Smith's prose? Are we to adopt a critical or a reverential attitude to the artwork? In Smith's *On Beauty*, as opposed to Scarry's, or Laird's, are we in the presence of beauty, or of the idea of beauty?

The paratexts set the terms of the dispute between Kipps and Belsey, and they frame, too, the other central question that the novel asks, which is woven throughout with the contemplation of aesthetic beauty. That is, the question of love. The academic dispute between Belsey and Kipps is balanced at all times against a more domestic discord – that between Howard Belsey and his wife Kiki, as they struggle to rebuild their marriage after Howard's affair with a colleague, Claire Malcolm. The discovery that her husband has lied to her, that he has broken whatever the bond of trust is that lies at the heart of a monogamous relationship, leads Kiki to reappraise the foundation not only of her relationship with Howard, but of her life itself. 'I staked my *life* on you', Kiki says to Howard. 'I staked my *life*' (p. 207). '*I staked my whole life* on you. And I have no idea any more why I did that' (p. 206). As Kiki earlier says to Carlene Kipps, the wife of her husband's arch enemy with whom Kiki establishes a peculiarly intimate relationship, her husband's infidelity has left her uncertain what the purpose and meaning of her life is. Carlene insists that the meaning of life is love. 'I lived because I loved *this* person', Carlene tells Kiki, as she insists that Kiki's life, too, is indissolubly bound with another's. 'You staked your *life*', Carlene says to Kiki, providing her with the terms that she later employs in her row with Howard. 'You gave somebody your *life*' (p. 177). But such stakes seem suddenly cancelled by the discovery that the love that underwrote them was false, or not what it appeared to be. 'Right now' Kiki says to Carlene, 'I'm trying to understand what my life's been *for*, and what it *will* be for' (p. 176). Can we make our love for others, for a single other person, the basis of our life? Does love, as Martha Nussbaum argues in *Love's Knowledge*, afford us knowledge, of ourselves and of others?[15] That is the question the novel asks. Can we embark on a life shared with someone else, that involves folding our own hopes and desires into theirs, that merges our future with theirs, and our children's futures? And can we ground that project on something as vaporous as love?

These two questions – the question of love and the question of aesthetic beauty – are, as I have said, intimately interwoven in Smith's novel, and this interweaving is given a premonitory form in the intertexts. It is not only that the various acknowledgements and dedications reflect the thematic concerns of the novel that they frame, it is that, in crossing over the boundary lines of the novel, in setting up channels of communication between author and narrator, between the outside and inside of the text, they create the conditions in which it becomes possible to think about the stakes both of beauty and of love. When Smith writes in the acknowledgements that both her book and her life are dedicated to Laird, we cannot but hear an echo of Kiki's assertion that she has staked her life on Howard's. Similarly, when she writes 'It's Nick who knows that "time is how you spend your love",' this gesture does not remain as a private, extratextual message to her husband, but becomes bound up with the internal mechanics of the text, and part of its striving to understand how we spend our love in the time-span of a shared life. The quotation marks in Smith's acknowledgements indicate this is a quotation from Laird – the line is taken from his poem 'The Last Saturday in Ulster' – but it soon becomes apparent that they are also marking a quotation from the novel that they frame.[16] The words are spoken in the novel in the voice of Howard Belsey, who denies their truth: 'He just did not believe', Howard thinks, 'that time is how you spend your love' (p. 302). And then, Laird's own poetic reflection on beauty, in the poem from which Smith borrows her title, appears in its entirety in the novel itself, where it is attributed to Claire Malcolm, the academic poet with whom Howard has his affair ('Oh, it's just old crap' (p. 154), Claire says). Laird's poetic thinking about beauty is absorbed into the novel's imagined world, as is Smith's declaration of love for him, a love upon which she declares herself to be willing to stake her life. And in performing this act of absorption, in allowing the boundaries between author and narrator, between the outside and the inside of the text, between the real and the imagined, to waver, to leak, the novel prepares the ground for the kind of thinking it wants to do, a kind of thinking in which beauty and love become part of the same movement, part of the same idea. For the novel to animate that idea, for us to see into the place where love and beauty are conjoined, and where love might be spent in the form of a shared life, we have to enter into this hinterland, this suspended region in the borders of the imagined world that it is the task of realism to body forth, the 'nowhere' that realism must supress if it is to inaugurate and realise itself. It is in this region, neither in the world nor out of it, neither real nor unreal, neither original nor copy, neither art nor the idea of art, that we might approach the meaning of love, and the meaning of beauty, as these mutually constitute one another.

II Kink

For a novel to think about beauty, this might suggest, or at least for Smith's novel to think about beauty, it is necessary to deactivate its apparatuses, its capacity to present us with a world in which, in Coetzee's terminology, ideas are properly embedded in things. 'Speech is beautifully useless', Laird writes in 'On Beauty', 'The beautiful know this'.[17] Beauty is related to uselessness, to a lapsing of the terms and conditions of use, and this lapsing has to do, as Elaine Scarry writes in her essay *On Beauty*, with the perception that beauty does not reside in itself, but comes about in the urge it instils in us to *replicate* it. When Scarry asks herself, at the opening of *On Beauty*, 'What is the felt experience of cognition at the moment one stands in the presence of a beautiful boy or flower or bird?', it is this desire for replication that she offers as an immediate response. 'Beauty', she says, 'brings copies of itself into being'. This is both its effect and its nature. 'It makes us draw it, take photographs of it, or describe it to other people'.[18] The beauty of a beautiful thing exceeds its own thingness, and is found, or asserts itself, in the copies that it engenders. As the narrator of Proust's *A la recherche* puts it, we 'become aware of the beauty of one thing only in another thing'.[19]

This migration of beauty outside of itself into its echoes or duplications is mirrored, in Smith's *On Beauty*, in the effects I have been tracing, in the tendency of fictional prose to weaken the bonds by which, in Coetzee's words, 'ideas are tied to the speakers by whom they are enounced'.[20] To think about beauty is to enter into a kind of shadow thinking, in which thought is found not in itself but in its replication. And if the idea of beauty requires us attend to this sense that beauty brings copies of itself into being, then there is no more insistent form of replication, in Smith's novel, than her reproduction of *Howards End*, the *hommage* she pays to that novel as an acknowledgement of her life-long 'love of E. M. Forster'. This duplication is at work, as I have said, in the opening sentence, an opening which sets Smith's own prose at a distance from itself, which casts its own genesis into the throes a former genesis. And from that opening on, Forster's novel inhabits every sentence of the text, so that we can see through the fabric of Smith's novel, at all times, to Forster's, which lies beneath it, like an underimage beneath a painted canvas.

Take, for example, the shared moment in which the plot machines of both novels are set in motion by an accidental theft. In *On Beauty*, this moment comes when the Belseys – Howard and Kiki, and their children, Jerome, Zora and Levi – attend a recital of Mozart's *Requiem*. The scene opens with a characterization of the ways in which the various members of the family respond to Mozart's music. Kiki is the kind of listener who understands music by converting it into story, into literary narrative. The *Requiem* is about 'apes and mermaids'. It is about a pit of damnation – 'your death is waiting for you in that pit' (p. 69). It is also about 'every person who has changed you during your time on this earth: your many lovers; your family, your enemies, the nameless, faceless woman who slept with your husband; the man you thought you were going to marry; the man you did' (p. 69). Kiki's older son Jerome, a sweet, lovelorn boy who has fallen in desperate and unrequited love with Monty Kipps's beautiful daughter Victoria, is the kind of listener who hears only the music, the music which has no reference outside itself. As he listens, Jerome simply sits and weeps (p. 70). Kiki's intellectual daughter Zora is an academic listener, one who must decode or anatomise the music in order to understand it. She listens to the music while simultaneously 'concentrating on her Discman, through which a recording of the voice of a Professor N. R. A. Gould carefully guided her through each movement' (p. 70). Howard, the professional debunker of the ideology of the aesthetic, sleeps through the performance, but feels qualified to declare, when it is over and the family are preparing to leave, that the *Requiem* is 'fine'; 'I just prefer music which isn't trying to fake me into some metaphysical idea by the back door' (p. 72). It is as the family are leaving, as Howard and Kiki are disagreeing over the genius of Mozart ('I don't know what you're talking about', Kiki says to Howard, 'It's like God's music or something' (p. 72)) that the accidental theft occurs. Sitting next to Zora in the auditorium is a young black man named Carl. He too has with him a Discman that contains a disc of his own music, a blend of Hip Hop and spoken word poetry. As Zora gets up to leave, she takes his Discman rather than her own because, naturally, 'they're *exactly* the same' (p. 74).

This accident, unashamedly contrived, is the device that allows Smith to initiate one of the elements of the plot, in which the wealthy, cosmopolitan, racially diverse Belsey family encounter a poor but gifted black musician, in order to test how far it is possible to meet across the dividing lines of race, class and economic privilege. Kiki, an African American woman whose great-great-grandmother was a 'house-slave', is married to a white academic, and lives in a large house bequeathed to her grandmother by a 'benevolent white doctor', a bequest which has made her, she thinks, 'middle-class' (p. 17). As she listens to the *Requiem*, she thinks with pride that her son Jerome is a 'young black man of intelligence and sensibility'. 'How many other young black men would even come to an event like this', she thinks to her herself, 'I bet there isn't one in this entire crowd' (p. 70). But of course, there is, and the accidental theft brings the wealthy Belsey children into social contact with a black man who is not middle class, who does not have the privilege of wealth and education. The third Belsey child, Levi, sees the mistake, and calls after Zora as she leaves with Carl's Discman. Together they listen to the disc in the machine, to ascertain that the Discman that Zora has taken does in fact belong to Carl (Levi admires Carl's music: 'it's tight man. There's a nice flow there' (p. 75)). The Discmans are returned to their rightful owners, and the connection is established.

The scene, as I say, is frankly contrived (Frank Kermode, in a warm and admiring review of Smith's novel, regards this particular scene as an aesthetic failure).[21] But whatever we make of its contrivance, and of what Smith is doing in fashioning it so clunkily, we cannot read it outside of its relation with the original scene from *Howards End* which it reprises, and which inhabits it like a spirit, or a ghost (and which is also, in Kermode's estimation, an aesthetic failure, 'facetious' and 'trivial' (np)). In Forster's novel the scene turns around the Schlegel family's trip to the theatre to attend a recital of Beethoven's *Symphony No 5*. The Schlegels – a liberal, left-leaning family whose progressive politics are founded on an equally progressive conception of the social value and function of the arts – are the model for Smith's Belseys. As the Belseys' politics are framed in opposition to the Kipps's, so Forster's Schlegels have their own counterparts in the form of the Wilcox family, who are politically right wing, emotionally illiterate, and aesthetically and intellectually conservative. Where the Schlegels are cosmopolitan intellectuals, focused on the 'inner life' of the mind, the Wilcoxes are practical people, emotionally and financially invested in empire and in 'civilization', committed to the business of the 'outer life'.[22] So when Forster presents us with the spectacle of the Schlegels listening to a Beethoven concert, it gives him the opportunity to characterize the ways in which each member of the family understands the music, as it touches on their conception of the 'inner life', and of how art makes the inner life expressive. Meg, the eldest sibling in the family, and, since the death of both parents, the de facto head of the household, listens to the music like Jerome. She 'can see only the music' (p. 31). Helen, Meg's younger sister, listens like Kiki. She can 'see heroes and shipwreck in the music's flood' (p. 31). Where Kiki sees a drama of apes and mermaids and final judgement, Helen sees a 'goblin walking quietly over the universe' and the prospect of anarchy, of 'Panic and emptiness! Panic and emptiness!' (p. 33). The youngest Schlegel sibling, a drily intellectual boy by the name of Tibby, listens like Zora. Tibby is 'profoundly versed in counterpoint, and holds the full score open on his knee' (p. 31). It is in the midst of this drama of listening that the theft occurs which brings the Schlegels into contact with a character from a different social class to their own. Here, it is the theft not of a Discman but of an umbrella, and the victim of the theft is a young man, Leonard Bast, living on the verge of poverty, striving to educate himself while working as a clerk in an insurance company. Helen leaves the concert early taking with her Leonard's umbrella, rather than her own. Meg brings Leonard back to their house in Wickham place and tells her sister that 'you've been taking this gentleman's umbrella' (p. 41). 'I do nothing but steal umbrellas', Helen says, 'I am so very sorry!'. The umbrella is restored to its rightful owner. The connection is established.

Smith's orchestration of this meeting across cultural difference is laid, in this way, across Forster's, and draws on Forster's thinking about the means by which art and beauty, in its abstract form, relate to the world of real things, a world shaped by an unequal distribution of wealth and cultural privilege. 'It will be generally admitted', Forster's narrator declares, in a lightly satirical vein, 'that Beethoven's Fifth Symphony is the most sublime noise that has ever penetrated into the ear of man' (p. 31). Beethoven of all musicians, and music of all the arts, affords the least contaminated, most transcendent form of expression; but, the narrator goes on, 'you are bound to admit that such a noise is cheap at two shillings' (p. 31). Art may be pure and disinterested, Forster's narrator suggests, but those who consume it are not, and in the passage from aesthesis to intellection, from the withheld beauty of the score to the reality of the performance, the real world, in which shillings are not evenly dispersed, intervenes. As Meg thinks to herself later, her forms of listening and thinking are determined by her income, by the fact that she stands on a small island of private wealth. 'I stand each year upon six hundred pounds, and Helen upon the same' she says 'and all our thoughts are the thoughts of six-hundred-pounders, and all our speeches' (p. 62). Leonard does not stand upon such an island, and so when he listens to music at a concert, or looks at a painting, or reads Ruskin's *Stones of Venice*, Forster's narrator suggests, he can't lift his thinking clear of the sea of his poverty, he can't 'forget about his stolen umbrella' (p. 40). 'Yes, the umbrella was the real trouble. Behind Monet and Debussy the umbrella persisted, with the steady beat of a drum' (p. 40). Forster's dramatization of the different ways in which his characters listen to Beethoven, whether they hear 'only the music', or follow the score, or turn the music into melodrama, or hear only the steady pulse of a stolen umbrella, is thus part of his interest in the way that art is made real, made part of the world – and so, for the progressive Schlegels, bound up with society's ills, with the unfreedom of women, economic apartheid, the uneven distribution of wealth. Meg and Helen are committed to doing what they perceive to be social good, to making the world better, and they think of art, of beauty, as a means of achieving those goals. They want women to have the vote. They want Leonard to have access to the 'inner life' granted to 'six-hundred-pounders'. And their belief in art, their insistence that one should 'take poetry seriously' (p. 77), arises from their conviction that art can transform the world, that aesthetic beauty might be the province of a kind of real political hope, 'hope', as the narrator repeatedly puts it, 'on this side of the grave' (pp. 107, 215, 348).

When Smith lays the concert scene in *On Beauty* over this same scene in *Howards End*, she animates the same questions that drive Forster's novel – How do we represent socio-political difference in fiction? Can access to art and to education help to overcome such differences? Can the artwork itself be the province of a more democratic and just form of social relation? – and she does so by inflecting those questions through a different socio-political prism; not England in 1910, but America in the early twenty-first century. It is true that this is a clunky moment in both texts (one in which the thinness and snobbery of Forster's depiction of Leonard's autodidacticism is most painfully apparent). It is a moment when, in Forster's novel, the ideas that drive the novel are stated so plainly, so didactically, that they threaten to become fatally divorced from the imagined scenario in which they are embedded. But if Smith takes the risk of following Forster's contours in this scene ('it is a fault completely out of character in this gifted novelist' Kermode writes in a somewhat paternalistic mode, 'and Forster has led her into it'),[23] she does so because the thinking that she is setting out to do – about beauty and the idea of beauty – resides in this echoing itself, this sense that Smith's novel has a kind of reflection in Forster's. And if this duplication is at work at this critical moment in both texts, then we can see it sustained throughout *On Beauty*, as the two novels enter into a kind of communion with one another, in which each lifts the other. At each of the weightbearing moments of *On Beauty* – at those moments when the relation of aesthetics to politics, or of beauty to love, or of one person to another, comes under the most intense scrutiny – the skin of Smith's prose goes clear, so we can see the Forster beneath. It is not just that Smith's plot follows Forster's, but that her field of gestures, the texture and kinks of her imagined world, are inhabited and spooked by those of Forster's. Smith's characters will sometimes quote Forster's, in a fashion that empties them out, that makes us conscious of the fabrication of Smith's world, its status as a copy or duplication. Jerome travels to the Kipps's family house in London before the opening of the novel, where he falls in love with Monty Kipps's daughter Victoria. He writes to his father, 'I have no idea how you're going to take this one, but we're in love!! The Kipps girl and me' (p. 7). The email is a near quotation of the letter sent by Helen to her sister, from the Wilcox's house, to tell her that she has fallen in love with one of the younger Wilcoxes, Paul. 'I do not know what you will say: Paul and I are in love' (p. 4). The declaration of love, as it reaches across the divide between the two families in both novels, thus reaches too across the divide between Smith and Forster, in a way that makes the reality effect of both novels tremble. When Jerome is staying at the Kipps's house, he finds that he is drawn to the Kipps as a family, almost as much as he is drawn to Victoria. 'It wasn't *about* a girl', Smith's narrator says, 'or, rather, it wasn't about *just* the girl. Jerome had fallen in love with a family' (p. 44). Whatever we make of this claim, its status and its effects are determined not only by Jerome's thinking (as the character in whom these thoughts, in Coetzee's terms, are 'embedded'), but by the mirroring between this line, and its counterpart in Forster – the moment when Helen discovers that, 'the truth was that she had fallen in love, not with an individual, but with a family' (p. 22). Helen finds, when she is at the Wilcox's, that the Wilcox worldview, long held by the Schlegels to be barbaric, verboten, has in fact a kind of fascination for her. 'When Mr Wilcox said that one sound man of business did more good to the world than a dozen of your social reformers', the narrator says, 'Helen had swallowed the curious assertion without a gasp, and had leant back luxuriously among the cushions of his motor-car' (pp. 22–23). When Jerome has the same realisation, he responds with the same gesture of submission, of release, as if his body is inhabited and animated by Helen's. 'When Monty suggested that minority groups too often demand equal rights they haven't earned', Smith's narrator says, 'Jerome had allowed this strange new idea to penetrate him without complaint and sunk further back into the receiving sofa' (p. 44).

The correspondence that Smith establishes in this way, between *On Beauty* and *Howards End*, opens a kind of passage between them, a strangely fissile kind of connecting ground which is the condition for the mode of thinking about beauty that both novels reach for. And if we can feel something like this effect at work throughout Smith's novel – this 'double-voicing', as Mikhail Bakhtin puts it, that is 'fraught with dialogue' – it is in the meetings between women at the heart of both novels where it is most pronounced, and most productive.[24] The central relationship in *On*

Beauty, its wellspring of uncontaminated love, is not between Kiki and Howard, but between Kiki and Monty Kipps's wife, Carlene (a meeting that takes place against the flow of their husbands' enmity). They meet on only a handful of occasions, but each time they do there is a charge to their encounter, a sense that they are remaking each other, that they are encountering a particular kind of beauty that they find only in each other, and that Carlene seeks to enshrine in the form of a gift – an Hector Hippolyte painting, *Maitresse Erzulie*, that Carlene leaves to Kiki after her death. Their meetings have a kind of magic to them, a sense that in each other's presence they are both possessed of something larger than themselves, a sense that their dialogue embraces 'everything I cannot say and I never hear said. The bit I cannot touch' (p. 94). And this magic is drawn not just from their contact with each other, but from their contact with their Forsterian counterparts, Meg Schlegel and Ruth Wilcox.

Consider their first meeting. Carlene and Kiki meet when Carlene moves from London to Kiki's small American town, and they discover a common sensibility, forged partly by their shared anxiety about the brief love affair between Jerome and Victoria. Carlene sees that Kiki has been concerned, as she was, by the relationship. 'It's interesting to me', Carlene says. 'You were worried too, about their meeting again, Jerome and my Vee [….] I was too [….] It's a silly thing, but I knew I didn't want them to meet again. Why *was* that?' (p. 170). This meeting is a version of the same encounter between Meg and Mrs Wilcox, early in *Howards End*. Mrs Wilcox moves from Howards End to a house on the same London street as the Schlegels. Meg goes to visit her, and they discover an affinity which is based partly on their shared anxiety about the brief love affair between Helen and Paul Wilcox. 'You've been worrying too', Meg says to Mrs Wilcox. 'I can see that you have. You felt as I do: Helen mustn't meet him again [….] Now why?' (p. 70). The meeting between the women here, the Forsterian connection, takes place against the current of their shared scepticism about the possibility of love overcoming difference, a meeting against the flow of social relations that is doubled in the dialogue that we can hear between Smith and Forster. Or consider their last encounter. Carlene and Kiki go Christmas shopping together (Kiki tells Carlene to take her name off the list of presents Carlene sets out to buy, 'but the name stayed on, although no present was written beside it' (p. 266)). After the shopping spree, Carlene invites Kiki to travel with her to her house in the country, an invitation which Kiki initially refuses, and then accepts; but when she turns up at the train station, she finds that Carlene has been joined by the other Kipps, and so the trip is cancelled, and the two never meet again. This meeting, again, is an echo of the last meeting between Meg and Mrs Wilcox. The two go shopping together to buy the presents on Mrs Wilcox's Christmas list (Meg's 'name remained at the head of the list, but nothing was written opposite it' (p. 83)). Mrs Wilcox invites Meg to travel with her to Howards End, an invitation Meg initially refuses, and then accepts; but when Meg arrives at Kings Cross, she finds that Mrs Wilcox has been joined by her family, and so the trip is cancelled, and the two never meet again. In dying (discreetly, in the hiatus between this chapter and the next) Mrs Wilcox gives Meg the gift that she failed to give in life, the gift that was not written against Meg's name on her Christmas list. Where Carlene leaves a note after her death bequeathing her Hippolyte portrait to Kiki ('please enjoy this painting. It needs to be loved by someone like you' (p. 430)), Mrs Wilcox leaves a note, written in pencil, that declares 'I should like Miss Schlegel (Margaret) to have Howards End' (p. 100).

The magic that graces the relationship between Kiki and Carlene in Smith's novel is generated by this duplication, this increasingly eerie sense of doubling. If, as Scarry writes, beauty brings copies of itself into being, then the beauty that illuminates Smith's novel, its capacity to give expression to 'everything I cannot say', is conjured from its replication of Forster's. In allowing Mrs Wilcox's voice to shine in Carlene's, Smith produces what Bakhtin calls an 'authentic double-voicedness'. This is a force, Bakhtin writes, that 'generates novelistic prose dialogues', but which, even though it gives rise to novel voice, 'is not exhausted in these dialogues and remains in the discourse, in language, like a spring of dialogism that never runs dry'.[25] Mrs Wilcox is a source from which Carlene's voice flows, as from a spring that never runs dry. But if Smith doubles Forster's voice in this way, it is central to everything I have to say here that the duplication works both ways. In doubling Mrs Wilcox's voice, in shadowing it or extending it in the way that she does, Smith is only giving expression to a form of duplication that is already at work in Forster, a duplication that is intrinsic to Forster's singular encounter both with beauty, and with love. The figure of Mrs Wilcox in Forster's novel owes her beauty, her peculiar empathic grace, not to her *character*, but to a certain distance from her own form of being that is the province, in Forster, of aesthetic possibility – a distance that Smith's doubling works to amplify. One can see this distance at work when we first encounter Mrs Wilcox at Howards End, an ethereal figure, 'trailing noiselessly over the lawn', with 'a wisp of hay in her hands' (p. 21). The wisp of hay is a recurrent feature of Mrs Wilcox's bearing (indeed, it recurs obliquely in Smith's novel when we first meet Carlene, whose face is 'framed' by 'stray wisps' of hair (p. 40)), and suggests that she is closer to unconscious than conscious things. 'She seemed to belong', the narrator says, 'not to the young people and their motor, but to the house, and to the tree that overshadowed it' (p. 40). Like all beautiful things, she does not reside quite in herself, but in these approximations or renditions of her – the house, the wisp of hay, the wych elm tree which stands beside the house at Howards End, and with whose shadowed and branched form, at dusk, the house is often entangled. Mrs Wilcox is dispersed in the things with which she is associated, so that she is never quite at rest, never quite distilled; and it is this gap, this disjoining between spirit and the forms in which spirit knows itself, that shapes all of the novel's encounters with her, and that makes Meg's meeting with her so powerful and transformative. For Meg, to stand in her presence, in the shifting light of her bedroom – in the 'flicker of the fire, the quiver of the reading-lamp upon their hands, the white blur from the window' (p. 74) – is to enter into the space, restless and unmade, that is opened by the idea of beauty, the ground that lies between an abstraction and its objectification, between thought and thing.[26] Mrs Wilcox puts strange, oblique propositions to Meg – 'I – I wonder whether you ever think about yourself'; 'I almost think you forget you're a girl' – which draw her into this space, a space in which each woman meets the other, outside of the terms in which they habitually recognise or embed themselves. 'Mrs Wilcox and daily life', Meg thinks, are 'out of focus', so 'one or other must seem blurred' (p. 79). To meet her is to enter into this blurred space, to see by an 'inward light' (p. 102), into the space where the 'unseen' impacts upon the 'seen' (p. 102), where visible forms reach towards a beauty which exceeds their expressive power.

It is this capacity for forms to harbour the possibility of a relation that lies beyond them – that dismantles them even as it animates them – that lies at the heart of Forster's conception of aesthetic beauty. Mrs Wilcox occupies the territory, as Samuel Beckett later puts it, where 'seen and unseen meet', and in so doing she embodies the work of literature itself.[27] 'Literature and art', Meg says to Mrs Wilcox, 'have what one might call the kink of the unseen about them' (p. 79), and it is this kink, like the 'kink in the brain' (p. 285) of Mrs Avery, the deranged housekeeper of Howards End, that is the motor of Forster's imaginative possibility. Such a conception of beauty, beauty as broken connection, sits, throughout *Howards End*, at an angle to the ideals of progressive art that are espoused, at least early in the novel, by the Schlegels, and that animate Leonard Bast's painful programme of self-improvement. Leonard believes that a literary education is a means to class advancement, to getting one's 'hands on the ropes' (p. 55), as, in Anahid Nersessian's terms, the 'social purpose' of an aesthetic education in the twentieth-century university 'was to provide access to class power and acculturate individuals to it'.[28] Leonard is guided in his conception of the means by which learning might enlarge and fortify the mind by his study of the most prominent Victorian thinkers of moral aesthetics, Matthew Arnold and John Ruskin. He is reading Ruskin, he tells his wife Jacky, because it will provide him with the key to an understanding of beauty, of proportion, that will allow him to lead a balanced and well-proportioned (and more prosperous) life. 'I care a good deal about improving myself by means of Literature and Art, and so getting a wider outlook' (p. 54), he tells Jacky, suggesting that it was by reading Ruskin's *The Stones of Venice* that he might 'see life steadily' and 'see it whole' (p. 55). This steadiness and wholeness is drawn not from Ruskin but from Arnold, and from Arnold's poem 'To a Friend', where the poet offers up thanks to the 'even balanc'd soul' of his friend, 'Who saw life steadily and saw it whole'.[29] But it is in *The Stones of Venice*, and in Ruskin's capacity to discover in the principles of architectural beauty a kind of moral proportion, that Leonard finds a model of the 'wider outlook' he seeks. In his study of Venetian architecture, Ruskin materialises Arnold's 'even balance' in the figure of the arch, the architectural feature that bears weight, and that spans the gulf between things. The arch bears within it what Ruskin calls the 'arch line' – the 'ghost or skeleton of the arch; or rather the spinal marrow of the arch'.[30] The arch line is what makes the arch steady and whole – it is 'the moral character of the arch, and the adverse forces are its temptations; and the voussoirs, and what else we may help it with, are its armour and its motives to good conduct' (pp. 125–126). 'There is a great deal of nicety in calculating it with precision' Ruskin goes on, extending his metaphor. But 'in arch morality and in man morality' there is 'a very simple and easily to be understood principle, – that if either arch or man expose themselves to their special temptations or adverse forces, *outside* of their voussoirs or proper and appointed armour, both will fall' (p. 126).

Leonard strives to fashion his moral character on Ruskin's arch line; but Forster's aesthetic theory, his idea of beauty, looks to a radically different model of connection, one which seeks to move past the Victorian moralism of Ruskin and Arnold. The possibility of beauty, the possibility that the shared apprehension of beauty might be a means of spanning the gulf between people and things, between one person and another, lies for Forster in that very distance, that kinked relation between idea and form, between thought and thing, that gleams in the white blur of Mrs Wilcox's window. As Leonard and the Schlegels listen to Beethoven at the opening of the novel, as Leonard struggles to hear the music over the steady drumbeat of his missing umbrella, Forster suggests that the beauty of the music is not captured in any particular form of listening – neither in Meg's purism, nor in Tibby's academicism, nor in Helen's literariness – but in the suspended space of translation itself, in the uncrossed gulf between the invisible *geist* of the music, and the forms, various and multiple, that the music takes. Meg expresses her frustration with Helen's need (and Kiki's need) to turn music into something else, to turn it into language or painting, in order to be able to apprehend it. 'Helen's one aim', she says, 'is to translate tunes into the language of painting, and pictures into the language of music'. 'What *is* the good of the arts', Meg demands, 'if they're interchangeable? What *is* the good of the ear if it tells you the same as the eye?' (p. 39). This is a Forsterian question – *the* Forsterian question – and it strikes at the heart of Forster's novelisation of aesthetic possibility. The ear, Meg thinks, attends to a different world than the eye, a soundworld, not a lightworld. Helen wants to read across from one to another, to find in aesthetics a form of conduit that brings light and sound together. Meg insists on their particularity – and in so doing she strikes an echo of the work of the young Karl Marx, as he strives, in his mid-twenties, to prepare the philosophical ground for his dawning historical materialism. 'A musical ear', Marx writes in 1844, and 'an eye for the beauty of form', respond to different stimuli, as all the senses 'come into being only through the existence of *their* objects'.[31] The 'peculiarity' of each sense belongs to the 'peculiar mode of its objectification' (p. 353). 'An object', Marx writes, in terms which closely resemble Meg's, 'is different for the *eye* from what it is for the *ear*, and the eye's object *is* different from the *ear's*' (p. 353).

This is a quietly devastating observation. The things of the world come to being as they come to thought and sensation, and they come to being *differently*, for the eye, the ear, the fingertips, the tongue. This, for Marx in 1844, is an effect of the 'human self-estrangement' that is a consequence of 'private property' (p. 348). The possibility that the differing objects of ear and eye might have a common 'essence' is forestalled by the estrangement brought about by capital – an estrangement that it is the task of communism to overcome. '*Communism*'. Marx writes, 'is the *positive* supersession of *private property* as *human self-estrangement*' (p. 348). In the absence of such supersession, we are presented with a world whose possibility unity – whose steadiness, and wholeness – lies beneath its perceived disunity. 'It is true', Marx writes, 'that thought and being are *distinct*, but at the same time they are in *unity* with one another' (p. 351), and it is this unity and disunity that Forster traces in the Schlegels' listening to Beethoven, this recognition that the forms of unity promised by aesthetic experience are bound to the disunity that it reveals, the gulf between eye and ear. Helen tries to uncover the unity that underwrites aesthetic forms; Meg attends to the disunity of the object as it is given aesthetic form: and beauty, for Forster, lies in this difference, in the capacity to apprehend this relation between thought and being both in its unity and its disunity. It is the nature of beauty, as we form an idea of it, to bring this distance from itself that dwells in the object to knowledge and thought. We might think here not only of Marx, but also of Wittgenstein, in Scarry's rendition, at the opening of her essay *On Beauty*: 'Wittgenstein says that when the eye sees something beautiful, the hand wants to draw it'.[32] Beauty does not build a bridge over these differences. It does not make the world steady or whole. If we should 'take poetry seriously', then this is not because it can educate us, or lift us clear of the abyss, or free us from our self-estrangement, but because it delivers us to this frightening gulf, between the eye and the ear, between the hand and the eye, in which our estrangement from the objects of the world is given an unmeasured form.

III Gleam

Forster's insistence on this broken connection, this unbreachable gulf, drives his thinking, and constitutes what Zadie Smith calls his 'quiet, Forsterish' radicalism.[33] So when Smith lays her novel like a gauze over Forster's, the beauty of the gesture is that it brings to thought precisely the gulf, precisely the broken junction, between beauty and the copies that beauty makes of itself, that it is the task of both novels to approach. When Carlene's voice summons the ghost of Mrs Wilcox's, we glimpse, in the dialogue that is set in motion, Bakhtin's 'spring of dialogism' that gives rise to a voice that is not contained in the words in which it speaks, but enters into the voice of the novel, something close to what Maurice Blanchot has called the 'neuter' ('we hear in the narrative form', Blanchot writes, 'something indeterminate speaking').[34]

This voice, sounding in the unsewn seams between Smith and Forster, offers a response to one of the questions that both novels ask – the question of love. The question of how we are to make of our love, for *this* person, the foundation of our being; of what it means to stake our life on our love for another. This is a question of particular concern for the novelist, Forster writes in *Aspects of the Novel*. When a novelist 'creates' his or her characters, he writes, "love" in any or all of its aspects becomes important in his mind'.³⁵ Love, and the possibility of truly loving relations between people, lies at the heart of the novel form for Forster, and Kiki's question – how do we spend our love in shared time, how do we find our own life lived out in that of another person – is the novel's question. 'How much time does love take' (p. 59), Forster asks, and his answer is characteristic of his gentle radicalism.³⁶ We cannot measure love, he says. We cannot place it in time or in sequence, we cannot make it the basis of a legal union, still less of a civilization. We cannot suborn it to any regulated model of sexuality or desire or propriety. 'All history, all our experience, teaches us that no human relationship is constant', and so if we seek to formalise it, to legislate for it, we destroy it.³⁷ If a relationship is 'constant', he writes, 'it is no longer a human relationship but a social habit' and 'the emphasis in it has passed from love to marriage'.³⁸ To be alive as a novelist to the shifting terms of all relations is to enter into the flux that characterises our relation not only to others, but to ourselves. In his 1939 essay 'What I Believe', composed in the shadow of world war, he writes that 'there is something incalculable in each of us'. 'We don't know what we are like', he says. 'We can't know what other people are like. How, then, can we put any trust in personal relations, or cling to them in the gathering political storm?'.³⁹ The novelist has to be true, Forster thinks, to the incalculable, the unformalised, which makes our relations with one another unstable and fragmentary, not stable and whole. But if this is so, it is the basis of everything that Forster has written, the very basis of what he believes, that love, even in its incalculability, is the condition of shared life, of the democracy which is threatened, in 1939, by the gathering political storm; and that the novel as a form is able to give a kind of expression to this love, in all its irregularity, its incalculability. How can we put any trust in personal relations, as the flimsy basis for a democracy on which we will stake our lives? 'In theory we cannot', he says. 'But in practice we can and do. Though A is not unchangeably A, or B unchangeably B, there can still be love and loyalty between the two'.⁴⁰

When Smith tunes the relation between Carlene and Kiki, in *On Beauty*, to that between Meg and Mrs Wilcox in *Howards End*, she coaxes this love into being, this love that is the province of political hope, of Forster's 'hope this side of the grave', even as it refuses to adopt a stable political form. The connection between Smith's novel and Forster's, in taking place outside of the bounds of both novels, in the space of the unbridged gulf between them, partakes of that love and loyalty that persists between people, even though they do not know themselves, or each other. The passage that she opens between the two novels is Smith's way of expressing her love of E. M. Forster, a way of spending the love that she finds lying latent in Forster's fiction itself. 'Time is how you spend your love', Smith says, in Nick Laird's voice, and as she does so we can hear the terms in which both novels jointly tell the time that love takes. This is the love between Carlene and Kiki, as it resonates with the love between Kiki and Howard, between Smith and Laird, Smith and Forster, Meg and Mrs Wilcox. It is perhaps above all the love that lies deepest in the groundless foundations of *Howards End* – Meg's love for her sister, which eludes all given political languages and regulations, but is the basis for the novel's expression of political hope. When Helen becomes pregnant, towards the close of the novel, and when the world turns against her in hypocritical disgust – when Meg's emotionally stunted husband Henry Wilcox turns against her, despite his own infidelities – Meg sets aside all conventional morality for the truth of her love for her sister. 'However piteous her sister's state', Meg thinks, 'she knew that she must be on her side. They would be mad together if the world chose to consider them so' (p. 302). The place in which Meg offers her sister shelter, of course, is Howards End, both the house that Mrs Wilcox bequeaths to Meg, and the novel that Forster bequeaths to Smith, and to us. Howards End becomes a kind of fortress – 'she was fighting for women against men', Meg thinks. 'If men came into Howards End, it should be over her body' – a fortress built of that vaporous stuff that is the sinew of literary connection in Forster. Howards End is bequeathed to Meg by Mrs Wilcox, even if it is scarcely 'credible' that 'the possessions of the spirit can be bequeathed at all' (p. 102), and the bequest is not only the house but the imagined space that Mrs Wilcox makes possible – the 'inward' space where Meg and Mrs Wilcox meet, where seen and unseen meet, the 'inner life' that makes being thinkable, even if it cannot be made visible, or palpable. Because their 'inner life was so safe', Meg thinks, she and her sister are proof against the cruelty of the world. They can offer each other a love and a loyalty that the Wilcoxes 'outer life' can't touch. 'There are moments when the inner life actually 'pays', when years of self-scrutiny, conducted for no other purpose, are suddenly of practical use' (p. 204). 'Such moments', she goes on, 'are still rare in the West' (p. 204). Like the deferred coming together of Aziz and Fielding at the close of *A Passage to India*, such a connection does not have a political space or time to unfold, and does not have a recognised currency.[41] It is in the novel form itself that this connection might be made – not the sturdy moral arch that Ruskin finds in the stones of Venice, but the vaporous connection forged only in fiction. It is in the kinked passages that the artwork makes thinkable that we can conceive of the 'rainbow bridge that should connect the prose in us with the passion'. 'Without it', Forster writes, without this conjunction between the inner life and the outer, the abstract and the material, 'we are meaningless fragments, half monks, half beasts, unconnected arches that have never joined into a man'. But 'with it love is born' (p. 194).

In building its own kind of rainbow bridge between *On Beauty* and *Howards End*, made out of her love of E. M. Forster, Smith's novel works as a kind of test of this capacity for art, for aesthetic beauty, to reach beyond itself, to bring people, places and times that are divorced from one another, or antipathetic to one another, into some kind of displaced conjunction. Can the work of a white man writing in 1910 come into meaningful contact with the work of a black woman writing in 2005? Can the broken relations between the Schlegels, the Wilcoxes and the Basts come into any meaningful alignment with the broken relations between the Belseys and the Kipps, or the Belsey children and Carl the street rapper? Do these relations, across historical divides, across divides between race, and class, and nation, bear any structural resemblance to the other relations that *On Beauty* sets in play – between philosophy and literature, between music and painting, between prose and poetry? For Dorothy Hale, in her penetrating 2012 reading of *On Beauty*, the answer to these questions is a kind of no. The importance of Smith's novel, in Hale's reading, lies in its demonstration of the *specificity* of subject positions and of archaeologies of thought, not in their translatability. When Elaine Scarry's *On Beauty* makes an appearance in Zadie Smith's, Hale suggests, we see not a coming together of philosophy and literature, but a manifestation of their incompatibility. 'If Smith's repetition of Scarry's title prepares us for a novel of ideas', Hale writes, 'the novel quickly teaches us that the novel's idea of an idea is different from the philosopher's'.[42] Fiction and philosophy cleave apart here rather than together, and what is more, their separation derives, in this instance, from their different conceptions of the means by which ideas migrate past their own fields of force and conditions of possibility. Scarry's philosophy leads her towards an attempt to identify the 'fundamental qualities of beauty' (p. 815), while Smith's fiction leads her to the representation of lived experience. 'Whereas Scarry seeks primarily to describe the 'felt experience of cognition' that unites all human beings of every culture in their experience of beauty, Smith portrays the particularity and contingency of each individual's apprehension of beauty' (p. 815). In a contradiction that is intrinsic to the novel form, Hale writes, the ethical capacity of the novel to be attentive to others, to those who speak from subject positions other than the novelist's own, emerges from its singular alertness to the embeddedness of subject positions in their own particular space and time. This is why, in Hale's estimation, Smith's novel is concerned not with communicability but with specificity. 'Any abstract idea a character might hold about the operation or value of cognition' Hale writes, 'is shown to be inseparable from an individual's social position within a particular cultural formation' (p. 815).

It is for this reason – that the novel as a form is committed to depicting the 'socially constructed act of cognition' (p. 825) – that it has so often seemed resistant to or at odds with the claims of aesthetic beauty. 'The constitutive sociality of the novel's representational project', Hale writes, 'has always put it in tension with the formal control and effects that would most often call forth praise of its beauty' (p. 817). Hale argues that Smith's 'understanding of the art of the novel as a perspectival endeavour and an ethical task' means that it 'seems a mistake to ask, "Is *On Beauty* beautiful?"' (p. 842) – and of course this suspicion of beauty, this sense that the aesthetic question of the beautiful is at odds with the novel's ethical and political concerns, is everywhere in evidence in *On Beauty*. The satirical tone of Smith's novel, its light comic touch, is expressive of its wry scepticism concerning the uses of beauty, and of the critical languages we bring to it. Forster's Leonard, in a moment of terrible literalism, dies under an avalanche of the books he was reading to save his life; Smith's Carl meets no such fate, but there is no place for him in Smith's twenty-first-century university, which is not a space for critical thinking about beauty but rather a bankrupt bastion of privilege, which can only deface or misrecognise the object of its study. The university is a 'precious thing', Elaine Scarry writes in *On Beauty*, and to 'misstate, or even merely understate, the relation of the universities to beauty is one kind of error that can be made'. The university, she writes, in a line that Smith takes as an epigraph, 'is among the precious things that can be destroyed',[43] and the university of *On Beauty* is a university in the process of being destroyed, a 'university', as Bill Readings puts it in 1994, 'in ruins'.[44] The Humanities professors, Howard among them, have all, in different ways, disavowed the idea of beauty – in Howard's case in an attempt to develop a properly political understanding of the ways in which beauty has served political power. 'Art', Howard tells his students in his introductory class on Rembrandt, is the 'western myth with which we both console ourselves and make ourselves' (p. 155). In Victoria Kipps's rendition – in her description of his class in which for comic effect she replaces the concept of beauty with the word 'tomato' – his scepticism becomes simply bathetic. 'That's what I *love* about your class', she says. 'It's properly intellectual':

> The tomato is just totally revealed as this phoney construction that can't lead you to some higher truth – nobody's pretending the tomato will save your life. Or make you happy. Or teach you how to live or *ennoble* you or be *a great example of the human spirit*. Your tomatoes have got nothing to do with *love* or *truth*. They're not fallacies. They're just these pretty pointless tomatoes that people, for totally selfish reasons of their own, have attached cultural – I should say *nutritional* – weight to. (p. 312)

The question, for Howard, in Victoria's pastiche, of 'what's so beautiful about this tomato' is reduced to the less elevated question of 'who decided on its worth' (p. 312). But even as *On Beauty* satirises the university, and the critical languages that we bring to beauty, its dialogue, not only with Forster, but with its other guiding spirits, Scarry, Laird, Schama, Rembrandt, turns around a kind of thinking about beauty, about the idea of beauty, which does have to do with those things that Howard's tomato does not, which does have something to do with love, and truth.[45] As Hale writes, if it is a mistake to ask if *On Beauty* is beautiful 'it is equally an error to ignore the question of beauty – beauty as a question' (p. 842) – a question that Smith poses by bringing discrete voices, art forms and disciplines into contact with each other, and approaching the spaces that open between them as the disappearing terrain of beauty itself.

It is in the novel's closing scene, in which Howard gives a valedictory lecture to his faculty, that this question – of the relation of beauty to political, historical and ontological difference – is given its sharpest expression. The lecture is on Rembrandt, the subject of Howard's life's work. All his colleagues are there. As he stands at the lectern, he sees that Kiki is in the audience too, Kiki who has left him because of his serial adultery. 'She wore a scarlet ribbon threaded through her plait', Howard sees, 'and her shoulders were gleaming' (p. 442). It feels like a moment to summarise a career, a moment to seek redemption, or justify the living of a life. But as Howard stands to speak, as the lights go down and Rembrandt's paintings appear projected on the screen behind him, he realises he has left the copy of his lecture on the front seat of his car, parked several blocks away. He clicks through his slide show in excruciating silence, painting after painting, until he comes to his final image, *Hendrickje Bathing*, Rembrandt's painting of his unmarried partner, Hendrickje Stoffels. The painting depicts Hendrickje standing in a stream, ankle deep, holding her white smock clear of the water (see Figure 6.1). She is looking down at the water, in a beautiful, contained abstraction. Rembrandt painted it in 1654, when Hendrickje was pregnant with their child.

III Gleam

Figure 6.1 Rembrandt van Rijn, *Woman Bathing in a Stream (Hendrickje Stoffels?)*, 1654, oil on oak, National Gallery, London, 61.8 × 47 cm.

Howard, struck dumb without his script, can only croak out the title, and the date. '*Hendrickje Bathing*, 1654'. It is as if the painting is required to speak for itself, while the audience is left vainly 'waiting for elucidation' (p. 442). It is as if, as Walter Pater puts it in one of the most influential statements ever made on thinking about beauty, 'gathering all we are into one desperate effort to see and touch, we shall hardly have time to make theories about the things we see and touch'.[46] Smith's narrator describes the image: Hendrickje 'looked away, coyly, into the water. She seemed to be wondering whether to wade deeper. The surface of the water was dark, reflective – a cautious bather could not be certain of what lurked beneath' (p. 442). All the speechless Howard can do is magnify the image, so the 'woman's fleshiness filled the wall', so we can see that 'her hands were imprecise blurs, paint heaped on paint and roiled with the brush', and we can see her skin, 'rendered in all its variety', 'chalky whites and lively pinks, the underlying blue of her veins' (p. 443).

It is hard not to see in this scene an insistence on the untranslatability of beauty, and on the impotence of the critical languages that we have to account for it – an insistence that, in Pater's words, 'theory, or idea, or system [...] has no real claim on us' (p. 120). But if Smith is making this gesture here, this disavowal of a certain model of critique, this moment does not privilege the artwork over the idea of the artwork, beauty over the idea of beauty. It does not suggest that we should simply look, and hold our peace. Rather, it puts the idea of beauty into motion, as all artworks do, as all acts of critical thinking do – as it is the task and gift of the university to do. It may be the case, as Timothy Bewes has recently argued, that the relation between the artwork and our critical idea of it is one that cannot be established, that remains open and undecided. The 'relation between writing and criticism', Bewes wites in *Free Indirect*, is 'an interstice that cannot be bridged'.[47] But if this is so, if there is no Ruskinian arch between aesthetic beauty and the languages we bring to it, this broken connection itself, as Bewes writes, can become 'its own order of thought' (p. 96), the order of thought that is latent in the novel form. Rembrandt's painting, in Smith's rendition, does not rest in itself, is not complete in itself. Even if the beauty of this portrait lies in Hendrickje's total absorption, in the sense that, as she looks down at the water, she is wrapped in the beauty of herself, the power of the painting is that such absorption, the adequacy to itself of the beautiful thing, is inseparable from its opposite – its openness to that which it is not, its condition as duplication, as the copy of itself that it brings into being. Hale is sceptical of the purpose or effectiveness of this closing scene, of its capacity to open the subject positions it depicts to critique, or to possibility. She wonders why Smith's novel should close with an episode told from the perspective of a sexually confused middle aged white man. 'What does it mean', Hale asks, 'that a novel that displays its capacity to write a new cultural narrative, Kiki's narrative, falls into the same old story, the Updikean-Bellowian-Rothian male midlife-crisis sexual romp'.[48] Why does a novel that shows such perspectival mobility abandon the promise of inhabiting Kiki's 'interiority', in favour of this 'old story'? For Hale, this moment has echoes with earlier failures in the history of the novel to reach under the skin of the objectified other. William Faulkner, in *The Sound and the Fury*, is able, Hale writes, to 'make vivid the interiorities of three white men' (p. 820). But this capacity reaches a kind of limit in his representation of the 'African American servant' Dilsey. In his depiction of Dilsey, Faulkner abandons interior monologue, in favour of a heightened aesthetic description of Dilsey's 'outside', of the body that he 'drapes over her' like a cloak (p. 822). 'Deprived of her inside view, the novelist adorns her outside with a portentous linguistic performance', a self-consciously lyrical beauty that is a compensation for its failed 'aesthetics of alterity' (p. 821).

The closing invocation of Rembrandt's portrait of Henrdrickje might partake of this failure, this sense that the novel tradition, even in Smith's hands, defaults to a white male perspective, and prefers to see black women from the outside. But if this is so, Smith's attention here to the junction between the inside and outside of being is tuned to the gulf that opens between these states, the gulf that the idea of beauty makes thinkable. In layering Howard's looking at Kiki over Rembrandt's looking at Hendrickje, Smith prises open the space and the time in which beauty and love come to possibility in art. We see in Smith's rendition of the painting not Hendrickje, or not just Hendrickje, but Rembrandt painting Hendrickje, and it is in the gulf between a woman enclosed in the being of herself, and the desire she provokes in him (and us) to capture that being, to share it, to enter into it, that the beauty of this painting lies. We don't see here Hendrickje's flesh, her hands, her face, we see instead the paint – paint heaped on paint, roiled with the brush – that lies over her form like a veil or a gauze. Even as this moment in Smith's novel is one in which criticism falls silent, in which Howard's professional scepticism falters before the beauty of art, it nevertheless turns around an open gulf, between the abstract idea of the artwork and its materiality, that is the source both of beauty itself, and of our capacity to think critically about it, to form an idea of it. In following the movement of the painting, in translating, as Forster would put it, the language of painting into the language of fiction, the prose reaches into the heart of the painterly moment, the aesthetic moment, in which beauty gives itself to and withholds itself from the forms in which we know it. The painting comes to view in Smith's rendition as a drama of surface and depth. The reflective surface of the water hides whatever might lie beneath. The white and pink of Hendrickje's skin lays over the blue of her veins, the hidden anatomical network exposed to such dramatic effect in Rembrandt's great painting *The Anatomy Lesson of Dr Tulp* (after which Smith names the second section of her novel) (see Figure 6.2). But *Hendrickje Bathing* does not anatomise, any more than *The Anatomy Lesson* does. *The Anatomy Lesson* offers to peel back the skin of the partly dissected corpse that lies in the foreground of the painting, to show us how muscles and tendons materialise the movement of mind – the abstract mental activity we see reflected in the face of the surgeon, Dr Tulp, as he operates the biological apparatus of the corpse's arm with his forceps. But the painting cannot

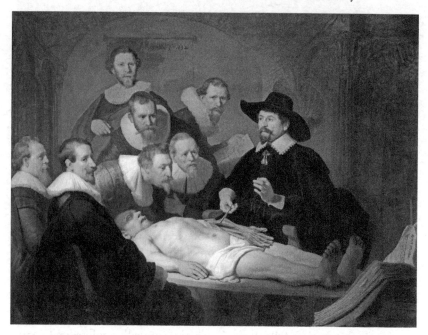

Figure 6.2   Rembrandt van Rijn, *The Anatomy Lesson of Dr Tulp*, 1632, oil on canvas, Mauritshuis, The Hague, 216.5 cm x 169.5 cm.

reveal the interiority of mind, suggesting instead that the place where interiority meets with its material exterior recedes always from view, and is thinkable only as disjunction, the disjunction that Marx finds between thinking and being, between the essence of a thing and its objectification, the 'interstice' that Bewes finds between writing and criticism. In the *Anatomy Lesson*, in *Hendrickje Bathing*, Rembrandt is not, as Claire Malcolm puts it in a phoney exchange with Kiki, 'digging into the canvas to get what's really in those faces' ('He doesn't want you to look at the faces', Claire, says, in a limply second-hand take on Rembrandt's portraiture, 'he wants you to look at the *souls*' (p. 54)). Rather, he is laying the surface, of face and of paint, over what lies beneath that surface, to open us to the space of the junction itself – what Simon Schama has called 'the material and conceptual interior of art-making'.[49] What the painting reveals is not a metaphysical interior, but the space that comes to thought in the time of viewing and reading, the kinked, unmeasured time (in art and in literature, in eye and in ear) in which beauty reveals itself to us, in which the unseen meets with the seen.[50]

III Gleam

This is the time, in Smith and in Forster, both of love and of beauty. 'How much time does love take?', Forster asks, and this ending to Smith's novel – its most aesthetically heightened passage – is an answer to this question. We look at Hendrickje's skin, its pinks and whites. Howard looks at the gleaming skin of Kiki's shoulders, seen across the gulf both of a lecture theatre, and of a marital estrangement. And Smith's novel reaches for a means of timing this looking, of seeing how it might contain both a life that *has been* staked on others, and a way of imagining, through an encounter with beauty, a life that *will be* staked on others, a life that might be animated by what Forster calls 'truer relations', which gleam with the same gleam that shines, for Howard, in Kiki's distantly naked skin.[51] As we look through the narrator's eyes at the dark, reflective water in Rembrandt's painting, Howard looks at his wife across the lecture theatre (a performative arena that catches another faint echo of Rembrandt's *Anatomy Lesson*). 'Howard looked at Kiki. In her face, his life' (p. 442). The time of a shared life is held in the opening contours of a face. This is the discovery of this moment in Smith's novel. Shared life gleams in the forms in which we reveal ourselves to each other. A shared past, a shared future, is threaded into these forms, and it is the work of beauty, its nature and its effect, to put these forms into the kind of suspension, the kind of openness which allows us to see how we meet each other across them, even though we do not know ourselves, or each other. As Smith reaches towards Forster, to find a common ground that they share beneath their differences, she is reaching towards the 'truer relationships' that, Forster writes, lie 'beyond the limits that fetter us now'.[52]

One of the more subterranean links between Smith's and Forster's novels – in which we can see both writers reaching towards those 'truer relationships' that lie beyond the distorting limits of their own time and place – is in the idea they share of the unborn baby, the baby that the world will not welcome. This is Helen's baby, in *Howards End*, and Hendrickje's baby, in *On Beauty*, hidden beneath the clothes and skin and paint of Rembrandt's portrait. Forster's novel ends with a utopian vision of collective living, in which Helen's baby is brought up at Howards End, under the collective care of Helen, Meg, and a reformed Henry Wilcox. The gleam of truer relations is given form and substance here, as the Wilcoxian defence of property and of propriety yields to a Schlegelian image of communal life that, as Marx puts it, is found in the 'supersession of *private property* as *human self-estrangement*'.[53] Mrs Wilcox leaves Howards End to Meg, against the diktats of property law, and in the teeth of the perception that the possession of the spirit cannot be bequeathed at all, that the 'soul' has no 'offspring' (p. 102); when Mr Wilcox repeats the bequest, when he says to the other Wilcoxes that 'I leave Howards End to my wife absolutely' (p. 360), Forster's novel imagines a form of community that looks past the fetters of private property, towards the offspring of the soul, towards a form of shared life that is not deformed by the class and gender relations that shape English culture in 1910. 'I feel', Meg says at the novel's close, 'that our house is the future as well as the past' (p. 359).

On Beauty ends with no such utopian vision, and offers no revealed future to Hendrickje's unborn baby, no imagined world in which the deformations of private property, or the inequalities of race and class and gender, have been overcome. But the closing scene, the magnified image of Hendrickje standing uncertain in the stream, the image of Kiki's gleaming shoulders as she stands distant in the lecture theatre, suggests that aesthetic beauty, aesthetic experience, is gravid with its own kind of futurity. To attend to beauty, Kant writes in the *Critique of Judgement*, is to find oneself bound into a community of others, as the expression – 'this thing is beautiful' – is one which presupposes the assent of others who share your belief in the beauty of that thing. If one 'calls the object beautiful', he writes, 'one lays claim to the consent of every one'.[54] Beauty is communal; as Sianne Ngai writes, it 'presupposes other minds'.[55] As Smith's novel brings Rembrandt into contact with Forster, Kiki into contact with Mrs Wilcox, Hendrickje's baby into contact with Helen's, it fashions a community made of this shared witnessing of beauty, a community that looks towards its own offspring. As we look, in *On Beauty's* final line, at Hendrickje's painted skin, the 'chalky whites and lively pinks, the underlying blue of her veins and the ever present human hint of yellow', Smith finds in Rembrandt's portrait of his lover and their unborn child an 'intimation of what is to come' (p. 443).

2022

PART II

On Literary History

CHAPTER 7

The Threshold of Vision
The Animal Gaze in Beckett, Sebald and Coetzee

I

What is the nature of the boundary or threshold across which the act of looking takes place?

This boundary can be thought of in various different ways and assumes many different configurations, but it is difficult, perhaps very difficult, to preserve a concept of vision, or of looking, that does not involve some such demarcation or borderline. At its most denuded, one might think of the threshold between the looker and the looked at as the corneal membrane itself, that transparent skin that separates the organ of looking from the object of the gaze. One only has to imagine what happens if this skin is removed, the consequent release of the vitreous and aqueous humour, the unsightly excretion of the eye's vile jelly, to realise how indispensable this boundary is.[1] This is an intimate boundary, as intimate as it is indispensable, and, with the eardrum, constitutes one of those sites at which the nature of the relationship between the mind and the world is at its most precarious, at which the film that keeps the thinking monad sealed and entire is at its most fragile.[2] Partly as a result of this intimacy, any understanding of the nature of this threshold involves us in ethical thinking, as well as in those aesthetic and political questions that have tended to be associated with the act of looking. To attend to the slim, clear boundary that intervenes between he or she or that which looks, and that which is looked upon, is necessarily to think about the forces which shape distinctions between self and other, and between self and world – the distinctions that lie at the foundation of all political and ethical structures. The threshold of vision is where such distinctions are at their most nearly invisible (lying almost below the threshold of the visible); but it is also the borderline upon which rest all of the other distinctions that allow for political and ethical thought and life.

The threshold of vision is summoned in any thinking of the aesthetics of alterity; but if this is so, the modern and contemporary period has seen a shift in the terms in which the literary imagination navigates this boundary, this threshold – a shift that can be mapped onto the unfolding relations between Samuel Beckett, J. M. Coetzee and W. G. Sebald. My contention here is that these three writers together offer what might be thought of as a new theory of vision, a thinking and a poetics of looking that suggests an emergent set of broader ethical possibilities that arise from their work, and that have stirring implications for the way that we understand the possibilities of contemporary literary expression more generally. Further, I will argue here that these writers' approach to the question and experience of vision is intimately entwined with their attention to the gaze of the animal. All three writers, I suggest, are preoccupied by what happens when a human looks into the eyes of an animal, and by what John Berger calls the 'narrow abyss of non-comprehension' across which such a gaze must pass.[3] The threshold of vision bears the weight of all ethico-political relations conducted in the realm of the visible, and the question of animal rights as balanced against human rights is only one among many such relations. But for all three of these writers, the encounter between human and animal is peculiarly charged, and has wide reaching consequences for a broader set of questions about responsibility, ipseity, alterity, hybridity, and the possibility of imagined community itself.

One can begin to address this shared concern by tracing, in an appropriately Sebaldian-arachnid metaphor, a web of connections between Beckett, Coetzee and Sebald, that touches either directly or obliquely both on the act of looking, and on the gaze of the animal. The first radial of this web is formed by an essay on Beckett by Coetzee, which was delivered to a conference in Tokyo in 2006, and subsequently published in a volume entitled *Borderless Beckett*.[4] Entitled 'Eight Ways of Looking at Samuel Beckett', the essay presents a series of meditations on what Coetzee calls Beckett's 'philosophical dualism' (p. 19). The essay reflects on how Beckett understands the experience of being composed at once of a mind and of a body, and on how Beckett's thinkers, or 'intelligences', might seek to free themselves from the closed cells of their minds, not only to take ownership of their bodies, but also to penetrate into the mind of another, another human, or another animal. For Coetzee's Beckett, in this essay, to think is merely to mark out the closed threshold of one's own consciousness. To think is to test the limits of thinking and to find them sealed. The mind, Coetzee suggests, that 'huge brain of homo sapiens, developed to bear the weight of so much consciousness' (p. 21), has produced only a consciousness of the tautological self referentiality of thought. Consciousness of self, which we require such a vast neural processor to generate, produces only the consciousness that one cannot free oneself from the constraints of self-hood. The mark of this failure, as performed by Beckett's intelligences, Coetzee suggests, is the unthinkable otherness of the other, and particularly of the animal other. 'What is missing from Beckett's account of life?' Coetzee asks at the beginning of meditation four, before answering his own question, in a manner that caused some discomfort in the Japanese lecture hall in which he originally delivered this talk. 'Many things', he replies, 'of which the biggest is the whale' (p. 21). The whale, 'huge in its rage, huge in its death agony' (p. 22), the harpooned whale whose 'blood bubbles and seethes for furlongs behind him, till the rays of the sun, reflected from it, reddens the face of its killers' (p. 22). This huge mountain of ancient being is absent from Beckett's starved and depleted mindscapes, and this absence, Coetzee suggests, signals the failure of a dying imagination whose only subject is its own death, not that of the other, not that of the hunted whale. We are left, he suggests, to imagine what Beckett's 'account of life' would be like if it had managed somehow to include the animal other. 'What if Beckett had had the imaginative courage to dream up the whale', Coetzee asks the by now faintly embarrassed delegates and dignitaries in the Tokyo lecture hall,

> What if Beckett had had the imaginative courage to dream up the whale, the great flat featureless front (front, from Latin frons, forehead) pressed up against the fragile bark in which you venture on the deep; and behind that front, the great, scheming animal brain, the brain that comes from another universe of discourse, thinking thoughts according to its own nature, beyond malign, beyond benign, thoughts inconceivable, incommensurate with human thought? (p. 24)

We cannot answer this question, Coetzee implies, because Beckett's poetic apparatus cannot accommodate the whale, not just because he is lacking in imaginative courage, but because he does not have the tools, the hardware. Herman Melville's Ahab seethes and boils in his attempt to penetrate that white wall, that blank white front behind which the whale brain mysteriously moves. 'If man will strike', Ahab cries in chapter 36 of *Moby Dick*, 'strike through the mask! How can the prisoner reach outside except by thrusting through the wall? To me, the white whale is that wall, shoved near me' (p. 22).[5] Ahab and Melville have harpoons to strike through the mask, but Beckett's 'creatures', those pale, impotent inheritors of Melville's legacy, do not. 'Why do these creatures not grasp their harpoon and hurl it through the white wall?', Coetzee asks, again: 'Answer: because they are impotent, invalid, crippled, bed-ridden .... Because they do not have harpoons, only pencils at most' (p. 23).

This failure, for Coetzee, this deficit of imaginative courage, is balanced in some limited fashion against the penetrative power of the gaze, a penetrative power that is also, at this late stage in the evolution of literary looking, on its last leg. Beckett's manikins do not throw harpoons at the white walls of their cells because, Coetzee writes, 'they and the intelligences behind them believe that the only tool that can pierce the white wall is the tool of pure thought. Despite the evidence of their eyes that the tool of pure thought fails again and again and again' (p. 23). The eyes, the thresholds of the mind, give evidence that the borders of the mind are sealed, unassailable, that thinking cannot think its way beyond the white wall of the skull. But even as the eyes submit this evidence of the failure of thought to penetrate, or to pierce, they also offer a compromised, perhaps misleading passage from mind to world, what the narrator of *The Lost Ones* would call a 'way out'.[6] Beckett shares with Kafka, that writer who so often thought with the mind of an animal, a piercing gaze that comes to us not in words but in photographs, in the iconic images of the writers themselves as they regard us from the page. Do these famous photographed gazes, Coetzee asks, lead us to believe after all that there is some traffic, in Kafka and in Beckett, between here and there? 'Are we misled', Coetzee asks, 'by the famous photograph of [Kafka], with the brilliant, dark eyes that seem to bespeak piercing insight into realms invisible and to hint that their owner does not belong in this world, not wholly?' (pp. 30–31). And Beckett, Coetzee goes on, 'Beckett had his own variety of piercing gaze. Like photographs of Kafka, photographs of Beckett show a man whose inner being shines like a cold star through the fleshly envelope' (p. 31). Coetzee seems disinclined to grant Beckett's photographed gaze this power. To see in images of Beckett's and Kafka's eyes thresholds to another realm would be to be 'misled', to elect to forget that, in the context of Beckett's so called 'philosophical dualism', in which the mind is a sealed, distinct entity, 'no photograph will ever tell the truth' (p. 31), no photograph will ever capture or reveal the workings of the mind, as hidden to us as the great scheming brain of the whale, pressed against the white wall of the forehead.

But despite this disinclination, Coetzee's essay nevertheless builds on the possibility that the gaze might travel beyond itself, might exceed the limits of the 'fleshly envelope', that something in the gaze can cross the corneal threshold to penetrate into the space of the other. The title of Coetzee's essay already suggests some such congress. 'Eight Ways of Looking at Samuel Beckett', of course, employs an optical metaphor to capture the encounter here between Coetzee and Beckett. Imagine how different this essay would be if Coetzee offered eight ways of *reading* Beckett, or eight ways of *thinking* about him. These staged meditations are visual encounters, even if the essay closes with the assertion that 'no photograph will ever tell the truth', even if the essay insists at all times on the incapacity of a look to pass, through the eyes, from one mind to another. And if the title suggests that what Coetzee is doing with Beckett is looking at him, rather than thinking about him or reading him, then the essay also calls, equally clearly, to another form of literary looking and image making, in which the capacity of the gaze to commingle mind with incommensurate mind is regarded with perhaps less scepticism. Coetzee's title, of course, evokes Wallace Stevens's poem, 'Thirteen Ways of Looking at a Blackbird', a poem which is at its heart about the capacity of the gaze to cross the species barrier, and a work which forms a second radial in the web of connections I am seeking to trace here. Stevens's poem, his act of looking, opens with the image of an eye:

> Among twenty snowy mountains,
> The only moving thing
> Was the eye of the blackbird.[7]

Already, in this opening movement, the subject and object of looking are entangled. We assume it is us, or the poet, or some combination of both, who looks at the blackbird, but all the movement in the scene upon which we gaze is generated by the eye of the blackbird, as it looks upon us, upon the snowy scene. As the poem moves through its phases, this entanglement of gaze with gaze becomes the centre of the poem, a kind of pool of shared vision, around which it circles. The mind of the poet, or of the poem, is composed both of human and of bird. 'I was of three minds' the poet writes, 'like a tree / in which there are three blackbirds', and the consubstantial trinity composed of bird and human minds suggested here is picked up later in the poem, in the fourth stanza:

> A man and a woman
> Are one.
> A man and a woman and a blackbird.
> Are one. (p. 35)

This unity suggests that for Stevens's poet the difficulty is not how to think one's way into the mind of the blackbird, but rather how to think without following the involuted trace of the blackbird's thought, as it spirals through his own, and through her own. 'I know noble accents', the poet writes, 'And lucid, inescapable rhythms',

> But I know, too,
> That the blackbird is involved
> In what I know. (p. 36)

I am not at this point going to expand any further on how Stevens's conjuring of a gaze shared by man, woman and bird speaks to Coetzee's ways of looking at Samuel Beckett, or on how the fluidity of the human-bird encounter in Stevens balances against the blocked encounter between human and whale in Coetzee's Beckett. I will come back to this later, but want now to move from the avian gaze that is obliquely involved in Coetzee's looking at Beckett, to a similarly avian encounter between Beckett and W. G. Sebald, an encounter which stretches the third radial of my web of connections. I would suggest that Beckett's gaze shines, to use Coetzee's expression, through Sebald's work, animating it in a certain way, but if this is often a pale kind of animation, one that could easily go unremarked, there is a moment in Sebald's work at which Beckett's gaze comes as it were to the surface. In Sebald's collaboration with Jan Peter Tripp, entitled *Unrecounted*, Beckett's gaze is included as one of the Tripp lithographs, to which Sebald attaches a short piece of verse.[8] The lithographic image is of Beckett's eyes, his gaze directed past our right shoulder. We see part of the aquiline bridge of his nose, the wings of the eyebrows hooding his gaze, and the beginning of wrinkled brow, the whole cased tightly in a rectangle, as if Beckett is peering at us, or past us, through a letter box, from the other side of a door or a threshold. The eyes are glassy, pin sharp. This is, unmistakably, the gaze of a bird. Sebald's verse responds to this birdishness:

> He will cover
> you with his
> plumage
> &
> under his wing then
> you will rest (p. 79)
>
> [Er wird Dich
> bedecken mit
> seinem Gefieder
> &
> unter seinem
> Flügel dann
> ruhest Du aus] (p. 108)

The plumage and wing in Sebald's verse are bird accoutrements, which add to the hawkishness that is already there in the lithographic image.

But if verse and image together suggest the gaze of a bird, what is striking about this passage in *Unrecounted* is how difficult this gaze is to meet. It does not evoke the commingling of bird and animal mind suggested by Stevens's poem, but seems instead much closer to that blank opposition between human and whale imagined by Coetzee. The shining of Beckett's eyes does not project, in Coetzee's phrase, Beckett's 'inner being' out of the 'fleshly envelope'; rather, their glassiness appears hard and brittle, reflecting our gaze back at us, the corneal coat acting here most emphatically as a barrier, much more reflective surface than window. Sebald's poem registers this aversion, this failure to meet Beckett face to face. The verse reflects the unavailability of Beckett's gaze – both its glassy impenetrability, and its obliqueness – by positioning itself underneath Beckett, rather than in front of him. The poem demands to be 'covered' by Beckett, to be sheltered beneath his wing, and in so doing draws attention to its own printed status as footnote. If the rectangle within which Beckett's gaze is contained suggests that the page is a window – that it might offer an opening of sorts through which a gaze might pass – Sebald's verse restates the opacity of the page. The verse does not reach through the page towards the gaze but settles itself beneath it, behind it, relinquishing the ethical challenge and promise of the face to face.

This engagement, or failure to engage with Beckett's avian gaze has a rich resonance in Sebald's work more widely, and provides the last threads of the web of connections I want to make here. Throughout Sebald's work, he is drawn periodically to the gaze of the animal, a gaze which is often reproduced photographically or pictorially in the pages of his novels. In *Vertigo*, for example, the narrator includes a photograph of a man on horseback, in which the gaze of both human and animal is trained on the viewer, remarking that 'horses often have a somewhat crazed look in their eyes'.[9] And Sebald's novel *Austerlitz* is shot through with animal gazes, with the collective gaze of a group of deer, the crazed gaze of a porcelain horse, and the gazes of nocturnal animals, including an owl, that the narrator encounters at the opening of the novel at a nocturama in Antwerp.[10] The repeated return to the gaze of the animal in Sebald is motivated in part by his fascination with the possibility of finding in this gaze a kind of communication with a mode of thought that is apparently unavailable to us, a fascination that he shares with Coetzee. When the narrator of *Austerlitz* finds himself drawn to the wide stare of the 'denizens of the Nocturama' (p. 3), he is struck by this sense that the eyes of the animal seem to carry a kind of special knowledge, in a fashion that again recalls Coetzee, and his thoughts on the penetrating quality of Beckett's and Kafka's gazes. 'All I remember of the denizens of the Nocturama', Sebald's narrator writes, 'is that several of them had strikingly large eyes, and the fixed inquiring gaze found in certain painters and philosophers who seek to penetrate the darkness which surrounds us purely by means of looking and thinking' (p. 3). As, for Coetzee, Beckett seeks to 'pierce the white wall' of his selfhood, and perhaps of the page, with the 'tool of pure thought', and as Beckett and Kafka are gifted with 'eyes that bespeak piercing insight into realms invisible', so for Sebald, the animal and the philosopher both offer us a gaze that seems to pierce, to penetrate the darkness, to open some kind of passage from the known to the unknown, the seen to the unseen, the self to the radically other. But it is key to all I have to say here that for Sebald, as for Coetzee, it is not the case that this gaze offers quite the kind of communication, the kind of commingling, that Stevens imagines as he looks in thirteen ways at his blackbird. The gaze of the animal in Sebald, laden as it is with the unthinkable, does not yield itself to ours, just as the thought of Wittgenstein remains to us a foreign thought, even as we try to think in its language. The eye of the animal remains, as Shane Weller remarks in relation to Beckett's approach to the animal gaze, 'unreadable'.[11] When Austerlitz encounters, with his friend Marie, that family of deer whose gazes are reproduced as images in the text, he suggests precisely this disjuncture between human and animal, this failure to communicate that is contained in the very act of looking, and in the kind of uncanny congress that is conjured by the animal gaze. 'Marie particularly asked me to take a photograph of this beautiful group', Austerlitz recalls,

> and as she did so, said Austerlitz, she said something which I have never forgotten, she said that captive animals and we ourselves, their human counterparts, view one another *à travers une brèche d'incompréhension*. (p. 368)

The animal gaze in Sebald might offer some access to the mind of the other, might offer us some kind of passage across that breach of incomprehension that exists between us and them, but it does so only by bringing that breach to the surface of the page, by giving Berger's 'abyss of non-comprehension' a kind of frozen form. Just as Beckett's gaze remains glassily impenetrable to us, even as it shines so penetratingly, so when the mind of the animal, the mind of the philosopher, reaches towards us, their human counterparts, it carries with it a foreignness, an unreadability, that shines a darkness on us. Wittgenstein's gaze, like the glassy gaze of the owl in the Antwerp Nocturama, might 'seek to penetrate the darkness which surrounds us merely by means of looking and thinking' (p. 3), but the narrator suggests that this penetrating gaze produces also a kind of isolation, as if it is kept behind glass. The narrator observes a striking resemblance between Wittgenstein and Austerlitz himself, the protagonist of the novel, and the mind into whose coils the narrative seeks to penetrate. 'Whenever I see a photograph of Wittgenstein somewhere or other', the narrator says,

> I feel more and more as if Austerlitz were gazing at me out of it, and when I look at Austerlitz it is as if I see in him the disconsolate philosopher, a man locked into the glaring clarity of his logical thinking as inextricably as into his confused emotions, so striking is the likeness between them. (p. 56)

The clarity of Wittgenstein's thought, like the clarity of Beckett's shining avian gaze reproduced in *Unrecounted*, like the clarity of the gaze of owl, of deer, of horse, is a clarity which is also somehow locked in, closed off, vitrified.

So, when Sebald and Coetzee look in their different ways at Beckett, when they meet or fail to meet his penetrating gaze, they mobilise a set of related questions about the nature of the visual encounter as it is staged in the literary work. For both Coetzee and Sebald the act of looking at Beckett, or of looking at Beckett looking back at us, involves an encounter with the other, with the workings of a foreign mind, a mind incommensurate with our own. For both writers this encounter has to do with the nature of the clear, glassy threshold that intervenes between looker and looked at, particularly with its qualities as a reflective barrier as opposed to its qualities as a transparent passageway. And for both writers, the encounter is thought of as owing something to, or being in some way entangled with, the encounter with the animal, as if to look at Beckett is to look across that breach of incomprehension that yawns in Sebald between the human and the nonhuman. The Stevens poem that haunts Coetzee's view of Beckett suggests the forsaken possibility of a form of looking that produces an intimate unity with the thing looked at. It suggests that the threshold that divides human from animal might somehow dissolve in the moment of looking, and that our ethical and political understanding of our relations with the animal, and with the radically other, might be tuned to this possibility, to the apprehension that 'A man and a woman and a blackbird. / Are one' (p. 35). But if both Coetzee and Sebald are drawn to the possibility of this sundering of the threshold of vision, what they find when they look at Beckett is that his gaze both offers a form of congress, offers to penetrate or pierce that white wall against which we are pressed, and denies that congress; that his gaze at once brings radically separate entities into a new and intimate proximity, and restates their separation, their incommensurateness. I suggested at the beginning of this essay that these three writers together offer a new poetics of vision, and if this is the case, then such a poetics is built on this peculiar combination of the disjunct and the conjoint, this capacity to find the communicative transparencies of the gaze in the midst of its reflective opacities.

II

It is in Beckett's work itself that this poetics of looking – the gaze that he offers to and elicits from Sebald and Coetzee – finds an initial form. The looking that Sebald and Coetzee perform in *Unrecounted* and in 'Eight Ways of Looking at Samuel Beckett' finds itself somewhat eerily prefigured, for example, in Beckett's early novel *Murphy*, when Murphy searches for a kind of quarantined, contactless contact with the alien mind of a lunatic mental patient, named Mr Endon (in whose name we can hear condensed the contradiction between the desire to stop and the imperative to continue that brings *The Unnamable* to its shattering conclusion).[12] Murphy becomes obsessed with the vacant mind of Mr Endon, thinking of it as itself a place of asylum, as a place where he might find himself at once entirely at home and absolutely adrift, and the means of establishing this homecoming in exile is through the unshared sharing of a gaze that is at once close and distant, at once penetrating and closed. At one point in the novel, Murphy positions himself right in front of Mr Endon – we are told that he 'took Mr Endon's head in his hands and brought the eyes to bear on his, or rather his on them, across a narrow gulf of air, the merest hand's breadth of air'[13] – and as he gazes into Mr Endon's empty eyes, the focus of the narrative is on the surface of the eyeball itself, the threshold which negotiates the contact between the minds of Murphy and Mr Endon. 'Approaching his eyes still nearer', the narrative goes on, Murphy focuses with intensity on the eyeball, discovering not ingress to the other, but rather a reflected version of himself, finding 'in the cornea, horribly reduced, obscured and distorted, his own image' (p. 140). The reflective surface of Mr Endon's eye, like that of Beckett's eyes in *Unrecounted*, signals the impenetrability of the threshold of vision, its impassability. The glassiness of Mr. Endon's eyeball causes Murphy to bounce off him, denying him entry into that seductively quiet mind behind the corneal threshold. But if the reflective surface of Mr Endon's eye holds Murphy off, it also offers him a kind of intimate access, a haven inside the very space of his mental absence, allowing a coming together of Murphy and Mr Endon that transgresses that boundary between self and incommensurate self, even as it is disarticulated by it. 'Seeing himself stigmatized in those eyes that did not see him', the narrative goes on,

> Murphy heard words demanding so strongly to be spoken that he spoke them, right into Mr Endon's face, Murphy who did not speak at all in the ordinary way unless spoken to, and not always even then.
> 'the last at last seen of him
> himself unseen by him
> and of himself'
> A rest.
> 'The last Mr Murphy saw of Mr Endon was Mr Murphy unseen by Mr Endon. This was also the last Murphy saw of Murphy.'
> A rest.
> 'The relation between Mr Murphy and Mr Endon could not have been better summed up [than] by the former's sorrow at seeing himself in the latter's immunity from seeing anything but himself.
> A long rest.
> 'Mr Murphy is a speck in Mr Endon's unseen.' (p. 140)

The gaze that is shared between Murphy and Mr Endon here produces a peculiar conjunction of the seen and the unseen, of the remote and of the intimately near. Murphy finds himself housed within Mr Endon's eyeball itself, within that peculiarly alien mind space whose very glassy impenetrability is what allows for such hyper-proximity. To use T.S. Eliot's haunting formulation in his poem 'Marina', Murphy's distance from Mr Endon here paradoxically brings him closer to Mr Endon than the mechanisms of vision can allow. He is at once, as Eliot puts it, 'more distant than the stars and nearer than / the eye'.[14] Seeing himself blindly reflected in Mr Endon's eye, Murphy finds himself at home within the solipsism of the other, finds himself *in* the immunity of the autistic other to the world, or to its 'own other'.[15] Becoming a 'speck in Mr Endon's unseen', he crosses that white wall that Coetzee finds intervening between mind and mind, but only because that wall is so glassily intact, only because this *becoming* other is also a peculiarly radical distancing *from* the other.

Throughout Beckett's writing career, this blocked face to face reasserts itself, building an ethic of reciprocity that is founded on the simultaneous unity and disunity forged at the nearly invisible threshold of vision. The meeting between Watt and Sam in *Watt*, between the fences of their respective pavilions;[16] the meeting of the lovers in *Krapp's Last Tape*, in which the man asks the woman to open her eyes to him, to 'let me in';[17] the reprise of this relationship in the later novella *Company*, in which the lovers find themselves entangled in the space of the eyeball, 'eyes in each other's eyes';[18] each of these relationships is predicated on the possibility that the threshold of vision opens itself to the other by sealing itself against the other. This kind of optical encounter is everywhere in Beckett's work; but the quality of the ethical possibilities that arise from it are given a privileged expression in relation specifically to the gaze that is shared between human and animal. That Coetzee and Sebald experience looking at Beckett in terms of looking at an animal, or at a bird, is symptomatic of the peculiar kind of hybridity that is summoned in Beckett's poetics of vision, the peculiar extra-human reach of the uncommunicative community that is forged in the space of the Beckettian gaze.

It is in *Malone Dies* that this disjunct conjunction of the human and animal gaze is at its most productive, and in this novel too that the negotiation of the simultaneously open and closed threshold of vision is at its most delicate and inventive. Perplexingly, it is also this novel that Coetzee seems consciously or unconsciously to repress in his assessment of the capacity of Beckett's creatures to strike through Ahab's 'mask', to penetrate the white wall that separates the animal from the human mind. 'Why do these creatures not grasp their harpoon and hurl it through the white wall?' Coetzee asks. 'Because they do not have harpoons, only pencils at most' (p. 23). But of course Malone, one of Beckett's more prolific wielders of a pencil, does have a harpoon of sorts, which he does use to penetrate the white surface of the page, if not the white wall of a whale's forehead. Malone panics mid-way through his narrative, having dropped the exercise book in which he writes his narrative with a dwindling pencil. 'The exercise-book had fallen to the ground', he writes. 'I took a long time to find it. It was under the bed. How are such things possible? I took a long time to recover it. I had to harpoon it. It is not pierced through and through, but it is in a bad way'.[19] Now in a sense Coetzee's neglect of this harpooning moment in *Malone Dies* may have little impact on his or our understanding of Beckett's encounter with the animal, or on his capacity to imagine the mind of the other, to have the imaginative courage to 'dream up the whale' (p. 24). But I suggest that this moment in *Malone Dies*, at which Malone damages his notebook in his struggle to recover it from beneath his bed, is in fact at the heart of the novel's exploration of the role of the written page – the written page as white wall – in bringing together and separating discrete and incommensurable minds, and in gaining access to the minds both of the human and of the animal other. When Malone scrapes at the white page of his notebook with his quasi-harpoon, he calls not only to Ahab's violence against the white whale, but also to an interest in murderous violence against the animal other than runs throughout the novel. And in doing so, he helps to set the balance in the novel between a violence against the animal as absolute other, and a desire to penetrate lovingly into the space of the other, a combination of violence and love that is lavished both upon the body of the animal, and upon the material body of fiction itself that is represented here by Malone's notebook.

To pursue this line of argument, it is necessary to attend to the representation of the written page itself in *Malone Dies*, to the status of the page as threshold between one mind and another, between author and creature, between human and animal. The page that is torn as Malone grapples with his exercise book is, of course, the page upon which Malone writes his narrative, the narrative which tells both the story of Malone's dying, and the stories that he writes about his characters – Saposcat and then Macmann – as he dies ('I write about myself', Malone says 'with the same pencil and in the same exercise-book as about him' (p. 208)). The central drama of the novel is, in a sense, the drama of the relationship between these stories – the story that Malone tells about himself as he lies dying, and the stories that he tells about his creatures, in order to pass the time as he dies. The novel is above all the story of the exhaustion of the possibility of storytelling, and in performing this exhaustion, Malone seeks at once to fall victim to it – to 'die' as a fictional character – and in some difficult sense to survive it, to become the narrative consciousness that is left behind, in what Malone calls the 'blessedness of absence' (p. 222) after prose narrative itself has run out. In this drama, the role of the page – its opacity, its transparency, it permeability – is crucial. Malone wants in one mood to allow the page to act as a kind of barrier between himself as godly author and those fictional others of whom he writes. He wants to feel himself separated from them by the white wall of the page, to hide in peace and isolation on the other side of the text as they play out their inconsequential tragedies and comedies under an imagined sky. But at the same time, Malone wants the page-barrier between himself and his stories to collapse, freeing the minds of Malone, of Sapo, of Macmann into the same written space, allowing the kind of unity in difference that is imagined between Murphy and Endon. He takes a certain perverse delight in allowing that clear sky under which Sapo walks to come asunder, to reveal the machinations of a god like Malone on the other side of the sky, half-heartedly pulling the strings. Repeatedly the page shifts from acting as an opaque barrier between the writer and his creatures to acting as a plane upon which author and subject merge – from figuring as a closed to an open threshold. Malone will congratulate himself upon having achieved a separation from his offspring – 'Nothing is less like me', Malone says proudly of Sapo, 'than this patient, reasonable child' (p. 193) – only to concede that perhaps he and his creatures are in fact somehow the same, born of the same lead applied to the same page. 'I wonder', Malone writes, breaking off from one of his descriptions of Sapo, 'if I am not talking yet again about myself' (p. 189). The violence that Malone commits against his exercise book is committed also against the fragile partitions that divide this novel, that divide the mind of the author, or deviser, from those which he devises, and that divide those devised minds from each other. And, if the harpoon image calls to mind the Melvillian tearing of the white wall between human and animal, between Ahab and the whale, then here also the piercing of the white page suggests a kind of coming together of different orders of being. 'I think I shall be able to tell myself four stories', Malone says at the beginning of his narrative: 'One about a man, another about a woman, a third about a thing and finally one about an animal, a bird probably' (p. 181). Much of the energy of the novel is devoted to keeping these stories separate from one another, but part of the pleasure of the text is found in the sundering of these partitions, the recognition, as Malone moves further into the shadow of death, that these stories are in fact all one, that, to recall Wallace Stevens, 'A man and a woman and a blackbird. / Are one'.

So, the rending of the page by harpoon calls, if obliquely, to the process by which the novel performs a coming together of human and animal and thing. Throughout the novel the possibility of this union can be felt, and, as I have already suggested, the violent tearing of the wall by harpoon is balanced always against another kind of commingling of human and animal that is conducted at the level of the gaze. Saposcat, for example, shares with the Beckett of Sebald's *Unrecounted* a distinctly avian gaze, and thinks with an avian mind. His eyes, like those of Murphy before him, are a bird's eyes, are 'pale and unwavering as a gull's',[20] and he longs to identify himself with a bird's movement of mind and body. 'He loved the flight of the hawk', Malone writes in an obliquely Yeatsian mode, 'and could distinguish it from all others. He would stand rapt, gazing at the long pernings, the quivering poise, the wings lifted for the plummet drop, the wild reascent, fascinated by such extremes of need, of pride, of patience and solitude' (p. 191).[21] As Steven Connor and others have noted, this avian gaze reflects the other animal gazes, and the other bird and animal motifs, that recur throughout the novel.[22] The unwavering eyes of the gull are reflected in the bulging eyes of Lambert's dead mule, the animal eye that old Lambert, expert exploiter and slaughterer of beasts, claims to be able unerringly to read. Lambert, who has a renowned knack for the elegant sticking of pigs, boasts how he can see in the eye of his mule the capacity for work, for devotion to its human master. 'In the case of mules', Lambert opines,

> it is the eye that counts, the rest is unimportant. So he looked the mule full in the eye, at the gates of the slaughter-house, and saw it could still be made to serve. And the mule returned his gaze, in the yard of the slaughter house [....] The look in his eye, Lambert said, was like a prayer to me to take him. It was covered with sores, but in the case of mules one should never let oneself be deterred by senile sores. (pp. 212–213)

The brutalized gaze of this mule is in turn reflected in the averted gaze of an ass in a photograph owned by Malone ('It is an ass', he says' 'taken from in front and close up [...] they naturally tried to make it raise its head, so that its beautiful gaze might be impressed in the celluloid' (p. 252)), which is in turn reflected in the image of a bird that adorns the box which contains a fountain pen bought for Sapo by his father ('A bird, its yellow beak agape to show that it was singing, adorned the lid' (p. 211)).

Malone Dies, seen in a certain light, is about the exchange of these gazes, about the capacity for the novel to erect and then to dismantle the material and imagined boundaries that separate its various zones, to allow material from one side of the threshold that separates looker from looked at, human from animal, to flow across the boundary and into the space of the other. But if it examines and performs this capacity, it does so not by imagining the kind of unity between man, woman and bird expressed by Wallace Stevens, but by developing the simultaneous unity and disunity first intuited in that gaze unshared by Murphy and Mr Endon. One moment in Beckett's oeuvre at which this kind of commune is at its most intense comes as Sapo sits in the Lambert's kitchen, in the gathering dusk. The growing darkness in the kitchen, as Sapo prepares to leave the Lamberts' for the evening, is registered here as part of the novel's wider interest in thresholds, in those variously sealed and porous boundaries that intervene between discrete places, that hold the mind and the gaze in place. 'The room was dark in spite of the door and window open on the great outer light', Malone writes:

> Through these narrow openings, far apart, the light poured, lit up a little space, then died, undiffused. It had no steadfastness, no assurance of lasting as long as day lasted. But it entered at every moment, renewed from without, entered and died at every moment, devoured by the dark. And at the least abatement of the inflow the room grew darker and darker until nothing in it was visible any more. For the dark had triumphed. And Sapo, his face turned towards an earth so resplendent that it hurt his eyes, felt at his back and all about him the inconquerable dark, and it licked the light on his face. (p. 203)

Sapo sits, at this point of the narrative, right on the threshold of vision, right on that fugitive boundary between the visible and the invisible, at that place, as Beckett's narrator puts it in *Murphy*, where 'seen and unseen meet' (p. 157). He sits at that threshold that is marked also by his creator Malone, as he lies writing in his bed, by his window that looks also onto the 'great outer light' (p. 203). Malone's window, like the white wall of the page, and like the corneal coat of the eyeball, separates one geography from another, forming an opaque sheet through which the light cannot readily travel. 'It is never really light in this place', Malone writes, 'never really light. The light is there, outside, the air sparkles, the granite wall across the way glitters with all its mica, the light is against my widow, but it does not come through' (p. 221). So, as Sapo sits on that vaporous threshold between light and dark, he sits also on the threshold between Malone and his stories, that boundary between devised and deviser that is also the white wall of the page and the clear skin of the eye. And as he sits in this gloaming, that trembling threshold is crossed by the hesitant step of a bird, by the subject perhaps of one of those stories that Malone never gets round to telling, and by that alien animal agent with whom Sapo himself has such a peculiar and intense affinity. 'It sometimes happened', we are told,

> before Sapo decided to go, that a hen, taking advantage of the open door, would venture into the room. No sooner had she crossed the threshold than she paused, one leg hooked under her breech, her head on one side, blinking, anxious. (p. 203)

This bird is joined by others, who advance from the light into the dark, who 'shone an instant in the light, grew dimmer and dimmer as they advanced, and finally vanished' (p. 204), or another still who hesitates uncertain in the doorway, 'poised irresolute on the bright threshold', before walking in with 'little hesitant steps, stopping often to listen, opening and shutting her little black bright eyes' (p. 204).

It is this strangely beautiful encounter between human and bird, across the disappearing boundary of the page, and across the simultaneously open and closed threshold of vision, that characterises the ethical power of Beckett's gaze to summon forms of community between minds that remain irreducibly other, even in the midst of their congress. As Sapo's favourite grey hen crosses from the resplendent light of the evening to the darkness of the Lambert's kitchen, she passes across the imaginary boundary that the novel seeks to interrogate between mind and world, between mind and mind. There is a real, unguarded beauty in her briefly gleaming passage from light to dark, and in the transit of her bird mind across

Malone's strangely opaque window. In this transit, the broad trajectory of the novel towards Malone's death and towards the failure of fiction, the failure of narrative, is counterbalanced by the possibility of a poetic becoming that rises from the ashes of Malone's storytelling. But what is most striking about this communion is that it emerges not in spite of the failure of Malone's storytelling, but as a consequence and a corollary of it. As the grey hen passes across this threshold she passes not into a new kind of visibility – she does not achieve that imagistic apotheosis offered to the blackbird in Stevens's poem – but rather vanishes in the thick dark of the Lamberts' kitchen. The crossing of the threshold of vision, like the harpooning of the white wall of the page, is an act that violates the organs of looking and the apparatus of narration. To pass across this threshold is to release something from within the eye, to allow it to leak out across the field of vision. This produces a wonderful liquid intimacy, but also of course a blindness, a merging of self and other that is also a destruction of the boundary that allows vision to take place at all. It produces that strange merging of the staring eye with that upon which the eye stares, that recurs with increasing urgency throughout Beckett's later works, that emerges in his late work *Worstward Ho* as two 'black holes', 'agape in unseen face', black holes that allow for the passage of the liquid of vision 'Out from soft through skull', the black hole of the pupil that expands and expands to absorb all into its dark looking, to absorb all into a surplus of vision that is also a deficit of vision, into a 'black hole agape on all. Inletting all. Outletting all.'[23] The piercing of the threshold of vision produces in Beckett, repeatedly, this flood of dark vision that passes from looker to looked at. And in *Malone Dies*, as in *Worstward Ho*, the merging of self and other, of human and animal in the expanded space of the dilated eye, produces a very particular kind of vision that is won from darkness and from failure, from the sundering of the distinctions that separate mind from mind.

III

When Coetzee and Sebald look at Samuel Beckett they enter into a gaze which suggests at once a blind failure to communicate – that failure to pierce the white wall that Coetzee finds in Beckett's limited imagination – and a new kind of seeing that emerges from such blindness, a kind of seeing that is at the heart of both Sebald's and Coetzee's work. In another late work, *Company*, Beckett famously gives a name to this kind of seeing, and in doing so suggests that it belongs to a long literary tradition. The narrator of Beckett's late novella says that the narrative voice itself sheds a dark light, a 'shadowy light 'that makes 'faintly luminous all his little void' – that makes his 'darkness visible'.[24] This dark light reaches back a long way, most notably perhaps to the Milton of *Paradise Lost*, who looks with fascinated awe upon the light that shines in hell, that makes the infernal 'darkness visible', and who pleads with his muse to lighten the burden of his own blindness.[25] 'What in me is dark', Milton pleads to his muse and to his God to 'Illumine' (p. 64). Both Coetzee and Sebald themselves engage with this tradition, reaching back through Beckett to Milton's bid for dark illumination. Coetzee's photographer protagonist in his late novel *Slow Man*, for example, finds that his 'greatest pleasure was always in [the] darkroom', where he experiences a 'little shiver of ecstasy' as 'the ghostly image emerged beneath the surface of the liquid, as veins of darkness on the paper began to knit together and grow visible'.[26] Similarly, Sebald's Austerlitz remarks that 'In my photographic work I was always especially entranced [...] by the moment when the shadows of reality, so to speak, emerge out of nothing on the exposed paper, as memories do in the middle of the night, darkening again if you try to cling to them, just like a photographic print left in the developing bath too long'.[27] Both Coetzee and Sebald here enter into a community of dark seers that include Beckett and Milton. But if Beckett's version of visible darkness might share something with Milton's, there is also something quite new about the way that Beckett's gaze mingles blindness and sight, something that has little in common with Milton's inspired transgression of the limits of mortal purview, and that opens a whole new set of aesthetic and ethical possibilities for Coetzee and Sebald. When Coetzee adapts, or to use his own expression in his 2009 book *Summertime* 'deforms' his medium,[28] in order to produce a conjoint human and animal voice, to see with eyes that belong at once to self and other, he does so in a Beckettian rather than a Miltonic spirit, in the spirit of that peculiar blocked unity that is produced in Beckett's lit dark. The new forms that Coetzee reaches for, that allow his female alter ego Elizabeth Costello, for example, to speak at once with Kafka's voice and with the voice of his ape human Red Peter, are fashioned to some degree from the dark light that gleams in Beckett's work.[29] And when Sebald seeks to make of the printed surface of the page a window which opens onto the other, onto the mind of an animal, or of a person long dead – when he seeks to bring the 'shadows of reality' to the photographic surface – it is in some sense Malone's window that he evokes, a window or threshold that owes its transparency to its reflective opacity, that opens a passage from darkness to light, from here to there, which is only passable to the extent that it is impassable, only open to the extent that it is closed.

There is an image in Sebald's *Austerlitz*, in which this coming together of human and animal at the very threshold of vision is given a visual form, one which ties together the threads that I have traced here between Beckett, Coetzee and Sebald. This image is a photograph, supposedly taken by Austerlitz himself, of a porcelain statue, a piece of bric a brac on sale in a bazaar in Terezín (p. 276), a town which Austerlitz visits in his attempt to rediscover his own past, and to swim against the historical current, back to the dark heart of the Holocaust, and to the ghetto at Terezín, which is the last place that he knew his mother to have been. When Austerlitz peers through this window at the horse frozen in its terror, he feels as if he is looking back through time itself, back to the heart of the massacre, which continues to go on, just as the horse continues endlessly to rear on its hind legs. The statue, he thinks, has somehow 'survived the process of destruction' (p. 277), as Hamm and Clov survive the destruction of their world in Beckett's play *Endgame*.[30] In regarding this object as a kind of survivor, a remainder from a vanished past, this moment might partake of Sebald's larger attempt to recover a lost history from oblivion. Sebald's work as a whole performs a kind of merging, in which his narrators become remade as those who have been lost, finding themselves refashioned in the form of the dead, just as the narrative seeks to cross that breach of incomprehension that divides the human from the animal other. But what this image demonstrates with great elegance and precision is that the windows that Sebald opens onto the past, and into the space of the other, are not transparent windows, but are rather forged, as in the gaze exchanged by Murphy and Mr Endon, from a peculiar and difficult combination of the transparent and the opaque, the clear and the reflective. The photograph here gives us a kind of access to the statue of the rearing horse, as an object that has been recovered from the shadowed past, but it does so only by reaching across that shining threshold between the light and the dark that separates Malone from Sapo in *Malone Dies*, that shining skin that separates us from Beckett's gaze in *Unrecounted*, and by bringing that clear threshold itself under the jurisdiction of the visible. As the narrator looks through the shining window of the bazaar, as he photographs the dark interior, he finds that his own image is caught also in that reflective surface, and it is this semitransparent barrier that intervenes between the looker and the looked at that allows for a profound merging of man and animal, of looker and looked at, of now and then, a merging that owes its intensity precisely to that limpid surface that separates those agents that it joins. The shadowy reflection of Austerlitz, or perhaps in another register of Sebald himself, is aligned with the image of the horse, the staring eye of the animal with the ghostly eye of the photographer, as if here man and horse might become one. But this is much more Beckett's unity than it is Stevens's. The becoming one of man and horse that is envisaged here is achieved not by erasing the gulf that separates them, not by annihilating the white wall that intervenes between human and whale, but by bringing that threshold itself, in its simultaneously open and closed form, onto the surface of the page, making of the page itself a disappearing plane in which we are remodelled as them, here as there, now as then.

It is this peculiar address to the threshold of vision that shapes Sebald's ethics, as it shapes Coetzee's, and Beckett's, and that has a wider resonance in contemporary culture more generally. If contemporary political conditions require us to attend to geopolitical boundaries – and boundaries between the human and the nonhuman – that are becoming ever thinner and producing ever less friction, then this capacity to bring the space that intervenes between mind and mind to a kind of expression, to a kind of visibility and thinkability, takes on a particular ethical force. As changes in the political relations between self and other, between human and animal, mean, in Beckett's words, that 'our condition is to be thought again', then the trembling, skinless convergence that Beckett imagines at the threshold of vision, at the point where seen and unseen meet, gives a formless form to that thinking, a new 'way', as Beckett puts it, 'of being we'.[31]

2011

CHAPTER 8

The Anatomy of Realism
Cervantes, Coetzee and Artificial Life

> And so by life I'm slain,
> Unwelcome state that mingles life and death!
> Living I die, and as my breath
> Dies, death recalls me into life again.
> <div align="right">Cervantes, <i>Don Quixote</i>.[1]</div>

I Dulcinea and the Cave of Montesinos

At a critical moment in Cervantes's *Don Quixote*, Don Quixote acknowledges that the lady for whose love he has committed himself to knight errantry might not exist.

We are in Part II of the novel, and the Don is staying with the unfathomably cruel Duke and Duchess, who take malicious pleasure in encouraging Quixote in his delusions. The Duchess asks Don Quixote, with her customary archness, to describe the 'peerless Dulcinea', to 'delineate and describe the features of the lovely lady', and Don Quixote responds with his characteristic rhetorical excess. 'If I could pluck out my heart and place it before your highness's eyes on this table in a dish', he says, 'I should relieve my tongue of the toil of expressing what is almost inconceivable'. To 'describe and delineate the beauty of the peerless Dulcinea, exactly and feature by feature', he goes on, is a 'burden fitter for other backs than mine' (p. 679).

This is the Quixotic madness which affords the Duke and Duchess such sport – the incontinent adoration of ghosts and phantoms, the unchecked devotion to non-existent beauty. But to give an extra turn to the screw, the Duchess decides on this occasion to taunt Quixote with the fact of Dulcinea's non-existence, to present him with the base line of truth against which Quixote's fantasies must always be measured. She 'gathers', the Duchess says sweetly to Don Quixote, 'if my memory is correct, that your worship never saw the lady Dulcinea, and that this same lady does not exist on earth, but is a fantastic mistress, whom your worship engendered and bore in your mind, and painted with every grace and perfection you desired' (p. 680). The Duchess confronts Quixote here with the untruth of Dulcinea, and by extension of the whole contraption of knight errantry, not in order to cure him of his madness, as those who care for him seek to do, but rather to fan the flames of his disease, to encourage another hilarious protestation of chivalric devotion for the amusement of herself and her husband. But Quixote's response, almost uniquely in the novel, is not to deny the attack on his fantasy as a blasphemy, but rather to offer a moving reflection on the nature of his understanding of Dulcinea's reality and of his love for her, a reflection which allows a species of doubt to 'cloud', in Vladimir Nabokov's lovely phrase, the 'limpid heavens of his madness'.[2] 'There is much to say on that score', Don Quixote replies:

> God knows whether Dulcinea exists on earth or no, or whether she is fantastic or not fantastic. These are not matters whose verification can be carried out to the full. I neither engendered nor bore my lady, though I contemplate her in ideal form, as a lady with all the qualities needed to win her fame in all quarters of the world. (p. 680)

Here, for perhaps the only time in the novel, Don Quixote's love for Dulcinea – what Erich Auerbach calls his 'idée fixe' – coexists with his understanding of its unreality.[3] Auerbach writes that Quixote does have what he calls 'an understanding of actual conditions in this world' (p. 344) – that he is capable of wisdom and good judgement. But, Auerbach argues, such understanding 'deserts him as soon as the idealism of his idée fixe takes hold of him' (p. 344). This play between Quixote's wisdom and his madness is familiar to anyone who has read *Don Quixote*; but here, in Quixote's grave and wounded response to the Duchess's taunt, we are given access to a hidden seam in the novel, at which the ideal and the real are somehow joined, rather than simply opposed to one another, a place where Quixote can love, in the understanding that such love is not subject to full verification.

This, as I say, is a singular moment in the novel. But it is closely entwined with another episode, which ramifies throughout the second part of the narrative, in which Quixote again expresses doubt about the reality of his knighthood, and of his love for Dulcinea. The episode I have in mind is that which concerns Quixote's visit to the 'Cave of Montesinos' – in which he is lowered into a cave on a rope, where he believes himself to

1 Dulcinea and the Cave of Montesinos

have met a cast of characters drawn from his beloved books of chivalry, as well as his lady Dulcinea (who oddly asks to borrow some money). This is one of the more famous scenes in *Don Quixote*, and perhaps the most symbolically overloaded. The prospect of Quixote 'journeying through that nether region' 'hanging and dangling by a rope' (p. 615) makes reference to sources from Plato to Virgil to Homer to the Christian tradition. According to his squire Sancho, who lowers him into the cave, Quixote is underground for 'little more than an hour'; but Quixote himself insists that he 'stayed three days in those remote and secret regions' (p. 620), suggesting a powerful allusion to Christ's crucifixion and resurrection, which resonates in turn with Plato's reflections on the insufficiency of our perceptions of reality, embodied in the cave allegory in the *Republic*.[4] Quixote is buried alive, he is Orpheus visiting Eurydice, he is Christ risen; but what I want to focus on here is not the intricate mythical and theological resonances of this scene, but its role in Quixote's developing understanding of the reality of his visions. When Sancho queries his master's version of events – trusting his own time sense over Quixote's – Quixote is insistent that his experiences in the cave were real. 'For what I told you of', he says, 'I saw with my own eyes and touched with my own hands' (p. 621). But despite such confidence, there is something about this episode in the Cave of Montesinos that neither Quixote nor Benengeli – the 'historian' upon whose account Cervantes's novel is based – can quite accept. Written in the margin of Benengeli's history, the narrator says, in Benengeli's handwriting, there is the following disclaimer:

> I cannot persuade myself that all that is written in the previous chapter literally happened to the valorous Don Quixote. The reason is that all the adventures till now have been feasible and probable, but this one of the cave I can find no way of accepting as true, for it exceeds all reasonable bounds. (p. 624)

Benengeli cannot vouch for the authenticity of this scene, and nor, it seems, can Quixote himself. While Quixote is being lowered into the cave, and upon first beholding the underground paradise that he discovers there, he undergoes an initial kind of reality testing. 'I felt my head and my bosom', he says, 'to make certain whether it was my very self who was there or some empty and counterfeit phantom' (p. 615). But for the rest of the novel, and until his death bed denunciation of the entire idea of knight errantry, Quixote is plagued with doubts about whether the events in the cave, and his meeting with the impecunious Dulcinea, were real or imagined.

II Partly True and Partly False

These two episodes – Quixote's admission to the Duchess that he does not know if Dulcinea exists or not, and his confusing experiences in the Cave of Montesinos – are intricately woven together. Together that they allow us to feel for what I have called here the 'anatomy' of Cervantes's realism. Erich Auerbach, in his luminous response to *Don Quixote*, maintains a strict distinction, both in the novel and in our response to it, between the real and the ideal. The 'difficulty' that we have in judging the force of Quixote's idealism, Auerbach argues, arises from 'the fact that in Don Quijote's idée fixe we have a combination of the noble, immaculate, and redeeming with absolute nonsense'.[5] For idealism to have any purchase in the world, for it to be 'imagined [...] as intervening meaningfully in the actual state of things, stirring it up, pressing it hard', it has to enter into some kind of dialectical relation with things as they are. 'The will working for an ideal', Auerbach writes, 'must accord with existing reality at least to such an extent that it meets it, so that the two interlock and a real conflict arises' (p. 344). The quality of Cervantes's realism, for Auerbach, is determined by the failure of Quixote's idealism to enter in this way into a relationship with reality, to stir it up, or press it hard. That Quixote's wisdom, in Auerbach's view, is suspended the moment he enters into the fantasy world of knight errantry means that there is no dialogue between wisdom and the fantastical imagination, and so *Don Quixote* ends up mapping the separation between the real and the fantastic, rather than staging any kind of transformative meeting between the two. In the 'clashes' between 'Don Quijote and reality', Auerbach writes, 'no situation ever results which puts in question that reality's right to be what it is. It is always right and he wrong; and after a bit of amusing confusion it flows calmly on, untouched' (p. 345). Cervantes is responding, for Auerbach, to his perception that, in the early seventeenth century, the 'phenomena of reality had come to be difficult to survey' (p. 358); but his response does not bring the right of that reality to be what it is into question. Rather, it sets out to 'portray contemporary reality', by displaying the comic gap which opens between reality and a diseased or mistaken apprehension of it.

Auerbach maintains, then, a distinction between a reality which is simply itself, and an imagined landscape which loses its purchase on such reality; but the two episodes with which I have begun here tend to complicate this scenario. The Cave of Montesinos might offer itself as a kind of negative image of the quotidian Spain through which Quixote and Sancho travel; underneath the realist surface are these yawning chasms of myth,

II Partly True and Partly False

and Quixote's passage from the above to the below, trussed in Sancho's rope, is one which takes him across the boundary between Auerbach's real and ideal. Quixote is a kind of upside down kite, who is allowed to soar into the nether regions of fantasy, before being reeled back to the realism that comes with his deathbed rejection of knight errantry. As Auerbach puts it, 'dying, he finds his way back into the order of the world' (p. 357). But if the Cave of Montesinos is a negative image of Cervantes's realism, I would argue that it is also deeply interwoven with it. The repeated advice that Quixote receives throughout the novel – that his vision in the cave is partly true and partly false – suggests as much. The novel is set up to trace Quixote's passage into the underworld, to act as a kind of dipstick or litmus paper, which passes across the threshold between the true and the false, in order both to mark where the boundary between them might lie, and to establish or in some sense *enact* their mutual contamination. As Quixote finds himself in the cave he undergoes, as I have said, some reality testing, to determine whether 'it was my very self who was there or some empty and counterfeit phantom' (p. 615), and in that test we can immediately feel the crossing or blurring of Auerbach's line between the real and the imagined. This is surely an odd kind of test, one which makes of the 'very self' a kind of amalgam of being and non-being. He does not set out to assure himself here of the reality of his surroundings, but of his own perception of himself; the possibility he entertains is not that the Cave of Montesinos is unreal, but that he himself might be 'empty' and 'counterfeit'. He says to Sancho that he looked at the cave 'with my own eyes', touched it with 'my own hands', but he does so not simply or even primarily to ascertain that the cave before him is real, but to prove the existence of himself as the agent doing the perceiving. 'Touch, feeling and the coherent argument I had with myself', he says, 'assured me that I was there then just as I am here now' (p. 615). He can be sure that the Cave of Montesinos is real, only to the extent that he can be sure that he himself is real, either 'there' and 'then' in the cave, or 'here' and 'now', as he relates the story to Sancho. If the Cave of Montesinos is not real, then that unreality, he fears, would reside not in the cave but in his own self. The proof that he seeks of the reality of his visions leads him to put his own reality at stake, to suggest that his own being partakes of the same order of reality as that of the Cave of Montesinos. And as he has that naked conversation with the Duchess, in which we are given the most direct access we have to the condition of Quixote's mind – to the texture of his perception – we find that same amalgam emerges, that same fusion, in the 'very self', between the true and the false. As so often, Quixote's protestations of devotion to Dulcinea here take on an anatomical hue. To display to the Duchess the truth of his love would require him to cut out his heart, and place it on a dish for the Duchess' inspection. As he puts it a little later in the tale, his 'adoration' of Dulcinea is 'engraved and imprinted in the centre of my heart and in my innermost entrails' (p. 772). His love is imprinted in his biological being, fused with his biomatter; and yet, in this conversation with the Duchess, he is ready to acknowledge that this most material of loves has no real existence, that he has not seen Dulcinea with his own eyes, or touched her with his own hand.

In admitting this to the Duchess, in allowing for the possibility that the name that is branded into his entrails belongs to a 'fantastic' being, he performs a feat of strange self-cancellation, an odd disappearing trick. He says to the Duchess that to 'rob' him of his lady is to 'rob him of the eyes with which he sees' (p. 680), thus suggesting, again, that the nonbeing of the fantastical object is registered not in that object itself, but in the organs of sight with which the object is perceived; in the heartland of the knight's own self. A 'knight errant without a lady', he goes on, again evoking the cave allegory in Plato's *Republic*, is 'like a shadow without a body to cast it' (p. 680). So, in acknowledging that his lady might not have a real existence, he condemns himself to become that empty, counterfeit being that he encounters in the Cave of Montesinos. If his lady does not 'exist on earth', this conversation with the Duchess suggests, then a part of Don Quixote too will consign itself to non-existence.

III Cervantes, Coetzee and the Meaning of Contemporary Realism

To attend to the anatomy of Cervantes's realism, one has to find a means of accounting for this peculiar fusion between true and false, real and ideal, as it is registered in Quixote's own anatomy. Where, for Auerbach, writing in 1946, reading *Don Quixote* involves separating these elements out from each other, the shifts in our theoretical understanding, both of realism and of reality, have tended over the decades since *Mimesis* was published to sensitize us to the unreliability of such a distinction. Indeed, the critical and literary focus has been, over this time, increasingly trained not on the separation between the real and the imagined, but on their inter-relation, on the spectacle, as Quixote himself puts it, of 'nature combined with art, and art with nature' (p. 569). *Don Quixote* has become, accordingly, a rich resource for literature and philosophy which seeks to explore the possibility that reality itself is in some sense *made of* fiction, rather than

III Cervantes, Coetzee and the Meaning of Contemporary Realism

its antidote. Cervantes's novel appears to Mario Vargas Llosa, writing in 2005, not to enact the divergence between fiction and the real, as Auerbach suggests, but to perform the directly opposite movement. In *Don Quixote*, Vargas Llosa writes, 'reality, as if infected by [Quixote's] powerful madness, becomes less and less real' until 'it becomes pure fiction'.[6] The experiments that have attended the fiction of the later twentieth century, Vargas Llosa goes on, are thus indebted to Cervantes's erosion of the real. 'Although they may not know it', he writes, 'the contemporary novelists who play with form, distort time, shuffle and twist perspectives, and experiment with language, are all in debt to Cervantes' (p. 132). The great postmodernists and magical realists of the later twentieth century return again and again to Don Quixote, as a kind of origin, as Paul Auster does in *The New York Trilogy*, as Kathy Acker does in *Don Quixote: Which Was a Dream*. The fate of Cervantes's book in the last five decades has followed the pattern set out in Borges's extraordinary *Parable of Cervantes and the Quixote*. 'The whole scheme of the work', Borges writes in Auerbachian vein, 'consisted in the opposition of two worlds: the unreal world of the books of chivalry, the ordinary everyday world of seventeenth century Spain'.[7] But if Auerbach seeks to maintain this distinction, for the narrator of Borges's parable, literary history sees their gradual and inevitable convergence. Neither Quixote nor Cervantes, Borges writes, as they mapped the gulf between windmills and giants, between Mambrino's helmet and a barber's basin, between one hour and three days, could have known that 'the years would finally smooth away the discord' between them – that the legacy of Cervantes's work would be the discovery that 'in the beginning of literature is the myth, and in the end as well' (p. 278).

A tradition of sorts has emerged, then, in the passage from Borges and Acker to Auster, in which contemporary narrative experiments that explore the erosion of the reality effect, the collapse of realism into forms of self-conscious artifice, draw on Cervantes as an archetype. And it is tempting to understand J. M. Coetzee's quiet obsession with Cervantes as belonging to this tradition. It is easy to see Coetzee's relationship with Cervantes as part of that shift in our understanding of realism that one can trace in the passage from Auerbach to Auster. With the beginning of his 'late phase', or the period described by some as encompassing his 'Australian novels', Coetzee's work has become increasingly experimental, and increasingly concerned with anatomising its own mimetic procedures. The novels of this period – *Elizabeth Costello, Slow Man, Diary of a Bad Year, Summertime, The Childhood of Jesus* – have tended to complicate the (always complicated) realism of earlier fiction such as *Disgrace*, *The*

Master of Petersburg and *Foe*, and in so doing they have arguably shown a tendency to shift the balance of literary allegiance from Dostoevsky and Defoe to Cervantes. Recent essays by Urmila Seshagiri, James Aubrey and Maria J. López have traced this growing Cervantine influence in Coetzee's work. López quotes a 2002 interview, in which Coetzee says that 'I have read *Don Quixote*, the most important novel of all times, time and again, as any serious novelist must do', and suggests that this investment can be seen throughout his work, in *Age of Iron* and *Disgrace*, and then increasingly prevalently, in *Slow Man*, *Diary of a Bad Year* and *The Childhood of Jesus*.[8] And for all three critics, Coetzee's growing involvement with Cervantes is entangled with Borges's sense that literary history sees the cancellation of the Cervantine disjunction between the real and the fictional. For Aubrey, there is an originating connection between *Slow Man*'s 'metafictional strategies' and the novel's 'intertextual links to *Don Quixote*' as it is through this connection that Coetzee explores the 'construction of a fictional narrative', the 'power and importance of stories', and the 'complicated relationship between a writer and his or her characters'.[9] Similarly, for Seshagiri, it is Coetzee's engagement with Cervantes in *The Childhood of Jesus* that grants him access to the 'self-referential, impenetrable play of linguistic and narrative meaning', and to the 'arbitrariness immanent in language and literature';[10] and for López, Coetzee's late fiction contains within itself the 'voice' of Don Quixote himself, a voice, she writes, that is 'infinitely resistant to the constant and painful onslaughts of the real world' (p. 96).

So it is tempting, as I have said, to see Coetzee's relationship with Cervantes as part of that shift in our understanding of realism that one can trace in the passage from Auerbach to Borges to Acker and Auster. But if this is so, it is also the case that understanding the kinds of challenge to Auerbach's conception of mimesis that is presented by Coetzee's dialogue with Cervantes requires a searching attention to the anatomy of realism itself, an attention that might not sit very comfortably with the postmodern and magic realist traditions as characterised by Vargas Llosa, and that might require a significant rethinking of the ways in which fiction is bound to reality, both in Cervantes's work and in Coetzee's.

It is in his 2013 work *The Childhood of Jesus* that Coetzee's dialogue with Cervantes is most sustained, and it is here, too, that Coetzee comes closest to giving expression to the structure of his own realism.[11] This novel quotes a number of passages from *Don Quixote* – indeed it turns around precisely that connection in Cervantes's novel that I have already discussed, between the episode of the Cave of Montesinos, and Don Quixote's admission to the Duchess of Dulcinea's questionable existence. Coetzee's novel tells the story of the arrival of a man and a young boy in a peculiarly evacuated time and space – which might be Limbo, but which is also a kind of displaced state named Novilla – and it follows the attempt of both man and boy to adapt themselves to the conditions of this strange and estranged place, to weave a narrative that might explain their relation both to each other, and to their new home. At its heart, the novel sets out to explore what is called the 'mystery' of 'how we elect those we love' – the mystery that is at the heart, too, of *Don Quixote*.[12] The man, Simón, has taken the boy, David, into his care, and has for him a boundless parental love, despite having no (apparent) biological relationship with him. This phantom paternity is matched with a phantom maternity when man and boy encounter Inés – a woman who Simón (apparently) arbitrarily decides is David's mother, as Quixote arbitrarily decides that Aldonza Lorenzo is the 'peerless Dulcinea'.[13] As they settle down to life in Novilla, Simón sets out to teach David to read, and it is in the course of these reading lessons that Cervantes's novel is woven into Coetzee's. Simón reads to David from the opening of an expurgated child's version of the novel. He reads from the episode of the windmills ('*A windmill may be what you see, Sancho,* said Don Quixote, *but that is only because you have been enchanted by the sorceress Maladuta. If your eyes were unclouded, you would see a giant with four arms bestriding the road*' (p. 153)); from the Cave of Montesinos ('*But your honour,* said Sancho, *surely you are mistaken, for you were under the earth not three days and three nights but a mere hour at most*' (p. 163)); and finally David takes the book from Simón, and begins to read for himself, from the passage in which Quixote addresses the Duchess:

> 'God knows whether there is a Dulcinea in this world or not,' reads the boy, 'whether she is fatansical or not fatansical [....] These are not things that can be proved or disproved. [....] I neither engendered nor gave birth to her, but I venerate her as one should venerate a lady who has virtues that make her famous through all the world'. (p. 217)

Simón and David, then, use the *Quixote* as a primer, and in so doing they establish a set of connections between Novilla and La Mancha, connections which build a kind of bridge between the two places, and between the two novels. The process by which David learns to read doubles throughout as that by which both David and Simón learn to find their place in Novilla – to tune themselves to the nature of the reality that they encounter there; and so this tuning, this reality testing, passes through a quixotic prism – and more specifically through that peculiar, fugitive seam that runs through Cervantes's novel, the seam that is marked by the coming together of Dulcinea and the Cave of Montesinos. As David gazes at the pages of his abridged copy of *Don Quixote*, he is both learning the mechanics of reading, and investigating the process by which written language itself works. David's school teachers become convinced that he has some kind of dyslexia, because he appears to struggle to learn to read – they suggest to Simón that he is 'not able to read words in the right order', or 'not able to read from right to left' (p. 212). But it turns out that David can read perfectly well – as evidenced in his accurate reading of Quixote's discussion with the Duchess. David's difficulty turns out to be not with the rules, but with the rules behind the rules – with the precept that language presupposes and requires a community of readers who share a common understanding both of language and of reality. David insists that 'I want to speak my own language' (p. 186). 'I don't want to read your way', he says, 'I want to read my way' (p. 165). Simón takes on a kind of Wittgensteinian coaching role, insisting that it is not possible to have a 'private language', what Wittgenstein calls, in the *Philosophical Investigations*, a 'language which describes my inner experiences and which only I myself can understand'.[14] 'There is no such thing as one's own language', he says to David. 'Language has to mean something to me as well as to you, otherwise it doesn't count as language' (p. 186). But if Simón maintains the necessity of common understanding, David's experiments in reading insistently undermine him, suggesting a kind of private undertow, a rejection of a shared perception which is mingled with Don Quixote's own. David's reading of *Don Quixote* not only refuses to obey the conventions of reading, it also does so in league with Quixote's wilful misapprehension, his electing to see giants instead of windmills. Simón tells David that what he is doing when he reads in 'his way' is not reading at all – 'you can't read', he says; 'you can look at the page and move your lips and make up stories in your head, but that is not reading. For real reading you have to submit to what is written on the page. You have to give up your own fantasies' (p. 165). But David insists, like Quixote himself, that his own unschooled, unverified reading has its own legitimacy. Where the orthodox reader of *Don Quixote* might be expected to correct Quixote's misapprehensions – 'To Don Quixote, it is a giant he is fighting', Simón explains to David, but 'most of us […] will agree with Sancho that it is a windmill' – David refuses to correct Quixote in this way. 'He's not a windmill, he's a giant' (p. 153), David says, just as he suggests that '*really*' Quixote was 'under the ground three days and three nights' when he visited the Cave of Montesinos (p. 165). When David

III Cervantes, Coetzee and the Meaning of Contemporary Realism 179

teaches himself to read, he is schooling himself in reading *through* language to some private space, some nether region into which he might lower himself. 'There is a hole', he says to Simón. 'It's inside the page' (p. 166). To read, for David, is to address the page as an entry to an underground space. He sees not simply the words on the page, but also the space beneath them, where private names lie, where a private language is hidden – a language that he shares only with Don Quixote. Simón presents David with the word '*Quixote*', as it is written on the page ('there is *Quixote*, with the big *Q*' (p. 161)), but David refuses to read it, seeing it only as the sign for another name, as yet unrevealed. In the phrase that echoes throughout *Don Quixote*, a frustrated Simón begs David to see true – to 'come to your senses' (p. 160) – but David insists that *Quixote* is 'not his *real* name', any more than is Alonso Quixano – that one can only discern Don Quixote, can only *read* him, by suspending the business of naming altogether.

Simón, as I say, seeks to correct David, to bring him to his senses as the priest and the Bachelor seek to bring Quixote to his senses. But it soon becomes apparent, both to Simón and to the reader, that to find one's way in Novilla requires one to learn to read after David's fashion, to find the hole in the page where the true names are hidden. Novilla, as its name suggests, is a new space – a *tabula rasa* where everyone who arrives is 'washed clean' of their memories of a former life. It is a kind of postcolonial, postnational space, in which everyone is a migrant from history, seeking asylum from the way things actually are, or were. But, as its name also suggests, Novilla is a novel space, a space made out of fiction. Coetzee has recently written that 'access to the other world – a world distinct from and in many ways better than our own' is gained 'by giving the self up to fiction',[15] and the business of arriving in Novilla, like Costello's arrival 'at the gate' at the close of *Elizabeth Costello*, involves this kind of giving up, this surrender to the novel.[16] It is beautifully paradoxical that the currency adopted in Coetzee's Novilla is the 'real'. Money, of course is the least real of substances. It is one of those 'things', as Simón puts it, 'that are not just themselves' (p. 132). Money always stands in for something else; but money in Novilla, in referring not only to an abstract value but also to the currency of Cervantes's La Mancha, achieves a different kind of reality. The community in Novilla, trading as it does in the *real*, is summoned into being through its associations with a Cervantine economy, one which finds both value and reality endorsed through the capacity of things to become not simply what they are, but what we imagine them to be – an economy which continually questions, in Auerbach's phrase, 'reality's right to be what it is'.[17] One of the extraordinary achievements of *The Childhood of Jesus* is its capacity to summon a world which trembles constantly on the brink of a kind of transmutation, in which things seem always ready to yield to ideas, in which the reality of the surface covers thinly over the cavelike depths of myth, allegory, theology. As Quixote can look at an inn and see a castle, as he can look at a barber's basin and see 'Mambrino's helmet', so the peculiarly fissile reality of Novilla is ready always to reshape itself around the hidden name that it harbours, and to collapse into that Cervantine world that it encloses within it. If Mambrino's helmet appears to Sancho, and to the world, to be a barber's basin, this, Quixote declares, 'is no consequence to me, who knows what it really is' (p. 163); so, Simón can look at Inés – a woman neither he nor David have seen before – and *know* her to be David's mother, with a kind of innate knowledge that is simply immune to the claims of ordinary reality, a kind of knowledge whose 'verification' cannot be 'carried out to the full', which can be 'neither proved nor disproved'.[18] Simón is told his recognition of Inés is a 'delusion' (p. 84), as Quixote's recognition of the enchanted Dulcinea in Aldonza Lorenzo, or in the body of a La Manchan girl smelling of garlic, is a delusion; but, Simón says, 'I have no doubt that she is the boy's true mother'. 'It is not from the past that I recognise Inés, but from elsewhere. It is as if the image of her were embedded in me' (p. 98). If it is the case that, as Simón says to David, 'we are like ideas' (p. 133) – 'ideas are everywhere' he says, 'the universe is instinct with them. Without them there would be no universe, for there would be no being' (p. 115) – then the reality of Novilla is always ready to give way to this likeness.

The relations between Novilla and La Mancha suggest the victory of ideas over things. But if this is the case, it is so only to the extent that the opposite is also the case – to the extent that things exercise a kind of power over ideas. If one of the achievements of Coetzee's novel is its capacity to produce a reality which is, in Joyce's iridescent phrase, 'thought-tormented', then its other equally extraordinary achievement is to fashion this shifting allegorical ground out of the most tangible of stuff.[19] The air in Novilla can feel thin, 'somewhat starved' (p. 139) – as Simón complains, there is a sense that 'things do not have their due weight here' (p. 64), that 'our very words lack weight' (p. 65) – but against this insubstantiality, there is an obsessive attention in the novel to what is called 'the thing itself', a capacity to capture the weight, texture and grain of things in the language of the novel itself. When Simón arrives in Novilla, he takes a job as a stevedore, unloading heavy sacks of grain from a container ship to a dock, and there is in this occupation a kind of joy – the joy of feeling the weight of things pressed against one's body. As one of the other stevedores puts it, to 'hoist a load onto our shoulders, feeling the ears of grain in the bag shift as they take the shape of our body', allows us to keep in 'touch with the thing itself' (p. 113). Fully as much as the things in this novel offer themselves as ciphers for ideas, they insist upon being what they are. It may be that we 'partake of the ideal' (p. 133), that we are, like the universe itself, instinct with ideas; but we are also 'just brute things' (p. 132), bodies that are made of stuff, and that can be 'afflicted with death' (p. 133). If the novel captures the capacity of language to give expression to the idea, then it also and at all times suggests that language has an affinity with the body, with the brute things for which it stands.

IV Realism and Artificial Life in Cervantes and Coetzee

It is this contradiction between the real and the ideal, what Simón calls this 'double nature' (p. 133), that characterises Coetzee's realism, and that shapes his dialogue with Cervantes. Just as Don Quixote insists that his love for Dulcinea is 'imprinted' in his 'innermost entrails', so Simón declares that the image of Inés, as David's mother, is 'embedded' in him; in both novels, the reaching for the ideal – for the love of Dulcinea, or for the parents' love of their son – does not only involve the release from the material but also the immersion in it. Quixote declares that the purpose of his life is to strip away the material that obscures the idea. He will, he says, 'live in perpetual tears till I see Dulcinea in her pristine state' (p. 682). But what finally emerges from the labour of *Don Quixote* is the recognition that this pristine state is the *effect* of a besmirchment, is only imaginable as it enters into a struggle with the things of the world, with the garlicy body in which spirit is immured. The mechanics of Cervantes's realism, the mechanics of Coetzee's realism, are tuned neither to escape from the material to the ideal, or to enact the primacy of reality over fantasy – neither to allow reality to give way to pure fiction, or to demonstrate that fiction leaves reality, as Auerbach puts it, to 'flow calmly on, untouched'.[20] Rather, this is a realism that seeks to make the very space of this contact palpable, to bring that connective tissue that binds us to our bodies, that binds words to what words mean, that binds being to the idea of which being is made, into the sphere of the thinkable; to make the sinews of reality visible. A fear that runs through *The Childhood of Jesus* is that there is no such connective tissue; that there is only world and idea, and nothing to connect them to each other. If this novel is concerned, fundamentally, with the question of how and whom we love, then this question is intricately interwoven with the way that we approach the linguistic and philosophical binding mechanisms of the world. David's experiments with reading are an analysis at once of the anatomy of realism and of the anatomy of love – an exploration of that material which binds one person to another, which binds words to things, and which binds us to ourselves. To make the leap between world and idea is to risk falling – falling into the emptiness that is both a kind of epistemological insufficiency, and the loss of a loved one. Coetzee's work, at least since *The Master of Petersburg*, has evinced a certain obsession with this kind of falling, the dropping into 'plummeting darkness' (Coetzee 1999, 121), the 'plunging through the air' (21), that has stood in Coetzee's work, since *The Master of Petersburg*, for the loss of one's son, for the wracking grief that a parent feels for a dead child.[21] The mournful lines from Goethe's 'Erlkönig' that make their way into *The Childhood of Jesus* give a kind of bleak European colour to this threat. David sings, in Schubert's rendition of the Goethe:

> Who rides by night in the wind so wild?
> It is the father, with his child.
> The boy is safe in his father's arm,
> He holds him tight, he keeps him warm.[22]

The opening of the song suggests the protection that a father might offer his son, but calls irresistibly to Goethe's conclusion:

> Now struck with horror the father rides fast,
> His gasping child in his arm to the last,
> Home through thick and thin he sped:
> Locked in his arm, the child was dead.[23]

When David contemplates the leap from word to thing, he risks being wrenched from his father's grasp – he risks falling into death, as Dostoevsky's son Pavel slips from his father's grasp in *The Master of Petersburg*. But the difficult discovery of Coetzee's work – 'a truth', he writes, 'that wrings the heart' – is that this risk is what realism entails.[24] The truth, Coetzee's Dostoevsky recognises, is that 'we live most intensely while we are falling', when we cast ourselves into the 'plummeting darkness' that extends between 'here' and 'there'.[25] As much as *The Childhood of Jesus* expresses a fear of that falling, it recognises too that the novel urge is to plunge into this space, because it is here, in the midst of the fall, that we brush against the unbound fabric of love, the unbound fabric of being itself, and that we come closest to making such fabric thinkable. As David retreats into his private language, and as Simón becomes frustrated with his obstinate refusal of the protocols of shared life, an interval opens in the novel in

IV Realism and Artificial Life in Cervantes and Coetzee

which this space becomes suddenly available, this yawning gap between words, where all is lost, but also where the very possibility of the real might lie. 'He looks into the boy's eyes', the narrator says:

> For the briefest of moments he sees something there. He has no name for it. *It is like* – that is what occurs to him in the moment. Like a fish that wriggles loose as you try to grasp it. But not like a fish – no, like *like a fish*. Or like *like like a fish*. On and on. (p. 187)

As Simón looks into David's eyes here, he looks into that bottomless emptiness for which there is no name, the emptiness into which Dostoevsky's Pavel falls, the emptiness into which Goethe's son falls, the emptiness which threatens to swallow up the devout love for the child with which this novel is infused. But what he sees here also, for the briefest of moments, is the anatomy of shared being, upon which love, thought, and reality itself are based.

It is this glimpse that lies at the heart both of Coetzee's realism, and of Cervantes's – the glimpse of a seam between the word and the thing, between the real and the ideal, that is not itself nameable, but which grants the name its signifying, world-making, self-making power. We live most intensely, Coetzee's Dostoevsky says in *The Master of Petersburg*, when we are falling. The purest form of life, life in its pristine state, might reside in that plummeting dark, in the plunge to a space that contains no body, and no idea. The plunge into this space is what Don Quixote, bravest of knights, risks, as he prepares to lower himself into the Cave of Montesinos. The desire that thrills through the work both of Cervantes and Coetzee is the desire to give oneself to this uncontaminated being. For both writers, the ultimate drive is perhaps towards a kind of nudity, a kind of life which has, in Flaubert's resonant phrase, no 'external attachments', which is not weighted down with any of the crude, embarrassing appurtenances of being.[26] 'I would have wished', Cervantes writes of his novel in the prologue to *Don Quixote*, 'to present it to you naked and unadorned (monda y desnuda)'.[27] At the heart of *Don Quixote* is a kind of love, a kind of wisdom, that does not clothe itself in Chivalric rhetoric, any more than Dulcinea presents herself in the body of a peasant girl, and it is this spirit in its naked form that the book sets out to capture. Cervantes wants *Don Quixote* to be naked and unadorned, but he knows, from the beginning, that such nakedness is not possible, or at least that one can only aspire to nakedness by clothing oneself in the 'ornament' of a self-cancelling prologue, as much as in Quixano's rusty armour, or Mambrino's golden helmet. One is most alive when one is falling, but this kind of life does not come to thought without some kind of artificial extension, some kind of prosthetic, and in Cervantes, in Coetzee, the very possibility of realism emerges from this play between a naked life, a pristine life which has no extension, and the forms of artificial life, bound to us with that word 'like', with which we make for ourselves a shared world, a world that we can share with those we love.

This difficult play between the real and the artificial, in the very nucleus of realism itself, is caught perhaps most powerfully in the shared fascination in Cervantes and Coetzee with hands, and with eyes – those most intimate of bodily extensions. 'For what I told you of', Quixote says, as he insists on the reality of the Cave of Montesinos, 'I saw with my own eyes and touched with my own hands' (p. 621). The hands and the eyes are our means of touching and seeing, of reaching out to the world around us. But it is the central discovery of *Don Quixote* that, in heartland of the hand, and of the eye, there lies a kind of emptiness, a suspension of the very forms of reality that one seeks to verify when one feels, when one sees. Even if the prologue to Don Quixote is a falsehood, Cervantes's friend tells him as he frets about whether he should write it or not, he should not worry too much, because 'they cannot cut off the hand you wrote it with' (p. 28). Cervantes's bodily integrity, his friend tells him at the outset, cannot be compromised by the adornment, the ornament of *Don Quixote*. But the discovery of the novel is that the hand, the eye, require a narrative supplement, are not nakedly, simply themselves. To rob Quixote of his lady is to rob him of his eyes, as his eyes 'partake of the ideal', are made of the fantasy they gaze upon. And his hands, too, are made both of sinew and of fiction. 'Take this hand', Quixote says to one of his female admirers, 'that you may gaze on the structure of its sinews, the interlacement of its muscles, the width and capacity of its veins' (p. 393). The hand is offered here as the proof of a kind of bodily reality. This is the biological hand, but it is also of course the imagined hand of knight errantry, the hand with which he feels for the truth of the Cave of Montesinos, and which he pledges to his lady Dulcinea. 'Take this hand', he says,

> or rather this scourge of the world's malefactors. Take this hand, which no other woman's has touched, not even hers who has complete possession of my whole body. (p. 393)

Quixote's body is made of flesh, and it is made of his love of Dulcinea, and the two are twined together, just as eyes and hands in Coetzee's work are an amalgam of the real and the ideal. David has an accident at the close of *The Childhood of Jesus*, in which he burns his hand and is temporarily blinded by a flash of magnesium. The injury grants him access, as he thinks, to an invisible world, to the world perhaps that Quixote sees and feels, with his hands and eyes, in the Cave of Montesinos. The blindness that David suffers, like Quixote when he imagines himself to have become 'empty' and 'counterfeit', does not mean that he cannot see others around him, but that they cannot see him, that he has slipped out of the world, into that space in which Pavel plunges, into that space without name, that hole in the page. 'I keep telling you', David says, 'I can see, only you can't see me' (p. 274). But the doctor who treats David insists that his invisibility does not free him from his attachment to sinews, to the interlaced muscles which truss him, as Quixote in trussed in Sancho's rope. 'Aha', the doctor says,

> I get the picture. You are invisible and none of us can see you. But you also have a sore hand, which happens not to be invisible. So shall you and I go into my surgery, and will you let me look at the hand – look at the visible part of you? (p. 274)

V A True Living World

Coetzee reflects in 1987, in his acceptance of the Jerusalem prize, on how a twentieth-century South African writer can take lessons on reality, and on realism, from Cervantes, 'the first of all novelists'. 'How do we get', he asks, 'from our world of violent phantasms to a true living world'.[28] This is a question, he suggests, that Cervantes solved 'quite easily': 'He leaves behind hot, dusty, tedious La Mancha and enters the realm of faery by what amounts to a willed act of the imagination' (p. 98). To enter a 'true living world', Coetzee suggests here, one has to enter the world of the imagination. But if this suggests that reality somehow converges with myth, with fiction, he goes on to make one of the most striking statements that he has made about the craft of writing, and the nature of realism. If Cervantes can escape into a true living world, he asks, what prevents the South African writer from doing the same? What prevents him or her, he says,

> is what prevents Don Quixote himself: the *power* of the world his body lives in to impose itself upon him and ultimately on his imagination, which, whether he likes it or not, has its residence in his body. The *crudity* of life in South Africa, the naked force of its appeals, not only at the physical level but at the moral level too, its callousness and its brutalities, its hunger and its rages, its greed and its lies, make it as irresistible as it is unlovable. The story of Alonso Quixano or Don Quixote – though not, I add, Cervantes' subtle and enigmatic book – ends with the capitulation of the imagination to reality, with a return to La Mancha and death. We have art, said Nietzsche, so that we shall not die of the truth. (p. 99)

Don Quixote might 'come to his senses' on his death bed, might 'find his way back into the order of the world'; but, Coetzee suggests, *Don Quixote* undergoes no such readjustment. Cervantes's 'subtle and enigmatic book' refuses the pull of such reality, the 'naked force of its appeals'; but this does not mean that it abandons the world, whose power continues to impose itself upon it. Rather, *Don Quixote* offers a model, to the writers that come after Cervantes, of an imagination that is able to find the place where mind and world meet, where the invisible hand meets with the 'visible part of you'; to find this place, and to make it, for the briefest of moments, imaginable. To do so, though, means that the quivering stuff of naked, unadorned life, that we feel 'most intensely while we are falling', does not come to us unalloyed. To live is to couple the quickness of being with the artificial appendage, the dead hand, the biological carapace. As Quixote himself puts it, his love for Dulcinea inducts him into an 'Unwelcome state that mingles life and death'. 'And so', he says, 'by life I'm slain', 'living I die' (p. 980). Art might stop us from dying of the truth; but the anatomy of realism, as revealed by Cervantes, and by Coetzee, demands that it is also made of it, as the imagination binds itself to the dying things of the world.

2015

CHAPTER 9

Back Roads
Edgeworth. Bowen. Yeats. Beckett

I

At one point in Maria Edgeworth's novel *Castle Rackrent*, the hopelessly spendthrift landlord Condy Rackrent gallantly returns to his Irish ancestral home with a new bride, whose possession of fine jewellery and a large personal fortune, he fondly hopes, will save him from impending bankruptcy. On arrival at the house, the bride and groom find that, through neglect and consequent dilapidation, the front entrance is impassable. As a result, the servants gather to greet their new mistress not in the arcaded front hall, but jostling at the 'back gate'. The disappointed bride Miss Isabella asks her husband 'am I to walk through all this crowd of people, my dearest love?', and he replies 'My dear, there is nothing for it but to walk, or to let me carry you as far as the house, for you see that back road is too narrow for a carriage, and the great piers have tumbled down across the front approach; so there's no driving the right way, by reason of the ruins'. As Miss Isabella makes her way into the house through the cramped back kitchen, the narrator Thady Quirke recounts, with his customarily oblique glee, that the 'feathers on the top of her hat were broke going in at the low back door'.[1]

This moment in the novel makes a conjunction between thresholds, thoroughfares, and minority that finds echoes across the following centuries of Irish writing. The back road, the back gate, and the back door are signs, in this novel, of the failure of an Anglo-Irish tradition, signs that the major lines of communication, the forms of congress and community that have made the Anglo-Irish ascendancy possible, are now impassable. The back door through which the bewildered Miss Isabella is forced to pass cannot accommodate her feathered grandeur, a grandeur which is in any case starting to look a little fragile, a little ridiculous. It is Thady Quirke, and more importantly Thady's calculating son Jason, who are better accustomed to the back passageways, and more adroit in the navigating of minor routes. Jason Quirke's capacity to slip in by the back door, to enter the house as servant and leave it as master, is the central focus of Edgeworth's narrative. Jason's incremental and somehow inevitable prising of the house and of the land away from the exhausted grasp of his Protestant masters suggests that capital will pass, from now on, through the back doors, that the front entrances and driveways that the absentee landlords had allowed to fall into disrepair would never again be the main channels of commerce and power.

As Edgeworth writes the novel, in the months before the 1800 Act of Union, she suggests that this migration from front to back, from dominant to emergent, should be seen in the context of a larger shift in the balance of power. The homely tale of Thady's dogged devotion to his slovenly masters, and of Jason's canny betrayal of them, is a mildly cautionary one, but it is nevertheless possible to laugh at it because, Edgeworth insists, 1800 will inaugurate a new age in which the Quirkes and the Rackrents will speak to each other in an entirely new language. 'There is a time', Edgeworth writes in her preface to the novel,

> when individuals can bear to be rallied for their past follies and absurdities, after they have acquired new habits and a new consciousness. Nations as well as individuals gradually lose attachment to their identity, and the present generation is amused rather than offended by the ridicule that is thrown upon their ancestors.[2]

The new consciousness that Edgeworth invokes here, perhaps anticipating the 'uncreated conscience' that Joyce's Dedalus ascribes to his 'race' in *Portrait* over a century later,[3] will give rise to a new cosmopolitanism, in which the local struggle between dominant and emergent cultures in Ireland will become a charming irrelevance. 'When Ireland loses her identity by an union with Great Britain', Edgeworth goes on, 'she will look back with a smile of good-humoured complacency on the Sir Kits and Sir Condys of her former existence'.[4] This assured confidence that the Union will effect a transformative cultural renaissance, however, is always somewhat strained in Edgeworth's account. In her preface there is a curious temporal slippage – it is the 'present generation' who thinks with a new consciousness, and yet the Union is still in the future, and evoked in the future tense – which echoes or anticipates the temporal confusion of the novel itself. Thady's narrative begins on '*Monday Morning*' (p. 7), and Edgeworth explains in her glossary that this Monday marks a stalled time that is a feature of provincial Irish culture. Thady 'begins his Memoirs of the Rackrent family by dating *Monday morning*' Edgeworth explains in the glossary to the novel, because no great undertaking can be auspiciously commenced in Ireland on any morning but *Monday morning*. – 'Oh please God we live till Monday morning, we'll set the slater to mend the roof of the house – On Monday morning we'll fall to and cut the turf – On Monday morning we'll see and begin mowing – On Monday morning, please your honour, we'll begin and dig the potatoes,' &c.

All the intermediate days between the making of such speeches and the ensuing Monday are wasted, and when Monday morning comes it is ten to one that the business is deferred to *the next* Monday morning. (p. 99)

In a sense, the novel sets out to remedy this collapse of linear time into a single, eternal Monday. The narrative is peppered with footnotes in which the editor of Thady's narrative insists that the Monday in which Thady is marooned has well and truly passed away. Thady says, for example, that 'Sir Murtagh had no childer', and the editor politely points out at the foot of the page that 'this is the manner in which many of Thady's rank, and others in Ireland, *formerly* pronounced the word *Children*'.[5] This word 'formerly', meaning before the Act of Union, comes up time and again in the narrative, where it marks a gap between Thady's blindly static narrative and the editorial apparatus of glossary, preface and footnotes that reflects upon it, and that belongs to a post-Union culture that has re-entered historical time.[6] But in the preface, already, it is possible to detect this same stalling, this same confusion between past and future, between next Monday and last. The union which will build a new, broad road across the Irish Sea, allowing the comically circuitous back roads of Thady's narrative to pass into obscurity, has both already occurred in the preface, and is still to come, suggesting that the confident separation between the future and the past upon which the novel is predicated is in fact far from clear. The scholarly voice of the preface and the notes is infected, as a result of this temporal confusion, by the idiomatic provincial voice in which the narrative is told. The former should belong to a utopian period after the Union, the latter should fall away into the pre-Union gloom. But the possibility of a unified cosmopolitan perspective which would allow Ireland to join with Britain – to enter into modernity – seems always just beyond the novel's grasp. Edgeworth conceives of the Union not only as a political act, but also as a sundering of the imagination from the coils, the back roads of a pre-modern Irish identity. This imaginary sundering, though, belongs to a future which cannot quite arrive – which even the 1800 act of Union cannot deliver – whilst the editorial voice of *Castle Rackrent* is returned to a troubling complicity with the 'former' Irish culture which it tries to mock.

One sign of this failure in Edgeworth to detach the cosmopolitan from the provincial is the continuing resonance in Irish writing of the back – the back door, the back room, the back road. It is possible to draw a line from Edgeworth through Elizabeth Bowen to Samuel Beckett – to map a kind of back road – which suggests that there is something like a tradition to be found here, a tradition of the back, or of the minor; a shadow of the Anglo-Irish tradition plotted by W. J. McCormack in *From Burke to Beckett*.[7] To take some examples more or less at random, we might trace a line from Edgeworth's back road to Bowen's extraordinary ghost story 'The Back Drawing Room', to Beckett's late, nostalgic evocation of the 'dear old back roads' in *Company, Stirrings Still* and *...but the clouds...*.[8] In these instances, it might be argued, the back road or the back room is asked to carry the burden of an Irishness that has not yet been accommodated within the unified cosmopolitanism that Edgeworth was reaching for in 1800, but that is also unable to find a major language in which to articulate itself, or to put itself into the foreground. In both Bowen and Beckett, the failure of the kind of reconciliation that Edgeworth imagines in her preface to *Castle Rackrent* has produced a curious shroudedness in reference to Ireland, a kind of occlusion, as if Ireland can no longer be looked at other than squintwise, as if it can be named only through the suspension of the name. Where Edgeworth imagines that the back roads of Thady's narrative will fall into a kind of disuse as Ireland is refashioned and renamed through its union with Britain, these writers suggest instead that Ireland's difficult relationship with modernity and with Europe has led to a failure of reference, a failure that is already anticipated in the curious contradictions exhibited by Edgeworth's narrative. The Ireland imagined in Thady's story cannot be translated into the language of European modernity, as Brian Friel's play *Translations* attests, but neither is there a language available in which to preserve the rural culture to which Thady belongs. Rather, the naming of and reference to Ireland in these writers takes place in a hidden back room, stowed somewhere beneath a surface which tends towards placelessness and geographical anonymity.

This connection between Ireland and the minor, or the back, tends, in Elizabeth Bowen, to produce a certain spectrality. The spectral can be felt in many of her novels – especially *The Last September* – but it is in her short stories that she explores this relation between Ireland and the ghostly most effectively, and particularly in her story 'The Back Drawing Room' – a story explicitly about the ghostliness of the back. This story, despite the article in the title, is in fact a tale of two back drawing rooms. The first of these, in which the story opens, is the scene of an intimate gathering of cosmopolitan intellectuals, a salon of some kind, in a place which remains unnamed and unspecified, but which we are led to assume is in England, probably London. The conversation is lofty, self-conscious and pompous, and turns around the possibility of the survival of the soul after death. The question that the company are addressing as the story begins is whether it is fitness or tenacity that guarantees the survival of the soul; is it a Darwinian principle, or something more mysterious – some blind, willed tenacity – that allows a trace of life to linger on after the conditions of its possibility has lapsed. Into this company blunders an unnamed stranger – 'Somebody who came in late had brought him, with an apology'.[9] The stranger, who has none of the sophistication of the salonnière and her guests, misreads the tone of the conversation, and sees the discussion of the post-mortem soul as a cue for a ghost story; 'Hell', says one of the guests, 'bring in the Yule log, this is a Dickens Christmas' (p. 203).

It is the ghost story that the stranger tells, against the mocking protests of the other guests in the salon, that takes us to the story's second room; the back drawing room of an Irish big house that has been burnt down by Republicans during the troubles, but that has somehow lingered on, somehow survived the passing of its age through stubborn tenacity rather than Darwinian fitness. Everything in the story hinges round the seam that the stranger opens here between the two rooms, a conjunction that produces a number of contradictory effects. Bowen's story tells of the movement from the first room to the second, but it quickly becomes apparent that the journey from first to second, from front story to back story, is haunted, from the beginning, by a simultaneous movement in the opposite direction. As the mocking guests who repeatedly interrupt the stranger's story are quick to point out, this is a clichéd tale of a journey towards a haunted house, a journey from the real and the quotidian towards the spectral, the absent, the strange. 'What was the house like' one of the guests interjects: 'Was it very obviously haunted? *weren't* there any dark windows' (p. 206). But while the journey is, in one sense, from the real to the spectral, in another sense the story moves the other way, from the vague to the defined. Whilst the first back drawing room remains unlocated, adrift, the second room is located, from the beginning, in Ireland. The movement towards the centre of the stranger's story is one that takes us from placelessness to place. As the story and the journey continue, the anonymity of the story's setting is gradually broken, as the story moves from a generalised cosmopolitan locale, across the Irish Sea towards a realised space that becomes increasingly concrete, until the stranger himself is riding bumpily along on a bicycle on a country road that is given more substantiality, more descriptive colour, than anything that belongs to the shadowy environs of the first back drawing room. Indeed, the salonnière herself, Mrs. Henneker, registers this sense that the stranger's story is taking us across a threshold from vagueness to the vividness of a specific place, but even as she does so she registers also the opposite direction in which the stranger's story moves. The stranger begins his story by saying that last year he 'went over to Ireland', and Mrs Henneker interrupts him:

> 'Ireland', said Mrs Henneker, 'unforgettably and almost terribly afflicted me. The contact was so intimate as to be almost intolerable. Those gulls about the piers of Kingstown, crying, crying: they are an overture to Ireland. One lives in a dream there, a dream oppressed and shifting, such as one dreams in a house with trees about it on a sultry night'. (p. 203)

The stranger's fictional journeying towards the second back drawing room takes him over the threshold marked by Kingstown, a name which might be thought of, itself, as a monarchical English mask for the Irish Dun Laoghaire. For Mrs Henneker, this journey towards the heart of Ireland is a journey towards an intimacy, towards a kind of *contact* that is unbearable in its overwhelming presence. But at the same time, it is a journey towards a dream, a journey away from the real. As the story continues, this confusion between the dreamlike and the concrete becomes increasingly marked, until we arrive at the heart of the story, a dead centre composed at once of the real and the spectral, the clichéd and the original, the present and the absent.

As we enter this dead centre – the heart of the back – the word *back* starts to repeat itself uncontrollably, as if this infestation of the word is part of the haunting.[10] The stranger, out for the day on a bike ride in the Irish countryside, arrives at the ghostly big house, where he lets himself timidly into the hall (his bicycle has had a puncture, and he is looking to the house, as per the generic convention, for help and shelter from the rain). The house seems deserted, until 'a door at the back of the hall opened' (p. 207), and the figure of a woman appears. Losing his sense of propriety, as if hypnotised or possessed, the stranger follows the woman into 'a drawing room, a back drawing room' (p. 207). ('Here was I', the stranger says, reliving his bafflement with a quiet, ironic reference to his uninvited presence as narrator in the first back drawing room, 'Here was I, unintroduced, in a back drawing room, really quite an intimate room, where I believe only favoured visitors are usually admitted' (p. 208)). As the stranger enters this intimate back room, there is an immediate sense that both he and his narrative are becoming submerged, immersed in the backness of this place that seems lost to time and to history. With his entry into this ghostly dimension, the voices belonging to the first back drawing room that have been haranguing him and holding him back fall away, and a new voice starts to speak, as if from the back. Adding to the overwhelming sense of immersion, the unnamed voice suggests that the woman, who is now sobbing silently before the stranger on the couch, is 'drowning'. When the drowning woman looks up at the stranger, he says, he is startled, and the unnamed voice interrupts again, 'as if you had not known she had a face' (p. 208). This encounter between the stranger and the drowning woman, mediated by an unanchored voice coming from the back heart of the narrative (a voice belonging at once to the drowning woman and to Mrs Henneker, but also to neither), is one in which the back shows its face, in which we discover that the back does indeed have a face, if not one which is describable or thinkable or knowable. The sight of this face, the stranger says, 'made me feel the end of the world was coming':

> 'I couldn't speak to her again; she – she....'
> 'Beat it back'.
> 'Beat it back'. (p. 208–209)

With this repetition of 'beat it back' – a repetition in which the voice of the stranger merges hypnotically with the unnamed, dislocated voice – the story is over. The woman 'put down her face again', and the stranger 'went back into the hall', and out of the house, back along the country road to the cosmopolitan present, and to the first back drawing room in which he tells his tale (p. 209).

The convention of the ghost story within the story dictates that the return of the teller to the scene of telling effects a closure, in which the spectral or the monstrous that is encountered at the story's heart is neutralised. The return to the normative setting with which we began allows us to put things back together, as if waking from a dream, having exorcised our fear of the other which the story has both banished and assimilated. But in Bowen's story, the encounter with the back does not allow for such a return. The directional and spatial effects that are produced around the word back mean that return itself, coming back, becomes entangled with its opposite. The back becomes the face, returning becomes a form of going on. The drowning woman, the stranger and the unnamed voice all join in the mantra 'beat it back', and there is a suggestion that the spectral woman is somehow containing her grief, pushing it back beneath the surface of the story, to release the stranger back to the first back drawing room. But back has mingled with the front in this story, the back has been grafted on to the face, and to be beaten back is not only to be suppressed or enshrouded, but also to be revealed, to be brought out of hiding. As the story ends, there is no simple return to solidity of the first room from the slippy spectrality of the first. Rather, the boundary between front and back has been disturbed, disabling any interpretive attempt to distinguish the one from the other. The background has become part of the foreground, the minor has been spliced into the major, in such a way that both rooms become unplacable, suspended in relation to one another. The frame narrative does not enclose the stranger's story, but rather the two narratives, and the two rooms, lie adjacent to one another, in an unmappable and unframable side by side, connected and separated by that back door through which the stranger first glimpsed his drowning ghost.

Bowen herself offers what might be thought of as a diagnosis of this condition, this appearance on the face of the back. In her late collection *Pictures and Conversations*, she emphasises her own commitment to place in her writing, asking rhetorically 'Am I not manifestly a writer for whom places loom large?'.[11] But for Bowen this looming large of place does not mean that her writing is placed, or placable; place remains located in the back, even as it looms large. Whilst she is centrally interested in the regional, specific locations of her writing, she also insists that 'the Bowen terrain cannot be demarcated on any existing map'.[12] Her commitment to place sits alongside a curious failure of place, as, she says, 'I have thriven on the changes and chances, the dislocations and the contrasts which have made up so much of my life'.[13] These contrasts, these dislocations, are to some degree a symptom, she says, of the Anglo-Irish condition. She suggests that, 'possibly, it was England that made me a novelist', speculating that this might be so because it is her arrival in England as an Anglo-Irish immigrant that introduced her to the dislocations that motivate her writing. She says, of the moment of her arrival in England, that

> from now on there was to be (as for any immigrant) a cleft between my heredity and my environment – the former remaining, in my case, the more powerful. Submerged, the mythology of this 'other' land could be felt at work in the ways, manners and views of its people, round me.[14]

This evocation of a submerged land hidden beneath the surface of another suggests a rich resonance between this moment in Bowen's autobiographical sketch, and her earlier story. The drowning woman in 'The Back Drawing Room', herself a figure cloven, in mysterious ways, to the cosmopolitan figure of Mrs Henneker, becomes, through reference to Bowen's later essay, emblematic of a wider cultural condition. It is the fate both of the drowning woman and of displaced Anglo-Irish peoples to feel suspended, cleft between these two spaces that work such a strange influence upon one another. Maria Edgeworth's dream of union has become, in Bowen's rendering, a much more partial and uncanny cleaving. England and Ireland cleave together and asunder, their separation and their connection effected by the work of the back.

Indeed, Bowen herself suggests that this condition might be thought of as producing a tradition of Irish writing, a tradition born out of a certain deterritorialisation. 'To most of the rest of the world' she writes in *Pictures and Conversations*,

> we [Anglo-Irish] are semi-strangers, for whom existence has something of the trance-like quality of a spectacle. As beings, we are at once brilliant and limited; our unbeatables, up to now, accordingly, have been those who best profited by that: Goldsmith, Sheridan, Wilde, Shaw, Beckett. Art is inseparable from artifice: of that, the theatre is the home.[15]

Condemned to be 'semi-strangers' everywhere, this line of Irish playwrights have conjured a dramatic art from the necessity for artifice that such strangeness produces. The brilliance that Bowen finds in these writers is intimately related, for her, to their limits: it is the disabling, damaging effects of homelessness that produce a paradoxical, trance-like comfort with the uncomfortable, with the unaccommodating. Declan Kiberd, among others, has pursued this possibility in relation to Samuel Beckett, the last figure on Bowen's list. For Kiberd, Bowen's 'ladies and gentleman' betray a perhaps surprising resemblance to 'Beckett's clowns', in that, despite the disparity in means, both are dispossessed, both are products of what he calls 'empty, contextless space'.[16] Reading directly from Beckett's Anglo-Irish context to the placelessness of much of his writing, Kiberd suggests that Beckett 'set up shop in the void' in response to the uprootedness of the Anglo-Irish predicament.[17] The estrangement suffered by the middle class Protestant culture to which Beckett belonged is mirrored in the dislocation of Beckett's dramatic and fictional landscapes. Considering that Beckett belongs to a generation of Anglo-Irish who 'feel like strangers in their own country', it is 'small wonder that the protagonist of his early stories comes to conclude that his true home is "Nowhere as far as I can see".[18] This nowhere is given a particularly emphatic form of expression in Beckett's stage spaces, Kiberd suggests. Plays such as *Waiting for Godot*, he goes on, enact 'the amnesia which afflicts an uprooted people'.[19] Beckett's empty stage is representative of a landscape which, shorn of any historical identity which might place it or colour it, has become blank and unreadable. Didi and Gogo are 'presented as characters without much history', who find themselves adrift in a world which 'has no overall structure, no formal narrative'.[20]

Like Elizabeth Bowen, Kiberd seeks to read this alienation from a national consciousness as forming part of a national tradition. The 'nowhere' in which the Anglo-Irish find themselves living, and which for Kiberd is the location of Beckett's writing, is revealed to be not only a limit or a privation, but also an 'artistic blessing', since it 'would make of Beckett the first truly Irish playwright, because the first utterly free of factitious elements of Irishness'.[21] The removal of 'elements of Irishness', according to this argument, allows Beckett to become 'truly Irish'. An Irish tradition here is founded upon the disappearance of Ireland, because it is only through such disappearance, such failure of reference, that the experience of living in cultural suspension can be accurately or authentically evoked. Kiberd's neat folding of absence into presence here, his transformation of a lack into a surfeit, is familiar from a long tradition of Beckett criticism which has discovered value and meaning in Beckett's dramatic articulation of valuelessness and meaninglessness. But there is an important difference between Kiberd's sketch of a negative Irish tradition, and that briefly glimpsed by Bowen in *Pictures and Conversations*. Where Kiberd describes the Anglo-Irish as 'strangers', Bowen calls them 'semi-strangers'. In Bowen's writing, as well as in her criticism, the Anglo-Irish condition is not determined by a lack of reference, by 'empty contextless space', but by a troubling tension between location and dislocation, the strange and the familiar, belonging and alienation. She writes that the 'Bowen terrain' cannot be mapped, going on to describe it as 'unspecific'.[22] But despite this lack of specificity, she insists, there is something 'under the surface' that locates her writing, a network of references that holds her stories together.[23] Indeed, she is evidently frustrated that 'few people questioning me about my novels, or my short stories, show curiosity as to the places in them. Thesis-writers, interviewers or individuals I encounter at parties all, but all, stick to the same track, which by-passes locality'.[24] Such an assumption that locality doesn't matter offends Bowen's sense that place 'looms large' in her work, and misses the point that, for her, understanding the geopolitical imperative that drives her writing would provide something like a key to reading it. 'Since I started writing', she claims, 'I have been welding together an inner landscape, assembled anything but at random'.[25] It is the mysterious forces that dictate this unrandom assemblage, this mosaic drawn, she says, from references to Irish and English places, that 'predetermines the work', to a greater extent, even, 'than I may have known at the time'.[26]

If Bowen's writing might be thought of as part of a tradition that finds a national consciousness in the experience of dispossession, then, such a tradition has to accommodate at once her lack of geographical specificity, and her attachment to place, an attachment which expresses itself in submerged connections, in rooms and spaces secreted in the back. And to position Beckett within this tradition similarly requires us to respond to the semi-strange in his work, rather than simply the strange. To read Beckett's 'nowhere', as Kiberd does, as an Ireland for the dispossessed, an Ireland free of Irish elements, is to make light of a struggle between reference and failure of reference – what W. J. McCormack calls a 'vestigial referentiality'[27] – that runs throughout his oeuvre. It is to assume that Beckett speaks of Ireland by freeing himself from it – in Kiberd's terms freeing himself from it 'utterly' – when I would suggest that Beckett's relationship with Ireland is best imagined in terms of cleavage rather than either separation or union. To place Beckett within a minor tradition, to understand how a back road might run from Edgeworth to Bowen to Beckett, it is necessary to respond to the double implications of this cleavage, this joining and severing of the face to and from the back.

II

Such a cleavage, such a difficult conjunction between the surface of Beckett's prose and Bowen's 'inner landscape', has been at work from Beckett's earliest writings. From Beckett's first novel *Dream of Fair to Middling Women* to *Stirrings Still*, one can see a struggle in Beckett's work between a remembered Irish landscape, sodden with forms of infantile attachment (what Bowen calls the 'semi-mystical topography of childhood');[28] a cosmopolitan, European space, which offers political exile from such forms of locality; and an inner landscape, a back space, which is committed to the idea that it is possible to imagine a mind that lives in no place, and no time.[29] In the earliest prose, this struggle is made explicit. In *Dream of Fair to Middling Women*, the protagonist Belacqua describes himself as undergoing a threefold struggle between Europe, Ireland, and a dream of 'emancipation, in a slough of indifference and negligence and disinterest, from identity'.[30] 'At his simplest', the narrator says, Belacqua was 'trine':

> Centripetal, centrifugal and ... not. Phoebus chasing Daphne, Narcissus flying from Echo and ... neither [....] The chase to Vienna, the flight to Paris, the slouch to Fulda, the relapse into Dublin and ... immunity like hell from journeys and cities. (p. 120)

As Beckett's work continues, this three-way struggle becomes less explicit. Throughout the prose of the forties and early fifties, from *First Love* to *The Unnamable* the secreting of an Irish space beneath a universalised European surface becomes more covert, as Beckett's experiments with the threshold between the revealed and the hidden, between the face and the back, become more intricate. It is partly the growing complexity of Beckett's dramatisation of the relationship between the local and the universal, the located and the adrift, that leads to the perception that his work is placeless – the perception, lamented by Bowen in her own critical reception, that the local doesn't matter. The connection with place in Beckett becomes so obscured as to be barely perceptible; the very possibility of home, as in Beckett's late piece 'Neither', becomes 'unspeakable'.[31] As Beckett enters into his most austere phase, from the sixties onwards, it is easy to imagine that there has been a final purging of all detail, of all local colour – and it is of course true that there is not much scenery in the late stories, or in the late dramatic works ('All my lousy life I've crawled about in the mud', Estragon says to Vladimir, 'And you talk to me about scenery!').[32] But paradoxically enough it is in his concentrated, short late works that the threefold negotiation between Ireland, Europe and nowhere, first staked out by Beckett's footsore Belacqua, reaches its most concise expression. It is in the sparse plays for television *Ghost Trio* and *...but the clouds...*, and in the somewhat gentler late novella *Company*, that Beckett's poetics of the back, in relation to a submerged, unspeakable homeland, reaches its apogee.

Company is a work that is concerned in equal measure with the back and with the face.[33] The story tells of a hearer lying on his back in the dark, listening to a voice which speaks to him, from somewhere above his 'upturned face', telling him stories about his life.[34] These stories, unusually for a late Beckett work, are rich in geographical detail. The autobiographical content of the stories, their nostalgic evocation of Beckett's Irish childhood, is well documented.[35] For this reason, it might appear that in this work Beckett relents from the cruel austerity of his other late works, that he gives himself a break from all the sparseness, revealing the nostalgic attachment to place that has been there all along, but that he has been at great pains to hide, to disguise. It is easy to imagine that this story stages a return to homeland, to those Irish spaces that have lain hidden beneath the sparse, dislocated French language texts such as *Ping* and *The Lost Ones*. It is tempting to think that here we find that we are finally walking again along the 'Ballyogan Road', that 'dear old back road'.[36] Where Beckett's and Belacqua's European wanderings have left him stranded 'nowhere in particular on the way from A to Z', the sudden remembrance that the voice grants the hearer, at this late stage in life and career, allows him to 'say for verisimilitude the Ballyogan road', to find himself walking 'the Ballyogan Road in lieu of nowhere in particular'.[37] We are no longer in the bleached out desert space of *Imagination Dead Imagine*, but walking again hand in hand with our mother and father, towards Croker's Acres, or home from Connolly's Stores ('A small boy you come out of Connolly's Stores holding your mother by the hand. You turn right and advance in silence southward along the highway').[38]

The back road, as it surfaces in *Company*, suggests the persistence, in Beckett's sparsening imagination, of the minor Irish tradition I am tracing here; but if this is so, the historical power of the back, its capacity to call back, or in Bowen's terms to 'bend back' to a remembered past, is always conjoined with and troubled by its spatial orientation. The back, in *Company*, signals a return home to a remembered childhood, as it suggests the pre-modern rural seclusion of the back road, the minor route. The back road can only ever take you backwards to a place that is hidden, inaccessible, resistant to the claims of modernity. But the back in *Company* also names the bodily back upon which the hearer lies, as the voice recounts to him those memories that he so longs and so refuses to accept are his. 'A voice comes to one in the dark', the narrator says, in the opening line of the story, 'Imagine. To one on his back in the dark' (p. 5). This cleavage in the use of the word back – a going back and a lying on the back – complicates any attempt to locate the back, to place it or to assimilate it into the story's spatial economy. Much of the energy of the work is dedicated to finding a way of allowing the hearer to own these memories, to take them into his body, to make the voice itself *his* voice, carried on *his* breath. As *How It Is* is narrated by a 'voice once without qua qua on all sides then in me', an 'ancient voice in me not mine', so the voice of *Company* strives to make a home for itself inside the body of the hearer.[39] For this story to signal a return home, the body must become a cage for these memories, these 'past moments old dreams back again'.[40] The back and the face must form two sides of a closed unit – what Molloy calls a 'sealed jar' that can contain the narrative voice.[41] But the dynamics of the story do not allow for this bodily arrangement of back and face. Rather, the back is continually becoming the face, just as back and face become uncannily merged in Bowen's ghost story. Rather than forming a three-dimensional storage unit in which the voice might rest or dwell, back and face continually merge, or lie side by side in a peculiar, flat adjacency. As in Bowen's story, the back has a face here, and the face lies flatly on the back, or alongside the back. Any coming together, any melding of voice, body and memory into a single, self-identical subject, is stymied by the insistent collapse of back into face, of face into back. The fantasy of a return home, of a reclaiming of place and of self, gives way to a scenario in which zones lie side by side, seeking but unable to find a means of becoming a whole. The unnamed, dislocated space in which the hearer lies is brought into contact with the remembered Irish space, as the voice is brought into contact with the hearer, flirting continually with the prospect of *becoming* the hearer, of revealing its identity with the decommissioned body that lies on its back in the dark. But as much as the story yearns for a means of putting these zones together, of finding a voice, emanating from within the face, that can say 'yes I remember' (p. 12), there is no means of producing such a union. The zones cleave to one another, but cannot join, leaving the voice to float outside of the face which remains uncannily coterminous with the back.

It is in the paired television plays *…but the clouds…* and *Ghost Trio*, first broadcast in 1977, that this cloven relation between back and face is given its clearest visual manifestation.[42] Both these plays turn around the relationship between the bowed back and the revealed, uplifted face, and both try and fail to craft a form in which to join face and back in a single body. *Ghost Trio* depicts a closed grey room – the 'familiar chamber' – in which a seated figure is bowed over a cassette recorder which plays Beethoven's piano trio, *The Ghost*. The face of the figure can barely be seen, as it is covered by his matted hair; the faint light that falls upon him lies along the ridge of his bowed back. This closed figure is held in a tense relation to the three moments in the play when a face is suddenly, magically revealed – the face of a boy who comes to visit the figure in his room, and the face of the figure himself seen once reflected in a mirror that is hanging on the wall, and once at the end of the play, as he raises his head to face the camera in the closing moments. *… but the clouds…* is set not in an enclosed space, but in three different locales. The first is the place from which the narrator (M) apparently speaks, and consists of a near shot of a seated figure, in which it is only possible to make out his clasped hands. The second is a kind of vestibule in which M appears as character – M1. In this interstitial space, a circle of light surrounded by thick shadow, M1 acts out the movements described by M, as he moves between the 'roads' upon which he tramps by day which are located to the west, a closet in which he changes from tramping gear to robe and skullcap which is located to the east, and a 'sanctum' which is located in the

North. As M1 walks in his circle of light between roads, closet and sanctum, he adopts the bowed posture that he shares with the figure in *Ghost Trio*, the light again catching the curve of his bowed back. The third space is an entirely spectral dimension, and consists of a painfully tight close up of a woman's face, drowning in white light, her wide eyes, brimming with unshed tears, averted from the viewer's gaze.

This relationship between face and back is determined by the struggle, in both plays, to find a connection between the former and the latter. As in *Company*, and in Bowen's *Back Drawing Room*, both of these plays depict a scenario in which the voice has become disconnected from the body, has been expelled from the scene of its own bodily production. The movements from back to face, controlled in both cases by a voice which is located outside of the stage space, are symptomatic of this expulsion. In both cases, also, this movement is orchestrated by the haunting presence of a remembered space, and a remembered time, the absence or unavailability of which is partly what has led to this curious dislocation of face from back, of voice from body. Both plays are about broken channels of communication, which have condemned the figures on set to become isolated from a loved one and a loved time, and to be broken from themselves, to be cleft in two.

In *Ghost Trio*, this broken communication is evoked most immediately by the grey room in which the seated figure is enclosed. The box of faint light, commanded into being, as in *Company*, by the faint voice which describes it, is a televisual representation of those late prose spaces in which Beckett's bodies lie immured. There is a powerful sense here of incarceration, of the figure's absolute enclosure within his room – his profound separation from the voice which animates him, and from the boy who comes to visit him. But despite this suggestion that the box is sealed, a central focus of the play is of course the door – the 'indispensable door' (p. 408) – and the 'opaque' window (p. 408), which offer a compromised access to the outside, from which the boy visits and from which the voice speaks. Throughout the performance, the stage directions tell us, both door and window are 'imperceptibly ajar' (p. 408), suggesting that at all times there is some possibility of communication between inside and outside. Indeed, it is the exploration of this possible communication that is the main action of the play, as the figure moves around the room, opening door and window, peering into the shadowed space that surrounds him, gazing through these semi-opaque thresholds towards the places from which he has been cut adrift. This lost place and time is summoned by the Beethoven trio, which comes partly from the cassette recorder locked within the room, but also from those remembered places that lie beyond the window and the door. If there is an imperceptible connection between inside and outside in the play, the music, belonging to both frames at once, marks this connection out, suggesting both the availability of the past that the music summons, and its spectrality, its imperceptibility. The music suggests the partiality of the threshold, its function both as a closed and as an open boundary, and it is this uncertainty at the boundary, this undecidability, that gives the play such a strange, mysterious power. There is an extraordinary affect produced by the view that we are granted through the window to the darkness scored with rain, and through the door to the corridor, in which the boy appears, dressed in glistening oilskins. These views across the threshold, this near contact with an outside, suggest an epiphanal, Proustian encounter with lost time. The rain – always evocative, however obliquely, of an Irish landscape in Beckett's writing – seems to belong to the lost past itself, as Beethoven's music is located, still, in the remembered past, even as it is reproduced on that tinny cassette recorder. The boy, drenched in remembered rain, seems to have travelled through time itself to deliver his enigmatic negative; it is of course a spectre of himself that both boy and man encounter across this simultaneously open and closed threshold. But whilst these moments in the play at which door and window are opened might suggest Proustian remembrance, they are also moments at which the incommensurability between past and present, between the inside and the outside, is at its most emphatic. The play depicts a situation in which the possibility of a channel between the expelled and his homeland, the possibility of a back road that might take this stranded figure home, back to himself as child, is recognised only as a condition of its impossibility. The door that is imagined here is one that makes spaces which are radically divorced from one another – which belong in different dimensions in time and in space – magically adjacent. As in Deleuze and Guattari's reading of Kafka, in which 'two blocks on a continuous and unlimited line, with their doors far from each other, are revealed to have contiguous back doors that make the blocks themselves contiguous',[43] Beckett's door is a back door that summons adjacency, contiguity, from radical separation. But the price of such adjacency is that the back road itself is impassable, or passable only imperceptibly, as ghost or spirit.

In ...*but the clouds*... this call back to an Irish landscape, suggested by the teeming rain in *Ghost Trio*, becomes a much stronger nostalgia for homeland. The play is possessed by the spirit of Yeats's poem 'The Tower', and seeks, like that poem, to

> send imagination   forth
> Under the day's declining beam, and call
> Images and memories
> From ruin.[44]

The figure in Beckett's play, like the stranger in Bowen's story, calls images from ruin, in particular the image of the woman's face, as he vanishes in his little sanctum through the night. And he too sends his imagination forth, when the time comes,

> with break of day, to issue forth again, void my little sanctum, shed robe and skull, resume my hat and greatcoat, and issue forth again, to walk the roads. [*Pause.*] The back roads. (pp. 421–422)

The back roads here become both the locus of a remembered Irish landscape – the 'dear old back roads' of *Company* – and the route towards the recovery of such a landscape, the back road along which the imagination might return to its lost home. The figure in …*but the clouds*… relives the predicament of the protagonist of *Stirrings Still*, who is marooned in 'a strange place', 'seeking the way out. A way out. To the roads. The back roads'.[45] But this play, like *Ghost Trio*, is a play about broken channels of communication; the back road here offers only a partial access to rural Ireland, or to the woman's face that so magically appears in the deepening shade of the inner sanctum. The elements of which this play is composed – the bowed back of the male figure, the revealed face of the spectral woman, the disembodied voice that directs the action – resist the binding force of dramatic form. The play, like most of Beckett's work for television, experiments with the effect on the *mise-en-scène* of the failure of suture.[46] The role of suturing in television and film is to fuse a flat succession of adjacent images – the face and the back, for example – into an embodied, three-dimensional world. It is to stitch together a coherent life world out of a montage of discrete, unconnected images. But Beckett's film and television work pushes in the opposite direction, so that voice, music, body and space do not cohere into a recognisable unit but rather lie alongside each other in a manner that defies the perception of an integrated whole.

In …*but the clouds*…, this refusal of suture expresses itself most powerfully in the broken relationship between face and back. The editing together of the woman's silently mouthing face with the pacing, bowed figure of the man and with the extra-diegetic narrative voice prompt us to make of these elements a whole, prompt us to find a bodily harmony between face, back and voice. And indeed, the sense of contiguity that is produced by the play does suggest a certain coming together here, a coming together that Richard Bruce Kirkley describes as a 'fleeting moment of unified consciousness'.[47] The appearance of the woman's face, mouthing a Yeatsian effort to recollect, does suggest a kind of presence, a kind of bodily relationality between the man and the woman, as if the play is inventing a new body in which man, woman and memory might become united. But at the same time, this is an unthinkable body, conceived from a deeply uncanny form of suturing which performs discontinuity and separation as much as union and possession. The central moment of the play – the moment at which this cleft relation between man and woman expresses itself most forcefully – comes as the voice quotes the close of Yeats's poem – 'but the clouds of the sky ... when the horizon fades ... or a bird's sleepy cry ... among the deepening shades ...' (p. 422)[48] – in time with the woman's inaudible speech. This moment suggests an extraordinary coming together of woman, man, voice, and memory, a coming together that has an uncanny resonance with the moment in Bowen's story at which man and woman speak together, in their hypnotic injunction to 'beat it back'. The man's voice itself shapes to come from within the woman's lips, to emerge on her breath from some internal body space in which profoundly separate entities have become merged. This moment is one in which face and back, man and woman, Beckett and Yeats, bodily and spectral, Ireland and nowhere, reach for a kind of accommodation, a kind of union more complete, and more transformative of the very conception of identity, than any imagined by Edgeworth. But this accommodation, this new bodily relation, is deeply unsettling, disturbing the very boundaries of the thinkable, or of the perceptible. The body that is suggested here is not only one that holds together, but one that breaks apart, as the indispensable door in *Ghost Trio* marks the separation between adjacent spaces as well as their impossible contiguity. The body made of face and back in ...*but the clouds*... is one that suggests a different kind of thinking about the possibility of communication and community. It suggests an almost perceptible form in which separate entities, which remain profoundly alienated from one another, might share presence. But in suggesting this form, the play produces a collapse of the possibility of form itself. The placing of the Yeatsian voice within and outside the woman's spectral face makes tremble the boundaries and the thresholds which have allowed for the placing of a body within a place.

It is this simultaneous incorporation and rejection of a remembered voice and a remembered landscape that characterises Beckett's belonging to a minor Irish tradition. In ventriloquising Yeats's voice, Beckett keeps this tradition alive, through a Bowenesque tenacity that allows it to continue even after its enabling conditions have passed away, even in its deterritorialised, dispossessed state. But the formal means by which Beckett inherits this tradition are also those that undermine the very possibility of inheritance. In allowing his ghosts to speak, Beckett disrupts the spatial and temporal boundaries which allow us to position ourselves in space and time, suggesting a new accommodation between present and past, between body, voice and memory, for which there is not yet a major language. Anna McMullen suggests that 'placing Beckett's oeuvre within the frames of Irish and postcolonial studies troubles their boundaries', because 'Beckett's work performs a dislocation of the frames of nation, identity, or theory'.[49] It is this dislocation of the frame, this dismantling of the mechanisms of spatial and temporal orientation, that marks Beckett's inheritance of a minor tradition. For those who come after Beckett, it is necessary to find a way of belonging to this broken, dislocated tradition, to find a way of speaking with a voice that comes at once from within and outside the face.

2010

CHAPTER 10

Blind Seeing
Deathwriting from Dickinson to the Contemporary

I Light and Shadow in the World Picture

'This invention', Wallace Stevens writes, of 'this invented world' rests on the 'inconceivable idea of the sun'.[1] The world as we see and picture it relies on our conception of the sun's light, and of the relation between what is light and what is dark. Without the sun, which is itself 'inconceivable', we would have no conception of thought or of idea, no way of picturing ourselves and the world.

The light of the sun is the 'source', Sevens writes, of our idea of ourselves. One way of conceiving the history of the literary imagination is as a long attempt to approach this truth, so resistant to thought – that the idea of the sun is also the idea of the idea itself. This is what Hamlet means when he declares that his encounter with the limit conditions of life, with the dissolved boundary between being and not being, has left him 'too much i' th' sun'.[2] The sun makes seeing possible, so when we try to see it, or to think it, we try to think the possibility of thinking, to see the possibility of seeing.

This difficulty is as old as seeing, as old as thinking. It is the difficulty, Stevens writes, of how to 'be / In the difficulty of what it is to be'.[3] But it is perhaps the case that the time that we find ourselves in now is one in which the conditions of seeing, and the structures of being which these conditions determine, are shifting, before our eyes. Our understanding of the relation between the visible and the invisible – as it determines the relation between the human and the nonhuman, the thinkable and the unthinkable – is coming in our time under intense pressure. The conjoined forces that shape the contemporary moment – eco-crisis, info-technological revolution, shifts in the flow of global capital – are transforming the place of the human in the world, and the paradigms that have allowed us to conceive of it. The traditions of thought that have aligned the human with life and with light, in opposition to a world of animals and things which do not share our world view, and which come to visibility and thinkability through reflected human light – these traditions look precarious or exhausted, as humanism itself enters into a late crisis, and as our wasted environment is flung clear of the frame of any given human world picture.

It is as a response to this precarity, this exhaustion, that I will here propose a literary countertradition, one which has lain latent in literary and intellectual history, and which has sat at an angle to the passage of enlightenment thought, and the prevailing conception of the relation between the visible and the invisible, the human and the nonhuman. This is a tradition that emerges from a collapse or a suspension of these oppositions, a tradition that uncovers a form of visible darkness, and of blind seeing, that is a structuring principle of literary possibility, even as it tends to elude critical expression. To see by this light is to encounter a way of thinking and seeing that adjusts the principles of sight, that makes newly inconceivable our idea of the sun, and in so doing opens onto the possibility of a differently configured life world. To resee the junction between the light and the dark is at the same time to denature our understanding of the relation between life and death, to encounter death not as the opposite of life, but as a constituent part of its possibility. The writers of visible darkness that I attend to here are accordingly also deathwriters, writers who enter into the field of death, and find there not just the negation of being, but its very idea.

The writer whose work might come most immediately to mind, when thinking about the possibilities of a literature which brings death into the sphere of the thinkable, is Franz Kafka. His work, from beginning to end, takes place in the sphere of death, in a shrouded terrain where the relations between dreaming and waking, being and not being, have become uncertain or suspended. Kafka himself makes this dissolution in his work of the boundary between living and dying explicit, in a diary entry of 13th December 1914. He spent the day 'at Felix's', he writes:

> On the way home told Max that I shall lie very contentedly on my deathbed, provided the pain isn't too great. I forgot – and later purposely omitted – to add that the best things I have written have their basis in this capacity of mine to meet death with contentment.[4]

In an inversion of Woody Allen's witticism ('I don't want to achieve immortality through my work, I want to achieve it through not dying'), Kafka imagines a fundamental connection between the capacity to write, and the capacity to die; his work grants him not immortality, but the very possibility of dying, so 'in the death enacted I rejoice in my own death'.[5] As Maurice Blanchot puts it, in his discussion of that same diary entry,

Kafka's work is propelled by a peculiarly circuitous and contradictory relationship with the death that enables it – 'write to be able to die – die to be able to write'.[6] Kafka's protagonists, Blanchot writes, 'carry out their actions in death's space, and […] it is to the indefinite time of 'dying' that they belong'.[7]

In his discussion of Kafka's deathwriting, from 1955, Blanchot suggests that there is something anomalous about this discovery of a kind of generative principle in the experience of death. 'Naturally', Blanchot writes, Kafka's thinking here is 'in conflict with generally accepted ideas about art and the work of art'. 'To write in order not to die', Blanchot goes on, 'to entrust oneself to the survival of the work: this motive is apparently what keeps the artist at his task'.[8] It is a mark of Kafka's singularity that he should refuse such a fundamental principle or motive, that he should so effortlessly evacuate the weighty idea that art is about the prolongation or affirmation or consecration of life. This may be so; but what I will explore in this essay is the possibility that Kafka's work, whatever its singularity, belongs to a literary tradition which has found in the approach to realised death not only a form of negation, but also a means of producing a new kind of possibility, a means, as Emily Dickinson puts it in 1862, of inventing 'another way – to see'.[9] This shadowy tradition may stretch as far back as writing itself, may simply be a darkling version of Harold Bloom's 'western canon' or Erich Auerbach's 'western literature'; but I will trace it here only as far back as the beautifully deathbound verse of Emily Dickinson. There is, I will suggest, a line of influence or affinity, reaching from Dickinson to Beckett to a body of contemporary deathwriting, that evokes this counter-tradition, and that allows us to imagine a way of thinking about death, and its relationship to life, that might work against the 'generally accepted ideas' that Blanchot talks of in 1955; that might allow us to picture a different kind of life world, in which the 'survival of the work' rests not on the eradication of the dark and the deathly, but on a radically reconceived relation between the dark and the luminous, between the quick and the dead. At a time when our conception of the lifeworld is in an unprecedentedly deep crisis, when our capacity to picture the world as an environment in harmony with human modes of life is most attenuated, it becomes an urgent task to read for such a counter-tradition, to find new ways to see without the aid of human light.

To trace such a tradition is to approach the means by which we encounter enworlded being as a picture, as Adam and Eve find themselves pictured, for Stevens, in Eden (Eve 'made air the mirror of herself'; Adam and Eve 'found themselves / In heaven as in a glass').[10] For Martin Heidegger, it is this picturing forth that inaugurates modernity. 'The fundamental event of the modern age', he writes in his 1938 lecture 'The Age of the World Picture', is 'the conquest of the world as a picture'.[11] In contradistinction to medieval and ancient conceptions of the world, the 'modern age' is characterised by its conception of the world as pictorial representation, and what is more by human representation. 'The essence of the modern age', Heidegger writes, is that the world becomes a picture which is projected by 'man'. With the arrival of the world picture, 'man becomes that being upon which all that is, is grounded as regards the manner of its being and its truth' (p. 128). When world becomes picture, 'Man becomes the relational center of that which is as such'. In casting the world as a picture, 'man sets himself up as the setting in which whatever is must henceforth set itself forth [....] Man becomes the representative of that which is' (p. 132). It is for this reason that the rise of humanism, for Heidegger, coincides with the modern age, and with the age of the world picture. 'It is no wonder,' he writes, 'that humanism first arises where the world becomes picture':

> It would have been just as impossible for a humanism to have gained currency in the great age of the Greeks as it would have been impossible to have had anything like a world picture in that age. (p. 133)

For Heidegger, the conquest of the world by the human is intricately bound up with the emergence of a form of pictorial representation which allows us to shape the world that we inhabit, the world which 'is normative and binding for us' (p. 129).

Such a conception of the normative and binding world picture, of course, rests on a quite radical anthropocentrism. Heidegger's correlation between man and world is part of what Giorgio Agamben, in his 2002 work *The Open*, calls the 'anthropological machine' – the organising of the world around a human centre that has been, he argues, at the heart of western metaphysics, and that has provided 'the motor for man's becoming historical'.[12] To produce a picture of the world, Agamben's work suggests, we have been required to banish the nonhuman from the sphere of the human, to banish darkness from the light, to banish death from life. Ontology, anthropogenesis, the 'becoming human of the living being', has required us, repeatedly, to enforce distinctions between 'the human and the animal, between nature and history, between life and death'.[13] If this is so, however, it is central to Agamben's project to recognise that our own age sees the winding down of the anthropological machine. 'The end of philosophy', Agamben writes in *The Open*, and 'the completion of the epochal destinations of being mean that today the machine is idling' (p. 80). To think about the world now requires us to adapt a different kind of seeing, one that is not structured by Heidegger's world picture, and that does not posit the human as the 'relational center of that which is as such'. It requires us to learn to see with the eyes of what Agamben calls, in 2009, the 'true contemporary'. To rise to the challenge of the contemporary, Agamben writes in his essay 'What is the Contemporary', requires us to see not only the world picture, to see not only what is made visible and brought into the light, but also to see what is banished from the visible, what is excluded from representation. 'The contemporary', he writes, is 'he who firmly holds his gaze on his own time so as to perceive not its light but rather its darkness'.[14] 'The ones who can call themselves contemporary', Agamben goes on,

> are only those who do not allow themselves to be blinded by the lights of the century and so manage to get a glimpse of the shadows in those lights, of their intimate obscurity [....] The contemporary is the person who perceives the darkness of his time as something that concerns him, as something that never ceases to engage him. Darkness is something that – more than any light – turns directly and singularly toward him. (p. 14)

Our own contemporary moment, Agamben suggests, requires us to overcome those distinctions that have separated life from death, human from animal. It requires us to develop a new way of thinking about how death relates to life, how the pictured relates to the unpictured. But, if we are to glean a connection here between this contemporary requirement, and the tradition of deathwriting I am proposing here, we have to address a paradox that is at work in Agamben's understanding of contemporaneity, and that complicates any perception that Agamben's project is involved in simply dismantling or overcoming a Heideggerian anthropocentrism, or in discomposing Heidegger's world picture. This paradox lies in the perception that the experience of contemporaneity has *always* involved the discerning of a darkness within the sphere of the visible, a deathliness within the province of the living. 'All eras', Agamben writes, 'for those who experience contemporariness, are obscure. The contemporary is precisely the person who knows how to see this obscurity, who is able to write by dipping his pen into the obscurity of the present'.[15] Indeed, the no doubt correct idea that Agamben's project, in *The Open*, is devoted to overcoming the distinctions that have separated human from animal, is troubled by the possibility that, in Heidegger's own work, in his exercising of his own contemporaneity, these distinctions are already under a certain kind of erasure. Agamben writes in 2009 that 'the contemporary is the one whose eyes are struck by the beam of darkness that comes from his own time' – that seeing one's own time requires one to see outside the precincts of the word picture, of the world as it is made visible to us, as it binds and normalises us. But Heidegger, even as he outlines the conditions of world picturing in 1938, is already cognizant of the conjunction between light and dark which is part of the picture itself. The picture of the world includes a glimmer of what Heidegger calls the 'incalculable' – the latent possibility of world picturing itself that cannot be contained within any given picture of the world. 'This becoming incalculable', he writes, 'remains the invisible shadow that is cast around all things everywhere' when the world has been 'transformed into a picture'.[16] To know our historical moment, to 'safeguard into its truth', requires us, Heidegger writes, to see into this shadow, as it is 'by means of this shadow' that 'the modern world extends itself out into a space withdrawn from representation' (p. 136). 'Everyday opinion', Heidegger writes, 'sees in the shadow only the lack of light, if not light's complete denial. In truth, however, the shadow is a manifest, though impenetrable, testimony to the concealed emitting of light' (p. 154). To look only at that which is illuminated or pictured – to be, in Agamben's terms, 'blinded by the lights' of one's own time – Heidegger writes in 1938, 'can bring about nothing in itself other than self-deception and blindness in relation to the historical moment' (p. 136).

II Blind Seeing and Deathwriting in Emily Dickinson

So, the tradition that I am seeking to trace here is one that has grounded itself in this peculiar fusion between the light and the dark – in this conjunction between the living and the dead that has been at work within the very forms that have allowed us to conceive of the human, and to conspire in the rise of humanism. And I have chosen to locate the beginning of this tradition in the writing of Emily Dickinson because it is in her verse that the aesthetic embrace of death comes closer than in any other writing to the obsessive tracing of a failed distinction between the visible and the invisible, between blindness and sight. Across the range of her poetry, it is possible to see that her chief literary and philosophical preoccupation – the aesthetic encounter with death, the conjunction between death and writing that Kafka describes in 1914 – is thought through a repeated, obsessive concern with what we might call a blind seeing. It is as light itself darkens and darkness gleams, as seeing shades into and mingles with unseeing, that Dickinson's poetry reaches towards a conception of death as possibility. As Dickinson most famously puts it in 1862, she is committed not to picturing the world, but to a particular kind of unpicturing, a kind of ungraven poetics, what Harold Bloom calls a 'passion for unnaming'.[17] 'I would not paint – a picture', she writes, dedicating herself to what she calls 'bright impossibility', to a writing which can only illuminate a failure of the possibility of vison or luminosity – a kindling of the impossible which remains unthought, even as it comes forth into brightness.[18]

It is through this unpicturing, through the dismantling of the mechanics of vision, that her poetry penetrates the shadows in which Heidegger discovers the 'concealed emitting of light', and in which she approaches what Blanchot calls 'death's space'. To read Dickinson now, in relation to an environment shaped by climate change, is to attend newly to this unpicturing, and to acknowledge the challenge that her poetry presents to reading and to seeing – a challenge that is perhaps not met, in Paul de Man's resonant phrase, by any existing 'rhetoric of blindness'.[19] De Man belongs to a group of thinkers, including Blanchot and Derrida, who have collectively developed a deconstructive conception of the relation between blindness and sight. It is de Man's central claim, in *Blindness and Insight*, that 'critics' moments of greatest blindness with regard to their own critical assumptions are also the moments at which they achieve their greatest insight'[20]. For de Man, as for Derrida and for Blanchot, blindness is the empty content of any act of seeing or thinking – the 'negative movement that animates the critic's thought', the 'unstated principle that leads his [or her] language away from its asserted stand'[21]. Paul de Man writes that 'a certain degree of blindness is part of the specificity of all literature',[22] as Derrida suggests that a certain 'invisibility [...] inhabit[s] the visible', or 'come[s] to haunt it to the point of being confused with it'.[23] Such attentiveness to the conjunctions between the visible and the invisible make for rich resonances between Dickinson and deconstruction; but if this is so, it is also the case that the poetic tradition I am tracing here, in the light of ecological crisis, opens onto a condition that is less epistemologically evacuated than that which is imagined by de Man, or by Derrida, an ecological ground to being that can only come to expression under intense poetic pressure, and which does not yet have a philosophical or political vocabulary in which to express itself.

To gather a sense of this conjunction between deathwriting and blind seeing in Dickinson's verse, one can draw on examples from across her oeuvre. Take, for example, the opening of poem 869 in the Franklin edition:

> What I see not, I better see –
> Through Faith – My Hazel Eye
> Has periods of shutting –
> But, No lid has Memory – (p. 379)

II Blind Seeing and Deathwriting in Emily Dickinson

As readers of Dickinson have pointed out, this reads as a response to William Shakespeare's Sonnet 43.[24] Dickinson's speaker finds that seeing well involves the failure of sight, as Shakespeare writes that 'When most I wink, then do my eyes best see'. 'For all the day', Shakespeare's sonnet continues,

> They view things unrespected;
> But when I sleep, in dreams they look on thee,
> And, darkly bright, are bright in dark directed.[25]

Shakespeare's sonnet continues to play with this paradox to its end. The effect of looking on beauty is to make shadows bright, and to make brightness shadowy so that, in the concluding couplet,

> All days are nights till I see thee,
> And nights bright days when dreams do show thee me. (p. 756)

There is a light play of oppositions in Shakespeare's sonnet, in which the overcoming of the limits of daylight can only be expressed in terms of the conditions of seeing which the poet is seeking to supersede. To see the object of this poem is to stage a reversal between bright and dark; but as bright becomes dark, and dark becomes bright, the very opposition that drives the poem is peculiarly cancelled, and the difference between 'winking' and 'seeing', the difference upon which the poem depends, yields to a kind of unity, a poetic fusion between seeing and unseeing. The poet looks upon his loved one here with 'unseeing eyes' (l. 8), with 'sightless eyes' (l. 12), and the collapsing play between opposition and identity that the poem enacts allows for a kind of looking which can at once maintain and overcome this difference between blindness and sight.

Dickinson's poem performs a similar operation, and moves in step with Shakespeare's sonnet, towards a climax in which Dickinson's poet, like Shakespeare's, suggests that the seeing demanded by the loved one involves a more perfect kind of light, a brighter kind of brightness, than that which allows for conventional seeing. She beholds the 'Features so beloved', in the light of 'Faith' and 'Memory', she writes at the poem's close, 'Till jealous Daylight interrupt – / And mar thy perfectness' (p. 379). Mere daylight, in Dickinson and in Shakespeare, seems like night, like dimness, in comparison with the pristine light by which the loved one is beheld. But if there is a close accord between Dickinson and Shakespeare here, there is also a deep chasm between them, one which opens around the way that the two writers understand the oppositions that drive their verse.

Shakespeare balances the opposition between bright and dark against their apparent sameness; but Dickinson's verse, here and always, produces a bottomless gulf between seeing and unseeing, a borderless zone of non-knowing, that is the signature of her thinking and of her poetics, and which opens onto a kind of deathwriting that is uniquely her own. The first line, 'What I see not, I better see –', forces a schism within the idea of seeing itself – that 'internal difference', as Dickinson puts it in poem 320, 'Where the Meanings, are' (p. 143). She sees well when she is not seeing, so seeing, at its best, contains and emerges from unseeing; and the poem can do nothing to sustain or overcome this contradiction, this internal difference. It is only in a kind of living death – only, she writes, with 'all my sense obscured' (p. 379) – that she is able to achieve her blind seeing, because the gap that opens, within seeing itself, between seeing and not seeing, can only find itself thought, or poetically realised, in the space of Dickinsonian death – the space of the dash, when words are gone, when thinking outlives itself.

This relation between deathwriting and blind seeing emerges repeatedly in Dickinson's verse – so much so that it becomes the motor and the medium of her thinking. Take poem 428, in which death is imagined as a process by which 'We grow accustomed to the Dark', and learn to see in the night of nonbeing. 'The Bravest', she writes, 'grope a little',

> But as they learn to see –
>
> Either the Darkness alters –
> Or something in the sight
> Adjusts itself to Midnight –
> And Life steps almost straight. (p. 198)

Death is here imagined as an alteration of the dark, an alteration in which life itself impossibly persists, learning to hold itself 'almost straight' in the province of a poetically lit dark. Or take poem 484, 'From Blank to Blank –':

> From Blank to Blank –
> A Threadless Way
> I pushed Mechanic feet –
> To stop – or perish – or advance –
> Alike indifferent –
>
> If end I gained
> It ends beyond
> Indefinite disclosed –
> I shut my eyes – and groped as well
> 'Twas lighter – to be Blind – (pp. 221–222)

II Blind Seeing and Deathwriting in Emily Dickinson

Here, the groping encounter with not being – with the blank that stretches before the beginning of existence and after its end – takes place, as in 'We grow accustomed to the Dark', in the precinct of a lit or altered dark. The poem is impelled by the impossible recognition that blankness, as the unthinkable origin and destination of all being, can only come to us in the form of a sign, a sign which immediately and unerringly betrays the blankness that it seeks to represent, either in the form of a word or in the form of a dash. The metrical feet of the poem, and the bodily feet of the groping poet, can only crank out a mechanical testimony to the blankness that both being and poetry are – and by staging such testimony, deny it. The figure of blind seeing upon which the poem rests – "Twas lighter – to be Blind –' – is the apotheosis of this irresolvable antinomy. The phrase might suggest a response to the indifference that the poet feels; it is easier (lighter) just to stop trying to see one's being or make sense of one's condition, as the heaviness of those trudging feet can only be lightened by a kind of careless resignation to unthinking. But it also suggests that the impossible combination of living and dying that being in time is – a being which is generated by nothingness and leads to nothingness and is continually giving way to nothingness, even as it finds itself impossibly persisting, pushing itself forward – can only be seen by inventing a looking which is also an aversion of the gaze, by learning to see in a dark which remains dark, even as it alters, even as it adjusts itself to the conditions of visibility.

The poem which perhaps captures this assemblage of dying and blind seeing most sharply is poem 591, 'I heard a Fly buzz – when I died –':

> I heard a Fly buzz – when I died –
> The Stillness in the Room
> Was like the Stillness in the Air –
> Between the Heaves of Storm –
>
> The Eyes around – had wrung them dry –
> And Breaths were gathering firm
> For that last Onset – when the King
> Be witnessed – in the Room –
>
> I willed my Keepsakes – Signed away
> What portion of me be
> Assignable – and then it was
> There interposed a Fly –
>
> With Blue – uncertain – stumbling Buzz –
> Between the light – and me –
> And then the Windows failed – and then
> I could not see to see – (pp. 265–256)

The task of this poem is to open a blind space within seeing, in which the event of death might be allowed, against all the rules of life, to take place. The first line – 'I heard a Fly buzz – when I died –' – makes the impossible claim, common to all posthumous narration, that one's own death has been achieved (as Kaka rejoices in his enacted death), that one has been able to experience and outlive one's own dying. The following stanzas fall back from this claim, recasting the poet's death as the future moment towards which the poem is moving, as the mourners in the still room prepare for their grief, and as the poet herself manages her final affairs. But as the poem moves towards its climax, it comes ever closer to the rent in being that is torn by that opening line, working its way back into the crevasse between life and death, before and after, that has already swallowed it. The opening line inaugurates a shattering difference within the I itself; the I who hears the fly's buzz cannot be quite the same as the I who has died, as the buzzing is surely a prelude to the death that the dead I has already achieved. This difference within the speaking voice can be heard again in the third stanza as the poet 'Signed away/What portion of me be/Assignable'. Just as the poet of 'From Blank to Blank' experiences a prosthetic difference from herself, as she 'pushed' her 'mechanic feet' along her threadless way, so here the poet feels an unravelled distance from herself in the very signs she has for herself – the signs with which she gives a portion of herself away. And then, as we reach the extraordinary ending of the poem, as the fly 'interposes' between the dead I and the living I, or between the I and the signs by which it knows itself, this difference flies wide open, leading to one of the most intense figures of blind seeing in Dickinson's verse. The fly buzzes at the window, which marks the threshold between 'the light' and 'me'; perhaps, as the uncertain, stumbling buzz begins its buzzing, the window marks the boundary between a celestial light outside or beyond, and the living 'me' who lies still on her deathbed, in her still room, on this side of death. But 'then', as the 'Windows failed', the distinctions that have held the poem in place give way, returning us to an impossible naked gulf between living self and dead self, a gulf in which the visible and the invisible, seeing and unseeing, reach an awful, disjunct identity. As the poet finds that 'I could not see to see' (l. 16), she understands that she is already beyond the horizons of the room, already in the death that has happened in the poem's first line. As the windows fail, the dead I can no longer see into the room, into the body and the mind in which she carries out her last act of seeing, can no longer see into herself in order to see out of the window towards her dying light. But even as this failure offers itself as the final act of the poem (the poem is driven by those urgent markers of temporal progression, 'and then' (l. 11), 'and then' (l. 15), 'and then' (l. 15)), the poem tells us that it is also its opening impulse, and the very condition of seeing itself. To see is to conjure some conjunction between the I who lives in sequential time and the I who is already and always in the blank province of death; and the light by which we achieve such seeing is always riven by the darkness of dying, always dimmed by its connection with the shadowy 'portion' of the self which is not 'assignable', which cannot find itself illuminated by any kind of light.

III Total Object, Complete with Missing Parts

It is this kind of seeing that both Heidegger and Agamben have in mind, when they talk of a darkness which contains a 'light that, while directed towards us, infinitely distances itself from us',[26] or when they see shadows as a 'concealed emitting of light'.[27] Picturing, for Dickinson, as for Agamben and for Heidegger, *involves* a kind of unpicturing, is shot through or bound up with unpicturing. To find 'another way to see' is to learn to see this hidden communication between light and dark. As Dickinson puts it in 'The Tint I cannot take – is best', this kind of picturing requires us to understand that a 'portion' of the life world is resistant to visibility, to apportioning or assigning, and cannot take any representative or material tint, so that one can only picture the world, can only 'see it', when the 'Cheated eye / Shuts arrogantly – in the Grave' (p. 310). To see by this dark light is to see in the grave, to see in the space of death that Dickinson's verse so singularly, so miraculously summons to thought. And, if one can see a shared vocabulary of blind seeing, in this dialogue between Dickinson, Heidegger and Agamben, so too it is possible to see a submerged or minor literary heritage that has its roots in Dickinson, and that stretches this relation between death and 'bright impossibility' (348, l. 3) beyond Dickinson's own time, into the twentieth century, and on into our own contemporary moment.

Take the work of Samuel Beckett, which is engaged throughout in a certain slantwise dialogue with Dickinson's poetry – a dialogue which has so far largely eluded critical expression. There is a buried affinity between these two writers, a kind of shared mood and sensibility that causes a shock of recognition when reading from one to the other, as if, in Beckett's words, they emerge from the same 'profounds of mind. Of mindlessness'.[28]

Think, for example, of Beckett's 1946 French language poem La Mouche (which I give here also in Steven Connor's translation):

> entre la scène et moi
> la vitre
> vide sauf elle
>
> ventre à terre
> sanglée dans ses boyaux noirs
> antennes affolées ailes liées
> pattes crochues bouche suçant à vide
> sabrant l'azur s'écrasant contre l'invisible
> sous mon pouce impuissant elle fait chavirer
> la mer et le ciel serein[29]
>
> between the vista and me
> the pane
> void save it
>
> belly down
> strapped in its black guts
> crazed antennae, bound wings
> legs crooked mouthparts sucking on void
> slashing the blue crushing itself against the invisible
> under my helpless thumb it convulses
> sea and quiet sky[30]

The image here, in Beckett's poem, of a fly pressed against a window-pane calls irresistibly (for me at least) to Dickinson's 'I heard a Fly buzz – when I died'. 'La Mouche' reads almost as an anagram of Dickinson's poem, with the 'blue' of the 'Blue – uncertain – stumbling Buzz' reframed in the phrase 'sabrant l'azure', with the failure of sight that ends Dickinson's poem rendered as a 'crushing' 'against the invisible' ('s'écrasant contre l'invisible'), and with the interposing of the window between 'the light – and me' in Dickinson cast here as the installing of a 'pane' ('vitre') between 'la scène' and 'moi'.

Such a recreation of the elements of Dickinson's poem in 'La Mouche', of course, is no proof of 'influence', and indeed I have no interest in claiming that Beckett is knowingly referencing Dickinson here. I do not seek to reveal that Beckett has an active interest in Dickinson that has so far been missed by his critics, but rather to suggest that Beckett's literary thinking has a rich resonance with Dickinson's, one which underlies their manifest differences in cultural attitude and religious conviction. What the Dickinsonian cast to Beckett's poem does allow us to see is a kind of shared sensibility, a shared visual vocabulary, that is evident in a particular way in 'La Mouche', but which turns and glimmers throughout Beckett's oeuvre, from 'Serena 1' and *More Pricks than Kicks* in the early 1930s to

Worstward Ho and *Stirrings Still* in the 1980s. As Seven Connor and others have demonstrated, the image of the fly pressed against the window-pane recurs through Beckett's oeuvre, and each time it does it brings with it associations that evoke a Dickinsonian undertow to Beckett's writing, a pull towards a kind of blind seeing that he shares with her, and that opens onto the space of an instantiated, imagined death.[31]

Watt, written in 1944, contains an image of flies seeking the warmth and light that has a Dickinsonian pulse:

> The flies, of skeleton thinness, excited to new efforts by yet another dawn, left the walls, and the ceiling, and even the floor, and hastened in great numbers to the window. Here, pressed against the impenetrable panes, they would enjoy the light and warmth of the long summer's day.[32]

The fly pressed against the impenetrable pane here carries something from the fly crushed against the invisible in 'La Mouche', and prepares the ground for Beckett's later houseflies – in *Company*, for example, which focuses sharply on a 'live fly' that might provide some company to the lone protagonist of the novella, a 'live fly mistaking him for dead';[33] or in *All Strange Away*, where the narrator commands himself to imagine, to 'lodge a second in that glare', a 'dying common house or dying window fly'.[34]

Of course, there is nothing in particular to suggest that this recurrence of the 'window fly' in Beckett is associated with Dickinson's death fly (although one of the few essays to extend a comparison between Beckett and Dickinson reads the fly in *Company* as a cousin of the fly in 'I heard a Fly buzz – when I died').[35] But the associations that gather around the fly in these recurring passages are woven into a particular kind of thinking about death, about visibility and about the requirement that one brings death to visibility and perception as part of any attempt to picture the world – a kind of thinking that Beckett and Dickinson deeply share. Dickinson's fly, in interposing between the dead and living 'I', between 'the light' and 'me', and in marking that gap that opens up in seeing as the poet 'could not see to see', stumbles into the limit space that her entire work strains to make thinkable, the space underlying being, in which the oppositions that make being possible are both revealed and overcome. There is – there has to be – a space between darkness and brightness, between being alive and being dead, where these two conditions meet and separate; to think is to approach this zone of mingling and separation, to find oneself at once annulled and brought to being within it. Both Dickinson and Beckett know this, and for both the task of writing is to enter this zone, to enter the indefinition, the indifference, that it confers upon the thinker, while making of such indefinition, such indifference, the very difference and definition that allows us to maintain a subject position, and allows us to cast a picture of the world. Sharon Cameron, in what remains one of the most incisive readings of 'I heard a Fly buzz – when I died' remarks on just this attention in Dickinson to the commingling of dark and bright, of life and death, in terms which make the continuity between Dickinson and Beckett palpable. Dickinson's lyrics, Cameron writes, 'attempt to cross boundaries, to blur distinctions between life and death, time and timelessness, figure and its fulfilment, or to put it more accurately, to wear a passage between them';[36] and the force that allows her to cross such boundaries, to wear such a passage, is that of imagined, perceived death, an imagining of death that manages to conjure a continuity between bright and dark, between blindness and seeing. The last two lines of Dickinson's poem ('And then the Windows failed – and then / I could not see to see'), Cameron writes, forge a space in which 'death is survived by perception', and in which the poem 'penetrates to the invisible imagination which strengthens in response to the loss of visible sight' (p. 115).

For any reader of Beckett's work, this description of Dickinson's blind seeing is eerily prescient of the passage that Beckett's own writing wears from blank to blank, 'on', as he puts it, from 'nought anew',[37] from the 'unthinkable first to the no less unthinkable last'.[38] If for Dickinson, death is survived by perception, so for Beckett, the imagination continually outlives its own death. 'I don't know when I died', the narrator of *The Calmative* says at the opening of his narrative, in an impossible posthumous gambit which mirrors the opening of Dickinson's poem;[39] and Beckett's writing career, from the *Unnamable* on, is nothing more than an extended attempt to imagine the death of the imagination, to conjure a kind of seeing that continues, after the difference between seeing and unseeing, between living and dying, has been cancelled. As the narrator of *All Strange Away* imagines that Dickinsonian fly, pressed against the window-pane in the bright glare of a death that has already been died, the narrator summons this requirement, this demand that the Beckettian imagination lives on in the throes of its own death. 'Imagination dead imagine', the narrator says: 'Imagination dead imagine to lodge a second in that glare a dying common house or dying window fly, then fall the five feet to the dust and die or die and fall' (p. 172).

The light that shines in Beckett's work, from the 'darkness visible' of 'A Wet Night' to the 'unfading light' of 'Neither',[40] is drawn from this encounter with a perceived death, this capacity to open a glaring second in which the imagination imagines its own dying. In all of the 'rotunda texts'

III Total Object, Complete with Missing Parts

of the sixties and seventies, in *Imagination Dead Imagine*, *All Strange Away*, and then in *The Lost Ones, Company, Ill seen Ill Said* and *Worstward Ho*, the undifferentiated storyscapes are lit by a peculiar light, which is made of the shadows that it seems to vanquish, and which is won by an imagination that is working at and beyond the limits of its own conditions of possibility. The scene in *Company*, in which the protagonist lies 'on his back in the dark' in a placeless cylinder, listening to a 'voice' which tells him of his life, is periodically lit by precisely this light. The light, the narrator says, has 'no source', 'as if faintly luminous all his little void' – in the same way that the light in the rotunda of *Imagination Dead Imagine* comes from 'no visible source'.[41] The light in these works appears to saturate the space – so that in the rotunda of *Imagination Dead Imagine* 'all shines with the same white shine' (p. 182), and in the cylinder of *The Lost Ones* the light 'appears to emanate from all sides and to permeate the entire space as though this were uniformly luminous down to its least particle of ambient air'.[42] This lends these works a kind of brilliance, a shadowless quality, like the relentless illumination of a shopping mall, or of a rubber cell. But even as these works bask in omnipresent light, it is clear at all times that the light here is only another kind of darkness, that brightness is, as in Dickinson's 'We grow accustomed to the Dark –', simply an alteration of the dark. The brilliant light of Beckett's late works always holds a darkness within it, always trembles on the brink of revealing an identity with the dark that it opposes – this, the narrator of *Company* suggests, is a 'shadowy light' (p. 15), a light which simply makes the 'darkness visible' (p. 15).

To learn to see in this light requires one to develop a particular kind of blind seeing, one that we are taught too in reading Dickinson's verse, as she stumbles from blank to blank. When Beckett seeks to picture a world, when he reaches for what the narrator of *The Lost Ones* calls 'a perfect mental image of the entire system' (p. 204), he seeks to imagine a space in which everything is included, in which death is included in the sphere of life, in which dark is included in the sphere of light. As a young Beckett puts it, he seeks to imagine the artwork as a 'total object, complete with missing parts'.[43] And this requires him to understand that the picture of the world, in its fullness, includes those shadows that are concealed within Heideggerian light, just as any attempt to imagine being requires us to apprehend the thought that nonbeing is one of its constituent parts. Beckett's late works seek to produce pictures of completion, pictures of the totality. But what Beckett finds is that the harder we try to imagine the world in its blankness or in its completeness, in its fullness or in its emptiness, we find that there exists always a remainder, some deathly element or ingredient of life, some dark element of light, that cannot quite come to thought or expression; some difference from self that is a feature of the very grammar of being. The narrator of *Worstward Ho* – Beckett's most excruciating experiment in blind seeing – finds that the attempt to 'see all' produces not simply omnipresent light, but a kind of Dickinsonian blank, a flaw in being, in thinking, that runs right through its very fabric. To try to say everything, Beckett's narrator writes, produces only a kind of Dickinsonian unsaying, in which we are cast into unthought, into 'profounds of mindlessness' which are marked only by those 'Blanks for when words gone'.[44]

IV The Ponderous Spectacle of Things Ceasing to Be

It is in the lit darkness of our own contemporary moment that this fugitive affinity between Beckett and Dickinson, this latent tradition of blind seeing, comes to a kind of oblique perceptibility. There is a recognition, across a wide range of contemporary writers, that the task of making a picture of the world today involves us in the apprehension of a kind of darkness that is woven into the picturing mechanism itself – just as there is a growing sense that to think about life now, under contemporary conditions, requires us to re-see the junction between the living and the dead. As Jane Bennett argues in her 2010 book *Vibrant Matter*, there is an urgent imperative now to rethink the means by which life is distributed in matter, beyond the forms prescribed by humanist traditions – a rethinking which requires us to 'dissipate the onto-theological binaries of life/matter, human/animal'.[45] Our current predicament both allows and requires us to produce a new material account of the terrain that opens up between life and death, to overcome our habit, as Bennett puts it, of 'parsing the world into dull matter (it, things) and vibrant life (us, beings)';[46] and in doing so, we are led to resee the difficult boundary between the blind and the sighted, between the visible and the invisible.

This articulation of world picturing, with blind seeing, with a new kind of inclusive disjunction between life and death, can be found, as I have said, across the range of contemporary imaginings. But I will focus here on one example – Cormac McCarthy's novel of global death *The Road* – a novel which owes an explicit debt to Beckett, and an implicit one to Dickinson, as the originator of the mode of deathwriting I am seeking here to articulate. McCarthy's novel sets out to offer a picture of the world as an environment given over in its entirety to death. The man at the heart of the story is afforded, at one moment in the novel, a vision of this kind of planetary death. 'He walked out in the gray light', the narrator says,

> and stood and he saw for a brief moment the absolute truth of the world. The cold relentless circling of the intestate earth. Darkness implacable. The blind dogs of the sun in their running. The crushing black vacuum of the universe.[47]

This is a moment of blind seeing of some intensity, in which, in Wallace Stevens's terms, we 'see the sun again with an ignorant eye / And see it clearly in the idea of it'.[48] The grey light in which the man stands is cast by a blind sun; the absolute seeing that he is granted – his sudden grasping of the mechanical turning of a cosmic machine – is a vision that emerges from and takes place in implacable darkness. The moment of seeing itself is peculiarly annulled or proleptically cancelled, as it belongs to a model of looking and observing that, in the wake of whatever disaster has befallen the world, is now defunct. As the man puts it later in the novel, whatever world picture is granted here is one that no longer organises itself around the human as a relational centre; a picture of a world, Stevens writes, 'That has expelled us and our images'.[49] It is only 'in the world's destruction', McCarthy's narrator says, that it is 'possible at last to see how it was made' (p. 293).

McCarthy's novel sets out to produce this picture of borderless death; but in doing so, in setting out to imagine the process by which the human extinguishes itself entirely, McCarthy produces that same kind of remainder, that same possibility of new modes of seeing, new ways of understanding the relation between the dead and the living, that we find in Beckett, and in Dickinson. McCarthy's novel is drenched in Beckettian rhythms and allusions – it conducts itself throughout as an exercise in Beckettian thinking. Beckett's *Imagination Dead Imagine*, with which McCarthy's novel is in constant dialogue, opens with the declaration that, in whatever space the narrator is imagining, there is 'No trace anywhere of life',[50] and this phrase comes back repeatedly in *The Road*, like a mantra or an undertone. In this world, the narrator says, there is 'no sign of life' (p. 11); 'The roadside hedges were gone to rows of black and twisted brambles. No sign of life' (p. 20); there are 'No tracks in the road, nothing living anywhere' (p. 29); there is 'no smoke, no movement of life' (p. 82); there is 'No sign of life anywhere' (p. 216). As the man and the boy walk the road, as they push their mechanic feet along the 'black shape' of the road, 'running from dark to dark' (p. 279), they walk in the footsteps of all those tramping figures in Beckett, who in turn walk mechanically along that threadless way that Dickinson strings between blank and blank. In a rare moment of humour, McCarthy's boy asks his father 'What are our long term goals?' (p. 170), and in the question we can hear Beckett's grim dismantling of the Christian mechanics of hope, Dickinson's disclosure of the indefinition of the end. But, in reanimating these Beckettian, Dickinsonian rhythms, McCarthy's novel also produces that same furtive duplication, that same opening of wriggling difference within the static picture of the self-same, that moves in Beckett's imagination, that animates Dickinson's deathwriting. The boy asks his father at one point, perhaps as an adjunct to the question of 'long term goals', whether there is any other world, whether the world that they inhabit, in the last throes of its destruction, is the only world available to thought or to life. 'There could be people alive someplace else', the boy suggests:

> Whereplace else?
> I dont know. Anywhere.
> You mean besides on earth?
> Yes.
> I dont think so. They couldnt live anyplace else.
> Not even if they could get there?
> No. (pp. 260–261)

This question is at the heart of McCarthy's imagination, as it is central to Beckett's thinking, and to Dickinson's. It calls, perhaps faintly, to Dickinson's assertion that 'the Brain – is wider than the sky –' (p. 269) ('put them side by side', she says, 'The one the other will contain / With ease'), and much more loudly to that moment in Beckett's *Endgame* when another love-crazed father seeks some kind of escape from the world that contains us. In the post-apocalyptic wastes of *Endgame*, where the 'earth is extinguished',[51] where the 'waves' are 'lead' and the 'sun is zero' (p. 107), a desperate father asks Hamm for some bread, to keep his child alive for another day, and Hamm refuses him, pointing out that survival in this world is only a prolongation of a time that has already died. 'Use your head', Hamm tells the pleading man, 'I give you some corn',

> the colours come back into his little cheeks – perhaps. And then? [*Pause.*] I lost patience. [*Violently.*] Use your head, can't you, use your head, you're on earth, there's no cure for that! (p. 118)

For Beckett's Hamm, as for McCarthy's father, the world is all there is. The vision that McCarthy's father is granted of the 'absolute truth of the world' is a monologic vision, a 'total object', like the 'perfect mental image of the entire system' that lies at the heart of Beckett's *The Lost Ones*.[52] There is no place 'besides on earth', there is no cure for our worldedness. But what McCarthy's world picture discovers, like Beckett's, like Dickinson's, is that picturing itself contains always a kind of darkness, a kind of countersight that is woven into seeing, and that offers a death that is also, as in Dickinson, 'Another way – to see'.[53] The light that shines in McCarthy's novel is, like that in Beckett and in Dickinson, a dark kind of light, a light made of 'implacable darkness'. In another of those seams, in which McCarthy's world folds suddenly and totally into Beckett's, the light in *The Road* is describes as 'sourceless' – the 'faint light all about, quivering and sourceless, refracted in the rain of drifting soot' (pp. 13–14). This is the light that is cast when the sun is 'zero', and in both Beckett and McCarthy there is an echo here of the possibility of seeing that emerges from the dark light cast in Dickinson's verse. But, in the half-light of the tradition I am sketching here, this sourceless light, this light compounded of the darkness it withstands, is not the result of a theology, but instead the fugitive corollary to seeing and thinking itself, the obscurity that inhabits the act of picturing, and that carries a latent, unthought, ungraven future. McCarthy's father equates world seeing with world destruction. It is only 'in the world's destruction' that it might be 'possible to see how it was made'; but the kind of world seeing that McCarthy reaches for, the kind of seeing that we find in Beckett, and in Dickinson, is one that unearths a junction between the destruction of the world and its very possibility, the motor of its becoming. The father sees before him 'the sweeping waste, hydrotopic and coldly secular', but he sees also 'The ponderous counterspectacle of things ceasing to be' (p. 293) – the counterspectacle that accompanies all instances of the spectacle, and that harbours that Heideggerian 'shadow that is cast around all things everywhere'.[54]

V Another Way – To See

I have talked throughout this essay of a tradition, a tradition of 'blind seeing', one to which we have to tune ourselves if we are to conceive of the world picture today, in the wake of the human project, and under the conditions of the Anthropocene. I have used this word, because I cannot find another that names the kind of work that I am suggesting that we need to do, or that could be equal to the kind of history that might address the future that awaits us. But I hope that it is clear that a tradition of blind seeing is hardly a tradition at all, and that it resists just the kind of lucidity it calls for, as Susan Howe recognises when she traces the 'ambiguous paths of kinship' that connect her to Emily Dickinson, or as Deleuze and Guattari recognise when they try to conscript Kafka into a 'minor literature'.[55]

Harold Bloom declares, in *The Western Canon*, that the operation of recruiting Dickinson's slantwise thinking for the great tradition is unproblematic. 'Her canonicity', he writes, 'results from her achieved strangeness, her uncanny relation to the tradition'.[56] Her 'Sublime', he goes on, 'is founded upon her unnaming of all our certitudes into so many blanks; and it gives her, and her authentic readers, another way to see, almost into the dark' (p. 309). That Bloom can rehearse the jargon of authenticity, while blithely laying claim to Dickinson's poetics of unnaming, indicates, I think, how weak this gesture of incorporation is, how it fails to respond to the kind of thinking that Dickinson's poetry demands, or to see in the kind of light that it casts. Seeing 'almost into the dark' is not, I would suggest, what Dickinson's poetry does; rather, it opens a buried junction between blindness and sight, an impossible meeting ground which sets the conditions for seeing itself, for being itself. To imagine a tradition to which such seeing belongs requires us to rethink the tradition itself, to suspend the cultural forms that have bound us and normalised us. Heidegger argues as much, when he offers a proleptic rebuke to Bloom's canon, and to the work of tradition more generally. The shadow which accompanies the world picture, which is in fact a 'concealed emitting of light' points, Heidegger writes, 'to something else, which it is denied to us of today to know'.[57] To 'experience' and 'ponder' this counterspectacle, requires us, Heidegger writes, to resist the 'flight into tradition' which 'can bring about nothing in itself other than self-deception and blindness in relation to the historical moment' (p. 136). If we are to see by the light of Dickinsonian darkness, or by the light that shines in Beckett's shade, then we need to learn to think a tradition, while resisting the flight into tradition – while recognising that world seeing today requires us to think beyond the human forms that have bound us. 'Reflection', Heidegger writes, 'transports the man of the future into that "between" in which he belongs to Being and yet remains a stranger amid that which is' (p. 136). To reflect on the world picture today requires us to achieve just this between-ness, and just this estrangement. To see with the eyes of the blind, as McCarthy and Beckett and Dickinson ask us to do, requires us to see this strangeness amid that which is, to see, as Wallace Stevens puts it, 'that we live in a place / That is not our own and, much more, not ourselves'.[58]

2017

CHAPTER 11

Mere Being
Imagination at the End of the Mind

> In this same interlude it doth befall
> That I, one Snout by name, present a wall;
> And such a wall as I would have you think
> That had in it a crannied hole or chink,
> Through which the lovers Pyramus and Thisbe
> Did whisper often, very secretly.
> William Shakespeare, *A Midsummer Night's Dream*.[1]

I

Does the contemporary moment require us to produce a new means of imagining the foundations of being, the ground of shared life?

We might begin to address this question, as it develops over the course of the twentieth century, by turning to Wallace Stevens, whose work constitutes one of the most sustained explorations we have of the meeting between mind and world, between idea and thing. In his late poem 'A Clear Day and no Memories', Stevens imagines a state of pure being, purged of any of the specificities that individuate us, that distinguish one person from another, one place from another, one time from another. 'Today', he writes,

> the air is clear of everything.
> It has no knowledge except of nothingness
> And it flows over us without meanings,
> As if none of us had ever been here before
> And are not now.[2]

This is the kind of being that remains when all the memories of being have been erased, the kind of being that Stevens thinks of, in one of the last and most beautiful poems he wrote, as 'mere being'. How can we have knowledge of a world without us in it, without the meanings that we make? How can we imagine a bare and unencumbered being, a being uncontaminated by the imagination? What do we see when we look past the edge of things, past the textured places that we inhabit in thought and memory and imagination, to some place beyond, and behind, and underneath? Do we see nothing? 'Of Mere Being' suggests not, suggests that there is a place beyond the far horizon, the last limit, that there is a 'palm at the end of the mind':

> The palm at the end of the mind,
> Beyond the last thought, rises
> In the bronze decor,
>
> A gold-feathered bird
> Sings in the palm, without human meaning,
> Without human feeling, a foreign song.
>
> You know then that it is not the reason
> That makes us happy or unhappy.
> The bird sings. Its feathers shine.
>
> The palm stands on the edge of space.
> The wind moves slowly in the branches.
> The bird's fire-fangled feathers dangle down.[3]

When we scrape human meaning away, this poem suggests, we find not just void, but desert space, unintelligible song.

It is perhaps difficult to do without such a concept – difficult to do without the idea that there is a ground to existence, a mere being, upon which all the perceived substances of our lives come to rest. It is difficult not to think that, if one could look past the edge of thought existence, one might find some creaturely life, some minimum condition of the viable, the vital. This is not simply, for Stevens, a response to the approach of death, a credulous falling back on a concept of persistent being; not simply a yearning for the artifice of eternity that Stevens borrows from Yeats, who imagines his own fire-fangled bird, 'set upon a golden bough', and required to 'sing / To Lords and Ladies of Byzantium / of what is past, or passing, or to come'.[4] This is not simply an attempt to ease the regret that Stevens expressed in a last fragment of verse left behind on his death, the regret that 'I have lived a skeleton's life, / As a disbeliever in reality, / A countryman of all the bones in the world'.[5] It is that thinking, imagining, opens onto a ground, a reality, from which it cannot escape, that is woven into it, that reveals itself when all that is extraneous to it is removed. We do not will mere being into existence as an antidote to a skeletal life, but find it there as the condition and pre-requisite of any minimal act of intellection. We find it there at the moments of greatest acuity, Stevens writes in his *Adagia*, the moments of 'clairvoyant observation' when we achieve that 'degree of perception at which what is real and what is imagined are one'.[6] As Simon Critchley puts it, it is the aim of Stevens's poetry, and particularly his later poetry, to see that 'things are what they are through an act of the mind', even though, at the same time, the reality of the thing resists the call of thought, that it resides, as the title of another late Stevens poem has it, not in 'Ideas about the Thing' but in 'the Thing itself'.[7] To read Stevens is to confront the fact, in all its wriggling complexity, that 'things merely are and that we are things too, things endowed with imagination'.[8]

Any thinking of the edge of space or the end of the mind, any attempt to approach the difficult junction between reality and imagination, has to address this concept that comes late in Stevens's writing life, the concept of mere being. To think the limits of life is to think the mere – not just as an imaginative exercise, but as a necessary condition of our relation to the political realities in which we live, and which determine our conception of the limit itself, as it scales and structures the inhabited world. For Stevens, the mere being he uncovers late in his writing life is not an abstraction, not an escape from reality, but an approach to the way that reality itself is structured. 'If we desire to formulate an accurate theory of poetry', he writes in *The Necessary Angel*, 'we find it necessary to examine the structure of reality, because reality is the central reference for poetry'.[9] The perception of resemblance, the poetic work of metaphor, lies at 'the base of appearance'. It is 'the creation of resemblance by the imagination', the discovery of resemblance 'between two or more parts of reality', or 'between something imagined and something real', that makes reality happen. Poetry 'binds together' the 'actual' world, even when it seems to disdain it, even or particularly when, as Critchley puts it, 'reality retreats before the imagination that shapes and orders it'.[10] This is why, Stevens writes to Barbara Church in 1949, 'more and more, one wants the voices of one's contemporaries – *today's* music, painting, poetry, thinking. I don't mean the voices of mere experimentalists, but the actual voices of our actual spirits'.[11] It is the task of the poet, Sevens writes to Peter Lee in 1951, to 'take his station in the midst of the circumstances in which people actually live, and to endeavour to give them, as well as himself, the poetry they need in those very circumstances'.[12]

Poetry is woven into the structure of reality, as the unintelligible song of mere being is woven into the processes that make our lives intelligible;

and if this is so, then it is perhaps the case for us, now, that the relation of mere being to the forces which are structuring our realities has become estranged, difficult to navigate. It is no doubt the case that this difficulty is a feature of contemporaneity more generally, that it is always difficult to see or measure oneself to one's own time. Such difficulty, such historical obduracy in any given contemporary moment is, perhaps paradoxically, a historical constant. But it seems true, also, to say that we are living now at a historical moment in which the gulf between reality and the imaginative forms in which it comes to thought – between the nakedness of mere being, and the various forms and commitments of collective social life – is unusually wide. Ours is a world and a time in which, as Auerbach says of Cervantes's seventeenth-century Spain, 'the phenomena of reality' have 'come to be difficult to survey and no longer possible to arrange in an unambiguous and traditional manner'.[13] It is a time at which the naked edges of things, the extremes where world and mind meet, the 'edge of space' that Stevens finds in 'Of Mere Being', impose themselves upon us, and derange us.

The causes and effects of this difficulty, of this derangement, are multiple, and unfold over different time scales. The most immediate agent of this estranging of the boundary between mind and world, between one person and another, as I write in the spring of 2021, is the Covid-19 pandemic. Both the global spread of a virus, and the state response to that spread, has shone a light on the way that the boundary itself functions under contemporary conditions. Pandemics, as J. M. Coetzee has noted (in the guise of one of his fictional alter egos), alert us to the limits of the human, and to the presence in our midst of inhuman forms of life. We see, in the drama of the pandemic, 'two forms of life each thinking about the other in its own way – human beings thinking about viral threats in the human way and viruses thinking about prospective hosts in a viral way'.[14] This inducts us into a new kind of knowledge about the ways in which human structures – global networks of communication and exchange – are inhabited by inhuman forces, which exploit them for inhuman ends. And it leads, also, to a defence of the human, at the level of the nation state. The imposition of lockdown across the globe (of varying kinds and intensity) has seen a hardening of the boundary between state and state, between person and person, between inside and outside. Lockdown safeguards the human, but it does so at the cost of revealing an underlying totalitarian structure at work under the surface of the state, whatever its system of government might be. The experience of self-ownership – that cornerstone, for Locke, of the democratic contract – appears, under these emergency conditions, to be merely ornamental, a privilege that is granted us when times are good, but which can be withdrawn under a state of exception. Lockdown re-enacted, in uncanny ways, the state response to plague in the seventeenth century so powerfully described by Michel Foucault in *Discipline and Punish*, a response which saw the 'penetration of regulation into even the smallest details of everyday life'.[15] Lockdown removes or suspends the political forms in which the sovereignty and autonomy of the political subject are couched, to reveal a biopolitical condition that subtends those forms; and this has happened at a time when other forces playing out over a longer historical term are reshaping the ways in which we conceive of the relations between person and person, between state and state. The biopolitical effects of the Covid pandemic resonate richly with the sense that we are entering now into a period both of geopolitical and of ecological crisis. The retreat behind a face mask occasioned by Covid has an odd congruence with the retreat behind a geopolitical border that takes the form of Brexit in the UK, or of the rise of right-wing nationalism across Europe and North-American. And looming over all forms of planetary life today is the temporally estranged unfolding of climate change. To ask how mind relates to world now, how human relates to environment, is to recognise that the terms in which we inhabit the planet are changing, beyond all measure. We cannot understand the nature of the partitions that organise contemporary spatial relations without acknowledging, as Dipesh Chakrabarty puts it, that climate change has seen the failure of the boundary between culture and nature, the boundary upon which all our forms of enworlding rest. Eco-crisis, Chakrabarty writes, has 'breached' the 'wall' that we erected between human and nature, unsettling our Heideggerian capacity to build, dwell and think, and in the process, 'a fundamental assumption of Western (and now universal) political thought has come undone'.[16]

The boundaries that determine our relation to our bodies, to our local communities, to nation and continent and globe, have become, under these circumstances, difficult to read. And it is in relation to this contemporary experience of the bounds of life – of the 'end of the mind' and the 'edge of space' – that I propose to trace what I will here call a literary tradition of mere being. There is, I will argue, a group of writers, of whom Wallace Stevens is one, whose work over the course of the last century or so has been dedicated to excavating the liminal place where mind meets with world, where imagination meets with reality, in order to develop a means of thinking the limit-boundary itself, of understanding how such world-making, mind-making limits shape all forms of shared experience.

This poetic impulse towards an encounter with mere being, in Stevens and in the tradition I am proposing more broadly, appears in the first instance to be a subtractive one, one which leads to and derives from a form of imaginative contraction. Stevens approaches the condition of mere being by removing all that is extraneous or additional to being, so we might catch a glimpse of what being is like when it is 'clear of everything'. To understand the limit, this thinking goes, to work our way towards a beginning or an ending, towards the end of the mind or the edge of space, it is necessary to undertake this sandpapering away, this removal of particularity so that we can gain some kind of access to the undifferentiated stuff, 'without human meaning', of which mere being is made – the plastic stuff of unspeciated life that underlies, precedes and survives the imposition of those boundaries and limits which we see hardening in our own time.

Stevens undertakes this act of poetic clearing, and one can see, too, that a version of this clearing, subtracting work can be found in a strain of imaginative work stretching back through the first decades of the twentieth century and the last decades of the nineteenth. For all their differences, for example, it is hard not to discern a common mere ground shared by Stevens and Virginia Woolf, a compulsion both writers share to expose the underside of being. Throughout her work Woolf returns to the image and the idea of a naked, prehistorical ground, a bare space, devoid of human culture, upon which cultural forms rest or accrete themselves. This space emerges in the early novel *Night and Day*, when Katherine Hilbery tries to see beneath the 'thick texture of her life' to what she calls an 'empty space', an 'empty land where all this petty intercourse of men and women, this life made up of the dense crossings and entanglements of men and women, had no existence whatever'.[17] It appears early in Woolf's writing, and then re-emerges, in every novel she writes – appearing, for example, in *Mrs Dalloway* when the narrator tries to see back 'through all ages', to 'when the pavement was grass, when it was swamp, through the age of tusk and mammoth, through the age of silent sunrise'.[18] Woolf's narrator looks to prehistoric, deculturated spaces, and she imagines, living in this denuded ground, a kind of bare, unspeciated being, a kind of minimal existence. In *Mrs Dalloway*, this being takes the form of a figure encountered by Peter Walsh and by Rezia Warren-Smith, as they both take their separate walks through Regent's Park. The figure is a homeless woman perhaps, but also a sexless and inanimate creature, who appears to them to be like a 'funnel', like a 'rusty pump', like a 'wind-beaten tree' (p. 90). The woman sings a 'frail quivering' song, a sound that issues from her ancient body, from 'so rude a mouth, a mere hole in the earth' (p. 90), and the song that she sings is surely the song that Stevens hears at the edge and end of things. Her song is a 'frail quivering sound',

> a voice bubbling up without direction, vigour, beginning or end, running weakly and shrilly and with an absence of all human meaning into
> ee um fah um so
> foo swee too eem oo – (p. 89)

This is the song of mere being, sung by a 'voice of no age or sex, the voice of an ancient spring sprouting from the earth' (p. 89); a song sung by a being like a 'wind-beaten tree for ever barren of leaves which lets the sound run up and down its branches' (p. 90), as the 'wind moves slowly in the branches' of Stevens's palm at the end of the mind, stirring the dangled feathers of a fire fangled bird. Woolf, like Stevens, makes this song audible not by translating it, not by lending it the human meaning that it lacks, but by removing the languages and forms that would cover it up, that would convert it into meaning by destroying its absence of meaning. *Mrs Dalloway* seeks to approach this place, this mere hole in the earth, by allowing the bonds which tie us to our subject positions, which equate us with our singular voces, to come undone. And this is the motion, the subtractive, untying impulse, that Samuel Beckett finds in Proust, and that he sees as the principle of his own mereward aesthetic. 'Man', Beckett writes, quoting Proust, 'is the creature who cannot come forth from himself';[19] and if we are to be true to this failure to come forth, Beckett suggests, we need an art that can gain access to our minimal, withdrawn being. 'The only fertile research', Beckett writes, 'is excavatory, immersive, a contraction of the spirit, a descent'. 'The artist is active', he says 'but negatively, shrinking from the nullity of extracircumferential phenomena, drawn in to the core of the eddy'.[20]

The artist of mere being is a contractive artist, one who scrapes away, reduces, minimises. The writers of the mere look to the minima, the barest conditions of being, and in so doing they work in the spirit of a philosophical tradition that finds, differently inflected, something approaching a substrate to life, which is not itself conscious being, but which underlies and enables it. This is the mere being that we find in the animals that rest unconsciously in themselves in Descartes ('animals', Descartes writes, 'have no mental powers whatsoever' as 'it is nature which acts in them').[21] It is the naked being we find in Freud's psychoanalysis, where structures of consciousness and forms of 'civilization' are laid over what Freud calls our 'feeble animal organism', our poor 'inch of nature'.[22] We find it in

Jung, when he declares that the 'sole purpose of human existence' is to transcend our bare animal natures, to 'kindle a light in the darkness of mere being'.[23] We find it in Heidegger, when he defines the animal as a being which 'merely has life', a phrase (rendered in Heidegger's German as 'einem Nur-Lebenden') which Derrida glosses as 'that which is living but no more, life in its pure and simple state'.[24] We find it in Agamben when he opposes 'political existence' to 'bare life' (declaring that 'there is politics because man is the living being who, in language, separates and opposes himself to his own bare life').[25]

The mere literary tradition I am tracing here resonates with this philosophy of mere life. But if this is the case, if Beckett and Stevens and Proust and Woolf are all in their various ways intent on unearthing some bare substructure that lies beneath what Beckett calls the 'mere shifting superficies' of being, it is my central proposal in this essay that the mere, as these writers conceive it, is not simply negative, subtractive, reductive.[26] Mereness is not an effect of shrinkage, or not only an effect of shrinkage, but the discovery of a kind of expansion that is won from contraction, a fullness of being that is amalgamated with an emptiness, in an amalgam that allows and requires its own understanding of limits, of boundaries, of the edge of space and mind. To understand the mere, as its possibility glimmers in these writers, one has to free oneself from a Cartesian or an Agambenian conception of human life as grounded on or overlying some fundamental animal or thingly life, to see instead a form of mere being which is interwoven with a fully realised life, part of its make-up, entwined with it rather than separable from it.[27]

This doubleness, this interweaving of subtraction and addition, is there, already, in the word itself, the word 'mere' – one of the group of words that fascinate Freud in his essay 'The Antithetical meaning of Primal Words'. 'Mere' is one of those antithetical words, in Freud's terms, 'that develops in ambivalence until it coincides with its opposite'.[28] In its earlier, now obsolete sense, 'mere' designates both purity – an unadulterated, unmixed state – and absoluteness, a form of perfect completion. This is the meaning captured in definition 4 in the *OED*, with a last recorded usage by Thomas de Quincey in 1838: 'That is what it is in the full sense of the term qualified'. This is mereness as a total coincidence of a thing with itself, in which the mere thing is 'nothing short' of itself, is 'perfect, absolute, sheer'. Consider the line in *Hamlet*, as Hamlet contemplates self-slaughter, a self-annihilation in which his flesh might 'melt, / Thaw, and resolve itself into a dew'.[29] How weary he is, he thinks, how stale, and flat, and unprofitable are the uses of the world to him:

> Fie on't, ah fie, fie! 'Tis an unweeded garden
> That grows to seed; things rank and gross in nature
> Possess it merely.[30]

This is mereness as absolute possession – here as the overwhelming of the world by things that are rank and gross in nature. But as the word evolves, as it develops in ambivalence, it tilts towards an opposite kind of sense. This is a sense that is contained within the original concept of a thing being precisely what it is, but now coincidence with self is experienced not as fullness and completeness, but rather as paucity, as bareness. The mere thing, in definition 5 in the *OED*, is one that has 'no greater extent, range, value, power, or importance than the designation implies'. The mere thing is 'barely or only what it is said to be'. This is the sense that is primary in Stevens's 'Of Mere Being' and that drives the contractive, subtractive movement in Stevens, in Woolf, in Beckett, toward some bare place that is just what it is, devoid of human meaning – the place that Beckett conceives in his minimal late work *Imagination Dead Imagine*. The merest place we can imagine is the place that we imagine when the imagination is dead – for Stevens a bird singing an unintelligible song in an empty plain, for Beckett two white bodies lying on a white ground, trembling on the brink of disappearance, 'all white in the whiteness'.[31]

II

The word mere itself, the mere word, touches on the condition I am seeking to characterise here, the condition of mere being, in which the possibility of a complete becoming is closely bound up with the work of subtraction, of denudation. The literary tradition I am proposing is one which finds in minima the intuition of a kind of maxima, one whose possibility lies beyond the limits of thinking as they are available to us now, or as they fetter us now. This is a mode of imagining whose capacity to capture a world lies not in addition, not in some urge towards comprehensiveness, but in the discovery of the full as a latent property of the empty, an imagining which finds a rich, shared being rising, beyond the last thought, from the contraction of things to their mere selves.

It is perhaps for this reason – that mereness consists of the amalgamation of the large with the small – that writers of the mere do not always or necessarily write slim or minimal works. Indeed, the writer who I will offer as an originator of the tradition I am proposing here might strike us as hardly, barely, mere at all, but rather somewhat bloated, somewhat protracted and prolix, more Brobdingnag than Lilliput. Henry James – the writer who inaugurates the kind of literary thinking I am tracing here – might not strike us immediately as a poet of the mere. A Jamesian sentence can sometimes feel that it might never end, that it defeats the capacity of the reading mind to contain or parse it, to hem it in. A Jamesian sentence can expand and expand, so its circumference moves beyond the reach of its own centre, like Yeats's falcon flying beyond the call of the falconer. But even if this is so, it is clear, I suspect, to most close readers of James that his work is concerned, at its heart, with the mere, the mere as the activating principle of his thinking – what he calls, in his preface to his 1899 novel *The Awkward Age*, the '*idée-mère*' (the mere idea, the mother of all ideas).[32] It is a constitutive feature of his imagination, James writes in that same preface, that his tendency towards proliferation is bound, in peculiar and fundamental ways, to his commitment to the slight, the underdeveloped. The bulky narrative of *The Awkward Age*, he writes, in presenting 'so considerable a mass' in relation to 'the germ sunk in it', is exemplary of the 'quite incalculable tendency of a mere grain of subject-matter to expand and develop and cover the ground' (p. 3). The extensive is peculiarly coterminous, in James's writing, with the restricted, as his oeuvre is composed, he writes, of 'long stories that had thoroughly meant to be short', and of 'short subjects that had underhandedly plotted to be long' (p. 4). As Vanderbank says, at a critical in *The Awkward Age*, mereness comes, in James, to denote the difficult junction between expansion and contraction, addition and subtraction: 'Mere', Vanderbank says. 'Mere, mere, mere. But perhaps it's exactly the mere that has made us range so wide' (p. 186).[33]

One can see an early exploration of this contradictory force at work in James's thinking, in his 1881 novel *The Portrait of a Lady*, James's first truly Jamesian novel. In the preface James wrote to this early novel late in his life he remarks that he composed his portrait of Isabel Archer with the express intention of making a monument out of her mereness. *Portrait*, he writes, is a 'square and spacious house' that is built around the 'single small corner-stone' of Isabel's quietly striving self.[34] His challenge, he recalls, was how to make a novelistic edifice that could rest, in all its spaciousness, on something so slight as Isabel's fine mind, what he calls her 'mere still lucidity' (p. 639), the 'mere slim shade' of her intelligence (p. 635). How, he asks, does the novelist endow the mere movement of mind with the 'high attributes of a Subject' (p. 634)? An immediate answer to this question, and one which sits quite comfortably with our received conception of what it is that novels do, is that James makes the movement of mind substantial and aesthetically arresting by producing a narrative apparatus which allows us to see deeply into what James calls the 'recesses' of consciousness, and so to make of the fleeting, disappearing turns of insolid thought something lasting, well-proportioned, solid (p. 55). It is the vocation of the novelist and of his or her close reader to see below what the narrator of James's story *In the Cage* calls the 'mere surface', and to hear the narrative harmonies that lie below what the narrator of *The Jolly Corner* calls the 'mere surface sound'.[35] The novel form, James writes, as he has inherited it from his predecessor and major influence George Eliot, is an apparatus designed to contain – within a mere envelope, beneath a mere surface – the unsounded depths of being in which, as James puts it, 'strange silent subjects float'.[36] 'Could there be', George Eliot's narrator asks of her character Gwendolen Harleth in *Daniel Deronda*, 'a slenderer, more insignificant thread in human history than this consciousness of a girl, busy with her small inferences of the way in which she could make her life pleasant?'.[37] The life of her female protagonists is slight, Eliot suggests, consisting, as she puts it most famously in *Middlemarch*, of 'unhistoric acts'.[38] The life that she consecrates in her depiction of Gwendolen Harleth, of Dorothea Brooke, is, she writes, a 'hidden life'[39] – but it is her conviction that it is this hidden life, contained and preserved in the novel form, that is the secret motor of the 'mighty drama' of those acts that we might more readily deem historical, of that 'good for which men are enduring and fighting'.[40] 'In these delicate vessels', she writes, in these slight personalities, preserved in prose, 'is borne onward through the ages the treasure of human affections'.[41] When James makes an aesthetic edifice of Isabel Archer's mere still lucidity, it is to this Eliotian conception of containment, of the hoarding of a deep hidden life within a slim container, that he turns. It is wonderful he writes, 'how absolutely, how inordinately, the Isabel Archers, and even much smaller fry, insist on mattering'. 'George Eliot has admirably noted it', he goes on, regrettably misquoting from *Daniel Deronda*: 'In these frail vessels is borne onward through the ages the treasure of human affection'.[42]

Portrait stores Isabel's mere intelligence inside its well-made architectural form, and it is the central task of James's novel to examine this conjunction, between a mind and its container, between the mere surface and the hidden depth, as it mutates under the pressure of Jamesian style. Accordingly, this junction itself, this passage between surface and depth, the revealed and the hidden, is materialised, early in the novel, in an appropriately architectural metaphor that provides the novel with one of its structuring devices. This metaphorical junction first appears when Isabel is at her grandmother's house in Albany, where she is visited by Mrs

Touchett – the wealthy aunt who takes Isabel under her wing, and removes her to Europe, thus setting the plot of the novel in motion. Mrs Touchett finds Isabel reading a book in a 'mysterious apartment' of the house 'which was called, traditionally, no one knew why, the office' (p. 24). This office sits on a peculiar faultline that runs through the novel – and that runs, as I shall argue, through Henry James's oeuvre as a whole. The house in Albany has the architectural oddity of being originally two houses that have been knocked into one, 'the party-wall having been removed and the rooms placed in communication'. The houses are connected internally by a 'sort of arched passage' (p. 23), but from the outside the house still appears to be two separate dwellings. 'There were two entrances', the narrator says, 'one of which had long been out of use, but had never been removed. They were exactly alike – large white doors, with an arched frame and wide sidelights' (p. 23). The office in which Mrs Touchett first encounters Isabel – the room in which Isabel has spent her childhood reading and thinking, the room in which, the narrator says, the 'foundation of her knowledge was really laid' (p. 25) – is shaped by its lying in some disappearing space between the two houses, which are now one. 'The place owed much of its mysterious melancholy' the narrator says,

> to the fact that it was properly entered from the second door of the house, the door that had been condemned [....]. She knew that this silent, motionless portal opened into the street; if the side-lights had not been filled with green paper, she might have looked out upon the little brown stoop and the well-worn brick pavement. But she had no wish to look out, for this would have interfered with her theory that there was a strange, unseen place on the other side – a place which became, to the child's imagination, according to its different moods, a region of delight or terror. (p. 25)

This door does not open onto the Albany street – Isabel had 'never opened the bolted door nor removed the green paper from its side-lights; she had never assured herself that the vulgar street lay beyond' (p. 25) – but looks instead onto a withdrawn space that is the locus in this novel of imaginative possibility, the place beneath the surface in which Isabel's mere still lucidity is stored. The novel seeks to preserve this withdrawn space – and it does so partly by modelling Isabel's character on its architectural principles. Isabel herself is figured as a single dwelling made of two houses, with the party wall removed (the 'arched passage' between the houses, the 'arched frame' of the condemned door, catching an echo of Isabel's maiden name). The strange, vague place on the other side of the condemned door doubles as what the narrator calls the 'depths' of Isabel's 'nature'. 'The depths of her nature', he says, 'were a very out of the way place, between which and the surface communication was interrupted by a dozen capricious forces' (p. 35). In this unseen place within her, we are told, there lies a 'great fund of life' (p. 35), squirrelled away, removed from circulation, and it is the impassioned calling of the novel to find a means of establishing some channel or passage that might allow surface and depth to come into communication with one another, that might allow Isabel (and James's novel) to draw on some of that fund of life that she has within her.

The plot of the novel is driven by this attempt, by Isabel's striving at once to preserve her hoard of inner life, and to find a means of spending it, of drawing on it both as a form of self-communion, and in order to share it with others, or with a loved other. The problem that impels the narrative is Isabel's reluctance to marry, despite receiving a brace of marriage proposals early in the novel from eligible men captivated by her intelligent beauty. 'I like my liberty too much', she says to the ardent men who propose to her – the tirelessly erect Caspar Goodwood, the gallant Englishman Lord Warburton. 'I don't wish to be a mere sheep in the flock; I wish to choose my fate and know something of human affairs'. 'If there is a thing in the world that I am fond of', she says, 'it is my personal independence'. Isabel has a sense of responsibility to the fund of life that is furled within her, a commitment that makes her easily proof against any temptation to marry for money, despite a lack if not of intellectual then of pecuniary funds. But even as this is so, it is the central contradiction in her character that her love of liberty coincides with a powerful desire to give that liberty away. 'Deep in her soul', the narrator says, '– it was the deepest thing there – lay a belief that if a certain light should dawn, she could give herself completely'. It is the tragedy of the novel that the character who loves Isabel perhaps most truly – her cousin, Ralph Touchett – in seeking to help her to preserve her liberty, her unspent selfhood, contrives, unknowingly, to help her to squander it. Ralph guards Isabel's fund of life almost as jealously as Isabel herself, and so comes to the decision to divide his inheritance from his fantastically wealthy father equally between them. Ralph assumes that money will allow Isabel to maintain her intellectual independence, or as he puts it to 'gratify her imagination' (p. 192) (as a means, he admits, of gratifying his own, of sustaining his own imaginative investment in her). 'If she has an easy income', he reasons, 'she will never have to marry for a support'. He gives her the gift of great wealth so that she can preserve her liberty; but the devastating irony of the novel is that this very gift exposes Isabel to the greed of the other man who comes closest to her – the cruel and callous art collector Gilbert Osmond. When the light dawns in which Isabel comes to give herself away, she chooses to give herself to Osmond, an unfeeling man who prizes her only as a commodity, a living artwork in which a capital fund is invested. It is Ralph's money that increases Isabel's value to Osmond, and so in increasing her capital worth, he conspires inadvertently in her spiritual bankruptcy.

   The novel traces these relations between Isabel, Ralph and Osmond, as they turn around the play between saving and squandering, between capital funds and a fund of spiritual life; and at each critical juncture, at each moment when she finds her inner life touching closely on theirs, the narrative registers something like an after image of that space that lies on the other side of the condemned door in Isabel's Albany house. When Osmond announces that 'I find I am in love with you', that 'I am thoroughly in love with you' (p. 325), Isabel feels herself to be standing at a junction, across which she can discern the outlines of a life shared with Osmond. As she looks towards that future, she looks through a version of the side lights of that Albany door, into the strange unseen space that lies beyond it. At this threshold, at this edge of space and of mind, the narrator says, her 'imagination halted'. 'Her imagination stopped, as I say; there was a vast vague space it could not cross – a dusky, uncertain tract which looked ambiguous, and even slightly treacherous, like a moorland seen in the winter twilight' (p. 328). Then, towards the end of the novel, as Isabel sits at Ralph's deathbed, she looks across this same tract, this same twilit region. She finds Ralph lying asleep, on a kind of open threshold between life and death. 'He might have passed away while she looked at him', the narrator says. 'He was already the figure and pattern of death' (p. 604); he has already resolved himself into a dew, has already become a countryman of all the bones in the world. He seems already to be in the region of death, a 'mere lattice of bones' (p. 604); but then he 'opened his eyes to greet her', and Isabel feels that she is looking deep into that death, that vague unseen space on the other side of a door, of a silent, motionless portal. He opened his eyes, and Isabel thinks that 'it was as if she were looking into immeasurable space' (p. 605), so that when he spoke 'his voice seemed to come from a distance' (p. 605). His voice, his eyes, are far away, belonging to that 'strange, unseen place on the other side'; but the seam that opens at this point in the novel brings that far space into an intense proximity with a nearness, a nearness that dawns as Isabel's mereness, the mere shade of her intelligence, flows into Ralph's, Ralph's mere, deathly lattice-work. They find themselves joined at the edges of their mere being, at the naked edge of eye and ear. 'He lay with his face turned towards Isabel, and his large unwinking eyes open into her own' (p. 605). 'His far-away voice was close to her ear' (p. 606).

Portrait turns, as I say, around this junction, the junction that we see in the Albany house at the opening of the novel, the junction and the passage between a mere surface and a behind, a below, a beyond. And the architectural form that James crafts here, in 1881, works as a foundation upon which his subsequent novels are laid. The central concerns of his fiction – how do we meet ourselves and each other across the barriers that are intrinsic to all forms of relational encounter; how does the distribution of capital and of social power, what one of James's late narrators calls the 'mere gross generalisation of wealth and force', work with and against such barriers – all gather around it.[43] It is there in *What Maisie Knew* (1897), as Maisie's slight being – her 'light little brain', her 'light vessel of consciousness' – sits at the tectonic faultline at which those who vie for custody of her meet.[44] 'Through the mere fact of presence', James writes in his preface to *What Maisie Knew*, Maisie, a child in the eye of an adult storm, acts as a junction, a party wall, 'bringing people together who would be at least more correctly separate; keeping people separate who would be at least more correctly together'.[45] It is there in *The Wings of the Dove* (1902), as Merton Densher, Kate Croy and Milly Theale balance capital funds against a fund of life, searching for an economy that could harmonise the novel's cross currents of wealth and of love. Densher and Kate are secretly engaged but too poor to marry; Milly Theale, dying of an unspecified illness, is wealthy, and in love with Densher. Is there a way of exploiting this pregnant situation, of employing Milly as a kind of arched passage that might bring Densher and Kate together, to secure them in what they call, throughout, 'our being as we are'?[46] When Milly dies, when, as Kate and Densher put it, she 'turns her face to the wall', can that wall, that dead end, become a kind of passageway, enabling a redirected flow of capital and of love?[47] It is there in *The Golden Bowl* (1904), as the novel traces the intensely intricate relations between Adam Verver and his daughter Maggie, and their respective spouses, Charlotte and Prince Amerigo. The four-way relations between them are all determined by Adam Verver's boundless wealth, against the flow of which runs a number of interweaving countercurrents. Verver purchases Prince Amerigo, as an ornate old-world gift for his American daughter Maggie; for the sake of symmetry, he then purchases the beautiful American Charlotte Stant (an old friend of his daughter's) to act as his own wife. The symmetry of the conjugal relations thus set up, though, is disturbed by the relations which run against its grain. Verver's marriage to Charlotte is a ploy, one suspects, that allows Adam to sustain the most important relationship in his life, that with his daughter Maggie. Maggie's relation, as stepdaughter, to Charlotte is shadowed by their prior relation as childhood friends. And the relations between the Ververs and their spouses are deranged most violently by the bond that exists between Amerigo and Charlotte – a love affair which precedes each of their marriages to a Verver, and which is then rekindled when they enter into their new relation as in-laws. As the novel sets up this matrix of financial, familial and erotic relations, it looks, again, to a kind of architecture that might allow for forms of conjunction, for passages along which redirected energies might flow. The lives that the four share, the narrator says, 'took on finally the likeness of some spacious central chamber in a haunted house, a great overarched and overglazed rotunda where gaiety might reign, but the door of which opened into sinister circular passages'.[48]

Portrait lays the foundations for this tectonics of personal relations, this meeting between one person and another, and between the surface of being and its depths. But if this is so, and if the terms in which *Portrait* conducts this analysis of relationality owe a clear debt to the nineteenth-century novel of interiority, it is my central argument here that James's fiction constitutes a radical rewiring of the relation between aesthetic surface and psychological depth, and that this rewiring is *inseparable* from his thinking of mereness, of mere being. His negotiation of this relation, in *Portrait*, is characterised by a hesitant and slow shift in the structure of realism, in which the mechanics of fictional self-containment – the aesthetic procedures which allow us to imagine ourselves as bounded within our own being – undergoes a transformation. The boundary line that hems being in, the glass case that contains within it, 'filled to the brim', the 'wine of consciousness', becomes, accordingly, James's central preoccupation.[49] He develops a fascination, in *Portrait*, with the dividing principle that metes being out – that asserts and organises the forms in which we compartmentalise ourselves – that is to last to the end of his writing career. At this early point, as I say, his attention to this principle still bears the stamp of the realism that he inherits from Eliot and from Dickens. The wall, here, is still the barrier to be overcome, in order to realise an investment in psychological depth. The political, aesthetic, libidinal desire of *Portrait* is still to find a way of passing through such walls, as the party wall is removed in the Albany house to bring discrete rooms into communication, and as the narrative strives to plumb the rich depths of Isabel's nature which capricious forces contrive to hide beneath her mere surface. But even if this is so, it is the case too that the wall itself, the partition, begins here to take on its own life, a life which is merged with the life of James's art. What begins to emerge in *Portrait*, and what grows with a strange insistence over the course of James's fiction, is the recognition that depth does not lie beneath surface, beneath the mere shifting superficies, but is a function of it. What *Portrait* constitutes, above all, is the hesitant origins of the Jamesian recognition that the mere surface is the province of depth, not its antithesis. The power of the closing deathbed scene, as Isabel finds herself drawn into an intense proximity with Ralph, their eyes in each other's eyes, arises from its discovery that mereness – the mere lattice of bones, the mere aesthetic surface – is not the opposite of the immeasurable, or not simply the opposite, but also a means of bringing the slight into contact with the vast, here into contact with there, of making the far-away voice press against the very skin of the ear. The wall, the dividing principle, the barrier, the tympanum, this is the obstacle to be overcome; but it is also, James starts to intuit at this early stage in the development of his style, the skin of the artwork itself, the mere living integument that does not divide but joins, registering in its surface the fine vibrations of difference that it overcomes.

It is for this reason that the figure of the wall emerges repeatedly in James's broader reflections on the capacity of the novel to imagine new forms of life, new forms of being. The artwork succeeds, James suggests both in his criticism and in his fiction, when it brings the wall to life, when it gives animation to the mere shifting superficies of the canvas or the page; the artwork fails when it is brought up against the dead wall, the wall untouched, untransfigured by life (the dead wall, perhaps, that James finds in Melville, and in Bartleby's 'dead wall revery').[50] This is what Isabel finds when the vague space of open possibility she divines on the other side of her Albany door yields to the cold reality of her marriage to Osmond. In her long night-time reflection on the state of her life and her marriage at the heart of the novel, she comes to the realisation that the 'infinite vista of a multiplied life' had been restricted to a 'narrow alley, with a dead wall at the end' (p. 447). This is the dead wall that appears in *The Aspern Papers* – 'you may push on through a breach', the narrator says, 'but you can't batter down a dead wall'.[51] It appears in James's earlier essay 'The Art of fiction', where he writes that an art which is deaf to the 'strange irregular rhythm of life' is one which 'leads us straight up to a dead wall'.[52] And it appears again much later in James's belated preface to *Portrait of a Lady*, where it is tied to the concept of the mere, as he makes his famous observation that the 'house of fiction' has 'not one window, but a million'. 'They are but windows', he writes, 'mere holes in a dead wall, disconnected, perched aloft; they are not hinged doors opening straight on life' (p. 632). The task for the artist, James suggests, is to make the mere wall itself, the mere window, a living conduit, like the living wall in Shakespeare's *A Midsummer Night's Dream*[53] – one which collapses the spaces and people it divides into each other, one whose very mereness allows for such collapse, such weightless tumbling of one thing onto another, of outside into inside, of back into face, of the dead into the living.

In *Portrait*, we can see the beginnings of this process, the beginnings of a form of expression which seeks to overcome the separation between the surface of the text and the depths that lie beneath the cover. When Isabel Archer's name is reflected in the architecture of the Albany house, in the arch of the passage, in the arch of the door frame, we see the faintest of indications that the depths of her nature are entering into a kind of conjunction with the revealed surface of the text itself, the house of fiction with its windows and doors. This is a process that happens time and again in James's work, as his character names become ensnarled in the thought contours of his novels (an entanglement that we see, too, when Isabel's mere lucidity is reflected in the name of her antagonist Madame Merle). The process of reference becomes bound up with that which is referred to, names with that which is named, as James starts, here, to adapt and transform the model of fiction as vessel that he inherits from Eliot. Here in *Portrait* we can see that the prose itself is seeking to reveal something of its structure, its mere lattice work of its bones, in order to draw depths into contiguity with surfaces, as if the structure itself is starting to rise to the surface, as if the internal scaffolding of the prose is starting here to uncover itself (as Beckett says of Proust that the 'scaffolding of his structure is revealed' at the close of *A la recherche*).[54] This process is partly what Leo Bersani has in mind when he writes that James's fiction 'is remarkably resistant to an interest in psychological depth'.[55] James demonstrates, Bersani writes, that 'the surfaces of our thought don't merely cover up the depths behind thought and speech'. Instead, James 'works towards a richly superficial art in which hidden depths would never ironically undermine the lives inspired by his own and his characters' "mere" ingenuities of design'.[56] We can see these mere ingenuities of design playing in the surface patterns of *Portrait*, interrupting the mode of mimetic reference to a world beyond the text which James inherits. And then, as James's work evolves, as his style develops, we see this structure becoming ever more prominent, so the mere architecture of the text starts to dominate, to shoulder aside everything extrinsic to it, as, in Sharon Cameron's terms, 'what is being contemplated by consciousness is something like itself'.[57] We start to see not an imagined world, containing imagined people, but the living structure of the imagination itself, what Lisa Robertson has recently theorised, in a different context, as a poetics of scaffolding. Scaffolding, Robertson writes, reveals to us how a structure works while allowing that structure to remain discomposed, keeping open channels between the spaces it demarcates. Scaffolding 'explains what a wall is without being a wall'. It crafts an 'inhabitable surface' that is 'neither inside nor outside'. It 'rhythmically exposes the vulnerability of the surface by subtracting solidity from form to make something temporarily animate'.[58] As the internal scaffolding rises to the surface in James, we start to see the formal oppositions that support his thinking and his imagining. We see the relation between the mere and the immense or unmeasured, that relation that comes to a climax as Isabel sits at Ralph's bedside; and we see too a host of other oppositions, organised around that wall that is not a wall, that mere open surface, that faultline that runs through James's fiction. We see not an imagined landscape, but a narrative architecture composed of the collapsed opposition between the inside and the outside, between the living and the dead, between the turned and the straight, between the back and the face, a set of oppositions that, once we are sensitised to them, we recognise as the very scaffolding of James's art.

We can see this structure rising as his work and his style evolve, so that by the time of the later work, *The Wings of the Dove*, *The Golden Bowl*, *The Jolly Corner*, this structure is almost all there is, this set of naked oppositions that continually threaten to demonstrate their identity. The dead wall of *Portrait* and of *The Aspern Papers* returns in *The Golden Bowl*, where its texture is now revealed to us, as it sits on that disappearing junction between one person and anther, between one place and another. Prince Amerigo encounters it in all its deadness, as he prepares to consummate his affair with Charlotte midway through the novel, as they set off on their outing to Gloucester. He tries to think his way into their coming relation, but, the 'result' of his speculation, he acknowledges, 'was too often to be confronted with a mere dead wall' (p. 287). The dead wall against which Amerigo bruises himself here is recreated in the novel's form, which cannot accommodate Amerigo and Charlotte's relation – an erotic bond which remains shrouded in a behind or a below. As Charlotte says to Amerigo in the novel's primal scene – in which the pair visit the shop where Maggie will later buy the golden bowl of the title, as a present for her father – what binds them lies beyond the reach of any form of reference. Perhaps, Amerigo says, he might buy Charlotte something as a 'small ricordo' of their attachment to each other. But she declines, telling him that 'A ricordo from you – from you to me – is a ricordo of nothing. It has no reference' (p. 104). Their relation achieves no consummation in the novel itself, remining instead obscene, offstage. It is rather in the midst of a meeting between Verver and his daughter (her name, Maggie

Verver, veering anagrammatically on the verge of the mere) that the novel imagines a form of conjunction that can summon all of the relations that the narrative maps into a kind of intense presence. At a critical moment in the novel, this conjunction takes the form of a living wall, a wall, in Robertson's sense, that is not a wall, a wall that does not separate but that unites. The narrative approaches, in this meeting between father and daughter, a region in which the auxiliary appurtenances of life are scraped away, and we see only this thin wall, this naked sheet of being, beyond the last thought, exposed to the air. 'This was the moment', the narrator says, as Maggie and Adam confront the spectre of their spouses' infidelity:

> This was the moment [...] in which it decidedly *most* hung by a hair that their thin wall might be pierced by the lightest wrong touch. It shook between them, this transparency, with their very breath; it was an exquisite tissue, but stretched on a frame, and would give way the next instant if either of them so much as breathed too hard.

The Golden Bowl is written to approach this exquisite tissue, to *be* this exquisite tissue. This is the tissue, the taut, stretched ear drum, that constitutes the mere ground of shared being. This moment reprises the critical point in *The Wings of the Dove,* when Milly Theale is brought face to face with the knowledge of her illness, from which she is separated by 'so thin a partition' (p. 196); in both moments the partition does not simply divide – does not divide Milly from her death, or Verver from his daughter, or Verver and Maggie from their spouses; rather it conjures an almost unthinkable proximity, in which these fields of consciousness are brought onto the same plane, a plane composed of what Amerigo calls a 'mere immensity', in which the oppositions between the mere and the immense, between the living and the dead, collapse into identity.

It is in the late work *The Jolly Corner* that this coming together, this fusing of difference on the mere plane of the work's surface, reaches its most concentrated expression – one which catches a last echo of that arched passage that James first intuits in the Albany junction at which two houses become one. Here, the compression of two dwellings into a single field is more intense, as Isabel's party wall has dissolved, to become integrated into the vaulted form of the story itself. The protagonist, Spenser Brydon, returns to the New York mansion of his childhood, on the 'jolly corner' of the title, after his long sojourn in Europe. In this house, shuttered and deserted, Brydon imagines that he might come into contact with the version of himself who lived there as a child, and who has led, he thinks, a parallel life, the American life that Brydon himself would have lived if he had not fled to become a European aesthete. The house contains, he imagines, a 'compartment of his mind never yet penetrated', and he stalks the rooms late at night trying to peer into this compartment, to catch a glimpse of that ghost of himself, the ghostly possibility of the imagination itself. He feels this other self, not buried beneath a veil, not hidden from him, but vibrating on the mere surface, etched into the mere being of the house itself,

> the mere sight of the walls, mere shape of the rooms, mere sound of the floors, mere feel, in his hand, of the old silver-plated knobs of the mahogany doors, which suggested the pressure of the palms of the dead. (p. 347)

He searches, night after night, for the person he feels to be contained in the overarched chamber of the house; and on the night that he succeeds in chasing this ghost down, in coming face to face with himself – or a powerfully estranged version of himself, 'disconnected from any possibility' – it is by the light of Isabel's shaded sidelights that the encounter takes place. He is standing in the twilit vestibule, looking to the door of the house that looks in turn out on to the vulgar street. The 'sidelights and the high fantracery of the entrance were glimmering straight into the hall' (p. 363), casting a light over the 'uncertain tract' at which Isabel's 'imagination stopped'. The 'thin admitted dawn', the narrator says, 'glimmering archwise over the whole outer door' makes a 'semicircular margin' in the 'vague darkness' of the hall, a 'penumbra, dense and dark' which is the 'virtual screen of a figure' – the alter ego for which Brydon has been hunting (p. 363). It is by this archwise light that Brydon – James's own alter ego, one feels – reaches towards a naked conjunction with self. This is a vibrating, disconnected self, one that is not contained in a frail vessel, or a golden bowl, but fashioned instead from the mere walls, the mere floors, the mere windows of the house of fiction.

III

It is James's capacity to fashion this coming together of surface and depth – of near and far, here and there – through his singular encounter with literary mereness, that places him at the foundation of the mere tradition I am proposing here.

In conducting this refashioning of the novel imagination in this way, it can appear that James participates in what we might think of as a weakening of the novel's purchase on reality, a kind of mereing of the form. When T. S. Eliot makes his pompous and inflated assertion in 1923 that the novel died somewhere near the beginning of the twentieth century – that the 'novel will no longer serve' – he is responding to a perception that James at once mastered the form, and completed it, exhausted it. 'The novel ended' Eliot writes, 'with Flaubert and James'.[59] James's development of the novel into an artform that is not a container for life but that is somehow life itself (what he calls in 'The Art of Fiction' a direct 'impression of life', and in a 1915 letter to H. G. Wells an 'extension of life') produces at once a fullness and an emptiness – that combination of the full and the empty that we can see at work in the concept of the mere.[60] It is a version of this problem that Sianne Ngai has elaborated in her essay on James in her 2020 book *Theory of the Gimmick*. Ngai reads in James's oeuvre a collapse of opposites into identity that has a family resemblance to that which I have been tracing here – the conjunction of the mere and the immeasurable, of deficit and excess. It is this fugitive identity of apparent oppositions that she sees as the secret principle of James's writing – a principle, too, that she identifies as the underlying logic both of the gimmick, and of capitalism as a whole. James's fiction is driven by what Ngai calls the 'contiguity of hyperbole and minimalism', which mirrors the tendency of the gimmick, in her reading, to do at once too much and too little, to do too much work and not enough.[61] Because, she writes, 'in the interior of the gimmick everything and nothing become strangely interchangeable' (p. 277), so James's overcoming of the opposition between abundance and scarcity maps perfectly on to the empty form of the capitalist gimmick. 'In showing how extravagance and impoverishment, hyperbole and austerity, and even "everything" and "nothing" are contiguous phenomena, James's "same secret principle" points to the "moving contradiction" of "capital itself"' (p. 304).

According to this reading, James's fiction is a symptom of the corrosive effects of capital on our capacity to apprehend the real, yielding a form in which the gaining, the hoarding of a fund of life becomes, insistently, its loss, its squandering. The most concentrated moment in James's oeuvre in which everything and nothing come into the same frame (a moment which Ngai does not address) would seem by this light to enact a failure of literary representation, or at least its reduction (or elevation) to the status of the gimmick. The moment comes in a discussion between Merton Densher and Kate Croy, in which they jointly contemplate the meaning of 'everything'. 'Oh – everything!', Densher says, 'Everything's nothing'.[62] Everything is nothing in the interior of the gimmick (and nothing everything); but the mere tradition I am suggesting here, that has an origin in James's antinomies, suggests that the combination of the full and the empty that the mere allows does not quite give way either to the exhaustion of the form that Eliot sees in James, or to the moving contradictions of Ngai's capitalist gimmick. Mereness in James, his approach to a condition of mere being, brings him close to a conception of 'everything' that looks beyond Ngai's gimmickry, and that suggests a radically new thinking of the boundary between the mere and the all, between the empty and the full, one which harbours the possibility of a shifted distribution of life, a different way of understanding the relation between being and the forms in which it is contained – what Marx calls the 'mere forms' assumed by capital.[63] 'Everything' in James comes to stand, repeatedly, and sometimes euphemistically, for sexual consummation, for the experience of intense erotic union between one person and another. Think of Densher arranging his secret liaison with Kate in his Rome flat: 'I'll do everything', he says to her.[64] Think of Amerigo, standing on the balcony at Matcham as he and Charlotte prepare to head off for their stolen afternoon in Gloucester. 'You shall have everything', he says to her.[65] Think of Madame de Vionnet confessing to Lambert Strether at the close of *The Ambassadors*, 'I want everything' ('Everything', Strether replies, 'Ah that's too much [...] or too little!').[66] This everything is always tied to nothing, to the nothingness of intense, shrouded desire; but it also works towards some kind of borderless meeting, some joining on a tissue of being, that moves past the contradictions of capital, that seeks another way of thinking about the fund of life, another way of understanding how it is stored, or saved, or shared.

It is this form that James bequeaths to the mere writers that come after him – a form adapted to give that 'everything' expression, even if such expression comes at the cost of a certain kind of psychological depth, or of the collapse of a surface-depth model of being into something like Bersani's rich superficiality. James passes on to those who come after him a transfigured novel art, one whose weakening capacity to reproduce reality is also the hesitant growth of a new way of imagining being, a shifted mode of relationality. The transformations in the texture of the word surface that come about in James's work find themselves reflected not only in a mere modernism – in the mere mouth of Woolf's singing woman, or the mereness of Gertrude Stein's tender objects, or the mere being of Wallace Stevens's verse. They are extended and developed too in the strand of experimental, estranged realism that proliferates in the second half of the twentieth century, in Ann Quin, in Christine Brooke-Rose, Natalia Ginzburg and Ingeborg Bachman, and they are tested, perhaps to their limits, in Beckett's fiction, as it reaches from the thirties towards the turn of the millennium. It is Beckett's task, over the decades of the twentieth century, to radicalise the movement towards the mere, the bare, that is one outcome of the failure of the model of realism that James inherits from George Eliot. If James's writing, even in its rich abundance, works towards that thin wall of being we find in *The Golden Bowl*, that sheet of tissue, stretched on a frame, trembling in the slightest breeze, then Beckett's work begins there, begins at the bare threshold of life. All those bowls and containers that run through James's work, exquisite art objects, frail vessels that seek to contain being while revealing a different model of storage, a newly forged relation between the cup and wine; these are defunct from the beginning in Beckett's work, where they already demonstrate that our given apparatuses for containing life have become inoperable. 'The individual,' Beckett writes in 1931, at the outset of his writing career, 'is the seat of a constant process of decantation', but if this is so, the vessel cannot quite hold the contents.[67] 'The whisky', he writes, 'bears a grudge against the decanter'.[68] This is what Beckett's Molloy thinks to himself, as he lies in Lousse's garden, a way station on his interminable journey towards his mother (his *idée-mère*). 'Yes', Molloy says, 'there were times when I forgot not only who I was, but that I was, forgot to be. Then I was no longer that sealed jar to which I owed my being so well preserved, but a wall gave way and I filled with roots and tame stems'.[69] Beckett's work pares back and back, to get as close as one can to that wall, the wall that is not a wall, the porous boundary that lies between the inside and outside of being. It is that thin wall, that exquisite tissue, that is reached at the climax of Beckett's mid-century trilogy – the climax, in a sense, of his struggle with the novel form. 'Perhaps that's what I am', the unnamable narrator says:

> The thing that divides the world in two, on the one side the outside, on the other the inside, that can be as thin as foil, I'm neither one side nor the other, I'm in the middle, I'm the partition, I've two surfaces and no thickness, perhaps that's what I feel, myself vibrating, I'm the tympanum, on the one hand the mind, on the other the world, I don't belong to either.[70]

It is this exposed surface, this thin partition, this mere sheet of being, that is the plane upon which the mere writers of our time are required to work. Beckett's writing has brought us to the space of the limit itself, the limit that is hardening in our time, the limit between one place and another, between one person and anther, between the living and the dead. Writing for Beckett is a process of exposing that junction, a process that has brought us to what Beckett calls, in his very late work *Worstward Ho*, the 'meremost minimum'.[71] Mere writing now – in the unbearably exposed surfaces of J. M. Coetzee's late work, or the broken, partial fragments by writers such as Jenny Offill and Diane Williams – has to work with this emptying form, composed of two surfaces with no thickness. If there is a decanter for being now, then it is what Diane Williams calls, in the title of a 2016 story, a 'Mere Flask'.[72] We have only mere forms to work with, mere flasks; but if this is true, this is not because the form itself will no longer serve, or because the artwork has folded into the capitalist gimmick. It is because the structures of being themselves, the paradigms which have enabled us to occupy the world, to live within the container of ourselves, are also changing, beyond all recognition. Being itself, mere being, has become alienated from the political and material forms which have structured reality, making it difficult to inhabit ourselves, making it difficult to rationalise the relation between self and self, between self and world.

As Isabel sits by the bedside of the dying Ralph, it is tempting to think that she is seeing into the future, seeing through the shifting terrain of the novels that James is sill to write, and towards our own moment, at which the relation between mind and world has become so newly estranged, at which the wall, as Chakrabarty puts it, between the human and the inhuman has been breached. She is afforded a vision of the end of the mind that James summons to thought, an end of mind and edge of space in which everything is divined through its contiguity with nothing. 'Oh Ralph' she says, 'you have been everything!'. 'I would die myself, not to lose you'.[73] Her own death seems to Isabel to be not just the negation of life, but some route to its shared persistence, and Ralph's response catches that thought, and amplifies it. 'You won't lose me', Ralph replies, 'you will keep me' (p. 606). Underneath the realism of this scene, its pathos, is the dawning Jamesian recognition that fiction – mere fiction – harbours such junctions, such contiguities, between death and life, between squandering and salvaging, keeping and losing. The richly realised space of the death chamber, organised around a human conception of what it is to dwell, is inhabited here by this other form of life, this other structure of reality that does not obey a human imperative, and whose stirring disturbs the limits of our imaginative capacities. Isabel's willingness to die in order to live calls forward to Milly Theale's recognition that her life, too, runs at a strange angle to death. 'Since I've lived all these years as if I were dead', she says, 'I shall die, no doubt, as if I were alive'.[74] We can feel, as Ralph lies in his death chamber, as Milly turns her face to the wall, the rising of a mere form, another distribution of the living and the dead, that offers a way of seeing the world, a way of being as we are, that lies, still, beyond the last thought.

2021

PART III
On the Contemporary

CHAPTER 12

Imagining the Future in the British Novel

I will live in the Past, the Present, and the Future. The Spirits of all Three shall strive within me.

Charles Dickens, *A Christmas Carol*.[1]

How do we make pictures of the future, at a time when futurity itself is difficult to frame? How do we make pictures of a *national* future, at a time when the capacity to imagine the nation state as an organising category has come under quite intense pressure?

To address the question of the British novel now is to pose these questions – questions which have assumed a degree of urgency, as we head towards the third decade of the twenty-first century. This is a time at which the forces that have driven British culture and politics since the Thatcher Regan era are playing themselves out to a tired close – washing up on the bleak shore of Brexit. It is a time, too, at which we are required to look towards new political and imaginary formations, ones whose outlines now are difficult to discern.

To address the nature of this transition – this 'interregnum', in Antonio Gramsci's famous phrase, between the old and the new, in which a 'great variety of morbid symptoms' appear – I will begin by considering four interventions made by world leaders at key moments in recent British history.[2]

The first of these is perhaps the most famous, and reflects the national tone in Britain in the eighties, under Margaret Thatcher. 'And you know', Thatcher says in an interview with *Woman's Own* in 1987, 'there's no such thing as society. There are individual men and women and there are families'.[3] Thatcherism, the Iron Lady herself suggests here, requires the dismantling of collective forms of community, as the model of free trade upon which monetarism relies sees each person as a single entity, an individual man or woman, competing with others for advantage and for capital. As David Harvey argues, it 'proposes that human well-being can best be advanced by liberating individual entrepreneurial freedoms and skills within an institutional framework characterized by strong private property rights, free markets and free trade'.[4] It is the role of government not to build communities, but to oversee unfettered competition between free individuals, who should be encumbered as little as possible by the state, or any other collective institutions. 'No government', Thatcher says in that same interview, 'can do anything except through people, and people must look after themselves first' (np).

Fast forward fourteen years, to Brighton in October 2001, and to Tony Blair's speech to the Labour Party Conference, less than a month after the terrorist attacks that took place in New York on September 11. Blair, for many political commentators, is Margaret Thatcher's heir, his 'third way' a means of adapting a centre-left commitment to social justice to the orthodoxies and demands of free trade.[5] But here, as Blair quickly (slickly, perhaps) adapts his conception of benign globalization to the seismic shifts in the world order caused by 9/11, his account of 'society' could not diverge more widely from Thatcher's. Thatcher says there is no such thing as society; Blair insists that the only way of overcoming the evils of terrorism – or the dissent of any group who violently opposes 'our way of life' – is to imagine that there is no outside to society, that globalization sees the production of an all-encompassing world community. It was immediately clear to Blair that the atrocities of 9/11 posed a significant threat to the consensus that history was moving towards the ever more complete hegemony of the global market place. The attacks seemed to offer evidence, even to neo-conservative ideologues such as Francis Fukuyama, that there was a real and effective resistance to the very concept of western democracy – but for Blair in 2001 the response to such resistance was not to lose faith in the concept of the global community, but to see it as the only solution to the experience of deprivation and alienation that led to the attacks in the first place.[6] It is the power of community – the very possibility of people and governments working together to create inclusive societies that Thatcher decried in 1984 – that Blair offers as the palliative to the unrest manifest in the 9/11 attacks. Blair acknowledges that there are 'critics' who doubt that 'the world' can be a 'community'. 'Nations act in their own interest', he admits, 'of course they do', just as individuals act in their own interests, apart from the claims of 'society'. But the 'lessons' of globalization, he insists, are that 'our self-interest and our mutual interest are today inextricably woven together'.[7] We must not kick against such forms of connection, out of some fear that in doing so we expose ourselves to hostile forces outside the family or outside the nation; rather we must accelerate the historical movement towards co-dependence. The 'problem' that comes to light on September 11, he argues, is 'not that there is too much [globalization]; on the contrary there's too little of it' (np). The way to overcome the violence of global terrorism is not to defend western nations against hostile opponents, but to recognise a global common cause (an argument made recently, from a rather different perspective, by Judith Butler).[8] 'The starving, the wretched, the dispossessed', he says, as he winds up to his emotional peroration, 'the ignorant, those living in want and squalor from the deserts of Northern Africa to the slums of Gaza, to the mountain ranges of Afghanistan: they too are our cause' (np).

Fast forward, again, to 2016, the annus horribilis for what we have become used to calling the 'liberal elite'. Blair's showy investment in the power of global community gave way quickly to military aggression – to US and allied wars fought in Iraq and Afghanistan, on spurious grounds, to defend the interests of the west against the ill-defined threat of Islamic terrorism.[9] The combination of military action in the aftermath of 9/11, with the economic crisis of 2008, derailed the forms of consensus that underwrote late twentieth-century globalization – the forms of global community that Blair sought to endorse in 2001. In North America, this denunciation of globalization takes the form of nationalism and protectionism, manifest in the figure of Donald Trump. Where Blair declared, in 2001, that 'our self-interest and our mutual interest are today inextricably woven together', Trump insists, throughout his 2016 election campaign, and in the 2017 speech he gave on his inauguration as President of the United States, that national self-interest must be opposed, directly, to any wider global concerns, economic, political or ecological. 'We assembled here today', Trump declares on 20 January 2017,

> are issuing a new decree to be heard in every city, in every foreign capital and in every hall of power – from this day forward a new vision will govern our land – from this day forward it is going to be only America first – America first.[10]

Where, for Blair, it is necessary to recognise that the people of Afghanistan are not our enemies but 'our cause', for Trump, reaping the dubious benefits of failed military operations in Afghanistan and Iraq, it has become clear that we must denounce the claims of all countries other than our own. 'We must protect our borders', he says, 'from the ravages of other countries, making our products, stealing our companies and destroying our jobs' (np).

Globalization gives way, in North America, to nationalism and protectionism; and in the UK we see the ugly twin of Trumpism in the form of UK nationalism, a version of the nationalism now spreading across the continent of Europe, and threatening the forms of consensus that were forged in the wake of World War II. The phenomenon of 'Brexit', still underway as I write, offers arguably the biggest challenge to the possibility of global integration, and the most dangerous assertion of European nationalism, since 1945.[11] As the UK Prime Minister Theresa May puts it, in a speech given in October 2016, Brexit marks the end of the idea that communities can extend across national boundaries, the idea that self-interest and mutual interest might be woven together.[12] In 'Brexit Britain', May declares, in an echo of Trump's 'America First' doctrine, it will no longer be possible for 'employers' to prioritise international concerns over the concerns of the nation – over 'the people down the road, the people they pass in the street'. In Brexit Britain, she declares, 'if you believe you're a citizen of the world, you're a citizen of nowhere. You don't understand what the very word 'citizenship' means'.[13]

The shifts in the idea of community that these interventions represent can be felt throughout contemporary British cultural life, its structure of feeling. The British novel of the last decades has been shaped by the movement from Thatcher's dismantling of the post-war welfare state, to the forms of globalism represented by Blair's hollow utopianism, to the uncertain challenge to such globalism represented by 9/11, economic crisis and the waning of US power. One can see that many of the energies that animate the fictional imagination in the period – that determine the evolution of postcolonial and postmodern forms, as well as the tension in the British novel between cosmopolitanism and localism – are shaped by this trajectory. The novel of the late twentieth century – from the postmodern inventiveness of Rushdie, Amis and Carter, to the nationalism of Irivine Welsh, Janice Galloway and the earlier James Kelman, to the watchful British realism of a novel such as Ian McEwan's *Atonement* – is determined to a significant degree by the movement that one can discern from Thatcherism to Blairism, from the forms of consensus that were developed in the post-war decades, to the neoliberal globalization of the model of western democracy that both Thatcher and Blair sought to endorse and extend. Both Zadie Smith's *White Teeth* and Ian McEwan's *Atonement*, in their different ways, are the products of that consensus, of that balance that is struck, at the close of the century, between the national and the international – the world view that is determined by the proposition, still self-evident to Blair in the immediate aftermath of 9/11, that 'our self-interest and our mutual interest' are 'inextricably woven together'. But, even as Blair makes that speech in Brighton in 2001, this balance was already changing, and the relation between national and global, the quality and texture of democratic sovereignty, was being redrawn. As Blair put it, rather hauntingly, in his 2001 speech, the 'kaleidoscope has been shaken, the pieces are in flux'. 'Soon', Blair says in 2001, 'the pieces will fall'.[14] It seems likely that the phenomena of Trump and Brexit are one way that the pieces have fallen, one of the new patterns that has formed from that shake of the kaleidoscope. A political legacy of 9/11 is a resurgent, right wing nationalism. But if this is the political response to that upheaval, the literary response, both in the British novel and more broadly, has been to seek new models for the production of national identities, and new ways of thinking about how historical forms of commitment and belonging relate to the strange new world to come, a world that seems no longer to accord with the paradigms and orthodoxies that stretched from the post-war to the turn of the century. British fiction's uncertain strain of postmodernism is one of the formal means by which the novel reflected the passage towards late century globalization – a cosmopolitan postmodernism that finds an exemplary model in Smith's *White Teeth*. But 9/11 was a trigger for a widespread waning of postmodernism as a cultural dominant, and with it the emergence of a generation of writers who were seeking to produce new narrative models of community, and of democracy.[15] The hermeneutic of suspicion adopted by late century postmodernism gives way to the perception that the novel has a responsibility to fashion new forms in which we might bring our shared histories into contact with a differently constituted public sphere, one which does not correspond to the models of political sovereignty bequeathed to us by the last century.

One of the ways in which this responsibility makes itself felt in the British post-millennial novel is in the perception, shared across a wide range of writers, that the novel has the capacity, and possibly the duty, to gestate images of the future, pictures of a world to come that might escape the narrow horizons thrown up by regressive twenty-first-century nationalisms. It is the case, of course, that these nationalisms themselves are also committed to the production of the future. As Trump puts it, in a chilling passage in his 2017 inauguration speech, 'now we are looking only to the future' (np). Like all radical political projects, the task of 'making America great again', or of freeing Britain from the cold clutch of the European Union, involves the adoption of a year zero, a revolutionary calendar, which projects us into a time which begins anew on 20th January 2017, or on a 'Brexit day' currently envisaged to take place in March 2019.[16] But the rise of twenty-first-century western nationalism, while it might gesture towards a future, towards a new beginning that rejects the legacies of Obama, or of Blair, is also an avowedly reactionary movement, a movement that is anchored firmly in the past, in the version of the US enshrined in the constitution, or in the fantasy of Britain as an imperial power, splendid in its isolation. It is against this version of the future, a future that is shaped by exclusive conceptions of a narrowly shared national past, that the post-millennial novel offers to produce pictures of futurity which are unstructured, which might open a space in which to envisage forms of imagined community that are not hemmed in by existing national boundaries and discriminations.

Across the range of British fiction written in the wake of 9/11, one can see these images of the future recurring – images which require the reinvention of the forms in which we have conceived of prose realism, and which suggest a new set of terms with which to represent and imagine our environments. We might think for example, of David Mitchell's *Cloud Atlas*, a novel which is, in the words of the novel's narrator, 'gravid with the ancient future'[17] – a novel whose elaborate Russian doll structure, story within story within story, is designed to reach towards a world of distant futurity which lies at its heart, a distant futurity which stretches and dismantles the nested forms in which we encounter the time to come. Or we might think of Zadie Smith's *NW*, a novel that turns around the passing from one generation to the next, and that tries to imagine how we form a bridge between these generations, how we fashion a form of prose that brings a past generation into delicate contact with the generations to come. The novel's title suggests its regionalism, its interest in a specific corner of Northwest London, and its belonging to a long history of realism that has sought to capture the history and atmosphere of a specific place. But, in a chance echo of Theresa May's brutal refusal of cosmopolitanism ('if you're a citizen of the world, you are a citizen of nowhere'), Smith's title refers also to the designation 'nowhere' – a fascination with empty space, with unmade time, which grows throughout the novel, and comes to signify the space of the future itself, the utopian 'no place' in which we meet the generation to come. Encountering the naked future, shorn of its connections with the past, Smith's novel discovers, involves 'going nowhere' (Smith, 2012: 318), a peculiar negation of the postcode which declares the novel's allegiance to place, to nationhood.[18] Or we might think of Julian Barnes's 2011 novel *The Sense of an Ending*, which imagines the future as an encounter with the next generation, a generation whose relation to us we struggle to understand or narrativise, and to whom we remain, in Barnes's bleak vision, deaf and blind.

Imagining the Future in the British Novel 261

This preoccupation with an immanent futurity – the sense that we are surrounded by a latent, untensed time that we cannot quite grasp, waiting for an instrument to arrive that might measure it, a language that might articulate it – is a structuring feature of post-millennial narrative life. And in responding to this prospect of a strangely unreadable future, in adapting formal structures with which to capture it, one can see that the contemporary novel is involved in a refashioning of the legacies not only of realism, but also of modernism, and the postmodernism that we associate with the late twentieth century. If our present predicament requires us to construct new ways of imagining community – a fresh means of understanding how shared life is embedded in collective pictures of a national past, while also entering into international, diasporic conjunctions that belong to an unforeseen future – then the means by which the novel reaches for such images is in large part through a critical engagement with a history of form.

One might glimpse the nature of this critical engagement, and see too its deployment across the range of British contemporary fiction, by attending to a perhaps surprising symmetry that is discernible between the post-millennial work of Ian McEwan and Ali Smith, a symmetry that arises from a relationship with the commingled spirits of Dickens and of Joyce that both writers share, despite McEwan's and Smith's manifold differences from each other both in form and in temperament. It is in his 2014 work *The Children Act* that McEwan most fully extends this dialogue with Dickensian realism and Joycean modernism, as a means of imagining the future – the future as manifest, in this novel, in the figure of the child.

The opening of McEwan's novel announces a debt to Dickens:

> London. Trinity term one week old. Implacable June weather. Fiona Maye, a High Court judge, at home on Sunday evening, supine on a chaise longue.[19]

This opening ventriloquises the first lines of Dickens's 1853 novel *Bleak House*:

> London. Michaelmas Term lately over, and the Lord Chancellor sitting in Lincoln's Inn Hall. Implacable November weather.[20]

In sharing its opening with *Bleak House* in this way, *The Children Act* announces a kinship with the earlier novel, a kinship which deepens as the novel progresses. Dickens's great novel stands in part as a rebuke to the law, which becomes barbarous when it is ensnared in its own laborious processes and vested interests rather than serving the interests of the citizens it is designed to protect. But it is also a rich meditation on the relationship between the law and literary fiction, as both discursive forms work at the junction between naked being in the world, and that being as it is given spatial and temporal extension, as it is brought forth into the sovereignty of subjecthood, as opposed to bare life. The famous figure of Jo the crossing sweeper, in *Bleak House*, is the closest Dickens comes to a representation of bare life – of a being that does not have the sovereignty granted either by law or by narrative. Jo, as he puts it himself, 'don't know nothink' (p. 235), and is entirely dead to the call of written language, to the discursive signs in which we encode our being. His, the narrator writes, is a 'wonderfully strange' being, one which appears human, but which, without language, cannot partake of human time, or human space. How strange, the narrator thinks, 'to be like Jo', to

> shuffle through the streets, unfamiliar with the shapes, and in utter darkness as to the meaning, of those symbols, so abundant over the shops, and at the corners of the streets, and on the doors, and in the windows! To see people read, and to see people write, and to see the postmen deliver letters, and not to have the least idea of all that language – to be, to every scrap of it, stone blind and dumb. (p. 236)

Dickens's project in *Bleak House* is to imagine a literary means of granting discursive power to the kind of naked being that he discovers in the figure of Jo, without that power becoming corrupted by legal and political institutions which serve their own interests rather than the common good. Standing as a blank opposite to Jo is the despicable lawyer Vholes, a man so versed in the cruel and empty letter of the law that he has almost no body, and certainly no literary soul; he has a surplus of legal language, to counterbalance Jo's utter lack. And between these opposites is Esther Summerson, whose gentle narrative becoming is an experiment in the process by which a well-balanced and crafted realism can found being in language, without such foundation becoming a servitude or a fixity: language as the gift of self-determination, rather than language as the imposing of a tyrannical law.

The Children Act opens with its obeisance to Dickens in part because it too is interested in the relationship between law and fiction (which, as McEwan has recently suggested, are 'rooted in the same ground'), and in particular in the question of how legal or literary forms might grant us the freedom to enter into a future that is at once legally or discursively controlled, and open to our own creative capacities and caprices.[21] The Children Act of 1989, after which McEwan's novel is named, decrees that 'when a court determines any question with respect to ... the upbringing of a child ... the child's welfare shall be the court's paramount consideration', and *The Children Act* turns around the difficulties and contradictions that this legislation sets in train.[22] As McEwan's protagonist the judge Fiona Maye puts it, 'the duty of the court was to enable the children to come to adulthood and make their own decisions about the sort of life they wanted to lead' (p. 38). The law protects the child, and looks after his or her interests, in such a way that maximises his or her capacity to reach an age when they can think for themselves. But the cases that McEwan's novel is interested in are those in which the rights of the child to self-determination are in conflict with their own wellbeing, in which the law has to set one freedom against another, in order to *shape* the future that the child will enter. This takes the form, early in the novel, of a case of conjoined twins named Matthew and Mark. Mark is healthy and autonomous, but Matthew cannot live independently, as he has a body that does not function – a damaged brain and a heart that barely squeezes. Here, the law does not simply protect a child's life, but has to create it, to step in and determine how the narrative of a life is linked to, and written upon, the child's body. The judge has to decide whether the just course is to separate the twins, or to leave them conjoined. 'Separating the twins', Fiona recognises, 'would be to kill Matthew. Not separating them would, by omission, kill both' (p. 27). The simple calculus, and the hospital's wish, is to perform the surgery that separates the twins – as one life spared is better than both lives lost. But the legal case is more demanding. How does the law legitimise the decision to withdraw life from one being, in order to confer it on another; what power is it granting itself when it decides that the experience of sovereignty denied to Dickens's Jo, the narrative of discrete selfhood, should be granted to one biopolitical assemblage, and not another?

In this early case – and then in the case that forms the central plot of the novel, concerning a young Jehovah's Witness with Leukaemia – Fiona's judgement is that the law should step in, and shape the child's future in accordance with its own definition of wellbeing, even if that means prioritising a stronger, more viable subject over a weaker one, or prioritising the decision making power of the adult over that of the child. In the case of the Jehovah's Witness, named Adam, this involves the legal instruction that Adam's leukaemia should be treated by blood transfusion, despite the fact that it is against his religious principles to allow 'blood products' to 'enter his body' (p. 65). As Adam's father puts it, Adam's decision to refuse the transfusion is driven by his sense that his biological being is a discrete and sacred gift from God. 'You have to understand', the father says, 'that blood is the essence of what's human. It's the soul, it's life itself' (p. 75). Adam is nearly old enough to act as an adult, so the law, in requiring him to accept treatment, is imposing its own view of the boundaries of the sovereign being (it is porous, and thus can accept blood from another body without losing its uniqueness) over those held by the Adam himself, a subject nearing his majority. Even though Fiona can see that Adam is lucid and able to think for himself, she cannot accept that his interests are served by allowing him to take a sovereign decision that will end his life. His 'welfare', Fiona decrees, invoking the Children Act of 1989, 'is better served by his love of poetry, by his newly found passion for the violin, by the exercise of his lively intelligence and the expressions of a playful, affectional nature, and by all of life and love that lie ahead of him' (p. 123).

In making this judgement, Fiona acts both as an agent of the law, and as a kind of author, a narrator of the life that 'lies ahead' for Adam. As *Bleak House* offers a narrative framework within which characters can come to self-determined being (in which Esther ends up living out the life and love ahead of her in a perfect (but miniature!) duplicate of the Bleak House in which she was brought up by her guardian (p. 891)), Fiona's judgement offers Adam a benign narrative of life, love and poetry. This granting of a narrative shape to being in time is the gift of realism. But what is most striking about *The Children Act*, and what makes it such a compelling reflection on the history of form, is that the narrative implicit in Fiona's judgement – the narrative that has its genesis in the Dickensian opening of the novel – is slowly dismantled as the novel moves through its tightly controlled phases. The judgement, coming at the end of act three of this five act drama, marks the climax of a certain realist logic, in which a past generation is able to set the terms in which a future generation comes to language and to being. But from this point on, another logic starts to insinuate itself in the narrative, and with it a completely different model of futurity; and as this other logic begins to surface, so the influence of Dickens begins to give way to the influence of Joyce, and the legacies of realism give way to the legacies of modernism. Fiona's judgement, in leading to Adam's treatment, grants him a new lease of life and of health. His body starts to regenerate itself (Fiona admires the 'whorls of his healthy young dark brown hair' (p. 167)), and, as Adam writes to Fiona, he recovers his vitality, 'getting stronger all the time' (p. 140). Fiona has granted him this strength, this health; but the legal and fictional processes by which one generation makes the space in which the next might flourish are disturbed, in McEwan's novel, by a certain refusal of narrative sequence. Adam, armed with his new strength, does not want to look forwards for life and love, but rather looks backwards, to Fiona, with whom he has fallen in love; and Fiona, suffering from childlessness and lovelessness, feels herself drawn to the child, not as a member of a future generation which she has set free, but as the extension of her own present, as someone who can give her the love that she half unconsciously craves.

At a critical moment in the second half of the novel, as one temporal logic begins to give way to another, this meeting between generations takes the form of a kiss, nearly a chaste kiss, but also 'more than a mother might give her grown up son':

> Over in two seconds, perhaps three. Time enough to feel in the softness of his lips that overlay their suppleness, all the years, all the life, that separated her from him. (p. 169)

From this point on, the question that drives McEwan's novel is how we might capture the years, and the life, that separate one generation from the next, years and life that don't obey the narrative trajectory of a realist plot, but that lie in the interstices, a kind of lived time that resists our narrative powers; that defies our models of responsibility, of prudence, of sequence; that does not have a language with which to express itself. And as this question comes to the fore, the model upon which it rests is no longer *Bleak House*, but *The Dead*, a text which begins to make itself felt in *The Children Act* with a vibrant, lyrical intensity. *The Dead* is itself concerned, above all, with the turning of the generations – with the ways in which the dead impose themselves on the living, through the perpetuation of models of community sustained by national myth. Gabriel Conroy's after-dinner speech, at his Aunt's Christmas party in Dublin, sets a nostalgic lament for a passing Dublin community against an acknowledgement that there is a coming international generation, which disrupts such forms of belonging. His Aunts are the last bastions, he says, of a 'tradition of genuine warm-hearted courteous Irish hospitality', a tradition which is threatened by a 'new generation' which is 'growing up in our midst, a generation actuated by new ideas and new principles'.[23] The Irish tradition, which lends the story a rich, festive warmth, is sustained by the folk music that runs through the story, by the strains of the 'Lass of Aughrim' that Gabriel finds his wife listening to, with a strange, rapt intensity, at the turn of a staircase. The new generation takes its cue from what Gabriel calls the 'thought-tormented music' of Robert Browning's difficult verse – the prosodic accompaniment to a 'sceptical and [...] a thought-tormented age' (p. 183). But these oppositions – Ireland versus Europe, tradition versus modernity – are radically upset at the close of the story, as Gabriel misreads the intense, distracted mood that the 'Lass of Aughrim' has kindled in his wife, Gretta. He sees that 'there was colour on her cheeks and that her eyes were shining', and a 'sudden tide of joy went leaping out of his heart' (p. 191), as the memory of their shared life together, captured in the strains of distant music, is mingled with a surge of present desire for her. He thinks to himself that perhaps 'her thoughts had been running with his', that 'she had felt the impetuous desire that was in him, and then the yielding mood had come on her' (p. 197). The music, he thinks, has produced in them both a moment of shared belonging, nourished by a collective national mythology. But, as the story comes to a softly crushing end, Gretta reveals that she is moved by the music to recall not the life she shares with Gabriel, but the life that she has *not* lived, with a delicate boy named Michael Furey, a figure from her past who died for his love of her. The 'Lass of Aughrim' has conjured not community, but a great distance between Gretta and Gabriel, between the dead and the living, the past and the future, a distance that yields the story's closing image, an image which has come to mark the threshold between realism and modernism.[24] Gabriel stands at the window, reflecting on the snow falling 'all over Ireland', falling 'on every part of the dark central plain, on the treeless hills, falling softly on the Bog of Allen and, farther westward, softly falling into the dark mutinous Shannon waves' (p. 202). The imagined prospect of such cold community leads him to a gesture of national belonging, a commitment to that Irish tradition that he (insincerely) celebrated at his Aunts' party. 'The time had come', he thinks, 'to set out on his journey westward' (p. 202). But whatever evocation of a shared time and space this homeward, backward journey is, it is of a piece, too, with the difficult futurism of a thought-tormented age. In the very moment that he travels westward, he heads, too, towards an ecstatic dismantling of being that he finds in the broken distance that opens between himself and his wife, a distance which no music can cross, no myth can overcome: 'His soul swooned slowly as he heard the snow falling faintly through the universe and faintly falling, like the descent of their last end, upon all the living and the dead' (p. 203).

To understand the modernism that Joyce invents after *Dubliners* – to understand how *Ulysses* produces forms which sustain a mythological and historical past, while opening themselves also to a form of dismantled being, a being that belongs to a future that has not already been made – it is necessary to approach this moment at the end of *The Dead*, a moment when a lyrical epiphany brings a commitment to a shared past into contact with a swooning surrender to the groundlessness of being. And it is this moment, this turning to that is a turning away, that animates McEwan's novel, as he approaches the space that opens between Fiona and Adam, a space between generations that cannot come under the jurisdiction of the law. As McEwan's novel draws to a close, the elements of *The Dead*, which have been gathering under the skin of the narrative throughout its second half, rise to the surface, producing a strangely intense moment of double-voicing. Fiona learns, during a public recital of Bach, and of a Yeats ballad that she had earlier sung with Adam, that Adam's leukaemia had returned, that having reached his majority he was able to refuse treatment, and that as a result he has died. As Gretta says of her young lover that 'I think he died for me' (p. 199), so Fiona discovers that Adam chooses death over the future that she had made for him, the future to which she had propelled him. On her return to the flat that she shares with her estranged husband Jack, Fiona enters into the same unstructured distance that opens between Gabriel and Gretta. As Gabriel feels a closeness to his wife on their return to their room at the end of the evening – as he is overcome, as he puts it, by his 'clownish lust' (p. 199) for her – so Jack expects a reconciliation with Fiona after her triumphant recital. He is in an 'elevated state, excited by her performance, and by what he thought lay ahead' (p. 206). But rather than sex, which might 'make everything easy between them once more' (p. 207), the evening ends in what Fiona thinks of as a 'great distance' (p. 208), filled by the spectre of Adam, the 'very strange and beautiful young man' (p. 208) who had died for love of her. The novel closes in semi-darkness, with rain rather than snow outside the window, as the 'great rain-cleansed city beyond the room settled to its softer nocturnal rhythms' (p. 213), and Fiona and Jack look upon the future of a marriage which will have to accommodate the ghost of a boy who chose, through love, to renounce 'all of love and life that lay ahead'.

The effect of this Joycean presence at the close of the novel is magical, endowing the prose with an epiphanal grace that McEwan's style rarely reaches – taking the prose beyond itself, as McEwan himself suggests music can sometimes take us beyond ourselves, in 'those rare moments when musicians together touch something sweeter than they've ever found before in rehearsals or performance, when their expression becomes as easy and graceful as friendship or love'.[25] But, of course, this magical presence, this peculiar collaboration, is bound up with the contradiction, explored both in *The Dead* and *The Children Act*, between presence and distance, between the communal and the estranged. In summoning *The Dead* with such intensity, McEwan's novel calls to a moment in the history of the novel at which the very possibility of community – and the very possibility that realist fiction can access and sustain such community – yields to the perception that communal experience is shadowed by an estrangement, a statelessness that it cannot overcome; when national identity meets what Stephen Dedalus famously called the 'uncreated conscience of my race'.[26] The end of *The Dead* produces a new, tormented affinity between community and estrangement, and suggests the first stirrings of a Joycean modernism that can give expression to such affinity, and in doing so produce a model of becoming in time that slips by the nets of narrative sequence. As it is reanimated in *The Children Act*, it offers a means of reflecting on the questions that drive McEwan's novel – how legal institutions and literary fiction bring the future into contact with the present and the past, how we can enable the future without predetermining it. *The Children Act* imagines a relationship between Fiona and Adam that does not quite belong to any of the conventions or the forms that structure it. Adam is not the child that Fiona longs for, nor the lover, and she is neither his mother nor his god. Their contact, caught in the short seconds of their kiss, does not have a temporal, theological or juridical form in which to ground itself. But it does suggest an encounter between the past and the future – loving, open, undecided – that cannot quite take place in a realist mode, and that resides in the strange semantic shifting that happens, in *The Children Act*, when Dickensian narrative sequence gives way to Joycean hauntology, to a dialogue with the past that happens outside of the sequential protocols of storytelling, and that engenders a different mode of futurity.

McEwan's prose summons a modernist forebear, in order to gesture towards a future that is beyond the sequential power of realism to conjure. But his own formal range remains peculiarly narrow – there is a soft dissolution, as the novel moves from its Dickensian opening to its Joycean conclusion, that is beguiling to the same extent that it is denied by the well-made realism of the narrative. It is in the work of Ali Smith, and particularly in her seasonal cycle beginning with the novels *Autumn* and *Winter*, that one can see an address to the future which is conducted through formal experiment as well as through historical critique, a future which, she has recently argued, is made 'negotiable' by the power of fiction.[27] In these novels, written at speed under the pressure of the passing moment, as if in 'real time', Smith seeks to respond to the seismic political upheavals of 2016 and 2017 – the Brexit campaign, Trump's election, the murder of Jo Cox, the Grenfell fire – producing an almost overwhelmingly vivid picture of the zeitgeist, of a year in which the socio-economic consensus that has held since the Thatcher-Regan era has been suddenly dismantled. The novels offer the first developed fictional depiction of the fever that has gripped the UK since the referendum of June 2016 – in which, as Smith's narrator puts it, 'All across the country, there was misery and rejoicing' ('All across the country, people looked up Google: *what is EU?* All across the country, people looked up Google: *move to Scotland*').²⁸ But, despite this deep investment in the present, both *Winter* and *Autumn* suggest that, to understand our current predicament – the peculiar season in which we are living – we need to see it as part of a logic that has been unfolding in the UK since the election of Thatcher in 1979. The intense focus on 2016–17 loops back repeatedly to absorb the longer history of the national present. Theresa May's denial of the possibility of world citizenship in 2016 is cast as an echo of Thatcher's own manifesto; we've been refusing the larger possibility of community, a character in *Autumn* says, 'since Thatcher taught us to be selfish and not just to think but to believe that there's no such thing as society'.²⁹ And the timeline of *Winter* begins, in a sense, with its beautifully evocative depiction of the establishment of the Greenham Common women's peace camp in the early eighties ('Come with me now back to an early sunny Saturday morning in September 1981, to a piece of English common land fenced off by the American military in agreement with the British military' (p. 143)).

Smith's novels depict a turbulent present, by producing a looping set of histories that locate it, that help us to focus it. But what connects Smith's cycle, with an almost uncanny insistence, to McEwan's dramatisation of the contemporary in *The Children Act*, is that both seek to capture the experience of passing time through an act of ventriloquism, which merges the voice of Dickens with that of Joyce. *The Children Act* begins by quoting the opening of *Bleak House*; the beginning of *Autumn* ('It was the worst of times, it was the worst of times' (p. 3)) echoes the famous opening of *A Tale of Two Cities* ('It was the best of times, it was the worst of times');³⁰ and the beginning of *Winter* ('God was dead: to begin with' (p. 3)) echoes the opening of *A Christmas Carol* ('Marley was dead, to begin with').³¹ These opening homages to Dickens then resonate through Smith's novels, as *Bleak House* resonates through *The Children Act*, so one can feel a Dickensian presence in every line, acting as a foundation to the narratives, to the turning of Smith's seasons. The exploration of revolutionary time in *Autumn* is impelled by Dickens's response to the French Revolution in *A Tale of Two Cities* – the revolutionary experience that both Dickens and Smith think of as being 'recalled to life';³² and *Winter* is, at its heart, a story of Christmas redemption that works as a retelling of *A Christmas Carol*. As in *The Children Act*, however, the legacy of Dickens is interwoven with an equally powerful Joycean bequest. The dazzling opening sequence of

Autumn depicts Daniel Gluck, the ancient guru figure who presides over the novel, being reborn on a strip of beach, and as Gluck experiences this Dickensian recall to life, it is impossible not to feel the presence of *Ulysses*, stirring within the language. With Gluck's first return to consciousness, as an 'old man [who] washes up on a shore' (p. 3), he is inhabited by figure of the drowned man who floats off the shore throughout Joyce's novel, the 'bag of corpsegas sopping in foul brine', the 'corpse rising saltwhite from the undertow';[33] and as he rejuvenates, as his youthful body grows around him and he finds himself standing on a 'sandy stony strand, the wind distinctly harsh' (p. 4), he becomes the young Dedalus, 'walking into eternity along Sandymount strand' (who is himself composed of 'dead dust', of the 'dead breaths I living breathe', and who is himself clothed in the 'strandentwining cable of all flesh').[34] *Ulysses* attends Daniel Gluck's narrative birth, and then, later in the novel as Gluck finds himself unrequitedly in love with Pauline Boty – the sixties British pop artist who is another of the novel's guiding figures – it is *The Dead* which offers the framework to Smith's narrative, that allows the dead to speak. Gluck stands outside Boty's house, 'in the rain in the back yard,' as Michael Furey stands outside Gretta's house in *The Dead*, as Adam stands outside Fiona's hotel in the rain in *The Children Act*. As he does so, Gluck thinks to himself that

> there is a famous short story, The Dead, by James Joyce, in which a young man stands at the back of a house and sings a song on a freezing night to a woman he loves. Then this young man, pining for the woman, dies. He catches a chill in the snow, he dies young. Height of Romanticism! That woman in that story for the rest of her life, has that young man's song always riddling through her like woodworm. (p. 97)

Smith, like McEwan, draws both on a realist and on a modernist tradition, to capture the presence of the past, which is riddled through us like woodworm. But where McEwan stages a gradual move from the former to the latter, allowing a realist conception of duration to dissolve into the Joycean epiphany with which *The Children Act* ends, Smith's novel cycle refuses any such linear history of form, offering instead a dizzying blend of ages and styles, crunching Dickens together with Joyce, as well as with a vast range of other influences, voices and images, from Barbara Hepworth, to Pauline Boty, to Elvis, to Paddington Bear. Just as the chronological passage from 2016 to 2017, from Autumn to Winter, is repeatedly disrupted by the appearance of jumbled images and sequences from the past – from Greenham in 1981, or from Christmases past that continually interfere with the unfolding of Christmas present in *Winter* – so the shifting influences that shape Smith's narrative are never clearly distinguished from one another, but can be felt jostling against each other in every line. It is as if, for Smith, the experience of this present season, the temporal quality of our own passing moment, does not have a form in which it might be given shape. The past mingles with the present, one voice mingles with another, in a way that defies the protocols of narrative sequence. As Smith's narrator says – of Daniel Gluck's regeneration, but also of the writing of *Autumn* itself – 'here's an old story so new that it's still in the middle of happening, writing itself right now with no knowledge of where or how it will end' (p. 181).

The novelty of this gesture, of course, is questionable, as if even novelty itself, in Smith's rendition of it, starts to feel stale. This shapeless mix of the old and the new, the high and the low, the realist and the modernist, might appear quite familiar, overly familiar, another staging of the hybridity of formal styles that is a staple feature of classic postmodernism, and that Jacques Derrida calls 'bricolage'.[35] As the character Art says, in *Winter*, this is a familiarity which could become rather wearisome. 'It is the dregs, really', he says, 'to be living in a time' when it is mandatory to be 'post-postmodern consciouser-than-thou' (p. 158). The perennial return of postmodern bricolage might resemble what another character thinks of as the reassuring reappearance of the same Christmas songs every midwinter, which mark 'the rhythm of passing time, yes, but also, and more so, the return of time in its endless and comforting cycle' (p. 39). If, as the Dickensian opening of *Winter* has it, we are surrounded by the signs of cultural as well as ecological death ('the earth', we hear, is 'also dead' (p. 5)), then this is perhaps because the literary and visual forms with which we have narrated the passing of time – even those postmodern forms which seemed, late last century, to be so revolutionary – have lost their freshness, have become recycled commodities as tinny as the horribly familiar strains of George Michael's *Last Christmas*. 'God was dead: to begin with' the narrator of *Winter* says,

> And romance was dead. Chivalry was dead. Poetry, the novel, painting, they were all dead, and art was dead. Theatre and cinema were both dead. Literature was dead. The book was dead. Modernism, postmodernism, realism and surrealism were all dead. (p. 3)

But if Smith's cycle is concerned with recycling, with the deathly return of the old, the shining of every morning's sun on Samuel Beckett's 'nothing new',[36] then it is equally invested in the future, in the imperative that we imagine a time to come that has not already been seen, that does not belong to cyclical time, but that glimmers on the other side of a seasonal, temporal threshold, unclothed by any hand-me-down narrative form. Even as her restless investment in the chopped up histories of narrative form produce a feeling of déjà vu, a reanimation of the ghosts of modernism and of postmodernism, of Dickens and of Joyce, she brings such histories into contact with a futurity, an open narrative horizon, that remakes them, as old stories are always made new just as they are in the middle of happening. What marks Smith's aesthetic above all, not only in *Autumn* and *Winter* but in earlier works, such as *How to Be Both* and *The Accidental*, is its singular, characteristic attention to the ways in which time inhabits material, the forms which allow a temporal consciousness to act within, to cleave to, the bodies and environments in which it recognises itself. In *Autumn*, the narrative explores the process by which Gluck's mind is given rejuvenated form, encased in flesh, or, in one of the novel's recurring fantasies, in a body of green wood, a flowering pine (echoed in his 'pining' for Paul Boty). In *Winter*, the fascination with the sculpture of Barbara Hepworth leads to a repeated figuring of body as stone, and the dwelling inside the body as a dwelling inside stone. There is no other contemporary novelist who works with such idiosyncratic precision at the boundary where art meets with its materials (with stone or wood or canvas), or where mind meets with body. When a character in *Winter*, reflecting on 'mind, matter, the structure of reality', thinks that 'mind and matter are mysterious and, when they come together, bounteous' (p. 303), he is stating a credo of Smith's work – her recurrent fascination with 'meeting' that runs through her work at least since her 2007 novel *Girl Meets Boy*. Smith seeks to reveal that junction at which mind meets with matter, at which one person meets with another, and this junction is the place, too, peculiarly fugitive and groundless, where the past meets with the future. The seasons may make this meeting point cyclical, may give a rhythm and a familiarity to the passing of time; indeed Smith is deeply attuned to this rhythm, and to the gathered mythologies that give a history to the transformative contact of old and new. But even as the turning of the seasons accords to such a rhythm, it also thrusts us into a strange flaw in the 'structure of reality', a suspended space between the gathered past and the empty future, a space that is 'like two weatherfronts meeting, like the coming season getting ready midway through the old one to make itself heard'.[37]

It is this temporal and material junction, this suspended ground between weather fronts, that Smith seeks to bring to thought and to form in her novel cycle, and that marks the far limit of the British novel now in its striving to imagine the future. In reaching to the future, *Autumn* and *Winter* are guided in part by the spirit of Dickens, and particularly by the spirits that speak in Dickens's *A Christmas Carol*. It is one of the great gifts of the realist novel, as it is brought to a particular form of perfection by Dickens, that it gives a shape to passing time, and allows us to bring the future into contact with the past. This is the gift that is given to Scrooge by the spirits that visit him on Christmas Eve. 'I will honour Christmas in my heart', Scrooge promises at the end of the novel, as he is confronted with the bankruptcy of his own stunted refusal of passing time. 'I will live in the Past, the Present and the Future. The Spirits of all three shall strive within me' (p. 77). It is this capacity, to extend oneself in time, that Smith is searching for in her novel cycle, as we look to bridge the gap between the future and the past opened by the revolutions of Trumpism, and of Brexit. Trump declares, in January 2017, that 'we are looking now only to the future', that his own revolution requires us to reject the past. Smith's novels offer a direct rebuke to this address to the future. We need now, like Scrooge, to feel both the future and the past striving within us. Only by working with both imperatives can we see past the current crisis in the passage of world history. But if this is so, what Smith's cycle suggests – what the British novel now suggests, as it experiments with formal means of imagining the future – is that we need a new mechanism with which to address the turning of the seasons, the passage from shared past to unknown future, from adult to child. Smith takes Theresa May's declaration, that 'if you believe you're a citizen of the world, you're a citizen of nowhere', as an epigraph to *Winter*, and it is difficult to resist the feeling that all the novel's energies are directed against this sentiment; there must be, Smith's novel cycle suggests, ways of extending citizenship across the globe, ways of imagining shared worlds, that are not reducible to the hegemony of the west offered by Blair, at the turn of the current century, as a phoney cure to the experience of dispossession. But if Smith's aesthetics are directed by this urge towards citizenry, towards shared worlds, she also counterintuitively shares something of May's sentiment here. It may be that, to be a citizen of the world now, we need also to be a citizen of nowhere, the no place that has haunted the novel's utopian imagination since Thomas More's 1516 work *Utopia*. Scrooge feels past, present and future striving within him, and Dickens crafts a literary form that resolves such striving into sequence. Smith, however, suggests that, it is necessary now for us to give expression not only to accommodations between the past and the future, but also to gulfs between them, gulfs that can only be experienced as a kind of nowhere, a wasteland between a shared past and a future that may grow out of our collective past, but which does not belong to it, or follow from it.

It is this attention – to a communal nowhere that, like Zadie Smith's *NW*, lies between generations, between the past and the future – that makes Smith's novel cycle so timely, so attuned to the state of the British novel now. 'The book was dead', Smith's narrator thinks at the opening of *Winter*, 'Modernism, postmodernism, realism and surrealism were all dead' (p. 3). This may be so – it may be the case that the passage from realism to modernism to postmodernism that is reanimated in McEwan and in Smith has led to a postmillennial wasteland, a stony ground in which no roots clutch and no branches grow, and to which we can offer only a heap of broken images. But for Smith and McEwan, and for a generation of British novelists working now, at a transitional moment in the passage of world history, it is only by clearing such a passage, by imagining what it would be to be a citizen of nowhere, that we can craft the forms in which we can look to the future, while feeling our shared past strive within us.

The book is dead; long live the book.

2019

CHAPTER 13

Shallow Intensity
Neoliberalism and the Novel

How does the late twentieth-century novel offer a critical response to the pervasive phenomenon of neoliberalism?

We might begin to address this question by attending to a key moment in Philp Roth's novel *The Human Stain*, at which the protagonist Coleman Silk pays a visit to the small-town American university at which he was once Dean of Humanities. He has not been back to the campus since he retired in disgrace, having been accused, falsely as he sees it, of using a racist slur against two African American students. As he walks towards the campus, he overhears a discussion among a number of male faculty members sitting in the sun on a park bench. The topic of conversation is the ongoing sexual scandal surrounding Bill Clinton and Monica Lewinsky, the scandal which is one of the reference points of the novel's title, the human stain in question being in part the famous stain left by the presidential semen on Monica Lewinsky's dress. The conversation, in its repellent bantering misogyny, turns around what it was that attracted Clinton to Lewinsky. He could see the kind of person she was, the men agree, 'a total narcissist', an 'exhibitionist, corrupted by privilege'.[1] He could read her – 'if he can't read and outfox Monica Lewinsky, the guy *shouldn't* be president' (pp. 147–148). It was not, they speculate, that he was blinded by her or seduced by her – on the contrary it was her very obvious limitations that attracted him to her. 'That she was totally corrupt and totally innocent, of course he saw it. The extreme innocence was the corruption' (p. 148). Innocence is somehow equated, in the figure of Lewinsky, with corruption, a woven combination of opposites that is replicated across a number of political contradictions that Lewinsky seems, to these men, to embody. 'That was her force' one of the men says, that combination:

> That she had no depth, that was her charm at the end of his day of being commander in chief. The intensity of the shallowness was its appeal. Not to mention the shallowness of the intensity. (p. 148)

275

This moment touches on many of the questions that propel *The Human Stain*, and that preoccupy the later twentieth-century novel more generally, as it is shaped by the collective forces of neoliberalism. The passage is in part about the politics and aesthetics of reading – a chief preoccupation of Roth's novel, and a central focus of contemporary critical thinking about what it is that literature does. Clinton can read Lewinsky, he can understand her specific combination of innocence and corruption, because his job requires him to be an analyst – a close reader – of the forms which corruption and innocence take in the late twentieth century. 'He could read her', one of the men says (at the opening of a chapter entitled 'What Do You Do with the Kid Who Can't Read'). 'If he can't read Monica Lewinsky, how can he read Saddam Hussein?' (p. 147). The rhetorical logic here is that a President who can't negotiate a trivial incident – a tame affair with an intern – could hardly be expected to manage a matter of major geopolitical significance – the relation between Clinton's administration and Saddam Hussein's regime, as it influences the globally critical balance of power in the Middle East. Of course Clinton should be able to read Lewinsky; he devotes his exhausting days as commander in chief to the task of critical analysis, whose stakes are immeasurably higher than those which determine the quaint intricacies of his heavy petting with Monica. But, at the same time, the scale which underlies this rhetoric, which opposes the weightily geopolitical to the trivially domestic, is disturbed or deranged by the prospect of Lewinsky herself, who seems to require a different model of reading, both of Clinton and of us. She collapses the distinction between the innocent and the corrupt, between the shallow and the intense, Roth's novel suggests, because she herself, in her relation to Clinton, is the symptom of a loss of historical perspective, in which we can no longer easily distinguish between the superficial and the profound, between surface and depth. This was the summer of 1998, the narrator Nathan Zuckerman says at the opening of the novel, the summer in the historically evacuated endgame of a century and a millennium, the summer in which 'terrorism' as 'the prevailing threat to the country's security' was 'succeeded by cocksucking', and the gravity normally accorded to geopolitics was squandered on the spectacle of a 'virile, youthful middle-age president and a brash, smitten twenty-one-year-old employee carrying on in the Oval Office like two teenage kids in a parking lot' (p. 2). This was 'the summer when a president's penis was on everyone's mind' (p. 2).

To read Monica Lewinsky's shallow intensity, to understand how intensity can be shallow, and shallowness can be intense, Roth's novel proposes, requires us to rethink the antinomial relationship between these terms. And if this moment touches on the novel's concern with reading, it activates too its wider thematic and political focus – the means by which the deep psychic and historical structures that determine identities are attached to the surfaces in which those identities present themselves to the world, and specifically the ways in which identity relates to the colour of one's skin. Coleman Silk is forced out of his university position, by his own account, because he was falsely accused of racism against two African American students; the irony as he sees it is that he himself, despite his self-presentation as a white Jew, is in fact – African American. The university administration's reading of the 'racist' incident – according to which a powerful white man abuses his privilege to discriminate against African American students – thus masks an entirely different set of active forces, which have led Coleman to disguise his own racial identity in order to gain access to the white enclave of the university administration, the very racist enclave that is now preparing to expel him for his perceived racism. Zuckerman is fascinated by this turn of events, and drawn to the writerly task of recovering Coleman's African American history from the white Jewish cloak which has occluded it, in part because it allows him to reflect on the way in which the legible surfaces – of things, of people – relate to the deep histories they contain. It is when Zuckerman visits Coleman in his house on a warm evening early in the novel, to find him in a loose and euphoric mood listening to music with his shirt off, that this act of narrative reclamation is set in motion, this adjustment of the relation between the surface and the depth. Being close to him in such an intimate setting, being given this 'exhibition of his body's suntanned surface' (p. 21), allows for one of the several close readings of Coleman's body as text that recur throughout the novel, and that carry such powerful racist overtones. There is an intense homoerotic quality to the meeting, at which Coleman and Zuckerman end up dancing in each other's arms to Frank Sinatra, and this eroticism is grounded in Zuckerman's fascinated attention to Coleman's body. 'Coleman wore a pair of denim shorts and sneakers', Zuckerman says, and nothing else:

> From behind, this man of seventy-one looked to be no more than forty – slender and fit and forty. Coleman was not much over five eight, if that, he was not heavily muscled, and yet there was a lot of strength in him, and a lot of the bounce of the high school athlete was still visible, the quickness, the urge to action. (p. 15)

Zuckerman is drawn to a close examination of this lithely compact body, just as Coleman's various lovers are throughout the novel – as his lover Steena later thinks that 'there was nothing about his body that she had not microscopically absorbed, nothing about this extensive surface imprinted with his self-cherishing evolutionary uniqueness [...] that she had not registered' (p. 113) – but even as he is so drawn, he is intrigued not only as a potential lover but also as a reader. Looking at the suntanned skin, Zuckerman sees also a 'small, Popeye-ish, blue tattoo situated at the top of his right arm, just at the shoulder joining – the words "U.S. Navy" inscribed between the hooklike arms of a shadowy little anchor and running along the hypotenuse of the deltoid muscle' (p. 22). Text and muscle come together here, the body offering itself up to be read, as Jeanette Winterson stages the joining of body and text in her influential 1992 novel *Written on the Body*. But Zuckerman, novelist that he is, is struck by the sense that this image of skin as text does not suggest legibility, but rather obscurity, the uncertain seam between skin and history in which the secret of Coleman's race is hidden. The tattoo, Zuckerman thinks to himself, as he is drawn, unknowing, into the task of novelising Coleman's past, is a

> tiny symbol, if one were needed, of all the million circumstances of the other fellow's life, of that blizzard of details that constitute the confusion of a human biography – a tiny symbol to remind me why our understanding of people must always be at best slightly wrong. (p. 22)

Zuckerman is drawn erotically and intellectually to the task of reading Coleman's body, of finding in the human stain of that tattoo – ink becoming part of the living human body – a means of recovering a lost history, or bringing a secret out of hiding. But if he is compelled in this way, it is the case, too, that the terms in which Zuckerman and Roth understand the capacity of the novel to establish a legible relation between surface and depth have been profoundly recast by the historical forces that have taken us to this strangely disoriented end of the millennium, to this tilted late condition, in which surface and depth, the shallow and the intense, enter into new relations with one another – the forces put in motion by the historical passage of neoliberalism. Zuckerman's reflection here on the unknowability of other people has a rich novelistic heritage. We can hear, in this invocation of the 'blizzard of details' that constitute a life, an echo of George Eliot's famous reflection on the sublime variousness of the world, in her 1872 novel *Middlemarch*. 'If we had a keen vision and feeling of all ordinary human life', Eliot's narrator writes, 'it would be like hearing the grass grow and the squirrel's heart beat, and we should die of that roar which lies on the other side of silence'.[2] The blizzard of details, for Zuckerman and for Eliot's narrator, does not make for rich narrative experience, but overwhelms narrative altogether. And we can hear, too, an echo from an earlier moment in the history of the novel, from Jane Austen's transformative 1815 work *Emma*. Austen's novel famously narrates Emma's progression from blindness to insight, from error to rectitude, from the artificial to the real, as this takes the form of her gradual realisation that she loves her avuncular family friend Mr Knightley. It is in satisfied recognition of this progress towards revelation that Mr Knightley declares, at the end of the novel, 'My Emma, does not every thing serve to prove more and more the beauty of truth and sincerity in all our dealings with each other'.[3] But even as Mr Knightley celebrates the beauty of natural truth telling, Austen's narrator gently corrects him. 'Seldom', the narrator says, 'very seldom, does complete truth belong to any human disclosure; seldom can it happen that something is not a little disguised, or a little mistaken' (p. 354). Austen's narrator, like Roth's nearly two centuries later, acknowledges that 'our understanding of people must always be at best slightly wrong'.[4]

The uncertain relation between seeing and mis-seeing is woven into the very mechanics of the novel. But if one can hear this dialogue with the novel form at this moment in *The Human Stain*, as Zuckerman studies Coleman's smooth seventy-one year old skin, one can see, too, that Roth's novel is witnessing a deep transformation in the way that the novel, under late twentieth-century conditions, responds to the faultiness of its own medium. For Austen, for Eliot, the novel functions as a machine that converts the uncontainable variety of reality – the blizzard of details – into a narrative shape. Its magic, as Austen shows more clearly than any writer before her, is that it can make of the uncertain relation between word and thing, between signifier and signified, the means to produce the most vivid pictures of reality, the means, as Eliot puts it, to undertake the 'difficult task of knowing another soul'.[5] Austenian irony, narrative irony more generally, is powered by the sense that language is always at a remove from reality, always double, that it very seldom constitutes a medium of complete truth; but it wins from its doubleness its own kind of novelistic truth. There is a mismatch between surface and depth, between what we say and what we mean. But the novel of interiority, as it draws on the capacity of language to mediate between the separate spheres of mind and body, of surface and depth, of appearance and reality, has allowed us to make a home for ourselves in a world from which we are always partly estranged. At this moment in *The Human Stain*, though, as Zuckerman recognises that Coleman's skin presents to him a text that he cannot read – as a history of racism remains detached from the forms in which it is written – Roth exposes a malfunction of the terms in which surface and depth have adhered to one another in the work of prose fiction, a sudden expiry of the novel's capacity to map the relations between the trivial and the profound, the shallow and the intense.

One cannot understand the novel of the later twentieth century without addressing this problem, this refiguring of the relations between surface and depth, shallowness and intensity; and one cannot measure the stakes of this refiguring without reckoning with the economic, political and aesthetic effects of the new cultural-economic logic that rises to dominance in the 1970s, and that has come to be known by the name of neoliberalism. We can see the outline of this relation, between the dawn of neoliberalism and the history of the novel form, by overhearing a quiet conversation between Muriel Spark and David Harvey concerning the effects of the various economic crises that cluster around 1973. In works such as *The Condition of Postmodernity* and *A Brief History of Neoliberalism*, Harvey has developed an influential account of the ways in which the economic transformations that occur in the early seventies – most notably the US withdrawal in 1973 from the Bretton Woods agreement that kept the US dollar pinned to a notional gold standard – have given rise to a neoliberal cultural logic. The Bretton Woods agreement, established in the immediate aftermath of the second world war, was a mechanism, Harvey explains, for the development of what he calls 'embedded liberalism'.[6] This is the form of liberal economics in which advanced economies balance the free movement of capital against the requirement, established in the wake of the war, that nation states co-operate with one another to regulate markets. The logic of neoliberalism, however, as it develops from the early seventies, requires that capital is increasingly freed from any of the regulatory frameworks imposed upon it by the state. The fundamental principle of neoliberalism, for Harvey, is that the market should operate with maximum freedom and minimum constraint, because 'market exchange' as Paul Treanor puts it, becomes 'an ethic in itself, capable of acting as a guide to all human action, and substituting for all previously held ethical beliefs'.[7] The post-war consensus that the sovereign state should impose some kind of social control over the global economy thus gives way to the belief that the social good is actually guaranteed not by political intervention but by free-market economics, and so to the increasing compulsion to free capital from any shackles that governments might lay upon it, and from any forms in which it might be weighed down. If the political forces operating in the immediate post-war gave rise to a form of embedded liberalism, then the 'neoliberal project', Harvey writes, 'is to disembed capital from these constraints', a disaggregation of capital from its material forms that is given its clearest manifestation in the breakdown of the Bretton Woods agreement.[8] 'Since 1973', Harvey writes in *The Condition of Postmodernity*, 'money has been "de-materialized" in the sense that it no longer has a formal or tangible link to precious metals [...] or for that matter to any other tangible commodity'. The 'de-linking of the financial system', he goes on, 'from active production and from any material monetary base calls into question the reliability of the basic mechanism whereby value is supposed to be represented'.[9]

Neoliberalism for Harvey, then, is the economic process whereby capital is freed from the constraints of nation states, in order to act as its own kind of sovereign agent. But if neoliberalism is an economic project, it is also a political one, one whose effects can be felt in every area of cultural life – a fact that is given novelistic expression by Muriel Spark, remarkably early in the history of neoliberalism, in her 1976 novel *The Takeover*. Written in a self-consciously fragile realist mode, this novel seeks to understand how the economic crises of 1973, and the neoliberal structures that arose from them, might have effects on a wider logic of representation. Spark's novel, dramatising the troubles of a group of moneyed expats struggling to understand the impact of the 1973 oil crisis on their wealth and privilege, is a response to the narrator's perception that the breakdown of Bretton woods has brought about 'the deterioration of money in general', 'the collapse of money as a concept'.[10] In seeking to respond to this collapse, what the novel both explores and in its own way demonstrates, is that Harvey's 'de-linking' of capital 'from any monetary base' has an equivalent in a de-linking of word from world, of text from body, a dismantling of the representational forms that allowed us to embed our sense of value and of signification in a reliable correspondence between thought and thing. What the collapse of Bretton Woods brings about, the narrator says, is a total transformation in the psychic structure of reality. The truth that the moneyed friends are trying to grasp is that a

> complete mutation of our means of nourishment had already come into being where the concept of money and property were concerned, a complete mutation not merely to be defined as a collapse of the capitalist system, or a global recession, but such a sea-change in the nature of reality as could not have been envisaged by Karl Marx or Sigmund Freud. (p. 97)

David Harvey and Muriel Spark here are both responding to the same phenomenon – the perception that the freedom of capital from its material forms produces a shift in the way that reality is perceived and constituted. And the way that we understand the relationship between neoliberalism and the novel is determined by how we read the novel's reaction to this shift, how we think the novel gives expression at a superstructural level, to use a hoary Marxist formulation, to transformations in the economic base. In Spark's novel this takes the form of a peculiar wobble in the quality of the realism, an anti-mimetic effect brought about by the 'complete mutation' in representational forms caused by the 'collapse of money as a concept'. As the character Hubert puts it, when the 'concepts of property and material possession' are revealed to be a product of 'lying, deception and fraud', then our broader mechanisms of faithful representation are also disabled. If everything is fraud and deceit, then 'deceit has no meaning, lies do not exist, fraud is impossible' (p. 138). We see the beginning of the process which leads us to the world of 'alternative facts' and of 'fake news' that characterises our own grievous moment in the history of neoliberalism. Rudy Giuliani notoriously declared in August 2018, when explaining why Donald Trump should not testify to the Mueller inquiry, that 'truth isn't truth'; Hubert, in *The Takeover*, offers an early echo of this chilling sentiment, asserting that 'truth is not literally true'.[11] Spark's response to the untruthfulness of the truth is to develop a realist narrative mode that oversees a malfunction in the reality effect – and one can see that the novel form more generally, in the passage from the seventies to the turn of the century, offers itself as a vehicle with which to explore the crisis in representation set in motion by the neoliberalisation of capital. All of the major developments in the history of the novel in this period are touched by this close relation between narrative form and the anti-representational logic of neoliberalism. From J.G. Ballard's *Crash*, to Angela Carter's *The Bloody Chamber*, to Salman Rushdie's *Midnight's Children*, to Don DeLillo's *White Noise*, to Toni Morrison's *Beloved*, to Chris Kraus's *I Love Dick*, the formal inventiveness of the novel is powered, to some degree, by the energy that is released by the freeing of capital from its material base. As the narrator of Martin Amis's grotesque novel *Money* puts it, the epistemological crisis that novel enacts began 'when money went wrong' in 1973.[12] Realities are performative, as Chris puts it in Chris Kraus's *I Love Dick*, because 'money's abstract'.[13] Or as DeLillo's narrator puts it in *Underworld*, 'capital burns off the nuance in a culture', exposing us to the 'attenuating influence of money that's electronic and sex that's cyberspaced'.[14]

The later twentieth-century novel can thus seem to act as the cultural expression of an underlying neoliberal logic, Sinn Fein to neoliberalism's IRA. The free-market economic forces that decouple capital from its material base are mirrored in the anti-representational narrative forces that decouple textual surface from historical or psychological depth. And if there is such a close accord between neoliberalism and the novel, then that accord finds a ready articulation in the critical language that comes to dominance in that same period between the seventies and the nineties – the critical language of postmodernism. For David Harvey, and even more influentially for Fredric Jameson, postmodernism named the process by which cultural forms gave expression to the cultural logic of late capitalism. Postmodernism happens, Jameson writes in *Postmodernism: Or the Cultural Logic of Late Capitalism*, when the 'economic system and the cultural "structure of feeling" somehow crystallized in the great shock of the crises of 1973'.[15] The collapse of the opposition between the shallow and the intense that one can see at the end of the century in Roth's *The Human Stain* is, for Jameson, part of a wider postmodern economy of meaning, in which a whole range of what he calls 'postmodern antimonies' (change and stasis, surface and depth, the trivial and the profound) turn out not to be in opposition at all, but secretly identical with each other.[16] Postmodern cultural forms oversee what Jameson famously calls a 'waning of affect' on the one hand, and a 'flatness or depthlessness' on the other, in which narrative forms, including the novel, give expression to the failure of the oppositional relations between signifier and signified, between textual surface and historical depth, that had characterized earlier periods in cultural history.[17] Mirroring the 'complete mutation' identified by Spark in *The Takeover*, Jameson argues that postmodern forms articulate a 'fundamental mutation both in the object world itself – now become a set of texts or simulacra – and in the disposition of the subject'.[18] The loss of the surface-depth model leads to 'a new kind of superficiality in the most literal sense, perhaps the supreme feature of all the postmodernisms'.[19] This superficiality – this intense shallowness – is the mark of the loss of affect, the loss of the sense that our artforms bear witness to some kind of embedded and embodied feeling, registered in deep psychic structures. 'The very concept of expression', Jameson writes, 'presupposes indeed some separation within the subject, and along with that a whole metaphysics of inside and outside, of the worldless pain within the monad, and the moment in which, often cathartically, that "emotion" is then projected out and externalised'.[20] Postmodernism, as a cultural expression of a neoliberal logic which dismantles the relations between thought and thing, oversees the lapsing of this separation in the self – the separation between Coleman's suntanned skin and his secret identity – as our artforms give up any pretension to being 'the outward dramatization of inward feeling'.[21]

Postmodernism, through this optic, is the cultural expression of a neoliberal structure of feeling, that comes into focus for Jameson at the end of the millennium; but if it is the historical progression towards a 'late' cultural moment that gives rise to postmodernism, then postmodernism itself also seemed to herald the end of a certain kind of historical logic. The process by which neoliberal economics have become, in David Harvey's words, 'hegemonic as a mode of discourse', appeared to many to have brought us, too, to what Francis Fukuyama famously, and famously hubristically, called 'the end of history'.[22] As Fredric Jameson put it early in the current century, in one of his most famous utterances, 'it is easier to imagine the end of the world than to imagine the end of capitalism'.[23] But while the end of the cold war, the dominance of the US as a single superpower, and the triumph of free market economics, allowed for the critical emergence of postmodernism as a late twentieth-century structure of feeling, the new century has seen a series of historical convulsions which have offered a radical challenge to the ways in which we have conceptualised late capitalism, and late culture more generally. If postmodernism was fuelled by a perception that the engine of history has stalled, the dramatic shifts in the production of world spaces in the twenty-first century – from the aftermath of 9/11, to the market crash of 2008, to American decline and the rise of China and India as superpowers, to the growing climate emergency, to the pandemic of 2020 – have contributed to the much discussed waning of postmodernism as a cultural dominant. And with the waning of postmodernism, it has become necessary to rethink the relation between neoliberalism and the cultural forms which give expression to it. It is not enough, critics such as Walter Benn Michaels have argued, for the postmodern novel to offer a critical response to neoliberal conditions that is also a symptom of such conditions – not enough to be content with a performance of intense shallowness as our only means of responding to the forces that are rendering our cultural experience shallow. Such a tight relation between the 'economic system' and the 'cultural "structure of feeling"' does not give rise, Benn Michaels argues, to a postmodern mode of critique, so much as it signals the end of critique altogether, the folding of the novel into the neoliberalism that it sets out to diagnose. The Humanities departments that teach these novels, he writes, are not the 'hotbeds of leftism' that they believe themselves to be, but are more like the 'research and development division of neoliberalism'.[24] Some of the most celebrated novels of the period – from Toni Morrison's *Beloved* to Jonathan Franzen's *Corrections*, to Philip Roth's *The Plot Against America* – for all their differences, have something in common, something which allows us to group these texts together under the heading of what Benn Michaels calls the 'neoliberal novel'. What they share, he suggests, is their tendency to endorse a neoliberal economic logic through a failure to critique it. These novels, he suggests, trade in personal stories of individual suffering or trauma or pleasure – Monica and Bill making out in the Oval Office rather than American power protecting its economic interests in the Middle east – because the novel of the period has reneged on its duty to expose the real economic drivers of our cultural condition. The recent explosion of books about historical injustice – novels exploring the trauma of the Holocaust or of slavery – comes about because shared historical suffering is a distraction from real contemporary inequality. 'No move is more characteristic of the neoliberal novel', he writes, 'than the substitution of cultural difference for [...] class difference'.[25]

Benn Michaels response to this perception – that the neoliberal novel has lost its critical power – is to suggest that the novel itself is bankrupt, obsolete. He hopes that the economic crash of 2008 will spell the end of neoliberal triumphalism, and with it the end of the neoliberal novel. 'Maybe', he suggests, an 'upside of the collapse of a Thatcherite economy will be the disappearance of this entirely Thatcherite genre'. There'll be 'no more books like *The Corrections*'. There'll be 'no memoirs, no historicist novels', and 'a lot of other novels will have to go, too'.[26] Benn Michaels welcomes a bonfire of the novel vanities. But for other more sober minded critics and theorists, the clear and pressing problem of the critical failures of the novel under neoliberalism requires not a bonfire but a new way of understanding critique, and the novel's contemporary capacity to perform it. There is a wave of scholars writing now who are seeking, after the decline of the languages of postmodernism, to develop new critical ways of understanding both neoliberalism itself, and the art forms that have arisen in response to it. The contemporary proliferation of new forms of reading – surface reading, mere reading, distant reading – is a part of this new wave, a response to the perception that the dominance of a neoliberal logic does not mean that our art forms have become complicit with the marketplace, so much as it requires us to develop new ways of understanding how art and economics are bound together. It might suggest, as Rita Felski has argued, that we are entering into a new era of critical thinking that she characterises as 'post-critique', or it might prompt us, like Sianne Ngai, to the conclusion that we need a new set of aesthetic categories with which to grasp our contemporary modes of expression. For Mitchum Huehls, in an implicit rejoinder to Benn Michaels' scepticism about the contemporary novel's capacities for critical work, it is 'too easy' to conclude that the contemporary novel has become 'merely symptomatic of neoliberalism's capacious grasp'.[27] It seems to him more likely that 'many contemporary authors who at first glance might appear to be abandoning politics are actually entirely rethinking what politics looks like in our neoliberal age' (p. xi). Shallowness has not become simply identical with intensity, this thinking goes, but has entered into a different relationship with it, which can only be seen through a fresh critical lens. As Rachel Greenwald-Smith has influentially argued, it may be that 'one of the most important legacies of postmodernist experimentation might in fact be the denaturalization of this binary'. It is not that affect has waned, but that it has migrated. 'What if what we see in postmodernist fiction are fleshed-out non-humans, warmth without depth, embodiment as a form of surface subjectivity?'.[28] It's not, perhaps, that the novels of the late twentieth century 'will have to go', but that we need a new means of reading them, as Bill needs to find a way of reading Monica's shallow intensity, as Zuckerman reaches for a means of reading Coleman's tanned skin, or his tattoo declaring his allegiance to the US navy.

To begin to imagine such a mode of reading, we might take as an example James Kelman's stunning 1994 novel, *How Late It Was How Late*. This is a novel concerned, both centrally and elliptically, with the condition of lateness, with the fin de millennial perception that we have reached a late stage, culturally, politically, economically. The protagonist Sammy, an impoverished ex-convict living precariously in Glasgow and trying to stay out of the way of the police, comes back repeatedly to his feeling that it is late, that things are late. 'Ah, fuck it', he thinks, 'life, it can be awkward. And time passes. Then it's too late'.[29] 'It's getting a bit late for games, and he's getting a bit too auld to be playing them anyway' (pp. 204–205). 'A bus was coming; he put out his hand; too late. There ye are; fucking time; fucking late again' (p. 246). Kelman's novel is set in a late medium; but this is not quite the lateness that Harvey diagnoses, or Jameson. There is no grand DeLillian theorising, no attempt to give a critical quality to this late time. Rather, the novel depicts lateness as complete, borderless disorientation, a groping in the dark. The novel opens in media res with the story, told exclusively in Sammy's demotic third person, of a fight. Sammy wakes up on the street after a long and heavy drinking binge, to find himself surveilled by two plain clothes policemen. He walks up to them and punches one of them, inadvisedly perhaps, whereupon he is taken into a close and severely beaten. 'They had him,' he says, 'they fucking had him, the two of them, one hand gripping the back of his neck and another on his left wrist and another yin twisting his right arm all the way up his fucking back and it was pure fucking agony like it was getting wrenched off man' (p. 6). We don't see the beating that Sammy is given. 'Ye're as well drawing a curtain here', he says, 'nay point prolonging the agony' (p. 6). But it is so horrific, so grotesquely violent, that it nearly kills him. He wakes in a prison cell in terrible pain and confusion, with strange effects in his vision. 'His fucking eyes', he thinks, 'there was something wrong with them, like if it had still been daylight and he was reading a book he would have had double-vision or something' (p. 9). He passes out, and when he reawakens he can no longer see. 'Then he scratched his cheek. Just at the bone beneath where his right eye should have been, then closing the eye and putting his finger on the lid, then opening it and closing it and for fuck sake man nothing, he couldnay see nothing' (p. 10).

The rest of the novel takes place in the darkness to which that beating delivers Sammy, and our understanding of the novel's critical and aesthetic texture, its relation to the lateness in which it is set, is determined by that darkness. Sammy's blindness is an effect of state violence; and in a sense this in itself serves a critical function, offering the kind of brutal depiction of the violence of neoliberal inequality that Benn Michaels suggests the contemporary novel has largely forsaken. *How Late* is one of the more powerful dramatisations of state violence written in the last half century (one of the others being Kelman's later novel *Translated Accounts*). There are few novels which live through the subjection of the poor and the precarious to the brutality of the neoliberal state with such intensity. But if that is so, what is so extraordinary about this novel is that the terms in which it dissects the violence of late culture are also, and at every moment, symptomatic of that lateness. There is no critical move outside of the condition to which Sammy is condemned, no Lukácsian corrective, no moment of redress. This is a narrative voice, descendant of the alienated voice in Kafka or in Beckett, that can find no traction, no alternative to the logic which grips it, as those policemen grip Sammy at the opening of the novel, preparing to beat him nearly to death. Like Gregor Samsa waking to find himself transformed from salesman to cockroach, Sammy does not even exhibit much surprise at the loss of his sight, or at the terrible damage done to his body. 'The auld life was definitely ower now man', he thinks, 'it was finished, fucking finished' (p. 11); but he contemplates the end of his old life from a kind of distance, as Gregor contemplates the end of his, as Gregor wonders dispassionately how he is going to get to work now he is an insect ('He lay in his former position, sighing, and watched his little legs struggling against each other more wildly than ever').[30] 'Now he was chuckling away to himself', Sammy says, in the first hours of his blindness, 'How the hell was it happening to him!'. 'He started thinking about it; this was a new stage in life, a development. A new epoch!' (p. 11).

There is, then, despite its intensity, a certain affectlessness to this novel, as Sammy chuckles to himself at the condition he is in, a certain disconnect that is the cause and effect of the violence it witnesses. And if Sammy's own relation to his beaten body is disjointed in this way, then the story that the novel goes on to tell, of Sammy's attempt to live in the 'new epoch' to which the beating has delivered him, is a story of affectlessness, a story of the dismantling of the apparatuses of embodied perception that is the work of the neoliberal state. One of the plotlines of the novel concerns Sammy's attempt to apply for state aid, for disability benefit, as his blindness makes it impossible for him to work. He visits the doctor who is responsible for registering him as blind, explaining to him that he can't work on building sites if he can't see. 'A lot of things ye do are up high doctor', he says, 'eh … there isnay any floors; nay walls, nay ceilings. Ye're in the middle of building them so … they're not there yet. Sammy shrugged. If ye cannay see ye're liable to fall off' (p. 223). This is a peculiarly moving moment in the novel. The lack of walls and ceiling, the unmade state that Sammy describes, names both the partly built environment of the labourer's workplace, and the condition to which his blindness has delivered him, that sense that his body's place in the world has been suddenly erased. His visit to the doctor is an appeal to the state – the state, of course, whose law-enforcers blinded him in the first place – to help him to embed himself again in a fully built environment, with walls and ceilings, and to help him embed himself in his own body. It is a first principle of the democratic condition, as Jonathan Locke tells us, that we all have a 'property in our own person'.[31] But the response of the doctor to Sammy's plea is a radical denial of this democratic principle, and a symptom of a failure of the bonds that tie bodies to minds, that ground ideational structures in material things. The doctor begins by giving Sammy a cod lesson in the priority of the soul over the body, telling him that 'it is to the soul that the very special sense of sight belongs'. 'Sensation,' he goes on, 'doesn't occur in view of the soul's presence in the parts that serve as external sense-organs but in view of its actual presence in the brain, where it employs a governing sensory faculty' (p. 222). Sensation has no manifestation in real bodies, the doctor tells Sammy, before going on to refuse to verify that Sammy is blind. 'What are ye saying', Sammy says, 'Are ye saying that you dont really think I'm blind?'. 'It isnt for me to say', the doctor replies.

The refusal of the state to recognise Sammy's condition is a corollary of the alienation that the novel performs in its own voice – the total enclosure of the narrative in a consciousness that cannot fling itself clear of its own closed circuitry. The sealed nature of the narrative voice lives out the sense that there is no way that Sammy can show the inside of his head to others, to demonstrate how he is feeling, how he is perceiving the world. As Sammy's self-appointed 'rep' Ally puts it later in the novel, it is hard to prove that you are blind, when other people cannot know what or if you are seeing. 'See I mean', he says 'if it was a straightforward loss of what we might call an objective function, like a limb or something, then fair enough but the eyes are something else' (p. 295). What *How Late* suggests is that, under late conditions, we cannot share our view of the world. We cannot give ourselves to others to be read, as Coleman cannot give himself to Zuckerman to be read. Harvey's 'decoupling' of capital from material that is the signature of late historical time has allowed the material world more generally to float free from the forms in which we measure and value it, and so those who fall victim to the state, those whose poverty and precarity is an effect of the unequal distribution of wealth that powers the logic of capital, can gain no purchase on their own material conditions. The intensity of their suffering remains shallow. The peculiar alienation of the narrative voice in Kelman's novels (in *How Late*, as well as in *Translated Accounts* and *Kiron Smith boy*), like the dismantlement of Spark's realism in *The Takeover*, is a symptom of this shallowness. But if this is the case, what Kelman's novel tells us, so loudly it deafens us, is that shallowness, loss of traction, is itself an affect, even if one that requires us to develop a new way of understanding how we register affect, how inner consciousness is attached to outer forms, how surface is grafted to depth, how perception materialises itself. This altered affect is given an arresting form early in the novel, as Sammy awakens to his blindness. 'He shifted his head' he says as he wakes, 'and felt the pillow damp on his face'. While he has been sleeping, liquid has been running from his eyes, but of course he can't see it, so he doesn't know what it is, what it is that has been leaking from him. 'He hadnay been greeting', he thinks, 'just water must have been running out' (p. 24). 'Maybe it was fucking pus', he thinks. 'Maybe it was fucking yellow fucking mucus pus or something, rancid fucking liquid shit running out his body, out his eyes' (p. 24). His distance from his body is such that he cannot imagine what his own materiality consists of. But then he hits on another idea, a way of thinking about sight that resonates through *How Late*, and perhaps through the novel of the period more generally. 'Maybe' he says, 'it was the thing that gave ye sight, now he didnay have sight the thing had turned into pus, and here it was getting discharged, excess body baggage' (p. 24).

 The weightless concept of sight, here, is given a kind of substance, a kind of embodied thinghood, just at the moment when our modes of perception are most divorced from the material world that we fail to look upon. The novel – Kelman's novel, but also perhaps the novel more generally – is in a certain sympathy with Sammy's blindness. The novel is a blind medium, a medium that has to do without the visual, that transmits its thoughts in words directly to the mind, to that horrible doctor's 'governing sensory faculty'. The total enclosure of the narrative within the precinct of Sammy's thoughts is a mark of this privation. But if the narrative is blind, it is itself a substance that conjures the most intense forms of seeing, a kind of thing that gives ye sight. Writing at the end of the century, writing in the gloaming of the millennium, Kelman suggests that the real violence of late capitalism is that it destroys the apparatuses we have to see it, to appraise or critique its affects. But if this is so, the novel contains within itself also a kind of substance, the substance perhaps of fiction itself, which is its own form of seeing, a seeing that adjusts the relations between the subject and the object, between the shallow and the intense. If we are to discover in our time a means of reading the relation between neoliberalism and the novel, we have to find a way of seeing fiction, fiction as an agent at work in the world, casting its own slant of light.

2023

CHAPTER 14

To Carry Now Away
Happy Days in the Anthropocene

Sarah Ahmed's 2010 book *The Promise of Happiness* 'proceeds', she writes, by 'suspending belief that happiness is a good thing'.[1]

The idea of happiness, she argues, is both normative and normalising. It comes with 'straight conditions' (p. 100). To strive to live in a way that will lead to our own happiness, and that of those we love, is to live within the narrow horizons of a prescribed ideal of the good life. 'If we have a duty to promote what causes happiness, then happiness becomes a duty' (p. 7). Happiness comes about when we find a way of containing the energies of what Ahmed calls 'possibility' within a normative frame – when we train the unknowability of the future, and of other people, into a known path. This is why 'one of the primary happiness indicators is marriage' – marriage as the denial of the futurity of the future and the otherness of the other (p. 6). An ethical relation to the other, and to the future, Ahmed argues, involves us in a resistance to the demands and the promise of happiness, a refusal of the duties that what Stanley Cavell calls 'the pursuits of happiness' impose upon us.[2] 'Opening up possibility causes unhappiness', she writes, and so a 'revolutionary politics has to work hard to stay proximate to unhappiness' (p. 223).

One can see another version of this scepticism concerning the desirability of happiness at work in Aldous Huxley's 1932 novel *Brave New World*. Huxley imagines a future state in which information technology, recreational pharmaceuticals and totalitarianism combine to enforce a situation in which, in one of the repeated mantras that run through the novel, 'everybody's happy now'.[3] Under the jurisdiction of the novel's 'World State', happiness is guaranteed, because the state has engineered a perfect fit between human and environment. In Huxley's brave new world, as in Beckett's *Endgame*, there is 'no more nature', as nature itself has been subsumed into the realm of the technologized commodity.[4] Every inch of natural space has been adapted for the enforced leisure activities of the residents – 'electromagnetic golf', or 'centrifugal bumble-puppy'. The human has mastered the environment, and this absorption of nature into culture is reflected in the eradication of all other kinds of disjunction or alienation. The class system has been so finely engineered that the members of each class (Alpha, Beta, Epsilon and so on) feel that their class identification involves no constraint, and so there is no discontent, no striving for a better life. And erotic relations, too, have been arranged in such a way that there are no barriers to fulfilment. Marriage – Ahmed's primary happiness indicator – has been banished here, but only because the happiness-benefits it accrues have been universalised. It is not necessary to marry someone to gain sexual ownership of them, because, in this happily polyamorous place, consent has always already been given, and other people, whoever they are, are already our property. As another of those repeated mantras has it, 'everybody belongs to everyone else' (p. 109).

Huxley shows us this picture of compulsory happiness in order to demonstrate to us the banality of happiness as a category, or a social aim. The culture industry's capacity to answer our needs, Huxley suggests, to keep us entertained with elaborate games, or with pharmaceutical and pornographic narcotics, becomes a kind of totalitarianism, against which we have to guard ourselves by holding ourselves close to those things that make us unhappy, or at least that defer the gratification of our desires. If we get what we want, Huxley worries, we will find that it is unsatisfying, as he thinks that the purpose of living lies not in achieving our aims (an achievement, he supposes, which could only demonstrate to us how little that which we want is worth) but in striving against the obstacles that stand in our way. So both for Huxley and for Ahmed, writers who come from strikingly different political positions, it seems politically necessary to cultivate a scepticism about the good of happiness, to work hard to stay proximate to unhappiness. For both writers, happiness is a mark of the coincidence of self with other, self with state, a discovery of what one *wants* to do in the shape of what one is *expected* or *compelled* to do, and so is a weak sign of compliance or docility, rather than anything like an achieved political desire.

The happiness that both Huxley and Ahmed distrust is thus the politically debilitating happiness that arises from *fitness*. Both writers train their critical eye on the complexes that enforce that fitness – the culture industry for Huxley, compulsory heterosexuality for Ahmed.[5] But, while it is the case that both of these complexes are alive and well – probably as powerful now as they have ever been in determining the horizon of our collective desires – the current century has seen the emergence of another factor which determines the fit between human and environment, and which drastically shifts the terms in which we conceive of happiness as an accommodation with the future. I mean, of course, the emergence of climate change as a determining condition of contemporary cultural life. Huxley cannot conceive of any limits to the artificiality that he sees dawning in the early twentieth century – the capacity of human cultures and technologies to overcome nature, to bend all natural processes, from childbirth to aging, to the human technological will. But the passage from the twentieth to the twenty-first centuries has seen something like the opposite recognition, the discovery that the nature that human technologies repress comes back in the form of a brutally material environment that is increasingly unsuited to human habitation. The fitness that Huxley dreads in 1932 has become, in 2022, a radical unfitness, in which the human cultures that technologies reproduce become ever less capable of finding themselves attuned to the environments that sustain them. Under these circumstances, the conception of happiness, in Ahmed's terms, as a suborning of the future to the norms of the present, is drastically reframed. If happiness is a sign that the future is already inscribed in the normative terms of the present, then what becomes of the promise of happiness when the future becomes unthinkable, when the time to come can no longer be contained within a given picture of the good or happy life? What happens when happiness, considered as a fit between present and future, between the life you strive for and the life you are given, becomes structurally impossible? What becomes of the revolutionary political power of unhappiness, when the futural space in which the very possibility of happiness unfolds has been abolished?

It was in two connected theatrical productions I attended in the early summer of 2021 that these questions took on, for me, a new kind of clarity, a clarity that was no doubt derived in part from the particular circumstances of the time in which they took place. This was the summer when we were just beginning to look past the Covid-19 pandemic – an event that had brought about a global shut down of the happiness machine. The spread of a virus had led governments around the world to close down their economies, to suspend business as usual, delivering people in all continents of the globe to a peculiar, slack time, in which the pursuit of a futural happiness was suddenly and dramatically cancelled. We were no longer heading towards the beginnings and endings we had imagined – marriages were cancelled, as well as funerals – and were instead cast into our own static midst, in which we were confronted not with the people we were in the process of becoming, but with the people we already were. We found ourselves confined not only to our dwellings, but to a kind of unmoving present, and we found too – many of us – that we entered into a shifted relationship with our surroundings. The sight of abandoned city centres weirdly replicated around the world laid bare some principle of dwelling, some relation between human and environment, that the commerce of the everyday had disguised. As families of wild boar were seen roaming in city centres, as birdsong replaced the sound of traffic, lockdown opened some window on our current state, on the terms in which the human project (now so bewilderingly paused) intersects with the world spaces in which it unfolds.[6]

It was in the space of this pause, or just as we were seeking to free ourselves from it in order to re-enter the stream of moving time, that I attended both of the productions I will discuss here – productions which turn, at their heart, around the struggle to share happiness with others, and around an examination of the environments in which such shared happiness might become possible.

The first of these, a site specific piece entitled *Beckett in Folkestone*, was a theatrical re-enactment of Samuel Beckett's secret marriage, on 25 March 1961, to his long-standing partner Suzanne Déchevaux-Dumesnil.[7] The performance, which I attended with my partner Hannah on 12 June 2021, sets out to recreate the fortnight that Beckett spent in Folkestone in the run up to his marriage. Beckett married Suzanne, at least in part, in order to ensure that she would inherit his property, and rights to his work, after his death. Because French property law does not automatically acknowledge the rights of spouses to their partners' estate, Beckett and Déchevaux-Dumesnil decided to marry in England, so that Beckett's estate would be bequeathed according to British rather than French law; and Beckett was required to spend a fortnight in England before the ceremony, because this is the minimum period that would allow him to claim residency for the purposes of matrimony on British soil.[8]

Beckett in Folkestone relives those two weeks, from when Beckett arrived in the town, through his solitary time staying in a hotel, the evenings spent sitting over pints of Guinness in a local pub, up to the day of the marriage itself. Partly because of Covid restrictions, which made it difficult to stage events with large audiences, the piece was conceived in such a way that each audience member experiences the performance alone. The piece opens when you are ushered into a Folkestone hotel room, done up to resemble Beckett's room (his clothes in the wardrobe, his glasses on the nightstand, a somewhat overripe banana on the table). A 1960s black and white television in the hotel room plays a monologue, told from the perspective of the hotel receptionist who has developed a fascination with Beckett (or 'Mr Barclay', which is the pseudonym under which Beckett checked in). This monologue starts to tell the story of Beckett's marriage, which is then continued as we are ushered, alone, though the various sites in which the piece unfolds. We are given headphones on which the narrative continues as we walk along the Folkestone streets, following in Beckett's footsteps. We go to the local pub he visited, where we find another television which takes up the story again, from the perspective of a local journalist, who thinks he might have recognised Beckett (the journalist contacted John Calder to ask if he knew anything of Beckett's being in Folkestone – Calder, in on the secret, assured him that Beckett was on holiday in North Africa).[9] We finish up in a large municipal space (the local library), which recreates the registry office in which the wedding takes place (seen through the eyes of one of the formal witnesses to the wedding, a Mrs E Pugsley, who also speaks to us on a flickering black and white Ferguson television).

The piece, in the manner characteristic of immersive theatre, produced a peculiar collapse between now and then, between a sunny Folkestone in 2021, and the town that Beckett visited in 1961. The forces that were in the air that summer – not only the uncertain emergence from lockdown, but the still unfolding geopolitical consequences of Brexit, and the developing awareness of a new viral logic ushered in by the pandemic – were merged, in edgeless ways, with Beckett's period of waiting for Suzanne. We were supposed to experience the performance alone, so we could enter into the spirit of Beckett's solitude; but timings were mixed up on the day of our visit, so Hannah and I went through the routine together – sitting in Beckett's hotel room together, walking the streets side by side, sitting together in the mocked up registry office. We ended up eating lunch, on a sparklingly sunny afternoon, in a pub garden that looked over the sea. It was such a clear day that we could see right across the channel to the northern coast of France – the France to which Beckett and Suzanne were even then returning, the France from which we had banished ourselves, in the shoddy post-imperial tantrum with which we had exited the European Union.

This way of experiencing the piece – both alone and together, as we listened to the same story on separate headphones – felt a little rebellious, as if we had disobeyed the rules. But it added in a peculiar way to its effect. The story of Beckett's marriage that emerges here is of a union that is also a separation. Beckett's desire to ensure that Suzanne inherited his estate had been quickened, the performance suggested, by the fact that his affair with the English translator and script editor Barbara Bray had started at that time to become more serious. They had become close in 1957, and by 1961 Bray was preparing to move to Paris, as their relationship deepened into a partnership that would last until Beckett's death in 1989. So, whatever gesture of commitment the marriage to Déchevaux-Dumesnil entailed, *Beckett in Folkestone* suggested, it was also an arrangement that allowed Beckett the freedom to commit himself, at the same time, to Bray. Binding oneself to another as a way of partly freeing oneself from that other. The theatrical dynamics of the piece – the way in which it wove solitude into company, now into then, the fictional into the real – resonated with this sense, that sharing a life and insulating oneself from the person whose life you share, might be part of the same movement. A resonance, unmistakably, that fed on its echoes with the time we were in, the hesitant movement towards a post-Covid sociality, the mourning, after Brexit, for an entente cordiale that had been lost. And if these resonances were at work throughout the piece, then the moment they reached their greatest intensity was the moment we learnt that, during this empty fortnight, this odd, stalled junction between France and England, between Déchevaux-Dumesnil and Bray, Beckett was tinkering with the second draft of a play – the play that was to become *Happy Days*.

Happy Days, Beckett's most acute portrait of a marriage, was in the air throughout the performance of *Beckett in Folkestone*. And it is a performance of that play, which I attended, also with Hannah, on the 26 June 2021, that is the second performance that I will discuss here. The performance was at the Riverside Studios, directed by Tevor Nunn, starring Lisa Dwan. The simple experience of travelling to London that day – of sitting outside by the Thames, having a drink before the performance in the soft light of a summer evening – felt, after the wilderness of Covid, like paradise enough. But nothing prepared us, either Hannah or me, for the intensity of the experience, electric from the moment that the stage is lighted, and we see Winnie, buried in her mound.

The run up to that opening was strange enough. Lingering Covid precautions meant that the seating arrangements were designed to allow for an element of social distancing. The auditorium was sparsely furnished with chairs that were locked together in pairs. Each of these coupled seats was marooned in a little pool of emptiness, so as the audience arrived we found ourselves separated into pairs, mostly it seemed into couples, feeling that same isolation, that same yoking together, that we had all just been through, privately and collectively.[10] So when the lights came on, and we saw Winnie, buried in the earth, compelled to talk, constantly, to Willie, her only companion – a sight that always, however often we have seen a performance of the play, causes a lurch of dread and nameless recognition – each of us, in our island twosomes, saw ourselves.

To see *Happy Days* at that moment, and in the immediate aftermath of *Beckett in Folkestone*, was to see it as a reflection on the means by which the forms and rhetorics of shared life survive the revelation – always already known but ruthlessly supressed – that they are fundamentally incompatible with the material realities of living. We know, don't we, and always have, from earliest memory, that the stories we tell ourselves to 'give us the impression that we exist' are at a remove from the condition of being immured in a body, of being 'plunged in it beyond recall' – the condition that *Happy Days* reveals with such force.[11] This revelation drew some of its power from its inescapable relation to the pandemic. A central element of the pandemic experience was the raw recognition that our bodies are not expressions or extensions of our own being – not vehicles of our consciousness over which we have control and jurisdiction – but rather earthen casements in which we are inescapably embedded. To be locked in our houses was to discover that our bodies are not really our own property but are instead vectors in a disease. It was to be buried in our biopolitical selves, as Winnie is buried in her mound. To watch *Happy Days* in 2021 was to see an articulation of this pandemic truth – but the play also captures a much wider element of contemporary planetary experience, and opens up a much deeper gulf between the languages of communal life, and the material conditions of contemporary existence. It is impossible to watch this play in the 2020s and not to see it as a dramatisation of the catastrophe of climate change – a catastrophe with which the pandemic itself is deeply entwined. The forces that gave rise to the pandemic – the intensive exploitation of natural resources for agricultural and/or pharmaceutical use, combined with the global mobility of the population – are also those that have driven eco-crisis, and that have caused the climate emergency. To see Winnie, now, buried in the scorched earth, drenched in a blaze of hellish light, is to see a world that has come to an end, a world whose climate is no longer in the remotest sympathy with the mantras, repetitions and routines of human life. 'The heat is much greater', Winnie says, in her brightly matter of fact way. It is getting hotter, drier, more and more unforgiving. Things burst spontaneously into flames. 'With the sun blazing so much fiercer down', Winne says,

> and hourly fiercer, is it not natural things should go on fire never known to do so, in this way, spontaneous like. [*Pause.*] Shall I myself not melt perhaps in the end, or burn, oh I do not mean necessarily burst into flames, no, just little by little be charred to a black cinder all this – [*ample gesture of arms*] – visible flesh.[12]

Winnie is buried in the stuff of herself, the stuff of an earth that is drying and burning, and, as the earth becomes less and less inhabitable, the human resources that she has to help her through the day become less and less effective. She has her bag. She has her cosmetics, to make her a 'Bit more human' (p. 156). She has her classics. What is that wonderful line? Something something laughing wild amid severest woe. She has her mercies. 'Ah yes. Many mercies. Great mercies' (p. 140). Above all, she has her Willie. 'Just to know you are there', she says to him, as he cowers somewhere out of sight behind her mound, 'within hearing and conceivably on the semi-alert is … er … paradise enow' (pp. 150–151). As she burns under a blazing sky, buried in an unhuman earth, she gathers around herself the tattered remains of a culture that no longer has the remotest relevance to her situation, and whose only remaining expressive power is the irony of that irrelevance. What are the classics to her? What is mercy? What is companionship? What is happiness, when the world in which happiness or unhappiness has any bearing has burned irrecoverably away?

These questions were in the air, as Hannah and I sat on our tethered chairs, and then, after the performance, sat over drinks in a bar, where we lingered for so long that we nearly missed the last train home. What does this play say about the possibility of companionship – the companionship between Winnie and Willie, or the triangular relations between Beckett, Déchevaux-Dumesnil and Bray that were preoccupying Beckett in 1961, as he tinkered with his script in his Folkestone hotel room? How does it conceive of the condition of marriage, what Devorah Baum calls the 'post-nuptial wilderness of the happy-ever-after'?[13] Does companionship, fidelity, infidelity become an irrelevance as the earth is scorched? Do the classics become a joke? Is literature in the Anthropocene an impossibility? What is that wonderful line? With something something and a flask of wine, and thou beside me singing in the wilderness, wilderness is paradise enow.[14] And if companionship is an impossibility, if literature is an irrelevance, if love is a weak joke, why did this play we had just seen, Hannah and I, why did it make us both feel so happy?

It was some time after we went to that performance, some time in 2022, that I found a kind of response to that question, in the form of a letter that Beckett wrote to Barbara Bray on 17 March 1958, as their relationship was becoming closer, or, to speak in the old style, as they were falling in love. Beckett is replying to a letter from Bray, in which she tells him of the sudden death of her estranged husband, John Bray. I will quote the letter in full:

Dear Barbara

Far from being troubled by your letter I am very touched that you should tell me about your great sorrow. I wish I could find something to comfort you. All I could say, and much more, and much better, you will have said to yourself long ago. And I have so little light and wisdom in me, when it comes to such disaster, that I can see nothing for us but the old earth turning onward and time feasting on our suffering along with the rest. Somewhere at the heart of the gales of grief (and of love too, I have been told) already they have blown themselves out. I was always grateful for that humiliating consciousness and it was always there I huddled, in the innermost place of human frailty and lowliness. To fly there for me was not to fly far, and I'm not saying this is right for you. But I can't talk about solace of which I know nothing. And beyond all courage and reasonableness I am sure that for the likes of you and me at least it's the "death is dead and no more dying" that makes it possible (just) to go on living. Forgive this wild stuff, I'm not a one to turn to in time of trouble. Work your head off and sleep at any price and leave the rest to the stream, to carry now away and bring you your other happy days.

Affectionately Sam[15]

This is a strange way to express a desire to comfort a grieving woman with whom you find yourself to be falling in love. There is an audible tone of defensive refusal in the letter, which resonates with letters that Beckett wrote to other women with whom he had erotic relationships around the same time. His declaration that 'I can't talk about solace', and 'I'm not a one to turn to in time of trouble' carries an echo of Beckett's earlier correspondence with Pamela Mitchell, which was characterised by Beckett's desire to keep the relationship alive, while ensuring that Mitchell was held at arm's length. In a letter of 6 August 1954, which Daniela Caselli quotes in her compelling close analysis of the Mitchell correspondence, Beckett warns Mitchell that he can't make her happy. 'The notion of happiness has no meaning at all for me any more', he writes, 'All I want is to be in the silence'. 'You will be happy one day and thank me for not involving you any deeper in my horrors'.[16] Both in the Mitchell correspondence, and in this letter to Bray, one can hear Beckett's insistence on his own shortcomings as a means of refusing intimacy – an insistence which in its repetition starts to look rote. But what is so striking about this letter to Bray (coming so early in their relationship) is that this reflex defensiveness is combined with the beginnings of a communicative urge, almost unique in Beckett's correspondence, one which works against his isolationist tendency, and which takes him towards the possibility of a kind of shared thinking with Bray that lasts until his death.

The most striking mark of this genesis – the beginning of what amounts to a collaboration – is the early appearance of the title of his later play, as if we are witnessing here the birth of Winnie's mordant optimism. It is true that the evocation here of happy days to come reads like a cruel joke – it is hard to see how a time that feasts on our suffering could be the vehicle that will take us to our other happy days. This closing gesture has affiliations with Beckett's defensiveness, his rote refusal of consolation. But it also marks the beginning of a discussion with Bray, in which, as Xander Ryan has recently shown, the scenario of *Happy Days* – the conceit of Winnie's bright cheeriness in the face of implacable woe – starts to take shape.[17] As the play is being written, late in 1960, we see Beckett trying out snatches of dialogue in progress with Bray, testing and adapting its feel and balance. He writes on 10 October 1960 to say that 'I put the tip of my little finger into the imbedded female solo machine, to the extent of writing a few stage directions and a scrap of dialogue':

<u>She</u> (loud)   Can you hear me?
<u>He</u> (off, loud)   Yes.
<u>She</u> (less loud) And now?
<u>He</u> (" ")   Yes.
<u>She</u> (soft)   And now?
<u>He</u> (" ")   Yes.
<u>She</u> (very soft) And now?
<u>He</u> (" ")   Yes.[18]

Beckett's conception of proximity, his testing of the range of Willie's earshot, is conducted here in dialogue with Bray, as if the growth of the Winnie-Wille complex is shaped by that between Beckett and Bray. The testing of sound as it carries over distance, which has recurred insistently in Beckett's writing at least since *First Love*, becomes here bound up with the voice that Beckett and Bray share in their correspondence, the voice that Beckett is trying to sound by listening to her.[19] When Beckett writes to Bray a couple of weeks later, on 28 October 1960, that the Willie figure 'should be as close to a mere ear as possible', we might hear an echo of the *Unnamable* narrator ('perhaps that's what I feel, myself vibrating, I'm the tympanum, on the one hand the mind, on the other the world, I don't belong to either').[20] We also hear Beckett opening himself to Bray, making of himself a mere ear.

The 17 March 1958 letter is the beginning of *Happy Days*, and the beginning of Beckett's and Bray's collaboration on the script (of which, sadly, only Beckett's half survives). But what is most remarkable about this letter is that, even here, so early in their correspondence, Beckett's relationship with Bray is becoming densely interwoven with the fabric of his writing, and of his literary thinking, as if the correspondence, from the beginning, touches closely on the junction that Beckett's writing works towards, the junction between one person and another, between human and environment, between body and earth. The picture he paints here, for example, of the 'old earth turning onward' ('I can see nothing for us but the old earth turning onward') resonates with a series of planetary images that run through his middle works, images that are integral to his picturing of a denuded or dehumanised earth. We can hear Molloy's reflections on planetarity as he lies in Lousse's garden. 'My life', Molloy says, as he sinks, like Winnie, into the soil, 'became the life of this garden as it rode the earth of deeps and wildernesses'.[21] As he merges with the earth, Molloy says, he can feel the 'labour of the planet rolling eager into winter'.[22] Or we can hear the narrator of *The Unnamable*, waiting for the agony of living to stop, thinking of the moment when the 'earth revolves no more', and 'time ends its meal and pain comes to an end'.[23] We can glimpse the dead earth of *Endgame*. 'The earth is extinguished', Clov says, 'though I never saw it lit'.[24] And then, the image of an aging planet comes back with a condensed force much later, in a short piece that trails other associations, too, from the 1958 letter to Bray. *Fizzle 6*, composed in the early seventies, and barely 300 words long, quotes directly from the letter in its opening line: 'Old earth, no more lies'.[25] The story tells of a man standing at a window at nightfall, watching as cockchafers hatch from eggs that have lain for long years underground (buried in that 'old earth'), so they might live their short, inhuman life. 'They take to wing, rise from my little oaktree and whirr away, glutted, into the shadows' (p. 238). The glutted cockchafers are feasting on brief time, as time feasts on us, and their ravenousness calls to mind the Shakespeare sonnet that Beckett alludes to in his letter to Bray. When Beckett writes to Bray that 'Death is dead and no more dying', he evokes the closing couplet of Sonnet 146:

> So shalt thou feed on death, that feeds on men,
> And death once dead, there's no more dying then.[26]

The guzzling of the cockchafers ('three years in the earth', the narrator thinks, 'then guzzle guzzle') is a feasting on death that leads the narrator, standing at his window, to a reflection on the passing of moments, and the possibility of happiness. 'For an instant', he says,

> I see the sky, the different skies, then they turn to faces, agonies, loves, the different loves, happiness too, yes, there was that too, unhappily. Moments of life, of mine too, among others, no denying, all said and done. Happiness, what happiness, but what deaths, what loves. (p. 238)

Fizzle 6 gathers together those images of an aging planet that recur in Beckett's writing, and merges them with his 1958 letter to Bray, so that the pieces together summon a kind of time in which grief and happiness, living and dying, become part of a composite, a kind of assemblage that resists our attempts to think it or measure it. But if *Fizzle 6* is a condensation of the thinking that appears in embryo in 1958, it is in *Happy Days* itself that it is given it fullest dramatic expression. When we see Winnie buried in her mound as the lights come up, what we see, what powers that lightning strike of immediate recognition, is an adjusted relation between the human and the 'old earth', an adjusted relation which carries within it a new worldview, a new form of life. What we see is something that we have long seen. What is that immortal line? 'O woe is me, t'have seen what I have seen'.[27] We see that what Heidegger called the world picture – the pictorial terms in which we have cast and framed the relation between human and planet – is lapsing, or has lapsed.[28] The world picture is predicated on the idea that human is figure, earth is ground. The human oversees the earth, like the figures in the paintings of Caspar David Friedrich who contemplate the land and the sky, bringing it into a German Romantic focus (see Figure 14.1). But the capacity to focus, to compose, to picture, has deserted us as we see Winnie, not contemplating the earth, or standing in relief against it, but buried in it, becoming it. The flash of recognition that the image produces, as the bell rings and the stage lights come up, is drawn from this revelation of a mingling of human and earth, a joining that signals the failure of a worldview, the collapse of a paradigm of enworlding. When we see Winnie buried to her waist at the opening of the first act, our eye is drawn immediately to that place where waist emerges from earth, distinguishing itself from it, merging itself with it. The only time that Winnie feels pain in the play is when she is made conscious, herself, of this difficult junction, this difficult zone of indifferentiation. No pain, she says throughout the play. No better, no worse, no change, no pain. That is what she finds so wonderful. But, leaning back in an attempt to see Willie, hidden somewhere behind the mound, she feels some grievous friction, some sore chaffing against the stuff in which she is encased. Giving up on her search for Willie, she 'turns back painfully front'. 'The earth is very tight today', she says, 'can it be that I have put on flesh?' (p. 149).

Figure 14.1 Caspar David Friedrich, *Two Men Contemplating the Moon*, 1830s, oil on canvas, Galerie Hans, Hamburg, 35 cm x 44.5 cm.

Everything that happens in *Happy Days* turns around this difficult place where the tight earth clasps the human form, where human and earth separate and join. It is this relation that produces the dominant effect of the play – the effect whereby the tattered remains of human culture appear purely anachronistic, as the distinction between human and earth loses its organising power. The experience of happiness, of love, even of the passing of time, relies, the play suggests, on a paradigmatic opposition between human and earth – between culture and nature – and so, when that opposition fails, the experience it underwrote, as immortalised in one's classics, becomes unthinkable. The possibility of happiness, Beckett writes in his 1958 letter to Bray, relies on the perception that we are carried on a stream of time. It is the measured passing of time that will 'carry now away and bring you your other happy days'.[29] But *Happy Days* presents us with a scenario in which the stream that might carry now away has dried up in the relentless heat, delivering us to an unchanging, unmoving now, in which all the forms which might make experience readable to us have withered away. Now; this is the most important word in *Happy Days*, the static block around which the rhythms of the play swirl, the mound in which it is buried. 'The day is now well advanced', Winnie says (p. 151). But she knows that the day is not advanced, either well or ill, that the difference between late and early, between morning and night, between yesterday and tomorrow, has been cancelled, as the old story of passing moments – the fizzling 'moments of life' – grinds to a halt. To speak of tomorrow or of yesterday is to speak, with automatic smile, in the old style. 'The day is now well advanced. (Smile.) To speak in the old style. (Smile off.)' (p. 151). How are we to think about then, or now, Winnie asks herself, when the old earth no longer recognises such categories. 'Then', Winnie says, 'now… what difficulties here, for the mind' (p. 161). What do we do, as we dwell in this no time, this no space? No, now, enow; the play happens along the line that connects these words, that merges negation, with the unmoving present, with a kind of sufficiency, a sated enough. 'Open and close the eyes, Winnie, open and close, always that. (Pause.) But no. (Smile.) Not now. (Smile broader.) No no. (Smile off)' (p. 163). Perhaps her mind will eventually fail, she thinks, eventually switch itself off. Perhaps some stream will carry her away. 'If the mind were to go?' she thinks, but she knows that 'it won't of course. (Pause.) Not quite. (Pause.) Not mine. (Smile) Not now' (p. 161). Perhaps her eyes will one day 'close in peace' (p. 161). But no. No, no. (Pause). Not mine. (Smile). Not now.

This now, the now of *Happy Days*, is the now, also, that closes *Fizzle 6*, as the cockchafers take to the wing for the unmeasurable duration of their brief, extended life. 'No but now, now, simply stay still, standing before a window, one hand on the wall, the other clutching your shirt, and see the sky, a long gaze' (p. 239). It is the now that we all glimpsed in the stillness at the heart of the pandemic, the now that happens when time stands still, and our apparatuses for measurement turn to ash. It is the now to which climate change has delivered us – a now that we see when the structure of futurity, to speak in the old style, has failed. The difficult, elusive join between the mound and Winnie's waist, and then Winnie's neck, the place where we both become and resist the old earth, is the province of this now, the unmoving time, the dried up stream, which delivers us to an assemblage of human and nonhuman that does not speak in the old style. To be presented with such an alien assemblage, to witness the destitution of a world view and the evacuation of the languages of mercy, of happiness, of companionship, should feel like a gross impoverishment. To see, in Dwan's immaculately precise performance, the reduction of all responsive or affective states to an empty automatism, this should install in us a kind of death. Smile. To speak in the old style. Smile off. Dwan's performance captured the rhythms of the play so minutely that the routines and rituals of shared life became, there on the stage before us, a precisely choreographed machinery of futility. Winnie's smile is not a sign of happiness, not the somatic expression of an inner state, but part of a clockwork mechanism, that tells not a moving but a stilled time. It should make us feel unhappy. Or worse it should make us feel that the time when we could measure the difference between happiness and unhappiness, when we could accord a value to that difference, has passed away. But it is the peculiar magic of the play that it does not. For Hannah and me, in June 2021, as we were emerging from the dark of lockdown into the hellish light, it did not.

It is easy to think that this effect – the strange failure of unhappiness to appear, the strange feeling of joy that Dwan's performance gave us – is a response to the play's comedy. That the joy we feel is a bleak and wild laughter amid severest woe. That we are enjoying, with Winnie, a 'brief ... gale of laughter' when we 'happen to see the old joke again' (p. 145). 'His Grace and Most Reverend Father in God Dr Carolus Hunter dead in tub' (p. 142). But it is not that – or it is more than that. The rhythms of the play – the turning of its routines around a still time that does not pass according to a human chronology – not only yield a comic picture of futility but also nudge us towards another horizon of meaning altogether. The joining of Winnie's body with the earth signals at once the collapse of a worldview, and the emergence of an ecological thinking that does not yet have a style of its own, or a vocabulary, or a time signature, but that rides on the play's rhythms, like a bird on a thermal. It is some such thinking that we can see, in embryo, in Beckett's letter to Bray, the letter in which he refuses to comfort her, or to offer her solace. The happiness that Beckett invokes at the end of the letter – that which depends on the capacity of the stream to carry now away – is a sham happiness, one whose possibility the whole flow of the letter denies. This is the cosmetic happiness, built on an accommodation with the future, against which Ahmed directs her energies. But at the heart of the letter is another structure of happiness, another way of thinking about how the old earth turns – one, Beckett says so earnestly to Bray, as he feels his way towards her and towards her grief, that might not be 'right' for her. Against the onward flow of the 'stream', Beckett writes, there is an 'innermost place', where 'I always huddled', a place that lies too at the very foundation of his writing. 'Somewhere at the heart of the gales of grief (and of love too, I've been told) already they have blown themselves out'.[30] These gales, again, find a place in *Happy Days,* in the form of Winnie's gale of laughter. But this meteorology of affect, both in the letter and the play, turns around a still centre, where the storm is already over, where peace and grief and happiness are not still to come, but are already here, in a conjoined presence that is produced from the recognition that the emotive forces that drive them have already waned, already lapsed. This is the still centre that we see before us on the stage, that is conjured as both human and earth, both happiness and unhappiness, lose their bearings, their place in the world picture, and open themselves to another time signature, another imagining of shared being.

Barbara Bray, in an interview she gave towards the end of her life, talked of this way of thinking, this 'way of being we'.[31] Beckett's work, she says, turns around the possibility that we might escape from 'the world and its snares and all the rest of it, and for a few moments you are free'.[32] 'But how are you going to put that into words?', she says, 'that was the problem', the problem that drives Beckett's work (p. 897). How do we get to the still centre, where the gales of words have already blown themselves out? 'Trying to use words', Bray says, 'to get to the state where there are no words' (p. 897). This is the state that we see, in *Happy Days*, when 'words fail'. 'Words fail', Winnie says. 'Is that not so, Willie? Is not that so, Willie, that even words fail, at times?' (p. 147). Words fail, and leave us in that space that we see on the stage in *Happy Days*, that space which does not belong in the world picture, that space conjoined of nothing, and now, and enough. Bray says that she feels able, at the end of her life, when the gale is so nearly blown out, to have what she calls a 'wild guess' at what the word is, the word that we see when words fail, the word that Beckett reaches for in his late work *What is the Word*. 'I think', she says 'that the word was love' (p. 897).

I don't know if the word is love. It could as well be death. But it speaks of a way of sharing being, a way of understanding how the joy and pain of living alone and together can survive the lapsing of the terms which make joy and pain meaningful. It suggests why, as Hannah and I sat over our drinks on that June evening, and the time ticked on to the last train, we felt so happy. This is a happiness, a joy, for which we do not wait, that does not require us to be carried away on any stream, and that does not rely on any existing model of futurity. Rather, it lies in the stream itself, and embodies a principle of shared being that lies at the heart of Beckett's writing, both his drama and his prose. Ahmed writes, in *The Promise of Happiness*, that she can conceive of happiness outside of the heteronormative future only by 'insisting that such happiness is *not* what is shared'.[33] To sidestep the duty that happiness imposes on us, we must, she thinks, refrain from the demand that our happiness is shared by others, or theirs by us. Here, she might find some sympathy with Beckett, who tends to defend himself against the demands that love makes on him. He wishes, often, that Bray might find happiness. 'Forgive all my sadness & foolishness', he writes on 10 October 1958, 'and try and find some happiness somewhere'.[34] 'You know what I'd give', he writes on 4 March 1960, 'to know you happier or less unhappy'.[35] But he does not want that happiness to be binding for him. 'Don't wish happiness on me', he writes to Bray, 'I'm not fitted for it'. 'Don't talk to me' he writes, 'for God's sake about the duty of happiness'.[36]

Beckett seeks to refuse the duty of happiness that others impose upon him; but in its 'innermost place' his work reaches for a kind of shared being that survives that imposition, that finds happiness not in the promissory, in the future, but in some suspended life, interwoven with the ground, that calls to a shifted conception of dwelling, and of the terms in which we relate to ourselves and each other. Even as the stream carries now away, Beckett's work looks to a form of conjunction that speaks to us, now, as we try to understand what happiness means in the Anthropocene. This is a conjunction that Beckett finds, at a lyrical moment in his late play *Ohio Impromptu*, in the flowing stream of the Seine. How the stream moves and stays still, separates and joins. 'How in joyous eddies its two arms conflowed and flowed united on'.[37]

2022

CHAPTER 15

On Rereading Proust

... for this very reason it causes us suddenly to breathe a new air, an air which is new precisely because we have breathed it in the past ...

Marcel Proust, *A la Recherche du Temps Perdu*[1]

I

It is possible to trace a connection, as tenuous as it is persistent, between rereading and autobiography. The drama of rereading, in which we encounter the same work at different times in our life, takes place in the theatre of our own mind. When we talk or think of reading, it is possible (just) to indulge the fantasy that reading is an abstract activity, an operation performed by some placeless, timeless reader, of no fixed abode or complexion or inclination. When we talk or think of rereading, by contrast, we posit, unavoidably, both a specific scene of reading, and a specific reader; or more precisely we posit at least two scenes of reading, and at least two readers – the scene in which the reader reads for the first time, and that in which he or she reads for the second time. And as we do so we are led, by the same logic, to imagine that both readers, both the reader encountering the book for the first time, and the reader who is reading for a second time, or a third, must be ourselves. We can talk in abstract terms about what *a reader* may or may not encounter on reading a given book, and disguise from ourselves some of the absurdity involved in invoking such abstractions, but surely only we ourselves – only you, or I – know what cognitive process occurred when we read a given book for a second time, or a third, when the labile impressions formed on first reading, under whatever circumstances, were shifted or reconstituted or confirmed on the second reading, when we were necessarily older, and perhaps sadder, or happier, or less enchanted; or on the third, when we were necessarily closer to death, and perhaps greedier for consolation, or less discriminating, or sickened by living. Or nourished by it. To think critically about the idea of rereading is to unearth this continuity, hidden and troubling and untrustworthy, between criticism and autobiography.

Even as this is the case, though, the basis upon which this connection between rereading and autobiography is laid is very unstable, and tends to weaken under analysis. This is partly because the distinction, between reading and rereading, is itself weak, and subject to disappearance. Vladimir Nabokov perhaps has this problem in mind when he writes, in one of the better known formulations concerning rereading, that 'one cannot *read* a book: one can only reread it'.[2] It is native to the condition of the book, of all books, that they come into being in the fullest sense only when they are read, and so any act of reading is always doubled or divided by the 're' – by the reading that has come before, or by that which is still to come. To read is not to consume that which is read, as if the book is a commodity that we can ingest or use up. It is rather to encounter an experience whose willingness to yield itself to us is reliant on its capacity to withhold itself from us, its insistence on belonging partly in a past that we cannot return to, and partly in a future which we cannot attain. To read is always to reread, because reading itself is an activity whose very possibility depends on iterability. Reading is impossible without repetition, as repeatability is a condition of legibility. So, when Nabokov remarks on the identity between reading and rereading, he is not thinking, at all, of rereading as a specific experience – a given individual rereading a given work that they have read in the past – but as a universal condition of reading. Seen in this light, rereading, and the rereadability of all writing, does not lead us towards autobiography – towards the subjective experience of rereading a given book – but in the opposite direction, towards a concept of reading that would be forever free from any given instance, any given context in which that reading might actually take place. The rereadability of all writing means that writing itself always exceeds the limits of any particular reading.

This problem – that the concept of rereading leads us both to a specific instance of reading, and towards a general and universal condition of readability – can be seen as one of the central contradictions of literary and critical theory, as it has developed over the twentieth and twenty-first centuries. Nabokov makes his remark on rereading in the introduction to a series of lectures he gave at Wellesley College in the 1940s (which were posthumously published as *Lectures on Literature*), and he does so in order to suggest that rereading is a necessary condition of what he calls 'good' reading – serious, critically attentive reading. 'A good reader', he says, 'a major reader, an active and creative reader, is a rereader'.[3] We need to reread, he goes on, because the process of understanding a book, as opposed, say, to looking at a painting, is one that takes time, a laborious and extended process that 'stands between us and artistic appreciation'.[4] When reading a book, we 'have no physical organ (as we have the eye in regard to a painting) that takes in the whole picture and then can enjoy its details'. We do not see the book whole, as we see the painting; but, he says, 'at a second, or third, or fourth reading we do, in a sense, behave towards a book as we do towards a painting'.[5] Rereading for Nabokov is a process which allows us gradually to bring the shape, structure and form of the book out of hiding, to scrape away the obstacles that 'stand between' us and the work, so that we might see it complete, in its true nature.

In thinking of rereading in this way, as a means of revealing the pictorial structure of the work, Nabokov is rehearsing a version of rereading that is proposed by Virginia Woolf two decades earlier, in her 1922 essay, 'On Re-reading Novels', an essay in which she herself rehearses an argument made by Percy Lubbock, in his 1921 book *The Craft of Fiction*. Lubbock, like Nabokov, imagines that a serious or 'good' reading of a book should resemble the process by which we appreciate visual rather than narrative art. Reading is fleeting, momentary. 'Nothing', Lubbock writes, 'no power, will keep a book steady and motionless before us'. 'As quickly as we read it melts and shifts in memory'.[6] So, to combat this tendency for narrative to dissolve in the mind, it is necessary for us to develop a form of reading which will allow us to discern the static formal structure of the work, to behold what he calls the 'book itself'. 'We must hold it away from us', he writes, 'see it all in detachment, and use the whole of it to make the image we seek, the book itself'.[7] It is the particular gift of rereading, Woolf writes, in her 1922 response to Lubbock, to achieve this discrimination, to take in, as Nabokov puts it, the 'whole picture'. It is reading a book for 'a second time' that allows us, she says, to 'somehow discriminate',[8] to see what Lubbock calls, in Woolf's quotation, its 'defined shape, firm of outline', to see 'the book itself, as the form of the statue is the statue itself'.[9] Lubbock provides us, she suggests, with a critical 'method' which allows us to approach 'the solid and enduring thing to which we can hold fast when we attack a novel for the second time'.[10] 'Here is something', she says, in a rush of gratitude to Lubbock

> to which we can turn and turn again, and with each clearer view of it our understanding of the whole becomes more definite. Here is something removed (as far as may be) from the influence of our fluctuating and private emotions.[11]

I

It is easy to see, in this appeal to the solidity of form, the stamp of a new critical sensibility that is emerging in the 1920s, as Woolf and Lubbock are writing, and that underlies the subsequent development of literary criticism as a discipline. Woolf's relief at the prospect of a kind of reading that might allow her to liberate herself from 'fluctuating and private emotions' carries a distinct echo of Eliot's 1919 essay 'Tradition and the Individual Talent', upon which an entire critical institution is built. 'Poetry', Eliot writes, 'is not a turning loose of emotion, but an escape from emotion; it is not the expression of personality, but an escape from personality'.[12] Rereading, seen as Lubbock, Woolf, and Nabokov see it here, is precisely not bound up with the contingencies of a given act of reading, or with the particular mood or sensibility or biography of a given reader, but is the means by which we might attain a serious understanding of literature as objective, thing-like, immune to the vagaries of its mere readers. But even as Woolf appears to endorse Lubbock's account of the 'book itself' in her 1922 essay, there is something in her tone that belies a scepticism about his method, a scepticism which she makes explicit in a diary entry written the following year, on 15 October 1923. As she writes the entry, she says, she is deep in the process of composing *Mrs Dalloway* – 'I am now in the thick of the mad scene in Regents Park'.[13] She has made a 'discovery' that has impassioned her, and that leads to a growing excitement about what her new novel might achieve ('I own' she writes, with a winningly cautious modesty, 'I have my hopes for this book').[14] She treats her discovery with care and circumspection, in case it turns out to be false (as her hopes for *Mrs Dalloway* may be false): 'lor' love me', she writes, 'I've not re-read my great discovery, & it may be nothing important whatsoever'. But the discovery, if she can trust it, leads her to the conclusion that Percy Lubbock's method might after all be altogether wrongheaded. After a 'year's groping', she has discovered 'what I call my tunnelling process by which I tell the past by instalments, as I have need of it':

> This is my prime discovery so far; & the fact that I've been so long finding it, proves, I think, how false Percy Lubbock's doctrine is – that you can do this sort of thing consciously. One feels about in a state of misery – indeed I made up my mind to abandon the book – & then one touches the hidden spring.[15]

Woolf wants to belong to the new critical school, fashioned in part by modernists such as Eliot, that makes of the fluctuations of reading something solid and enduring, but the hesitant dawning of her own modernism won't let her. The passages in *Mrs Dalloway* set in Regent's Park, still lying on Woolf's desk, scintillatingly un-reread, take her not towards the establishing of a conscious design, a formal integrity to the work that rereading might reveal, but towards the hidden, the uncertain, the contingent. The scene that Woolf is 'in the thick of', in which Septimus Warren Smith and his wife Rezia brush past Peter Walsh and Clarissa Dalloway as they walk through London, each enclosed in their own separate worlds, is held together, famously, by a scene of reading. The scene begins when 'Lucrezia Warren Smith, sitting by her husband's side on a seat in Regent's Park' looks up to see an aeroplane come 'rushing out of the clouds', as a 'train comes out of a tunnel', writing words in the sky.[16] The written words hovering above the scattered cast of Woolf's novel might offer a means of bringing the separate histories it traces together, attaching them to the revealed literary form of the novel itself. But, in accordance with Woolf's nascent discovery, they do not. In an implicit denunciation of Lubbock's 'doctrine', the readers of this skywriting can do nothing to counteract the tendency for words to 'melt and shift in memory', but rather its very expressive power is found in that tendency itself, in the failure of reading to excavate an enduring form. The plane writes in a 'thick ruffled bar of white smoke which curled and wreathed upon the sky in letters', but it is hard to be sure what the letters are, or what word they spell. 'A C was it? An E, then an L? Only for a moment did they lie still: then they moved and melted and were rubbed out up in the sky, and the aeroplane shot further away and again, in a fresh space of sky, began writing a K, an E, a Y perhaps' (p. 20). The 'people in the Mall, in the Green Park, in Piccadilly, in Regent Street, in Regent's Park' all look up, all try to enter into a collective scene of reading; but all find that whatever the words are saying, they will not be fixed, they will not adhere to their own form as a painting might, or a statue. Septimus – a bad reader, perhaps – is certain that the words have a hidden, portentous meaning. 'So,' he thinks, 'looking up, they're signalling to me'. But it is the beauty of this message, meant just for him, that it won't take the form of 'actual words', won't yield itself to the labour of common reading. 'He could not read the language yet', Septimus thinks,

> but it was plain enough, this beauty, this exquisite beauty, and tears filled his eyes as he looked at the smoke words languishing and melting in the sky and bestowing upon him in their inexhaustible charity and laughing goodness one shape after another of unimaginable beauty and signalling their intention to provide him, for nothing, for ever, for looking merely, with beauty, more beauty! (p. 22)

In Woolf's work, and in these years from 1921 to 1923, one can see a schism opening between a critical doctrine, fashioned in part by the modernists themselves, which insists that rereading might grant us access to Woolf's 'solid and enduring thing', and a modernist method that accords to reading a kind of insolid inexhaustibility, in which the beauty, the very possibility of literature resides. This is a schism that grows wider as literary studies evolves over the subsequent decades, and as the contradictions inherent in the concept and practice of rereading play themselves out. Lubbock's materialisation of the reading process – his framing of rereading as a kind of viewing – thrives in the English academy where it develops into the new criticism of F. R. Leavis and I. A. Richards, and it remains an orthodoxy in the Anglo-American academy when Nabokov gives his lectures at Wellesley in the 1940s, and then at Cornell into the 1950s. But the attempt to fashion out of the act of rereading the basis of a stable literary form is always vulnerable to the tendency for rereading to become either a kind of autobiography – a subjective experience of the text that can make no claims to shared meaning – or a kind of radical undecidability, in which the responsibility for generating the meaning of a given text passes from the author, or from the text itself, to the reader (and thus to potentially limitless readers to come). Septimus might be a model of the first kind of reader – the paranoid reader, who believes that a text contains a message which is meant only for them, and which cannot pass beyond the confines of their own mind; but he is also a model for the second, the unguessable, inexhaustible reader, who never quite disentangles him or herself from the first. The critical method that Lubbock outlines in 1921 cannot for long hold these contradictory forces together, and over the second half of the twentieth century the passage of literary criticism opens an increasingly wide gulf between rereading as a critical practice, the text that offers itself for reading, and the reader him or herself who carries out the act of reading. Roland Barthes institutes a seismic shift in the history of criticism in 1968, when he declares that 'the birth of the reader must be at the cost of the death of the author', and the subsequent decades of literary thinking take place in the wake of this death and rebirth.[17] From Wolfgang Iser's (arguably doomed) attempts to make the unknowable reader the foundation of a kind of critical knowledge, to Jacques Derrida's invention of a 'signifying structure that critical reading should *produce*', to Eve Kosofsky Sedgwick's theorisation of paranoid and reparative models of reading, the history of critical thinking has been driven by the compulsion to reconceive the fractured relations between text, reading, and the figure (or sometimes body) of the reader.[18]

Woolf's slight essay 'On Re-reading Novels' thus contains within it a proleptic microhistory of what she calls the 'criticism of fiction', which is still, in 1922, 'in its infancy'.[19] She sees that rereading is an already unstable figure for the ways in which critical thinking will negotiate the relations between the literary text and the scenes in which it is read. And it is in this essay, too, that she makes the first generative connection between rereading and the work of Marcel Proust. The arrival of the critical reader who will 'press close' on the 'heels' of the novelist, Woolf thinks, is set to transform the novel form itself. 'We may expect the novel to change and develop as it is explored by the most vigorous minds of a very complex age'. 'What', she asks, 'have we not, indeed, to expect from M. Proust alone?'.[20] As it turned out, we did not have much more to expect from Proust. Woolf published her essay in the *TLS* on 20 July 1922; Proust died, in the act of revising the manuscript of *A la recherche*, on 18 November of that same year. But if Proust died on that day, with manuscript pages scattered on his bed, and his manuscript in notebooks piled on the mantelpiece, Woolf's intuition that the future of novel theory is bound up with the relation between Proust and his readers is nevertheless prescient. Jean Cocteau attended Proust's death chamber, and noted that, as Proust lay dead on his bed, 'that pile of paper on his left was still alive'.[21] His novel is a repository of life, and it is so because it is concerned, above all, with rereading. If the development of literary criticism is shaped by the shifting relation between text, reader and the act of rereading, then *A la recherche* is a continuous assessment of that relation, a living embodiment of the means by which the novel gives itself to its readers, again, and again, and again.

In part, Proust's novel conducts this analysis of rereading at a formal level, making of the text itself a kind of machinery of rereading. The novel is structured as a Künstlerroman, in which a young Marcel, inspired by a desire to write but doubtful of his talent as a writer, slowly approaches the moment when he reaches the maturity that will allow him to convert his hesitant, fitful, intermittent life into art. Over the three thousand or so pages of this extraordinarily long novel, the Marcel in the difficult process of becoming makes his way towards the Marcel who has already become, the Marcel who has acted, throughout, as the narrator. It is only at the end of this laborious journey, when Marcel attends a party at the house of the Prince de Guermantes in the closing section of *Time Regained*, that this meeting finally occurs. At every stage along the way, Marcel frets about his incapacity to write, and fears that he will fail to fulfil his vocation. As a young boy, walking along the Guermantes way in his beloved Combray, he dreams that he might capture his being in poetry, that he might 'some day [...] become a writer'. But when 'I tried to discover some subject to which I could impart a philosophical significance of infinite value, my mind would stop like a clock, my consciousness would be faced with a blank' (I, 189). He dreads, he says, 'this black cavity which gaped in my mind when I ransacked it for the theme of my future writings' (I, 189). Then later, as an adolescent, having been given permission by his father to pursue a literary career, he finds, again, that he simply can't begin. 'If only I had been able to start writing!', he thinks. But however serious his intentions, he finds himself distracted by other things, so 'what always emerged in the end from all my efforts was a virgin page, undefiled by any writing' (II, 151). And then later again, as an older man, nearing the end of his journey towards himself, he is still worrying away at the same concern, at the 'thought of my lack of talent for literature – a defect which I had first discovered, so I supposed, long ago on the Guermantes way' (III, 886). 'If ever I thought of myself as a poet', he thinks, 'I know now that I am not one' (III, 886). So, when he finally meets himself at the close of the novel, and finally assumes the role not of character but of narrator, the meeting takes the form of a long deferred epiphany, in which all of those doubts are swept away. All that work of self-becoming was only a prelude to this moment when Marcel realises that the subject of his work, the theme of his writings which was secreted in the black cavity of his mind, was that passage itself, that intermittent progress through the years. That 'moment from long ago', he thinks, the moment when he sits as a child reading in his garden at Combray and dreaming of becoming a writer, 'still adhered to me and I could still find it again, could retrace my steps to it merely by descending to a greater depth within myself' (III, 1106). Now he has the theme of his writing, he simply has to live that life again in his art. 'Yes', he thinks to himself, 'upon this task the idea of Time which I had formed to-day told me it was time to set to work. It was high time' (III, 1091). 'The life that we live in half-darkness', he thinks, 'can be illumined'. That passing life 'can be restored to its true pristine shape', 'can be realised within the confines of a book!' (III, 1088). The black cavity of the mind, the virgin page, the blank consciousness, the stopped clock, they are all lying not behind him but before him, waiting for the tide of writing to sweep over them, gathering them up into the completed work. As we have been reading, we have been living with that blankness, that terrible black cavity of the mind, and now, now we simply have to reread, reread in the light of Marcel's epiphany which will carry all before it.

The formal structure of the novel produces this compulsion to reread, but rereading is also an action that Marcel repeatedly rehearses in the novel, a feature of its architecture which resonates with that formal compulsion, realising it in the embodied scenes it depicts. Marcel continually rereads himself as he progresses, continually returns to scenes that have been narrated, to test for their changing meaning as they unfold and recur within him – and all these ongoing forms of revision, of self-inspection, are held within an overarching act of rereading that reaches, like a vaporous bridge, from the overture to the closing scene in the library at the Guermantes party. The overture to the novel turns around Marcel's recounting of an evening on which it is agreed that his mother might spend the night sleeping with him in his bedroom. It is Marcel's greatest dread at this early point in his life that he will be separated from his mother, that something will happen to prevent her from kissing him goodnight – the kiss that is all that enables him to endure the long night spent without her. On this one evening, exceptional, unrepeatable, he has become so upset, so sick for love of his mother, that his father waives his normal prohibition on maternal love, saying to Marcel's mother the magic, unbelievable words, 'stay in his room' (I, 39), 'go and comfort him' (I, 40). His mother stays with him, and to help him to sleep she reads to him from George Sand's novel *François le Champi*. The sound of Sand's prose in his mother's voice has for Marcel a miraculous effect, one which makes of this vanishingly short night – this inexplicable lifting of the iron law of solitude, this rescinding of our banishment from the object of our love – something lasting. 'I knew that such a night could not be repeated', Marcel says:

> The strongest desire I had in the world, namely, to keep my mother in my room through the sad hours of darkness, ran too much counter to general requirements and to the wishes of others for such a concession as had been granted to me this evening to be anything but a rare and artificial exception. (I, 46)

He knows that 'tomorrow night my anguish would return and Mama would not be by my side', but listening to her reading voice 'my aching heart was soothed; I let myself be borne upon the current of this gentle night on which I had my mother by my side' (I, 46). The sentences of Sand's novel 'seemed to have been composed for her voice' (I, 45), so that in his mother's reading the words become containers in which that night is distilled, vessels which preserve 'all the sweetness to be found in generosity, all the melancholy to be found in love'. Reading *François le Champi* aloud to him, his mother 'breath[es] into this quite ordinary prose a kind of emotional life and continuity'. This life, this continuity, acts for Marcel as a 'bridge' that might carry him, he says, 'across the terrifying abyss that yawned at my feet' (I, 26). So it feels like a necessity, like a fate demanded by the structure of *A la recherche*, that countless years later, a million words later, as the aged Marcel stands in the Guermantes library, and the scenes of his life come rushing back to him in preparation for the epiphany that will usher in the beginning of the work, this act of reading should return. He is standing before the Prince's bookshelves, and sees, among the rare first editions, a copy of George Sand's *François le Champi*, a printed volume in which his mother's reading voice is preserved, in which that night when she stayed by his side, against all the forces that separated her from him, is still continuing, and in which he himself, as the avidly listening child, the child sick for love of his mother, is living on. 'The memory of what had seemed to me too deep for understanding in the subject of *François le Champi* when my mother long ago had read the book aloud to me, had been reawakened' (III, 919). Standing beside him as he reads is a stranger. 'The stranger was none other than myself, the child I had been at that time, brought to life within me by the book', and the older Marcel becomes an aftereffect of that younger self, a mirage who wants to be remade by him, 'wants to be seen only by his eyes, to be loved only by his heart, to speak only to him' (III, 920).

In reaching in this way across the vast terrain of the novel, the figure of rereading offers to make of the book a kind of whole, as Nabokov and Lubbock imagine that rereading might present us with a work entire. Marcel, inspired by his rediscovery of *François le Champi*, imagines that he might assemble an entire library comprising only of first editions – by which he means not the version in which a given book first appeared, but 'the edition in which I read it for the first time' (III, 923). He would 'pick from the bookshelf *François le Champi*', he says, and 'immediately there rises within me a child who takes my place, who alone has the right to spell out the title *François le Champi*, and who reads it as he read it once before, with the same impression of what the weather was like in the garden' (III, 921). It is this effect, he says, which 'illuminated for me not only the old groping movements of my thought, but even the whole purpose of my life and perhaps of art itself' (III, 923). To read rereading in Proust, as Gérard Genette argues in his reading of *A la recherche*, is to glimpse this opening before us of a revealed edifice. To read Proust, Genette writes, echoing Nabokov, is 'really to reread; it is already to have reread, to have traversed the book tirelessly in all directions, in all its dimensions' (p. 23). The rereading that Proust conceives of for Marcel, and that he demands of us, evokes what Genette calls a

> simultaneous perception of the total unity of the work, a unity which resides not solely in the horizontal relations of continuity and succession, but also in the relations that may be called vertical or transversal, those effects of expectation, or response, of symmetry, or perspective, which prompted Proust himself to compare his work to a cathedral.[22]

Rereading grants to narrative art, for Genette, the architectural solidity that Lubbock finds in statuary. But if this is so, it is intrinsic to rereading – both the act of rereading itself, and rereading as Proust imagines and narrates it – that it undoes, at every moment, the work of simultaneity that it evokes. Paul de Man is thinking of Genette's structuralism when he writes that the dramatization of reading in Proust raises the 'possibility of including the contradictions of reading in a narrative that would be able to contain them'.[23] But for de Man, such a possibility is always forsaken. The process by which the text rolls into itself, so it is recuperated by its own act of rereading, is one, de Man writes, which continually asserts the non-identity of the elements that it seeks to make identical, a non-identity that becomes the central discovery of the work. The novel is built around the meeting of Marcel as character with himself as narrator, a meeting in which the dispersal of self over time will be overcome by the gathering work of form – the gathering work through which time is 'regained'. As he stands at the Guermantes party, feeling the epiphany sweep over him, it is this meeting that Marcel envisages. He will dedicate himself from now on, he thinks, to the writing of his great work, which can finally begin. He will lock himself away, cancel all engagements. 'I should have the courage' he says, 'to reply to those who came to see me or tried to get me to visit them that I had, for necessary business which required my immediate attention, an urgent, a supremely important appointment with myself' (III, 1035). But it is inscribed in every sentence of this work, it is the very engine of its possibility, that this meeting can never happen, that the distance it seeks to cross is, in de Man's terms, 'unbridgeable'.[24] The meaning of the work does not reside, de Man suggests, in Genette's revealed unity, but rather in the failure of this convergence, in the recognition that 'what we call time is precisely truth's inability to coincide with itself'.[25] The sweeping of the tide of writing over the terrain of the novel – the novel's demand that the passage of time that leads up to the moment of writing should be reread, and thus redeemed, in its wake – never overcomes the intermittence that powers it. The 'black cavity' which 'gaped' in Marcel's mind, which separates him from himself and in which his unwritten novel is stored, remains, on rereading, a cavity. It can never be filled in. It must remain a cavity, because its emptiness, the undefiled blankness of the 'virgin page', is the very quality which drives us towards the moment of overcoming, the moment of convergence between character and narrator whose failure to occur, whose deferral to a future, prompts us to reread, to propel ourselves, again, towards the possibility that we might at last overcome the contradictions of reading, the contradictions of living. Rereading names at once the promise that we might overcome our failure to coincide with ourselves and with each other, and the discovery, once again, and as if for the first time, that we cannot.

II

It is perhaps for this reason – that *A la recherche* appears at once to stage a triumphant recovery of self and to endlessly defer such a recovery – that Proust's novel compels its readers to make of rereading a form of introspection. We are compelled to reread, because the novel brings us close to the process by which we seek, endlessly, to coincide with ourselves. In her 2016 essay, 'How the French Reread Proust', Laure Murat offers an exemplary account, both of the means by which Proust's novel produces a uniquely powerful compulsion to reread ('rereading Proust is something akin to an addiction' the 'title to reread above all others'), and of the tendency to experience rereading as self-discovery.[26] Murat's essay supplies a long list of readers whose relation to Proust leads them to confessional accounts of their own scenes of reading ('the first time reading Proust made me feel as if I were drunk'; 'The first time, I read it at 18, like a crime novel, a beach book [....] I reread the *Remembrance* around 35, more slowly and carefully this time').[27] The contradiction with which I began this essay – between rereading as autobiography and rereading as undecidability – becomes, in *A la recherche*, the motor of narrative possibility. The impossibility of achieving a final sculptural form, of reaching the moment when the text is conclusively read, not only causes the reading to continually escape from the reader, but also compels us, as readers, to continually impose our own life upon it, as Marcel experiences the loss of self, in those closing scenes at the Guermantes party, as self-possession. The narrator himself, aptly enough, anticipates this double movement – anticipates it, and absorbs it into the economy of the work. 'In reality', he says, 'every reader is, while he is reading, the reader of his own self. The writer's work is merely a kind of optical instrument which he offers to the reader to enable him to discern what, without this book, he would perhaps never have perceived in himself' (III, 949).

In my own case, my reading of Proust bridged the gap between early adulthood and the onset of later middle age. I first read *A la recherche* in the spring of 1994, when I was in my mid twenties. I was living in Brighton, a seaside town on the south coast of England, trying and failing to write a PhD thesis on Samuel Beckett's fiction. For a number of reasons, both intellectual and personal, I was finding the task of writing a doctoral dissertation impossibly hard. I had submitted a halting early chapter to my supervisor – an exacting man who intimidated me, and whom I revered – which had come back to me annotated with the scant remark 'fail again, fail better'. My work felt to me thin and artificial, and my life was in a state of transition which I could not understand or even properly acknowledge. My mother's sixteen year marriage to my stepfather had ended the previous year in dire acrimony – an event which was more significant for me than I realised at the time – and I myself had met a woman with whom I was falling in love. With these conflicting currents at work within me – the undiagnosed grief caused by the end of my mother's marriage, and the agitated, precarious happiness we feel when we are newly in love – I decided to abandon my thesis, which had in any case barely begun. I went to my supervisor to tell him of my decision. Fine, he said. Give yourself some time off. But before you leave for good, take a month or two to read Proust. It'll change your life.

I did as he suggested, and spent those months, February, March, April, reading Proust's novel in Scott Moncrieff's translation, revised by Terence Kilmartin. Released from the burden of work I read the novel with a peculiar freedom. I did not read at my desk, but in bed, or on the sofa. I read by day, waiting under the skin of my mind for the evening, which I would spend with the woman I had newly met, whose presence worked its way into every scene. I read large swathes of the novel soaking in my large and rather antique cast-iron bath, in which the water quickly cooled. I was never to write literary criticism again, so I could read without a pen in my hand – or at least the pen that I held, with which I annotated the text, was no longer the pen of a critic, or of a student. My reading, of Swann's excruciating, obsessive love of Odette, and then of Marcel's cruel, selfish love of Gilberte and of Albertine, became an index to my own experience of self-loss – of extension through loss – that is the condition of infatuation, of infatuation becoming love. Love, in Proust, is an agent at once of duplication and division, of enlargement and diminishment. It is a force which expels you from the domain of your own being into the being of another, while also imprisoning you in your own self. Swann, recognising that he is falling in love with Odette, is 'obliged to acknowledge that now [...] he was no longer the same man, was no longer alone even – that a new person was there beside him, adhering to him, amalgamated with him' (I, 249–250). The new person beside him is not Odette – or not only Odette – but the person who Swann becomes when he loves Odette, and the question that he asks himself here, the question that Proust's novel asks, is whether it is possible to experience this division in the self as an addition to being, or whether love is only a form of egotism, of solipsism. Does love 'correspond to anything outside itself' (I, 258)? This is a question that recurs throughout *A la recherche*. In loving, do we give ourselves to another, or do we seek to absorb the loved person into our own mental life, to restore the unity of our own ego that the experience of love, as painful as it is exhilarating, has destroyed? Is it true, as Leo Bersani suggests, that when Marcel feels that he 'most intensely needs someone else, he is, in reality, astonishingly unaware of the other person, and seems to be pursuing an elusive fantasy in himself?'[28] As I read, my reading became a conversation with the narrator about what kind of duplication love entails, what kind of bridge it is possible to build between one person and another, or between different versions of our self. The narrator speaks to us directly, towards the close of the novel, addressing us as '"My" readers'. 'I should not ask them to praise me or censure me, but simply to tell me whether "it is really like that"' (III, 1089). 'I should ask them', he writes, 'whether the words that they read within themselves are the same as those which I have written' (III, 1089).

There is a deeply uncanny charge to this address to the reader, this reaching of the narrator into the private, withdrawn space in which his words have their real life, in the reader's mind. Who oversees this peculiarly groundless relationship between the words that 'Marcel' writes, and the words that we read – the printed words that I read in the spring of 1994? Do the words one reads within oneself correspond with anything outside themselves? What correspondence was there, between Marcel's experience and analysis of love and the strange thing that was happening to me, as I found my own life amalgamated with another's? These questions felt bound up with the life that I was then living, the life in which I had lost whatever concept of family my mother's marriage had represented to me, the life in which I myself was falling in love, the life in which I was suddenly no longer a student of literature. And they felt bound up, too, with the thinking that I had been trying to do, the thinking about Beckett's fiction that had lately failed – failed better, or worse ('Or better worse. Fail worse again. Still worse again).[29] *A la recherche*, I was discovering, was among other things a work of aesthetic theory (despite Marcel's own insistence that 'A work in which there are theories is like an object which still has its price tag on' (III, 916)) – a work of theory which addressed the same problems that I was tracing in Beckett's work.[30] How can we make of a rigorous refusal of shared life a form of company? That was the question I had been trying to ask in my abandoned PhD, and here, in Proust's long novel, I found the same question addressed, in terms which seemed to resolve or at least restate some of the difficulties in Beckett's work which had come to seem intractable to me. Proust's thinking predicted Beckett's, and provided him, too, with a bank of images and gestures, whose provenance in Proust I was only now discovering. It was a strange disordering of sequence, to find shapes, lines, scenes I knew from Beckett lying already in Proust, waiting to be found. (Once, as a young child, I had lifted from my father's shelves, after his death, a copy of Alistair Maclean's thriller about racing car drivers and heroin smuggling entitled *The Way to Dusty Death*. I had no idea what heroin was, so the plot was mostly opaque to me. But it was a peculiar feeling, a decade or so later, to find Macbeth lamenting that 'all our yesterdays have lighted fools / The way to dusty death' – a feeling that I remembered now as I discovered Beckett's origins in Proust, and yesterday revealed its odd continuity with tomorrow, and tomorrow, and tomorrow).[31] I had been turning a line from *The Unnamable* over and over in head, through the previous months: 'What doesn't come to me from me has come to the wrong address'.[32] A comic short-circuit of a line, that seemed to admit of no entry to the text, no breaking of the seal in which the narrative is enclosed; but I found now that it was already formulated in Proust, in *Swann's Way*, as Marcel waits to receive a letter from Gilberte that will never come. Desperate to hear from her, to feel as if he exists for her, Marcel composes his own letter in Gilberte's voice, which he compulsively rereads. 'Every evening I would beguile myself by imagining this letter, believing that I was actually reading it, reciting each of its sentences in turn' (I, 443). In this deranged way he communes with Gilberte, but then 'suddenly I would stop in alarm. I had realised that if I was to receive a letter from Gilberte, it could not, in any case, be this letter, since it was I myself who had just composed it'. How can we receive a letter from a correspondent that lies truly beyond the pale of our own ego, that does not write in our voice, that does not belong to our '*field* of possibilities' (I, 443)? How do we give ourselves the 'impression that I was receiving something that had not originated from me, something real, something new, a happiness external to my mind, independent of my will, a true gift of love' (I, 444)? This is Marcel's question, as it is the question that drives *The Unnamable*. It is the question that shapes bodily attitude in Beckett from the beginning to the end, that composes our relations with ourselves and each other. It is asked as an old man is visited by a boy – both a stranger and himself at a younger age – in Beckett's late television play *Ghost Trio*.[33] It is asked in the early story, *First Love*, as the narrator regards Lulu, the object of his unenchanted love, and wonders where the line might be drawn between her and him. Lulu stands by the window, to display her pregnant body to the narrator: 'She had drawn back the curtain for a clear view of all her rotundities. I saw the mountain, impassable, cavernous, secret'. He sees, ranged behind her, the mountains, and the sea, 'the lights, the lighthouses and lightships my father had named for me, when I was small, and whose names I could find again, in my memory, if I chose'.[34] Lulu's body is both within and outside the circuit of the narrator's self-regard, as she stands against a landscape shaped by the narrator's love for his father (the story's other *premier amour*). But how strange to find the origin of Lulu's pose in Marcel's Albertine (who has, herself, an origin in Gilberte, as Marcel much later declares that 'my love for Albertine' was 'already inscribed in my love for Gilberte' (III, 942)). On the climactic night in the Grand Hotel at Balbec, the night that Marcel first tries to kiss Albertine, he finds her, like Lulu, framed against the landscape, which mirrors the 'rotundities' of Albertine's body. 'Beyond her, through the window, the valley lay bright beneath the moon'. 'The sea [...] was visible through the window as well as the valley, the swelling breasts of the first of the Maineville cliffs' (I, 995).

To read Proust that spring – to find Beckett's work pre-empted there – was to begin to see a logic of connection, of connection won through separation, that seemed to reshape the world around me (it'll change your life, my supervisor had said). The aesthetic theory that Proust develops in *A la Recherche* offered to account for the strange, nearly unreadable relations that the work contains, between Marcel and those he loves or fails to love, between the narrator and his readers, between Proust and Beckett. A fabric of connection in which solitude is woven into company, made of the very same stuff, in which the letters that come from outside the self are woven together with those that we read inside ourselves. As I reached the late scene in the library, and then the final scene in which Marcel joins the Guermantes party to find the cast of the novel gathered together as if in fancy dress – all of them, Marcel included, clothed in the organic disguise of their own aged and dying bodies – this fabric seemed to me nearly palpable, nearly tangible. To articulate it, to find out how this Proustian fabric is at work in Beckett, in those Beckettian forms that had eluded me, that still eluded me, that elude me still, seemed now to be necessary. So I returned to my desk, to my thesis, and built a shaky argument about Beckett's invention of a literary politics that was based, mostly implicitly, on the junction that I had found in Proust, the junction that was also a barrier. Sitting back at my desk, I found myself restarting my life, a life now shared with someone else, someone I loved with less agitation, less precarity. I got on with writing. I got on with living. I – we – had children. I wrote books – I wrote the essays that are collected in this volume – that were built on that difficult ground. A 'ground', Beckett writes, 'unfit for loads', where there was never 'any upright thing, nor any true foundation, but only these leaning things, forever lapsing and crumbling away'.[35] I built my relations with the people I love on these foundations – as they built theirs with me – lapsing foundations which were shaped by the conviction that the self is porous and unstable and open to others, even or especially where it appears to be most impermeable. I did not return to Proust, did not reread him for years, for decades, even as his novel continued to unfold in me, to separate and join in that unique, unending rhythm. I did not reread him until the later months of 2018, when I was led, perhaps as a half-conscious response to my mother's death earlier that year, to go to my shelves and find the three volume copy that I had read in the spring of 1994 – in Marcel's first edition, the edition in which I had first read it.

It was only on this rereading, on this return to the text after the elapsing of the intervening years, that the novel truly happened to me, that I could really begin to see the fabric of which it is composed. I reread partially in 2018, and then more systematically in the autumn of 2022, both times in the same three volumes, both times making new annotations over those I had made in my twenties with my unaccustomed, my unstudious pen. I read, for much of the time, in the bath, with my pen in my hand (a habit I have never lost), and as I did so I could feel the cooling water of my old iron bath, could feel myself as an older man, clothed in my older body, laid over that younger self, who was agitatedly, precariously happy. My rereading contained within it, like a liquid, the years that lay between us, that lay between an older man with most of his life behind him, and a younger man with most of his life ahead of him. The first time I opened the volume to reread – the first time I lay in the bath and read 'For a long time I used to go to bed early' (I, 3) – was, itself, a Proustian moment, an unmistakably and groundshakingly Proustian moment, a moment at once inside and outside the book that I held in my hands, carefully so as not to get it wet. It was, like all Proustian moments, an experience at once of gathering together and of falling apart, of gaining and losing time. The book offered itself as a container of those intervening years, promising to bring back the time and the self that were lost, or that were deadened by the narrative protocols of memory, by regulated forms of sociality. But the dizzying means by which a moment in the past comes into borderless contact with a moment in the present is also unavoidably an experience of loss, in which neither moment can maintain its proper place, in which we do not overcome passing time but are delivered to its dissolving medium, to the 'abyss of not-being' (I, 6) that lies unfathomably between each moment and the next. To encase the liquid of time in this novel shaped container is to feel that the self has been recuperated, reanimated, to find oneself immersed in the water of our youth as in a long, an unbelievably long bath; but only at the cost of the recognition, always known but now *lived*, that we are not ourselves at any given moment, that the fiction of the persistent self involves an airy dilation of mind over time, a dilation in which every moment is lost to a moment in the past, or a moment still to come.

Rereading delivered me to this experience, in a way that reading along never could, as if Proust's novel requires a long stretch of forgetfulness to achieve its effect of possession, as if, as Bersani puts it, 'the condition of self-possession is self-forgetfulness'.[36] And in doing so, it enabled me to gain a new imaginative and haptic access to the medium of connection that Proust's novel fashions – partly because that medium itself is built on the hinged structure of reapprehension, a structure that rereading reveals, unearths, makes vividly real. Being cast, as I lay in the bath, into a moment of Proustian recollection, one which contained a lived life within it, revealed to me with a new intensity both the terms in which involuntary memory occurs in Proust, and the aesthetic forms that he crafts in order to make of such an experience – of the simultaneous recovery and loss of our own past selves – a form of literary possibility. My experience of rereading followed the pattern of each of those moments of involuntary memory that the narrator recounts over the longue durée of the work, over what Kate Briggs has recently theorised, in a brilliant book of that title, as the 'long form' of the novel.[37] Each of these moments – from Marcel's tasting of the madeleine soaked in tea, to his view of the church steeples of Martinville from the back of a moving carriage, to the shifting appearance of three trees from another moving carriage in Balbec, to the sight of hawthorn in Combray and Balbec, to the dank smell of a public toilet, to the movement of Marcel's body as he bends over to unbutton his boots in the Grand Hotel, to the shifted distribution of his body weight as he stands on some uneven paving stones outside the Guermantes hotel – involves the same combination of gain and loss, of self-recovery and self-annihilation. Each involves the collision of two moments, separated by a gulf of time – a coming together in which an 'old, dead moment' has been brought back to life, 'raised up out of the very depths of my being', by the 'magnetism of an identical moment' in the present (I, 50). When Marcel tastes the madeleine as an older man, and finds himself in the unbidden presence of himself as a young boy drinking tea with his aunt Leonie in her house in

Combray, the narrator provides us with the language of simultaneous loss and gain that he develops over the rest of the novel. The experience produces great happiness, an 'all-powerful joy' (I, 48). But this joy is provoked by an encounter with something closely resembling death. 'What an abyss of uncertainty', the narrator says,

> whenever the mind feels overtaken by itself; when it, the seeker, is at the same time the dark region through which it must go seeking, and where all its equipment will avail it nothing'. (I, 49)

In the coming together of these moments, he says, the mind is brought 'face to face with something that does not yet exist, to which it alone can give reality and substance, which it alone can being into the light of day' (I, 49). It is this same apprehension of nonexistence that moves Marcel, as he sees the steeples of Martinville from the back of a moving carriage, and is cast into the unbound relation between time, space and distance that the vision affords, the sense that the golden steeples veering and shifting in the sun have a 'mobility', a 'luminosity' that they lose as soon as we fix them in spatial and temporal position (I, 196). He has this same feeling on seeing three trees from Mme Villparisis's carriage. 'I could see them plainly', he says, 'but my mind felt that they were concealing something which it could not grasp' (I, 771). It is this same feeling that grants Marcel a sudden surge of happiness, when the fusty smell of a damp toilet 'filled me with a pleasure of a different kind from other pleasures', one which was 'rich with a truth that was lasting, unexplained and sure', which contained an 'underlying reality which it had not yet disclosed to me' (I, 531). It is what provokes the 'upheaval of my entire being' (II, 783), when Marcel leans down to unbutton his boots, on his return to Balbec after his grandmother's death, and feels his body repeating the same gesture, in the same place, as when she was still alive, so that it is only then, as his body finds this earlier version of itself preserved within it, that he 'became conscious that she was dead' (II, 783). The gesture brings his earlier self back, so

> the self that I then was, that had disappeared for so long, was once again so close to me that I still seemed to hear the words that had just been spoken, although they were now no more than a phantasm. (II, 784)

'I could not understand', the narrator says, 'I struggled to endure the anguish of this contradiction'. On the one hand, the experience brings his grandmother back, so that he feels 'an existence, a tenderness, surviving in me as I had known them', and on the other, such recovery itself is the vehicle that allows him to fully register her loss, so his 'bliss' is 'shot through with the certainty, throbbing like a recurrent pain, of an annihilation that had effaced my image of that tenderness, had destroyed that existence' (II 785). And, finally, it is this same contradiction that recurs, gathers, becomes overwhelming, as Marcel 'tripped against the uneven paving stones' on his way to the Guermantes party, and is overwhelmed by the flooding return of a 'whole instant of my life' which, 'pure and disembodied, caused me to swell with happiness' (III, 899). He feels the 'same happiness', he says, 'which at various epochs of my life had been given to me by the sight of trees which I had thought that I had recognised in the course of a drive near Balbec, by the sight of the twin steeples of Martinville, by the flavour of a madeleine dipped in tea' (III, 899).

This combination of recovery and loss – which is bookended by the moment of rereading in the Guermantes' library, through which the night Marcel spent with his mother by his side is magically restored to him – is the essence of the Proustian experience. It is through such moments – like the moment that I encountered as I reread that line, 'For a long time I used to go to bed early' – that Marcel approaches what he calls the 'contradiction of survival and annihilation' that he feels 'so strangely intertwined within me' (II, 786); the 'agonising synthesis of survival and annihilation' (II, 787); the 'incomprehensible contradiction between memory and nonexistence' (II 796). But if this contradiction, this lapsing, tumbling gathering and falling, is what we mean by the adjective 'Proustian', this is only one half of what Beckett famously calls the 'Proustian equation', the other being the aesthetic theory that Marcel develops over the course of the narrative, in a kind of counterpoise to those moments of involuntary memory which punctuate it. The aesthetic experience which Marcel theorises – and which is balanced against the simultaneously joyous and agonising experience of involuntary memory – is itself, perhaps paradoxically, composed of the same elements. As involuntary memory is driven by the coming together of moments that are at once identical and non-identical, so Proustian aesthetics turn around the conjoining of different elements, whose difference persists even as it is overcome. It is this sameness in difference that provides the terms in which Swann falls in love with Odette, and which supplies him, as the narrator puts it, with the 'aesthetic basis of Odette's beauty' (I, 44). Famously, Swann finds his obsession with Odette baffling because, he says, she isn't his 'type'; but he becomes attuned to her beauty when he finds it duplicated, cast beyond itself. As Henry James's novel *The Wings of the Dove* turns around a startling likeness between its protagonist Milly Theale and Bronzino's portrait of Lucrezia, so *Swann in Love* turns around a similarity Swann divines

Figure 15.1 Sandro Botticelli, *The Trials of Moses* [detail], 1481–1482, fresco, Sistine Chapel, Rome, 348.5 cm × 558 cm.

between Odette and Botticelli's portrait of Jethro's daughter, Zipporah (see Figure 15.1).[38] Seeing the painting reflected in her countenance, seeing that 'traces of the old fresco were apparent in her face and her body', allows Swann to see beyond the 'mere sight of her in the flesh' (I, 245), towards some coming together of art and life, through which each is transformed. 'Although his admiration for the Florentine masterpiece was doubtless based on his discovery that it had been reproduced in her', he thinks, 'the similarity enhanced her beauty also, and made her more precious' (I, 244). He 'placed on his study table, as if it were a photograph of Odette, a reproduction of Jethro's daughter', so he can concentrate on this mutually illuminating resonance, and love Odette through this out-of-time reproduction of her – so he can 'adapt to the idea of a living woman what he had until then felt to be beautiful on aesthetic grounds' (I, 245).

Swann's love is grounded in a conception of aesthetic beauty, one in which art and life are brought into a unity that is always divided; and this is the basis upon which each of the invented representatives of aesthetic expression that recur through *A la recherche* come to rest. The music of

Vinteuil, the painting of Elstir, the prose of Bergotte; these are all driven by forms of non-identity that each medium preserves as a principle of its possibility. Swann's response to Odette's beauty is shaped by his admiration of Botticelli, but of course the medium in which his love is preserved is not painting but music, and specifically the little phrase that Swann hears in Vinteuil's sonata – a passage of music which he thinks of as the 'national anthem of their love' (I, 238). He hears, one evening at the Verdurins, the phrase begin to stir 'below the delicate line of the violin part', a phrase that he can only conjure in metaphorical terms. He discerns the phrase 'beginning to emerge in a sort of liquid rippling of sound, multiform but invisible, smooth yet restless, like the deep blue tumult of the sea, silvered and charmed into a minor key by the moonlight' (I, 227). The phrase moves him, but he can't approach it in itself, as sound, but rather he is led to translate it into an image, or a kind of architecture, like Genette's cathedral. 'He could picture to himself its extent, its symmetrical arrangement, its notation, its expressive value; he had before him something that was no longer pure music, but rather design, architecture, thought' (I, 228). The phrase becomes sculpted thought, and in doing so it attaches itself to Odette, like Botticelli's fresco before it, so that Swann's love of Odette is merged with the phrase, becomes one with it. The phrase, he thinks, becomes a 'confidante of his love', so that, even though it 'consists in being incommunicable', he feels that his love has been 'captured and made visible by the little phrase' (I, 379), as Marcel later finds that he associates with the music of Vinteuil 'the memory of one person only, which was Albertine' (III, 260). It is the music's difference from itself – its capacity at once to be 'the same and something else' (III, 261) – that makes it a fit medium for the preservation both of Swann's love, and of Marcel's. And so, too, with 'Bergotte's books', which, Marcel tells us, 'I constantly re-read' (I, 337), the power of the literary imagination resides not in its own form, in Lubbock's 'the book itself', but in its capacity to make links between different things, that remain different beneath their similarity, so that the reader 'would see the new relationships between things' (II, 338), and hear in Bergotte's voice 'vital links which the ear did not at once distinguish' (I, 594). Bergotte's books and Vinteuil's music recreate that collision of different things that provokes involuntary memory – and it is in Elstir's painting that this process becomes perhaps most powerfully embodied. 'I was able to discern', Marcel says of his fascinated regard of Elstir's painting, 'a sort of metamorphosis of the objects represented' that is 'analogous to what in poetry we call metaphor' (I, 893). Things, in Elstir's paintings, are freed from their positions in space and time, as the steeples of Martinville veer and shift when Marcel looks at them from the back of a carriage, so that in Elstir's painting of the harbour of Carquethuit, 'the eye should discover no fixed boundary, no absolute line of demarcation between land and sea' (I, 895). There is a mobility to the world as Elstir sees and represents it, that builds on the metaphorical structure that underlies the work of Bergotte and of Vinteuil, and that makes Elstir's paintings evocative of Marcel's love for Albertine. It is Elstir who introduces Marcel to Albertine, and it is Elstir's painting that frames the scene in which Marcel's love for her reaches a crisis – in which he realises that Albertine has erotic attachments to women (and to none other than Mlle Vinteuil, the musician's daughter). Sitting in his room in the hotel at Balbec, looking at the view through the window of the same Balbec beach and cliff that lay behind Albertine on the night that he first tries to kiss her, Marcel sees not the view, or not just the view, but the scene, as well, of Albertine's imagined liaison with Mlle Vinteuil, an imagined scene that torments him with jealousy, and leads him to tell his mother that he intends to marry Albertine. The view through the window wavers and bends, the view of the Balbec seascape overlying the scene of Albertine's infidelity, one 'no more than a dim veil drawn over the other, superimposed upon it like a reflexion' (II, 1167); a superimposition that leads Marcel to make a connection between the scene he sees 'behind Albertine' – the 'blue mountains of the sea' – and 'a study that Elstir had made of a sunset effect' (II, 1154).

Art, like involuntary memory, is fuelled by the identity of the non-identical; but it is the central claim of Marcel's aesthetic theory that art, unlike involuntary memory, can make of these convergences a new world, one in which the chance effects of recovery provoked by a taste, or a sight, or a gesture, are in some fashion contained, or preserved. The fabric of connection I had found in the novel on first reading, that had lain between the view from Proust's window and the view from Beckett's, is built on this capacity of the artwork to make of non-identity the basis of a form of expression. Proust's novel traces the spatial and temporal forces that separate people from each other and from themselves – the forces that separate the two moments that lie alongside each other in an episode of involuntary memory, that separate Swann from Odette, or that separate Marcel from his mother, from Gilberte, from Albertine. Most compulsively, it traces the forces that separate us from ourselves, as Swann's love for Odette leads him to feel that 'a new person was there beside him, adhering to him, amalgamated with him' (I, 249–250), and as Marcel finds, on rereading George Sands, that standing beside him is a 'stranger' who 'was none other than myself' (III, 920). The artwork reproduces this side-by-side – suggests that it is this separation itself, this cleaving at the heart of being, that is the province both of love and of beauty. If love corresponds to anything outside itself, if aesthetic beauty escapes the confines of any individual judgement, then they do so because they arise from this gulf that the artwork opens, this abyss of not-being, in which 'each artist' finds him or herself to be the 'native of an unknown country' (III, 258). The artwork traces this force of separation, but as it does so – in the work of Bergotte, Vinteuil and Elstir, but most of all in Proust's novel, as it absorbs all three – it discovers in that separation itself the means of overcoming or sublimating it. The double sided fabric of the work, like the genetic strand of Vinteuil's little phrase, runs as a twisting ribbon through the junctions it traces, making of love and beauty both a loss and a gain of being. As Marcel stands in the Hotel Guermantes at the close of the novel, and his epiphany gathers within him, it is this fabric that he finally sees and understands, this capacity of the artist to 'become aware of the beauty of one thing only in another thing'; to become aware of this difference that is native to love and to aesthetic beauty at the same moment that he finds the key to overcoming that difference, 'reuniting' those divided things 'to each other, liberated from the contingencies of time, within a metaphor' (III, 925). With his life lying behind him, with the revealed ground of his novel stretching before him, he comes to the recognition that 'through art alone are we able to emerge from ourselves, to know what another person sees of a universe which is not the same as our own' (III, 932).

III

Our reading of Proust's novel – our understanding of the kind of critical and aesthetic work it is able to do – rests on our response to this possibility, that art might overcome the differences that it witnesses. Can the fabric of the work, the twisting seam that the narrator generates from his amalgamation of Vinteuil, Elstir and Bergotte – of music, painting and fiction – summon a fullness of being from its division? Can it imagine a form of love, a form of beauty, that corresponds to something outside itself? Can it open onto a 'field of possibilities', an arena of social relations in which we can picture forms of shared life, in which we can live in a universe that is not our own?

The narrator's own response to this question, at the triumphant close of the novel, might seem to be an emphatic yes. As the waves and waves of epiphanic recollection roll over the narrator, the novel's art offers to recapture lost time, presenting to the narrator a 'pure and disembodied form' that 'caused me to swell with happiness' (III, 901). All those moments of involuntary memory that occur throughout the text, that are always joyous, that always cause a swelling, giddying feeling of happiness, are also always transitory, so happiness returns to unhappiness, the ecstasy of love returns to jealousy and distrust and egotism, the possibility of the unity of two things (moments, places, people) yields to the division, the disunity, of which it is composed. But the aesthetic revelation that is granted to the narrator at the novel's close, that allows him to set out on the project of writing the work, offers to make of that transitory sensation something lasting, or in Virginia Woolf's terms, 'something permanent'.[39] The mobile work that Marcel envisages – at once auditory, pictorial, narrative – promises to create what the narrator calls a 'community of minds' (I, 572), a community that he suggests, much earlier in the novel, might be summoned into being by the music of Beethoven, as 'the quartets themselves' invent the conditions of their own reception (giving a kind of birth to the 'persons capable of appreciating' them (I, 572)). The act of rereading that encompasses the novel – that recovers the rare and exceptional night that Marcel spends with his mother by his side and sustains it indefinitely – contains this aesthetic community within it, as my own rereading contains those years of my life that reach from 1994 to 2022, giving them an aesthetic shape and unity that they borrow from Proust's novel. The novel acts as a 'vase enclosing our spiritual nature', in which 'all our inner wealth, our past joys, all our sorrows, are perpetually in our possession' (II, 784). The artworks that it contains – the artwork that it is – allow us at once to recover our own being, to make of that distant stranger we see beside us our own true self, and to see into the being of others, as they are intertwined with our own. It is 'thanks to art', the narrator says at the close of the novel, that 'instead of seeing one world only, our own, we see the world multiply itself and we have at our disposal as many worlds as there are original artists' (III, 932).

The fabric of the artwork performs this magic, binding us to ourselves at the same time as it binds us to others, providing the terms in which we might both achieve a fullness of being, and find that fullness embodied in our commingling with other people, living in other worlds. Such, in any case, appears to be the conclusion of the narrator at the novel's orchestral close. He means it, too, as he feels and lives his epiphany at the Guermantes party, and he means us to feel with him this certainty, to live with him in this revelation, in the vaulted chamber of this swelling, happy joy. But we cannot grasp the texture of what I am insisting on calling the fabric of the artwork in Proust without recognising that its capacity to bring this joy, to grant us this communion with ourselves and with those we love, is woven into dissolution, as survival is woven into annihilation, as containment is a form of dispersal rather than its antidote. The artwork is a braid, plaited together from sound and colour and voices heard in the mind. Its composite nature is what grants it its beauty, but this beauty rests on the decomposition that is integral to all acts of composition. As Marcel feels his artwork gathering within him at the novel's close, he feels closest to a declaration of faith in the transformative potential of the aesthetic. But it is here, too, that the junction on which the novel rests, whose presence can be discerned in every sentence of the work, is most fully exposed. It is as Marcel asserts his readiness to begin his life's work that we can see most deeply into the gulf that runs through the work between the retrospective and the prospective, between what Emily Dickinson beautifully calls the 'thought behind' and the 'thought before'. 'The thought behind, I strove to join / Unto the thought before –'.[40] It is in this gulf that the fabric of the artwork forms, in this weather front that opens between two climatic zones, between the life that we have just seen Marcel live and the life that he is about to recreate in his work. The trembling, pulsating artwork, as it is imagined and embodied in Proust, owes its being to its belonging to both of these zones, to its capacity at once to bring them together and to sunder them in two, to instigate, as Dickinson puts it, a 'Cleaving in my Mind' through which being is cloven together and cloven apart at the same time and by the same grace.[41] The artwork sits between weather fronts, where it condenses and evaporates, gathering and dispersing like a cloud formation ('Do you see yonder cloud that's almost in shape of a camel?').[42] The very process by which the fabric of the work condenses into the already written, by which it makes palpable or tangible the meeting between a time that is past and a time that is to come, is also the process by which it evaporates into the yet to be written, freeing the elements that it ties together, the climatic zones that it brings into contact, to their difference from each other, their non-identity which can never be overcome, the non-identity of which the fabric itself is composed.

It is for this reason – that the Proustian artwork owes its expressive power to its intense proximity to the meeting ground between time past and time to come, between remembrance and futurity – that it acts so persistently as a diagnostic tool with which to read the condition of criticism, and to test the critical possibility of literature itself. This is why Woolf was so prescient, in 1922, to see that Proust's work touches closely on the process by which rereading determines the shifting historical meaning of literary fiction. The history of twentieth century literary criticism is a history of the means by which critical formulations materialise the literary possibilities that always exceed them, that melt and shift like the cloudy words that form in the London sky in Woolf's *Mrs Dalloway*. Successive movements in that evolution each find themselves endorsed by Proust's novel, as the novel itself functions as a machine to bring its future readings into contact with its own formal architecture. Genette seizes on the models of containment that Proust imagines – the 'vase' in which our spiritual natures are decanted, or the 'thousand sealed vessels' (III, 903) in which our memories are preserved – to ratify his own conception of a structural aesthetics, in which *A la recherche* becomes a cathedral whose solidity and unity is emboldened with each rereading. Gilles Deleuze reads the same text, and finds not a form of Christian architecture, but something much more ... Deleuzian. 'The Search is not constructed like a cathedral or like a gown, but like a web'.[43] Paul de Man reads the same text, and finds that rereading does not usher us into the space of a cathedral, or into the sticky rhizomatic filaments of a spiderweb, but into the dismantled space of reading per se. *A la recherche*, he writes, is an 'allegory of reading' that 'narrates the impossibility of reading'.[44] It shows us that 'it is forever impossible to read Reading'[45] – and de Man makes of this demonstration, of this impossibility, his own reading of reading.

For so many of the major figures of twentieth century theory – not only Deleuze, de Man and Genette, but Roland Barthes, Jacques Derrida, Leo Bersani, Walter Benjamin, Julia Kristeva – Proust sits in this way within and beyond the limits of their thinking, allowing a new thought to come into contact with the history of thinking from which it departs, and which it extends. As so often, Proust contains a figure for this effect in his novel, a message to the future readers who will continue to find their thought forming in the climate generated by his. 'It is essential', the narrator says, 'that the work [...] should create its own posterity' (I, 572). Speaking at once from and to the future that the novel creates – the contemporaneity that it continues, endlessly, to summon, for each new 'community of minds' – the novel addresses its readers to come, urging them to be equal to the novel's thinking that is still, peculiarly, ahead of them, as the structure of the narrative takes it past that horizon on which it continually condenses into form. As the novel, at its close, demands to be reread, so it projects itself forwards into the moment that it will be read again, and into the *environment* in which it will be read again, so no particular reading could ever exhaust it. 'And so it is essential', the narrator says, 'that the artist (and this is what Vinteuil had done), if he wishes his work to be free to follow its own course, should launch it, there where there is sufficient depth, boldly into the distant future' (I, 572). Proust's novel follows its course through the twentieth century, which is also the course of literary thinking, as Proust's readers continually strive to catch up with him, 'pressing close on his heels', drawing their thinking from the atmosphere that he creates.[46] All who have read the novel recognise that atmosphere – the particular light of the garden at Combray in which the young Marcel sits reading; the particular gloom of his bedroom, where he waits in trembling anxiety for his mother to come and kiss him goodnight, and from which he hears the tinkling of the garden gate which signals that the dinner party is over, that Swann, the family's guest, has left for the evening, and that 'Mama would presently come up stairs' to be with him. This is an atmosphere drenched in recollection, heavy with the weight of lived life, so that time moves slowly though a resistant medium; but this weight, its specific density, comes from its belonging at once in the past and in the future, as Marcel hears that same bell ringing in his ears in the closing paragraphs of the novel, so 'yes, unmistakably I heard those very sounds, situated though they were in a remote past' (III, 1105). It is the singular contemporaneity of Proust's novel that this bell is always about to ring, that Swann is always about to depart, that our 'strongest desire', which runs so counter to the general requirements and to the wishes of others, is always about to be appeased, even though the same bell is ringing, too, in the distant past. If the novel is a container, if it is a chamber, or a cathedral, it is one that is always reforming, always collapsing and rebuilding around the contemporaneity that it harbours, that it helps to bring into being. It expresses the futurity that powers Genette's structuralism, and Barthes' poststructuralism, and the deconstruction of de Man and of Derrida; and it speaks to, of the future that is dawning for us now (if futures dawn), as we seek new languages with which to articulate our own discomposed contemporaneity, a contemporaneity which, as Giorgio Agamben puts it, is hidden in the 'obscurity of the present'.[47]

It is this capacity, for *A la recherche* to speak to us of our own occurring moment, to usher us past the stretched horizon of the twentieth century into the time that we are entering now, that Eve Sedgwick has in mind, in the essay she writes on Proust in the closing months of her life, entitled 'The Weather in Proust'. 'For many readers of Proust', she writes, 'the textual experience of the *Recherche* seems to give access to a radically fruitful double movement: into an acutely enriched space of reverie, and outward with an enriched interest in the daily-changing climates of reality'.[48] We can see in this doubly enriched movement a version of the contradiction with which I began this essay, and to which I have returned periodically throughout it. The force which propels the reader towards introspection and 'reverie', and which makes of reading Proust a kind of auto-reading, is also the force that takes us beyond ourselves, into the contingency, the unknowability of the scene of reading. The weather, for Sedgwick, is a mark of that unknowability, a feature of that ever changing world into which the mind is projected on each rereading, on each fresh act of intellection. Marcel thinks that, each time he rereads *François le Champi*, he will be returned to himself as a child ('there rises within me a child who takes my place'), and will recover the 'same impression of what the weather was like in the garden' (III, 921). But Sedgwick's reading of the weather in Proust places as much emphasis on what the weather is like on the occasion of rereading as on that of the initial reading, as Proustian weather – what Sedgwick calls 'Proustian reality' – is forged in this coming together of internal memoryscapes and the meteorology of the present, and of the future inscribed in rereading.[49] This is why, Sedgwick argues, Marcel's father is so obsessed with the weather, and is so often to be seen diligently 'consulting the barometer';[50] and it is why, she suggests, Marcel himself has a barometer inside him, an atmospheric pressure gauge which grants him an uncanny sensitivity to the climate in which Proust's book will be read. The fabric of the artwork in Proust is the ground in which the weather outside us meets with the weather inside us, and in which the weather of rereading intersects with the weather in the garden at Combray when Marcel first reads George Sands. But if this is the case, it is also true, as is clear in every line of Sedgwick's essay, written in the shadow of her death, that the passage of the current century has changed, irrevocably and immeasurably, the relation of human cultures to the weather. We have passed a tipping point in what Dipesh Chakrabarty calls the 'climate of history', after which human worlds (and the weather inside us) can no longer coincide with external meteorological conditions, after which the terms in which we imagine the relation between climate and history have been irreversibly dismantled.[51]

Sedgwick gives us a model, in an earlier essay published in her collection *Touching Feeling*, for how Proust might respond to this non-coincidence, this failure of our own private being to match with the world in which we are required now to live. Reading the late scene at the Guermantes party, in which Marcel is bewildered by the sight of his old friends clothed in the brutal disguise of old age, she notes that this kind of time-shock would be unlikely to befall anyone who was more in tune than Marcel with a normative passage of time, a regulated climate of history. 'Isn't it worth pointing out', she asks, that the complete temporal disorientation that initiates him onto this revelatory space would have been impossible in a heterosexual *père de famille*, in one who had meanwhile been embodying, in the form of inexorably "progressing" identities and roles, the regular arrival of children and grandchildren?[52]

For Sedgwick it is Marcel's 'queerness' – the homoerotic current that flows always beneath his attractions to Gilberte and Albertine – that casts him outside of a normative model of unfolding time, into what she calls a 'deroutinized temporality'.[53] Proust's writing, she suggests, is alert to a non-coincidence of time with itself that is a feature of what Jack Halberstam has theorised as 'queer time', and that is a feature of the communities to which Sedgwick herself belongs.[54] Her friendships, with those fifteen years younger than herself, with those fifteen years older than herself, are organised around principles of desire and of community that lie outside what she proposes as a '"normal" generational narrative', in which 'in another fifteen years, I'd be situated comparably to where my sixty-year-old-friend is, while my thirty-year-old friends would be situated comparably to where I am'.[55] Not only because homosocial communities tend to be organised outside of familial narratives, but also because of the relation between queer communities and precarity, minority, and, since the advent of HIV, illness, her own friendships, she says 'are likely to differ from that model'. In Sedgwick's case, this difference is compounded by her diagnosis of advanced breast cancer which means that 'I have little chance of ever being the age the age my older friend is now'.[56] 'On this scene', Sedgwick writes, 'an older person doesn't love a younger as someone who will someday be where she is now, or vice-versa'. Friends are brought into a kind of contact with one another that lies outside of regulated forms of temporality, so they 'slide up more intimately alongside one another than can any lives that are moving forward according to the regular schedule of the generations'. They encounter one another 'as the present fullness of a becoming whose arc may extend no further'.[57]

Proust's novel, Sedgwick suggests, is attuned to these forms of becoming – these relations between people that lie outside of regulated models of time, and these forms of desire that run counter to the general requirements. His writing performs a discrepancy between the weather inside us and the weather outside us – between what she calls the 'will of the subject' and the 'weather of the world'.[58] The artwork in Proust, she writes, offers a surface on which these two things might come into contact, on which we might inscribe the non-regulated terms in which we relate to one another. Vinteuil's 'little phrase' 'condenses outside' of Marcel, while 'it effects his internal geography as well'.[59] 'Everything in Proust', she says 'depends on the ratio or relation between an internal object and an ambient surround'.[60] Sedgwick's illness opens a gulf between these things, estranging her from a regulated 'arc of becoming'. Her belonging to forms of community that are at an angle to normative familial narratives opens a gulf between these things. And it is the case, too, as she implies in 'The Weather in Proust', that the weather itself oversees a widening gulf between subjective life and the environments in which it unfolds (a gulf that becomes the central concern of Jenny Offill's 2020 novel *Weather*). The years that are encompassed in my own act of rereading Proust – the years that are contained in the passage from 1994 to 2022 – are years in which the weather, the climate, has changed. They are years in which what Wallace Stevens calls the 'mere weather', the 'mere air', has become a medium of disjunction.[61] They are years, in John Ashbery's phrase, of 'crazy weather'. 'It's this crazy weather we've been having', Ashbery writes, that has estranged us, has undone the bonds that hold our environments together, so that the 'sky calls / to a deaf earth'.[62] Climate change has ushered in a radical disjunction between the time of human culture and the time of the planet, one in which all of us are subject to forms of deroutinized temporality, in which the time of the teenager has become unmoored from the time of the middle aged man, and from the time of the grandmother. How do we assemble ourselves now? How do we contain ourselves within the bounds of ourselves? Those twenty-eight years of my own life, 'realised', as Marcel puts it, 'within the confines of a book', are years in which our capacity to assemble our lives, to gather together both ourselves and those we love into a space of plenitude, has been transformed, changed utterly. Not only has climate change discomposed our relation to futurity, but the industrial-technological production of the public sphere (with which climate change is so intimately interwoven) has transformed the material and discursive terms in which we encounter ourselves, and time ourselves. If we imagine a container for the self now, a storage unit 'filled with a colour, a scent, a temperature' from our past, in which the 'extraordinarily diverse atmospheres' that have formed within us 'over the whole range of our years' (III, 903) might be distilled; if we imagine such a thing, we do not tend to think of the storage facility as Genette's cathedral, or as Deleuze's web. We think of it, I suspect, as the 'Cloud'. Not Shakespeare's cloud, that resembles a camel or a whale. Not Woolf's clouds of writing, forming in the sky over London. But the Cloud, owned by the mega-corporations who control the weather now, powered by banks of computers in the desert, burning countless tonnes of carbon so our lives, our memories, can be stored, in a term we have come bewilderingly to accept as perfectly natural, 'remotely'.

III

To read Proust now is to read him in the daily-changing climate of this reality – a reality shaped by corporate owned information technologies and by a planetary environment which is asserting its resistance to the logic of human cultures. It is to bring Marcel's past, the distant childhood in which he hears the ringing of the garden gate bell, into contact with the time in which he is about to hear that bell again, and again, and again. It is to bring my own past, in which I lay in my iron bath, trying to quell the agitation within me of love and hope so I could concentrate on my reading, into contact with the world that is happening now, the world in which my children, born of that love, will have to find their way. The fabric of the Proustian artwork brings these moments together, brings them into a kind of contact which is made, more miraculously with each reading, of their difference from one another. The bell of Marcel's childhood is different from the bell that he hears at the novel's close, that we hear with him, each time we feel that ending sweep over us. The lives of my children will unfold in a different climate to the one in which my own life has been lived. Nothing could or should make those different things the same. But it is the boundless beauty of Proust's novel, the possibility that it harbours, that it can reanimate the past by making it a part of the future that it meets, that it can allow a kind to historical thinking in which the past that we recover is made anew, at every moment, by the changing world in which that past is brought to life. Proustian remembrance does not look back, to a paradise that has been lost. Rather it unfolds in the weather of today, in the atmosphere in which we – you, and I – are living now. Each time we read Proust, we find that we 'breathe a new air'. But this, magically, is an 'air which is new precisely because we have breathed it in the past' (III, 903). It is this impossibility, that a new air might be at once the same as and different from an air that we have already known and breathed, that Proust's novel makes possible. That something can be new and old, lost and recovered, divided and joined, all at the same time and in the same breath; it is impossible, of course. That time can gain weight and colour in the chambers of our collective memory; it is impossible. But it is also strangely, palpably possible. It is the possibility of literature itself.

2022

Notes

Introduction

1. Samuel Beckett, *Proust and Three Dialogues with Georges Duthuit* (London: Calder, 1965), p. 125.
2. William Davies and Helen Bailey, eds., *Beckett and Politics* (Basingstoke: Palgrave, 2021), p. 6: 'This first phase of critical work on Beckett and the political in the early 2000s reaches its apogee with the publication of Peter Boxall's 2002 essay, "Samuel Beckett: Towards a Political Reading"'.
3. For key examples of first wave of Beckett criticism, see Martin Esslin, *The Theatre of the Absurd* (London: Penguin, 1968); Hugh Kenner, *Samuel Beckett: A Critical Study* (Berkeley: University of California Press, 1968); Ruby Cohn, *Samuel Beckett: The Comic Gamut* (New Jersey: Rutgers University Press, 1962). For examples of the second wave see Steven Connor, *Samuel Beckett: Repetition, Theory and Text* (Oxford: Blackwell, 1988); Leslie Hill, *Samuel Beckett: In Different Words* (Cambridge: Cambridge University Press, 1990); Carla Locatelli, *Unwording the World: Samuel Beckett's Prose Works after the Nobel Prize* (Philadelphia: University of Pennsylvania Press, 1990).
4. Kwame Anthony Appiah, 'Is the Post- in Postmodernism the Post- in Postcolonial?', in *Critical Inquiry*, vol 17, no 2 (Winter, 1991) pp. 336–357, p. 342.
5. Fredric Jameson proposed postmodernism as a 'cultural dominant' in his essay 'Postmodernism, or the Cultural Logic of Late Capitalism', in *New Left Review*, vol 146 (July, 1984), pp. 53–92: 'it seems to me essential to grasp "postmodernism" not as a style, but rather as a cultural dominant', p. 56.
6. Fredric Jameson, 'The End of Temporality', in *Critical Inquiry*, vol 29, no 4 (Summer, 2003), pp. 695–718, p. 704.
7. Francis Fukuyama, *The End of History and the Last Man* (New York: Free Press, 2006), p. 67. For Alexandre Kojève's Hegelian account of the end of history, see Alexandre Kojève, *Introduction to the Reading of Hegel* (New York: Basic Books, 1969), trans. James H. Nichols, Jr., ed. Allan Bloom.
8. Jameson, 'End of Temporality', p. 704. For Jameson's more recent and somewhat quixotic attempt to imagine a utopian future, see Fredric Jameson, et al., *An American Utopia: Dual Power and the Universal Army* (London: Verso, 2016).
9. Francis Fukuyama, 'The West has Won', *The Guardian* (11 October, 2001), www.theguardian.com/world/2001/oct/11/afghanistan.terrorism30.

Notes to pages 5–8 341

10. Jameson, 'End of Temporality', p. 709. Jameson outlines his concepts of waning of affect and weakening of historicity in the *New Left Review* essay, 'Postmodernism, or the Cultural Logic of Late Capitalism', which he later expands in his book length *Postmodernism, or, The Cultural Logic of Late Capitalism* (London: Verso, 1991).
11. Samuel Beckett, *Molloy*, in Samuel Beckett, *Molloy, Malone Dies, The Unnamable* (London: Calder, 1994), p. 40.
12. Samuel Beckett, *The Lost Ones*, in Samuel Beckett, *The Complete Short Prose, 1929–1989* (New York: Grove Press, 1995), pp. 202–223, p. 223.
13. Theodor Adorno, 'Trying to Understand *Endgame*', in Theodor Adorno, *Notes to Literature*, vol 1 (New York: Columbia University Press, 1991), trans. Shierry Weber Nicholsen, pp. 241–275, p. 243.
14. Jacques Derrida, *Acts of Literature* (New York: Routledge, 1991), ed. Derek Attridge, p. 61.
15. See Theodor Adorno, 'Reconciliation Under Duress', in Ernst Bloch, et al., eds., *Aesthetics and Politics* (London: Verso, 1980), trans. Ronald Taylor, pp. 151–176.
16. Fukuyama, *The End of History*, p. 35.
17. Virginia Woolf, 'Character in Fiction', in Virginia Woolf, *The Essays of Virginia Woolf: Volume III, 1919–1924* (London: Hogarth Press, 1988), ed. Andrew McNeillie, pp. 421, 422.
18. Jean Baudrillard, *The Spirit of Terrorism and Requiem for the Twin Towers* (London: Verso, 2002), trans. Chris Turner, pp. 44–45.
19. Bruno Latour, 'Why Has Critique Run out of Steam? From Matters of Fact to Matters of Concern', in *Critical Inquiry*, vol 30 (2004), pp. 225–248, p. 228.
20. Coetzee, *Diary*, p. 19.
21. For two accounts of the global politics both of 9/11, and of the US military response, see Lawrence Wright, *The Looming Tower: Al-Qaeda's Road to 9/11* (London: Penguin, 2007), and Jason Burke, *The 9/11 Wars* (London: Penguin, 2011).
22. For Blair's justification of military aggression in support of western democracy and global capitalism, see his speech to the Labour Party conference in Brighton, on 2 October 2001. It is published in full in *The Guardian* here: www.theguardian.com/politics/2001/oct/02/labourconference.labour6. I discuss the speech in Chapter 12, pp. 255–274.
23. George W. Bush used this phrase many times. See for example his State of the Union address, of 2006, online at https://georgewbush-whitehouse.archives.gov/news/releases/2006/01/20060131-10.html.
24. Tony Blair, 'Why We Must Not Abandon the People of Afghanistan – For Their Sakes and Ours', *Tony Blair Institute for Global Change*, 21 August 2021, online at https://institute.global/tony-blair/tony-blair-why-we-must-not-abandon-people-afghanistan-their-sakes-and-ours, np.
25. For an influential account of the consequences of the 2008 crash, see Adam Tooze, *Crashed: How a Decade of Financial Crises Changed the World* (London: Penguin, 2018).

26. For a concise account of the relation between neoliberalism and the collapse of the Bretton Woods agreement, see David Harvey, *A Brief History of Neoliberalism* (Oxford: Oxford University Press, 2005). I discuss this further, in Chapters 12 and 14, pp. 255–274, 291–307.
27. Jean François Lyotard, *The Postmodern Condition: A Report on Knowledge* (Manchester: Manchester University Press, 1984), trans. Geoff Bennington and Brian Massumi, p. 37.
28. See Timothy Morton, *Ecology without Nature: Rethinking Environmental Aesthetics* (Cambridge: Harvard University Press, 2007); Wai Chee Dimock, *Through Other Continents: American Literature across Deep Time* (Princeton: Princeton University Press, 2006); Ursula K. Heise, *Sense of Place and Sense of Planet: The Environmental Imagination of the Global* (Oxford: Oxford University Press, 2008); Timothy Clark, 'Derangements of Scale', in Tom Cohen, ed., *Telemorphosis: Theory in the Era of Climate Change* (London: Open Humanities Press, 2012).
29. Amitav Ghosh, *The Great Derangement: Climate Change and the Unthinkable* (Chicago: The University of Chicago Press, 2016), pp. 9, 8.
30. Richard Powers, 'The Seventh Event' *Granta* no 90 (2005), pp. 58–74, p. 66.
31. Noam Chomsky, *Hegemony or Survival: America's Quest for Global Dominance* (London: Penguin, 2004). p. 236.
32. See Jeremy Green, *Late Postmodernism: American Fiction at the Millennium* (Basingstoke: Palgrave, 2015).
33. Rita Felski, *The Limits of Critique* (Chicago: University of Chicago Press, 2015), p. 186. See Elizabeth S. Anker and Rita Felski, eds., *Critique and Post-Critique* (Durham: Duke University Press, 2017). See also Rita Felski, *Hooked: Art and Attachment* (Chicago: Chicago University Press, 2020), where, in Ben Highmore's reading, Felski seeks to 'imagine a post-critical attention to art (broadly conceived) that can hang on to our first-person response to works [...] while ensuring that such attention isn't a flight from the social but a more capacious form of contact with it'. Ben Highmore, 'Promiscuous Attachments', in *New Formations*, vol 103 (2021), pp. 181–184, p. 182.
34. For the most influential work on metamodernism, see David James and Urmila Seshagiri, 'Metamodernism: Narratives of Continuity and Revolution', in *PMLA*, vol 129, no 1 (January, 2014), pp. 87–100, and Robin Van den Akker, Timotheus Vermeulen, and Alison Gibbons, eds., *Metamodernism: Historicity, Affect, and Depth After Postmodernism* (Lanham: Rowman and Littlefield, 2017). For the 'new sincerity', see Adam Kelly, 'David Foster Wallace and the New Sincerity in American Fiction', in David Hering, ed., *Consider David Foster Wallace: Critical Essays* (Los Angeles: Sideshow Media, 2010), pp. 131–146.
35. John Guillory, *Professing Literature: Essays on the Organization of Literary Study* (Chicago: University of Chicago Press, 2022), p. xiii.
36. Hamid Dabashi, *Europe and Its Shadows: Coloniality after Empire* (London: Pluto, 2019), p. 9.

37. Priyamvada Gopal, 'On Decolonisation and the University', in *Textual Practice*, vol 35, no 6 (2021), pp. 873–899, p. 878. See also Priyamvada Gopal, *Insurgent Empire: Anticolonial Resistance and British Dissent* (London: Verso, 2019).
38. Sianne Ngai, *Theory of the Gimmick: Aesthetic Judgment and Capitalist Form* (Cambridge: Harvard University Press, 2020), p. 33. See also Sianne Ngai, *Our Aesthetic Categories: Zany, Cute, Interesting* (Cambridge: Harvard University Press, 2012).
39. See Alberto Toscano and Jeff Kinkle, *Cartographies of the Absolute* (Winchester: Zero Books, 2015), p. 27.
40. Toni Morrison, 'Unspeakable Things Unspoken: The Afro-American Presence in American Literature', in Toni Morrison, *Mouth Full of Blood: Essays, Speeches, Meditations* (London: Chatto and Windus, 2019), p. 178.
41. Wallace Stevens, 'Of Mere Being', in Wallace Stevens, *The Palm at the End of the Mind: Selected Poems and a Play* (New York: Vintage, 1990), ed. Holly Stevens, p. 398.
42. Beckett, *Proust*, pp. 69–70.
43. Ludwig Wittgenstein, *Tractatus Logico-Philosophicus* (London: Routledge, 2001), trans. D. F. Pears and B. F. McGuinness, 41.
44. Don DeLillo, *The Body Artist* (London: Picador, 2001), pp. 34–35.
45. Don DeLillo, *Zero K* (London: Picador, 2016), p. 20.
46. Louis Althusser, 'Ideology and Ideological State Apparatuses', in Louis Althusser, *Essays on Ideology* (London: Verso, 1984), p. 51.
47. Margaret Atwood, *Oryx and Crake* (London: Virago, 2009), p. 43, p. 78.
48. Cormac McCarthy, *The Road* (London: Picador, 2007), p. 93.
49. J. M. Coetzee, *Elizabeth Costello* (New York: Viking, 2003), p. 67.
50. Don DeLillo, *The Word for Snow* (New York: Karma Glenn Horowitz, 2014), p. 21.
51. Jacques Derrida, 'Passions: "An Oblique Offering"', trans. David Wood, in David Wood, ed., *Derrida: A Critical Reader* (Oxford: Blackwell, 1992), pp. 5–35, p. 6.
52. Timothy Bewes, *Free Indirect: The Novel in a Postfictional Age* (New York: Columbia University Press, 2022), p. vii.
53. Bewes, *Free Indirect*, p. vii; Gilles Deleuze, *Cinema II: The Time Image* (London: Continuum, 2005), trans. Hugh Tomlinson and Robert Galeta, p. 166.
54. J. M. Coetzee, *The Childhood of Jesus* (London: Harvill Secker, 2013), 217.
55. J. M. Coetzee, 'Jerusalem Prize Acceptance Speech', in J. M. Coetzee, *Doubling the Point: Essays and Interviews* (Cambridge: Harvard University Press, 1992), ed. David Atwell, p. 98.
56. Coetzee, *Elizabeth Costello*, p. 70.
57. Derrida, 'Passions', p. 6.
58. For the original scene from which these words are drawn, see Cervantes, *The Adventures of Don Quixote* (London: Penguin, 1950), trans. J.M. Cohen, p. 680.

344 Notes to pages 20–29

59. Walter Benjamin, 'Theses on the Philosophy of History', in Walter Benjamin, *Illuminations* (London: Pimlico, 1999), trans. Harry Zorn, p. 254.
60. John Donne, 'Batter My Heart, Three-Personed God', in John Donne, *The Complete English Poems* (London: Penguin, 1986), p. 315.
61. Coetzee, *Diary of a Bad Year*, p. 96.
62. Samuel Beckett, *Happy Days*, in Samuel Beckett, *The Complete Dramatic Works* (London: Faber, 2006), p. 145.
63. Dante Alighieri, *Inferno* (London: Penguin, 1984), trans Mark Musa, p. 383.
64. Dante Alighieri, *Purgatorio* (Oxford: Oxford University Press, 1961), trans John D. Sinclair, p. 441, 'pure and ready to mount to the stars'; Dante Alighieri, *Paradiso* (Oxford: Oxford University Press, 1961), trans. John D. Sinclair, p. 485: 'the Love that moves the sun and the other stars'. For readings of Dante's presence in *The Lost Ones*, see Daniela Caselli, *Beckett's Dantes: Intertextuality in the Fiction and Criticism* (Manchester: Manchester University Press, 2005), pp. 183–200, and Joseph Long, 'Divine Intertextuality: Samuel Beckett, *Company, Le Dépeupleur*', in *Samuel Beckett Today/Aujourd'hui*, vol 9 (2000), pp. 145–157. I owe this observation about the closing of all three volumes of the *Comedy* to Long's essay.
65. Samuel Beckett, *Waiting for Godot*, in Beckett, *Complete Dramatic Works*, p. 42.
66. See Voltaire's *Candide*, where Leibniz's claim, in the *Theodicy*, that we are living in the best of all possible worlds, is satirised in the figure of Pangloss, who argues that 'since everything must be made for a purpose, everything must be for the best possible purpose' (Voltaire, *Candide* (London: Penguin, 2001), p. 2).
67. Samuel Becket, *Worstward Ho*, in Samuel Beckett, *Nohow On: Company, Ill Seen Ill Said, Wostward Ho* (London: Calder, 1992), p. 118.
68. J. M. Coetzee, 'Eight Ways of Looking at Samuel Beckett', in J. M. Coetzee, *Late Essays, 2006–2017* (London: Harvill and Secker, 2017), p. 212.
69. Emily Dickinson, 'We grow accustomed to the Dark -', and 'What I see not, I better see -', in Emily Dickinson, *The Poems of Emily Dickinson* (Cambridge: Harvard University Press, 1998), ed. R. W. Franklin, p. 198, p. 379.
70. Virginia Woolf, *Between the Acts* (Oxford: Oxford University Press, 2008), p. 137.
71. Walter Benjamin, *The Arcades Project* (Cambridge: Harvard University Press, 1999), trans. Howard Eiland and Kevin McLaughlin, p. 463.
72. Marcel Proust, *Remembrance of Things Past* (London: Penguin, 1983), 3 vols., trans. C. K. Scott Moncrieff and Terence Kilmartin, vol 1, p. 443.
73. Proust, *Remembrance*, vol 3, p. 1088.
74. Water Benjamin, 'The Image of Proust', in Benjamin, *Illuminations*, p. 206.
75. Dickinson, *Poems*, p. 198.
76. Dickinson, *Poems*, p. 198.

1 A Sort of Crutch

1. Herman Melville, *Billy Budd, Sailor (An Inside Narrative)*, in Herman Melville, *Melville's Short Novels* (New York: Norton, 2002), ed. Dan McCall, p. 111.

2. Herman Melville, *Moby Dick* (Oxford: Oxford University Press, 2008), p. 55.
3. John Donne, *The Complete English Poems* (London: Penguin, 1986), p. 294.
4. Avital Ronell, *Stupidity* (Chicago: University of Illinois Press, 2003), p. 100. Ronell quotes Barbara Johnson, *The Critical Difference: Essays on the Contemporary Rhetoric of Reading* (Baltimore: Johns Hopkins University Press, 1980), p. 94.
5. Voltaire, *Candide* (London: Penguin, 2001), p. 2.
6. See Victor Hugo, *Les Misérables* (London: Penguin, 1982). The obsessive detective Javert is wedded to the letter of the law, insisting that 'if facts did their duty they would simply reinforce the law'; he is forced to accept, though, at the close of the novel that 'it was abominable that true fact should wear so distorted a face' (p. 1108).
7. Nicholas Royle, *Veering: A Theory of Literature* (Edinburgh: Edinburgh University Press, 2011), p. 166.
8. Herman Melville, *Bartleby, The Scrivener: A Story of Wall Street*, in Melville, *Melville's Short Novels*, p. 32.
9. Melville, *Moby Dick*, p. 55.
10. For an archive of Melville's marginalia in his copies of Shakespeare, see https://melvillesmarginalia.org/Browser.aspx. For a classic account of Shakespeare's influence on Melville, see Charles Olson, *Call Me Ishmael: A Study of Melville* (San Francisco: City Light Books, 1947), pp. 35–73.
11. Virginia Woolf, *Between the Acts* (Oxford: Oxford University Press, 2008), p. 137.
12. William Shakespeare, *Hamlet*, in William Shakespeare, *The Complete Works* (Oxford: Clarendon Press, 1988), p. 669.
13. William Shakespeare, 'Sonnet 43', in Shakespeare, *Complete Works*, p. 756.
14. Emily Dickinson, *The Poems of Emily Dickinson* (Cambridge: Harvard University Press, 1998), p. 379.
15. Samuel Beckett, *Malone Dies*, in Samuel Beckett, *Molloy, Malone Dies, The Unnamable* (London: Calder, 1994), p. 222.
16. See Katie Chenoweth, *The Prosthetic Tongue: Printing Technology and the Rise of the French Language* (Philadelphia: University of Pennsylvania Press, 2019).
17. Michael Paul Rogin, *Subversive Genealogy: The Politics and Art of Herman Melville* (Berkeley: University of California Press, 1983), p. 209.
18. Melville, *Bartleby*, p. 27.
19. Toni Morrison, 'Unspeakable Things Unspoken: The Afro-American Presence in American Literature', in Toni Morrison, *Mouth Full of Blood: Essays, Speeches, Meditations* (London: Chatto and Windus, 2019), p. 179.
20. Melville, *Moby Dick*, p. 168.
21. W. E. B. Du Bois, *The Souls of Black Folk* (Oxford: Oxford University Press, 2007), p. 8
22. Frantz Fanon, *Black Skin White Masks* (London: Pluto, 1986), trans. Charles Lam Markmann, p. 101.
23. Edward W. Said, *Orientalism* (London: Penguin, 2003), p. 3.
24. James Baldwin, *Another Country* (London: Penguin, 2011), p. 61.
25. Fanon, *Black Skin*, p. 85.

26. David Marriott, *On Black Men* (Edinburgh: Edinburgh University Press, 2000), p. 66. Baldwin, *Notes*, p. 113.
27. James Baldwin, *Notes of a Native Son* (London: Penguin, 2017), p. 113.
28. See James Baldwin, *Down at the Cross: Letter from a Region in My Mind*, in James Baldwin, *The Fire Next Time* (London: Penguin, 2017), pp. 19–89.
29. James Baldwin, *My Dungeon Shock*, in Baldwin, *Fire Next Time*, p. 17.
30. Baldwin, *Another Country*, p. 297.
31. Morrison, 'Unspeakable Things', p. 179.
32. Dickinson, *Poems*, p. 310.
33. Morrison, 'Unspeakable Things', p. 179.
34. Ralph Ellison, *Invisible Man* (London: Penguin, 1965), p. 6.

2 Samuel Beckett

1. [Since this essay was published in 2002, a significant body of criticism has emerged which has addressed the critical lacuna that this essay is identifying. Emilie Morin's *Beckett's Political Imagination* (Cambridge: Cambridge University Press, 2017) was extremely influential in shifting the prevailing consensus concerning Beckett's politics; William Davies and Helen Bailey's 2021 collection *Beckett and Politics* suggests the range and vitality of readings of Beckett's politics in the early 2020s].
2. For the most thoughtful and persuasive account of indifference in Beckett's work, see Leslie Hill, *Beckett's Fiction: In Different Words* (Cambridge: Cambridge University Press, 1990).
3. Beckett, *Worstward Ho*, p. 101.
4. See Vivian Mercier, *Beckett/Beckett* (Oxford: Oxford University Press, 1977).
5. Eoin O'Brien, *The Beckett Country* (Dublin: Black Cat Press, 1986), p. xix.
6. O'Brien, *Beckett Country*, p. xix.
7. James Knowlson, 'Foreword', in O'Brien, *Beckett Country*, p. xvi.
8. See, for example, Ludovic Janvier, 'Place of Narration/Narration of Place', in Ruby Cohn, ed., *Samuel Beckett: A Collection of Criticism* (New York: McGaw Hill, 1975), p. 101, where it is suggested that, in the fictional space of *Watt*, 'a few residual traces of Dublin and countryside remain but reality is dissolving as though an anchor were raised, permitting the work to set out slowly toward its own myth'.
9. For an analysis of the dialectic between 'physical space' and 'mental space', and for an examination of the ideological and theoretical conditions that have led to the invisibility of this dialectic, see Henri Lefebvre, *The Production of Space* (Oxford: Blackwell, 1991), trans. Donald Nicholson-Smith. The 'most recent hypothesis' about the production of space, Lefebvre writes in the 1970s, in the 'Plan of the Present Work', is content to 'cheerfully commandeer social space and physical space and reduce them to an epistemological (mental) space – the space of discourse and of the Cartesian *cogito*'. His own work, he writes, sets out to ask 'what connection exists between this abstract body, understood

simply as a mediation between 'subject' and 'object', and a practical and fleshy body conceived of as a totality complete with spatial qualities (symmetries, asymmetries) and energetic properties (discharges, economies, waste)' (p. 61).
10. See Leslie Hill, '"Up the Republic!": Beckett, Writing, Politics', *Modern Language Notes*, vol 112, no 5 (1997), pp. 909–298; Leslie Hill, 'Beckett, Writing, Politics: Answering for Myself', in Peter Boxall, ed., *Beckett/Aesthetics/Politics*, a special issue of *Samuel Beckett Today/Aujourd'hui* (Amsterdam: Rodopi, 2000), pp. 215–221.
11. See, for example, Maurice Blanchot, 'Where Now? Who Now?', in Maurice Blanchot, *The Sirens' Song: Selected Essays by Maurice Blanchot* (Bloomington: Indiana University Press, 1982), ed. Gabriel Josipovici, pp. 192–198; Gilles Deleuze, 'The Exhausted', in Gilles Deleuze, *Essays Critical and Clinical* (London: Verso, 1998), trans Daniel W. Smith and Michael A. Greco, pp. 152–174.
12. Maurice Blanchot, *The Space of Literature* (Lincoln: University of Nebraska Press, 1982), trans. Ann Smock, p. 105.
13. James Joyce, *Portrait of the Artist as a Young Man* (Oxford: Oxford University Press, 2000), p. 202.
14. Blanchot, 'Where Now?', p. 195.
15. Blanchot, *Space of Literature*, p. 185.
16. Israel Schenker, 'A Portrait of Samuel Beckett, the Author of the Puzzling *Waiting for Godot*', *New York Times*, 6 May 1956, p. 3.
17. Blanchot, 'Where Now?', p. 198.
18. Fredric Jameson, *The Seeds of Time* (New York: Columbia University Press, 1994), p. 4.
19. Seamus Deane, *Celtic Revivals: Essays on Modern Irish Literature 1880–1980* (London: Faber, 1985), pp. 131–132.
20. Beckett, *Worstward Ho*, pp. 121, 125.
21. Blanchot, *Space of Literature*, p. 110.
22. Beckett, *Worstward Ho*, pp. 121–122.
23. Maurice Blanchot, 'The Narrative Voice or the Impersonal "He"', in Blanchot, *Sirens' Song*, p. 297.
24. Lefebvre, *Production of Space* p. 61.
25. Beckett, *Molloy*, p. 54.

3 A Leap Out of Our Biology

1. DeLillo, *The Body Artist*, p. 124.
2. Don DeLillo, *Point Omega* (London: Picador, 2010), p. 3.
3. Don DeLillo, *Cosmopolis* (London: Picador, 2003), p. 5.
4. Don DeLillo, 'The Starveling', in Don DeLillo, *The Angel Esmerelda: Nine Stories* (London: Picador, 2011), p. 188.
5. Wittgenstein, *Tractatus*, p. 41.
6. Roland Barthes, *Mythologies* (London: Paladin, 1973), trans. Annette Lavers, p. 153.

Notes to pages 69–80

7. Don DeLillo, *Americana* (London: Penguin, 1989), p. 257.
8. Don DeLillo, *Great Jones Street* (London: Picador, 1998), pp. 188, 246.
9. Don DeLillo, *End Zone* (London: Penguin, 1986), p. 88.
10. Daniel Grausam, *On Endings: American Postmodern Fiction and the Cold War* (Charlottesville: University of Virginia Press, 2011), p. 109.
11. Don DeLillo, *Underworld* (London: Picador, 1999), p. 786.
12. DeLillo, *End Zone*, p. 232.
13. Don DeLillo, 'In the Ruins of the Future', in *The Guardian* (22 December, 2001), www.theguardian.com/books/2001/dec/22/fiction.dondelillo, np.
14. Beckett, *Proust*, pp. 69–70.
15. Don DeLillo, *Running Dog* (London: Picador, 1999), p. 74.
16. DeLillo, *Underworld*, p. 11.
17. Don DeLillo, *Libra* (London: Penguin, 1988), p. 181.
18. DeLillo, *Underworld*, p. 63.
19. Duvall has a section on DeLillo's 'major novels' in his *Cambridge Companion to Don DeLillo*, which he lists as *White Noise*, *Libra* and *Underworld*. See John Duvall, ed., *The Cambridge Companion to Don DeLillo* (Cambridge: Cambridge University Press, 2008).
20. See Edward Said, *On Late Style: Music and Literature against the Grain* (London: Bloomsbury, 2007). See Margaret Atwood, *Alias Grace* (London: Virago, 1997), Margaret Atwood, *The Penelopiad* (Edinburgh: Canongate, 2006), and Philip Roth, *Exit Ghost* (London: Vintage, 2008). For a discussion of posthumous narration in the contemporary novel, see Alice Bennett, 'Unquiet Sprits: Death Writing in Contemporary Fiction', in *Textual Practice*, vol 23, no 3 (2009). For a discussion of posthumous narration in Atwood, see John O'Neill, 'Dying in a State of Grace', in *Textual Practice*, vol 27, no 4 (2013).
21. DeLillo, *The Word for Snow*, p. 21.
22. David Cowart, 'DeLillo and the Power of Language', in Duvall, ed., *Cambridge Companion to Don DeLillo*, p. 156. Mark Osteen has also noted the effect whereby Mr Tuttle's 'tautologies gleam with evanescent lucidity'. See Mark Osteen, 'Echo Chamber: Undertaking *The Body Artist*', in *Studies in the Novel*, vol 18, no 1–2 (2009), pp. 72–87, p. 73.
23. Virginia Woolf, *To the Lighthouse* (London: Grafton, 1977), p. 151.
24. DeLillo, *Point Omega*, p. 67.
25. DeLillo, *The Body Artist*, p. 91.
26. See John A. McClure, 'Postmodern/Post-Secular: Contemporary Fiction and Spirituality', in *Modern Fiction Studies*, vol 41, no 1 (1995), pp. 141–164, p. 44; Amy Hungerford, 'Don DeLillo's Latin Mass', in *Contemporary Literature*, vol 47, no 3 (2006), pp. 343–380, p. 345.
27. Don DeLillo, *The Names* (London: Picador, 1999), p. 7.
28. Henry James, *The Middle Years*, in Henry James, *The Tales of Henry James* (New York: Norton, 2003), eds. Christof Wegelin and Henry B. Wonham, p. 214.
29. DeLillo, *Zero K*, p. 43.
30. [DeLillo made this remark in a personal correspondence with me, which has since been published. See Don DeLillo and Peter Boxall, 'The Edge of the

Future: A Discussion with Don DeLillo', in Katherine Da Cunha Lewin and Kiron Ward, eds., *Don DeLillo: Contemporary Critical Perspectives* (London: Bloomsbury, 2019), pp. 159–164.]
31. DeLillo and Boxall, 'Edge of the Future', p. 163.
32. For two extended examinations of Beckett's depiction of closed and open rooms in his late television work, see Kumiko Kiuchi, 'Oxymoronic Perception and the Experience of Genre: Samuel Becket's *Ghost Trio*, ...*but the clouds*... and Beyond', in *Journal of Beckett Studies*, vol 18, nos 1–2 (2009), pp. 72–87, and Katherine Weiss, 'Animating Ghosts in Samuel Beckett's *Ghost Trio* and ...*but the clouds*...', in *Journal of Beckett Studies*, vol 18, nos 1–2 (2009), pp. 105–122.
33. Samuel Beckett, *Ghost Trio*, in Beckett, *Complete Dramatic Works*, p. 408.
34. Samuel Beckett, *Imagination Dead Imagine*, in Beckett, *Complete Short Prose*, p. 182.
35. Martin Heidegger, *The Fundamental Concepts of Metaphysics: World, Finitude, Solitude* (Indiana: Indiana University Press, 1995), trans. William McNeill and Nicholas Walker, p. 177.
36. DeLillo and Boxall, 'Edge of the Future', p. 162.
37. Beckett, *Proust*, p. 101.
38. Wittgenstein, *Tractatus*, p. 42.
39. DeLillo, *Americana*, p. 257.
40. See Martin Heidegger, 'The Way Back into the Ground of Metaphysics', in Walter Kaufmann, ed., *Existentialism from Dostoevsky to Sartre* (London: Meridian, 1968).
41. See Alexander Pope, 'An Essay on Man', in Alexander Pope, *The Major Works* (Oxford: Oxford University Press, 2006), p. 281; Johann Wolfgang von Goethe, *Elective Affinities* (London: Penguin, 2005), trans. R. J. Hollingdale, p. 216.
42. Heidegger, 'The Way Back into the Ground of Metaphysics', p. 158.
43. For Heidegger's definitive discussion of the production of a 'world picture', see Martin Heidegger, 'The Age of the World Picture', in Martin Heidegger, *The Question Concerning Technology and Other Essays* (New York: Harper, 1977), trans. William Lovitt.
44. For her discussion of 'vibrant matter', see Jane Bennett, *Vibrant Matter: A Political Ecology of Things* (Durham: Duke University Press, 2010).
45. Samuel Beckett, *How It Is* (London: Calder, 1996), p. 10.
46. DeLillo and Boxall, 'Edge of the Future', p. 164.
47. DeLillo and Boxall, 'Edge of the Future', p. 164.

4 A More Sophisticated Imitation

1. William Shakespeare, *Hamlet*, in William Shakespeare, *The Complete Works* (Oxford: Clarendon, 1988), p. 669.
2. Michel de Montaigne, *The Complete Essays* (London: Penguin, 2003), trans. M. A. Screech, p. 11.

3. Kazuo Ishiguro, *Klara and the Sun* (London: Faber, 2021), p. 121.
4. Rebecca L. Walkowitz, 'Ishiguro's Floating Worlds', in *ELH*, vol 68, no 4 (2001), pp. 1049–1076, p. 1052.
5. See Ishiguro, *Klara and the Sun*, p. 103.
6. Thomas Pynchon, *The Crying of Lot 49* (London: Vintage, 2000), p. 10. For a reproduction of Varo's painting, see Janet A. Kaplan, *Unexpected Journeys: The Art and Life of Remedios Varo* (London: Vintage, 1988), p. 21.
7. Edith Wharton, *The House of Mirth* (Oxford: Oxford University Press, 1999), p. 132. For a reproduction of Reynolds's portrait, see Mark Hallett, *Reynolds: Portraiture in Action* (New Haven: Yale University Press, 2014), p. 263.
8. Henry James, *The Wings of the Dove* (London: Everyman, 1997), p. 147. For a reproduction of Bronzino's portrait, see Charles McCorquodale, *Bronzino* (London: Jupiter, 1981), colour plate IV.
9. Oscar Wilde, *The Picture of Dorian Gray* (London: Penguin, 1985), p. 136.
10. See for example Charles Maturin, *Melmoth the Wanderer* (Oxford: Oxford University Press, 2008), where the vast mechanics of the plot are set in motion by an encounter with a portrait in the attic, in which 'only the eyes had life' (p. 18). See Edgar Allan Poe, 'The Oval Portrait', in Edgar Allan Poe, *The Complete Tales and Poems of Edgar Allan Poe* (New York: Castle Books, 2002), p. 249, in which a painter captures 'life itself' in a portrait, but only at the cost of the death of the sitter. See also Sheridan LeFanu, 'Schalken the Painter', in Sheridan LeFanu, *The Hours After Midnight* (London: Leslie Frewin, 1975), pp. 37–73. For a reading of the recurrence of portraiture in the Gothic tradition, see Michael Peled Ginsburg, *Portrait Stories* (New York: Fordham University Press, 2015).
11. George Eliot, *Daniel Deronda* (Oxford: Oxford University Press, 2009), pp. 20, 597.
12. Jane Austen, *Emma* (Oxford: Oxford University Press, 2008), p. 38.
13. Cervantes, *Don Quixote*, p. 641.
14. Kazuo Ishiguro, *An Artist of the Floating World* (London: Faber, 1987), p. 169.
15. Kazuo Ishiguro, *The Unconsoled* (London: Faber, 1995), p. 186.
16. Kazuo Ishiguro, *Never Let Me Go* (London: Faber, 2006), p. 26.
17. See Franz Kafka, *The Trial* (London: Penguin, 1994), trans. Idris Parry, where many of the scenes in *The Unconsoled* have a kind of origin. The darkness of the cinema in *The Unconsoled*, for example, is prefigured in the 'intense darkness' of the Cathedral in a late sequence in *The Trail* (p. 159); and the tendency for one space to open oddly onto another in *The Unconsoled* is prefigured in episodes in *The Trail*, in which, for example, K will discover that a 'long passage' stretches from the studio of a painter to the heart of the dreaded court' (p. 129).
18. See Gilles Deleuze and Félix Guattari, *Kafka: Toward a Minor Literature* (Minneapolis: University of Minnesota Press, 1986), trans. Dana Polan, p. 8, where they argue that in Kafka's fiction 'the indistinction of inside and outside leads to the discovery of another dimension, a sort of adjacency marked by halts, sudden stops where parts, gears, and segments assemble themselves'.

5 A Cleaving in the Mind

1. [Since this essay was published in 2010, Kelman's body of twenty-first-century fiction has grown, to include *Mo Said She Was Quirky* (2012), *Dirt Road* (2016) and *God's Teeth and Other Phenomena* (2022)].
2. Theodor Adorno, 'Commitment', in Ernst Bloch, et al., eds., *Aesthetics and Politics* (London: NLB, 1977), trans. Francis McDonagh, pp. 177–195, p. 190.
3. Georg Lukács, *The Meaning of Contemporary Realism* (Monmouth: Merlin Press, 2006), p. 92. See also Georg Lukács, 'Realism in the Balance', in Ernst Bloch, et al., eds., *Aesthetics and Politics* (London: NLB, 1977), trans. Rodney Livingstone, pp. 28–59.
4. Lukács, *Meaning of Contemporary Realism*, p. 83.
5. Lukács, *Meaning of Contemporary Realism*, p. 80.
6. Adorno, 'Commitment', p. 191.
7. Adorno, 'Commitment', p. 191.
8. Adorno, 'Commitment', p. 191.
9. Adorno, 'Commitment', p. 191.
10. Adorno, 'Commitment', p. 194.
11. For comparison, see the development of Scottish dialect in Lewis Grassic Gibbon, *Sunset Song* (London: Penguin, 2007). Ali Smith notes in her introduction to the novel that Gibbon's 'hybrid of English and Scots stretches what language can do and is expected to do' (Ali Smith, 'Introduction', p. xvii).
12. Adorno, 'Commitment', p. 190.
13. [For two brilliant works which seek to rethink the politics and aesthetics of abstraction, forthcoming as I write, see Jeff Wallace, *Abstraction in Modernism and Modernity* (Edinburgh: Edinburgh University Press, 2023), and Richard Godden, *Punctuating Capital: Towards a Narrative Poetics for the Financial Turn* (Oxford: Oxford University Press, 2023).]
14. For an account of Kelman's place in the 'new Scottish renaissance', see Christie L. March, *Rewriting Scotland* (Manchester: Manchester University Press, 2002), pp. 4–7.
15. James Kelman, *You Have to Be Careful in the Land of the Free* (London: Penguin, 2004), p. 379.
16. James Kelman, *Some Recent Attacks* (Stirling: A. K. Press, 1992), p. 81.
17. For a discussion of Kelman's relation to postcolonial writing, see Carole Jones, '"Acting the Part of an Illiterate Savage": James Kelman and the Question of Postcolonial Masculinity', in *Journal of Postcolonial Writing*, vol 45, no 3 (2009), pp. 275–284. For a discussion of the relation between Scottish writing and the postcolonial tradition, see Michael Gardiner, '"A Light to the World": British Devolution and Colonial Vision', in *Interventions*, vol 6, no 2 (2004), pp. 264–281.

18. Samuel Beckett, *Fizzles*, in Beckett, *Complete Short Prose*, pp. 224–228, 238–239.
19. James Kelman, *Translated Accounts* (London: Secker and Warburg, 2001), pp. 314–315, 89–96.
20. Kelman, *Translated Accounts*, p. 133.
21. Dickinson, *Poems*, p. 379.
22. Kelman, *Translated Accounts*, p. 133.
23. Kelman, *Kieron Smith, Boy*, p. 2.
24. Kelman, *Careful*, p. 374.
25. Rimbaud makes these comments in his famous letter to Paul Demeny, 15 May 1871, quoted in Enid Starkie, *Arthur Rimbaud* (London: Faber, 1961), p. 122.

6 Zadie Smith, E. M. Forster and the Idea of Beauty

1. Karl Marx, *Economic and Philosophical Manuscripts*, in Karl Marx, *Early Writings* (London: Penguin, 1992), trans. Rodney Livingstone and Gregor Benton, p. 353.
2. Zadie Smith, *On Beauty* (London: Penguin, 2005), p. 3.
3. E. M. Forster, *Howards End* (London: Penguin, 2012), p. 1.
4. Ian McEwan, *The Children Act* (London: Jonathan Cape, 2014), p. 1.
5. Charles Dickens, *Bleak House* (Oxford: Oxford University Press, 1998), p. 11.
6. Zadie Smith and Ian McEwan, 'Zadie Smith Talks with Ian McEwan', in Ryan Roberts, ed., *Conversations with Ian McEwan* (Jackson: University of Mississippi Press, 2010), p. 108.
7. J. M. Coetzee, *Elizabeth Costello* (New York: Viking, 2003), p. 9.
8. Samuel Beckett, *The Unnamable*, in Beckett, *Molloy, Malone Dies, The Unnamable*, p. 418.
9. George Eliot, *Daniel Deronda* (Oxford: Oxford University Press, 2009), p. 3.
10. H. J. Blackham, *Six Existentialist Thinkers* (London: Routledge, 1952), p. 118.
11. The epigraph to *Howards End*, 'Only connect…', appears in the main body of the text, when Meg thinks to herself that 'only connect' was the 'whole of her sermon' (p. 195).
12. See Simon Schama, *Rembrandt's Eyes* (London: Allen Lane, 1999).
13. Nick Laird, 'On Beauty', in Nick Laird, *To a Fault* (New York: Norton, 2006), p. 59.
14. See, for example, Dorothy Hale's essay '*On Beauty* as Beautiful? The Problem of Novelistic Aesthetics by Way of Zadie Smith', in *Contemporary Literature*, vol 53, no 4 (2012), pp. 814–844, which engages extensively with the paratexts in *On Beauty*.
15. Martha C. Nussbaum, *Love's Knowledge: Essays on Philosophy and Literature* (Oxford: Oxford University Press, 1990).
16. Nick Laird, 'The Last Saturday in Ulster', in Laird, *To A Fault*, p. 61.
17. Laird, *To A Fault*, p. 58.
18. Elaine Scarry, *On Beauty and Being Just* (London: Duckworth, 2006), p. 3.
19. Proust, *Remembrance*, vol 3, p. 925.

20. Coetzee, *Elizabeth Costello*, p. 9.
21. Frank Kermode, 'Here She Is', in *London Review of Books*, vol 27, no 19 (October, 2005). Online at www.lrb.co.uk/the-paper/v27/n19/frank-kermode/here-she-is.
22. The Schlegels, Meg thinks, share a richly realised 'inner life' (p. 203); the Wilcoxes, in contrast 'led a life that she could not attain to – the outer life of "telegrams and anger"' (p. 107).
23. Kermode, 'Here She Is', np.
24. M. M. Bakhtin, *The Dialogic Imagination: Four Essays* (Austin: University of Texas Press, 1981), trans. Caryl Emerson and Michael Holquist, p. 330.
25. Bakhtin, *Dialogic Imagination*, p. 330.
26. For a searching analysis of the connections and disjunctions between thoughts and things, see Leo Bersani, *Thoughts and Things* (Chicago: University of Chicago Press, 2015).
27. Samuel Beckett, *Murphy* (London: Picador, 1973), p. 157.
28. Anahid Nersessian, 'For Love of Beauty: Literary Criticism in Troubled Times', in *NLR*, vol 133/134 (2022), pp. 1–32, p. 4.
29. Matthew Arnold, 'To a Friend', in Matthew Arnold, *The Poems of Matthew Arnold 1840–1867* (London: Humphrey Milford, 1913), p. 40.
30. John Ruskin, *The Stones of Venice* (London: George Allen and Unwin, 1925), 3 vols, vol 1, p. 125.
31. Marx, *Early Writings*, p. 353.
32. Scarry, *On Beauty*, p. 3.
33. Zadie Smith, 'E. M. Forster, Middle Manager', in Zadie Smith, *Changing My Mind: Occasional Essays* (London: Hamish Hamilton, 2009), pp. 14–27, p. 14.
34. Maurice Blanchot, *The Infinite Conversation* (Minneapolis: University of Minnesota Press, 1993), trans. Susan Hanson, p. 380.
35. E. M. Forster, *Aspects of the Novel* (London: Penguin, 2005), p. 62.
36. Forster, *Aspects of the Novel*, p. 59.
37. Forster, *Aspects of the Novel*, p. 63.
38. Forster, *Aspects of the Novel*, p. 63.
39. E. M. Forster, 'What I Believe', in E. M. Forster, *Two Cheers for Democracy* (London: Edward Arnold, 1972), pp. 65–73, p. 65.
40. Forster, 'What I Believe', p. 65.
41. See the close of E. M. Forster, *A Passage to India* (London: Penguin, 2005), p. 289, where 'half kissing him', Aziz says to Fielding that 'you and I shall be friends'; but 'not yet', and 'not there'.
42. Hale, '*On Beauty* as Beautiful?', p. 815.
43. Scarry, *On Beauty*, p. 8; Smith *On Beauty*, p. 127.
44. See Bill Readings, *The University in Ruins* (Cambridge: Harvard University Press, 1996). This book came out after Bill Readings' death in a plane crash, in 1994.
45. See Briana G. Brickley, '*On Beauty* and the Politics of Academic Institutionality', in *Ariel: A Review of International English Literature*, vol 48, no 2 (2017), pp. 73–100, for a reading of Smith's critique of the university in *On Beauty*. Brickley argues that the novel 'ultimately theorizes a complicated,

intersectional aesthetics not to indict the neoliberal university as a cultural hegemon that limits beauty and difference but to reflect on how the institution is a space of tension, discontinuity, and contradiction' (p. 96).
46. Walter Pater, *The Renaissance: Studies in Art and Poetry* (Cambridge: Cambridge University Press, 2011), p. 237.
47. Bewes, *Free Indirect*, p. 96.
48. Hale, '*On Beauty* as Beautiful?', p. 836.
49. Schama, *Rembrandt's Eyes*, p. 558.
50. For my own extended reading of this painting as a representation of a relation between mind and mater, see Peter Boxall, *The Prosthetic Imagination: A History of the Novel as Artificial Life* (Cambridge: Cambridge University Press, 2020), pp. 34–39.
51. Forster, *Howards End*, p. 107.
52. Forster, *Howards End*, p. 348.
53. Marx, *Early Writings*, p. 348.
54. Immanuel Kant, *Critique of the Power of Judgement* (Cambridge: Cambridge University Press, 2000), trans. Paul Guyer, p. 101.
55. Ngai, *Theory of the Gimmick*, p. 18.

7 The Threshold of Vision

1. See William Shakespeare, *King Lear*, in Shakespeare, *Complete Works*, p. 963, where Cornwall blinds Gloucester: 'Out, vile jelly! Where is thy lustre now?'.
2. For a reflection on the ear drum as a boundary (between mind and world, and between philosophy and literature), see Jacques Derrida, 'Tympan', in Jacques Derrida, *Margins of Philosophy* (New York: Harvester, 1982), trans. Alan Bass, pp. ix–xxix. For Beckett's poetic musings on the ear drum as boundary, see *The Unnamable*, where the narrator imagines that 'I'm neither one side nor the other, I'm in the middle, I'm the partition, I've two surfaces and no thickness, perhaps that's what I feel, myself vibrating, I'm the tympanum, on the one hand the mind, on the other the world, I don't belong to either'. Beckett, *The Unnamable*, p. 386.
3. John Berger, 'Why Look at Animals?', in Geoff Dyer, ed., *John Berger: Selected Essays* (London: Bloomsbury, 2001), p. 260.
4. See J. M. Coetzee, 'Eight Ways of Looking at Samuel Beckett', in Minako Okamuro, et el., eds., *Borderless Beckett/ Beckett sans frontières* (Amsterdam: Rodopi, 2008), pp. 19–31. As will be clear from the following account, I was present at the conference at which Coetzee delivered this essay as a keynote address. [This essay was subsequently published in Coetzee, *Late Essays*, pp. 202–217].
5. Melville, *Moby Dick*, p. 167.
6. Beckett, *The Lost Ones*, p. 206.
7. Wallace Stevens, 'Thirteen Ways of Looking at a Blackbird', in Wallace Stevens, *Selected Poems* (London: Faber, 2010), p. 34.

8. See W. G. Sebald and Jan Peter Tripp, *Unrecounted* (New York: New Directions, 2004), pp. 78–79.
9. W. G. Sebald, *Vertigo* (London: Vintage, 2002), trans. Michael Hulse, p. 190.
10. See W. G. Sebald, Austerlitz (London: Penguin, 2001), trans. Anthea Bell, p. 369, p. 276, p. 3.
11. See Shane Weller, 'Beckett and Animality', in Okamuro, et al., eds., *Borderless Beckett*, p. 219.
12. See Beckett, *The Unnamable*, p. 418, 'I can't go on. I'll go on'.
13. Beckett, *Murphy*, p. 139.
14. T. S. Eliot, 'Marina', in T.S. Eliot, *Selected Poems* (London: Faber and Faber, 1954), p. 103, ll. 18–19.
15. For Beckett's dramatisation of the attempt to become one's 'own other', see Samuel Beckett, *Rockaby*, in Beckett, *Complete Dramatic Works*, pp. 431–442. The play follows a woman's search with 'famished eyes' for another like herself – 'a little like' – until she reaches the decision to become 'her own other', p. 441. For a reflection on the political significance of this phrase, in relation to Beckett's engagement with feminism, see Mary Bryden, *Women in Samuel Beckett's Prose and Drama: Her Own Other* (Basingstoke: Macmillan, 1993).
16. See Samuel Beckett, *Watt* (London: Calder, 1976), pp. 154–162.
17. Samuel Beckett, *Krapp's Last Tape*, in Beckett, *Complete Dramatic Works*, p. 221.
18. Samuel Beckett, *Company*, in Beckett, *Nohow On*, p. 39.
19. Beckett, *Malone Dies*, p. 209.
20. Beckett, *Murphy*, p. 5; Beckett, *Malone Dies*, p. 192.
21. The 'pernings' of Sapo's hawk here call to mind Yeat's 'Sailing to Byzantium', where the poet calls to his 'sages' to 'perne in a gyre, / And be the singing masters of my soul'. Yeats, *Poems*, p. 217.
22. See Steven Connor, 'Beckett's animals', in *Journal of Beckett Studies*, no. 8 (1982), pp. 29–44.
23. Samuel Beckett, *Worstward Ho*, in Beckett, *Nohow On*, pp. 126, 127.
24. Beckett, *Company*, p. 15.
25. John Milton, *Paradise Lost* (Harlow: Pearson Longman, 2007), ed. Alastair Fowler, p. 64.
26. J. M. Coetzee, *Slow Man* (London: Secker and Warburg, 2005), p. 65.
27. Sebald, *Austerlitz*, p. 109.
28. J. M. Coetzee, *Summertime: Scenes from Provincial Life* (London: Harvill Secker, 2009), p. 242.
29. See Coetzee, *Elizabeth Costello*, particularly 'The Philosophers and the Animals', pp. 59–90, in which Costello gives a lecture in which she says, 'I felt a little like Red Peter myself' (p. 62).
30. See Samuel Beckett, *Endgame*, in Beckett, *Complete Dramatic Works*.
31. Samuel Beckett, 'The Capital of the Ruins', in Beckett, *Complete Short Prose*, p. 278, p. 277.

8 The Anatomy of Realism

1. Cervantes, *Don Quixote*, p. 906.
2. Vladimir Nabokov, *Lectures on Don Quixote* (London: Weidenfeld and Nicolson, 1983), ed. Fredson Bowers, p. 57.
3. Erich Auerbach, *Mimesis: The Representation of Reality in Western Literature* (Princeton: Princeton University Press, 2003), trans. Willard R. Trask, p. 343.
4. See Plato, *The Republic* (London: Penguin, 2007), trans. Desmond Lee, pp. 240–248.
5. Auerbach, *Mimesis*, pp. 343–344.
6. Mario Vargas Llosa, 'A Novel for the Twenty-First Century', in *Harvard Review*, vol 28 (2005), trans. Johanna Damgaard Liander, pp. 125–136, p. 126.
7. Jorge Luis Borges, *Labyrinths* (London: Penguin, 1970), trans. Donald A. Yates, p. 278.
8. Maria J. López, 'Miguel de Cervantes and J.M. Coetzee: An Unacknowledged Paternity', in *Journal of Literary Studies*, vol 29, no 4 (2013), pp. 80–97, p. 81.
9. James Aubrey, '"For Me Alone Paul Rayment Was Born": Coetzee's *Slow Man*, *Don Quixote*, and the Literature of Replenishment', in *Peer English*, vol 6 (2011), pp. 93–106, p. 99.
10. Urmila Seshagiri, 'The Boy of La Mancha: J. M. Coetzee's *The Childhood of Jesus*', in *Contemporary Literature*, vol 54, no 3 (2013), pp. 643–654, p. 648.
11. [Since this essay was written, Coetzee has extended the *Jesus* books into a trilogy, comprising *The Childhood of Jesus*, *The Schooldays of Jesus* and *The Death of Jesus*. Cervantes is a structuring presence throughout the trilogy, as evidenced by the epigraph to *Schooldays*, taken from *Don Quixote*: J. M. Coetzee, *The Schooldays of Jesus* (London: Harvill Secker, 2016), np: 'Algunos dicen: Nunca segundas partes fueron buenas'].
12. Coetzee, *Childhood of Jesus*, p. 95.
13. Cervantes, *Don Quixote*, p. 36.
14. Ludwig Wittgenstein, *Philosophical Investigations* (Oxford: Blackwell, 2001), trans G. E. M. Anscombe, p. 256.
15. Seshagiri, 'The Boy of La Mancha', p. 647.
16. Coetzee, *Elizabeth Costello*, pp. 193–225.
17. Auerbach, *Mimesis*, p. 345.
18. Cervantes, *Don Quixote*, p. 680.
19. James Joyce, *Dubliners* (Oxford: Oxford University Press, 2000), p. 160.
20. Auerbach, *Mimesis*, p. 345.
21. J. M. Coetzee, *The Master of Petersburg* (London: Vintage, 1999), p. 121, p. 21.
22. Johann Wolfgang von Goethe, *Selected Poems* (London: Calder, 1983), ed. and trans. Christopher Middleton, p. 87.
23. Goethe, *Selected Poems*, p. 87.
24. Coetzee, *Master of Petersburg*, p. 121.
25. Coetzee, *Master of Petersburg*, p. 121.
26. Gustave Flaubert, *The Selected Letters of Gustave Flaubert* (London: Hamish Hamilton, 1954), trans. Francis Steegmuller, p. 131.

Notes to pages 183–195 357

27. Cervantes, *Don Quixote*, p. 26; Cervantes, *Don Quijote de la Mancha* (London: Hirschfeld Brothers, 1928), p. xviii.
28. Coetzee, *Doubling the Point*, p. 98.

9 Back Roads

1. Maria Edgeworth, *Castle Rackrent* (Oxford: Oxford University Press, 1964), pp. 46–47.
2. Edgeworth, *Castle Rackrent*, p. 5.
3. James Joyce, *Portrait*, p. 276.
4. Edgeworth, *Castle Rackrent*, p. 5.
5. Edgeworth, *Castle Rackrent*, p. 18. Edgeworth's emphasis.
6. For a striking account of temporality in *Castle Rackrent*, which suggests that the novel's 'strange, fractured, and unstable narrative, is *the* symptomatic discrepancy of the nineteenth century novel', see Seamus Deane, *Strange Country: Modernity and Nationhood in Irish Writing since 1790* (Oxford: Clarendon, 1997), pp. 38–41.
7. See W. J. McCormack, *From Burke to Beckett: Ascendancy, Tradition and Betrayal in Literary History* (Cork: Cork University Press, 1994).
8. Beckett, *Company*, p. 18; Samuel Beckett, *Stirrings Still*, in Beckett, *Complete Short Prose*, p. 260; Samuel Beckett, *…but the clouds…* in Beckett, *Complete Dramatic Works*, p. 422.
9. Elizabeth Bowen, 'The Back Drawing Room', in Elizabeth Bowen, *Collected Stories* (London, Vintage, 1999), p. 200.
10. For her own reflections on the operations of the back, see Elizabeth Bowen, 'The Bend Back', in Elizabeth Bowen, *The Mulberry Tree: Writings of Elizabeth Bowen* (London: Vintage, 1999), ed. Hermione Lee, pp. 54–60. For David Wills' book length reflections on the back, see David Wills, *Dorsality: Thinking Back through Technology and Politics* (Minneapolis: University of Minnesota Press, 2008).
11. See Elizabeth Bowen, *Pictures and Conversations* (New York: Knopf, 1975), reprinted in Bowen, *The Mulberry Tree*, p. 282.
12. Bowen, *The Mulberry Tree*, p. 282.
13. Bowen, *The Mulberry Tree*, p. 283.
14. Bowen, *The Mulberry Tree*, p. 276.
15. Bowen, *The Mulberry Tree*, p. 276.
16. Declan Kiberd, *Inventing Ireland: The Literature of the Modern Nation* (London: Vintage, 1996), p. 377. For a nuanced reading of Bowen's and Beckett's belonging to a shared tradition, see W. J. McCormack, 'Infancy and History: Beckett, Bowen and Critical Theory', in McCormack, *From Burke to Beckett*, pp. 375–433.
17. Kiberd, *Inventing Ireland*, p. 531.
18. Kiberd, *Inventing Ireland*, pp. 530, 531.
19. Kiberd, *Inventing Ireland*, p. 539.

20. Kiberd, *Inventing Ireland*, p. 538.
21. Kiberd, *Inventing Ireland*, p. 531.
22. Bowen, *The Mulberry Tree*, p. 282.
23. See Bowen, *The Mulberry Tree*, where Bowen says that the places in her stories are scattered between England and Ireland, noting that 'Nothing (*at least on the surface*) connects them' (my italics).
24. Bowen, *The Mulberry Tree*, p. 281.
25. Bowen, *The Mulberry Tree*, p. 282.
26. Bowen, *The Mulberry Tree*, p. 283.
27. McCormack, *From Burke to Beckett*, p. 413.
28. Bowen, 'The Bend Back', p. 55.
29. There are a number of recent studies which have reassessed Beckett's relationship with Ireland, and moved past the older model of a universal or placeless Beckett. See, for example, Eion O'Brien, *The Beckett Country* (Dublin: Black Cat Press, 1986), John P. Harrington, *The Irish Beckett* (New York: Syracuse University Press, 1991), David Lloyd, 'Writing in the Shit: Beckett, Nationalism and the Colonial Subject', in David Lloyd, *Anomalous States: Irish Writing and the Post-Colonial Moment* (Dublin: The Lilliput Press, 1993), pp. 41–58, Sinead Mooney, '"Integrity in a Surplus": Beckett's (Post-) Protestant Politics', in Peter Boxall, ed., *Beckett/Aesthetics/Politics, Samuel Beckett Today/Aujourd'hui*, vol 9 (Amsterdam: Rodopi, 2000), pp. 223–237, Peter Boxall, 'The Existence I Ascribe: Memory, Invention and Autobiography in Beckett's Fiction', in *The Yearbook of English Studies*, vol 30 (2000), pp. 137–153. Anna McMullen contributes to this reassessment, and offers an excellent survey of such approaches; see Anna McMullen, 'Irish/Postcolonial Beckett', in Lois Oppenheim, ed., *Palgrave Advances in Samuel Beckett Studies* (Basingstoke: Palgrave, 2004), pp. 89–109. [See p. 346, n 1 above for an account of more developments in the critical construction of a political Beckett, that have unfolded in the years since this essay was published].
30. Samuel Beckett, *Dream of Fair to Middling Women* (London: Calder, 1993), p. 121.
31. Beckett, *Complete Short Prose*, p. 258.
32. Beckett, *Waiting for Godot*, in Beckett, *Complete Dramatic Works*, p. 57.
33. For a reading of the back in *Company*, and in Beckett's work more generally, see Nicholas Royle, 'Back', in *Oxford Literary Review*, vol 18 (1996), pp. 145–157.
34. Beckett, *Company*, p. 12.
35. See, for example, James Knowlson, *Damned to Fame: The Life of Samuel Beckett* (London: Bloomsbury, 1996), pp. 651–653.
36. Beckett, *Company*, p. 18.
37. Beckett, *Company*, p. 18.
38. Beckett, *Company*, p. 8.
39. Beckett, *How It Is*, p. 7.
40. Beckett, *How It Is*, p. 7.
41. Beckett, *Molloy*, p. 49.

42. The discussion of these plays refers throughout to the version broadcast by the BBC on 17 April 1977.
43. Deleuze and Guattari, *Kafka: Toward a Minor Literature*, p. 73.
44. W. B. Yeats, 'The Tower', in W. B. Yeats, *Collected Poems* (London: Picador, 1990), p. 219. For a fuller reading of the relationship between the Yeats poem and ...*but the clouds*..., see Richard Bruce Kirkley, 'A *catch in the breath*: Language and Consciousness in Samuel Beckett's ...*but the clouds*...', in *Modern Drama*, vol 35, no 4 (December 1992), pp. 607–616.
45. Samuel Beckett, *Stirrings Still*, in Beckett, *Complete Short Prose*, p. 260.
46. For a discussion of cinematic suturing, see Stephen Heath, 'On Suture', in Stephen Heath, *Questions of Cinema* (Basingstoke: Macmillan, 1981), pp. 76–112, and Kaja Silverman, 'Suture', in Kaja Silverman, *The Subject of Semiotics* (New York: Oxford University Press, 1983), pp. 194–236.
47. Kirkley, 'A *catch in the breath*', p. 615.
48. Yeats, 'The Tower', p. 225.
49. McMullen, 'Irish/Postcolonial Beckett', p. 107.

10 Blind Seeing

1. Wallace Stevens, 'Notes Toward a Supreme Fiction', in Wallace Stevens, *Selected Poems* (London: Faber, 2010), p. 85.
2. Shakespeare, *Hamlet*, p. 657.
3. Stevens, 'Notes Toward a Supreme Fiction', p. 86.
4. Franz Kafka, *Diaries, 1910–1923* (New York, Schoeken, 1980), ed. Max Brod, p. 321.
5. Eric Lax, *On Being Funny: Woody Allen and Comedy* (New York: Manor Books, 1975), p. 232. Kafka, *Diaries*, p. 321.
6. Maurice Blanchot, *The Space of Literature* (Lincoln: The University of Nebraska Press, 1982), trans. Ann Smock, p. 94.
7. Blanchot, *Space of Literature*, p. 92.
8. Blanchot, *Space of Literature*, p. 94.
9. Emily Dickinson, 'The Tint I cannot take – is best –', in Dickinson, *Poems*, p. 310.
10. Stevens, 'Notes Toward a Supreme Fiction', p. 88.
11. Martin Heidegger, 'The Age of the World Picture', in Martin Heidegger, *The Question Concerning Technology and Other Essays* (New York: Harper, 1977), trans. William Lovitt, p. 134.
12. Giorgio Agamben, *The Open: Man and Animal* (Stanford: Stanford University Press, 2004), trans. Kevin Attell, p. 80.
13. Agamben, *The Open*, p. 79.
14. Giorgio Agamben, 'What is the Contemporary?', in Giorgio Agamben, *Nudities* (Stanford: Stanford University Press, 2011), trans. David Kishik and Stefan Pedatella, p. 13.
15. Agamben, 'What is the Contemporary?', p. 13.
16. Heidegger, 'Age of the World Picture', p. 135.

17. Harold Bloom, *The Western Canon: The Books and School of the Ages* (London: Papermac, 1996), p. 295.
18. Dickinson, *Poems*, p. 157.
19. See Paul de Man, 'The Rhetoric of Blindness', in *Blindness and Insight: Essays in the Rhetoric of Contemporary Criticism* (London: Routledge, 1983), second edition, pp. 102–141. There are a number of different rhetorical forms in which the relation between blindness and sight has been couched. Paul de Man's work is part of a deconstructive rhetoric of blindness; for a recent book which addresses the question from a disability studies perspective, see Georgina Kleege, *Sight Unseen* (New Haven: Yale University Press, 1999).
20. de Man, *Blindness and Insight*, p. 109.
21. de Man, *Blindness and Insight*, p. 103.
22. de Man, *Blindness and Insight*, p. 141.
23. Jacques Derrida, *Memoirs of the Blind: The Self-Portrait and Other Ruins* (Chicago: University of Chicago Press, 1993), trans. Pascale-Anne Brault and Michael Naas, p. 51.
24. See Páraic Finnerty, *Dickinson's Shakespeare* (Amherst: University of Massachusetts Press, 2006), pp. 118–119.
25. William Shakespeare, 'Sonnet 43', Shakespeare, *Complete Works*, p. 756.
26. Agamben, 'What is the Contemporary', pp. 14–15.
27. Heidegger, 'Age of the World Picture', p. 154.
28. Beckett, *Ohio Impromptu*, p. 448.
29. Samuel Beckett, 'La Mouche', in Samuel Beckett, *Collected Poems* (London: Calder, 1986), p. 45.
30. Steven Connor, *Beckett, Modernism and the Material Imagination* (Cambridge: Cambridge University Press, 2014), pp. 50–51.
31. See Steven Connor, 'Making Flies Mean Something', in Connor, *Beckett, Modernism and the Material Imagination*, pp. 48–62.
32. Samuel Beckett, *Watt* (London: Calder, 1976), p. 236.
33. Samuel Beckett, *Company*, in Samuel Beckett, *Nohow On* (London: Calder, 1992), p. 22.
34. Samuel Beckett, *All Strange Away*, in Samuel Beckett, *The Complete Short Prose 1929–1989* (New York: Grove Press, 1995), p. 172.
35. Mary F. Cantanzaro, 'More Than a Common Pest: The Fly as Non-human Companion in Emily Dickinson's 'I Heard a Fly Buzz When I Died' and Samuel Beckett's *Company*', in Anna-Teresa Tymieniecka, ed., *From Sky and Earth to Metaphysics* (New York: Springer, 2015), pp. 157–162.
36. Sharon Cameron, *Lyric Time: Dickinson and the Limits of Genre* (Baltimore: The Johns Hopkins Press, 1979), p. 135.
37. Beckett, *Company*, p. 12.
38. Beckett, *How It Is*, p. 153.
39. Samuel Beckett, *The Calmative*, in Samuel Beckett, *The Expelled and Other Novellas* (London: Penguin, 1980), p. 51.
40. Samuel Beckett, 'Neither', in Beckett, *Complete Short Prose*, p. 258.
41. Beckett, *Company*, p. 15; Beckett, *Imagination Dead Imagine*, p. 182.

42. Beckett, *The Lost Ones*, p. 215.
43. Beckett, *Proust*, p. 101.
44. Samuel Beckett, *Worstward Ho*, in Beckett, *Nohow On*, p. 124.
45. Jane Bennett, *Vibrant Matter: A Political Ecology of Things* (Durham: Duke University Press, 2010), p. x.
46. Bennett, *Vibrant Matter*, p. vii.
47. Cormac McCarthy, *The Road* (London: Picador, 2007), p. 138.
48. Stevens, 'Notes Toward a Supreme Fiction', p. 85.
49. Stevens, 'Notes Toward a Supreme Fiction', p. 85.
50. Beckett, *Imagination Dead Imagine*, p. 182.
51. Beckett, *Endgame*, p. 132.
52. Beckett, *The Lost Ones*, p. 204.
53. Dickinson, *Poems*, p. 310.
54. Heidegger, 'Age of the World Picture', p. 135.
55. See Susan Howe, *My Emily Dickinson* (Berkeley: North Atlantic Books, 1985), p. 1, and Deleuze and Guattari, *Kafka: Toward a Minor Literature*.
56. Harold Bloom, *The Western Canon: The Books and School of the Ages* (London: Papermac, 1996), p. 308.
57. Heidegger, 'Age of the World picture', p. 136.
58. Stevens, 'Notes Toward a Supreme Fiction', p. 88.

11 Mere Being

1. William Shakespeare, *A Midsummer Night's Dream*, in Shakespeare, *Complete Works*, p. 330.
2. Wallace Stevens, 'A Clear Day and No Memories', in Wallace Stevens, *The Palm at the End of the Mind: Selected Poems and a Play* (New York: Vintage, 1990), p. 397.
3. Wallace Stevens, 'Of Mere Being', in Stevens, *A Palm at the End of the Mind*, p. 398.
4. W.B. Yeats, 'Sailing to Byzantium', in Yeats, *Collected Poems*, p. 218.
5. Wallace Stevens, 'As You Leave the Room', in Stevens, *The Palm at the End of the Mind*, pp. 395–396. See Samuel French Morse, *Wallace Stevens: Poetry as Life* (New York: Pegasus, 1970), pp. 219–222, for a discussion of this poem's genesis.
6. Wallace Stevens, *Opus Posthumous* (New York: Knopf Doubleday, 1989), p. 192.
7. Simon Critchley, *Things Merely Are: Philosophy in The Poetry of Wallace Stevens* (London: Routledge, 2005), p. 5. Wallace Stevens, 'Not Ideas about the Thing but the Thing Itself', in Stevens, *The Palm at the End of the Mind*, pp. 387–388.
8. Critchley, *Things Merely Are*, p. 6.
9. Wallace Stevens, *The Necessary Angel: Essays on Reality and the Imagination* (New York: Vintage, 1965), p. 71.
10. Stevens, *The Necessary Angel*, p. 72. Critchley, *Things Merely Are*, p. 6.
11. Wallace Stevens, *The Letters of Wallace Stevens* (London: Faber, 1966), ed. Holly Stevens, p. 659.

12. Stevens, *Letters*, p. 711.
13. Auerbach, *Mimesis*, p. 358.
14. Coetzee, *Diary of a Bad Year*, p. 68.
15. Michel Foucault, *Discipline and Punish* (New York: Vintage, 1995), trans. Alan Sheridan, p. 198.
16. Dipesh Chakrabarty, 'The Climate of History: Four Theses', in *Critical Inquiry*, vol 35, no 2 (2009), pp. 197–222, p. 221, p. 207. For Heidegger's essay, 'Building Dwelling Thinking', see Martin Heidegger, *Poetry, Language, Thought* (New York: Harper, 1971), trans. Albert Hofstadter.
17. Virginia Woolf, *Night and Day* (London: Penguin, 1982), p. 86.
18. Virginia Woolf, *Mrs Dalloway* (New York: Knopf, 1993), p. 90.
19. Beckett, *Proust*, p. 66.
20. Beckett, *Proust*, p. 65.
21. René Descartes, *A Discourse on the Method* (Oxford: Oxford University Press, 2006), p. 48.
22. Sigmund Freud, *Civilization and Its Discontents*, in Sigmund Freud, *Civilization, Society and Religion* (London: Penguin, 1991), trans. James Strachey, p. 279, p. 280.
23. Carl Jung, 'On Life after Death', in Carl Jung, *Memories, Dreams, Reflections* (New York: Pantheon, 1973), ed. Aniela Jaffé, p. 326.
24. Martin Heidegger, *Being and Time* (Oxford: Blackwell, 1962), trans. John Macquarrie and Edward Robinson, p. 396. Martin Heidegger, *Sein und Zeit* (Tübingen: Verlag, 1963), p. 346. Jacques Derrida, 'The Animal That Therefore I Am (More to Follow)', in *Critical Inquiry*, vol 28, no 2 (Winter, 2002), trans. David Wills, pp. 369–418, p. 391.
25. Giorgio Agamben, *Homo Sacer: Sovereign Power and Bare Life* (Stanford: Stanford University Press, 1998), trans. Daniel Heller-Roazen, p. 8.
26. Beckett, *Proust*, p. 47.
27. For a careful reading of 'mere living' in Coetzee's fiction, one which warns that '"Mere living" should not be confused with Giorgio Agamben's notion of "bare life"', see Arthur James Rose, *Cynical Cosmopolitans? Borges, Beckett, Coetzee* (PhD thesis: Leeds: Leeds University, 2014), p. 223.
28. Sigmund Freud, *The Uncanny*, in Sigmund Freud, *Art and Literature* (London: Penguin, 1990), trans. James Strachey, p. 347.
29. Shakespeare, *Hamlet*, p. 657.
30. Shakespeare, *Hamlet*, p. 657.
31. Beckett, *Imagination Dead Imagine*, p. 182.
32. Henry James, *The Awkward Age* (London: Penguin, 1987), p. 5.
33. My thanks to Merve Emre for drawing my attention to this passage.
34. Henry James, *The Portrait of a Lady* (London: Penguin, 2011), p. 633.
35. Henry James, *In the Cage*, in Henry James, *Complete Stories: 1892–1898* (New York: The Library of America, 1996), eds. David Bromwich and John Hollander, pp. 835–923, p. 877. Henry James, *The Jolly Corner*, in James, *The Tales of Henry James*, p. 352.
36. James, *The Middle Years*, p. 213.

37. Eliot, *Daniel Deronda*, p. 102.
38. George Eliot, *Middlemarch* (London: Penguin, 1994), p. 838.
39. Eliot, *Middlemarch*, p. 838.
40. Eliot, *Daniel Deronda*, p. 103.
41. Eliot, *Daniel Deronda*, p. 103.
42. James, *Portrait of a Lady*, p. 634.
43. James, *The Jolly Corner*, p. 343.
44. Henry James, *What Maisie Knew* (London: Penguin, 1985), p. 164, p. 26.
45. James, *What Maisie Knew*, p. 25.
46. James, *The Wings of the Dove*, p. 77.
47. James, *The Wings of the Dove*, p. 358.
48. Henry James, *The Golden Bowl* (London: Penguin, 2009), p. 536.
49. James, *The Golden Bowl*, p. 567.
50. Melville, *Bartleby*, p. 18. The dead wall recurs throughout Melville's story, and appears finally at the close, when Bartleby lies against the 'dead-wall'(p. 32) of the prison, where he meets his own death.
51. Henry James, *The Aspern Papers and Turn of the Screw* (London: Penguin, 1984), p. 70.
52. Henry James, 'The Art of Fiction', in Henry James, *The Future of the Novel: Essays on the Art of Fiction* (New York: Vintage, 1956), ed. Leon Edel, pp. 3–27, p. 19.
53. See Shakespeare, *A Midsummer Night's Dream*, p. 330.
54. Beckett, *Proust*, p. 11.
55. Leo Bersani, *A Future for Asyntax: Character and Desire in Literature* (London: Marion Boyars, 1978), p. 130.
56. Bersani, *A Future for Asyntax*, p. 132.
57. Sharon Cameron, *Thinking in Henry James* (Chicago: University of Chicago Press, 1989), p. 7.
58. Lisa Robertson, *Occasional Work and Seven Walks from the Office for Soft Architecture* (Toronto: Coach House Books, 2011), p. 134, p. 140. My thanks to Mae Losasso, who suggested to me this conjunction between James and Lisa Robertson.
59. T. S. Eliot, 'Ulysses, Order and Myth', in *The Dial* (November, 1923), pp. 480–483, pp. 482–483.
60. James, 'The Art of Fiction', p. 9. Henry James, *Selected Letters* (Cambridge: Harvard University Press, 1987), ed. Leon Edel, p. 431. For a developed reading of the impression and impressionism in Henry James, see John Scholar, *Henry James and the Art of Impressions* (Oxford: Oxford University Press, 2020).
61. Ngai, *Theory of the Gimmick*, p. 277.
62. James, *The Wings of the Dove*, p. 59.
63. See Karl Marx, *Capital* (Hertfordshire: Wordsworth, 1987), trans. Samuel Moore and Edward Aveling, p. 104, where Marx describes 'money and commodities' as the 'mere forms which [capital] assumes and casts off in turn'.
64. James, *Wings of the Dove*, p. 336.

65. James, *The Golden Bowl*, p. 293.
66. Henry James, *The Ambassadors* (London: Penguin, 2008), pp. 438–439.
67. Beckett, *Proust*, p. 15.
68. Beckett, *Proust*, p. 22.
69. Beckett, *Molloy*, p. 49.
70. Beckett, *The Unnamable*, p. 386.
71. Beckett, *Worstward Ho*, p. 103.
72. Diane Williams, 'A Mere Flask Poured Out', in Diane Williams, *The Collected Stories of Diane Williams* (New York: Soho, 2018), pp. 715–716.
73. James, *Portrait*, p. 606.
74. James, *Wings of the Dove*, p. 136.

12 Imagining the Future in the British Novel

1. Charles Dickens, *A Christmas Carol and Other Christmas Books* (Oxford: Oxford University Press, 1998), p. 77.
2. Antonio Gramsci, *Selections from the Prison Notebooks of Antonio Gramsci* (London: Lawrence and Wishart, 1971), tans. Quentin Hoare and Geoffrey Nowell Smith, p. 276.
3. Margret Thatcher, 'Interview for Woman's Own', in *Woman's Own* (31 October, 1987), np. A transcript of the interview is available at www.margaretthatcher.org/document/106689.
4. David Harvey, *A Brief History of Neoliberalism* (Oxford: Oxford University Press, 2005), p. 2.
5. For a theoretical account of Blair's third way, see Anthony Giddens, *The Third Way: The Renewal of Social Democracy* (Hoboken, Wiley, 2013).
6. For Fukuyama's famous account of the hegemony of the west, see Francis Fukuyama, *The End of History and the Last Man*. For Fukuyama's immediate, and defensive, response to 9/11, see his essay in *The Guardian*, 'The West has Won'. For a more trenchant response to US hegemony, see Noam Chomsky *Hegemony or Survival*. [For a discussion of Fukuyama, Chomsky and the fate of the end of history thesis, see the introduction to the present volume, pp. 1–26].
7. Tony Blair, 'Speech to the Labour Party Conference', in *The Guardian* (2 October, 2001), np. A transcript of the speech is available in *The Guardian*, online at www.theguardian.com/politics/2001/oct/02/labourconference.labour6.
8. See Judith Butler, *Precarious Life: The Powers of Mourning and Violence* (London: Verso, 2004), p. 3, p. 2, where Butler argues that we need to pit 'long range prospects for global co-operation' against 'the binarism that Bush proposes, in which only two positions are possible – "Either you're with us or you're with the terrorists"'.
9. For an account of the relation between 9/11 and the wars in Afghanistan and Iraq, see Jason Burke, *The 9/11 Wars*.

10. A transcript of Donald Trump's 2017 inauguration speech is available in the *Guardian*, online at www.theguardian.com/world/2017/jan/20/donald-trump-inauguration-speech-full-text.
11. [Since the time that I wrote this essay, we have seen the first major military conflict in Europe since 1945 – in the invasion of Ukraine by Russia – which has dated this comment.]
12. [Again, this has been overtaken by events. Theresa May was UK Prime Minister from 2016 to 2019, when she was succeeded by Boris Johnson.]
13. Theresa May, 'Conference Speech', in *The Telegraph* (5 October, 2016), np. Available online at www.telegraph.co.uk/news/2016/10/05/theresa-mays-conference-speech-in-full/
14. Blair, 'Speech to the Labour Party Conference', np.
15. For two accounts of the passing of postmodernism in the current century, see Jeffrey T. Nealon, *Post-Postmodernism, or the Cultural Logic of Just-in-Time Capitalism* (Stanford: Stanford University Press, 2012), and Josh Toth, *The Passing of Postmodernism: A Spectroanalysis of the Contemporary* (Albany: SUNY Press, 2010).
16. [Britain finally left the European Union at 23:00 GMT on 31 January 2020.]
17. David Mitchell, *Cloud Atlas* (London: Hodder & Stoughton, 2004), p. 510.
18. Zadie Smith, *NW* (London: Penguin, 2012), p. 318. For a fuller reading of the status of 'nowhere' in Smith's novel, see Peter Boxall and Bryan Cheyette, *The Oxford History of the Novel in English: British and Irish Fiction since 1940* (Oxford: Oxford University Press, 2016), pp. 580–586.
19. McEwan, *The Children Act*, p. 1.
20. Dickens, *Bleak House*, p. 11. [For another reflection on this dialogue between McEwan and Dickens, see pp. 117–118 above].
21. Ian McEwan, 'The Law versus Religious Belief', In *The Guardian* (5 September, 2014), np. Available online at www.theguardian.com/books/2014/sep/05/ian-mcewan-law-versus-religious-belief.
22. The Children Act is quoted in the epigraph to McEwan, *The Children Act*, np.
23. James Joyce, *The Dead*, in Joyce, *Dubliners*, p. 183.
24. There is a wealth of critical literature devoted to this closing image of *The Dead*. For a helpful summary of positions, and for a powerful reading in its own right, see Emer Nolan, *James Joyce and Nationalism* (London: Routledge, 1995), pp. 24–36.
25. Ian McEwan, *Saturday* (London: Jonathan Cape, 2005), p. 171.
26. Joyce, *Portrait of the Artist*, p. 276.
27. Ali Smith, '"Vital, Witty, Formidably Blithe": Ali Smith on Muriel Spark at 100', in *The Guardian* (29 January, 2018), np. Online at www.theguardian.com/books/2018/jan/29/ali-smith-on-muriel-spark-at-100. [Since the writing of this essay, Smith has published the final two titles in her cycle: Ali Smith, *Spring* (London: Hamish Hamilton, 2019), and Ali Smith, *Summer* (London: Hamish Hamilton, 2020).]
28. Ali Smith, *Winter* (London: Hamish Hamilton, 2017), p. 59.
29. Ali Smith, *Autumn* (London: Hamish Hamilton, 2016), p. 112.

30. Charles Dickens, *A Tale of Two Cities* (Oxford: Oxford University Press, 1998), p. 7.
31. Dickens, *A Christmas Carol*, p. 9.
32. Smith, *Autumn*, p. 213; Dickens, *A Christmas Carol*, p. 14.
33. James Joyce, *Ulysses* (London: Penguin, 1986), p. 41.
34. Joyce, *Ulysses*, p. 42, p. 32.
35. For Derrida's discussion of bricolage, see Jacques Derrida, 'Structure, Sign and Play in the Discourse of the Human Sciences', in David Lodge and Nigel Woods, eds., *Modern Criticism and Theory: A Reader*, 3rd edition (London: Routledge, 2008), pp. 211–224.
36. Beckett, *Murphy*, p. 5.
37. Smith, *Winter*, p. 268.

13 Shallow Intensity

1. Philip Roth, *The Human Stain* (London: Vintage, 2001), p. 147.
2. Eliot, *Middlemarch*, p. 194.
3. Austen, *Emma*, p. 365.
4. Roth, *Human Stain*, p. 22.
5. Eliot, *Middlemarch*, p. 119.
6. Harvey, *A Brief History of Neoliberalism*, p. 11.
7. Paul Treanor, quoted in Harvey, *A Brief History of Neoliberalism*, p. 3.
8. Harvey, *A Brief History of Neoliberalism*, p. 11.
9. David Harvey, *The Condition of Postmodernity: An Enquiry into the Origins of Cultural Change* (Oxford: Blackwell, 1990), p. 297.
10. Muriel Spark, *The Takeover* (London: Macmillan, 1976), p. 10, p. 147.
11. Giuliani's comment can be seen here: www.youtube.com/watch?v=CljsZ7lgbtw. Spark, *The Takeover*, p. 138.
12. Martin Amis, *Money* (London: Vintage, 2011), p. 7.
13. Chris Kraus, *I Love Dick* (London: Serpent's Tail, 2016), p. 71.
14. DeLillo, *Underworld*, p. 785.
15. Jameson, *Postmodernism*, pp. xx–xxi.
16. For Jameson's elaboration of this antinomial tendency in postmodern thought, see Fredric Jameson, 'The Antinomies of Postmodernism', in Fredric Jameson, *The Seeds of Time* (New York: Columbia University Press, 1994), pp. 1–71. See also Fredric Jameson, *The Antinomies of Realism* (London: Verso, 2013).
17. Jameson, *Postmodernism*, p. 9.
18. Jameson, *Postmodernism*, p. 9.
19. Jameson, *Postmodernism*, p. 9.
20. Jameson, *Postmodernism*, p. 11.
21. Jameson, *Postmodernism*, p. 12.
22. David Harvey, 'Neoliberalism as Creative Destruction', in *The Annals of the American Academy of Political and Social Science*, vol 610 (March, 2007), pp. 22–44, p. 23.

23. Fredric Jameson, 'Future City', in *New Left Review*, vol 21 (May/June, 2003), p. 76.
24. Walter Benn Michaels, *The Trouble with Diversity: How We Learned to Love Identity and Ignore Inequality* (New York: Holt, 2006), p. 200.
25. Walter Benn Michaels, 'Going Boom', in *BookForum*, online at www.bookforum.com/print/1505/the-economic-collapse-points-up-how-little-our-literary-world-has-to-say-about-social-inequality-3274, np.
26. Benn Michaels, 'Going Boom', np.
27. Mitchum Huehls, *After Critique: Twenty-First-Century Fiction in a Neoliberal Age* (Oxford: Oxford University Press, 2016), p. xi.
28. Rachel Greenwald Smith, 'Postmodernism and the Affective Turn', in *Twentieth Century Literature*, vol 57, nos 3/4 (2011), p. 428.
29. James Kelman, *How Late It Was, How Late* (London: QPD, 1994), p. 151.
30. Franz Kafka, *Metamorphosis and Other Stories* (London: Minerva, 1992), trans. Willa and Edwin Muir, p. 13.
31. John Locke, *Second Treatise of Government* (Oxford: Oxford University Press, 2016), p. 15.

14 To Carry Now Away

1. Sara Ahmed, *The Promise of Happiness* (Durham: Duke University Press, 2010), p. 13.
2. See Stanley Cavell, *Pursuits of Happiness: The Hollywood Comedy of Remarriage* (Cambridge: Harvard University Press, 1981).
3. Aldous Huxley, *Brave New World* (London: Flamingo, 1994), p. 67.
4. Beckett, *Endgame*, p. 97.
5. For a more recent examination of the relation between happiness and same sex desire, see Kevin Brazil, *Whatever Happened to Queer Happiness* (London: Influx Press, 2022).
6. For an account of the resurgence of bird life in cities during the pandemic, see Elizabeth Anne Brown, 'Many Birds Flocked to Cities during COVID-19 Lockdowns', in *National Geographic* (22 September, 2021), online at www.nationalgeographic.com/animals/article/birds-moved-to-urban-areas-during-covid-lockdowns-anthropause.
7. *Beckett in Folkestone* is written by Helen Oyeyemi, Rupert Thomson and Eimear McBride. It stars Jade Anouka (receptionist), Russell Tovey (local journalist) and Harriet Walter (E. Pugsley). For a review of the production, see Alison Flood, 'Samuel Beckett's Secret Wedding in Folkestone Inspires Festival 60 Years On', in *The Guardian* (2 June, 2021), online at www.theguardian.com/culture/2021/jun/02/samuel-beckett-secret-wedding-folkestone-inspires-festival-60-years-on.
8. The story of the marriage is largely drawn from James Knowlson's biography of Beckett. See James Knowlson, *Damned to Fame: The Life of Samuel Beckett* (London: Bloomsbury, 1996), pp. 480–484.

9. Knowlson, *Damned to Fame*, p. 484.
10. Devorah Baum, in her 2023 book *On Marriage*, describes attending the same performance of *Happy Days* with her husband. She notes that the 'socially distanced seating meant our twosome did look as dismayingly hitched to each other and nobody else as did the pair we had come along to watch', Devorah Baum, *On Marriage* (London: Hamish Hamilton, 2023), p. 280. Thanks to Devorah for giving me access to an early proof edition of this (marvelous) book.
11. Beckett, *Waiting for Godot*, p. 64. Beckett, *Molloy*, p. 111.
12. Beckett, *Happy Days*, p. 154.
13. Baum, *On Marriage*, p. 280.
14. Omar Khayyam, *The Rubaiyat of Omar Khayyam* (Auckland: The Floating Press, 2009), p. 24.
15. Beckett, *Letters 1957–1956*, p. 119.
16. Daniela Caselli, *Insufferable: Beckett, Gender and Sexuality* (Cambridge: Cambridge University Press, 2023), np. Thanks to Dani for giving me access to a proof copy of this book.
17. Xander Ryan, '"To Talk Alone": Beckett's Letters to Barbara Bray and the Epistolary Drama of *Happy Days*', in *Samuel Beckett Today / Aujourd'hui*, vol 31, no 1 (2019), pp. 163–177.
18. Beckett, *Letters 1957–1956*, p. 365.
19. See Samuel Beckett, *First Love*, in Beckett, *The Expelled and Other Novellas*, p. 30, where the narrator tries to discover how far from his lover's house he has to travel before he can no longer hear the cries of his newborn child: 'I began playing with the cries, a little in the same way as I had played with the song, on, back, on, back, if that may be called playing'.
20. Beckett, *The Unnamable*, p. 386. Beckett, *Letters 1957–1956*, p. 360.
21. Beckett, *Molloy*, p. 49.
22. Beckett, *Molloy*, p. 49.
23. Beckett, *The Unnamable*, p. 384.
24. Beckett, *Endgame*, p. 132.
25. Samuel Beckett, *Fizzle 6*, in Beckett, *Complete Short Prose*, p. 238.
26. William Shakespeare, 'Sonnet 146', in Shakespeare, *The Complete Works*, p. 769.
27. Shakespeare, *Hamlet*, p. 670.
28. See Heidegger, 'The Age of the World Picture', pp. 115–154.
29. Beckett, *Letters 1957–1956*, p. 119.
30. Beckett, *Letters 1957–1956*, p. 119.
31. Samuel Beckett, 'Capital of the Ruins', in Beckett, *Complete Short Prose*, p. 277.
32. Marek Kędzierski, 'Barbara Bray: In Her Own Words', in *Modernism and Modernity*, vol 18, no 4 (2011), pp. 887–896, p. 897.
33. Ahmed, *The Promise of Happiness*, p. 100.
34. Beckett, *Letters 1957–1956*, p. 171.
35. Beckett, *Letters 1957–1956*, p. 310.
36. Beckett, *Letters 1957–1956*, p. 310.
37. Samuel Beckett, *Ohio Impromptu*, in Beckett, *Complete Dramatic Works*, p. 446.

15 On Rereading Proust

1. Marcel Proust, *Remembrance of Things Past* (London: Penguin, 1983) 3 vols., trans. C. K. Scott Moncrieff and Terence Kilmartin, vol 3, p. 903. All further page references to this text will be included in the text, with volume and page number.
2. Vladimir Nabokov, *Lectures on Literature* (London: Weidenfeld and Nicolson, 1980), ed. Fredson Bowers, p. 3.
3. Nabokov, *Lectures on Literature*, p. 3.
4. T. J. Clark, in his magnificent reading of Poussin, *The Sight of Death: An Experiment in Art Writing* (New Haven: Yale University Press, 2006), gives a very eloquent testimony to the fact that our understanding of a painting does unfold over time, just as our reading of a novel does.
5. Nabokov, *Lectures on Literature*, p. 3.
6. Percy Lubbock, *The Craft of Fiction* (London: Jonathan Cape, 1954), p. 1.
7. Lubbock, *Craft of Fiction*, p. 6.
8. Virginia Woolf, 'On Re-reading Novels', in Virginia Woolf, *The Essays of Virginia Woolf: Volume III, 1919–1924* (London: Hogarth Press, 1988), p. 341.
9. Lubbock, *Craft of Fiction*, p. 24. Woolf, 'On Re-reading Novels', p. 339.
10. Woolf, 'On Re-reading Novels', p. 341.
11. Woolf, 'On Re-reading Novels', pp. 341–342.
12. T. S. Eliot, *Selected Essays* (London: Faber, 1999), p. 21.
13. Virginia Woolf, *The Diary of Virginia Woolf: Volume II, 1920–1924* (London: Hogarth Press, 1978), ed. Anne Olivier Bell, p. 272.
14. Woolf, *The Diary of Virginia Woolf*, p. 272.
15. Woolf, *The Diary of Virginia Woolf*, p. 272.
16. Woolf, *Mrs Dalloway*, p. 22, p. 21.
17. Roland Barthes, *Image Music Text* (London: Fontana Press, 1977), trans. Stephen Heath, p. 148.
18. See Wolfgang Iser, *The Implied Reader: Patterns of Communication in Prose Fiction from Bunyan to Beckett* (Baltimore: Johns Hopkins University Press, 1987), and Wolfgang Iser, *The Act of Reading: A Theory of Aesthetic Response* (Baltimore: Johns Hopkins University Press, 1991). Jacques Derrida, *Of Grammatology* (Baltimore: Johns Hopkins Press, 1997), trans. Gayatri Chakravorty Spivak, p. 158. See Eve Kosofsky Sedgwick, 'Paranoid Reading and Reparative Reading, or, You're So Paranoid, You Probably Think This Essay Is About You', in Eve Kosofsky Sedgwick, *Touching Feeling: Affect, Pedagogy, Performativity* (Durham: Duke University Press, 2003), pp. 123–152.
19. Woolf, 'On Re-reading Novels', p. 339.
20. Woolf, 'On Re-reading Novels', p. 344.
21. William C. Carter, *Marcel Proust: A Life* (New Haven: Yale University Press, 2000), p. 809.
22. Gérard Genette, *Figures III*, quoted in Joseph Frank, 'Spatial Form: Some Further Reflections', in *Critical Inquiry*, vol 5, no 2 (1978), pp. 275–290, p. 290. My attention was drawn to this passage in Genette by Matei Calinescu's

book *Rereading* (New Haven: Yale University Press, 1993), where it is quoted, on p. 23. I am indebted to Calinescu's excellent book for much of my thinking about rereading in this essay.
23. Paul de Man, *Allegories of Reading: Figural Language in Rousseau, Nietzsche, Rilke, and Proust* (New Haven: Yale University Press, 1979), p. 72.
24. de Man, *Allegories of Reading*, p. 78.
25. de Man, *Allegories of Reading*, p. 78.
26. Laure Murat, 'How the French Reread Proust', in *Literary Hub* (11 July, 2016), np. Online at https://lithub.com/how-the-french-reread-proust/.
27. Murat, 'How the French Reread Proust', np.
28. Leo Bersani, *Marcel Proust: The Fictions of Life and Art* (Oxford: Oxford University Press, 2013), p. 88.
29. Beckett, *Worstward Ho*, p. 102.
30. Marcel's dismissal of literature which contains its own theory as a 'gross impropriety' (III, 916) is the prompt for Patrick Bray's analysis of the theoretical novel, *The Price of Literature: The French Novel's Theoretical Turn* (Evanston: Northwestern University Press, 2019).
31. William Shakespeare, *Macbeth*, in Shakespeare, *Complete Works*, p. 998.
32. Beckett, *The Unnamable*, p. 353.
33. [For a discussion of this moment in *Ghost Trio*, see pp. 201–204 above.]
34. Beckett, *First Love*, pp. 28–29.
35. Beckett, *Molloy*, p. 40.
36. Bersani, *Marcel Proust*, p. 225.
37. Kate Briggs, *The Long Form* (London: Fitzcarraldo, 2023).
38. See James, *The Wings of the Dove*, p. 147. [For a fuller reading of this passage, see pp. 91–92 above.]
39. Woolf, *To the Lighthouse*, p. 151.
40. Dickinson, *Poems*, p. 379.
41. Dickinson, *Poems*, p. 379. [For a reading of this poem, see p. 108 above.]
42. Shakepseare, *Hamlet*, p. 674.
43. Gilles Deleuze, *Proust and Signs* (Minneapolis: University of Minnesota Press, 2000), trans Richard Howard, p. 182.
44. de Man, *Allegories of Reading*, p. 77.
45. de Man, *Allegories of Reading*, p. 77.
46. Woolf, 'On Re-reading Novels', p. 344.
47. Agamben, *Nudities*, p. 13.
48. Eve Kosofsky Sedgwick, *The Weather in Proust* (Durham: Duke University Press, 2011), p. 34.
49. Sedgwick, *The Weather in Proust*, p. 6.
50. Sedgwick, *The Weather in Proust*, p. 8.
51. See Chakrabarty, 'The Climate of History: Four Theses', pp. 197–222.
52. Sedgwick, *Touching Feeling*, p. 148.
53. Sedgwick, *Touching Feeling*, p. 148.
54. See Jack Halberstam, *In a Queer Time and Place* (New York: New York University Press, 2005).

55. Sedgwick, *Touching Feeling*, p. 148.
56. Sedgwick, *Touching Feeling*, pp. 148–189.
57. Sedgwick, *Touching Feeling*, p. 149.
58. Sedgwick, *The Weather in Proust*, p. 34.
59. Sedgwick, *The Weather in Proust*, p. 18.
60. Sedgwick, *The Weather in Proust*, p. 32.
61. Stevens, *Selected Poems*, p. 90.
62. John Ashbery, 'Crazy Weather', in John Ashbery, *Collected Poems 1956–1987* (Manchester: Carcanet, 2010), p. 503.

Bibliography

Acker, Kathy, *Don Quixote: Which Was a Dream* (New York: Grove Press, 1986).
Adorno, Theodor, 'Commitment', in Ernst Bloch, et al., eds., *Aesthetics and Politics* (London: NLB, 1977), trans. Francis McDonah, pp. 177–195.
Adorno, Theodor, *Negative Dialectics* (London: Routledge, 1990), trans. E. B. Ashton.
Adorno, Theodor, *Notes to Literature* (New York: Columbia University Press, 1991), 2 vols., trans. Shierry Weber Nicholsen.
Agamben, Giorgio, *Homo Sacer: Sovereign Power and Bare Life* (Stanford: Stanford University Press, 1998), trans. Daniel Heller-Roazen.
Agamben, Giorgio, *Nudities* (Stanford: Stanford University Press, 2011), trans. David Kishik and Stefan Pedatella.
Agamben, Giorgio, *The Open: Man and Animal* (Stanford: Stanford University Press, 2004), trans. Kevin Attell.
Ahmed, Sara, *The Promise of Happiness* (Durham: Duke University Press, 2010).
Akker, Robin Van den, Timotheus Vermeulen, and Alison Gibbons, eds., *Metamodernism: Historicity, Affect, and Depth after Postmodernism* (Lanham: Rowman & Littlefield, 2017).
Althusser, Louis, *Essays on Ideology* (London: Verso, 1984).
Amis, Martin, *Money* (London: Vintage, 2011).
Anker, Elizabeth S., and Rita Felski, eds., *Critique and Post-critique* (Durham: Duke University Press, 2017).
Appiah, Kwame Anthony, 'Is the Post- in Postmodernism the Post- in Postcolonial?', in *Critical Inquiry*, vol 17, no 2 (Winter, 1991), pp. 336–357.
Arnold, Matthew, *The Poems of Matthew Arnold 1840–1867* (London: Humphrey Milford, 1913).
Ashbery, John, *Collected Poems 1956–1987* (Manchester: Carcanet, 2010).
Atwood, Margaret, *Alias Grace* (London: Virago, 1997).
Atwood, Margaret, *Oryx and Crake* (London: Virago, 2009).
Atwood, Margaret, *The Penelopiad* (Edinburgh: Canongate, 2006).
Aubrey, James, '"For Me Alone Paul Rayment Was Born": Coetzee's *Slow Man*, *Don Quixote*, and the Literature of Replenishment', in *Peer English*, vol 6 (2011), pp. 93–106.

Auerbach, Erich, *Mimesis: The Representation of Reality in Western Literature* (Princeton: Princeton University Press, 2003), trans. Willard R. Trask.
Austen, Jane, *Emma* (Oxford: Oxford University Press, 2008).
Auster, Paul, *The New York Trilogy* (London: Faber, 1987).
Bakhtin, M. M., *The Dialogic Imagination: Four Essays* (Austin: University of Texas Press, 1981), trans. Caryl Emerson and Michael Holquist.
Baldwin, James, *Another Country* (London: Penguin, 2011).
Baldwin, James, *The Fire Next Time* (London: Penguin, 2017a).
Baldwin, James, *Notes of a Native Son* (London: Penguin, 2017b).
Ballard, J. G., *Crash* (London: Fourth Estate, 2014).
Barnes, Julian, *The Sense of an Ending* (London: Jonathan Cape, 2011).
Barthes, Roland, *Image Music Text* (London: Fontana Press, 1977), trans. Stephen Heath.
Barthes, Roland, *Mythologies* (London: Paladin, 1973), trans. Annette Lavers.
Baudrillard, Jean, *The Spirit of Terrorism and Requiem for the Twin Towers* (London: Verso, 2002), trans. Chris Turner.
Baum, Devorah, *On Marriage* (London: Hamish Hamilton, 2023).
Beckett, Samuel, *Collected Poems* (London: Calder, 1986).
Beckett, Samuel, *The Complete Dramatic Works* (London: Faber, 2006).
Beckett, Samuel, *The Complete Short Prose, 1929–1989* (New York: Grove Press, 1995).
Beckett, Samuel, *Dream of Fair to Middling Women* (London: Calder, 1993).
Beckett, Samuel, *The Expelled and Other Novellas* (London: Penguin, 1980).
Beckett, Samuel, *How It Is* (London: Calder, 1996).
Beckett, Samuel, *The Letters of Samuel Beckett, vol III: 1957–1965* (Cambridge: Cambridge University Press, 2014), eds. George Craig, Martha Dow Fehsenfeld, Dan Gunn, and Lois More Overbeck.
Beckett, Samuel, *Molloy, Malone Dies, The Unnamable* (London: Calder, 1994).
Beckett, Samuel, *More Pricks than Kicks* (London: Picador, 1974).
Beckett, Samuel, *Murphy* (London: Picador, 1973).
Beckett, Samuel, *Nohow On: Company, Ill Seen Ill Said, Wostward Ho* (London: Calder, 1992).
Beckett, Samuel, *Proust and Three Dialogues with Georges Duthuit* (London: Calder, 1965).
Beckett, Samuel, *Watt* (London: Calder, 1976).
Benjamin, Walter, *The Arcades Project* (Cambridge: Harvard University Press, 1999), trans. Howard Eiland and Kevin McLaughlin.
Benjamin, Walter, *Illuminations* (London: Pimlico, 1999), trans. Harry Zorn.
Benn Michaels, Walter, 'Going Boom', in *BookForum*, online at www.bookforum.com/print/1505/the-economic-collapse-points-up-how-little-our-literary-world-has-to-say-about-social-inequality-3274.
Benn Michaels, Walter, *The Trouble with Diversity: How We Learned to Love Identity and Ignore Inequality* (New York: Holt, 2006).
Bennett, Alice, 'Unquiet Sprits: Death Writing in Contemporary Fiction', in *Textual Practice*, vol 23, no 3 (2009), pp. 463–479.

Bennett, Jane, *Vibrant Matter: A Political Ecology of Things* (Durham: Duke University Press, 2010).
Berger, John, 'Why Look at Animals?', in Geoff Dyer, ed., *John Berger: Selected Essays* (London: Bloomsbury, 2001), pp. 259–273.
Bersani, Leo, *A Future for Asyntax: Character and Desire in Literature* (London: Marion Boyars, 1978), p. 130.
Bersani, Leo, *Marcel Proust: The Fictions of Life and Art* (Oxford: Oxford University Press, 2013).
Bersani, Leo, *Thoughts and Things* (Chicago: University of Chicago Press, 2015).
Bewes, Timothy, *Free Indirect: The Novel in a Postfictional Age* (New York: Columbia University Press, 2022).
Blackham, Harold John, *Six Existentialist Thinkers* (London: Routledge, 1952).
Blair, Tony, 'Speech to the Labour Party Conference', in *The Guardian* (2 October 2001).
Blair, Tony, 'Why We Must Not Abandon the People of Afghanistan – For Their Sakes and Ours', Tony Blair Institute for Global Change (21 August, 2021), https://institute.global/tony-blair/tony-blair-why-we-must-not-abandon-people-afghanistan-their-sakes-and-ours.
Blanchot, Maurice, *The Infinite Conversation* (Minneapolis: University of Minnesota Press, 1993), trans. Susan Hanson.
Blanchot, Maurice, *The Sirens' Song: Selected Essays by Maurice Blanchot* (Bloomington: Indiana University Press, 1982), ed. Gabriel Josipovici.
Blanchot, Maurice, *The Space of Literature* (Lincoln: University of Nebraska Press, 1982), trans. Ann Smock.
Bloch, Ernst, et al., *Aesthetics and Politics* (London: Verso, 1980), trans. Ronald Taylor.
Bloom, Harold, *The Western Canon: The Books and School of the Ages* (London: Papermac, 1996).
Borges, Jorge Luis, *Labyrinths* (London: Penguin, 1970), trans. Donald A. Yates.
Börsch-Supan, Helmut, *Caspar David Friedrich* (New York: George Brazille, 1974), trans. Sarah Twohig.
Bowen, Elizabeth, *Collected Stories* (London: Vintage, 1999).
Bowen, Elizabeth, *The Last September* (New York: Knopf, 1964).
Bowen, Elizabeth, *The Mulberry Tree: Writings of Elizabeth Bowen* (London: Vintage, 1999), ed. Hermione Lee.
Bowen, Elizabeth, *Pictures and Conversations* (New York: Knopf, 1975).
Boxall, Peter, ed., *Beckett/Aesthetics/Politics*, Samuel Beckett Today/Aujourd'hui, vol 9 (Amsterdam: Rodopi, 2000).
Boxall, Peter, 'The Existence I Ascribe: Memory, Invention and Autobiography in Beckett's Fiction', in *The Yearbook of English Studies*, vol 30 (2000), pp 137–153.
Boxall, Peter, *The Prosthetic Imagination: A History of the Novel as Artificial Life* (Cambridge: Cambridge University Press, 2020).

Boxall, Peter and Bryan Cheyette, *The Oxford History of the Novel in English: British and Irish Fiction since 1940* (Oxford: Oxford University Press, 2016).
Bray, Patrick, *The Price of Literature: The French Novel's Theoretical Turn* (Evanston: Northwestern University Press, 2019).
Brazil, Kevin, *Whatever Happened to Queer Happiness* (London: Influx Press, 2022).
Brickley, Briana G., '*On Beauty* and the Politics of Academic Institutionality', in *Ariel: A Review of International English Literature*, vol 48, no 2 (2017), pp. 73–100.
Briggs, Kate, *The Long Form* (London: Fitzcarraldo, 2023).
Brontë, Charlotte, *Jane Eyre* (New York: Norton, 2001).
Brown, Elizabeth Anne, 'Many Birds Flocked to Cities during COVID-19 Lockdowns', in *National Geographic* (22 September, 2021).
Bryden, Mary, *Women in Samuel Beckett's Prose and Drama: Her Own Other* (Basingstoke: Macmillan, 1993).
Burke, Jason, *The 9/11 Wars* (London: Penguin, 2011).
Butler, Judith, *Precarious Life: The Powers of Mourning and Violence* (London: Verso, 2004).
Calinescu, Matei, *Rereading* (New Haven: Yale University Press, 1993).
Cameron, Sharon, *Lyric Time: Dickinson and the Limits of Genre* (Baltimore: The Johns Hopkins Press, 1979).
Cameron, Sharon, *Thinking in Henry James* (Chicago: University of Chicago Press, 1989).
Cantanzaro, Mary F., 'More Than a Common Pest: The Fly as Non-human Companion in Emily Dickinson's "I Heard a Fly Buzz When I Died" and Samuel Beckett's *Company*', in Anna-Teresa Tymieniecka, ed., *From Sky and Earth to Metaphysics* (New York: Springer, 2015), pp. 157–162.
Carter, Angela, *The Bloody Chamber* (London: Vintage, 2006).
Carter, William C., *Marcel Proust: A Life* (New Haven: Yale University Press, 2000).
Caselli, Daniela, *Beckett's Dantes: Intertextuality in the Fiction and Criticism* (Manchester: Manchester University Press, 2005).
Caselli, Daniela, *Insufferable: Beckett, Gender and Sexuality* (Cambridge: Cambridge University Press, 2023).
Cavell, Stanley, *Pursuits of Happiness: The Hollywood Comedy of Remarriage* (Cambridge: Harvard University Press, 1981).
Cervantes, Miguel de, *The Adventures of Don Quixote* (London: Penguin, 1950), trans. J. M. Cohen.
Cervantes, Miguel de, *Don Quijote de la Mancha* (London: Hirschfeld Brothers, 1928).
Chakrabarty, Dipesh, 'The Climate of History: Four Theses', in *Critical Inquiry*, vol 35, no 2 (2009), pp. 197–222.
Chenoweth, Katie, *The Prosthetic Tongue: Printing Technology and the Rise of the French Language* (Philadelphia: University of Pennsylvania Press, 2019).

Chomsky, Noam, *Hegemony or Survival: America's Quest for Global Dominance* (London: Penguin, 2004).
Clark, T. J., *The Sight of Death: An Experiment in Art Writing* (New Haven: Yale University Press, 2006).
Clark, Timothy, 'Derangements of Scale', in Tom Cohen, ed., *Telemorphosis: Theory in the Era of Climate Change* (London: Open Humanities Press, 2012), 148–166.
Coetzee, J. M., *Age of Iron* (London: Penguin, 2010).
Coetzee, J. M., *The Childhood of Jesus* (London: Harvill Secker, 2013).
Coetzee, J. M., *The Death of Jesus* (London: Vintage, 2021).
Coetzee, J. M., *Diary of a Bad Year* (London: Vintage, 2008).
Coetzee, J. M., *Disgrace* (London: Vintage, 2000).
Coetzee, J. M., *Doubling the Point: Essays and Interviews* (Cambridge: Harvard University Press, 1992), ed. David Atwell.
Coetzee, J. M., *Elizabeth Costello* (New York: Viking, 2003).
Coetzee, J. M., *Foe* (London: Penguin, 1987).
Coetzee, J. M., *Late Essays, 2006–2017* (London: Harvill and Secker, 2017).
Coetzee, J. M., *The Master of Petersburg* (London: Vintage, 1999).
Coetzee, J. M., *The Schooldays of Jesus* (London: Harvill Secker, 2016).
Coetzee, J. M., *Slow Man* (London: Secker and Warburg, 2005).
Coetzee, J. M., *Summertime: Scenes from Provincial Life* (London: Harvill Secker, 2009).
Cohn, Ruby, ed., *Samuel Beckett: A Collection of Criticism* (New York: McGaw Hill, 1975).
Cohn, Ruby, *Samuel Beckett: The Comic Gamut* (New Jersey: Rutgers University Press, 1962).
Connor, Steven, *Beckett, Modernism and the Material Imagination* (Cambridge: Cambridge University Press, 2014).
Connor, Steven, 'Beckett's Animals', in *Journal of Beckett Studies*, no 8 (1982), pp. 29–44.
Connor, Steven, *Samuel Beckett: Repetition, Theory and Text* (Oxford: Blackwell, 1988).
Critchley, Simon, *Things Merely Are: Philosophy in The Poetry of Wallace Stevens* (London: Routledge, 2005).
Dabashi, Hamid, *Europe and Its Shadows: Coloniality after Empire* (London: Pluto, 2019).
Davies, William and Helen Bailey, eds., *Beckett and Politics* (Basingstoke: Palgrave, 2021).
Deane, Seamus, *Celtic Revivals: Essays on Modern Irish Literature 1880–1980* (London: Faber, 1985).
Deane, Seamus, *Strange Country: Modernity and Nationhood in Irish Writing since 1790* (Oxford: Clarendon, 1997).
Deleuze, Gilles, *Cinema II: The Time Image* (London: Continuum, 2005), trans. Hugh Tomlinson and Robert Galeta.

Deleuze, Gilles, *Essays Critical and Clinical* (London: Verso, 1998), trans Daniel W. Smith and Michael A. Greco.
Deleuze, Gilles, *Proust and Signs* (Minneapolis: University of Minnesota Press, 2000), trans Richard Howard.
Deleuze, Gilles and Félix Guattari, *Kafka: Toward a Minor Literature* (Minneapolis: University of Minnesota Press, 1986), trans. Dana Polan.
DeLillo, Don, *Americana* (London: Penguin, 1989).
DeLillo, Don, *The Angel Esmerelda: Nine Stories* (London: Picador, 2011).
DeLillo, Don, *The Body Artist* (London: Picador, 2001).
DeLillo, Don, *Cosmopolis* (London: Picador, 2003).
DeLillo, Don, *End Zone* (London: Penguin, 1986).
DeLillo, Don, *Great Jones Street* (London: Picador, 1998).
DeLillo, Don, 'In the Ruins of the Future', in *The Guardian* (22 December, 2001), www.theguardian.com/books/2001/dec/22/fiction.dondelillo.
DeLillo, Don, *Libra* (London: Penguin, 1988).
DeLillo, Don, *Mao II* (London: Vintage, 1992).
DeLillo, Don, *The Names* (London: Picador, 1999).
DeLillo, Don, *Point Omega* (London: Picador, 2010).
DeLillo, Don, *Ratner's Star* (London: Vintage, 1991).
DeLillo, Don, *Running Dog* (London: Picador, 1999).
DeLillo, Don, *Underworld* (London: Picador, 1999).
DeLillo, Don, *White Noise* (London: Picador, 1999).
DeLillo, Don, *The Word for Snow* (New York: Karma Glenn Horowitz, 2014).
DeLillo, Don, *Zero K* (London: Picador, 2016).
DeLillo, Don and Peter Boxall, 'The Edge of the Future: A Discussion with Don DeLillo', in Katherine Da Cunha Lewin and Kiron Ward, eds., *Don DeLillo: Contemporary Critical Perspectives* (London: Bloomsbury, 2019), pp. 159–164.
de Man, Paul, *Allegories of Reading: Figural Language in Rousseau, Nietzsche, Rilke, and Proust* (New Haven: Yale University Press, 1979).
de Man, Paul, *Blindness and Insight: Essays in the Rhetoric of Contemporary Criticism*, 2nd edition (London: Routledge, 1983).
Derrida, Jacques, *Acts of Literature* (New York: Routledge, 1991), ed. Derek Attridge.
Derrida, Jacques, 'The Animal That Therefore I Am (More to Follow)', in *Critical Inquiry*, vol 28, no 2 (Winter, 2002), trans. David Wills, pp. 369–418.
Derrida, Jacques, *Margins of Philosophy* (New York: Harvester, 1982), trans. Alan Bass.
Derrida, Jacques, *Memoirs of the Blind: The Self-Portrait and Other Ruins* (Chicago: University of Chicago Press, 1993), trans. Pascale-Anne Brault and Michael Naas.
Derrida, Jacques, *Of Grammatology* (Baltimore: Johns Hopkins Press, 1997), trans. Gayatri Chakravorty Spivak.
Derrida, Jacques, 'Passions: "An Oblique Offering"', trans. David Wood, in David Wood, ed., *Derrida: A Critical Reader* (Oxford: Blackwell, 1992), pp. 5–35.

Derrida, Jacques, 'Structure, Sign and Play in the Discourse of the Human Sciences', in David Lodge and Nigel Woods, eds., *Modern Criticism and Theory: A Reader*, 3rd edition (London: Routledge, 2008), pp. 211–224.
Descartes, René, *A Discourse on the Method* (Oxford: Oxford University Press, 2006).
Dickens, Charles, *Bleak House* (Oxford: Oxford University Press, 1998).
Dickens, Charles, *A Christmas Carol and Other Christmas Books* (Oxford: Oxford University Press, 1998).
Dickens, Charles, *Great Expectations* (Oxford: Oxford University Press, 2008).
Dickens, Charles, *A Tale of Two Cities* (Oxford: Oxford University Press, 1998).
Dickinson, Emily, *The Poems of Emily Dickinson* (Cambridge: Harvard University Press, 1998), ed. R. W. Franklin.
Dimock, Wai Chee, *Through Other Continents: American Literature across Deep Time* (Princeton: Princeton University Press, 2006).
Donne, John, *The Complete English Poems* (London: Penguin, 1986)
Du Bois, W. E. B., *The Souls of Black Folk* (Oxford: Oxford University Press, 2007).
Duvall, John, *The Cambridge Companion to Don DeLillo* (Cambridge: Cambridge University Press, 2008).
Edgeworth, Maria, *Castle Rackrent* (Oxford: Oxford University Press, 1964).
Eliot, T. S., *Selected Essays* (London: Faber, 1999).
Eliot, T. S., *Selected Poems* (London: Faber and Faber, 1954).
Eliot, T. S., 'Ulysses, Order and Myth', in *The Dial* (November, 1923), pp. 480–483.
Eliot, George, *Daniel Deronda* (Oxford: Oxford University Press, 2009).
Eliot, George, *Middlemarch* (London: Penguin, 1994).
Ellison, Ralph, *Invisible Man* (London: Penguin, 1965).
Esslin, Martin, *The Theatre of the Absurd* (London: Penguin, 1968).
Fanon, Frantz, *Black Skin White Masks* (London: Pluto, 1986), trans. Charles Lam Markmann.
Fanon, Frantz, *Peau noire, masques blancs* (Paris: Éditions du Seuil, 1952).
Felski, Rita, *Hooked: Art and Attachment* (Chicago: Chicago University Press, 2020).
Felski, Rita, *The Limits of Critique* (Chicago: University of Chicago Press, 2015).
Finnerty, Páraic, *Dickinson's Shakespeare* (Amherst: University of Massachusetts Press, 2006).
Flaubert, Gustave, *The Selected Letters of Gustave Flaubert* (London: Hamish Hamilton, 1954), trans. Francis Steegmuller.
Flood, Alison, 'Samuel Beckett's Secret Wedding in Folkestone Inspires Festival 60 Years On', in *The Guardian* (2 June, 2021).
Forster, E. M., *Aspects of the Novel* (London: Penguin, 2005).
Forster, E. M., *Howards End* (London: Penguin, 2012).
Forster, E. M., *A Passage to India* (London: Penguin, 2005).
Forster, E. M., *Two Cheers for Democracy* (London: Edward Arnold, 1972).
Foucault, Michel, *Discipline and Punish* (New York: Vintage, 1995), trans. Alan Sheridan.

Frank, Joseph, 'Spatial Form: Some Further Reflections', in *Critical Inquiry*, vol 5, no 2 (1978), pp. 275–290.
Franzen, Jonathan, *The Corrections* (London: Fourth Estate, 2002).
Freud, Sigmund, *Art and Literature* (London: Penguin, 1990), trans. James Strachey.
Freud, Sigmund, *Civilization, Society and Religion* (London: Penguin, 1991), trans. James Strachey.
Friel, Brian, *Translations* (London: Faber, 1981).
Fukuyama, Francis, *The End of History and the Last Man* (New York: Free Press, 2006).
Fukuyama, Francis, 'The West Has Won', *The Guardian* (11 October, 2001), www.theguardian.com/world/2001/oct/11/afghanistan.terrorism30.
Gardiner, Michael, '"A Light to the World": British Devolution and Colonial Vision', in *Interventions*, vol 6, no 2 (2004), pp. 264–281.
Ghosh, Amitav, *The Great Derangement: Climate Change and the Unthinkable* (Chicago: The University of Chicago Press, 2016).
Gibbon, Lewis Grassic, *Sunset Song* (London: Penguin, 2007)
Giddens, Anthony, *The Third Way: The Renewal of Social Democracy* (Hoboken, Wiley, 2013).
Ginsburg, Michael Peled, *Portrait Stories* (New York: Fordham University Press, 2015).
Godden, Richard, *Punctuating Capital: Towards a Narrative Poetics for the Financial Turn* (Oxford: Oxford University Press, 2023).
Goethe, Johann Wolfgang von, *Elective Affinities* (London: Penguin, 2005), trans. R. J. Hollingdale.
Goethe, Johann Wolfgang von, *Selected Poems* (London: Calder, 1983), ed. and trans. Christopher Middleton.
Gopal, Priyamvada, *Insurgent Empire: Anticolonial Resistance and British Dissent* (London: Verso, 2019).
Gopal, Priyamvada, 'On Decolonisation and the University', in *Textual Practice*, vol 35, no 6 (2021), pp. 873–899.
Gramsci, Antonio, *Selections from the Prison Notebooks of Antonio Gramsci* (London: Lawrence and Wishart, 1971), trans. Quentin Hoare and Geoffrey Nowell Smith.
Grausam, Daniel, *On Endings: American Postmodern Fiction and the Cold War* (Charlottesville: University of Virginia Press, 2011).
Green, Jeremy, *Late Postmodernism: American Fiction at the Millennium* (Basingstoke: Palgrave, 2015).
Greenwald Smith, Rachel, 'Postmodernism and the Affective Turn', in *Twentieth Century Literature*, vol 57, no 3/4 (2011), pp. 423–446.
Guillory, John, *Professing Literature: Essays on the Organization of Literary Study* (Chicago: University of Chicago Press, 2022).
Halberstam, Jack, *In a Queer Time and Place* (New York: New York University Press, 2005).

Hale, Dorothy, '*On Beauty* as Beautiful? The Problem of Novelistic Aesthetics by Way of Zadie Smith', in *Contemporary Literature*, vol 53, no 4 (2012), pp. 814–844.
Hallett, Mark, *Reynolds: Portraiture in Action* (New Haven: Yale University Press, 2014).
Harrington, John P., *The Irish Beckett* (New York: Syracuse University Press, 1991).
Harvey, David, *A Brief History of Neoliberalism* (Oxford: Oxford University Press, 2005).
Harvey, David, *The Condition of Postmodernity: An Enquiry into the Origins of Cultural Change* (Oxford: Blackwell, 1990).
Harvey, David, 'Neoliberalism as Creative Destruction', in *The Annals of the American Academy of Political and Social Science*, vol 610 (March, 2007), pp. 22–44.
Heath, Stephen, *Questions of Cinema* (Basingstoke: Macmillan, 1981).
Heidegger, Martin, *Being and Time* (Oxford: Blackwell, 1962), trans. John Macquarrie and Edward Robinson.
Heidegger, Martin, *The Fundamental Concepts of Metaphysics: World, Finitude, Solitude* (Indiana: Indiana University Press, 1995), trans. William McNeill and Nicholas Walker.
Heidegger, Martin, *Poetry, Language, Thought* (New York: Harper, 1971), trans. Albert Hofstadter.
Heidegger, Martin, *The Question Concerning Technology and Other Essays* (New York: Harper, 1977), trans. William Lovitt.
Heidegger, Martin, *Sein und Zeit* (Tübingen: Verlag, 1963).
Heidegger, Martin, 'The Way Back into the Ground of Metaphysics', in Walter Kaufmann, ed., *Existentialism from Dostoevsky to Sartre* (London: Meridian, 1968), pp. 150–161.
Heise, Ursula K., *Sense of Place and Sense of Planet: The Environmental Imagination of the Global* (Oxford: Oxford University Press, 2008).
Highmore, Ben, 'Promiscuous Attachments', in *New Formations*, vol 103 (2021), pp. 181–184.
Hill, Leslie, 'Beckett, Writing, Politics: Answering for Myself', in Peter Boxall, ed., *Beckett/Aesthetics/Politics*, a special issue of *Samuel Beckett Today/Aujourd'hui* (Amsterdam: Rodopi, 2000), pp. 215–221.
Hill, Leslie, *Samuel Beckett: In Different Words* (Cambridge: Cambridge University Press, 1990).
Hill, Leslie, '"Up the Republic!": Beckett, Writing, Politics', in *Modern Language Notes*, vol 112, no 5 (1997), pp. 909–298.
Howe, Susan, *My Emily Dickinson* (Berkeley: North Atlantic Books, 1985).
Huehls, Mitchum, *After Critique: Twenty-First-Century Fiction in a Neoliberal Age* (Oxford: Oxford University Press, 2016).
Hugo, Victor, *Les Misérables* (London: Penguin, 1982).
Hungerford, Amy, 'Don DeLillo's Latin Mass', in *Contemporary Literature*, vol 47, no 3 (2006), pp. 343–380.
Huxley, Aldous, *Brave New World* (London: Flamingo, 1994).

Iser, Wolfgang, *The Act of Reading: A Theory of Aesthetic Response* (Baltimore: Johns Hopkins University Press, 1991).
Iser, Wolfgang, *The Implied Reader: Patterns of Communication in Prose Fiction from Bunyan to Beckett* (Baltimore: Johns Hopkins University Press, 1987).
Ishiguro, Kazuo, *An Artist of the Floating World* (London: Faber, 1987).
Ishiguro, Kazuo, *Klara and the Sun* (London: Faber, 2021).
Ishiguro, Kazuo, *Never Let Me Go* (London: Faber, 2006).
Ishiguro, Kazuo, *A Pale View of Hills* (London: Faber, 1982).
Ishiguro, Kazuo, *Remains of the Day* (London: Faber, 1996).
Ishiguro, Kazuo, *The Unconsoled* (London: Faber, 1995).
James, David and Urmila Seshagiri, 'Metamodernism: Narratives of Continuity and Revolution', in *PMLA*, vol 129, no 1 (January, 2014), pp. 87–100.
James, Henry, *The Ambassadors* (London: Penguin, 2008).
James, Henry, *The Aspern Papers and Turn of the Screw* (London: Penguin, 1984).
James, Henry, *The Awkward Age* (London: Penguin, 1987).
James, Henry, *Complete Stories: 1892–1898* (New York: The Library of America, 1996), eds. David Bromwich and John Hollander.
James, Henry, *The Future of the Novel: Essays on the Art of Fiction* (New York: Vintage, 1956), ed. Leon Edel.
James, Henry, *The Golden Bowl* (London: Penguin, 2009).
James, Henry, *The Portrait of a Lady* (London: Penguin, 2011).
James, Henry, *Selected Letters* (Cambridge: Harvard University Press, 1987), ed. Leon Edel.
James, Henry, *The Tales of Henry James* (New York: Norton, 2003), eds. Christof Wegelin and Wonham Henry B.
James, Henry, *What Maisie Knew* (London: Penguin, 1985).
James, Henry, *The Wings of the Dove* (London: Everyman, 1997).
Jameson, Fredric, et al., *An American Utopia: Dual Power and the Universal Army* (London: Verso, 2016).
Jameson, Fredric, *The Antinomies of Realism* (London: Verso, 2013).
Jameson, Fredric, 'The End of Temporality', in *Critical Inquiry*, vol 29, no 4 (Summer, 2003), pp. 695–718.
Jameson, Fredric, 'Future City', in *New Left Review*, vol 21 (May/June, 2003), pp. 65–81.
Jameson, Fredric, 'Postmodernism, or the Cultural Logic of Late Capitalism', in *New Left Review*, vol 146 (July, 1984), pp. 53–92.
Jameson, Fredric, *Postmodernism, or, The Cultural Logic of Late Capitalism* (London: Verso, 1991).
Jameson, Fredric, *The Seeds of Time* (New York: Columbia University Press, 1994).
Janvier, Ludovic, 'Place of Narration/Narration of Place', in Ruby Cohn, ed., *Samuel Beckett: A Collection of Criticism* (New York: McGaw Hill, 1975), pp. 96–110.
Johnson, Barbara, *The Critical Difference: Essays on the Contemporary Rhetoric of Reading* (Baltimore: Johns Hopkins University Press, 1980).

Jones, Carole, '"Acting the Part of an Illiterate Savage": James Kelman and the Question of Postcolonial Masculinity', in *Journal of Postcolonial Writing*, vol 45, no 3 (2009), pp. 275–284.
Joyce, James, *Dubliners* (Oxford: Oxford University Press, 2000).
Joyce, James, *Portrait of the Artist as a Young Man* (Oxford: Oxford University Press, 2000).
Joyce, James, *Ulysses* (London: Penguin, 1986).
Jung, Carl, *Memories, Dreams, Reflections* (New York: Pantheon, 1973), ed. Aniela Jaffé.
Kafka, Franz, *Diaries, 1910–1923* (New York: Schoeken, 1980), ed. Max Brod.
Kafka, Franz, *Metamorphosis and Other Stories* (London: Minerva, 1992), trans. Willa and Edwin Muir.
Kafka, Franz, *The Trial* (London: Penguin, 1994), trans. Idris Parry.
Kant, Immanuel, *Critique of the Power of Judgement* (Cambridge: Cambridge University Press, 2000), trans. Paul Guyer.
Kaplan, Janet A., *Unexpected Journeys: The Art and Life of Remedios Varo* (London: Vintage, 1988).
Keats, John, *Selected Poems and Letters of Keats* (Oxford: Heinemann, 1966), ed. Robert Gittings.
Kędzierski, Marek, 'Barbara Bray: In Her Own Words', in *Modernism and Modernity*, vol 18, no 4 (2011), pp. 887–896.
Kelly, Adam, 'David Foster Wallace and the New Sincerity in American Fiction', in David Hering, ed., *Consider David Foster Wallace: Critical Essays* (Los Angeles: Sideshow Media, 2010), pp. 131–146.
Kelman, James, *The Busconductor Hines* (Edinburgh: Polygon, 1984).
Kelman, James, *A Chancer* (Edinburgh: Polygon, 1985).
Kelman, James, *Dirt Road* (Edinburgh: Canongate, 2016).
Kelman, James, *A Disaffection* (London: Picador, 1990).
Kelman, James, *God's Teeth and Other Phenomena* (San Francisco: PM Press, 2022).
Kelman, James, *Greyhound for Breakfast* (London: Secker & Warburg, 1987).
Kelman, James, *How Late It Was, How Late* (London: QPD, 1994).
Kelman, James, *Kieron Smith, Boy* (London: Hamish Hamilton, 2008).
Kelman, James, *Mo Said She Was Quirky* (London: Hamish Hamilton, 2012).
Kelman, James, *Not Not While the Giro* (Edinburgh: Polygon, 1983).
Kelman, James, *Some Recent Attacks* (Stirling: AK Press, 1992).
Kelman, James, *Translated Accounts* (London: Secker & Warburg, 2001).
Kelman, James, *You Have to Be Careful in the Land of the Free* (London: Penguin, 2004).
Kenner, Hugh, *Samuel Beckett: A Critical Study* (Berkeley: University of California Press, 1968).
Kermode, Frank, 'Here She Is', in *London Review of Books*, vol 27, no 19 (October, 2005), www.lrb.co.uk/the-paper/v27/n19/frank-kermode/here-she-is.
Khayyam, Omar, *The Rubaiyat of Omar Khayyam* (Auckland: The Floating Press, 2009).

Kiberd, Declan, *Inventing Ireland: The Literature of the Modern Nation* (London: Vintage, 1996).
Kirkley, Richard Bruce, 'A *catch in the breath*: Language and Consciousness in Samuel Beckett's *...but the clouds...*', in *Modern Drama*, vol 35, no 4 (December, 1992), pp. 607–616.
Kiuchi, Kumiko, 'Oxymoronic Perception and the Experience of Genre: Samuel Becket's *Ghost Trio*, *...but the clouds...* and Beyond', in *Journal of Beckett Studies*, vol 18, nos 1–2 (2009), pp. 72–87.
Kleege, Georgina, *Sight Unseen* (New Haven: Yale University Press, 1999).
Knowlson, James, *Damned to Fame: The Life of Samuel Beckett* (London: Bloomsbury, 1996).
Kojève, Alexandre, *Introduction to the Reading of Hegel* (New York: Basic Books, 1969), trans. James H. Nichols, Jr., ed. Allan Bloom.
Kraus, Chris, *I Love Dick* (London: Serpent's Tail, 2016).
Laird, Nick, *To a Fault* (New York: Norton, 2006).
Latour, Bruno, 'Why Has Critique Run out of Steam? From Matters of Fact to Matters of Concern', in *Critical Inquiry*, vol 30 (2004), pp. 225–248.
Lax, Eric, *On Being Funny: Woody Allen and Comedy* (New York: Manor Books, 1975).
LeFanu, Sheridan, 'Schalken the Painter', in Sheridan LeFanu, ed., *The Hours After Midnight* (London: Leslie Frewin, 1975), pp. 37–73.
Lefebvre, Henri, *The Production of Space* (Oxford: Blackwell, 1991), trans. Donald Nicholson-Smith.
Lewin, Katherine Da Cunha and Kiron Ward, eds., *Don DeLillo: Contemporary Critical Perspectives* (London: Bloomsbury, 2019).
Lloyd, David, *Anomalous States: Irish Writing and the Post-Colonial Moment* (Dublin: The Lilliput Press, 1993).
Locatelli, Carla, *Unwording the World: Samuel Beckett's Prose Works after the Nobel Prize* (Philadelphia: University of Pennsylvania Press, 1990).
Locke, John, *Second Treatise of Government* (Oxford: Oxford University Press, 2016).
Long, Joseph, 'Divine Intertextuality: Samuel Beckett, *Company, Le Dépeupleur*', in *Samuel Beckett Today/Aujourd'hui*, vol 9 (2000), pp. 145–157.
López, Maria J., 'Miguel de Cervantes and J. M. Coetzee: An Unacknowledged Paternity', in *Journal of Literary Studies*, vol 29, no 4 (2013), pp. 80–97.
Lubbock, Percy, *The Craft of Fiction* (London: Jonathan Cape, 1954).
Lukács, Georg, *The Meaning of Contemporary Realism* (Monmouth: Merlin Press, 2006).
Lukács, Georg, 'Realism in the Balance', in Ernst Bloch, et al., eds., *Aesthetics and Politics* (London: NLB, 1977), trans. Rodney Livingstone, pp. 28–59.
Lyotard, Jean François, *The Postmodern Condition: A Report on Knowledge* (Manchester: Manchester University Press, 1984), trans. Geoff Bennington and Brian Massumi.
Maclean, Alistair, *The Way to Dusty Death* (London: William Collins, 1973).

March, Christie L., *Rewriting Scotland* (Manchester: Manchester University Press, 2002).
Marriott, David, *On Black Men* (Edinburgh: Edinburgh University Press, 2000).
Marx, Karl, *Capital* (Hertfordshire: Wordsworth, 1987), trans. Samuel Moore and Edward Aveling.
Marx, Karl, *Early Writings* (London: Penguin, 1992), trans. Rodney Livingstone and Gregor Benton.
Maturin, Charles, *Melmoth the Wanderer* (Oxford: Oxford University Press, 2008).
May, Theresa, 'Conference Speech', in *The Telegraph* (5 October, 2016).
McCarthy, Cormac, *The Road* (London: Picador, 2007).
McClure, John A., 'Postmodern/Post-Secular: Contemporary Fiction and Spirituality', in *Modern Fiction Studies*, vol 41, no 1 (1995), pp. 141–164.
McCormack, W. J., *From Burke to Beckett: Ascendancy, Tradition and Betrayal in Literary History* (Cork: Cork University Press, 1994).
McCorquodale, Charles, *Bronzino* (London: Jupiter, 1981).
McEwan, Ian, *Atonement* (London: Vintage, 2001).
McEwan, Ian, *The Children Act* (London: Jonathan Cape, 2014).
McEwan, Ian, 'The Law versus Religious Belief', in *The Guardian* (5 September, 2014).
McEwan, Ian, *Saturday* (London: Jonathan Cape, 2005).
McMullen, Anna, 'Irish/Postcolonial Beckett', in Lois Oppenheim, ed., *Palgrave Advances in Samuel Beckett Studies* (Basingstoke: Palgrave, 2004), pp. 89–109.
Melville, Herman, *Melville's Short Novels: Bartleby, The Scrivener, Benito Cereno, Billy Budd, Sailor* (New York: Norton, 2002), ed. Dan McCall.
Melville, Herman, *Moby Dick* (Oxford: Oxford University Press, 2008).
Melville, Herman, *Typee: A Peep at Polyneisan Life* (Evanston: Northwestern University Press, 1968).
Mercier, Vivian, *Beckett/Beckett* (Oxford: Oxford University Press, 1977).
Milton, John, *Paradise Lost* (Harlow: Pearson Longman, 2007), ed. Alastair Fowler.
Mitchell, David, *Cloud Atlas* (London: Hodder & Stoughton, 2004).
Montaigne, Michel de, *The Complete Essays* (London: Penguin, 2003), trans. M. A. Screech.
Mooney, Sinead, '"Integrity in a Surplus": Beckett's (Post-) Protestant Politics', in Peter Boxall, ed., *Beckett/Aesthetics/Politics, Samuel Beckett Today/Aujourd'hui*, vol 9 (Amsterdam: Rodopi, 2000), pp. 223–237.
More, Thomas, *Utopia* (Cambridge: Cambridge University Press, 2002), trans. Robert M. Adams.
Morin, Emilie, *Beckett's Political Imagination* (Cambridge: Cambridge University Press, 2017).
Morrison, Toni, *Beloved* (London: Vintage, 2014).
Morrison, Toni, *Mouth Full of Blood: Essays, Speeches, Meditations* (London: Chatto & Windus, 2019).
Morse, Samuel French, *Wallace Stevens: Poetry as Life* (New York: Pegasus, 1970).

Morton, Timothy, *Ecology without Nature: Rethinking Environmental Aesthetics* (Cambridge: Harvard University Press, 2007).
Murat, Laure, 'How the French Reread Proust', in *Literary Hub* (11 July, 2016).
Nabokov, Vladimir, *Lectures on Don Quixote* (London: Weidenfeld and Nicolson, 1983), ed. Fredson Bowers.
Nabokov, Vladimir, *Lectures on Literature* (London: Weidenfeld and Nicolson, 1980), ed. Fredson Bowers.
Nealon, Jeffrey T., *Post-Postmodernism, or the Cultural Logic of Just-in-Time Capitalism* (Stanford: Stanford University Press, 2012).
Ngai, Sianne, *Our Aesthetic Categories: Zany, Cute, Interesting* (Cambridge: Harvard University Press, 2012).
Ngai, Sianne, *Theory of the Gimmick: Aesthetic Judgment and Capitalist Form* (Cambridge: Harvard University Press, 2020).
Nolan, Emer, *James Joyce and Nationalism* (London: Routledge, 1995).
Nussbaum, Martha C., *Love's Knowledge: Essays on Philosophy and Literature* (Oxford: Oxford University Press, 1990).
O'Brien, Eoin, *The Beckett Country* (Dublin: Black Cat Press, 1986).
Offill, Jenny, *Weather* (London: Granta, 2020).
Okamuro, Minako, et al., eds., *Borderless Beckett/Beckett sans frontières* (Amsterdam: Rodopi, 2008).
Olson, Charles, *Call Me Ishmael: A Study of Melville* (San Francisco: City Light Books, 1947).
O'Neill, John, 'Dying in a State of Grace', in *Textual Practice*, vol 27, no 4 (2013), pp. 651–670.
Oppenheim, Lois, ed., *Palgrave Advances in Samuel Beckett Studies* (Basingstoke: Palgrave, 2004).
Osteen, Mark, 'Echo Chamber: Undertaking *The Body Artist*', in *Studies in the Novel*, vol 18, nos 1–2 (2009), pp. 72–87.
Pater, Walter, *The Renaissance: Studies in Art and Poetry* (Cambridge: Cambridge University Press, 2011).
Plato, *The Republic* (London: Penguin, 2007), trans. Desmond Lee.
Poe, Edgar Allan, *The Complete Tales and Poems of Edgar Allan Poe* (New York: Castle Books, 2002).
Pope, Alexander, *The Major Works* (Oxford: Oxford University Press, 2006).
Proust, Marcel, *Remembrance of Things Past* (London: Penguin, 1983) 3 vols., trans. C. K. Scott Moncrieff and Terence Kilmartin.
Pynchon, Thomas, *The Crying of Lot 49* (London: Vintage, 2000).
Readings, Bill, *The University in Ruins* (Cambridge: Harvard University Press, 1996).
Robertson, Lisa, *Occasional Work and Seven Walks from the Office for Soft Architecture* (Toronto: Coach House Books, 2011).
Rogin, Michael Paul, *Subversive Genealogy: The Politics and Art of Herman Melville* (Berkeley: University of California Press, 1983).
Ronell, Avital, *Stupidity* (Chicago: University of Illinois Press, 2003).
Rose, Arthur James, *Cynical Cosmopolitans? Borges, Beckett, Coetzee* (PhD thesis, Leeds: Leeds University, 2014).

Roth, Philip, *Exit Ghost* (London: Vintage, 2008).
Roth, Philip, *The Human Stain* (London: Vintage, 2001).
Roth, Philip, *The Plot Against America* (London: Jonathan Cape, 2004).
Royle, Nicholas. 'Back', in *Oxford Literary Review*, vol 18 (1996), pp. 145–157.
Royle, Nicholas, *Veering: A Theory of Literature* (Edinburgh: Edinburgh University Press, 2011).
Rushdie, Salman, *Midnight's Children* (London: Vintage, 2006).
Ruskin, John, *The Stones of Venice* (London: George Allen and Unwin, 1925), 3 vols.
Ryan, Xander, '"To Talk Alone": Beckett's Letters to Barbara Bray and the Epistolary Drama of *Happy Days*', in *Samuel Beckett Today/Aujourd'hui*, vol 31, no 1 (2019), pp. 163–177.
Said, Edward W., *On Late Style: Music and Literature against the Grain* (London: Bloomsbury, 2007).
Said, Edward W., *Orientalism* (London: Penguin, 2003).
Scarry, Elaine, *On Beauty and Being Just* (London: Duckworth, 2006).
Schama, Simon, *Rembrandt's Eyes* (London: Allen Lane, 1999).
Schenker, Israel, 'A Portrait of Samuel Beckett, the Author of the Puzzling Waiting for Godot', *New York Times* (6 May, 1956).
Scholar, John, *Henry James and the Art of Impressions* (Oxford: Oxford University Press, 2020).
Sebald, W. G., *Austerlitz* (London: Penguin, 2001), trans. Anthea Bell.
Sebald, W. G., *Vertigo* (London: Vintage, 2002), trans. Michael Hulse.
Sebald, W. G. and Jan Peter Tripp, *Unrecounted* (New York: New Directions, 2004).
Sedgwick, Eve Kosofsky, *Touching Feeling: Affect, Pedagogy, Performativity* (Durham: Duke University Press, 2003)
Sedgwick, Eve Kosofsky, *The Weather in Proust* (Durham: Duke University Press, 2011).
Seshagiri, Urmila, 'The Boy of La Mancha: J. M. Coetzee's *The Childhood of Jesus*', in *Contemporary Literature*, vol 54, no 3 (2013), pp. 643–654.
Shakespeare, William, *The Complete Works* (Oxford: Clarendon Press, 1988).
Silverman, Kaja, *The Subject of Semiotics* (New York: Oxford University Press, 1983).
Smith, Ali, *The Accidental* (London: Penguin, 2007).
Smith, Ali, *Autumn* (London: Hamish Hamilton, 2016).
Smith, Ali, *Girl Meets Boy* (Edinburgh: Canongate, 2008).
Smith, Ali, *How to Be Both* (London: Hamish Hamilton, 2014).
Smith, Ali, 'Introduction', in Lewis Grassic Gibbon ed., *Sunset Song* (London: Penguin, 2007), pp. xi–xxiii.
Smith, Ali, *Spring* (London: Hamish Hamilton, 2019).
Smith, Ali, *Summer* (London: Hamish Hamilton, 2020).
Smith, Ali, '"Vital, Witty, Formidably Blithe": Ali Smith on Muriel Spark at 100', in *The Guardian* (29 January, 2018).
Smith, Ali, *Winter* (London: Hamish Hamilton, 2017).

Smith, Zadie, *Changing My Mind: Occasional Essays* (London: Hamish Hamilton, 2009).
Smith, Zadie, *NW* (London: Penguin, 2012).
Smith, Zadie, *On Beauty* (London: Penguin, 2005).
Smith, Zadie, *White Teeth* (London: Penguin, 2001).
Smith, Zadie and Ian McEwan, 'Zadie Smith Talks with Ian McEwan', in Ryan Roberts, ed., *Conversations with Ian McEwan* (Jackson: University of Mississippi Press, 2010), pp. 108–133.
Spark, Muriel, *The Takeover* (London: Macmillan, 1976).
Starkie, Enid, *Arthur Rimbaud* (London: Faber, 1961).
Stevens, Wallace, *The Letters of Wallace Stevens* (London: Faber, 1966), ed. Holly Stevens.
Stevens, Wallace, *The Necessary Angel: Essays on Reality and the Imagination* (New York: Vintage, 1965).
Stevens, Wallace, *Opus Posthumous* (New York: Knopf Doubleday, 1989).
Stevens, Wallace, *The Palm at the End of the Mind: Selected Poems and a Play* (New York: Vintage, 1990), ed. Holly Stevens.
Stevens, Wallace, *Selected Poems* (London: Faber, 2010).
Thatcher, Margaret, 'Interview for Woman's Own', in *Woman's Own* (31 October, 1987).
Tooze, Adam, *Crashed: How a Decade of Financial Crises Changed the World* (London: Penguin, 2018).
Toscano, Alberto and Jeff Kinkle, *Cartographies of the Absolute* (Winchester: Zero Books, 2015).
Toth, Josh, *The Passing of Postmodernism: A Spectroanalysis of the Contemporary* (Albany: SUNY Press, 2010).
Vargas Llosa, Mario, 'A Novel for the Twenty-First Century', in *Harvard Review*, vol 28 (2005), trans. Johanna Damgaard Liander, pp. 125–136.
Voltaire, *Candide* (London: Penguin, 2001).
Walkowitz, Rebecca L., 'Ishiguro's Floating Worlds', in *ELH*, vol 68, no 4 (2001), pp. 1049–1076.
Wallace, Jeff, *Abstraction in Modernism and Modernity* (Edinburgh: Edinburgh University Press, 2023).
Weiss, Katherine, 'Animating Ghosts in Samuel Beckett's *Ghost Trio* and *…but the clouds…*', in *Journal of Beckett Studies*, vol 18, nos 1–2 (2009), pp. 105–122.
Weller, Shane, 'Beckett and Animality', in Okamuro, Minako, et al., eds., *Borderless Beckett/ Beckett sans frontières* (Amsterdam: Rodopi, 2008), pp. 211–221.
Wharton, Edith, *The House of Mirth* (Oxford: Oxford University Press, 1999).
Wilde, Oscar, *The Picture of Dorian Gray* (London: Penguin, 1985).
Williams, Diane, *The Collected Stories of Diane Williams* (New York: Soho, 2018).
Wills, David, *Dorsality: Thinking Back through Technology and Politics* (Minneapolis: University of Minnesota Press, 2008).
Winterson, Jeanette, *Written on the Body* (London: Jonathan Cape, 1992).
Wittgenstein, Ludwig, *Philosophical Investigations* (Oxford: Blackwell, 2001), trans G.E.M. Anscombe.

Wittgenstein, Ludwig, *Tractatus Logico-Philosophicus* (London: Routledge, 2001), trans. D. F. Pears and B. F. McGuinness.
Woolf, Virginia, *Between the Acts* (Oxford: Oxford University Press, 2008).
Woolf, Virginia, *The Diary of Virginia Woolf: Volume II, 1920–1924* (London: Hogarth Press, 1978), ed. Anne Olivier Bell.
Woolf, Virginia, *Mrs Dalloway* (New York: Knopf, 1993).
Woolf, Virginia, *The Essays of Virginia Woolf: Volume III, 1919–1924* (London: Hogarth Press, 1988), ed. Andrew McNeillie.
Woolf, Virginia, *Night and Day* (London: Penguin, 1982).
Woolf, Virginia, *To the Lighthouse* (London: Grafton, 1977).
Wright, Lawrence, *The Looming Tower: Al-Qaeda's Road to 9/11* (London: Penguin, 2007).
Yeats, W. B., *Collected Poems* (London: Picador, 1990).

Index

11 September 2001, 6–8, 106, 256, 258–259, 284
2008 economic crash, 8, 257, 284

Acker, Kathy, 175
Act of Union (1800), 188–189
Adorno, Theodor, 5, 104–105
Afghanistan, invasion of, 7, 257
Agamben, Giorgio, 209–211, 217, 234, 335
Ahmed, Sara, 291–293, 305–306
America, decline of, 284
Amis, Martin, *Money*, 282
Anglo-Irish tradition, 187, 190, 194–196
animal gaze, 155–157, 162–163, 167–168
antinomy, 56–57
Appiah, Kwame Anthony, 2
Arnold, Matthew, 133
Ashbery, John, 338
Attridge, Derek, 5
Atwood, Margaret, 74
   Oryx and Crake, 15
Aubrey, James, 176
Auerbach, Erich, 170, 172–174, 176, 179, 181, 230
Austen, Jane, 279
   Emma, 93–94, 279
Auster, Paul, 175

Bachman, Ingeborg, 249
back, concept of, 190, 192–194, 199
Bailey, Helen, 2, 346
Bakhtin, Mikhail, 129, 131, 135
Baldwin, James, 42–43
   Another Country, 42–43
   Fire Next Time, The, 43
Ballard, J. G., *Crash*, 282
Barnes, Julian, *The Sense of an Ending*, 260
Barthes, Roland, 68, 313, 334–335
Baudrillard, Jean, 7
Baum, Devorah, 298, 368
beauty, 118, 122–124, 131–135, 139–146, 331
Beckett, Samuel, 83, 113, 168, 234, 249–250
   All Strange Away, 219, 221
   antinomy in, 57, 59

Bray, Barbara, relationship with, 295, 298–302, 305–307
…but the clouds…, 190, 198, 200–204
Company, 80, 159, 165, 190, 198–200, 219, 221
criticism on, 1–2, 5–6, 47–53, 57–59, 105, 150–153, 157, 195–196, 346
cultural specificity of, 49–52, 58, 195–199, 202
Dickinson and, 217–220
Dream of Fair to Middling Women, 197
Endgame, 5, 167, 224, 291, 301
First Love, 198, 300, 322, 368
Fizzle 6, 301, 304
Fizzles, 107
Footfalls, 52
Ghost Trio, 81, 198, 200–202, 204, 322
happiness in, 303, 305, 307
Happy Days, 20, 296–298, 300–306
How It Is, 52, 85, 199
Ill seen Ill said, 221
Imagination Dead Imagine, 53, 82, 199, 221, 223, 235
Krapp's Last Tape, 159
light in, 220–222
Lost Ones, The, 5, 20–24, 152, 198, 221
Malone Dies, 34, 160–165, 167
marriage, 294–295
Mitchell, Pamela, relationship with, 299
Molloy, 5, 62, 199, 250, 301, 324
'Mouche, La', 217–218
Murphy, 132, 158–159, 164, 167, 271
negation in, 53–55, 58–61
Nohow On, 52
Not I, 52
Ohio Impromptu, 307
photographs of, 152, 154
Ping, 198
political reading of, 1–2, 47–49, 51–52, 60–62
Proust, anticipation by, 321–323
Proust, criticism on, 72, 233, 244, 327
Rockaby, 355
Shakespeare and, 301

389

Index

Beckett, Samuel (cont.)
    silence in, 48
    Stirrings Still, 52, 190, 197, 203
    tautology in, 15, 72, 81
    Unnamable, The, 52–55, 158, 198, 250, 300–301, 322, 354
    Waiting for Godot, 22, 52, 198
    Watt, 52, 159, 219, 346
    Worstward Ho, 23, 49, 59–60, 165, 221–222, 250
    See also Beckett in Folkestone
Beckett in Folkestone, 294–296
being, 39, 42, 227–230, 232–234, 251
Benjamin, Walter, 20, 25, 334
    Arcades Project, The, 25
Benn Michaels, Walter, 284–285, 287
Bennett, Jane, 84, 222
Berger, John, 150
Bersani, Leo, 244, 321, 325, 334
Bewes, Timothy, 16–17, 142, 144
black experience, 41–43
Blackham, H. J., 119
Blair, Tony, 8–9, 256–258
Blanchot, Maurice, 53–57, 59, 61, 135, 207, 212
blindness. *See* vision
Bloom, Harold, 212, 225
Borges, Jorge Luis, 175–176
Botticelli, Sandro, 328
Bowen, Elizabeth
    'Back Drawing Room, The', 190–194, 199, 204
    Last September, The, 190
    Pictures and Conversations, 194–195
    place in, 194, 196–197, 358
Bray, Barbara, 295, 298–302, 305–307
Bretton Woods agreement, 9, 280–281
Brexit, 9, 231, 258–259, 269, 295–296
Briggs, Kate, 325
Brontë, Charlotte, *Jane Eyre*, 113
Brooke-Rose, Christine, 249
Bush, George W., 8

Cameron, Sharon, 220, 244
capitalism, 3, 9, 12, 56, 248, 283, 290. *See also* neoliberalism
Carter, Angela, *The Bloody Chamber*, 282
Caselli, Daniela, 299
Cavell, Stanley, 291
Cervantes, *Don Quixote*, 17–19, 94
    Cave of Montesinos episode, 170–173, 183
    criticism on, 174–175
    prologue, 183–184
    reality in, 169–174, 180–181, 183–185
    See also Coetzee, J. M., Cervantes and
Chakrabarty, Dipesh, 231, 251
Chenoweth, Katie, 34
Children Act 1989, 262

Chomsky, Noam, 11
Clark, T. J., 369
climate change, 10, 16, 86, 231, 284, 293, 297, 304, 336, 338
Clinton, Bill, 275–276
Cloud, the, 338
Coetzee, J. M., 16, 18–21, 124, 165–167, 182
    11 September 2001, comments on, 7
    Cervantes and, 17, 175–180, 185–186, 356
    Childhood of Jesus, The, 17, 19, 24, 175–184
    criticism on, 176
    Diary of a Bad Year, 20, 175
    'Eight Ways of Looking at Samuel Beckett', 24, 150–153, 155–157, 160
    Elizabeth Costello, 16, 18, 118–120, 124, 166, 175, 179
    grief in, 182
    Jesus books, 17, 356
    late style of, 175, 250
    Master of Petersburg, The, 182–183
    pandemics in, 230
    realism in, 118, 175–176, 181–186
    Slow Man, 166, 175
    Summertime, 166, 175
Connor, Steven, 162, 219
contradiction, 56–57
Covid-19 pandemic, 87, 230–231, 284, 293, 295–297, 304
Critchley, Simon, 229

Dabashi, Hamid, 12
Dante, *Divine Comedy*, 21
darkness, 26, 33–34, 44, 166, 210, 217, 221–222, 224, 226, 287
Davies, William, 2, 346
de Man, Paul, 212, 318, 334–335
Deane, Seamus, 57, 60
death, 207–208, 211, 214, 216, 219–220, 222, 306
Deleuze, Gilles, 17, 53, 61, 98, 202, 225, 334
DeLillo, Don
    Americana, 69
    Body Artist, The, 15, 63, 67, 75–77, 79–80, 82, 85, 348
    consciousness in, 76, 78, 85–86
    Cosmopolis, 65
    End Zone, 69–74
    Great Jones Street, 69
    history in, 70–74
    late style of, 63–66, 68, 80, 84
    Names, The, 77
    Point Omega, 64–67, 74, 76, 78–80
    Ratner's Star, 80
    Running Dog, 72
    scantness in, 82–83
    'Starveling, The', 64, 68, 80

tautology in, 63–64, 66–75, 80–83, 85
time in, 75–78
Underworld, 67, 71, 73, 80, 113, 282
White Noise, 282
Word for Snow, The, 16
Zero K, 15, 78–86
depth. *See* surface and depth
Derrida, Jacques, 5, 16, 19, 212, 234, 271, 313, 334–335
Descartes, René, 233
Dickens, Charles, 17
   Bleak House, 117, 261–262, 264
   Christmas Carol, A, 269, 273
   Great Expectations, 112
   Tale of Two Cities, A, 269
Dickinson, Emily, 26, 34, 44, 108, 115, 211, 217, 225
   'Brain – is wider than the sky –, the', 224
   'From Blank to Blank', 214–216
   'I felt a Cleaving in my Mind', 333
   'I heard a Fly buzz – when I died –', 215–220
   'There's a certain Slant of light', 214
   'Tint I cannot take – is best, The', 208, 217
   'We grow accustomed to the Dark', 24, 214, 221
   'What I see not, I better see', 24, 212–214
   See also Beckett, Samuel, Dickinson and
Donne, John, 20, 29
Du Bois, W. E. B., 41
Duvall, John, 73
Dwan, Lisa, 304

economic crash. *See* 2008 economic crash
Edgeworth, Maria, *Castle Rackrent*, 187–190
   footnotes, 189
   preface, 188–189
Eliot, George
   Daniel Deronda, 93, 119, 237
   Middlemarch, 237, 278–279
Eliot, T. S., 247
   'Marina', 159
   'Tradition and the Individual Talent', 311
Ellison, Ralph, *The Invisible Man*, 45

fake news, 282
Fanon, Frantz, 41–43
   Black Skin, White Masks, 46
Faulkner, William, *The Sound and the Fury*, 142
Felski, Rita, 11, 13, 285
fitness, 292
Flaubert, Gustave, 183
Forster, E. M., 120
   art in, 134
   Aspects of the Novel, 135
   Howards End, 117, 120, 124, 126–138, 145, 352
   Passage to India, A, 137, 353
   'What I Believe', 136

Foucault, Michel, 231
Franzen, Jonathan, *Corrections, The*, 284
Freud, Sigmund, 233–234
Friedrich, Caspar David, 302
Friel, Brian, *Translations*, 190
Fukuyama, Francis, 3–6, 8–9, 256, 284
futurity, 76, 259–261

gaze. *See* animal gaze; vision
Genette, Gérard, 317, 334–335
Ghosh, Amitav, 10
gimmick, the, 12, 248
Ginzburg, Natalia, 249
Giuliani, Rudy, 282
globalization, 3, 8, 256–258
Goethe, Johann Wolfgang von, 84, 182
Gopal, Priyamvada, 12–13
gothic fiction, 92
Gramsci, Antonio, 255
Grausam, Daniel, 70
Green, Jeremy, 11
Greenwald-Smith, Rachel, 286
Guattari, Félix, 98, 202, 225
Guillory, John, 11

Halberstam, Jack, 337
Hale, Dorothy, 138, 140, 142
happiness, 291–294, 303, 305–307
Harvey, David, 256, 280–281, 283–284, 289
Heidegger, Martin, 225, 234
   light and, 212, 217, 226
   world picture, concept of, 208, 211, 302
   worldlessness, concept of, 82, 84
Hill, Leslie, 53
history, end of, 3–6, 9, 22, 76, 284
Howe, Susan, 225
Huehls, Mitchum, 285
Hugo, Victor, *Les Misérables*, 31, 345
Hungerford, Amy, 77
Huxley, Aldous, *Brave New World*, 291–293

imagination, 61, 95, 229, 231, 244, 247
   death of, 85, 220, 235
Iraq, invasion of, 7, 257
Ireland, 58, 188–190, 192, 196. *See also* Anglo-Irish tradition; Beckett, Samuel, cultural specificity of
Irishness, 190, 196
Iser, Wolfgang, 313
Ishiguro, Kazuo, 95
   art in, 94–97, 100–101
   Artist of the Floating World, The, 95–98, 101
   Kafka and, 98, 100
   Klara and the Sun, 87–90, 94, 97–98, 100–103
   Never Let Me Go, 88, 95, 97, 99, 101

Ishiguro, Kazuo (cont.)
  novel form and, 90, 100, 103
  Pale View of Hills, A, 95
  Remains of the Day, 95
  Unconsoled, The, 95–101, 350

James, Henry, 235, 243–245, 247–249
  Ambassadors, The, 249
  'Art of Fiction, The', 243, 248
  Aspern Papers, The, 243
  Awkward Age, The, 236
  everything, concept of, 249
  Golden Bowl, The, 241, 245–246, 249
  In the Cage, 237
  Jolly Corner, The, 237, 246–247
  novel form and, 237, 247
  Portrait of a Lady, The, 236–245, 251
  wall, figure of, 243, 245–247
  What Maisie Knew, 241
  Wings of the Dove, The, 91–92, 241, 246, 248, 251, 327
Jameson, Fredric, 3–4, 12, 56–57, 283–284
Janvier, Ludovic, 346
Johnson, Barbara, 30
Joyce, James, 180
  Dead, The, 265–268, 270
  Portrait of the Artist as a Young Man, 54, 188, 268
  Ulysses, 266, 270
Jung, Carl, 234

Kafka, Franz, 98, 100, 104, 207–208, 216
  Metamorphosis, 287
  photographs of, 152
  Trial, The, 98, 350
Kant, Immanuel, *Critique of Judgement*, 146
Kelman, James, 104–105
  Disaffection, 105
  How Late It Was How Late, 286–290
  Kieron Smith, Boy, 104–116, 289
  Translated Accounts, 104–110, 112, 115–116, 287, 289
  You Have to Be Careful in the Land of the Free, 104–109, 111–112, 116
Kermode, Frank, 126, 128
Khayyam, Omar, *Rubaiyat*, 298
Kiberd, Declan, 195–197
Kirkley, Richard Bruce, 204
Knowlson, James, 50
Kojève, Alexandre, 4, 6, 9–10
Kraus, Chris, *I Love Dick*, 282
Kristeva, Julia, 334

Laird, Nick, 119, 121, 123–124
Latour, Bruno, 7

Lefebvre, Henri, 346
Lewinsky, Monica, 275–276
literary politics. *See* Beckett, Samuel, political reading of; political fiction
López, Maria J., 176
love, 122–123, 130, 135–138, 145, 181–183, 306, 320, 324, 331
Lubbock, Percy, *The Craft of Fiction*, 310–311, 313
Lukács, Georg, 104–105
Lyotard, Jean-François, 9

Maclean, Alistair, *The Way to Dusty Death*, 322
Marriott, David, 43
Marx, Karl, 134, 144–145, 249
Marxism, 12
Maturin, Charles, *Melmoth the Wanderer*, 350
May, Theresa, 258, 260, 269, 273
McCarthy, Cormac
  Beckett and, 222–225
  Dickinson and, 222–225
  Road, The, 15, 222–225
McClure, John, 77
McCormack, W. J., 190, 197
McEwan, Ian, 261, 274
  Atonement, 258
  Children Act, The, 117–118, 261–265, 267–270
  Dickens and, 117, 261–262
  Joyce and, 261, 264–265, 267
McMullen, Anna, 205
Melville, Herman, 32–34, 43–44
  Bartleby the Scrivener, 32, 40, 243
  Benito Cereno, 34–40, 44–46
  Billy Budd, 29–33, 44
  Moby Dick, 29, 32, 41, 44–45, 151
memory. *See* Proust, Marcel, involuntary memory in
Mercier, Vivian, 49
mere, concept of, 229, 233–236, 240, 242–243, 248
Milton, John, *Paradise Lost*, 166
Mitchell, David, *Cloud Atlas*, 260
modernism, 91–92, 266, 274
Monday morning, 188
Morin, Emilie, 346
Morrison, Toni, 24, 40, 44–45
  Beloved, 282, 284
Murat, Laure, 319

Nabokov, Vladimir, 170, 309, 313
nationalism, 9, 231, 258–259
neoconservatism, 4
neoliberalism, 8, 258, 278, 280–288
new criticism, 313
Ngai, Sianne, 12–13, 146, 248, 285

novel
  blindness and, 290
  form, 90, 100, 103, 237, 247
  late twentieth-century, 279–280
  neoliberalism and, 281–286, 290
  twenty-first-century British, 258–261, 274
Nussbaum, Martha, 122

O'Brien, Eoin, 50–51
Offill, Jenny, 250
  Weather, 338
openings (of novels), 117–120
Osteen, Mark, 348

pandemic. *See* Covid-19 pandemic
Pater, Walter, 141–142
Plato, *Republic*, 171, 174
Poe, Edgar Allan, 102, 350
political fiction, 104–106. *See also* Beckett, Samuel, political reading of
Pope, Alexander, 84
portraiture, 90–95
postcolonialism, 2, 11, 258
post-critique, 11
postmodernism, 2–3, 9, 11, 56, 91, 258–259, 271, 274, 283–284
poststructuralism, 2
Powers, Richard, 10, 16
prosthesis, 30, 32–33, 37, 40–41, 44, 84–85, 89–90
Proust, Marcel, 25, 234
  A la recherche du temps perdu, 113, 124, 314–323, 325–339
  aesthetic theory of, 321, 323, 327–332
  Beckett, anticipation of, 321–323
  Beckett's criticism on, 72, 233, 244, 327
  criticism and, 333–335
  death, 314
  involuntary memory in, 325–327, 329–330, 332
  music in, 329
  reading in, 25, 315–319, 329, 332, 334
  readings of, 319–320, 324
  Woolf's criticism on, 314, 333
  writing in, 314–315, 318
Pynchon, Thomas, *The Crying of Lot 49*, 90

Quin, Ann, 249

race and power, 35–36, 38–41, 46
reading, 178, 308–312, 315–318, 325, 332
  critical forms of, 312–313, 333
  new forms of, 285
  politics of, 276
Readings, Bill, 139
realism, 91, 104, 123, 174–176, 181–186

authenticity and, 106
development of, 94
experimental forms of, 249
ideas and, 118
portraiture and, 93
time and, 273
transformation of, 242, 274
reason, 16, 18
Rembrandt, 120
  Anatomy Lesson of Dr Tulp, The, 120, 143
  Hendrickje Bathing, 120, 140, 142–143
rereading, 308–313, 315–318, 325, 332–333
Rimbaud, Arthur, 115
Robertson, Lisa, 244
Ronell, Avital, 30
Roth, Philip, 74
  Human Stain, The, 275–280, 283, 286
  Plot Against America, The, 284
Royle, Nicholas, 32
Rushdie, Salman, *Midnight's Children*, 282
Ruskin, John, *The Stones of Venice*, 133
Ryan, Xander, 300

Said, Edward, 42, 74
Sand, George, 316
Scarry, Elaine, 121, 124, 131, 135, 138–139
Schama, Simon, 120, 144
Sebald, W. G., 17, 155–158, 165–167
  Austerlitz, 155–157, 166–168
  Unrecounted, 154–155, 158, 167
  Vertigo, 155
Sedgwick, Eve Kosofsky, 313, 335–338
Seshagiri, Urmila, 176
Shakespeare, William
  Hamlet, 33, 45, 206, 234, 302, 333
  Macbeth, 322
  Midsummer Night's Dream, A, 243
  sonnets, 33, 213–214, 301
sight. *See* vision
Smith, Ali, 261, 272–274
  Accidental, The, 272
  Autumn, 268–272
  Dickens and, 269, 273
  Girl Meets Boy, 272
  How to Be Both, 272
  Joyce and, 269
  Winter, 268–274
Smith, Zadie
  art in, 121, 139–144
  Forster and, 117, 120, 124–127, 131, 135–136
  McEwan, Ian, comments on, 117
  NW, 260, 274
  On Beauty, 117–131, 135–136, 138–146
  university, satire of, 139–140
  White Teeth, 258

Soviet Union, collapse of, 9
Spark, Muriel, 280
　Takeover, The, 281–283, 289
Stein, Gertrude, 249
Stevens, Wallace, 206, 223, 226–229, 231–234, 249, 338
　Adagia, 229
　'As You Leave the Room', 228
　'Clear Day and no Memories, A', 227
　Necessary Angel, The, 229
　'Not Ideas about the Thing but the Thing Itself', 229
　'Of Mere Being', 228, 230, 235
　'Thirteen Ways of Looking at a Blackbird', 153–154, 157, 162
sun, the, 206
surface and depth, 143, 237, 239, 241–244, 277–279, 283
Swift, Jonathan, 21

tautology, 15, 23, 68, 72. *See also* DeLillo, Don, tautology in
Thatcher, Margaret, 255, 258, 269
theory wars, 2
Treanor, Paul, 280
Trump, Donald, 257, 259, 273, 282

Ukraine, invasion of, 9
utopianism, 1, 57, 62, 145, 273

Vargas Llosa, Mario, 175–176
vision, 152–153, 157–158, 206, 212–217, 226, 290
　threshold of, 149–150, 158–159, 165
Voltaire, *Candide*, 31, 344

Walkowitz, Rebecca, 89
weather. *See* climate change
west, the, 8–9
Wharton, Edith, *The House of Mirth*, 91–92
whiteness, 41, 44–45, 82
Wilde, Oscar, *The Picture of Dorian Gray*, 92
Williams, Diane, 250
Winterson, Jeanette, *Written on the Body*, 278
Wittgenstein, Ludwig, 15, 68, 83, 135, 156, 178
Woolf, Virginia, 75, 232–234
　Between the Acts, 24
　December 1910, 6
　Mrs Dalloway, 232, 249, 311–313
　Night and Day, 232
　'On Re-reading Novels', 310, 313
　Proust, criticism on, 314, 333
　To the Lighthouse, 332
world picture, concept of, 208–212, 222, 224–226, 302

Yeats, W.B.
　'Sailing to Byzantium', 228, 355
　'Tower, The', 202, 204